DICTIONARY *of* NAVAL ABBREVIATIONS

DICTIONARY *of* NAVAL ABBREVIATIONS

DEBORAH W. CUTLER
THOMAS J. CUTLER

NAVAL INSTITUTE PRESS
ANNAPOLIS, MARYLAND

Naval Institute Press
291 Wood Road
Annapolis, MD 21402

Library of Congress Cataloging-in-Publication Data

Cutler, Deborah W., 1949-
Dictionary of naval abbreviations / Deborah W. Cutler, Thomas J. Cutler.— 4th ed.
p. cm. — (Blue and gold professional library series)
Rev. ed. of: Dictionary of naval abbreviations / compiled and edited by Bill Wedertz. 3rd ed. 1984.
ISBN 1-59114-152-4 (alk. paper)
1. United States. Navy—Abbreviations—Dictionaries. 2. United States. Navy—Acronyms—Dictionaries. 3. Naval art and science—Abbreviations—Dictionaries. 4. Naval art and science—Acronyms—Dictionaries. I. Cutler, Thomas J., 1947- II. Wedertz, Bill. Dictionary of naval abbreviations. III. Title. IV. Series.
V23.C86 2005
359'.003—dc22

2004023836

Printed in the United States of America on acid-free paper ♾
12 11 10 09 08 07 06 05 9 8 7 6 5 4 3 2
First printing

CONTENTS

To FSG*

Friends forever

*Francesca Schuler Guerin

PREFACE

The U.S. Navy is one of the world's great users and abusers of abbreviations. Read a naval message or listen to a staff briefing, and within a very short time you will find yourself in a sea of alphabet soup. Consider this sentence, for instance: "UNODIR, COMDESRON 9 will COMEX at 300700Z AUG using VTF and BD AMMO for all WEPSYS unless CASREP." A seasoned Sailor would be able to translate this message as: "Unless otherwise directed, the commander of destroyer squadron nine will commence the exercise at 7 o'clock in the morning on 30 August using variable time fuze and base detonating ammunition for all weapon systems unless they have been reported as nonfunctioning on a standard Navy casualty report." The brevity is commendable, but if the reader is not a professional Sailor, he or she might not understand much of this message.

The need for help is obvious, and that is exactly where this book comes in. It (and its companion volume, the *Dictionary of Naval Terms*) is written for Navy neophytes who want—indeed need—to be able to understand the language of their new profession. It is also written for outsiders, including, among others, journalists writing stories about the Navy, congressional staffers whose principals serve on naval related subcommittees, and academics studying naval history. Because the Navy has grown so large and so complex, this book is even written for seasoned veterans of the naval profession who, like fluent translators of foreign languages, must still occasionally look up a word to stay in the know.

Unofficial and slang terms are also an important part of naval vocabulary; we have included many of them here. If, for example, a young midshipman is told to avoid PDAs, she might wonder why the Navy is against something so useful as a personal digital assistant. Upon referring to this book, however, she would learn that PDAs stand for "public displays of affection," which her community frowns upon. We have used the qualifier Inf: to identify these terms as "informal." Some of these terms can be rather colorful, so readers are warned in advance that if these terms were movies, they would surely receive a "PG" or an "R" rating.

Because users of this book may come across old terms as well as new, this revision includes both historic and current terminology. But because terms often come and go, because changes within today's Navy are frequent, and because terms used by an organization that is so conscious of its heritage often overlap, it is beyond the scope of this work to determine whether a term is still in use or merely once was. It is hoped that such matters will be discernible in context.

While this *Dictionary of Naval Abbreviations* stands alone as a useful reference tool in "cracking the code" of the Navy's unique language, serious users will do well to avail themselves of (translated purchase) the similarly updated *Dictionary of Naval Terms* as well.

Finally, we acknowledge that creating a book of this type is inherently a subjective process and a giant task. No doubt we have failed on occasion, and some readers will discover that we have inadvertently omitted an important abbreviation, or we have consciously left one out in the interest of space. We submit our apologies in advance for such occurrences. More importantly, though, we encourage readers to help us make this a better resource by nominating other terms to include in the next edition and making suggestions about how we can improve this book. Send your correspondence to *tcutler@usni.org* or to *Deborah Cutler, c/o USNI Dictionaries, 291 Wood Road, Annapolis, MD 21402*.

DICTIONARY *of* NAVAL ABBREVIATIONS

A
Aerology (NAO code)
Annually
Answer
Arctic/Antarctic
Auxiliary

A&E
Analysis and Evaluation

A&I
Alteration and Improvement

A&R
Assembly and Repair

A&T
Acceptance and Transfer

A&WI
Atlantic and West Indies

A2D^{2}
Auxiliary Active Digital Display (sonar)

A-3
Polaris Missile

A/A
Analysis of Accounts
Angle of Attack

AA
Absolute Altitude
Acting Appointment
Active Adjunct
Airman Apprentice
All After
Anti-Aircraft
Anti Aircraft
Arlington Annex

AA&A
Armor, Armament, and Ammunition

AAA
Anti-Aircraft Artillery
Authorized Accounting Activity
Awaiting Aircraft Availability

AAAV
Advanced Amphibious Assault Vehicle

AAB
Aircraft Accident Board
Aviation Armament Bulletin

AABCP
Advanced Airborne Command Post

AABNCP
Advanced Airborne National Command Post

A/AC
Aft Across the Hatch

AAC
Anti-Aircraft Common (projectile)
Alaskan Air Command
Aviation Armament Change

AACS
Automated Access Control System

AADC
Advanced Avionic Digital Computer
Area Air Defense Commander

AADD
Auxiliary Active Digital Display (sonar)

AAE
Ancillary Armament Equipment
Arms, Ammunition, and Explosives

AAF
Atlantic Amphibious Force

AAFSS
Advanced Aerial Fire Support System

AAGP
Acoustic Analysis Guidance Product

AAH
Advanced Attack Helicopter

AAHA
Awaiting Action and Higher Authority

AAHM
Anesthetics and Certain Other Harmful Materials

AAI
Aircraft Accident Investigation
Angle of Approach Indicator

AAIS
Acoustic Automated Information System

AAL
Aircraft Approach Limitations
Aircraft Assignment Letter

AALC
Amphibious Assault Landing Craft

AALS
Acoustic Artillery Location System

AAM
Air-to-Air Missile

AAMG
Anti-Aircraft Machine Gun

AAMREP
Air-to-Air Missile Weapons System Flight Report

AAO
Artillery Air Observer
AUTOVON Assistance Operator

AAOC
Anti-Air Operations Center

AAP
Affirmative Action Plan
Allied Administrative Publication
Allowance Appendix Package
Analyst Assistance Program

AAPP
Affirmative Action Program Plan

AAR
Aircraft Accident Report

AARGM
Advanced Anti-Radiation Guided Missile

AASR
Airport and Airways Surveillance Radar

AATB
Advanced Amphibious Training Base

AATC
Advanced Air Training Command
Anti-Aircraft Training Center

AATRACEN
Anti-Aircraft Training Center

AATS
Armament Auxiliaries Test Set
Automatic Altitude Trim System (helicopters)

AAV
Airborne Assault Vehicle

AAW
Anti-Air Warfare

AAWC
Anti-Air Warfare Center
Anti-Air Warfare Commander

AAWEX
Anti-Air Warfare Exercise

AAWS
Automatic Attack Warning Systems

A/B
Afterburner
Air Blast

AB
Abbreviation
Able-Bodied (seaman)
Aerial Burst (bombs)
Afterburner
Air Base
Air Blast
All Before
Auxiliary Crane Ship
Aviation Boatswain's Mate
Crane Ship
Harbor Launch (USCG)

AB1
Aviation Boatswain's Mate First Class

AB2
Aviation Boatswain's Mate Second Class

AB3
Aviation Boatswain's Mate Third Class

ABAND
Abandoned

ABAR
Advanced Battery Acquisition Radar

ABBR
Abbreviation

ABC
Accounting and Budgetary Control
Advanced Base Components
Advanced Biomedical Capsule
American-British-Canadian
Argentina, Brazil, and Chile
Atomic, Biological, and Chemical (warfare or defense)
Chief Aviation Boatswain's Mate

ABCAIRSTD
American-British-Canadian Air Standardization Agreement

ABCCTC
Advanced Base Combat Communications Training Center

ABCD
Advanced Base Construction Depot

ABCM
Master Chief Aviation Boatswain's Mate

ABCS
Senior Chief Aviation Boatswain's Mate

ABD
Abbreviated Dial
Aboard
Advanced Base Dock
Airborne Division

ABDACOM
Advanced Base Depot Area Command
American, British, Dutch, Australian Command (World War II Pacific Allied command)

ABE
Aviation Boatswain's Mate (Launch and Recovery Equipment)

ABE1
Aviation Boatswain's Mate (Launch and Recovery Equipment) First Class

ABE2
Aviation Boatswain's Mate (Launch and Recovery Equipment) Second Class

ABE3
Aviation Boatswain's Mate (Launch and Recovery Equipment) Third Class

ABEAA
Airman Apprentice Striker for Aviation Boatswain's Mate (Launch and Recovery Equipment)

ABEAN
Airman Striker for Aviation Boatswain's Mate (Launch and Recovery Equipment)

ABEC
Chief Aviation Boatswain's Mate (Launch and Recovery Equipment)

ABECM
Master Chief Aviation Boatswain's Mate (Launch and Recovery Equipment)

ABECS
Senior Chief Aviation Boatswain's Mate (Launch and Recovery Equipment)

ABF
Aviation Boatswain's Mate (Fuels)

ABF1
Aviation Boatswain's Mate (Fuels) First Class

ABF2
Aviation Boatswain's Mate (Fuels) Second Class

ABF3
Aviation Boatswain's Mate (Fuels) Third Class

ABFAA
Aviation Boatswain's Mate (Fuels) Airman Apprentice

ABFAN
Aviation Boatswain's Mate (Fuels) Airman

ABFC
Chief Aviation Boatswain's Mate (Fuels)
Advanced Base Functional Components

ABFCM
Master Chief Aviation Boatswain's Mate (Fuels)

ABFCS
Senior Chief Aviation Boatswain's Mate (Fuels)

ABH
Above Burst Height
Aviation Boatswain's Mate (Aircraft Handling)

ABH1
Aviation Boatswain's Mate (Aircraft Handling) First Class

ABH2
Aviation Boatswain's Mate (Aircraft Handling) Second Class

ABH3
Aviation Boatswain's Mate (Aircraft Handling) Third Class

ABHAA
Aviation Boatswain's Mate (Aircraft Handling) Airman Apprentice

ABHAN
Aviation Boatswain's Mate (Aircraft Handling) Airman

ABHC
Chief Aviation Boatswain's Mate (Aircraft Handling)

ABHCM
Master Chief Aviation Boatswain's Mate (Aircraft Handling)

ABHCS
Senior Chief Aviation Boatswain's Mate (Aircraft Handling)

ABI
Aviation Billet Indicator

ABIOL
Advanced Base Initial Outfitting List

ABISL
Advanced Base Initial Support List

ABL
Above Base Line
Allocated Base Line
Automated Biological Laboratory

ABM
Anti-Ballistic Missile

ABN
Aerodrome Beacon
Airborne
VA/VAH Bombardier/Navigator (code)

ABOOW
Assistant Battalion Officer Of the Watch

ABPA
Advanced Base Personnel Administration

ABPG
Advanced Base Proving Ground

ABPO
Advanced Base Personnel Officer

ABPU
Advanced Base Personnel Unit

ABR
Additional Billet Requirements
Amphibian Boat Reconnaissance

ABRB
Advanced Base Receiving Barracks

ABRD
Advanced Based Receiving Depot

ABRES
Advanced Ballistics Reentry System

ABS
Absolute
Acrylonitrile Butadiene Styrene

ABSAP
Airborne Search and Attack Plotter

ABSD
Advanced Base Sectional Dock
Advanced Base Supply Depot

ABSLA
Approved Basic Stock Level of Ammunition

ABSTEE
Absentee

ABT
About

ABTF
Airborne Task Force

ABTU
Advanced Base Training Unit

ABUT
Abutment

ABV
Above

(AC)
Suffix added to an enlisted rate that indicates the individual is qualified as an Aircrewman.

A/C
Account
Air Conditioning
Aircraft

AC
Active Component
Adopted Child
Aircraft
Aircraft Commander
Airframe Change
Air Traffic Controller
Alternating Current
Altocumulus
Amphibious Corps
Atlas Centaur (rocket)

AC&I
Acquisition, Construction and Improvement

AC&W
Air Communications and Weather

AC1
Air Traffic Controlman First Class

AC2
Air Traffic Controlman Second Class

AC3
Air Traffic Controlman Third Class

ACA
Airlift Clearance Authority
Awaiting Combat Assignment

ACAA
Air Traffic Controlman Airman Apprentice

ACAD
Academy

ACAD CL YR
Academy Class Year

ACAL
Aircraft Configuration Allowance List

ACAN
Air Traffic Controlman Airman

ACAPS
Automated Costing and Planning System

ACAS
Aircraft Collision Avoidance System

ACAT
Acquisition Category

ACB
Amphibious Construction Battalion

ACBD
Active Commission Base Date

ACBWS
Automatic Chemical-Biological Warning System

ACC
Chief Air Controlman
Area Control Center
Accounting Category Code
Accumulation
Air Center Commander
Alternate Command Center
Altocumulus Castellanus (cloud formation)
Antarctic Circumpolar Current
Aural Comprehension Course
Automatic Chroma Control
Automatic Combustion Control

ACCB
Airframe Change Control Board

ACCESS
Afloat Cost Consumption Effectiveness Surveillance System
Automatic Computer Controlled Electronic Scanning System

ACCF
Area Communications Control Function

ACC/FWC
Automatic Combustion Control and Feedwater Control

ACCGAT
Accumulator Gating (NSSS)

ACCHAN
Allied Command Channel

ACCIS
Alpha Command and Control Information System (NATO)

ACCM
Master Chief Air Controlman

ACCS
Senior Chief Air Controlman

ACCT
Account

ACCTG
Accounting

ACCY
Accessory

ACD
Administrative Commitment Document
Advanced Copies Delivered
Aviation Commission Date

ACDA
Aviation Combat Development Agency

ACDIFDEN
Active duty in a flying status not involving flying

ACDIFDENIS
Active duty under instruction in a flying status involving operational or training flights

ACDIFINSPRO
Active duty under instruction in a flying

status involving proficiency flying

ACDIFNOPS
Active duty under instruction in a flying status involving operational or training flights

ACDIFOPS
Active duty in a flying status involving operational or training flights

ACDIFOTCREW
Active duty in a flying status involving operational or training flights as a crewmember

ACDIFOTINSNONCREW
Active duty under instruction in a flying status involving operational or training flights as a non-crewmember

ACDIFOTNONCREW
Active duty in a flying status involving operational or training flights as a non-crewmember

ACDIFPRO
Active duty in a flying status involving proficiency flying

ACDIV
Assault Craft Division

ACDO
Assistant Command Duty Officer

ACDT
Accident

ACDU
Active Duty

ACDUINS
Active Duty Under Instruction

ACDUOBLI
Active Duty Obligation

ACDUTRA
Active Duty for Training

ACE
Activity Civil Engineer
Aircraft Condition Evaluation
Allied Command, Europe
Atmospheric Control Experimentation
Automatic Checkout Equipment

ACEL
Aerospace Crew Equipment Laboratory

ACEORP
Automotive and Construction Equipment Overhaul and Repair Plant

ACEPD
Automotive and Construction Equipment Parts Depot

ACEUR
Allied Command, Europe

ACFAT
Aircraft Carrier Firefighting Assistance Team

ACFEL
Arctic Construction and Frost Effects Laboratory

ACFT
Aircraft

ACG
Airborne Coordinating Group

ACGM
Aircraft Carrier General Memorandum

ACHO
Aircraft Handlng Officer

ACI
Allocated Confirmation Identification

ACIM
Axis Crossing Interval Meter

ACINT
Acoustic Intelligence

ACIP
Aviation Career Incentive Pay

ACIS
Aeronautical Chart and Information Squadron
Automated Claims Information System

ACK
Acknowledge

ACKN
Acknowledge

ACL
Aeronautical Computer Laboratory
Aircraft Circular Letter
Automatic Carrier Landing

ACLANT
Allied Command, Atlantic

ACLS
Air Cushion Landing System
All-Weather Carrier Landing System
Automatic Carrier Landing System

ACM
Accumulator
Additional Crewmembers
Air Combat Maneuver
Drill Minelaying and Recovery Vessel

ACMI
Air Combat Maneuvering Instrumentation

ACMPM
Analytic Countered Minefield Planning Model

ACMR
Air Combat Maneuvering Range

ACMS
Automated Career Management System

ACN
Activity Control Number
Advance Change Notice

ACNO
Assistant Chief of Naval Operations

ACNO(COMM)/DNC
Assistant Chief of Naval Operations (Communications)/Director, Naval Communications

ACO
Administrative Contracting Officer
Attack Cut-Out

ACOB
Actual Current on Board (status)

ACOC
Area Communications Operations Center (DCS)
Automatic Control Operations Center

ACOCC
Atlantic Fleet Commander Operational Control Center

ACOFS
Assistant Chief of Staff

ACOG
Aircraft on Ground

ACOM
Area Cutover Manager

ACP
Airlift Command Post
Allied Communications Publication
Area Coordinating Paper

ACPT
Accept

ACPY
Accompany

ACR
Advanced Capabilities Radar
Aircraft Control Room
Airlift Control Radar
Allowance Change Request
Anti-Circular Run
Approach Control Radar

ACRE
Automatic Checkout and Readiness Equipment

ACRN
Accounting Classification Reference Number

ACRS
Across
Advisory Committee on Reactor Safeguards

ACS
Air Capable Ship
Assistant Chief of Staff
Auxiliary Crane Ship

ACSAP
Automated Cross-Section Analysis Program

ACS/FOR
Assistant Chief of Staff/Force Development

ACSI
Assistant Chief of Staff for Intelligence

ACSR
Aluminum Conductors, Steel-Reinforced

ACSS
Antilles Consolidated School System

ACT
Acting
Action
Active
Activity
Aircraft Commander Time
American College Test
Aviation Classification Test

ACTC
Air Combat Training Continuum

ACT/CONV
Activation/Conversion

ACTD
Advanced Concept Technology Demonstration

ACTDU
Active Duty

ACTDUTRA
Active Duty Training

ACTG
Advanced Carrier Training Group

ACTH
Arbitrary Correction to Hit

ACT/IC
Active/In Commission (vessel status)

ACT/IS
Active/In Service (vessel status)

ACT/OC
Active/Out of Commission (vessel status)

ACT/OS
Active/Out of Service (vessel status)

ACTREP
Activities Reporting (shipping)

ACTY
Activity

ACU
Academic Credit Unit
Armament Control Unit
Assault Craft Unit

ACV
Air Cushion Vehicle
Aviation General Purpose Ship

ACW
Anti-Carrier Warfare
Automated Keyed Continuous Wave

A/D
Acceptance and Delivery
Aerodrome
Analog-to-Digital

AD
Active Duty
Acoustic Decoupler
Aerodrome
Aircraft Depth (bomb)
Air Defense
Air Depot
Air-Start Diesel Engine
Aviation Machinist's Mate
Destroyer Tender

AD&C
Ammunition Distribution and Control

AD1
Aviation Machinist's Mate First Class

AD2
Aviation Machinist's Mate Second Class

AD3
Aviation Machinist's Mate Third Class

ADA
Active Duty Agreement
Actual Arrival Date
Advisory Area
Airborne Data Automation
Automatic Data Analyzer

ADAA
Aviation Machinist's Mate Airman Apprentice

ADAC
Acoustic Data Analysis Center

ADAKSARCOORD
Coast Guard Search and Rescue Coordinator, Adak (AK)

ADAL
Authorized Dental Allowance List

ADALCON
Advise All Concerned

ADAN
Aviation Machinist's Mate Airman

ADAP
Active Duty Assistance Program
Analog-Digital Automatic Program

ADAPTS
Air Deliverable Anti-Pollution Transfer System

ADAR
Advanced Design Array Radar

ADARCO
Advise date of reporting in compliance with these orders

ADAS
Automatic Data Acquisition System

Auxiliary Data Annotation Set

ADATS
Automated Data and Telecommunications Service (GSA)

ADAWS
Action Data Automation Weapons System

A-Day
Announcement Day

ADBD
Active Duty Base Date

ADC
Air Data Computer
Air Defense Capable
Air Defense Command
Assistant Defense Counsel
Automated Data Collection
Chief Aviation Machinist's Mate

ADCAD
Airways Data Collection and Dissemination

ADCAP
Advanced Capability

ADCASHAL
Advance Cash Allowance Authorized

ADCC
Air Defense Control Center

ADCEP
Advanced Structural Concept and Evaluation Program

ADCM
Master Chief Aviation Machinist's Mate

ADCNO
Assistant Deputy Chief of Naval Operations

ADCNO(CP/EEO)
Assistant Deputy Chief of Naval Operations (Civilian Personnel/Equal Employment Opportunity)

ADCOM
Administrative Command

ADCON
Advise All Concerned

ADCONSEN
With the Advice and Consent of the Senate

ADCOP
Associate Degree Completion Program

ADCS
Advanced Defense Communications System
Senior Chief Aviation Machinist's Mate

ADCSP
Advanced Defense Communications Satellite Program

ADCX
Auxiliary Dry Cargo Ship

ADD
Addition
Additional

ADDAS
Automatic Digital Data Assembly System

ADDC
Air Defense Direction Center

ADDEE
Addressee

ADDL
Additional
Aircraft Dummy Deck Landing

ADDN
Addition
Additional

ADDPLA
(And) to such additional places as may be necessary

ADDS
Advanced Data Display System
Air Development Delivery System

ADDU
Additional Duty

ADD UNIF ALW
Additional Uniform Allowance

ADE
Aircraft Data Entry

ADEE
Addressee

ADF
Automatic Direction Finder
Auxiliary Detonating Fuze

ADG
Degaussing Ship

ADI
Altitude-Direction Indicator
Area of Dominant Influence

ADIS
Automatic Data Interchange System

ADIU
Airborne Data Insertion Unit

ADIZ
Air Defense Identification Zone

ADJ
Adjusted
Adjutant

ADJ1
Aviation Machinist's Mate Jet Engine Mechanic First Class

ADJ2
Aviation Machinist's Mate Jet Engine Mechanic Second Class

ADJ3
Aviation Machinist's Mate Jet Engine Mechanic Third Class

ADJAA
Aviation Machinist's Mate Jet Engine Mechanic Airman Apprentice

ADJAN
Aviation Machinist's Mate Jet Engine Mechanic Airman

ADJC
Chief Aviation Machinist's Mate Jet Engine Mechanic

ADJG
Adjutant General

ADJ/PPR
Adjusted/Permanent Pay Record

ADJ/RCT
Adjusted/Reviewed Copy of Temporary Pay Record

ADJT
Adjutant

ADJ/TDA
Adjusted/Transcript Deserter's Account

ADL
Advance Distributed Learning
Armament Data List
Armament Datum Line
Authorized Data List

ADLS
Air Dispatch Letter Service

ADM
Acquisition Decision Memorandum
Admiral
Atomic Demolition Munition

ADMAT
Administrative-Material (inspection)

ADMIN
Administration
Administrative

ADMINO
Administrative Officer

ADMINSUPPU
Administrative Support Unit

ADMIRE
Automated Diagnostic Maintenance Information Retrieval

ADMIT
Aeronautical Depot Maintenance Industrial Technology

ADMRL
Applications Data for Material Readiness List

ADMS
Automatic Digital Message-Switching

ADMSC
Automatic Digital Message-Switching Center

ADMSG
Advise by Electronically-Transmitted Message

ADNOMOVPEN
Advised not to move dependents until suitable quarters located

ADNS
Automated Digital Network System

ADO
Advanced Development Objective
Associated Disbursing Officer

ADP
Acceptance Data Package
Air Defense Position

Air Delivery Platoon
Alternative Defense Posture
Automated Data Processing
Automatic Deletion Procedure

ADPBUD
Automatic Data Processing Budget

ADPE
Automatic Data Processing Equipment

ADPESO
Automatic Data Processing Equipment Selection Office

ADPM
Automatic Data Processing Machine

ADP/MIS
Automatic Data Processing/Management Information System

ADPPRS
Automatic Data Processing Program Reporting System (DOD)

ADPRES
Automatic Data Processing Program Reporting System

ADPS
Automatic Data Processing System

ADPSO
Automatic Data Processing Selection Office

ADPTOS
Automatic Data Processing Tactical Operation System

ADR
Advisory Route
Aeronautical Directive Requirements
Aircraft Direction Room
Aircraft Directive Requirements
Aircraft Discrepancy Report
Applied Data Research
Arrival Discrepancy Report

ADR1
Aviation Machinist's Mate Reciprocating Engine Mechanic First Class

ADR2
Aviation Machinist's Mate Reciprocating Engine Mechanic Second Class

ADR3
Aviation Machinist's Mate Reciprocating Engine Mechanic Third Class

ADRAA
Aviation Machinist's Mate Reciprocating Engine Mechanic Airman Apprentice

ADRAN
Aviation Machinist's Mate Reciprocating Engine Mechanic Airman

ADRC
Aviation Machinist's Mate Reciprocating Engine Mechanic

ADRNBN
Aerodrome Beacon

ADS
Accelerated Declassification Schedule
Advanced Declassification Schedule
Advanced Deployable System
Advanced Diving System
Aegis Display System
Air Defense Section
Assault Data System
Audio Distribution System

ADSC
Automatic Data Service Center

ADSD
Active Duty Service Date

ADSOC
Administrative Support Operations Center

ADSPO
Automatic Data Processing Selection Office

ADSTADIS
Advise Status and/or Disposition

ADSTAP
Advancement, Strength, and Training Planning

ADSUP
Automated Data Systems Uniform Practices

ADSW
Active Duty for Special Work

ADT
Active Duty Training
Amphibious Training Demonstrator
Automatic Detection and Tracking

ADTAKE
Advise Action Taken

ADTU
Auxiliary Data Translator Unit

ADU
Accumulation Distribution Unit
Aircraft Delivery Unit

ADV
Advance
Advanced

ADVAILTRANS
Advise appropriate command having cognizance of transportation when available for transportation

ADVAILTRANSCONUS
Advise appropriate command having cognizance of transportation when available for transportation to Continental Limits of the United States

ADVAILTRANSPOE
Advice (command designated) date available for transportation from port of embarkation

ADVAL
Advise availability

ADV-BR
Advanced Branch (training)

ADVCHG
Advance Change

ADVHED
Advance Headquarters

ADV/L
Advance Leave

ADVN
Advanced

ADV/P
Advanced Pay

ADVS
Advises

ADVSCOL
Advanced School

ADVSY
Advisory

ADVY
Advisory

ADWS
Automated Digital Weather Switch

AE
Ammunition Ship
Availability of Equipment
Aviation Electrician's Mate

AE1
Aviation Electrician's Mate First Class

AE2
Aviation Electrician's Mate Second Class

AE3
Aviation Electrician's Mate Third Class

AEA
Airborne Electronic Attack (aircraft)

AEAA
Aviation Electrician's Mate Airman Apprentice

AEAN
Aviation Electrician's Mate Airman

AEB
Air, Emergency Breathing

AEC
Atomic Energy Commission
Automated Electronic Classroom
Chief Aviation Electrician's Mate

AECC
Aeromedical Evacuation Control Center

AECL
Aircraft and Equipment Configuration List

AECM
Master Chief Aviation Electrician's Mate

AECS
Senior Chief Aviation Electrician's Mate

AED
Assurance Engineering Division

AEDA
Ammunition, Explosives, and Other Dangerous Articles

AEEL
Aeronautical and Electronic Engineering Laboratory

AEF
Advanced Electronics Field

AEFF
Assurance Engineering Field Facility

AEG
Active Element Group
Aeromedical Evaluation Group

AEI
Aerial Exposure Index

AEL
Allowance Equipage List
Small Ammunition Ship

AELW
Airborne Electronics Warfare (course)

AEM
Missile Support Ship

AEM AoA
Airborne Electronic Attack Analysis of Alternatives

AEN
Advance Evaluation Notice

AEO
Air Electronics Officer
Air Engineering Officer

AEOB
Advanced Engine Overhaul Base

AEOS
Aft Engineering Operating Station

AEP
Average-Evoked Potentials

AEPS
Aircraft Escape Propulsion System

AER
Aeronautics
Alteration Equivalent to Repair

AERC
Aircraft Engine Record Card

AERO
Aerographer
Aeronautical

AEROF
Aerological Officer

AEROG
Aerologist

AEROMED
Aeromedical
Aeromedicine

AERO R BN
Aeronautical Radio Beacon

AERO R RGE
Aeronautical Radio Range

AERP
Advanced Equipment Repair Program

AERREFRON
Aerial Refueling Squadron

AERS
Aircraft Equipment Requirement Schedule

AES
Advanced Encryption Standard

AESA
Active Electronically Scanned Array

AESC
Automatic Electronic Switching Center

AESR
Aeronautical Equipment Service Record

AEW
Airborne Early-Warning
Airborne Electronic Warfare

AEW/C
Airborne Early-Warning and Control

AEWRON
Fleet Air Reconnaissance Squadron

AEWS
Advanced Electronic Warfare System

AEX
Agreement to Extend Enlistment

AF
Air Force
Anti-Fouling (paint)
Audio Frequency
Automatic Following (radar)
Stores Ship

AF&S
Administrative and Financial Services

AFAADS
Advanced Forward Area Air Defense System

AFAITC
Armed Forces Air Intelligence Training Center

AFAVC
Atlantic Fleet Audio-Visual Center

AF/B
After Bulkhead in Hatch

AFB
Airframe Bulletin

AFC
Airframe Change
Automatic Frequency Control

AFCE
Automatic Flight Control Equipment

AFCM
Master Chief Aircraft Maintenanceman

AFCS
Adaptive (or Automatic) Flight-Control System

AFDB
Large Auxiliary Floating Drydock (Non-Self-Propelled)

AFDCB
Armed Forces Disciplinary Control Board

AFDK
After Dark

AFDL
Small Auxiliary Floating Drydock

AFDL(C)
Small Auxiliary Floating Drydock (Concrete)

AFDM
Medium Auxiliary Floating Drydock

AFDO
Assistant Fighter Direction Office

AFDS
Amphibious Force Data System
Auxiliary Fighter Director Ship

AF/E
After End of the Hatch

AFEB
Armed Forces Epidemiological Board

AFEM
Armed Forces Expeditionary Medal

AFES
Armed Forces Exchange Service

AFFD
Affirmed

AFFF
Aqueous Film-Forming Foam

AFFIRM
Affirmative

AFGU
Aerial Free Gunnery Unit

AFHPSP
Armed Forces Health Professional Scholarship Program

AFI
African-Indian (Ocean regional area)

AFIL
AMVER (Automated Mutual-Assistance Vessel Rescue) File

AFINSPATH
Armed Forces Institute of Pathology

AFIO
Agreement for Fighter Interceptor Operations

AFIP
Armed Forces Information Program
Armed Forces Institute of Pathology

AFJ
Armed Forces Journal (publication)

AFO
Artillery Forward Observer

AFOE
Assault Follow-On Echelon

AFOSS
Aviation Fuel Operational Sequencing Systems

AFP
Air Force Pamphlet
Armed Forces Police

AFPCB
Armed Forces Pest Control Board

AFPD
Armed Forces Police Department
Armed Forces Police Detachment

AFPDS
Armed Forces Production Distribution Service

AFPR
Armed Forces Procurement Regulations

AFQT
Armed Forces Qualification Test

AFR
Aircraft Flight Record

AFRADBIORSCHINST
Armed Forces Radiobiology Research Institute

A-Frame
A-Shaped Hydraulic Device for Overboarding Equipment

AFRBA
Armed Forces Relief and Benefit Association

AFRRI
Armed Forces Radiobiology Research Institute

AFRS
Automatic Flight Reference System

AFRSF
Atlantic Fleet Range Support Facility

AFRT
Armed Forces Radio and Television

AFRTS
Armed Forces Radio and Television Service

AFS
Combat Store Ship

AFSA
American Flagship Available

AFSC
Armed Forces Staff College

AFSSC
Armed Forces Supply Support Center

AFSTAFFCOL
Armed Forces Staff College

AFSU
Auxiliary Ferry Service Unit

AFSWP
Armed Forces Special Weapons Project

AFT
After

AFTA
Advanced First-Term Avionics

AFTI
Advanced Fighter Technology Integrator

AFTN
Aeronautical Fixed Telecommunications Network
Afternoon

AFW
Auxiliary Fresh Water

AFWA
Air Force Weather Agency

AFWL
Armed Forces Writers' League

AFWR
Atlantic Fleet Weapons Range

AFWST
Armed Forces Women's Selection Test

AFWTF
Atlantic Fleet Weapons Training Facility

AFY
Air Facility

A-G
Arresting Gear

A/G
Air-to-Ground (communications)

AG
Aerographer's Mate
Air Group
Armed Guard
General Auxiliary Ship
Miscellaneous Ship

AG1
Aerographer's Mate First Class

AG2
Aerographer's Mate Second Class

AG3
Aerographer's Mate Third Class

A/G/A
Air/Ground/Air

AGAA
Aerographer's Mate Airman Apprentice

AGACS
Automatic Ground-to-Air Communications System

AGAFBO
Atlantic and Gulf American Flag Berthing Operations

AGAN
Aerographer's Mate Airman

AGB
Icebreaker

AGBT
Airborne Expendable Bathythermograph Sonobuoy

AGC
Armed Guard Center
Automatic Gain Control
Chief Aerographer's Mate

AGCA
Automatic Ground-Controlled Approach

AGCL
Small Communications Ship

AGCM
Master Chief Aerographer's Mate

AGCS
Senior Chief Aerographer's Mate

AGCY
Agency

AGD
Attack Geometry Display
Axial Gear Differential
Seagoing Dredge

AGD/CSD
Axial Gear Differential/Constant-Speed Drive

AGDE
Auxiliary General Destroyer Escort
Escort Research Ship

AGDS
Deep Submergence Support Ship

AGE
Aerospace Ground Equipment
Automatic Ground Equipment

A-GEAR
Arresting Gear

AGEH
Hydrofoil Research Ship

AGER
Environmental Research Ship

AGF
Miscellaneous Command Ship

AGFCS
Automatic Gunfire Control System

AGFF
Auxiliary General Frigate
Frigate Research Ship

AGF/LCC
Amphibious Command Ship

AGFSRS
Aircraft Ground Fire Suppression and Rescue Systems

AGHS
Hydrofoil Research Ship

AGI
Adjutant General Inspection
Intelligence Collector (ship)

AGIC
Automatically-Generated Integrated Circuit

AGIO
Armed Guard Inspection Officer

AGIS
Armed Guard Inspection Service

AGL
Above Ground Level
Lighthouse Tender

AGM
Air-to-Ground Missile
Alternative Generator Model
Missile Range Instrumentation Ship

AGMR
Major Communications Relay Ship

AGN
Again

AGO
Air Gunnery Officer

AGOE
Advisory Group for Ocean Engineering (SNAME)

AGOR
Oceanographic Research Ship

AGOS
Air-Ground Operations School
Air Gunnery Officers School
Ocean Surveillance Ship

AGP
Motor Torpedo Boat Tender
Patrol Craft Tender

AGR
Air-to-Ground Ranging

AGS
Advanced Gun System
Alternating Gradient Synchrotron
Armed Guard School
Surveying Ship

AGSS
Auxiliary Research Submarine

AGT
Adage Graphics Terminal
Agent
Target Service Ship

AGTR
Adage Graphics Terminal
Technical Research Ship

AGY
Agency

A/H
Alter Heading

AH
Attack Heavy
Hospital Ship

AHD
Advanced Helicopter Development

AHP
Air, High Pressure
Evacuation Hospital Ship

AHRRN
Automatic Hydrologic Radio Reporting Network

AHRS
Altitude-Heading-Reference System

AHT
Acoustic Homing Torpedo

AI
Airborne Interceptor
Air Intelligence
Automated Instruction
Automatic Input
Awaiting Instruction

AIA
Action Item Assignment

AIB
Aircraft Instrument Bulletin

AIC
Advanced Intelligence Center
Airborne Intercept Control
Air Intercept Control

AICEM
Anti-Intercontinental Ballistic Missile

AICO
Action Information Control Officer

AICS
Advanced Interior Communications System
Air Intercept Control School

AIDE
Adapted Identification Decision Equipment

AIDJEX
Arctic Ice Dynamics Joint Experiment

AIDO
Air Intelligence Duty Officer

AIDS
Airborne Integrated Data Systems

AIE
Authorized in Excess

AIETA
Airborne Infrared Equipment for Target Analysis

AIEWS
Advanced Integrated Electronic Warefare System

AIF
Air Intelligence Force

AIFI
Automatic In-Flight Insertion

AIG
Address Indicator Group

AIG(A)
Assistant Inspector General for Auditing

AIL
Airborne Instrument Laboratory
Artificial Intelligence Laboratory (MIT)

AILAS
Automatic Instrument Landing Approach System

AILSS
Advanced Integrated Life-Support System

AIM
Advanced Induction Motors

AIMACO
Air Material Command

AIMD
Aircraft Intermediate Maintenance Department

AIMS
Air Traffic Control, Radar Beacon System, IFF, Military Secure System
American Institute of Merchant Shipping

AIMSO
Aircraft Intermediate Maintenance Support Office

AINO
Assistant Inspector of Naval Ordnance

AIO
Action Information Organization
Air Intelligence Officer

AIP
Aeronautical Information Publication
Anti-Surface Warfare Improvement Program
Aviation Indoctrination Program

AIR
Aircraft Inventory Record
Aviation Item Report

AIRACLIS
Air Activities Logistic Information Center

AIRAD
Airman Advisory

AIRANTISUBRON
Air Antisubmarine Squadron

AIRANTISUBRONDET
Air Antisubmarine Squadron Detachment

AIRARMUNIT
Aircraft Armament Unit

AIRCON
Automatic Information and Reservations Computer-Oriented Network

AIRDEFCOM
Air Defense Commander

AIRDEVRON
Air Development Squadron

AIRELO
Air Electrical Officer

AIREO
Air Engineering Officer

AIREP
Air Reports in Plain Language

AIREVACWING
Air Evacuation Wing

AIRFAC
Air Facility

AIRFAM
Aircraft Familiarization

AIRFERRON
Aircraft Ferry Squadron

AIRIS
Air-Stores-Issuing Ship

AIRLANT
Air Forces, Atlantic Fleet

AIRLMAINT
Airline-Like Maintenance

AIRMET
Airmen's Meteorological (condition)

AIRMG
Aircraft Machine Gunner

AIROPS
Air Operations

AIRPAC
Air Forces, Pacific Fleet

AIRSUPPTRAU
Air Support Training Unit

AIRTEVRON
Air Test and Evaluation Squadron

AIRTEVRONDET
Air Test and Evaluation Squadron Detachment

AIRTRANSRON
Air Transport Squadron

AIRTRARON
Air Training Squadron

AIS
Accelerated Inspection System
Advanced Information System
Aeronautical Information Service
Air Intelligence Service
Automated Information System

AISV
Amphibious Infantry-Support Vehicle

AIT
Autogenous Ignition Temperature

AITC
Action Training Information Center

AJ
Anti-Jamming
Applied Journalism (DINFOS department)
Attack Jet

AJA
Adjacent

AJCC
Alternate Joint Communication Center

AJTWC
Alternate Joint Typhoon Warning Center

AK
Aviation Storekeeper
Cargo Ship

AK1
Aviation Storekeeper First Class

AK2
Aviation Storekeeper Second Class

AK3
Aviation Storekeeper Third Class

AKA
Also Known As

AKAA
Aviation Storekeeper Airman Apprentice

AKAN
Aviation Storekeeper Airman

AKB
Auxiliary Cargo Barge
Auxiliary Cargo Lighter Ship

AKC
Chief Aviation Storekeeper

AKCM
Master Chief Aviation Storekeeper

AKCS
Senior Chief Aviation Storekeeper

AKD
Cargo Ship, Dock

AKF
Auxiliary Cargo Float-On/Float-Off
Refrigerated Cargo Ship

AK-FBM
Polaris Cargo Resupply Ship

AKL
Light Cargo Ship

AKN
Net Cargo Ship
Non-Mechanized Artillery Transport

AKR
Vehicle Cargo Ship

AKS
Stores-Issue Ship

AKSS
Cargo Submarine

AKV
Aircraft Ferry

A/L
Air Liaison

AL
Acquisition Logistician
Air Liaison
Approach and Landing (charts)
Arrival Locator
Lightship

ALAIRC
Alaskan Air Command

ALAM
Advanced Land-Attack Missile

ALARM
Alerting Long-Range Airborne Radar for Moving Targets

ALARR
Air-Launched Acoustical Reconnaissance

ALBI
Air-Launched Ballistic Intercept
Air-Launched Boost Intercept

ALBM
Air-Launched Ballistic Missile

ALC
Airborne Launch Control
American Language Course
Automatic Level Control

ALCAPP
Automatic List Classification and Profile Production

ALCC
Airborne Launch Control Center

ALCEP
AUTOSERVCOM Life Cycle Extension Program

ALCOM
Algebraic Complier
All Commands

ALCOMLANT
All Commands, Atlantic

ALCOMPAC
All Commands, Pacific

ALCON
All Concerned

ALCOR
ARPA/Lincoln Labs C-band Observable Radar

ALCPT
American Language College Placement Test

ALCS
Automatic Launch Control System

ALDP
Advanced Leadership Development Program

ALDPS
Automated Logistic Data Processing System

ALERTS
Airborne Laser Electronic Real-Time Surveillance

ALF
Aloft
Auxiliary Landing Field

ALFS
Advanced Low Frequency Sonar

ALG
Along

ALL/LL QTY
Allowance or Load List Quality

ALLOW
Allowance

ALLSTAT
All-Purpose Statistical Package

ALMAR
All Marine

ALMB
Air-Launched Missile Ballistics

ALMC
Air-Launched Missile Changes

ALMDS
Airborne Laser Mine Detection System

ALMILACT
All Military Activities

ALN
Ammunition Lot Number

ALNAV
All Navy

ALNAVSTA
All Naval Stations

ALNN
Air-Launched Non-Nuclear (ordnance)

ALNOT
Alert Notice

ALNW
Air-Launched Nuclear Weapon

ALO
Air Liaison Officer

ALOC
Allocate

ALOFT
Airborne Light Optical Fiber Technology

ALOT
Allotment

ALOTMT
Allotment

ALOTS
Airborne Lightweight Optical Tracking System

ALP
Air Liaison Party
Air, Low-Pressure
Automated Learning Process

ALPA
Airline Pilots Association

ALPEC
Ammunition Loading Production Engineering Center

ALPS
Automated Leave and Pay System

Automated Library Processing Services
Automated Linear Programming System

ALPURCOMS
All-Purpose Communication System

ALRE
Aircraft Launch and Recovery Equipment

ALREMP
Aircraft Launch and Recovery Equipment Maintenance Program

ALREP
Air-Launched Report
Analysis and Evaluation Report

ALRI
Airborne Long-Range Input

ALRT
Time-Ordered Alerts (NNSS)

ALS
Advanced Logistics System
Approach Lighting System
Automatic Landing System
Auxiliary Lighter Ship

ALSAM
Air-Launched Ship-Attack Missile

ALSEAFRON
Alaskan Sea Frontier

ALSEC
Alaskan Sector

ALSTACON
All Stations Continental (United States)

ALSTG
Altimeter Setting

ALT
Administrative Lead Time
Alteration/Improvement Proposal
Alterations
Alternate
Altimeter
Altitude

ALTAC
Algebraic Translator-Compiler

ALTAIR
ARPA Long-Range Tracking and Instrumentation Radar

ALTCOMLANT
Alternate Commander, Atlantic

ALTCOMLANTFLT
Alternate Commander, Atlantic Fleet

ALTFFL
Alternating Fixed and Flashing (light)

ALTFGFL
Alternating Fixed and Group-Flashing (light)

ALTFL
Alternating Flashing (light)

ALTGPOCC
Alternating Group-Occulting (light)

ALTN
Alternate

ALT PROG
Alternate Program

ALTRAN
Algebraic Translator

ALTREV
Altitude Reservation

ALTRV
Altitude Reservation

ALU
Arithmetic Logic Unit

ALUSLO
American Legation, United States Naval Liaison Officer

ALUSNA
American Legation, United States Naval Attaché

ALUSNOB
American Legation, United States Naval Observer

ALW
Allowance

ALWT
Advanced Lightweight Torpedo

A-M
Active Mariner

AM
Acquisition Manager
Air Medal
America
American
Amplitude Modulation

Ampoule
Aviation Structural Mechanic
Ocean Minesweeper

AMA
Air Material Area
ASROC Missile Assembly

AMAC
Aircraft Monitor and Control

AMAD
Aircraft Mounted Accessory Drive

AMAL
Authorized Medical Allowance List

AMAL/ADAL
Authorized Medical Allowance List/Authorized Dental Allowance List

AMAS
Advanced Mid-Course Active System

AMASCP
Air Material Area Stock Control Point

AMB
Aircraft Mishap Board
Ambulance
Armament Material Bulletin

AMC
Activity Mission Code
Air Mail Center
Armament Material Change
Atlantic Marine Center (NOAA)
Automatic Maneuvering Control
Aviation Maintenance Costs
Chief Aviation Structural Mechanic

AMCM
Airborne Mine Countermeasures
Master Chief Aviation Structural Mechanic

AMCS
Airborne Missile Control System
Senior Chief Aviation Structural Mechanic

AMD
Aircraft Maintenance Department
Air Movement Designator
Air Movement Directive
Aviation Maintenance Department

AMDAR
Aircraft Meteorological Data Relay

AMDO
Aeronautical Maintenance Duty Officer

AMDP
Aircraft Mmaintenance Delayed for Parts

AME
Angle-Measuring Equipment
Aviation Medical Examiner
Aviation Structural Mechanic (Safety Equipment)

AME1
Aviation Structural Mechanic (Safety Equipment) First Class

AME2
Aviation Structural Mechanic (Safety Equipment) Second Class

AME3
Aviation Structural Mechanic (Safety Equipment) Third Class

AMEAA
Aviation Structural Mechanic (Safety Equipment) Airman Apprentice

AMEAN
Aviation Structural Mechanic (Safety Equipment) Airman

AMEB
American Embassy

AMEC
Chief Aviation Structural Mechanic (Safety Equipment)

AMEND
Amendment

AMER
America
American

AMFAR
A Mulifunction S-band Array Radar

AMFINFOS
American Forces Information Service

AMFSV
Auxiliary Mobile Fuel-Storage Vessel

AMFUR
Amplified Failure and Unsatisfactory Report

AMG
Acquisition Management Guide

Aircraft Machine Gunner

AMGA
Award of Merit for Group Achievement

AMH
Aviation Structural Mechanic (Hydraulics)

AMH1
Aviation Structural Mechanic (Hydraulics) First Class

AMH2
Aviation Structural Mechanic (Hydraulics) Second Class

AMH3
Aviation Structural Mechanic (Hydraulics) Third Class

AMHAA
Aviation Structural Mechanic (Hydraulics) Airman Apprentice

AMHAN
Aviation Structural Mechanic (Hydraulics) Airman

AMHAZ
Ammunition and Hazardous Materials

AMHC
Chief Aviation Structural Mechanic (Hydraulics)

AMHD
Average Man-Hours per Day

AMHS
Automated Materials-Handling System

AMI
Airspeed Mach Indicator
Amalgamated Military and Technical Improvement Plan
Annual Military Inspection

AMIL
A Microprogramming Language (NRL)

AML
Advance Material List
Aeronautical Materials Laboratory
Applied Mathematics Laboratory

AMM
Anti-Missile Missile

AMMO
Ammunition

AMMRL
Aircraft Maintenance Material Readiness List

AMNS
Airborne Mine Neutralization System

AMO
Air Material Office
Area Monitoring Office
Aviation Medical Officer

AMP
Analytical Maintenance Program

AMPE
Automated Message Processing Equipment

AMPFUR
Amplified Failure and Unsatisfactory Report

AMPH
Amphibious

AMPHIB
Amphibious

AMPHIBEX
Amphibious Exercise

AMPI
Annual Military Personnel Inspection

AMPIR
Airborne Polarmetric Microwave Imaging Radiometer

AMPLE
Analytical Mode for Performing Logistic Evaluation

AMPN
Amplification

AMPS
Automatic Message-Processing System

AMR
Advanced Material Requirement
Auxiliary Machinery Room

AMRAAM
Advanced Medium-Range Air-to-Air Missile

AMRAD
Advanced Research Projects Agency Measurements Radar

AMS
Aeronautical Material Specification
Air Mass

Auxiliary Machinery Space
Minesweeper, High Speed

AMS1
Aviation Structural Mechanic Structures First Class

AMS2
Aviation Structural Mechanic Structures Second Class

AMS3
Aviation Structural Mechanic Structures Third Class

AMSA
Advanced Manned Strategic Aircraft

AMSAA
Aviation Structural Mechanic Structures Airman Apprentice

AMSAN
Aviation Structural Mechanic Structures Airman

AMSC
Acquisition Management Systems
Chief Aviation Structural Mechanic Structures

AMSD
Anti-Ship Missile Defense

AMSE
Aeronautical Material Support Equipment

AMSI
Atlantic Merchant Shipping Instructions

AMSL
Above Mean Sea Level

AMSO
Aeromedical Safety Officer

AMSP
Advanced Magnetic Silencing Project
Asbestos Medical Surveillance Program

AMSR
Aviation Maintenance-Supply Readiness

AMST
Advanced Medium STOL Transport

AMSU
Aeronautical Material Screening Unit
Amphibious Maintenance Support Unit

AMSULANT
Amphibious Maintenance Support Unit, Atlantic

AMSUPAC
Amphibious Maintenance Support Unit, Pacific

AMT
Amalgamated Military Technical Amount

AMTA
Audio-Monitored Talk Amplifier

AMTI
Airborne Moving-Target Indicator

AMTRACBN
Amphibious Tractor Battalion

AMU
Atomic Mass Unit

AMVER
Automated Mutual-Assistance Vessel Rescue

A/N
Aids to Navigation (USCG)

AN
Aids to Navigation (USCG)
Airman
Alphanumeric
Army-Navy (ordnance)
Net Laying Ship

ANA
Air Force-Navy Aeronautical (bulletin)

ANAL
Analog
Analysis

ANAPROP
Anomalous Propagation (radar)

ANCA
Allied Naval Communications Agent

ANCH
Anchorage

ANCH PROHIB
Anchorage Prohibited

AND
Air Force-Navy Design

ANDB
Air Navigation Development Board

ANDVT
Advanced Narrowband Digital Voice Terminal

ANEW
A New Antisubmarine Warfare System

ANF
Antinuclear Force

ANFE
Aircraft Not Fully Equipped

ANGLICO
Air and Naval Gunfire Liaison Company

AN(HS)
High School Airman

ANIP
Army-Navy Instrumentation Program

ANJSB
Army-Navy Joint Specifications Board

ANL
Annealed
Automatic Noise-Landing
Net Laying Ship

ANLYS
Analysis

ANMB
Army-Navy Munitions Board

ANMCC
Alternate National Military Command Center

ANMI
Allied Naval Maneuvering Instructions

ANMPO
Army-Navy Medical Procurement Office

ANNA
Army, Navy, National Aeronautics

ANNADIV
Annapolis Division

ANNFLYQUIRE
Annual Flying Requirement

ANN NO
Announcement Number

ANNREPT
Annual Report

ANO
Air Navigation Order

ANON
Anonymous

ANORS
Anticipated Not Operationally Ready (Supply)

ANP
Aircraft Nuclear Propulsion
Air Navigation Plan

ANS
Answer

ANSI
Assistant Naval Science Instructor

ANSIA
Army-Navy Shipping Information Agency

ANSO
Assistant Naval Stores Officer

ANT
Antenna
Antenna Height Entry (NNSS)

ANTARCTICDEVRON
Antarctic Development Squadron

ANTARCTICDEVRONDET
Antarctic Development Squadron Detachment

ANTDEFCOM
Antilles Defense Command

ANTI-C
Anti-Contamination (clothing)

ANTILOG
Antilogarithm

ANTISUB
Antisubmarine

ANTISUBFITRON
Antisubmarine Fighter Squadron

ANTS
Advanced Naval Training School

ANTU
Air Navigation Training Unit

ANX
Annex

ANZUK
Australia, New Zealand, and United Kingdom

ANZUS
Australia, New Zealand, and the United States

A/O
All Over the Hatch or Hold

AO
Acousto-Optic
Administrative Officer
Aerodrome Officer
Air Observer
Appointing Order
Area of Operations
Audit Organization
Aviation Ordnanceman
Oiler

AO1
Aviation Ordnanceman First Class

AO2
Aviation Ordnanceman Second Class

AO3
Aviation Ordnanceman Third Class

AOA
Amphibious Objective Area
Analysis of Alternatives
Angle of Attack
Atlantic Operating Area

AOAA
Aviation Ordnanceman Airman Apprentice

AOAN
Airman Striker for Aviation Ordnanceman

AOB
Advanced Operational Base

AOBS
Annual Officer Billet Summary

AOC
Agreed Operational Characteristics
Aircraft Operational Capability
Association of Old Crows
Aviation Officer Candidate
Chief Aviation Ordnanceman

AOCAN
Aviation Officer Candidate Airman

AOCC
Air Operations Control Center

AOCM
Aircraft Out-of-Commission for Maintenance
Master Chief Aviation Ordnanceman

AOCP
Aircraft Out-of-Commission for Parts
Aviation Officer Continuation Pay

AOCR
Aircraft Operating-Cost Report

AOCS
Aviation Officer Candidate School
Aviation Ordnance Control Station
Senior Chief Aviation Ordnanceman

AOD
Aerodrome Officer-of-the-Day

AODC
Allowance Officer Desk Code

AOE
Aerodrome of Entry
Fast Combat-Support Ship

AOES
Air-Ocean Environmental Specialist

AOG
Aircraft on Ground
Gasoline Tanker

AOH
Accepted on Hire
Aircraft Requiring Overhaul
Awaiting Overhaul

AOI
And-or-Invert (gate)

AOIL
Aviation Oil

AO(J)
Jumbo Oiler

AOL
Absent Over Liberty
Small Oiler

AOM
All Officers Meeting

AOML
Atlantic Oceanographic and Meteorological Laboratory

AOO
Aviation Ordnance Officer

AOP
Air Observation Post
Atomic Ordnance Platoon

AOQ
Average Outgoing Quality
Aviation Officers' Quarters

AOQL
Average Outgoing Quality Limit

AOR
Air Operations Room
Allowance Override Requirement
Area of Responsibility
Argon Oxygen Refining
Replenishment Oiler

AOS
Amphibious Objective Study

AOSO
Advanced Orbiting Solar Observatory

AOSS
Airborne Oil Surveillance System
Submarine Oiler

AOT
Transport Oiler

AOTU
Amphibious Operations Training Unit

AOV
APA items for Overseas Shipment

AOWS
Aircraft Overhaul Work-Stoppage

A/P
Airplane
Auto Pilot

AP
After Peak
Aft Perpendiculars
Air Patrol
Air Plot
Air Position
Air Publication
Anomalous Propagation (radar)
April
Armor-Piercing
Assumed Position
Attack Prop
Aviation Pilot
Transport (ship)

APA
Appropriation Purchases Account
Attack Transport Ship
Automatic Pulse-Analyzer

APACHE
Analog Programming and Checking

AP/AM
Anti-Personel/Anti-Material (cluster bomb)

APAR
Automatic Programming and Recording

APATS
Automatic Programmer and Test System

APB
Advanced Processor Build
Auxiliary Barracks Ship (Self-Propelled)

APBI
Advanced Planning Briefings for Industry

APC
Academic Potential Coding
Academic Profile Code
Activity Processing Code
Air Project Coordinator
Approach Power Compensator
Area of Position Control
Area of Positive Control
Armored Personnel Carrier
Automatic Phase Control
Small Coastal Transport

APCH
Approach

APCHE
Automatic Programmed Checkout Equipment

APCON
Approach Control

APCS
Approach Power Compensator System

APD
Advanced Planning Document
Air Procurement District
Destroyer Transport Ship
High-Speed Transport

APDM
Amended Program Decision Memorandum

APDP
Automatic Payroll Deposit Plan

APDSMS
Advanced Point Defense Surface Missile System

APEL
Aeronautical Photographic Experimentation Laboratory

APERS
Anti-Personnel

APEXER
Approach Indexer

APG
Advanced Pay Grade

APGC
Air Proving-Ground Center
Air Proving-Ground Command

APH
Casualty Transport Ship
Hospital Transport Ship

API
Area of Possible Incompatibility

APIX
Automated Personnel Information Exchange

APL
Allowance Parts List
Applied Physics Laboratory
Barracks Craft (Non-Self-Propelled)

APLO
Aerial Port Liaison Officer

APM
All Pilots Meeting
Assistant Project Manager
Mechanized Artillery Transport

APOB
Actual Projected On Board (allowance)

APOE
Aerial Port of Embarkation

APOTA
Automatic Positioning Telemetering Antenna

APP
Adjusted Performance Percentile
Advanced Procurement Plan
Appendix
Approach
Auxiliary Power Plant

APPAC
Aviation Petroleum Products Allocation Committee

APPAC-L
Aviation Petroleum Products Allocation Committee-London

APPCON
Approach Control

APP/DEP
Approach/Departure (controller)

APPL
Applicable
Applicant
Application

APPN
Appropriation

APPR
Approve

APPRES
Applied Research

APPROX
Approximately

APPS
Advanced Planning Procurement System
Applications
Automated Photogrammetric Positioning System

APPT
Appoint
Appointed
Appointment

APR
Alterations and Project Reports
April
Rescue Transport

APREQ
Approval Request

APROP
Appropriately
Appropriation

APS
Automatic Program System
Automatic Propulsion Control System
Auxiliary Power Supply
Submarine Transport Ship

APSA
Ammunition Procurement and Supply System

APSET
Aviation Personnel and Survival Equipment

APSS
Transport Submarine

APT
Armor-Piercing Tracer
Automatic Picture Transmission
Troop Barge, Class B

APTE
Automatic Production Test Equipment

APTES
Administrative Professional and Technical Evaluation System

APTS
Acoustic Proficiency Training Systems
Activity Providing Telephone Service

APU
Auxiliary Power Unit

APV
Transport and Aircraft Ferry

APWO
Assistant Public Works Officer

AQ
Aircraft Quality
Allowance Quality

AQ1
Aviation Fire Control Technician First Class

AQ2
Aviation Fire Control Technician Second Class

AQ3
Aviation Fire Control Technician Third Class

AQAA
Aviation Fire Control Technician Airman Apprentice

AQAN
Aviation Fire Control Technician Airman

AQCS
Senior Chief Aviation Fire Control Technician

AQD
Additional Qualification Designation

AQD/U
Additional Qualification Designation/Utilization

AQL
Acceptable Quality Level

AR
Aeronautical Requirement
Aircraft Requirement
Airman Recruit
Air Refueling
Air Rescue
Air Reserve
Amphibian Reconnaissance
Armor Reconnaissance
As Required (report frequency)
Repair Ship

ARA
Accelerated Readiness Analysis
Airborne Radar Approach
Aircraft Replaceable Assembly
Assigned Responsible Agency
Avionics Repairable Assemblies

ARAA
Aerodrome Radar Approach Aid

ARAC
Airborne Radar Approach Control (facility)

ARAPS
Area Requirements and Product Status

ARB
Air Registration Board
Air Reserve Base
Battle Damage Repair Ship
RVAH Bombardier/Navigator (code)

ARBS
Angular Rate Bombing System

ARC
Accessory Record Card
Acoustic Research Center
Acquisition Review Committee
Activity Readiness Code
Alcohol Recovery Center
Alcohol Rehabilitation Center
Area of Responsibility Center
Cable-Repairing Ship

ARCO
Airborne Remote-Control Operator
Auxiliary Resources Control Office

ARCP
Air Refueling Control Point

ARCTICSARCOORD
Coast Guard Search and Rescue Coordinator, Arctic

ARD
Alcohol Recovery Drydock
Alcohol Rehabilitation Drydock
Auxiliary Repair Drydock (Non-Self-Propelled)

ARDA
Analog Recording Dynamic Analyzer

ARDF
Applications Research and Defense Fund

ARDL
Small Auxiliary Floating Drydock (Non-Self-Propelled)

ARDM
Medium Auxiliary Repair Drydock (Non-Self-Propelled)

ARE
Aviation Readiness Evaluation

AREACORD
For the purpose of area coordination or to such other command designated by him in appropriate instructions

AREAPETOFF
Area Petroleum Office

ARF
Automatic Return Fire

ARFCOS
Armed Forces Courier Service

ARFCOSTA
Armed Forces Courier Station

ARFF
Aircraft Rescue and Fire Fighting

AR/FOR
Active Records/Fiche-Oriented Retrieval

ARFOR
Area Forecast

ARG
Amphibious Ready Group
Internal Combustion Engine Repair Ship

ARG-SLF
Amphibious Ready Group-Special Landing Force

ARGUS
Analytical Reports Gathering and Updating System
Automatic Routine Generation and Updating System

ARH
Anti-Radiation Homing
Heavy-Hull Repair Ship

ARHAWS
Anti-Radiation Homing and Warning System

AR(HS)
High School Airman Recruit

ARI
Arithmetic

ARIES
Airborne Reconnaissance Integrated Electronic System

ARIP
Air Refueling Initial Point
Automatic Rocket Impact Predictor

ARIS
Advanced Range Instrumentation Ship
Altitude and Rate Indicating System

ARL
Acceptable Reliability Level
Aeromedical Research Laboratory
Aeronautical Research Laboratory
Arctic Research Laboratory
Small Repair Ship

ARLAN
Arlington Annex

ARLEX
Arlington Annex

ARLIS
Arctic Research Laboratory Ice Station

ARLS
Automatic Resupply System

ARM
Anti-Radar Missile
Anti-Radiation Missile
Applied Research Motor
Armament
Heavy Machinery Repair Ship

ARMACS
Aviation Plans/Aviation Resources Management and Control System

ARMD
Armored

ARMGD
Armed Guard

ARMGRD
Armed Guard

ARMGRDCEN
Armed Guard Center

ARMM
Automatic Reliability Mathematical Model

ARMMS
Automated Reliability Maintenance Measurement System

ARMS
Automatic Remote Manned System
Automation Resource Management System

ARN
Around

ARNG
Arrange
Arrangement

ARO
Air Radio Officer
Auxiliary Readout

ARODS
Airborne Radar Orbital Determination System

AROICC
Area Resident Officer-in-Charge of Construction

AROU
Aviation Repair and Overhaul Unit

ARP
Aircraft Recommended Practice
Air Raid Precaution
Analytical Rework Program
Armament Release Panel

ARPA
Advanced Research Projects Agency

ARPARSCHCEN
Advanced Research Projects Agency Research Center

ARPAT
Advanced Research Projects Agency

ARPN
Aircraft and Related Procurement, Navy

ARPROIMREP
Upon Arrival Proceed Immediately and Report

ARPROPORICH
Upon Arrival Proceed to Port In Which

ARPROREP
Upon Arrival Proceed and Report

ARQ
Automatic Response to Query

ARR
Arrival
Arrive

ARREC
Armed Reconnaissance

ARREP
Arrival report

ARREPCOVES
Arrival reporting commanding officer of that vessel (duty indicated)

ARREPISIC
Arrival report to superior in command, if present, otherwise by message (duty indicated)

ARRL
Aeronautical Radio and Radar Laboratory

ARRV
Arrive

ARS
Advanced Reconnaissance Satellite
Advanced Record System
Air Rescue Service
Alcohol Recovery Service
Automatic Routing System
Salvage Ship

ARSD
Aviation Repair Supply Depot
Salvage Lifting Ship

ARSR
Air Surveillance Radar

ARSSS
Automated Ready-Supply Stores System

ARST
Salvage-Craft Tender

ARSV
Armored Reconnaissance Scout Vehicle

ART
Academic Remedial Training
Active Repair Time
Airborne Radiation Thermometer
Article

ARTC
Air Route Traffic Control
Alcohol Recovery Training Center

ARTCC
Air Route Traffic Control Center

ARTL
Awaiting Results of Trial

ARTRAC
Advanced Range Testing, Reporting and Control
Advanced Real-Time Range Control

ARTRON
Artificial Neuron

ARTS
Automated Radar Terminal System

ARTY
Artillery

ARTYLO
Artillery Liaison Office
Artillery Liaison Officer

ARU
Alcohol Rehabilitation Unit

ARV
Aircraft Repair Ship

ARVA
Aircraft Repair Ship Aircraft

ARVE
Aircraft Repair Ship Engines

ARVH
Aircraft Repair Ship Helicopter

A/S
Airspeed

AS
Aiming Symbol
Altostratus
Ammonia Service
Analytical Stereoplotter
Annual Survey
Auxiliary Steam
Aviation Support Equipment Technician
Submarine Tender

AS&SL
All Ships and Stations Letters

AS1
Aviation Support Equipment Technician First Class

AS2
Aviation Support Equipment Technician Second Class

AS3
Aviation Support Equipment Technician Third Class

ASA
Aviation Supply Annex

ASAA
Aviation Support Equipment Technician Airman Apprentice

ASAC
Altostratus and Altocumulus
Antisubmarine Air Controller

ASAMP
AUTODIN Subscriber Activation Management Plan

ASAN
Aviation Support Equipment Technician Airman

ASAP
Alcohol Safety Action Program
Antisubmarine Attack Plotter
As Soon As Possible

ASAR
Air Search Acquisition Radar
Air Search Attack Team
Anti-Satellite
Antisubmarine Attack Teacher
Automated Statistical Analysis Technique

ASAT
Air Search Attack Team
Anti-Satellite
Antisubmarine Attack Teacher
Automated Statistical Analysis Technique

ASATTU
Antisubmarine Attack Teacher Training Unit

ASB
Air Safety Board
Arctic Survey Boat (USCG)

ASBCA
Armed Services Board of Contract Appeals

ASBD
Active Service Base Date
Advanced Sea-Based Deterrent

ASC
Advanced Ship Concept
Air Support Control
Asset Status Card
AUTODIN Switching Center
Automated Service Center
Automatic Steering Control
Chief Aviation Support Equipment Technician

ASCA
Aircraft Stability Control Analyzer
Automatic Subject Citation Alert

ASCAC
Antisubmarine Classification and Analysis Center
Antisubmarine Combat Activity Center

ASCAC/TSC
Antisubmarine Classification and Analysis Center/Tactical Support Center

ASCAT
Antisubmarine Classification Analysis Test

ASCB
Aviation Command Screening Board

ASCC
Aviation Supply Control Center

ASCII
Automatic Synchronous Control of Intelligence Information

ASCM
Anti-Ship Cruise Missile
Master Chief Aviation Support Equipment Technician

ASCO
Air Service Coordination Office

ASCOMED
Air Service Coordination Office, Mediterranean

ASCOMM
Antisubmarine Warfare Communications

ASCOMMDET
Antisubmarine Warfare Communications Detachment

ASCOP
Advanced Submarine Control Program

ASCS
Altitude Stabilization and Control System
Automatic Stabilization Control System
Senior Chief Aviation Support Equipment Technician

ASCSR
Armed Services Commissary Store Regulations

ASCU
Air Support Control Unit
Armament Station Control Unit

ASD
Activity Support Date
Aircraft Statistical Data
Assistant Secretary of Defense
Aviation Supply Depot

ASDAR
Aircraft Satellite Data Relay

ASDARP
Aviation Supply Development and Readiness (program)

ASD(C)
Assistant Secretary of Defense (Comptroller)

ASDE
Air Surface Detection Equipment
Airport Surface Detection Equipment

ASDEC
Applied Systems Development and Evaluation Center

ASDEFORLANT
Antisubmarine Defense Forces, Atlantic

ASDEFORPAC
Antisubmarine Defense Forces, Pacific

ASDEVDET
Antisubmarine Development Detachment

ASD(HA)
Assistant Secretary of Defense (Health Affairs)

ASD(I)
Assistant Secretary of Defense (Intelligence)

ASDIC
Antisubmarine Detection Investigation Committee
Armed Services Documents Intelligence Center

ASD(ISA)
Assistant Secretary of Defense (International Security Affairs)

ASDIV
Advanced Systems Division

ASD(MRAL)
Assistant Secretary of Defense (Manpower, Reserve Affairs, and Logistics)

ASDO
Assistant Squadron Duty Officer

ASD(PA)
Assistant Secretary of Defense (Public Affairs)

ASD(R&D)
Assistant Secretary of Defense (Research and Development)

ASDS
Advanced Swimmer Delivery System

ASDV
Swimmer Delivery Vehicle Support Craft

ASE
Allowable Setting Error
Automatic Stabilization Equipment
Aviation Support Equipment Technician Electrical

ASE2
Aviation Support Equipment Technician Electrical Second Class

ASE3
Aviation Support Equipment Technician Electrical Third Class

ASEAA
Aviation Support Equipment Technician Electrical Airman Apprentice

ASEAN
Aviation Support Equipment Technician Electrical Airman

ASED
Aviation and Surface Effects Department
Aviation Service Entry Date

A/SEE
Antisubmarine Experimental Establishment

ASEG
All Services Evaluation Group

ASER
Armed Services Exchange Regulations

ASESB
Armed Services Explosive Safety Board

ASF
Activity Support File
Aeromedical Staging Facility
Aeronautical Staging Flight

AS(FBM)
Submarine Tender (Fleet Ballistic Missile)

A/SFDO
Antisubmarine Fixed Defenses Officer

ASFIR
Active Swept Frequency Interferometer Radar

ASG
Afloat Shopping Guide
Assign
Auxiliary Service Group

ASGD
Assigned

ASGN
Assign

ASH
Assault Support Helicopter
Aviation Support Equipment Technician Hydraulics and Structures

ASH2
Aviation Support Equipment Technician Hydraulics and Structures Second Class

ASH3
Aviation Support Equipment Technician Hydraulics and Structures Third Class

ASHAA
Aviation Support Equipment Technician Hydraulics and Structures Airman Apprentice

ASHAN
Aviation Support Equipment Technician Hydraulics and Structures Airman

ASHE
Aircraft Salvage Handling Equipment

ASHMS
Automatic Ship's Heading Measurement System

ASI
Airspeed Indicator
Annual Supply Inspection
Automatic Start Interrupt (NNSS)
Aviation Status Indicator

ASIF
Airlift Services Industrial Fund

ASIS
Ammunition Stores Issuing Ship
Amphibious Support Information System

ASL
Above Sea Level
Aeronautical Structures Laboratory
Approved Suppliers List
Atmospheric Sciences Laboratory
Salvage Tug

ASLADS
Automatic Shipboard Launch Aircraft Data System

ASLBM
Anti-Sea-Launched Ballistic Missile

ASLT
Assault

ASLTPHIBBN
Assault Amphibious Battalion

ASM
Administrative Support Manual
Air-to-Surface Missile
Aviation Support Equipment Technician Mechanical

ASM2
Aviation Support Equipment Technician Mechanical Second Class

ASM3
Aviation Support Equipment Technician Mechanical Third Class

ASMAA
Aviation Support Equipment Technician Mechanical Airman Apprentice

ASMD
Anti-Ship Missile Defense

ASMIS
Automated Ships Management Information System

ASMS
Advanced Surface Missile System

ASN
Assistant Secretary of the Navy
Average Sample Number

ASNE
American Society of Naval Engineers

ASN(FM)
Assistant Secretary of the Navy (Financial Management)

ASN(I&E)
Assistant Secretary of the Navy (Installation & Environment)

ASN(I&L)
Assistant Secretary of the Navy (Installation and Logistics)

ASN(MRA)
Assistant Secretary of the Navy (Manpower and Reserve Affairs)

ASN (RD&A)
Assistant Secretary of the Navy (Research, Development and Acquisition)

ASN(RDA)
Assistant Secretary of the Navy (Research, Development and Acquisition)

ASN(RE&S)
Assistant Secretary of the Navy (Research, Engineering and Systems)

ASN(RES)
Assistant Secretary of the Navy (Research and Development)

ASN(SL)
Assistant Secretary of the Navy (Shipbuilding and Logistics)

ASO
Air Signal Officer
Air Surveillance Officer
Area Safety Officer
Assistant Secretary's Office
Aviation Safety Officer
Aviation Supply Office

ASO/ICP
Aviation Supply Office/Inventory Control Point

ASOP
Automatic Operating and Scheduling Program

ASOS
Assistant Supervisor of Shipbuilding
Automated Surface Observing System
Automatic Storm Observation Service

ASP
Advanced Signal Processing
Advanced Study Project
Air Superiority Program
Ammunition Supply Point
Antisubmarine Patrol
Atmospheric Sounding Projectile

ASPB
Assault Support Patrol Boat

ASPCB
Armed Services Pest Control Board

ASPO
Avionics System Project Officer

ASPPO
Armed Services Procurement Planning Office

ASPR
Armed Services Procurement Regulations

A/SR
Air-Sea Rescue

ASR
Airborne Search Radar
Air Surveillance Radar
Air-Sea Rescue
Automatic Send-and-Receive (teletype)
Submarine Rescue Ship

ASRAP
Acoustic Sensor Range Prediction

ASRGN
Altimeter Setting Region

ASROC
Antisubmarine Rocket

ASROC(ERA)
Extended-Range Antisubmarine Rocket

ASRS
Automatic Storage Retrieval System

ASRT
Air Support Radar Team

ASS
Airborne Surveillance System
Transport Submarine

ASSA
Cargo Submarine

ASSC
Advanced Shipboard Satellite Communications
Airborne Systems Support Center

ASSES
Analytical Studies of Surface Effects of Submerged Submarines

ASSET
Advanced Solar Turbo-Electric Conversion
Aerothermodynamic Elastic Structural Systems Environmental Tests

ASSIST
Afloat Supply Systems Improvement and Support Team

ASSOTW
Airfield and Seaplane Stations of the World

ASSP
Area Supply Support Plan
Transport Submarine

ASST
Assist
Assistant

ASSTCOMNAVSECGRU
Assistant Commander Naval Security Group

ASSTNAVSEATECHREP
Assistant Sea Systems Command Technical Representative

ASSTSECDEF
Assistant Secretary of Defense

ASSTSECDEF(COMPT)
Assistant Secretary of Defense (Comptroller)

ASSTSECDEF(HELAFF)
Assistant Secretary of Defense (Health Affairs)

ASSTSECDEF(INTEL)
Assistant Secretary of Defense (Intelligence)

ASSTSECDEF(INTSECAFF)
Assistant Secretary of Defense (International Security Affairs)

ASSTSECDEF(MPRRESAFFLOG)
Assistant Secretary of Defense (Manpower, Reserve Affairs, and Logistics)

ASSTSECDEF(PUBAFF)
Assistant Secretary of Defense (Public Affairs)

ASSTSECDEF(RSCHDEV)
Assistant Secretary of Defense (Research

and Development)

ASSTSECNAV
Assistant Secretary of the Navy

ASSTSECNAVFINMGMT
Assistant Secretary of the Navy (Financial Management)

ASSTSECNAVINSTLOG
Assistant Secretary of the Navy (Installation and Logistics)

ASSTSECNAVMPRESAFF
Assistant Secretary of the Navy (Manpower and Reserve Affairs)

ASSTSECNAVRES
Assistant Secretary of the Navy (Research and Development)

ASSTSECNAVRESENGSYS
Assistant Secretary of the Navy (Research, Engineering, and Systems)

ASSTSECNAVSHIPLOG
Assistant Secretary of the Navy (Shipbuilding and Logistics)

ASSY
Assembly

ASTAB
Automated Status Board

ASTAC
Antisubmarine Tactical Air Controller

ASTADIS
Advise Status and/or Disposition

ASTAP
Acoustic Sensor Training Aids Program

ASTAPA
Armed Services Textile and Apparel Procurement Agency

ASTD
American Society for Training and Development

ASTDS
Antisubmarine Tactical Data System

ASTECS
Advanced Submarine Tactical ESM Combat System

ASTER
Antisubmarine Terrier (missile)

ASTIA
Armed Services Technical Information Agency

ASTIAB
Armed Services Technical Information Agency Bulletin

ASTOR
Antisubmarine Torpedo (rocket)

ASTOVL
Advanced Short Take-Off and Vertical Landing

ASTRO
Artificial Satellite, Time and Radio Orbit
Astronomical

ASTU
Air Support Training Unit

ASU
Administrative Screening Unit
Aircraft Scheduling Unit
Aircraft Starting Unit
Approval of Systems and Equipment for Service Use

ASUPT
Advaced Simulation in Undergraduate Pilot Training

ASUW
Antisurface Warfare

ASV
Aerothermodynamic Structure Vehicle
Anti-Surface Missile

ASVAB
Armed Services Vocational Aptitude Battery

ASW
Antisubmarine Warfare

ASWCCS
Antisubmarine Warfare Command and Control System
Antisurface Warfare Command and Control System
Auxiliary Sea-Water (system)

ASWCR
Airborne Surveillance Warning and Control Radar

ASWEPS
Antisubmarine Warfare Environmental Prediction System

ASWEX
Antisubmarine Warfare Exercise

ASWFITRON
Antisubmarine Warfare Fighter Squadron

ASWGRU
Antisubmarine Warfare Group

ASWICS
Antisubmarine Warfare Integrated Combat System

ASWO
Air Stations Weekly Orders

ASWOC
Antisubmarine Warfare Operational Center

ASWORG
Antisubmarine Warfare Operations Research Group

ASWR
Antisubmarine Warfare Radar

ASWRC
Antisubmarine Warfare Research Center

ASWS
Antisubmarine Warfare Systems

ASWSAG
Antisubmarine Warfare Systems Analysis Group

ASWSC&CS
Antisubmarine Warfare Ship-Command and Control System

ASWSP
Antisubmarine Warfare Systems Project

ASWSPO
Antisubmarine Warfare Systems Project Office

ASWSYSPROJOFC
Antisubmarine Warfare Systems Project Office

ASWTACSCOL
Antisubmarine Warfare Tactical School

ASWTC
Antisubmarine Warfare Training Center

ASWTNS
Antisubmarine Warfare Tactical Navigation System

ASWTRACEN
Antisubmarine Warfare Training Center

ASWTRO
Antisubmarine Warfare Test Requirements Outline

ASWTV
Antisubmarine Warfare Target Vehicle

A/T
Action Taken
Air Tracker
Anti-Torpedo
Attack Teacher

AT
Acceptance Trials
Active Training (reserves)
Air-Tight
Air Transmit
Allowance Type
Annual Training
Arming Time
Assortment
Aviation Electronics Technician
Awaiting Transfer
Tug

AT1
Aviation Electronics Technician First Class

AT2
Aviation Electronics Technician Second Class

AT3
Aviation Electronics Technician Third Class

ATA
Actual Time of Arrival
Administration, Training, and Advisor
Airport Traffic Area
Automatic Target Acquisition
Auxiliary Ocean Tug
Aviation Training Aids

ATAA
Aviation Electronics Technician Airman Apprentice

ATAB
Aviation Training Aids Branch

ATAC
Air Transport Advisory Council

ATAD
Absent on Temporary Additional Duty

Air Technical Analysis Division

ATAK
Attack

ATAN
Aviation Electronics Technician Airman

ATAP
Anti-Tank Armor-Piercing
Anti-Tank Personnel (bomb)

ATARS
Advanced Tactical Airborne Reconnaissance System

ATB
Aircraft Technical Bulletin
All Trunks Busy
Amphibious Training Base

ATBM
Advanced Tactical Ballistic Missile

ATC
Action Taken Code
Advanced Training Command
Air Traffic Control
Air Training Command
Air Transport Command
Assistant Trial Counsel
Chief Aviation Electronics Technician
(Mini)-Armored Troop Carrier

ATCA
Altitude Translation and Control Assembly

ATCC
Aircraft Traffic Control Center

ATCE
Ablative Thrust Chamber Engine

ATCH
Armored Troop Carrier (Helicopter)
Attach

ATCLO
Amphibious Training Command Liaison Officer

ATCM
Master Chief Aviation Electronics Technician

ATCO
Aircraft Traffic Control Officer
Air Traffic Coordinating Office

ATCOR
Air Traffic Coordinator

ATCOREU
Air Traffic Coordinator, Europe

ATCORUS
Air Traffic Coordinator, United States

ATCRBS
Air Traffic Control Radar Beacon System

ATCS
Senior Chief Aviation Electronics Technician

ATCU
Air Transportable Communications Unit

ATD
Academic Training Division
Actual Time of Departure
Advanced Technology Demonstration
Air Turbine Drive

ATDA
Augmented Target Docking Adapter

ATDLS
Advanced Tactical Data Link System

ATDR
Aeronautical Technical Directive Requirement

ATDS
Airborne Tactical Data System
Aviation Tactical Data System

ATE
Altitude Transmitting Equipment
Automatic Test Equipment

ATEP
Aegis Tactical Executive Program

ATF
Accession Transcription Form
Actual Time of Fall
Air Torpedo-Firing
Amphibious Task Force
Automatic Target Following
Aviation Training Form
Fleet Ocean Tug

ATFLIR
Advanced Targeting Forward-Looking Infrared Radar

ATFOS
Alignment and Test Facility for Optical Systems

AT/FP
Anti-Terrorism/Force Protection

ATG
Afloat Training Group
Amphibious Task Group

ATGSB
Admission Test for Graduate Study in Business

ATHODYD
Aero-Thermo-Dynamic-Duct

ATI
Average Total Inspection

ATIC
Aerospace Technical Intelligence Center

ATIS
Automatic Terminal Information Service

ATJ
Aviation Training Jacket

ATK
Attack

ATKCARAIRWING
Attack Carrier Air Wing

ATKRON
Attack Squadron

ATKRONDET
Attack Squadron Detachment

ATL
Aeronautical Turbine Laboratory
Atlantic
Awaiting Trial
(Ocean-Going) Tank Landing Craft

ATLAS
Automatic Tape Load Audit System

ATLD
Air-Transportable Loading Dock

AT/LR
Air Tracker/Long-Range

ATM
Air Turbine Motor
Altimeter Transmitter Multiplier
Atmosphere
Atmospheric Analyzer (system)

ATMP
Air Target Materials Program

ATMU
Aircraft Torpedo Maintenance Unit

ATN
Augmented Transition Network

AT NO
Atomic Number

ATO
Aircraft Transfer Order
Assisted Take-Off
Auxiliary Ocean Tug, Old

ATOM
Astronomical Telescope Orientation Mount

ATO/MDU
Air Tasking Order/Mission Data Update

ATOP
Automated Traffic Overload Protection

ATP
Acceptance Test Procedure
Allied Tactical Publication
Authority to Proceed
Authorized Test Procedure

AT/PERS
High-Explosive Antitank/Antipersonnel

ATR
Advanced Tactical Readout
Aircraft Trouble Report
Airline Transport Rating
Ammunition Transaction Report
Attenuated Total Reflectance
Automatic Tape Reader
Aviation Training Record
Rescue Ocean Tug

ATRB
Advanced Technology Review Board

ATRC
AEGIS Training Readiness Center

ATRS
Assembly Test-Recording System

ATS
Administrative Terminal System
Air-to-Ship
Air Traffic Services
Air Transportable Sonar
Air Turbine Starter
Salvage and Rescue Ship

AT/SR
Air Tracker/Short-Range

ATSS
Auxiliary Training Submarine

ATSU
Air Travel Security Unit

ATT
Advanced Technicians Test
Aviation Training Team

ATTC
Aviation Technical Training Center

ATTD
Attitude
Aviation Technical Training Division

ATTN
Attention

ATTNDIR
Attention Directed

ATTNINV
Attention Invited

ATTNINVRETGUIDE
Attention Invited NAVPERS 15891 Series, Navy Guide for Retired Personnel and Their Families

ATTR
Average Time to Repair

ATTRS
Automatic Tracking Telemetry Receiving

ATU
Advanced Training Unit
Amphibious Task Unit

ATV
All-Terrain Vehicle

AT VOL
Atomic Volume

ATWCS
Advanced Tomahawk Weapon Control System

AT WT
Atomic Weight

AU
Air University
Auditor
August

AUASM
Automatic Aimpoint Selection and Maintenance

AUDGENNAV
Auditor General of the Navy

AUDIT
Automated Unattended Detection Inspection Transmitter

AUG
Augment
August

AUGU
Augmenting Unit

AUL
Authorized Use List

AUM
Air-to-Underwater Missile

AUSS
Advanced Unmanned Search System

AUTEC
Atlantic Undersea Test and Evaluation Center

AUTH
Authority
Authorized

AUTHAB
Authorized Abbreviation

AUTHDELPHYSTRANS
If date of arriving port of embarkation as specified by cognizant transportation office and reporting date for physical examination do not agree, authorized to delay in reporting for physical until such time as will enable him to arrive at port of embarkation by specified date.

AUTHEXANDO
Authority granted to execute acceptance and oath of office for _____

AUTHGR
Authority Granted

AUTHPROBOUT
Authorized to proceed on or about _____

AUTHTRAV
Authorized to perform such travel via commercial and/or government transportation as may be necessary in proper performance of duties. While traveling via government air outside CONUS, Class Three priority is certified. Cost of this travel

chargeable (appropriation designated).

AUTO
Automatic

AUTODIN
Automatic Digital Network

AUTODIN EMOD
Automatic Digital Network-Evolutionary Modernization

AUTODIN ICCDP
Automatic Digital Network-Integrated Circuits Communications Data Processor

AUTOMAD
Automatic Adaption Data

AUTOMET
Automatic Correction of Meteorological

AUTONAV
Autonomous Navigation

AUTOPIC
Automatic Personal Identification Code

AUTOPROPS
Automatic Programming for Positioning System

AUTOSERVOCOM
Automatic Secure Voice Communications Network (DCS)

AUTOVON
Automatic Voice Network

AUTOWEAP
Automatic Weapon

AUW
Advanced Underseas Weapon
All Up Weight (gross)

AUWC
Advanced Underseas Weapons Circuitry

AUX
Auxiliary

A/V
Audio-Visual

AV
Audio-Visual
Seaplane Tender

AVAIL
Available

AVAL
Available

AVB
Advance Aviation Base Ship
Aviation Logistic Support Ship
Avionics Bulletin

AVBLTY
Availability

AVC
Automatic Volume Control
Avionics Change

AVCAD
Aviation Cadet

AVCAL
Aviation Consolidated Allowance List

AVCM
Master Chief Avionics Technician

AVCS
Advanced Video Camera System

AVD
Avoirdupois
Seaplane Tender (Destroyer)

AVE
Air Vehicle Equipment

AVELECTECH
Aviation Electronics Technician

AVERDISROP
Avert Disruption of Operations

AVF
All-Volunteer Force

AVF PAR
All-Volunteer Force/Program Action Request

AVG
Average
Aviation, General Purpose Ship

AVGAS
Aviation Gasoline

AVH
Aircraft Rescue Boat

AVLB
Armored Vehicle Launched Bridge

AVLD
Acoustic Valve Leak Detector

AVM
Airborne Vibration Monitor
Guided Missile Test Ship

AVMAINTECH
Aviation Maintenance Technician

AVN
Autovon
Aviation

AVN(CM)
Aviation Pay (Crewmember)

AVNL
Automatic Video Noise Limiting

AVNMATOLANT
Aviation Material Office, Atlantic

AVNMATORES
Aviation Material Office, Reserve

AVN(NCM)
Aviation Pay (Non-Crewmember)

AVO
Avoid Verbal Orders

AVOIL
Aviation Oil

AVOPTECH
Aviation Operations Technician

AVP
Small Seaplane Tender

AVR
Aviator

AVROC
Aviation Reserve Officer Candidate

AVS
Aviation Supply Ship

AVSAT
Aviation Satellite

AVT
Auxiliary Aircraft Landing Training Ship

AVTR
Aviator

AVVI
Attitude-Vertical Velocity Indicator

AW
Above Water
Airspace Warning
Air Warfare
All-Weather
Arc Weld
Armature Winding
Automatic Weapons
Aviation Antisubmarine Warfare Operator
Distilling Ship

AW1
Aviation Antisubmarine Warfare Operator First Class

AW2
Aviation Antisubmarine Warfare Operator Second Class

AW3
Aviation Antisubmarine Warfare Operator Third Class

AWAA
Aviation Antisubmarine Warfare Operator Airman Apprentice

AWACS
Airborne Warning and Control System

AWADS
Adverse Weather Aerial Delivery System

AWAN
Aviation Antisubmarine Warfare Operator Airman

AWARS
Airborne Weather and Reconnaissance System

AWB
Airborne Weapons Bulletin
Amphibious Warfare Branch

AWBER
Awaiting Berthing

AWC
Air Warfare Commander
Chief Aviation Antisubmarine Warfare Operator
VAW Airborne Intercept Controller

AWCLS
All-Weather Carrier Landing System

AWCM
Master Chief Aviation Antisubmarine Warfare Operator

AWCO
Area Wage and Classification Office

AWCREW
Awaiting Crew

AWCS
Automatic Weapons Control System
Senior Chief Aviation Antisubmarine Warfare Operator

AWD
Award

AWDISCH
Awaiting Discharge

AWDO
Air Wing Duty Officer

AWE
Accepted Weight Estimate
VAQ/ECM/ESM Evaluator

AWEA
Awaiting Weather

AWG
American Wire Gauge

AWK
Water Tanker

AWL
Absent With Leave

AWLAR
All-Weather Low-Altitude Route

AWLOAD
Awaiting Loading

AWM
Awaiting Maintenance

AWMCS
Aviation Weapons Movement Control System

AWN
Automated Weather Network

AWO
Administrative Watch Officer

AWOC
All-Weather Operations Committee

AWOL
Absent Without Leave

AWORD
Awaiting Orders

AWP
Awaiting Parts

AWR
Automated Work Request

AWRS
Automatic Weapons Release System

AWS
Advanced Wideband System
Aegis Weapon System
Air Weather Service
Amphibious Warfare School
Aviation Warfare Specialist

AWSAIL
Awaiting Sailing (orders)

AWSD
Air Warfare Systems Development

AWSM
Air Weather Service Manual

AWSP
Air Weather Service Pamphlet

AWST
Atomic Weapons Special Transport

AWSTA
All-Weather Station

AWT
Awaiting Trial

AWTOW
Awaiting Tow

AWY
Airway

AX
Planned Auxiliary, New Construction

AX1
Aviation Antisubmarine Warfare Technician First Class

AX2
Aviation Antisubmarine Warfare Technician Second Class

AX3
Aviation Antisubmarine Warfare Technician Third Class

AXAA
Aviation Antisubmarine Warfare Technician Airman Apprentice

AXAN
Aviation Antisubmarine Warfare Technician

Airman

AXBT
Airborne Expendable Bathythermograph

AXC
Chief Aviation Antisubmarine Warfare Technician

AXCS
Senior Chief Aviation Antisubmarine Warfare Technician

AY
Academic Year
Assembly

AZ
Aviation Maintenance Administrationman
Azimuth
Lighter-than-Air Aircraft Tender

AZ1
Aviation Maintenance Administrationman First Class

AZ2
Aviation Maintenance Administrationman Second Class

AZ3
Aviation Maintenance Administrationman Third Class

AZAA
Aviation Maintenance Administrationman Airman Apprentice

AZAN
Aviation Maintenance Administrationman Airman

AZC
Aviation Maintenance Administrationman

AZCM
Master Chief Aviation Maintenance Administrationman

AZCS
Senior Chief Aviation Maintenance Administrationman

AZRAN
Azimuth Range

B

B
Biennial (report frequency)
Boiler
Bombardier-Navigator (NAO code)

B&A
Bond and Allotment (system)

B&P
Bidding and Proposal (effort)

B&Q
Barracks and Quarters

B&W
Black and White
Bread and Water

B&WHB
Black and White Horizontal Bands (buoy markings)

B/A
Breaking Action

BA
Ball
Breaks Above
Budget Activity

BAAM
Basic Administration and Management (program)

BABS
Beam Approach Beacon System (radar)

BACE
Basic Automatic Check Equipment

BADC
Binary Asymmetric Dependent Channel

BADG
Battle Group Anti-Air Warfare Display

BADGE
Base Air Defense Ground Environment

BAF
Back-up Alert Force

BAGAIR
while traveling via air outside the United

States (number of pounds indicated).

BAH
Basic Allowance for Housing

BAI
Bearing-Range Indicator

BAIC
Binary Asymmetric Independent Channel

BAKS
Barracks

BAL
Balance
Ballistics
Boats and Landing Craft

BALDNY
Ballistic Density

BALLUTES
Balloon-Parachutes

BALWND
Ballistic Wind

BAM
Minesweeper (Ocean) British Lend-Lease

BAMBI
Ballistic Missile Boost Intercept

BAMP
Basic Analysis and Mapping Program

BAMS
Broad Area Maritime Surveillance (aircraft)

BANAVAVNOFFSCOL
Basic Naval Aviation Officers School

BAQ
Basic Allowance for Quarters

BAQ(AC)
Basic Allowance for Quarters for Adopted Child/Children

BAQ(DISRET)
Basic Allowance for Quarters Pending Disability Retirement

BAQ(F)
Basic Allowance for Quarters for Father

BAQ(H)
Basic Allowance for Quarters for Husband

BAQ(LC)
Basic Allowance for Quarters for Legitimate Child/Children

BAQ(M)
Basic Allowance for Quarters for Mother

BAQ(SC)
Basic Allowance for Quarters for Stepchild/Stepchildren

BAQ(W)
Basic Allowance for Quarters for Wife

BAR
Browning Automatic Rifle

BARCAP
Barrier Combat Air Patrol

BARO
Barometer

BARSTUR
Barking Sands Tactical Underwater Range

BAS
Basic Airspeed
Basic Allowance for Subsistence
Bleed Air System
Bomb Assembly Spares

BAS-BR
Basic Branch Training (course)

BASEOPS
Base Operations

BASIC
Battle Area Surveillance and Integrated Communications
Beginners All-Purpose Symbolic Instruction Code

BASICPAC
Basic Processor and Computer

BAT
Basic Air Temperature
Battalion
Battleship

BATDIV
Battleship Division

BATFOR
Battleship Force

BATS
Ballistic Aerial Target System

BATT
Battalion

BATT EFF PRIZE
Battle Efficiency Prize

BAVG
Aviation, General Purpose, British Lend-Lease Ship

BAYONGRP
Bayonne (NJ) Group

B/B
Baby Incendiary Bomb

BB
Back-to-Back
Battleship
Bottom Bounce
Breaks Below

BBB
Basic Boxed Base

BBC
Bareboat Charter
Boiler Blower Control

BBH
Battalion Beachhead

BC
Back Course (approach)
Bareboat Charter
Bathyconductograph
Battery Commander
Blind Copy
Block
Body Count
Bolt Circle
Bottom Contour

BCAPP
Battle Force Capability Assessment and Programming Process

BCC
Basic Cryptanalysis Course

BCD
Bad Conduct Discharge
Binary Coded Decimal

BCDD
Base Construction Depot Detachment

BCH
Beach

BCM
Become
Beyond Capability of Maintenance

BCN
Beacon
Bureau Control Number

BCP
Ballast Control Panel
Basic Control Program

BCST
Broadcast

BCU
Ballistics Computer Unit

BD
Base Detonating
Blowing Dust (weather symbol)
Board
Bomb Disposal
Bundle

BDA
Battle Damage Assessment
Bomb Damage Assessment

BDC
Bottom Dead Center

BDCNR
Board of Correction for Naval Records

BDE
Brigade

BDGC
Bad Conduct Discharge, General Court-Martial after Violation of Probation

BDGE
Brigade

BDHI
Bearing-Distance-Heading Indicator

BDI
Bearing Deviation Indicator

BDII
Battle Damage Indication Imagery

BDL
Baseline Demonstration Laser
Beach Discharge Lighter
Bundle

BDM
Bomber Defense Missile

BDP
Base Development Planning

BDRY
Boundary

BDS
Battle Dressing Station

BDSI
Bad Conduct Discharge, Sentence of Summary Court-Martial, Immediate

BDSP
Bad Conduct Discharge, Summary Court-Martial after Violation of Probation

BDU
Bomb Dummy Unit

BE
Bale
Base-Emitter
Beginning Event
Bombing Encyclopedia

BECO
Booster Engine Cut-Off

BED
Boat Engineering Department

BE/E
Basic Electricity and Electronics (course)

BE/E INLS
Basic Electricity and Electronics Individualized Learning System

BEER
Battery Exhaust Emergency Recirculation

BEES
Basic Electricity and Electronics School

BEF
Blunt End Forward

BEGR
Bore Erosion Gauge Reading

BEHSTU
Behavioral Skill Training Unit

BEIP
Boiler Efficiency Improvement Program

BEL
Bureau Equipment List

BEM
Back Emergency (speed)

BEMAR
Backlog of Essential Maintenance and Repair

BEMO
Bare Equipment Modernization Officers

BENEF
Beneficiary

BENG
Basic Engineering

BENNY SUGG
Beneficial Suggestion (program)

BEN SUG
Beneficial Suggestion (program)

BEOG
Basic Educational Opportunity Grant

BEQ
Bachelor Enlisted Quarters

BERSEAPAT
Bering Sea Patrol

BERSL
Behavioral Sciences Research Laboratory

BESS
Bottom Environmental Sensing System

BEST
Basic Electronics Training (program)
Behavioral Skill Training

BETS
Bullseye Engineering and Technical Services

BF
Back Full (speed)
Board Foot
Boat Foreman
Brazed Joint-Face Fed
Brought Forward

BFD
Inf: Big Fucking Deal

BFDK
Before Dark

BFE
Battlefield Exercise

BFIMA
Battle Force Intermediate Maintenance Activity

BFL
Bill of Lading
Bomb Fall Line

BFM
Basic Flight Maneuvers

BFR
Before
Briefer

BFRL
Basic Facilities Requirements List

BFTT
Battle Force Tactical Trainer

BFWTT
Boilerwater/Feedwater Test and Treatment

BG
Bag
Battle Group

BGIE
Battle Group Inport Exercise

BGLOC
Government Bill of Lading Office Code

BGM
Basegram

BGN
Begin

BGPHES
Battle Group Passive Horizon Extension System

BGPP
Beneficiary Government Production Program

BGRV
Boost Glide Reentry Vehicle

BH
Bunch

BHD
Bulkhead

BHN
Brinell Hardness Number (metals)

BHND
Behind

BHP
Brake Horsepower

BHQ
Brigade Headquarters

BI
Background Investigation
Biographical Inventory
Biological Inventory
Block-In
Brick

BIC
Business Initiatives Council (DOD)

BIFF
Battlefield Identification-Friend or Foe

BIM
Basic Industrial Materials (program)
Beacon Identification Methods
Blade Inspection Method

BINOVC
Breaks in Overcast

BIO
Branch Intelligence Officer

BIOPAC
Biological Packs

BIPAD
Binary Pattern Detector

BIPP
Briefings/Issues/Projects/Programs

BIRDCAP
Rescue Aircraft Combat Air Patrol

BIRDIE
Battery Integration and Radar Display Equipment

BIRO
Base Industrial Relations Officer

BIS
Bibliographic Information Sheet
Board of Inspection and Survey

BIST
Built-In Self-Test

BISTEP
Binary System

BIT
Binary Digit
Built-In Test

BITE
Built-In Test Equipment

BJM
The Bluejacket's Manual

BJN
Basic Jet Navigation

BJU
Beach Jumper Unit

BK
Book
Yardarm Blinker

BKS
Barracks

BKT
Blinker Tube

BKW
Breakwater

B/L
Bill of Lading

BL
Barrel
Base Line
Blank
Bomb Line

BL&P
Blind-Loaded and Traced (projectile)

BLC
Boundary Layer Control

BLD
Build

BLDG
Building

BLEU
Blind Landing Experimental Unit

BLIS
Base Level Inquiry System

BLKD
Blocked

BLO
Below
Bombardment Liaison Officer

BLP
Bombing Landplane

BLS
Base Loading System

BLT
Battalion Landing Team

BLU
Bomb, Live Unit

BLUE
Best Linear Unbiased Estimation

B/M
Bill of Material

BM
Back Marker
Battle Manning
Bench Mark
Boatswain's Mate

BM1
Boatswain's Mate First Class

BM2
Boatswain's Mate Second Class

BM3
Boatswain's Mate Third Class

BMA
Basic Maintenance Allowance

BMAA
Barracks Master-at-Arms

BMAC
Basic Medical Assistant Course

BMAT
Bill of Material

BMC
Chief Boatswain's Mate

BMCM
Master Chief Boatswain's Mate

BMCS
Senior Chief Boatswain's Mate

BMD
Ballistic Missile Defense
Base Maintenance Division

BMDO
Ballistic Missile Defense Organization

BMEP
Brake Mean Effective Pressure

BMEWS
Ballistic Missile Early Warning System

BMG
Browning Machine Gun

BMJ
Basic Military Journalist (DINFOS course)

BMNT
Beginning of Morning Nautical Twilight

BMOW
Boatswain's Mate-of-the-Watch

BMR
Basic Military Requirements
Basic Military Requirements
Beachmaster
Bomber
River Monitor

BMRL
Small River Monitor

BMS
Ballistic Missile Ship

BMSA
Boatswain's Mate Seaman Apprentice

BMSN
Boatswain's Mate Seaman

BMU
Beachmaster Unit

BMUP
Block Modification Upgrade Program

BN
Battalion
Bombardier Navigator
Bombing/Navigator

BNAO
Basic Naval Aviation Officers School

BN-CP
Battalion Command Post

BNDRY
Boundary

BNDY
Boundary

BNEP
Basic Naval Establishment Plan

BNTH
Beneath

BO
Back Order
Base Order
Black-Out
Block-Out
Buyer's Option

BOA
Basic Ordering Agreement
Break-Off Altitude

BOA-MILS
Broad Ocean Area Missile Impact Locating System

BOATSUPPU
Boat Support Unit

BOB
Barge on Board
Branch Office, Boston (ONR)
Bureau of the Budget

BOC
Billet Occupational Code
Branch Office, Chicago (ONR)

BOD
Basic Operational Data
Beneficiary Occupancy Date

B OF R
Board of Review

BOH
Break-Off Height

BOI
Boiler

BOL
Branch Office, London

BOM
Bill of Material
Bomb
By Other Means

BOMEX
Barbados Oceanographic and Meteorological Experiment

BOMID
Branch Office, Military Intelligence Division

BOOST
Broadened Opportunity for Officer Selection and Training

BOOW
Battalion Officer-of-the-Watch

BOP
Blow-Out Preventer

Branch Office, Pasadena (ONR)

BOQ
Bachelor Officers' Quarters

BO REL
Back Order Release

BORU
Boat Operating and Repair Unit

BOS
Base Operating Support
Basic Operating System

BOSN
Boatswain

BOSS-WEDGE
Bomb Orbital Strategic System-Weapon Development Glide Entry

BOSTONSARCOORD
Coast Guard Search and Rescue Coordinator, Boston (MA)

BOT
Beginning of Tape
Bottom

BP
Base Pay
Brazed Joint-Preinserted Ring
Budget Project

BPA
Basic Pressure Altitude
Blanket Purchase Agreement
Blanket Purchase Authority
Blocked Precedence Announcement

BPB
Base Planning Board

BPD
Barrels Per Day

BPDLS
Base Point Defense Launching System

BPDSMS
Base Point Defense Surface Missile System

BPED
Base Pay Entry Date

BPN
Budget Project Number
Bureau Project Number

BPO
Barracks Petty Officer
Base Post Office
Blood Program Office
Budget Project Officer

BPPG
Bureau Planned Procurement Guide

BPR
Bridge Plotting Room

BPS
Bits Per Second

BQC
Basic Qualification Course

BR
Back Reflection
Bar
Bomber Reconnaissance (aircraft)
Breeder Reactor
Briefing Room

BR&CL
Branch and Class

BR1
Boilermaker First Class

BRA
Bench Replaceable Assembly

BRAC
Base Closure and Realignment

BRAS
Ballistic Rocket Air Suppression

BRASO
Branch Aviation Supply Office

BRASS
Ballistic Range for Aircraft Survivability Studies

BRC
Base Recovery Course
Chief Boilermaker

BRCM
Master Chief Boilermaker

BRCS
Senior Chief Boilermaker

BRD
Underwater Mobile Submarine Radio Detection Finder

BRF
Brief

BRFA
Boilermaker Fireman Apprentice

BRFN
Boilermaker Fireman

BRG
Bearing
Bridge

BRIG
Brigade

BRINSMAT
Branch Officer, Inspector of Naval Material

BRIT
Britain
British

BRITE
Bright Radar Indicator Tower Equipment

BRK
Break

BRKN
Broken

BRL
Ballistic Research Laboratory
Barrel
Bomb Release Line
Boresight Reference Line

BRL/EEP
Bomb Release Line/End Exercise Point

BRM
Barometer

BRNAVCOMMSTO
Branch Navy Commissary Store

BRR
Brigade Receiving Room

BR/RL
Bomb Rack/Rocket Launcher

BRT
Bright

BRU
Boat Repair Unit

BRUSA
British-United States Agreement

BS
Backsight
Blowing Sand (weather symbol)
Bound Seam
Broadcast Station

BSA
Base Structure Annex

BSC
Billet Sequence Code
Broadcast Specialist Course (DINFOS)

BSD
Biological Sciences Division (ONR)

BSDC
Binary Symmetric Dependent Channel

BSIC
Binary Symmetric Independent Channel

BSO
Base Supply Officer
Bomb Safety Office

BSP
Billet Selection Program

BSQ
Bachelor Staff Quarters

BST
Bonded Spoon Type

BSU
Base Service Unit
Beach Support Unit
Boat Support Unit

BT
Ballistic Trajectory
Bathythermograph
Beam-riding Terrier (missile)
Begin Tape
Berth Term
Boilerman Technician
Bottle
Break
Break Transmission

BT1
Boilerman Technician First Class

BT2
Boilerman Technician Second Class

BT3
Boilerman Technician Third Class

BTB
Basic Test Battery
Bomb Thermal Battery

BTC
Chief Boilerman Technician

BTCM
Master Chief Boilerman Technician

BTCS
Senior Chief Boilerman Technician

BTDCPF
Bathythermograph Data Collecting and Processing Facility

BTDPAF
Bathythermograph Data Processing and Analysis Facility

BTE
Battery Terminal Equipment

BTFA
Boilerman Technician Fireman Apprentice

BTFN
Boilerman Technician Fireman

BTL
Beginning of Tape Level

BTM
Bench, Missile Test
Blast Test Missile

BTN
Between

BTR
Better

BTRY
Battery

BTU
British Thermal Unit

BTU/HR
British Thermal Unit per Hour

BTV
Blast Test Vehicle

BTWN
Between

BTY
Battery

B/U
Back-Up

BU
Back-Up
Builder
Buoy Boat (USCG)
Bureau
Bushel

BU1
Builder First Class

BU2
Builder Second Class

BU3
Builder Third Class

BUC
Chief Builder

BUCA
Builder Construction Apprentice

BUCM
Master Chief Builder

BUCN
Builder Constructionman

BUCS
Senior Chief Builder

BUD
Budget

BUD/S
Basic UDT/SEAL (training)

BUIC
Back-Up Intercept Control

BUL
Bulletin

BUM&S
Bureau of Medicine and Surgery

BUMED
Bureau of Medicine and Surgery

BUNO
Bureau Number

BUPS
Beacon, Ultra-Portable S (band)

BUR
Bureau

BUSANDA
Bureau of Supplies and Accounts

BUSH
Buy U.S. Here (contracts)

BUSL
Buoy Boat, Stern-Loading (USCG)

BUWC
Basic Underseas Weapons Circuit

BVE
Binocular Visual Efficiency

BVP
Beacon Video Processor

BVPS
Beacon Video Processing System

BVR
Beyond Visual Range

BW
Below Water
Biological Warfare
Butt Weld

BWAR
Budget Workload Analysis Report

B/WCC
Bomb to Warhead Conversion Components

BW/CW
Biological Warfare/Chemical Warfare

BW/FWT&TT
Boiler Water/Feedwater Test and Treatment Training

BWO
Backward Wave Oscillator

BWPA
Backward Wave Power Amplifier

BWR
Boiler Water Reactor

BWVB
Black and White Vertical Bands (buoy markings)

BX
Box

BY
Budget Year

BZ
Well Done

BZI
Beam Zero Indication

C

C
Can (buoy)
Circling
Clear (weather symbol)
Confidential
Controlled
Controller (NAO code)
Cylinder (buoy)

C&C
Command and Control
Communications and Control

C&CS
Communications and Control Subsystem

C&D
Cover and Deception

C&GS
Command and General Staff

C&M
Construction and Machinery

C&R
Convoy and Routing

C&S
Charges and Specifications
Clean and Sober

C&SS
Clothing and Small Stores

C^2D^2
Command and Control Development Division

C^2IF
Command and Control Information Flow

C^3
Command and Control and Communications

C1
Fully Mission Capable

C2
Command and Control

C2F
Commander Second Fleet

C2P
Next Generation Command and Control Processor

C-3
Poseidon Missile

C3
Command, Control, and Communications

C3CM
Command, Control, and Communications Countermeasures

C3F
Commander Third Fleet

C3I
Command, Control, Communications and Intelligence

C4I
Command, Control, Communications, Computers, and Intelligence

C4ISR
Command, Control, Communications, Computers, Intelligence, Surveillance, and Reconnaissance

C5RA
Combat Systems, Command, Control, Computers, and Communications Readiness Assessment

C/A
Civic Action
Contract Administration

CA
Cartridge
Civil Authorities
Closest Approach (NNSS)
Commercial Activity
Commercially Available
Compartment and Access
Construction Apprentice
Container Agreement
Contract Administration
Convening Authority
Cumulative Amount
Current Address
Heavy Cruiser

CAAC
Counseling and Assistance Center

CAAD
Counseling and Assistance Director

CAAR
Compressed Air Accumulator Rocket

CAB
Captured Air Bubble (boat)
Centralized Accounting and Billeting

CAC
Climate-Altitude Chamber
Combat Air Crew
Combined Action Company
Commander Air Center
Common-Access Cards
Contract Area Commander
Contract Administration Control
Cost Accounting Code

CAC&W
Continental Aircraft Control and Warning

CAC/FHS
Casualty Assistance Calls and Funeral Honors Support

CACHE
Computer-Controlled Automated Cargo Handling Envelope

CACO
Casualty Assistance Calls Officer

CACP
Casualty Assistance Calls Program

CAD
Cartridge-Actuated Device
Central Accounts Division
Central Aircraft Dispatch
Civic Action Detachment
Civil Affairs Division
Collective Address Designator
Component Advanced
Computer Address Decoder (NNSS)
Computer-Aided Design
Contract Award Date

CADC
Central Air Data Computer
Combined Administrative Committee
Computer-Aided Design Council

CADD
Combat Zone, Additional Withholding Tax
Current Active Duty Date

CADFISS
Computation and Data Flow Integrated Subsystem

CADIZ
Canadian Air Defense Identification Zone

CADM
Configuration and Data Management

CADNC
Computer-Aided Design and Numerical Control

CADPO
Communications and Data Processing Operation

CADRC
Combined Air Documents Research Center

CADRE
Completed Active Duty Requirements, Enlisted

CADRT
Computer-Aided Dead-Reckoning Table

CAE
Computer-Assisted Enrollment

CAF
Clerical, Administrative, and Fiscal
Combined Action Forces
Completed Assembly for Ferry
Contract Administration Functions

CAFAF
Commander Amphibious Forces, Atlantic Fleet

CAFPF
Commander Amphibious Forces, Pacific Fleet

CAFSU
Carrier and Field Service Unit

CAFT
Consolidated Advance Field Team

CAG
Carrier Air Group
Catapult and Arresting Gear
Civil Affairs Group
Combined Action Group
Guided Missile Heavy Cruiser

CAGO
Cargo in Apparent Good Order

CAI
Computer-Assisted Instruction

CAIC
Computer-Assisted Instruction Center

CAIG
Cost Analysis Improvement Group

CAIMS
Conventional Ammunition Integrated Management System

CAINS
Carrier Aircraft Inertial Navigation System

CAIRC
Caribbean Air Command

CAL
Caliber
Confined Area Loading

CALIBR
Calibration

CALS
Communications Area Local Station
Computer Lesson Service

CAL/VAL
Calibration and Validation

CAM
Channel Access Module
Computer-Aided Manufacturing
Content Addressable Memory
Contract Audit Manual (DCAA)
Cybernetic Anthropomorphous Machine

CAMAL
Continuous Airborne Missile-Launched and Low-Level (system)

CAMAS
Computer-Assisted Manpower Analyses System

CAMEL
Critical Aeronautical Material/Equipment List

CAMI
Continuing Action Maintenance Instructions

CAMP
Computer-Aided Mask Preparation
Computer Applications of Military Problems

CAMS
Commissioning Accession Management System
Communications Area Master Station

CAMSI
Canadian, American Merchant Shipping Instructions
Carrier Aircraft Maintenance Support Improvement

CAN
Canister

CANC
Cancel

CANDR
Convoy and Routing

CANEL
Connecticut Advanced Nuclear Engineering Laboratory

CANTRAC
Catalog of Naval Training Courses

CAN-UK-US
Canadian-United Kingdom-United States

CANX
Canceled

CAO
Change of Administrative Office
Civil Affairs Officer
Collateral Action Officer
Contract Administration Office

CAOC
Counter Air Operations Center

CAORF
Computer-Aided Operations Research Facility

CAOS
Completely Automatic Operational System

CAP
Capture
Combat Air Patrol
Combined Action Platoon
Command Action Program
Command Advancement Program
Communications Afloat Program
Contractor Assessment Program
Coriolis Acceleration Platform
Corrective Action Program
Current Assessment Plan

CAPCHE
Component Automatic Programmed Checkout

CAPCP
Civil Air Patrol Coastal Patrol

CAPDET
Commercial Activities Program Detachment

CAPDETREGOFF
Commercial Activities Program Detachment Regional Office

CAPE
Capability and Proficiency Evaluation
Communications Automatic Processing Equipment

CAPPI
Constant-Altitude Plan-Position Indicator

CAPRI
Compact All-Purpose Range Instrumentation
Computerized Advance Personnel Requirements Information

CAPSQ-N
Capital Area Personnel Services Office-Navy

CAPT
Captain

CAPTOR
Encapsulated Torpedo

CAPUC
Coordinating Area Production Urgency Committee

CAPWSK
Collision Avoidance, Proximity Warning, Station-Keeping

CAR
Caribbean
Carrier
Cloudtop Altitude Radiometer
Combat Action Ribbon
Configuration Audit Review

CARAEWRON
Carrier Airborne Early Warning Squadron

CARAEWTRARON
Carrier Airborne Early Warning Training Squadron

CARAIRSUPPDET
Carrier Air Support Detachment

CARAM
Content Addressable Random Access memory

CARANTISUBAIRGRU
Carrier Antisubmarine Warfare Air Group

CARANTISUBGRU
Carrier Antisubmarine Warfare Group

CARASGRURES
Reserve Carrier Antisubmarine Group

CARASWAIRGRU
Carrier Antisubmarine Warfare Air Group

CARB
Carburetor

CARBAGAIR
Baggage for Air Cargo

CARBASORD
Carry out Remainder of Basic Orders

CARBSEAFRON
Caribbean Sea Frontier

CARDIV
Carrier Division

CARE
Cause and Removal Error

CAREPAY
Centralized Automated Reserve Pay

CARF
Central Altitude Reservation Facility

CARGO
Consolidated Afloat Requisitioning Guide

CARIB
Caribbean (Sea)

CARIBDIV
Caribbean Division

CARIBSEAFRON
Caribbean Sea Frontier

CARINFOCEN
Career Information Center

CARINFRO
Career Information

CARP
Carpenter
Computer Air-Release Point

CARQUAL
Carrier Qualification

CARS
Country, Area, or Regional Specialist

CARSO
Country, Area, or Regional Staff Officer

CART
Cartridge
Central Automated Replenishment Technique
Central Automatic Reliability Tester
Combat-Ready Training
Command Assessment of Readiness and Training

CARTASKFOR
Carrier Task force

CARTU
Combat Aircraft Refresher Training

CAS
Calculated Airspeed
Carrier Air Support
Casualty
Civil Affairs Section
Close Air Support
Collision Avoidance System
Combined Antenna System
Completely Assembled for Strike
Contract Administration Services
Controlled American Source
Cost Accounting Standards

CASA
Commander Antarctic Support Activities

CASB
Cost Accounting Standards Board

CASCAN
Casualty Cancelled

CASCON
Casualty Control Station

CASCOR
Casualty Correction

CASCP
Caribbean Area Small Craft Project

CASCU
Commander Aircraft Support Control Unit

CASD
Carrier Aircraft Service Detachment

Carrier Air Support Detachment
Computer-Aided System Design

CASDAC
Computer-Aided Ship Design and Construction

CASDIV
Carrier Aircraft Services Division

CASDO
Computer Application Support and Development Office

CASDS
Carrier Aircraft Service Detachments
Computer-Aided Structural Detailing of Ships

CASE
Commission on the Accreditation of Service Experience
Computer-Aided System Evaluation
Counter-Agency for Sabotage and Espionage

CASEVAC
Casualty-Evacuee

CASEX
Casualty Exercise

CASINFOSUPPSYS
Casualty Information Support System

CASOFF
Control and Surveillance of Friendly Forces

CASP
Computer-Assisted Search Planning

CASPER
Contact Area Summary Position Report

CASREP
Casualty Report

CASS
Carrier Aircraft Support Study
Central Automated Support System
Command Active Sonobuoy System
Core Auxiliary Cooling System (reactors)

CAST
Computerized Automatic Systems Tester

CASU
Carrier Aircraft Service Unit

CASU(F)
Combat Aircraft Service Unit (Fleet)

CASUM
Civil Affairs Summary

CASWO
Confidential and Secret Weekly Orders

CAT
Carburetor Air Temperature
Cartridge Assembly Test
Catapult
Category
Civic Action Team
Clear Air Turbulence
Collect and Transmit
Combined Acceptance Trials
Compute of Average Transients
Crisis Action Team

CATCC
Carrier Air Traffic Control Center

CATCO
Carrier Air Traffic Control Officer

CATF
Commander Amphibious Task Force

CATG
Commander Amphibious Task Group

CATO
Computer for Automatic Teaching Operations
Cycloidal Activities in Two Oceans

CATOCOMP
Computer for Automatic Teaching Operations-Compiler

CATORES
Computer for Automatic Teaching Operations-Resident

CATS
Centralized Automatic Test System
Civil Affairs Training School
Communications and Tracking System

CATU
Combat Aircrew Training Unit

CAVCO
Consolidatd Audio-Visual Coordinating Office

CAVE
Consolidated Aquanaut Vital Equipment

CAVT
Constant Absolute Vorticity Trajectories

CAVU
Ceiling and Visibility Unlimited

CAW
Inf: Computer-Assisted War

CAWEX
Conventional Air Warfare Exercise

CAX
Cheltenham Annex

CB
Carbuoy
Center of Buoyancy
Circuit Breaker
Citizen's Band
Collector-Base
Common Battery
Construction Battalion
Crash Boat
Crew Boat (USCG)
Cumulonimbus
Seabee

CBA
Classified by Association

CBALS
Carrier-Borne Air Liaison Section

CBASS
Common Broadband Advanced Sonar System

CBC
Construction Battalion Center
Contraband Control
Large Tactical Command Ship

CBCMIS
Construction Battalion Center Management Information System

CBD
Construction Battalion Detachment

CBL
Cable Length
Central Bidder's List
Commercial Bill of Lading

CBLO
Chief Bombardment Liaison Officer

CBLS
Carrier-Borne Air Liaison Officer

CBMU
Construction Battalion Maintenance Unit

CBMUDET
Construction Battalion Maintenance Unit Detachment

CBN
Cabin
Carbine
Construction Battalion

CBNDET
Construction Battalion Detachment

CBO
Coding Board Officer

CBR
Chemical-Bacteriological-Radiological
Chemical-Biological-Radiological

CBRD
Construction Battalion Replacement Depot

CBRNE
Chemical, Biological, Radiological, Nuclear, and Enhanced Explosive

CBRP
Chemical, Biological, and Radiological Protection

CBT
Clinical Laboratory Technician
Combat
Computer-Based Training

CBTENGRBN
Combat Engineer Battalion

CBU
Cluster-Bomb Unit
Contact Back-Up

C/C
Change of Course

CC
Caption Code
Card Column
Cirrocumulus
Combat Command
Command Ship
Communications Controls
Company Commander
Computer Communications
Condition Code
Construction Corps
Control Center

Control Console
Correspondence Course
Cost Center
Cryptologic Center
Cubic Centimeter
Cushion Craft
Tactical Command Ship

CC2IP
CINC Command and Control Initiative

CCA
Carrier Controlled Approach
Configuration Change Actions

CCAC
Combined Civil Affairs Committee

CCAC/L
Combined Civil Affairs Committee-London

CCAC/S
Combined Civil Affairs Committee-Supply

CCAEP
Computer-Controlled Action Entry Panel

CCAM
Computer Communications Access Method

CCAO
Chief Civil Affairs Officer (United States-Britain)

CCAP
Conventional Circuit Analysis Program

CCB
Change Control Board
Combined Communications Board
Command and Control Boat
Configuration Control Board
Contraband Control Base
Contract Change Board

CCBD
Configuration Control Board Directive

CCD
Center for Career Development

CCDB
Contractor's Control Data Bank

CCDD
Command and Control Development Division

CCDL
Commander Cruiser-Destroyer Force, Atlantic

CCGI
Commodity Coordinated Group Items

CCI
Carrier-Controlled Intercept

CCIS
Command Control Information System

CCIU
Component Control Issue Unit

CCL
Communications Circular Letter
Communications Control Link
Convective Condensation Level

CCM
Combined Cipher Machine
Constant Current Modulation
Controlled Carrier Modulation
Counter-Countermeasures

CCMA
Civilian Clothing Maintenance Allowance

CCMC
Civilian Career Management Center

CCMU
Commander's Control and Monitoring Unit

CCN
Contract Change Notice

CCO
Combat Cargo Officer
Commercial Contracting Officer
Contract Change Order

CCOPS
Coordination and Control of Personnel Surveys

CCP
Cross-Check Procedure

CCPO
Centralized Civilian Personnel Office
Consolidated Civilian Personnel Office

CCPOFD
Consolidated Civilian Personnel Office Field Division

CCR
Capital Commitment Request
Closed-Circuit Radio
Coastal Confluence Region
Current Control Relay

CCRS
Computer-Controlled Receiving System

CCS
Combat Control System
Combined Chiefs of Staff
Component Control Section
Contract Change System

CCSB
Change Control Sub-Board

CCSC
Civil Affairs Staff Center

CCSD
Command Communications Service Designator

CCSF
Commander Caribbean Sea Frontier

CCSP
Contractor Claims Settlement Program

CCSS
Command and Control Shore Station

CCT
Coated Cargo Tanks (tankers)
Combined Cortical Thickness
Communications Control Team
Comprehensive College Test

CCTS
Combat Crew Training Squadron

CCTV
Closed-Circuit Television

CCU
Component Control Unit

CCWS
Common Cryptologic Workstation

C/D
Correction/Discrepancy

CD
Camouflage Detection (film)
Card Distribution
Certification Data
Classification of Defects
Code
Cold Drawn (steel)
Confidential Document
Conning Director
Contract Definition

CDA
Command and Data Acquisition (station)

CDAS
Catapult Data Acquisition System

CDC
Caribbean Defense Command
Classification Document Control
Command and Data-Handling Console
Common Distributable Changes
Contract Definition Concept
Control Data Center
Credit Code

CDCE
Command Disaster Control Element

CDCF
Command Disaster Control Force

CDCG
Command Disaster Control Group

CDD
Certification of Disability for Discharge

CDDL
Commander Cruiser-Destroyer Force, Atlantic

CDDP
Commander Cruiser-Destroyer Force, Pacific

CDE
Disaster Control Element

CDF
Class Determinations and Findings
Controlled Detonating Fuze

CDI
Classification Document Index
Collateral Duty Inspector
Course Deviation Indicator

CDIS
Commandant, Defense Intelligence School

CDL
Common Data Link

CDLMS
Common Data Link Management System

CDL-N
Common Data Link-Navy

CDN
Condition

CDO
Central Disbursing Officer
Command Duty Officer

CDOG
Combat Development Objective Guide

CDONSA
Coordinator, Department of the Navy Studies and Analyses

CDOVHL
Crash Damage Overhead

CDP
Career Development Program
Communications Data Processor
Compressor Discharge Pressure
Configuration Data Package
Contract Definition Phase
Cost Data Plan
Cross Deck Pendant
Customer Dividend Program

CDPG
Commander Disaster Preparedness Group

CDPI
Customer Dividend Program Indentification

CDPS
Communications Data Processing System

CDQAI
Collateral Duty Quality Assurance Inspector

CDQCP
Civil Defense Quality Check Program

CDR
Commander
Complete Design Release
Configuration Data Requirements
Critical Design Review

CDRC
Computation and Data Reduction Center

CDRE
Commodore

CDRJPAA
Commander Joint Military Postal Activity, Atlantic

CDRJPAALANT
Commander Joint Military Postal Activity, Atlantic

CDRJTE
Commander Joint Task Element

CDRL
Contractor Data Requirement List

CDS
Central Distribution System (publications)
Commander Destroyer Squadron
Construction Differential Subsidies
Control Distribution System (publications)

CDTC
Computer Detector Test Console

CDX
Control Differential Transmitter

CE
Construction Electrician

CE&TS
Contractor Engineering and Technical Services

CE1
Construction Electrician First Class

CE2
Construction Electrician Second Class

CE3
Construction Electrician Third Class

CEB
CNO Executive Board

CEC
Chief Construction Electrician
Civil Engineering Corps
Cooperative Engagement Capability

CECA
Construction Electrician Constructionman Apprentice

CECM
Master Chief Construction Electrician

CECN
Construction Electrician Constructionman

CECS
Senior Chief Construction Electrician

CEIL
Ceiling

CEN
Center
Central

CENNAVINTEL
Center for Naval Intelligence

CENTCOM
U.S. Central Command

CEO
Chief Executive Officer

CEP
Circular Error Probable

CEPCN
Construction Electrician (Power) Constructionman

CEQC
COMNAVMAR Environmental Quality Control

CER
Complete Engineering Release
Complete Engine Repair

CERAP
Control Center and Radar Approach

CERC
Centralized Engine Room Control

CERF
Commander Emergency Recovery Force

CERG
Commander Emergency Recovery Group

CERMET
Ceramic-to-Metal

CERPS
Centralized Expenditure and Reimbursement Processing System

CERRC
Complete Engine Repair Requirement Card

CERS
Civilian Engineering Squadron
Commander Emergency Recovery Section

CERT
Certificate
Certified

CERTQUAR
Obtain certification of non-availability of government quarters and government mess or officers mess open in accordance with Joint Travel Regulations, par. M 4551

CERU
Commander Emergency Recovery Unit

CES
Commission on Epidemiological Survey
Construction Electrician (Shop)

CES1
Construction Electrician (Shop) First Class

CES2
Construction Electrician (Shop) Second Class

CES3
Construction Electrician (Shop) Third Class

CESCA
Construction Electrician (Shop) Construction Apprentice

CESCN
Construction Electrician (Shop) Constructionman

CESE
Civil Engineering Support Equipment

CESF
Commander Eastern Sea Frontier

CESMIS
Civil Engineer Support Management Information System

CESP
Civil Engineer Support Program

CET
Combat Engineer Tractor
Construction Electrician (Telephone)

CET1
Construction Electrician (Telephone) First Class

CET2
Construction Electrician (Telephone) Second Class

CET3
Construction Electrician (Telephone) Third Class

CETCA
Construction Electrician (Telephone) Constructionman Apprentice

CETCN
Construction Electrician (Telephone) Constructionman

CETS
Contractor Engineering and Technical Services

CEU
Continuing Education Unit

CEV
Combat Engineer Vehicle
Convoy Escort Vehicle

CEW
Construction Electrician (Wiring)

CEW1
Construction Electrician (Wiring) First Flass

CEW2
Construction Electrician (Wiring) Second Class

CEW3
Construction Electrician (Wiring) Third Class

CEWCA
Construction Electrician (Wiring) Constructionman Apprentice

CEWCN
Construction Electrician (Wiring) Constructionman

CEWRC
Civilian Employee Welfare and Recreation Committee

CF
Cable-Firing
Cable-Fuzing
Carry Forward
Centrifugal Force
Complement Fixation
Concept Formulation
Confer
Cumulus Fractus

CFA
Cognizant Field Activity
Contractor-Furnished Accessories

CFAD
Commander Fleet Air Detachment

CFAE
Contractor-Furnished Aeronautical Equipment

CFAR
Constant False Alarm Rate

CFAW
Commander Fleet Air Wing

CFAWL
Commander Fleet Air Wings, Atlantic

CFAWP
Commander Fleet Air Wings, Pacific

CFC
Controlled Force Circulation (boilers)

CF/CD
Concept Formulation/Contract Definition

CFD
Contaminated Fuel Detector

CFDB
Concept Formulation Data Bank

CFE
Contractor-Furnished Equipment

CFF
Control Flip-Flop (NNSS)
Critical Flicker Fusion

CFFC
Commander, United States Fleet Forces Command

CF/HP
Constant-Flow/High-Pressure (oxygen system)

CFI
Certified Flight Instructor

CFM
Confirm
Contractor-Furnished Materials
Cubic Feet per Minute

CFN
Confirmation of Numbers

CFO
Commissioning and Fitting Out
Connection Fitting Out

CFOC
Contractor Fin Opener Crank

C-F/PCM
Course-Fine/Pulse Code Modulator

CFRD
Confidential and Formerly Restricted Data

CFS
Contract Field Services
Cubic Feet per Second

CFSR
Contract Funds Status Report

CFU
Control Functional Unit (data link)

CFWS
Coordinated Federal Wage System

CG
Capacity Gauge (depth)
Centerless Ground
Center of Gravity
Centigram
Coast Guard
Communications Group
Compressed Gas
Cost Growth
Guided-Missile Cruiser

CGC
Coast Guard Cutter

CGE
Cockpit Geometry Evaluation
College

CGFMF
Commanding General, Fleet Marine Force

CGMAW
Commanding General, Marine Air Wing

CGN
Guided Missile Cruiser (Nuclear-Powered)

CGOS
Combat Gunnery Officers School

CGRS
Central Gyro Reference System

CGSE
Common Ground Support Equipment

CGSEL
Common Ground Support Equipment List

cGy
Centigrays

C-H
Candle-Hour

CH
Channel
Chester
Chief of the _____
Children (AFRT code)

CHACOM
Chief of Naval Communications

CHAF(F)ROC
Chaff Rocket

CHAFFROC
Chaff Rocket

CHAMPION
Compatible Hardware and Milestone Program for Integrating Organizational Needs

CHAMPUS
Civilian Health and Medical Program of the Uniformed Services

CHAN
Channel

CHANSY
Charleston Naval Shipyard

CHAP
Chaplain
Chapter

CHARM
Civil Aeronautics Agency High-Altitude

CHAR-TRAN
Character Translation

CHASGRP
Charleston (SC) Group

CHATRA
Chaff Trajectory

CHAVMAINTECH
Chief Aviation Maintenance Technician

CHB
Cargo Handling Battalion

CHBOSN
Chief Boatswain

CHC
Chaplain Corps

CHCIVENG
Chief of Civil Engineers

CHDLG
Chief, Defense Liaison Group

CHDLG-INDO
Chief, Defense Liaison Group-Indonesia

CHEC
Checkered (buoy)

CHELECTECH
Chief Electronics Technician

CHEMBOMB
Chemical Bomb

CHESBAYGRU
Chesapeake Bay Group

CHESDIVNAVFACENGCOM
Chesapeake Division, Naval Facilities Engineering Command

CHESDIVSEACON
Chesapeake Division, Ocean Construction Platform

CHESDIVSUPPFAC
Chesapeake Division Support Facility

CHG
Change
Charge

CHGS
Changes

CHIL
Consolidated Hazardous Item List

CHINFO
Chief of Information

CHK/DEBT-LIST
Bad Checks and Indebtedness List

CHMDO
Chief, Military Equipment Delivery Team

CHMEDT
Chief, Mutual Defense Assistance Team

CHMILTAG
Chief, Military Technical Aid Group

CHNAVADVGRU
Chief, Naval Advisory Group

CHNAVDEV
Chief of Naval Development

CHNAVMARCORMARS
Chief, Navy-Marine Corps Military Affiliate Radio Station

CHNAVMAT
Chief of Naval Material

CHNAVMAT ERS
Chief of Naval Material Emergency Relocation Site Commander

CHNAVMIS
Chief, U.S. Naval Mission to ______ (country)

CHNAVRSCH
Chief of Naval Research

CHNAVSECJUSMAGTHAI
Chief, Navy Section, Joint United States Military Advisory Group, Thailand

CHNAVSECMAAG
Chief, Naval Section, Military Assistance Advisory Group

CHNAVSECMTM
Chief, Navy Section, Military Training Mission

CHNAVSECUSMILGP
Chief, Navy Section, United States Military Group

CHNAVTRASUPP
Chief of Naval Training Support

CHNOMISO
Chief, Naval Ordnance Management Information System Office

CHOP
Change of Operational Control

CHORI
Chief of Office of Research and Inventions

CH/RM
Chill Room (stowage)

CHSAMS
Chief, Security Assistance Management and Staff

CHT
Chemist
Collection, Holding and Transfer

CHU
Centrigade Heat Units

CHUM
Chart Updating Manual

CHUSDLG
Chief, United States Defense Liaison Group

CHUSNAVMIS
Chief, United States Naval Mission

C/I
Commercial/Industrial

CI
Cirrus
Configuration Inspection

Configuration Item
Control Indicator
Cost Inspector
Counterinsurgency
Critical Item
Cubic Inch

CIA
Central Intelligence Agency

CIAC
Career Information and Counseling

CIACT
Civilian Industrial Advisory Committee for Telecommunications
CNO Industry Advisory Committee for Telecommunications

CIB
COBOL Information Bulletin (publication)
Combat Information Bureau
Command Information Bureau
Communication Information Bulletin
Current Intelligence Brief

CIC
Clinical Investigation Center
Combat Information Center
Combat Intercept Control
Combined Intelligence Committee
Content Indication Code (AUTODIN)
Counter-Intelligence Corps (G-2)
Customer Identification Code

CICC
Clinical Investigation Control Center

CICO
Combat Information Control Officer

CICWO
Combat Information Center Watch Officer

CID
Change in Design
Command Information Division
Component Identification Description (number)

CIDNO
Contractor's Identification Number

CIDS
Consolidated Information on Data Schedule
Coordination of Direct Support

CIF
Central Intelligence File

CIG
Central Intelligence Group
Ceiling

CIGTF
Central Inertial Guidance Test Facility

CII
Component Identification Index
Configuration Identification Index

CIL
Critical Item List

CIM
Communications Improvement Memorandum

CIMMS
Civilian Information Manpower Management

CIMS
Civilian Information Management System
Communications Instructions for Merchant Ships

C-in-C
Commander-in-Chief

CINC
Commander-in-Chief

CINCAL
Commander-in-Chief, Alaska

CINCARIB
Commander-in-Chief, Caribbean

CINCEASTLANT
Commander-in-Chief, Eastern Atlantic Fleet

CINCENT
Commander-in-Chief, Allied Forces Central Europe

CINCEUR
Commander-in-Chief, Europe

CINCLANT
Commander-in-Chief, Atlantic

CINCLANT ABNCP
Commander-in-Chief, Atlantic Airborne Command Post

CINCLANT CAO
Commander-in-Chief, Atlantic Coordination of Atomic Operations

CINCLANTFLT
Commander-in-Chief, Atlantic Fleet

CINCLANTFLTRESAFFAIRS
Commander-in-Chief, Atlantic Reserve Affairs Officer

CINCLANTREP
Commander-in-Chief, Atlantic Representative

CINCMEDAFSA
Commander-in-Chief, Middle East/South Asia and Africa South of the Sahara

CINCNELM
Commander in Chief, U.S. Naval Forces, Eastern Atlantic and Mediterranean

CINCNORAD
Commander-in-Chief, North American Air Defense Command

CINCPAC
Commander-in-Chief, Pacific

CINCPACFLT
Commander-in-Chief, Pacific Fleet

CINCPACFLT ACE
Commander-in-Chief, Pacific Fleet, Alternate Command Element Commander

CINCPACFLT ECC
Commander-in-Chief, Pacific Fleet, Emergency Command Center Commander

CINCPACFLT ERS
Commander-in-Chief, Pacific Fleet, Emergency Relocation Site Commander

CINCPACFLT OAC
Commander-in-Chief, Pacific Fleet, Oceanic Airspace Coordinator

CINCPACFLTREP
Commander-in-Chief, Pacific Fleet Representative

CINCPACFLTREPPACMISTESTCEN
Commander-in-Chief, Pacific Fleet Representative, Pacific Missile Test Center

CINCPACHEDPEARL
Commander-in-Chief, Pacific Fleet Headquarters, Pearl Harbor (HI)

CINCPACREP
Commander-in-Chief, Pacific Representative

CINCSOUTH
Commander-in-Chief, Allied Forces Southern Europe

CINCSTRIKE
Commander-in-Chief, U.S. Strike Command

CINCUNC
Commander-in-Chief, United Nations Command

CINCUNCKOREA
Commander-in-Chief, United Nations Command, Korea

CINCUSNAVEUR
Commander-in-Chief, United States Naval Forces Europe

CINCUSNAVEURALT
Commander-in-Chief, United States Naval Forces, Europe, Alternate Commander

CINCUSNAVEUR ERS
Commander-in-Chief, United States Naval Forces, Europe, Emergency Relocation Site Commander

CINCUSNAVEUR IDHS
Commander-in-Chief, United States Naval Forces, Europe, Intelligence Data Handling System

CINCWESTLANT
Commander-in-Chief, Western Atlantic Area

CINOS
Centralized Input/Output System

CINTEX
Combined Import Training Exercise

CIO
Combat Intelligence Officer
Conference on the Inhabitants of the Ocean

CIOR
Interallied Confederation of Reserve Officers

CIOS
Combined Intelligence Objectives Subcommittee
Combined Intelligence Operations Section

CIP
Class Improvement Plan
Clinical Investigation Program
Coast-In Point
Combined Instrument Panel (submarines)
Computer Image-Processing

CIPC
Combined Intelligence Priorities Committee

(U.S.-Britain)

CIR
Circulator
Cost Information Reports

CIRCLTR
Circular Letter

CIRCUITROUTE
Circuitous Route

CIREP
Circular Error Probable

CIRO
Consolidated Industrial Relations Office

CIRVIS
Communications Instructions, Reporting Vital Intelligence Sightings

CIS
Cost Inspection Service
Curriculum and Instructional Standards

CI/SERE
Counterinsurgency/Survival, Evasion, Resistance, and Escape

CISP
Cast-Iron Soil Pipe

CISS
Casualty Information Support System

CIT
Catalog Input Transmittal
Center for Information Technology
Citation
Citizen

CITC
Computer Indicator Test Console

CITE
Compression Ignition and Turbine Engine (fuel)
Contractor Independent Technical Effort

CIU
Central Interpretation Unit

CIV
Civilian

CIVAFFAIRSGRU
Civil Affairs Group

CIVCLO
Civilian Clothing

CIV CONF
Civilian Confinement

CIV DEF
Civil Defendent

CIVEMP
Civilian Employee

CIVEMPAF
Civilian Employees of Non-Appropriated Fund Activities (record system)

CIVENGLAB
Civil Engineering Laboratory

CIV-M-MARP
Civilian-Mobilization-Manpower Allocation/Requirements Plan

CIVPERSADMSYS
Civilian Personnel Administration Services Record System

CIVPERS/EEODIRSYS
Civilian Personnel/Equal Employment Opportunity Directives System

CIVSUB
Civilian Substitution (program)

CIWS
Close-In Weapons System

CJTF
Commander Joint Task Force

CJTG
Commander Joint Task Group

CK
Cake
Check

C/L
Carrier Landing
Circular Letter

CL
Centerline
Class
Clearance
Coil
Light Cruiser

CLA
Certified Laboratory Assistant
Crew Loading Analysis

CLAC
Combined Liberated Areas Committee

CLAIMS
Conventional Ammunition Integrated Management System

CLAM
Chemical Low-Altitude Missile
Classification Management

CLAMP
Closed Loop Aeronautical Management

CLAS
Class
Classification
Classified
Classify

CLASP
Classification and Assignments within Pride Program

CLASSMATE
Computer Language to Aid and Stimulate Scientific, Mathematical, and Technical Education

CLC
Command and Control Ship
Communications Line Controller

CLCVN
Class Convening

CLDAS
Clinical Laboratory Data Acquisition System

CLEP
College-Level Examination Program

CLER
Clerical (aptitude test)

CLF
Civilian Labor Force
Combat Logistics Force
Commander Landing Force

CLG
Guided Missile Light Cruiser

CLGN
Guided Missile Light Cruiser (Nuclear Powered)

CLIFS
Costs, Life, Interchangeability, Function, and Safety

CLIP
Compiler and Language for Information Processing

CLK
Hunter-Killer Ship

CLL
Consolidated Load List

CLNC
Clearance

CLO
Campus Liaison Officer
Chief Learning Officer
Command Liaison Officer

CLOSENLJACKRET
Activity performing final separation procedures directed to close out enlisted jacket and forward it to NMPC (Code 38). In "Remarks" section of page 14 show effective date of retirement, grade in which retired, and provisions of law under which retired by reason of completion of more than ______ years service.

CLP
Command Language Program

CLR
Center of Lateral Resistance
Clear

CLSA
Cooperative Logistic Support Agreement

CLSD
Closed

CLSSA
Cooperative Logistics Supply Support Arrangement

CLTE
Commissioned Loss to Enlisted Status

CLUDACTDAT
Include accounting data on orders, transportation requests, and meal tickets covering such travel

CLUSA
Continental Limits, United States of America

CM
Celestial Mechanics
Centimeters
Chemical Milling
Circular Mil (wire measure)
Configuration Management

Construction and Machinery
Construction Mechanic
Contract Modification
Contractural Milestone
Controlled Minefield
Corrective Maintenance
Countermeasures
Courts-Martial
Cumulonimbus Mammatus
Minelayer Ship

CM&D
Countermeasures and Deception

CM1
Construction Mechanic First Class

CM2
Construction Mechanic Second Class

CM3
Construction Mechanic Third Class

CMA
Civil-Military Affairs
Clothing Maintenance Allowance
Court of Military Appeals

CMAA
Chief Master-at-Arms

CMB
Code Matrix Block

CMBD
Combined

CMBL
Commercial Bill of Lading

CMC
Chief Construction Mechanic
Commandant of the Marine Corps
Command Master Chief
Communication Multiplexor Channel

CMCA
Construction Mechanic Constructionman Apprentice

CMCM
Master Chief Construction Mechanic

CMCN
Construction Mechanic Constructionman

CMCO
Confidential Material Control Officer

CMCRL
Consolidated Master Cross Reference List

CMCS
Communications Monitoring and Control System
Senior Chief Construction Mechanic

CMD
Capital Military District
Command
Cruise Missile Defense

CMDCM
Command Master Chief Petty Officer

CMDN
Catalogue Management Data Notification

CMF
Coherent Memory Filter

CMG
Chief Marine Gunner

C/MH
Cost per Manhour

CMH
Congressional Medal of Honor

CMI
Computer-Managed Instruction

CMIO
Communications Material Issuing Office

CMIS
Court-Martial Index and Summary

CML
Commercial
Current Mode Logic

CMM
Configuration Management Manual

CMMG
Civilian Manpower Management Guides

CMMI
Civilian Manpower Management Instructions

CMML
Civilian Manpower Management Letters

CMN
Chairman
Commission

CMO
Configuration Management Office
Controlled Materials Officer
Court-Martial Officer
Court-Martial Orders

CMOOW
Company Midshipman Officer-of-the-Watch

C-MOS
Complementary-Metal Oxide Semiconductor

CMP
Camp
Contract Maintenance Plan
Corps of Military Police

CMPCTR
Computer Center

CMPI
Civilian Marine Personnel Instructions

CMR
Common Mode Rejection
Contract Management Region
Court-Martial Reports

CMRF
Capital Maintenance and Rental Funds

CMRR
Common Mode Rejection Rate

C/MRS
Calibration/Measurement Requirements Summary

CMS
Career Management Detailing System
Communications Security Material System

CMSS
Communications Security Material System
Compiler Monitor System
Crewmember Trainee

CMTC
Civilian Military Training Camp

CMTQ
Cruise Missile Tactical Qualification

CMV
Common Mode Voltage

CN
Can
Constructionman
Controller

CNA
Canadian Northwest Atlantic
Center for Naval Analyses
Chief of Naval Air
Computer Network Attack

CNAADTRA
Chief of Naval Air Advanced Training

CNAB
Commander Naval Air Bases

CNABTRA
Chief, Naval Air Basic Training

CNAF
Commander, Naval Air Forces

CNAG
Chief, Naval Advisory Group

CNAL
Commander Naval Air Forces, Atlantic

CNAP
Commander Naval Air Forces, Pacific

CNAR
Commander Naval Air Reserve

CNARESTRA
Chief of Naval Reserve Training

CNARF
Commander Naval Air Reserve Force

CNAT
Chief of Naval Air Training

CNATECHTRA
Chief of Naval Air Technical Training

CNATRA
Chief of Naval Air Training

CNATT
Chief of Naval Air Technical Training

CNAVAADTRA
Chief of Naval Air Advanced Training

CNAVADTRA
Chief of Naval Air Advanced Training

CNAVAIR
Chief of Naval Air

CNAVANTRA
Chief of Naval Air Advanced Training

CNAVRES
Chief of Naval Reserve

CNAVRESAIRLANTREP
Chief of Naval Reserve, Representative for Naval Air Forces, Atlantic

CNAVRESAIRPACREP
Chief of Naval Reserve, Representative for Naval Air Forces, Pacific

CNB
Commander Naval Base

CNBZN
Cannibalization

CNC
Central Navigation Computer
Change of Notice Card
Change of Notice Code
Chief of Naval Communications

CNCL
Cancel
Cancellation

CND
Chief of Naval Development

CND/CNA
Computer Network Defense and Attack

CNDO
Chief Navy Disbursing Officer

CNE
Collateral Nature of Effects

CNET
Chief of Naval Education and Training

CNETC
Commander Naval Education and Training Command

CNETLANTREP
Commander Naval Education and Training Command, Representative Coordinator for Atlantic

CNETPACREP
Commander Naval Education and Training Command, Representative Coordinator for Pacific

CNF
Central NOTAMS Facility
Commander Naval Forces

CNFA
Commander, U.S. Naval Forces, Azores

CNFJ
Commander, U.S. Naval Forces, Japan

CNFSD
Confused

CNG
Commander Northern Group

CNHAVRSCH
Chief of Naval Research

CNI
Chief of Naval Intelligence
Communications-Navigation Identification
Navy Installations Command

CNIC
Commander Naval Intelligence Command

CNL
Cancel
Cancellation

CNM
Chief of Naval Material
Commander Naval Forces, Marianas

CNMO
Canadian Naval Mission Overseas

CNMPC
Commander Naval Military Personnel Command

CNO
Chief of Naval Operations

CNOB
Commander Naval Operating Base

CNOBO
Chief of Naval Operations Budget Office

CNOCM
CNO-Directed Command Master Chief Petty Officer

CNO/RAAB
Chief of Naval Operations Reserve Affairs Advisory Board

CNP
Celestial North Pole
Chief of Naval Personnel

CNR
Carrier-to-Noise Ratio

Changes to Navy Regulations
Chief of Naval Research
Chief of Naval Reserve

CNRA
Commander Navy Recruiting Area

CNRC
Commander Navy Recruiting Command

CNSG
Consolidated Nuclear Steam Generator

CNSP
Causeway Section (Non-Self Propelled)

CNSTC
Commander Naval Service Training Command

CNSY
Charleston Naval Shipyard

CNSYD
Charleston Naval Shipyard

CNT
Certified Navy Twill
Continuation Pay for Medical/Dental Officers

CNTNTN
Continuation Pay for Medical/Dental Officers

CNTPS
Consolidated Naval Telecommunications Program System

CNTR
Center
Central

CNTRL
Central

CNTS
Chief of Naval Training Support

CNVA
Computer Network Vulnerability Assessment

CNWDI
Critical Nuclear Weapons Design Information

CNX
Cancel
Canceled

C/O
Care of
Change Order

CO
Central Office
Change Order
Coastal (route)
Combined Operations
Commanding Officer
Communications Officer
Company
Conscientious Objector
Container
Contracting Officer
Commander Officer

COAC
Chief Operating Area Coordinator

COB
Chief of the Boat
Committee of Combined Boards
Current on Board (status)

COBLU
Cooperative Outboard Baseline Logistics Update

COC
Certificate of Competency
Certificate of Conformance
Chief of Chaplains
Civilian Orientation Cruise
Combat Operations Center
Control Officer's Console

COCO
Coordinator of Chain Operations (USCG)

COD
Carrier Onboard Delivery
Close Order Drill

CODAC
Collateral Duty Alcoholism Counselor

CODAG
Combined Diesel and Gas (propulsion)

CODAN
Coded (Weather) Analysis

CODAP
Comprehensive Occupational Data Analysis Program
Control Data Assembly Program

CODAR
Coded Aircraft Report
Correlation Display Analyzing and Recording

CODASYL
Conference on Data Systems Languages

CODEL
Congressional Delegation

CODIPHASE
Coherent Digital Phased Array System

CODIS
Coded Discharge
Controlled Orbital Decay and Input System

CODIT
Computer Direct to Telegraph

CODIZ
Cable-Operated Zero Impedance

CODOG
Combined Diesel or Gas (propulsion)

COE
Certificate of Eligibility
Common Operating Environment

COEA
Cost and Operational Effectiveness Analysis

COED
Char Oil Energy Development (process)
Composition and Editing Display
Computer-Operated Electronic Display

COEEOCA
Commanders Equal Employment Opportunity Advisory Council

C OF A
Certificate of Airworthiness

COFC
Container on Flat Car (shipping)

COFS
Chief of Staff

COG
Cognizance
Course Over Ground

COGAG
Combined Gas Turbine and Gas Turbine (propulsion)

COGAGE
Combined Gas Turbine and Turbine Electric (propulsion)

COGAP
Computer Graphics Arrangement Program

COGARD
Coast Guard

COGARDACFTPROGOFF
Coast Guard Aircraft Program Office

COGARDADMINLAWJUDGE
Coast Guard Administrative Law Judge

COGARDAIRSTA
Coast Guard Air Station

COGARDANFAC
Coast Guard Aids to Navigation Facility

COGARDANT
Coast Guard Aids to Navigation Team

COGARDARSC
Coast Guard Aircraft Repair and Supply Center

COGARDAVDET
Coast Guard Aviation Detachment

COGARDAVTC
Coast Guard Aviation Training Center

COGARDAVTECHTRACEN
Coast Guard Aviation Technical Training Center

COGARDBASE
Coast Guard Base

COGARDBST
Coast Guard Boating Safety Team

COGARDCOMMSTA
Coast Guard Communications Station

COGARDCOSARFAC
Coast Guard Coastal Search and Rescue Facility

COGARDCOTP
Coast Guard Captain of the Port Office

COGARDCRUITOFF
Coast Guard Recruiting Office

COGARDEECEN
Coast Guard Electronics Engineering Center

COGARDEGICP
Coast Guard Inventory Control Points

COGARDEP
Coast Guard Depot

COGARDES
Coast Guard Electronic Shop

COGARDESM
Coast Guard Electronic Shop Minor

COGARDESMT
Coast Guard Electronics Shop Minor Telephone and Teletype

COGARDEST
Coast Guard Electronics Shop Major Telephone and Teletype

COGARDETNDBO
Coast Guard National Data Buoy Office Detachment

COGARDFOGSIGSTA
Coast Guard Fog Signal Station

COGARDFSTD
Coast Guard Fire and Safety Test Detachment

COGARDINST
Coast Guard Institute

COGARDISF
Coast Guard Icebreaker Facility

COGARDLOCOMFLETRAGRU
Coast Guard Liaison Officer, Commander Fleet Training Group

COGARDLOEPIC
Coast Guard Liaison Officer Eastern Pacific Intelligence Center

COGARDLOFEASTRACENPAC
Coast Guard Liaison Officer, Fleet Antisubmarine Warfare Training, Central Pacific

COGARDLONNAVDAMCONTRACEN
Coast Guard Liaison Officer, Navy Damage Control Training Center

COGARDLOREP
Coast Guard Liaison Officer Representative

COGARDLORMONSTA
Coast Guard LORAN Monitor Station

COGARDLTSTA
Coast Guard Light Station

COGARDMID
Coast Guard Marine Inspection Detachment

COGARDMILPAYDCEN
Coast Guard Military Pay Center

COGARDMIO
Coast Guard Marine Inspection Office

COGARDMRDET
Coast Guard Maintenance Repair Detachment

COGARDMSD
Coast Guard Marine Safety Detachment

COGARDMSO
Coast Guard Marine Safety Office

COGARDNDBO
Coast Guard National Data Buoy Office

COGARDNMLBS
Coast Guard National Motor Lifeboat School

COGARDNSF
Coast Guard National Strike Force

COGARDNSFGULF
Coast Guard National Strike Force, Gulf

COGARDNSFLANT
Coast Guard National Strike Force, Atlantic

COGARDNSFPAC
Coast Guard National Strike Force, Pacific

COGARDOCEANU
Coast Guard Oceanographic Unit

COGARDOMSTA
Coast Guard Omega Station

COGARDONSOD
Coast Guard Omega Navigation Systems Office Detachment

COGARDOPDAC
Coast Guard Operations Data Analysis Center

COGARDORDSUPPFAC
Coast Guard Ordnance Support Facility

COGARDPSDET
Coast Guard Port Safety Detachment

COGARDPSSTA
Coast Guard Port Safety Station

COGARDRADSTA
Coast Guard Radio Station

COGARDRANDDC
Coast Guard Research and Development Center

COGARDRECDEP
Coast Guard Records Depot

COGARDREPNAVREGMEDCEN
Coast Guard Representative, Naval Regional

Medical Center

COGARDREPSTUDREC
Coast Guard Representative, Student Records

COGARDREPTAMC
Coast Guard Representative, Tripler Army Medical Center

COGARDREPUSAFH
Coast Guard Representative, Student Records

COGARDREPUSPHS
Coast Guard Representative, United States Public Health Service Hospital

COGARDRESCEN
Coast Guard Reserve Center

COGARDRESTRACEN
Coast Guard Reserve Training Center

COGARDRIO
Coast Guard Resident Inspecting Officer

COGARDSHIPTRADET
Coast Guard Ship Training Detachment

COGARDSICP
Coast Guard Stock Inventory Control Point

COGARDSIU
Coast Guard Ship Introduction Unit

COGARDSTA
Coast Guard Station

COGARDSUPCEN
Coast Guard Support Center

COGARDSUPRTFAC
Coast Guard Support Facility

COGARDTRACEN
Coast Guard Training Center

COGARDTRATEAM
Coast Guard Training Team

COGARDVTS
Coast Guard Vessel Traffic System

COGAS
Combined Gas and Steam (propulsion)

COGB
Certified Official Government Business
Continuous Orbital Guidance System

COGOG
Combined Gas Turbine or Gas (propulsion)

COGP
Commission on Government Procurement

COGSA
Carriage of Goods by Sea Act

COH
Completion of Overhaul
Complex Overhaul

COHARDOCC
Coast Guard Operations Computer Center

COHO
Coherent Oscillator

COHQ
Combined Operations Headquarters

COI
Center of Influence
Communications Operation Instruction
Community-of-Interest
Contact of Interest
Course of Instruction

COIC
Combined Operational Intelligence Center

COIN
Counter-Insurgency
Counter-Insurgent (aircraft)
Counter-Intelligence

COINT
Commands Interested

COL
Collateral
College
Colonel
Column
Computer-Oriented Language
Cost-of-Living

COLA
Cost-of-Living Allowance

COLANFORASCU
Commanding Officer, Landing Force Air Support Control Unit

COLDS
Cargo Offload and Discharge System

COLIDAR
Coherent Light Detection and Ranging

COLL
Collect
Collection
Commanding Officer's Leave Listing

COLOD
Completed Loading

COLREGS
Collision Regulations (International Rules of the Road)

COLT
Cryptologic On-Line Trainer

COM
Prefix used with the short title of a command, indicating reference to the commander rather than to the command; *e.g.*, COMCRUDESLANT indicates Commander, Cruiser-Destroyer Force, Atlantic Fleet, not the force, which is CRUDESLANT.
Command
Commander
Commence
Commissioned Officers' Mess
Common
Computer Operated Microfilm

COMA
Court of Military Appeals

COMAAC
Commander Alaskan Air Command

COMAC
Continuous Multiple-Access Collator

COMADC
Commander Air Defense Command

COMAEWW
Commander Airborne Early-Warning Wing

COMAEWWING
Commander Airborne Early-Warning Wing

COMAIRASWING
Commander Air Antisubmarine Wing

COMAIRCANLANT
Air Commander, Canadian Atlantic Sub-Area

COMAIRPATGRU
Commander Air Patrol Group

COMAIRRECONGRU
Commander Air Reconnaissance Group

COMAIRRECONPATGRU
Commander Air Reconnaissance Patrol Group

COMALAIRC
Commander Alaskan Air Command

COMALSEAFRON
Commander Alaskan Sea Frontier

COMANTARCTICSUPPACT
Commander Antarctic Support Activities

COMANTDEFCOM
Commander Antilles Defense Command

COMAREASWFOR
Commander Area Antisubmarine Warfare Forces

COMARSURVRECFOR
Commander Maritime Surveillance and Reconnaissance Force

COMARSURVRECFORDET
Commander Maritime Surveillance and Reconnaissance Force Detachment

COMARSURVRECFORPASRAP
Commander Maritime Surveillance and Reconnaissance Force, Passive ASRAP Data

COMASWFORLANT
Commander Antisubmarine Warfare Forces, Atlantic

COMASWFORPAC
Commander Antisubmarine Warfare Forces, Pacific

COMASWGRU
Commander Antisubmarine Warfare Group

COMASWSUPPTRADET
Commander Antisubmarine Warfare Support Training Detachment

COMASWWINGPAC
Commander Antisubmarine Warfare Wing, Pacific

COMATKCARAIRWING
Commander Attack Carrier Air Wing

COMATKCARSTRIKEFOR
Commander Attack Carrier Strike Force

COMATKSUBFOR
Commander Attack Submarine Force

COMAZSECASWGRU
Commander Azores Sector Antisubmarine Warfare Group

COMB
Combination
Combine

COMBATFOR
Commander Battle Force

COMBATSYSENGDEVSITE
Combat System Engineering Development Site

COMBATSYSTECHSCOLCOM
Combat Systems Technical Schools Command

COMBSVCSUPPSCOLANT
Combined Services Support Program School, Atlantic

COMBSVCSUPPSCOLPAC
Combined Services Support Program School, Pacific

COMCARAIRWING
Commander Carrier Air Wing

COMCARAIRWINGDET
Commander Carrier Air Wing Detachment

COMCARAIRWINGRES
Commander Reserve Carrier Air Wing

COMCARANTISUBAIRGRU
Commander Carrier Antisubmarine Air Group

COMCARASWAIRGRU
Commander Carrier Antisubmarine Air Group

COMCARGRU
Commander Carrier Group

COMCARIBSEAFRON
Commander Caribbean Sea Frontier

COMCARIBSECASWGRU
Commander Caribbean Sector Antisubmarine Warfare Group

COMCARSTRIKEFOR
Commander Carrier Striking Force

COMCBLANT
Commander Naval Construction Battalions, Atlantic

COMCBLANTDET
Commander Naval Construction Battalions, Atlantic Detachment

COMCBLANT MLO
Commander Naval Construction Battalions, Atlantic, Material Liaison Office

COMCBPAC
Commander Naval Construction Battalions, Pacific

COMCEDEFOR/COMICEASWGRU
Commander Iceland Defense Force/Commander Iceland Antisubmarine Warfare Group

COMCENSECT/WESTSEAFRON
Commander Central Section/Western Sea Frontier

COMCM
Communications Countermeasures

COMCMDCOORDFOR
Commander Command and Coordination Force

COMCOGARDACTEUR
Commander Coast Guard Activities, Europe

COMCOGARDEUR
Commander Coast Guard Force, Europe

COMCOGARDFESEC
Commander Coast Guard Section Office, Far East Section

COMCOGARDGANTSEC
Commander Coast Guard Section Office, Guantanamo Section

COMCOGARDGRU
Commander Coast Guard Group

COMCOGARDLANT
Commander Coast Guard, Atlantic

COMCOGARDLANTWWMCCS
Commander Coast Guard World-Wide Military Command and Control System, Atlantic

COMCOGARDMARSEC
Commander Coast Guard, Maritime Section

COMCOGARDRON
Commander Coast Guard, Southeast Squadron

COMCORTDIV
Commander Escort Division

COMCORTRON
Commander Escort Squadron

COMCOSDIV
Commander Coastal Division

COMCOSURVFOR
Commander Coastal Surveillance Force

COMCRUDESGRU
Commander Cruiser-Destroyer Group

COMCRUDESLANT
Commander Cruiser-Destroyer Force, Atlantic

COMCRUDESLANTSUPPGRU
Commander Cruiser-Destroyer Force, Atlantic Support Group

COMCRUDESLANTSUPPGRUCHAR
Commander Cruiser-Destroyer Force, Atlantic Support Group, Charleston (SC)

COMCRUDESLANTSUPPGRUMPT
Commander Cruiser-Destroyer Force, Atlantic Support Group, Mayport (FL)

COMCRUDESLANTSUPPGRUNORVA
Commander Cruiser-Destroyer Force, Atlantic Support Group, Norfolk, Virginia

COMCRUDESPAC
Commander Cruiser-Destroyer Force, Pacific

COMD
Command

COMDESDEVGRU
Commander Destroyer Development Group

COMDESFLOT
Commander Destroyer Flotilla

COMDESGRU
Commander Destroyer Group

COMDESLANT
Commander Destroyers, Atlantic

COMDESLANTDET
Commander Destroyers, Atlantic Detachment

COMDESPAC
Commander Destroyers, Pacific

COMDESPACDET
Commander Destroyers, Pacific Detachment

COMDESRON
Commander Destroyer Squadron

COMDG
Commanding

COMDR
Commander
Commodore

COMDT
Commandant

COMDTAFSC
Commandant, Armed Forces Staff College

COMDTCOGARD
Commandant, Coast Guard

COMEASTCONRADREG
Commander Eastern Continental Air Defense Region

COMEASTLANT
Commander Eastern Atlantic Force

COMEASTSEAFRON
Commander Eastern Sea Frontier

COMEDCENT
Commander Central Mediterranean

COMEODGRU
Commander Explosive Ordnance Disposal Group

COMET
Computer-Operated Management Evaluation Technique
CONUS Meteorological Teletype

COMET II
CONUS Meteorological Teletype, Second Net

COMEX
Commence Exercise

COMEXDIV
Commander Experimental Division

COMFAIR
Commander Fleet Air

COMFAIRCARIB
Commander Fleet Air, Caribbean

COMFAIRDET
Commander Fleet Air Detachment

COMFAIRKEF
Commander Fleet Air, Keflavik (IC)

COMFAIRKWEST
Commander Fleet Air, Key West (FL)

COMFAIRMED
Commander Fleet Air, Mediterranean

COMFAIRMEDET
Commander Fleet Air, Mediterranean Detachment

COMFAIRWESTPAC
Commander Fleet Air, Western Pacific

COMFAIRWESTPACDET
Commander Fleet Air, Western Pacific Detachment

COMFAIRWINGNORLANT
Commander Fleet Air Wing, Northern Atlantic

COMFAIRWINGSLANT
Commander Fleet Air Wings, Atlantic

COMFAIRWINGSPAC
Commander Fleet Air Wings, Pacific

COMFEWSG
Commander Fleet Electronic Warfare Support Group

COMFEWSGDET
Commander Fleet Electronic Warfare Support Group Detachment

COMFISCS
Fleet Assitance Team Program of the Commander

COMFITAEWWINGPAC
Commander Fighter Airborne Early Warning Wing, Pacific

COMFITWING
Commander Fighter Wing

COMFLATWING
Commander Light Attack Wing

COMFLEACT
Commander Fleet Activities

COMFLEACTDET
Commander Fleet Activities Detachment

COMFLETACSUPPWING
Commander Fleet Tactical Support Wing

COMFLETRAGRU
Commander Fleet Training Group

COMFLETRAGRULANT
Commander Fleet Training Group, Atlantic

COMFLETRAGRUPAC
Commander Fleet Training Group, Pacific

COMGREPAT
Commander Greenland Patrol

COMGTMOSECTASWU
Commander Guantanamo (Bay, Cuba) Sector, Antisubmarine Warfare Unit

COMHASWING
Commander Helicopter Antisubmarine Wing

COMHAWSEAFRON
Commander Hawaiian Sea Frontier

COMHELSEACONWING
Commander Helicopter Sea Control Wing

COMHELWINGRES
Commander Reserve Helicopter Wing

COMHELWINGRESREPLANT
Commander Reserve Helicopter Wing, Atlantic Representative

COMICEASWGRU
Commander Iceland Antisubmarine Warfare Group

COMICEDEFOR
Commander Iceland Defense Force

COMICPAC
Commander Intelligence Center, Pacific

COMIDEASTFOR
Commander Middle East Force

COMIDF
Commander Iceland Defense Force

COMIFSDIV
Commander Inshore Fire Support Division

COMILDEPT
Commanding Officer Military Departments (USNS)

COMINCH
Commander in Chief, U.S. Fleet

COMINE
Commander Minecraft

COMINEDIV
Commander Minecraft Division

COMINEFLOT
Commander Mine Flotilla

COMINEGRP
Commander Mine Group

COMINEGRPOK
Commander Mine Group, Okinawa

COMINELANT
Commander Minecraft, Atlantic

COMINEPAC
Commander Minecraft, Pacific

COMINERON
Commander Mine Squadron

COMINEWARCOM
Commander Mine Warfare Command

COMINEWARINSGRU
Commander Mine Warfare Inspection Group

COMINST
Communications Instructions

COMINTICEPAT
Commander International Ice Patrol

COMISH
Commander Military Attaché

COMJUWTF
Commander Joint Unconventional Warfare Task Force

COMKWESTEVDET
Commander Key West Test and Evaluation Detachment

COMKWESTFOR
Commander Key West Force

COML
Commercial

COMLAIRAUTH
Where government aircraft is not available, travel via commerical aircraft authorized where necessary

COMLAIRDIR
Where government aircraft is not available, travel via commercial aircraft is directed

COMLANSHIPFLOT
Commander Landing Ship Flotilla

COMLANSHIPRON
Commander Landing Ship Squadron

COMLANTAREACOGARD
Commander, Atlantic Area Coast Guard

COMLANTCOMELINTCEN
Commander Atlantic Electronic Intelligence Center

COMLANTFLT
Commander, United States Atlantic Fleet

COMLANTFLTWPNRAN
Commander Atlantic Fleet Weapons Range

COMLATWINGPAC
Commander Light Wing, Pacific

COMLF
Commercial Line Feed

COMLO
Combined Operations Material Liaison Officer

COMLOGNET
Combat Logistics Network

COMLOGSUPPFOR
Commander Logistics Support Force

COMLOPS
Commercial Operations

COMLTRANSAUTH
Where government transportation is not available, travel via commercial transportation is authorized

COMLTRANSAUTHEXPED
Where government transportation is not available, travel via commercial transportation authorized where necessary to expedite completion of duty

COMM
Communication
Communications

COMMATVAQWINGPAC
Commander Medium Attack Tactical Electronic Warfare Wings, Pacific

COMMATWING
Commander Medium Attack Wing

COMMBN
Communications Battalion

COMMCEN
Communications Center

COMMDET
Commissioning Detail

COMMO
Commodore
Communications Officer

COMMOBSUPPUDET
Commander Mobile Support Unit Detachment

COMM RI
Communications Routing Indicator

COMMS
Communications

COMMSTA
Communications Station

COMMSYSTECH
Communications Systems Technician

COMMTECH
Communications Technician

COMNAB
Commander Naval Air Base

COMNATODEFCOL
Commandant, North Atlantic Treaty Organization Defense College

COMNAVACT
Commander Naval Activities

COMNAVACTUK
Commander Naval Activities, United Kingdom

COMNAVAIRES
Commander Naval Air Reserve

COMNAVAIRESFOR
Commander Naval Air Reserve Force

COMNAVAIRLANT
Commander Naval Air Forces, Atlantic

COMNAVAIRPAC
Commander Naval Air Force, Pacific

COMNAVAIRPACMATREP
Commander Naval Air Force, Pacific, Material Representative

COMNAVAIRPACREP
Commander Naval Air Force, Pacific Representative

COMNAVAIRSYSCOM
Commander Naval Air Systems Command

COMNAVAIRSYSCOM ERS
Commander Naval Air Systems Command, Emergency Relocation Site Commander

COMNAVAIRSYSCOMHQ
Commander Naval Air Systems Command Headquarters

COMNAVAIRTESTCEN
Commander Naval Air Test Center

COMNAVAIRTRANSWING
Commander Naval Air Transport Wing

COMNAVAIRTRANSWINGPAC
Commander Naval Air Transport Wing, Pacific

COMNAVBASE
Commander Naval Base

COMNAVBASEREP
Commander Naval Base Representative

COMNAVBEACHGRU
Commander Naval Beach Group

COMNAVBEACHPHIBREFTAGRU
Commander Naval Beach and Amphibious Refresher Training Group

COMNAVCOMM
Commander Naval Communications Command

COMNAVCRUITAREA
Commander Navy Recruiting Area

COMNAVCRUITCOM
Commander Navy Recruiting Command

COMNAVCRUITCOM QAT
Commander Navy Recruiting Command Quality Assurance Team

COMNAVDAC
Commander Naval Data Automation Center

COMNAVDISTWASHDC
Commander, Naval District Washington, District of Columbia

COMNAVEASTLANTMED
Commander U.S. Naval Forces Eastern Atlantic and Mediterranean

COMNAVEDTRACOM
Commander Naval Education and Training Command

COMNAVELEXSYSCOM
Commander Naval Electronic Systems Command

COMNAVELEXSYSCOM ALT
Commander Naval Electronic Systems Command Alternate Commander

COMNAVELEXSYSCOM ERS
Commander Naval Electronic Systems Command Emergency Relocation Site Commander

COMNAVELEXSYSCOMHQ
Commander Naval Electronic Systems Command Headquarters

COMNAVFACENGCOM
Commander Naval Facilities Engineering Command

COMNAVFOR
Commander Naval Forces

COMNAVFORAZORES
Commander U.S. Naval Forces, Azores

COMNAVFORCARIB
Commander Naval Forces, Caribbean

COMNAVFORCARIBDET
Commander U.S. Naval Forces, Caribbean Detachment

COMNAVFORFE
Commander U.S. Naval Forces, Far East

COMNAVFORICE
Commander U.S. Naval Forces, Iceland

COMNAVFORJAP(AN)
Commander, U.S. Naval Forces, Japan

COMNAVFORJAPAN
Commander U.S. Naval Forces, Japan

COMNAVFORKOREA
Commander U.S. Naval Forces, Korea

COMNAVFORKOREADET
Commander U.S. Naval Forces, Korea Detachment

COMNAVFORPHIL
Commander Naval Forces, Philippines

COMNAVINTCOM
Commander Naval Intelligence Command

COMNAVLEGSVCCOM
Commander Naval Legal Service Command

COMNAVLOGPAC
Commander Naval Logistics Command, Pacific

COMNAVMAR
Commander U.S. Naval Forces, Marianas

COMNAVMARIANAS
Commander U.S. Naval Forces, Marianas

COMNAVMED
Commander U.S. Naval Forces, Mediterranean

COMNAVMILPERSCOM
Commander Naval Military Personnel Command

COMNAVNAW
Commander U.S. Naval Forces, Northwest African Waters

COMNAVOCEANCOM
Commander Naval Oceanography Command

COMNAVOPSUPPGRU
Commander Naval Operations Support Group

COMNAVOPSUPPGRULANT
Commander Naval Operations Support Group, Atlantic

COMNAVOPSUPPGRUPAC
Commander Naval Operations Support Group, Pacific

COMNAVRESPERSCEN
Commander Naval Reserve Personnel Center

COMNAVRESSECGRU
Commander Naval Reserve Security Group

COMNAVSEASYCOM
Commander Naval Sea Systems Command

COMNAVSEASYSCOM ALT
Commander Naval Sea Systems Command Alternate Commander

COMNAVSEASYSCOM ERS
Commander Naval Sea Systems Command Emergency Relocation Site Commander

COMNAVSEASYSCOMHQ
Commander Naval Sea Systems Command Headquarters

COMNAVSECGRU
Commander Naval Security Group

COMNAVSPECWARGRU
Commander Naval Special Warfare Group

COMNAVSPECWARGRUDET
Commander Naval Special Warfare Group Detachment

COMNAVSUPPFOR
Commander Naval Support Force

COMNAVSUPPFORANTARACTICA
Commander Naval Support Force, Antarctica

COMNAVSUPPFORANTARCTICREP
Commander Naval Support Force, Antarctic Representative

COMNAVSUPSYSCOM
Commander Naval Supply Systems Command

COMNAVSUPSYSCOM ERS
Commander Naval Supply Systems Command Emergency Relocation Site Commander

COMNAVSUPSYSCOMHQ
Commander Naval Supply Systems Command Headquarters

COMNAVSURFGRUMED
Commander Naval Surface Group, Mediterranean

COMNAVSURFGRUMIDPAC
Commander Naval Surface Group, Mid-Pacific

COMNAVSURFGRUWESTPAC
Commander Naval Surface Group, Western Pacific

COMNAVSURFGRUWESTPACDET
Commander Naval Surface Group, Western Pacific Detachment

COMNAVSURFLANT
Commander Naval Surface Force, Atlantic

COMNAVSURFLANTDET
Commander Naval Surface Force, Atlantic Detachment

COMNAVSURFLANTREP
Commander Naval Surface Force, Atlantic Representative

COMNAVSURFPAC
Commander Naval Surface Force, Pacific

COMNAVSURFPAC ADP
Commander Naval Surface Force, Pacific Automatic Data Processing

COMNAVSURFPAC DET
Commander Naval Surface Force, Pacific Detachment

COMNAVSURFPAC DISCUS
Commander Naval Surface Force, Pacific Distributed Information System for CASREP/UNIT Status

COMNAVSURFPAC RES
Commander Naval Surface Force, Pacific Representative

COMNAVSURFRES
Commander Naval Surface Reserve Force

COMNAVTELCOM
Commander Naval Telecommunications Command

COMNET
Command Network
Computer Network

COMNLONTEVDET
Commander New London (CN) Test and Evaluation Detachment

COMNORASDEFLANT
Commander North Atlantic Antisubmarine Defense Force

COMNORSECT
Commander Northern Section

COMNORSECT/WESTSEAFRON
Commander Northern Section/Western Sea Frontier

COMNORSTRIKFOR
Commander Northern Striking Force

COMNORVATEVDET
Commander Norfolk, Virginia Test and Evaluation Detachment

COMNRCBPAC
Commander Naval Reserve Construction Battalions, Pacific

COMNRCF
Commander Naval Reserve Construction Force

COMNRCFREP
Commander Naval Reserve Construction Force Representative

COMNRIUWGRU
Commander Naval Reserve Inshore Undersea Warfare Group

COMNRPC
Commander Naval Reserve Personnel Center

COMNUWPNTRAGRULANT
Commander Nuclear Weapons Training Group, Atlantic

COMO
Commodore
Communications Officer

COMOCEANLANT
Commander Atlantic Ocean Sub-Area

COMOCEANSYSLANT
Commander Oceanographic Systems, Atlantic

COMOCEANSYSLANT OC
Commander Oceanographic Systems, Atlantic Operations Center

COMOCEANSYSPAC
Commander Oceanographic Systems, Pacific

COMOCEANSYSPAC MEC
Commander Oceanographic Systems, Pacific Main Evaluation Center

COMOMAG
Commander Mobile Mine Assembly Group

COMOPCONCEN
Commander Operational Control Center

COMOPDEVFOR
Commander Operational Development Force

COMOPTEVFORLANT
Commander Operational Test and Evaluation Force, Atlantic

COMOPTEVFORPAC
Commander Operational Test and Evaluation Force, Pacific

COMORTEXGRP
Commander Orange, Texas Group, Inactive Reserve Fleet, Atlantic

COMOT
Clerical, Office Machine Operation and Technical (evaluation system)

COMP
Component
Composite
Comptroller

COMPACAREACOGARD
Commander, Pacific Area Coast Guard

COMPACELINTCEN
Commander Pacific Electronic Intelligence Center

COMPACMISTESTCEN
Commander Pacific Missile Test Center

COMPAD
Combined Office, Material Procurement and Distribution

COMPASECT
Commander Panama Section

COMPASECTASWGRU
Commander Panama Section Antisubmarine Warfare Group

COMPASECT/CARIBSEAFRON
Commander Panama Section/Caribbean Sea Frontier

COMPASECT/WESTSEAFRON
Commander Panama Section/Western Sea Frontier

COMPASS
Compiler-Assembler
Computer-Assisted Classification and Selection of Navy Recruits

COMPATASWDEVGRU
Commander Patrol Antisubmarine Warfare Development Group

COMPATFOR
Commander Patrol Forces

COMPATFORSIXTHFLTDET
Commander Patrol Forces, Sixth Fleet Detachment

COMPATRECONFOR
Commander Patrol and Reconnaissance Force

COMPATWINGSLANT
Commander Patrol Wings, Atlantic

COMPATWINGSPAC
Commander Patrol Wings, Pacific

COMPATWINGSPACREP
Commander Patrol Wings, Pacific Representative

COMPCOURDET
Upon completion of instruction and when directed, detached (duty indicated). (Date on or about which these orders are effective may be indicated.)

COMP DEC
Comptroller's Decisions

COMPDESFLTSURG
Upon completion of duty you are hereby designated as a flight surgeon.

COMPET
Competitive

COMPEX
Competitive Evaluation Exercise

COMPGEN
Comptroller General

COMPHIBFOR
Commander Amphibious Force

COMPHIBFORLANT
Commander Amphibious Force, Atlantic

COMPHIBFORPAC
Commander Amphibious Force, Pacific

COMPHIBGRU
Commander Amphibious Group

COMPHIBGRUDET
Commander Amphibious Group Detachment

COMPHIBGRUEASTPAC
Commander Amphibious Group, Eastern Pacific

COMPHIBREADYGRU
Commander Amphibious Ready Group

COMPHIBRON
Commander Amphibious Squadron

COMPHIMRON
Commander Patrol Combatant Missile Hydrofoil Squadron

COMPL
Complete
Completed
Upon completion thereof

COMPORON
Composite Squadron

COMPRET
Upon completion return to duty station and resume regular duties

COMPRON
Composite Squadron

COMPRSECTASWU
Commander Puerto Rico Section Antisubmarine Warfare Unit

COMPS
Consolidated Military Pay System

COMPT
Comptroller

COMPTEM
Upon completion of temporary duty

COMPTEMDET
Upon completion of temporary duty, detached

COMPTEMDIRDET
Upon completion of temporary duty and when directed, detach

COMPTEMINS
Upon completion of temporary duty under instruction

COMPTOUR
Completing Tour

COMPTRADIRDET
Upon completion training and when directed, detached

COMPUERTORICOSECT
Commander Puerto Rico Section

COMPUERTORICOSECT/CARIBSEAFRON
Commander Puerto Rico Section/Caribbean Sea Frontier

COMPVANTRADET
Upon completion of advanced training, detached

COMRADE
Computer-Aided Design Environment

COMRATS
Commuted Rations

COMRATS PT
Commuted Rations, Proceed Time

COMRDNAVFOR
Commander Rapid Development Naval Force

COMRECONATKWING
Commander Reconnaissance Attack Wing

COMREDATKCARAIRWING
Commander Readiness Attack Carrier Air Wing

COMREL
Community Relations

COMRESDESRON
Commander Reserve Destroyer Squadron

COMRESPATWINGLANT
Commander Reserve Patrol Wing, Atlantic

COMRESPATWINGPAC
Commander Reserve Patrol Wing, Pacific

COMRESPATWINGPACDET
Commander Reserve Patrol Wing, Pacific Detachment

COMRIVSUPPRON
Commander River Support Squadron

COMRNCBLANT
Commander Reserve Naval Construction Battalions, Atlantic

COMRNCF
Commander Reserve Naval Construction Force

COMSAR
Commander Search and Rescue

COMSAT
Communications Satellite

COMSC
Commander Military Sealift Command

COMSCELM
Commander Military Sealift Command, Eastern Atlantic and Mediterranean

COMSCEUR
Commander Military Sealift Command, Europe

COMSCFE
Commander Military Sealift Command, Far East

COMSCGULF
Commander Military Sealift Command, Gulf

COMSCLANT
Commander Military Sealift Command, Atlantic

COMSCMED
Commander Military Sealift Command, Mediterranean

COMSCPAC
Commander Military Sealift Command, Pacific

COMSCSEA
Commander Military Sealift Command, Southeast Asia

COMSEABASEDASWWINGSLANT
Commander Sea-Based Antisubmarine Warfare Wings, Atlantic

COMSEC
Communications Security

COMSEC I
Communications Security, Phase I (course)

COMSER
Commission on Marine Sciences, Engineering and Resources

COMSERVFOR
Commander Service Force

COMSERVFORLANT
Commander Service Force, Atlantic

COMSERVFORPAC
Commander Service Force, Pacific

COMSERVGRU
Commander Service Force Group

COMSERVGRUDET
Commander Service Force Group Detachment

COMSERVLANT
Commander Service Force, Atlantic

COMSERVPAC
Commander Service Force, Pacific

COMSERVPACPETSCOL
Commander Service Force, Pacific Petroleum School

COMSERVRON
Commander Service Squadron

COMSN
Commission

COMSOLANT
Commander South Atlantic Force

COMSOSECT
Commander Southern Section

COMSOSECT/WESTSEAFRON
Commander Southern Section/Western Sea

Frontier

COMSPECBOATRON
Commander Special Boat Squadron

COMSPECBOATU
Commander Special Boat Unit

COMSTDIV
Commander Landing Ship Tank Division

COMSTRATSUBFOR
Commander Strategic Submarine Force

COMSTRIKEFLTLANT
Commander Strike Fleet, Atlantic

COMSUBDEVGRU
Commander Submarine Development Group

COMSUBDEVGRUDET
Commander Submarine Development Group Detachment

COMSUBDEVGRU UMV
Commander Submarine Development Group Unmanned Vehicles

COMSUBDEVRON
Commander Submarine Development Squadron

COMSUBDEVRONTRADET
Commander Submarine Development Squadron Training Detachment

COMSUBDIV
Commander Submarine Division

COMSUBFLOT
Commander Submarine Flotilla

COMSUBFRONDEF
Commander Sub-Frontier Defense

COMSUBFRONDEF/CHESBAYGRU
Commander Sub-Frontier Defense/Chesapeake Bay Group

COMSUBFRONDEF/DELGRU
Commander Sub-Frontier Defense/Delaware Group

COMSUBFRONDEF/GULFGRU
Commander Sub-Frontier Defense/Gulf Group

COMSUBFRONDEF/NEWENGRU
Commander Sub-Frontier Defense/New England Group

COMSUBFRONDEF/SOGRU
Commander Sub-Frontier Defense/Southern Group

COMSUBGRU
Commander Submarine Group

COMSUBGRUDET
Commander Submarine Group Detachment

COMSUBLANT
Commander Submarine Forces, Atlantic

COMSUBLANTREP
Commander Submarine Forces, Atlantic Representative

COMSUBPAC
Commander Submarine Forces, Pacific

COMSUBPAC CC
Commander Submarine Forces, Pacific Command Center

COMSUBPAC ECC
Commander Submarine Forces, Pacific Emergency Command Center

COMSUBPAC OTH
Commander Submarine Forces, Pacific, Over-the-Horizon Fleet Commander

COMSUBPACREP
Commander Submarine Forces, Pacific Representative

COMSUBREFITRAGRU
Commander Submarine Refit and Training Group

COMSUBRON
Commander Submarine Squadron

COMSUBSEATLANT
Commander Submarine Force, Eastern Atlantic

COMSUBTRAGRU
Commander Submarine Training Group

COMSUBTRAGRUHAWAREA
Commander Submarine Training Group, Hawaiian Area

COMSUBTRAGRUNORWEST
Commander Submarine Training Group, Northwest Area

COMSUBTRAGRUWESCO
Commander Submarine Training Group,

West Coast Area

COMSURFRON
Commander Surface Squadron

COMSURFWARDEVGRU
Commander Surface Warfare Development Group

COMSYSTO
Commissary Store

COMSYSTOREG
Commissary Store Region

COMSYSTOREGDET
Commissary Store Region Detachment

COMTAC
Communications/Tactical (publications)

COMTACGRU
Commander Tactical Air Control Group

COMTACRON
Commander Tactical Air Control Squadron

COMTACSUPPWING
Commander Fleet Tactical Support Wing

COMTACWINGSLANT
Commander Tactical Wings, Atlantic

COMTAIWANPATFOR
Commander Taiwan Patrol Force

COMTONGRU
Commander Tongue Point Group, Inactive Fleet, Pacific Fleet

COMTRALANT
Commander Training Force, Atlantic

COMTRAN
Commercial Translator

COMTRAPAC
Commander Training Force, Pacific

COMTRAWING
Commander Training Air Wing

COMUNPWRTRAGRULANT
Commander Nuclear Power Training Group, Atlantic

COMUNPWRTRAGRUPAC
Commander Nuclear Power Training Group, Pacific

COMUNWPNTRAGRULANT
Commander Nuclear Weapons Training Group, Atlantic

COMUNWPNTRAGRUPAC
Commander Nuclear Weapons Training Group, Pacific

COMUPWRTRAGRUPAC
Commander Nuclear Power Training Group, Pacific

COMUSAFSO
Commander United States Air Forces, Southern Command

COMUSFAC
Commander United States Facility

COMUSFORAZ
Commander United States Forces, Azores

COMUSFORCARIB
Commander United States Forces, Caribbean

COMUSFORCARIBREP
Commander United States Forces, Caribbean Representative

COMUSFORICE
Commander United States Forces, Iceland

COMUSFORJAPAN
Commander United States Forces, Japan

COMUSFORKOREA
Commander United States Forces, Korea

COMUSFORMAR
Commander United States Forces, Marianas

COMUSMACTHAI
Commander United States Military Assistance Command, Thailand

COMUSMILGRU
Commander United States Military Group

COMUSNAVFORCONAD
Commander United States Naval Forces, Continental Air Defense Command

COMUSNAVPHIL
Commander United States Naval Forces, Philippines

COMUSNAVSO
Commander United States Naval Forces, Southern Command

COMUSTDC
Commander United States Taiwan Defense

Command

COMWESTSEAFRON
Commander Western Sea Frontier

COMZ
Communications Zone

COMZONE
Communications Zone

CON
Concrete
Confidential
Conical
Constant
Consul
Control

CONAC
Contractor Acceptance Records

CONACTD
Continuous Active Duty

CONAD
Continental Air Defense Command

CONAG
Combined Nuclear and Gas (propulsion)

CONALOG
Contact Analog (non-digital computer)

CONAS
Commanding Officer, Naval Air Station

CONASAERO
These orders constitute assignment to duty in part of aeronautical organization of the Navy

CONC
Concentrate
Concrete

COND
Condition

CONDEF
Contract Definition

CONDUCTVIEW
Command delivering orders is directed to conduct an interview as required by current NAVMILPERSINST 1300.26 prior to delivery

CONELRAD
Control of Electromagnetic Radiation (civil defense)

CONESTAB
Connection Establishment

CONEX
Container Express

CONF
Conference
Confidential
Confinement

CONFBUL
Confidential Bulletin

CONFLAG
Conflagration Control

CONF-MH
Confidential-Modified Handling

CONFORM
Concept Formulation

CONGRATS
Congratulations

CONGRINT
Congressional Interest
Letter of Congressional Interest

CONOPS
CONUS Operations

CONPLAN
Operations Plan in Concept Format

CONPRESDU
Continue Present Duties

CONREP
In Connection with Replenishment

CONSHELF
Continental Shelf

CONSOL
Consolidate

CONSOLREC
Consolidated Recreation

CONSPIC
Conspicuous

CONST
Construction

CONSTELEC
Construction Electrician

CONSTRUCTS
Control Data Structural System

CONSUB
Continuous Submarine Duty Incentive Pay

CONT
Continue
Continued

CONTAREX
Conventional Targeting Exercise

CONTD
Continued

CONTFLDSERV
Contract Field Service

CONTN
Contain

CONTR
Contract
Contractor

CONTREAT
Continue Treatment (medical)

CONUBS
Compact Nuclear Brayton System

CONUS
Continental United States

CONV
Convict
Convicted
Conviction

CONVATE
Connection Reactivation

CONVERS
Connection Conversion

CONVEX
Convoy Exercise

CONVL
Conventional

CONVN
Convenient

CO-OP
Cooperative

COOP
Contingency of Operations Planning
Cooperative Observations Program

COOPLAN
Contingency of Operations Planning

COORD
Coordinate
Coordination

COORS
Communications Outage Restoral Section

COP
Coast-Out Point
Commanding Officer's Punishment
Common Operational Picture
Continuation of Pay
Control for Operational Programs
Co-Pilot

COPARS
Contractor-Operated Spare Parts Store

COPE
Computer Operating and Programming Environment
Continuous Officer Professional Education

COPI
Computer-Oriented Programmed Instruction

COPNORSA
A certified copy of these orders with all endorsements shall be forwarded to Naval Officer Record Support Activity, Omaha, NE 68111

COPP
Combined Operations Pilotage Party

COPRESTRA
Within 30 days after completion separation processing, forward copy of these orders and intended new address to Commander Naval Air Reserve Training, Glenview, IL

COR
Cargo Outturn Reporting
Change Order Request
Circular of Requirements
Communication Operating Requirements
Contracting Officer's Representative
Corner
Corps
Correction

CORA
Conditioned-Response Analog

CORCONU
Corrosion Control Unit

CORCY
Corrected Copy

CORD
Cascade Orifice Resistor Device
Coordinate
Coordination
Coordination of Research and Development
Coordinator

CORDIC
Coordinate Rotation Digital Computer

CORDPO
Correlated Data Printout

CORDS
Civil Operations Revolutionary Development Support

COREP
Combined Overload and Repair Control

CORES
Cooperative Radiation Effects Simulation (program)

CORPS
CASREP and Outstanding Repair Parts

CORR
Correct
Correction
Correspondence

CORRESP
Correspondence

CORSCHOPSDET
Commanding Officer, Research Operations Detachment

CORT
Escort

CORTDIV
Escort Division

CORTRON
Escort Squadron

CORTS
Conversion of Range and Telemetry Systems

COS
Central Operations System
Chief of Staff
CO2 Removal System

COSA
Combat Operational Support Aircraft

COSAG
Combined Steam and Gas (proplusion)

COSAL
Coordinated Shipboard Allowance List

COSAR
Compression Scanning Array Radar

COSBAL
Coordinated Shore-Based Allowance List

COSD
Combined Operations Support Depot

COSDIV
Coastal Division

COSFLOT
Coastal Flotilla

COSMD
Combined Operations Signal Maintenance Depot

COSMO
Combined Operations Signal Maintenance Officer

COSO
Combined Operations Signal Officer

COSRIVDIV
Coastal River Division

COSRIVRON
Coastal River Squadron

COSRIVRON MST
Coastal River Squadron Mobile Support Team

COSRON
Coastal Squadron

COSSAC
Chief of Staff, Supreme Allied Command

COSSACT
Command Systems Support Activity

COT
Cockpit Orientation Trainer
Consecutive Overseas Tours
Consolidated Operability Test
Coordinated Operability Test

COTA
Certification as Occupational Therapy Assistant
Confirming Telephone or Message Authority of ______

COTAR
Correlation Tracking and Ranging

COTAT
Correlation Tracking and Triangulation

COTC
Commander Fleet Operational Training Command

COTCLANT
Commander Fleet Operational Training Command, Atlantic

COTCPAC
Commander Fleet Operational Training Command, Pacific

COTCPACSUBCOM
Commander Fleet Operational Training Command, Pacific Subordinate Command

COTR
Contracting Officer's Technical Representative

COTS
Commercial-Off-the-Shelf
Cargo Offload and Transfer System

COTS/NDI
Commercial Off-the-Shelf/Non-Development Items

COUSS
Commanding Officer, United States Ship (name of ship)

COV
Covered
Covers

COVE
Committee on Value and Evaluation

COW
Chief Of the Watch
Inf: Commanding Officer's Wife

COWAN
Coalition-Wide Area Network

COWS
Change Order Work Sheet

COY
Company

COZI
Communications Zone Indicator

CP
Capsule
Command Post
Constant Pressure
Contact Preclude
Continental Polar (air mass)
Control Post

CP&AA
Components, Parts, Accessories, and Attachments

CPA
Central Program Agent
Closest Point of Approach
Cost Planning and Appraisal
Critical Path Analysis

CPAD
Central Pay Accounts Division

CPAF
Cost-Plus-Award Fee

CPAM
CNO Program Analysis Memorandum

CPC
Coastal Patrol Boat
Computer Program Components
Crafts, Protective and Custodial (series)

CPCU
Custody Pending Completion of Use

CPD
Constant Pressure Date

CPDF
Central Personnel Data File

CPE
Contractor Performance Evaluation
Cytopathic Effect

CPEB
Central Physical Evaluation Board

CPEG
Contractor Performance Evaluation Group

CPES
Contractor Performance Evaluation System

CPF
Central Program Facility

CPFF
Cost-Plus-Fixed Fee

CPFG
CNO Policy and Fiscal Guidance

CPG
Commander Amphibious Group

CPHC
Central Pacific Hurricane Center

CPI
Crash Position Indicator

CPIC
Coastal Patrol and Interdiction Craft
Combined Photographic Interpretation Center

CPIF
Cost-Plus-Incentive Fee

CPI/FDR
Crash Position Indicator/Flight Data Recorder

CPL
Corporal
Crash Position Locator

CPM
Cards Per Minute
Counts Per Minute
Critical Path Method
Cycles Per Minute

CPMS
Communications Procedures Management System
Computerized Performance Monitoring System

CPO
Chief Petty Officer
Component Pilot Overhaul

CPOA
Completion of Post Overhaul Availability

CPOC
Chief Petty Officer of the Command

CPOIC
Chief Petty Officer-in-Charge

CPOW
Chief Petty Officer-of-the-Watch

CPP
Commander Amphibious Force, Pacific

CPPC
Cost-Plus-Percentage-of-Cost

CPPS
Critical Path Planning and Scheduling

CPPSO
Consolidated Personal Property Shipping Office

CPR
Commander Amphibious Squadron
Component Pilot Rework
Continuing Property Records
Cost-Performance Report

CPS
Certificate of Prior Submission
Collective Protection System
Consolidated Package Store
Contract Plant Services
Conversational Programming System
Corps
Cycles Per Second

CPSR
Contractor Procurement System Review

CPSS
Component Percentage Shipping Schedule

CPT
Co-Pilot Time
Critical Path Technique (PERT)

CPTR
Capture

CPU
Central Processing Unit

CPX
Command Post Exercise

C/Q
Certificate of Assignment to Quarters

CQ
Carrier Qualifications
Change of Quarters
Commercial Quality
Constraint Qualification

CQAP
Component Quality Assurance Program

CQC
Contractor Quality Control

C/Q (NOT)
Certificate of Assignment to Quarters Not Issued

CQS
Common Query System

C/Q (TERM DATE)
Termination of Assignment to Quarters

C/R
Change of Rating
Change of Request

CR
Cold-Rolled (steel)
Conference Room
Congenic Resistant
Construction Recruit
Continuous Rod
Control Relay
Crate
Creditable Record
Crypto Top Secret

CRA
Composite Research Aircraft

CRAB
Caging, Retention, and Airborne Boresight

CRACC
Communications and Radar Assignment Coordinating Committee

CRAE
Combat-Readiness Assessment Exercise

CRAF
Civil Reserve Air Fleet

CRAFTY
Conscientious, Responsible, Aboveboard, Faultless, Timely, Yeomanly

CRAG
Carrier Replacement Air Group
Combat Readiness Air Group

CRAM
Card Random Access Memory
Compression, Retrieval, and Maintenance (of data)
Contractual Requirements Recording Analysis and Management

CRASP
COSAL Requisitioning and Status Procedures

CRAW
Combat Readiness Air Wing

CRB
Computer Resources Board
Control Review Board

CRBRP
Clinch River Breeder Reactor Plant

CRC
Central Requirements Committee
Communication Readiness Certification
Core Removal Coding

CRCC
Cyclic Redundancy Check Code

CRD
Classified Restricted Data

CRDF
Cathode Ray Direction Finding

CRDL
Collateral Recurring Document Listing (DIA)

CRDM
Control Rod Drive Mechanism (reactors)

CRDS
Component Repair Data Sheet

CREDIT
Cost-Reduction Early-Decision Information Techniques

CREO
Career Reenlistment Objectives

CRES
Corrosion Resistant Steel

CRF
Career Recruiter Force
Cryptographic Repair Facility

CRI
Code Relationship Index

CRIL
Consolidated Repairable Item List

CRIO
Communications Security Regional Issuing Office

CRITHOUS
Advised of Critical Housing Shortage

CRITIC
Critical Intelligence

CRO
Cathode-Ray Oscilloscope
Cathode-Ray Tube Readout
Civilian Repair Organization

CROV
Constant Run Out Valve

CRP
Civilian Requirements Plan
Controllable and Reversible Pitch (propeller)
Coordinated Reconnaissance Plan
Corrugated Ribbon Packing
Cost-Reduction Program

CRPI
Card Reader-Punch Interpreter (unit)

CRPL
Central Radio Propagation Laboratory

CRPM
Combined Registered Publications Memoranda
Communications Registered Publications Memorandum

CRS
Calibration Requirements Summary
Canister Round Simulator
Course

CRSD
Contractor Required Shipment Date

CRSE
Course Interval (NNSS)

CRT
Cathode-Ray Tube
Combat-Readiness Training

CRTN
Correction

CRU
Complete Capability Response Unit
Composite Reserve Unit
Cruiser

CRUD
Corrosive Radioactive Undetermined Deposit

CRUDESFLOT
Cruiser-Destroyer Flotilla

CRUDESLANT
Cruiser Destroyer Force, Atlantic

CRUDESPAC
Cruiser Destroyer Force, Pacific

CRUDIV
Cruiser Division

CRUIT
Recruit
Recruiting

CRUITSTA
Recruiting Station

CRWO
Coding Room Watch Officer

CRYPTO
Cryptographic

C/S
Call Sign
Certificate of Service
Change of Speed
Chief of Staff

CS
Carrier Suitable
Cirrostratus
Civil Service
Cloud Shadow
Commissaryman
Communications Station
Continuous Strip (film)
Contractor Sensitization
Coolant Sampling
Culinary Specialist

CS1
Culinary Specialist First Class

CS2
Culinary Specialist Second Class

CS3
Culinary Specialist Third Class

CSA
Configuration Status Accounting

CSAB
Combined Shipping and Adjustment Board (United States-Britain)

CSAC
Central Ships Alignment Console

CSAR
Combat Search and Rescue
Communication Satellite Advanced Research
Configuration Status Accounting Report

CSBL
Consolidated Site Base Loading

CSC
Central Security Control
Chief Culinary Specialist
Civil Service Commission
Combined Shipbuilding Committee
Continuous Service Certificate

CSCA
Control Surface Decontamination Area

C-SCAN
Carrier System for Controlled Approach of Naval Aircraft

CSCCE
Combat Systems Casualty Control Exercise

CSCL
Care of Ship Checkoff List

CSCM
Master Chief Culinary Specialist

CSCS
Senior Chief Culinary Specialist

C/SCSC
Cost-Schedule Control Systems Criteria

CSD
Constant-Speed Drive
Crew Systems Department

CSDIC
Combined Services Detailed Interrogation Center

CSDIC-NOI
Combined Services Detailed Interrogation Center-Non-Operational Intelligence

CSDP
Coordinated Ship Development Plan

CSDPP
Combat Systems Data Processing Project

CSDRBL
Considerable

CSDTS
Common Shipboard Data Terminal Set

CSE
Common Support Equipment
Critical Specifications Elements

CSED
Consolidated Ships Electronic Design
Coordinated Ship Electronics Device

CSF
Caribbean Sea Frontier

CSG
Carrier Strike Group
Close Support Gun

CSGMP
Cross-Scan Ground Map Pencil

CSI
CONUS Sustainiing Increment
Customer Satisfaction Index

CSID
Combat Systems Integration Department

CSI-DET
CONUS Sustaining Increment Detachment

CSIGO
Chief Signal Officer

CSL
Commander Service Force, Atlantic
Complete Service Life
Component Save List

CSM
Calendar Maintenance Supervisor
Command Security Manager
Contractor Support Milestones

CSMP
Current Ship's Maintenance Project

CSMS
Computerized Specifications Management

CSN
Nuclear Strike Cruiser

CSO
Chief Staff Officer
Club Safety Officer
Combat Systems Officer

CSOOW
Combat Systems Officer of the Watch

CSOSS
Combat Systems Operational Sequencing System

CSP
Causeway Section Powered
Coherent Signal Processor
Commander Service Force, Pacific
Command Selector Panel
Concurrent Spare Parts
Contractor Standardization Plan

CSPD
Central Still-Photo Depository

CSPM
Communication Security Publication Memorandum

CSR
Continuous Sampling Run
Contract Status Report
Current Sensitive Relay

CSRA
Civil Service Reform Act

CSRF
Commissary Store Reserve Fund

CSRFG
Commissary Store Reserve Fund Grant

CSRR
Combat Systems Readiness Review

CSS
Combat Systems Support
Common Skills Shops
Consolidated Support System
Contractor Support Services

CSSA
Culinary Specialist Seaman Apprentice

CSSM
Computer System Security Manager

CSSN
Culinary Specialist Seaman

CSSO
Common Support Services Office
Computer System Security Officer

CSSP
Combined Services Support Program

CSSQT
Combat Systems Ships Qualification Trials

CST
Coast
Coding Speed Test

CSTA
Cross-Scan Terrain Avoidance

CSTDD
Combat Systems Test Development Director

CSTEX
Combat Systems Training Exercise

C-STOL
Controlled Short Take-Off and Landing

CSTOM
Combat Systems Tactical Operations Manual

CSTT
Combat Systems Training Team

CSTV
Control System Test Vehicle

CSU
Circuit-Switching Unit

CSV
Capacity Selector Value

CSWC
Crew-Served Weapons Captured

CSWR
Conversation Specifications and Work Requirements

CT
Card Type
Carton
Cartridge
Central Time
Circuit Theory
Combat Team
Combined Trials
Contact (approach)
Continental Transformer
Control Transformer
Cryptologic Technician

CTA
Control Area
Cryptologic Technician (Administrative)

CTA1
Cryptologic Technician (Administrative)

CTA2
Cryptologic Technician (Administrative) Second Class

CTA3
Cryptologic Technician (Administrative) Third Class

CTAC
Chief Cryptologic Technician (Administrative)

CTACM
Master Chief Cryptologic Technician (Administrative)

CTACS
Senior Chief Cryptologic Technician (Administrative)

C/TB
Cargo/Tanker Branch

CTC
Contract Task Change

CTDO
Central Technical Doctrine Officer
Central Technical Documents Office
Central Training Documents Office

CTDS
Code Translation Data System

CTE
Chief Test Engineer
Commander, Task Element
Contractor Technical Evaluation

CTF
Carrier Task Force
Commander, Task Force

CTFM
Continuous Transmission, Frequency Modulated

CTG
Commander, Task Group

CTI
Contractor Training Instruction
Cryptologic Technician (Interpretive)

CTI1
Cryptologic Technician (Interpretive) First Class

CTI2
Cryptologic Technician (Interpretive) Second Class

CTI3
Cryptologic Technician (Interpretive) Third Class

CTIC
Chief Cryptologic Technician (Interpretive)

CTICM
Master Chief Cryptologic Technician (Interpretive)

CTICS
Senior Chief Cryptologic Technician (Interpretive)

CTIM
Cooked Therapeutic In-Flight Meals

CTIS
Carrier Terminal Information Services

CTM
Cryptologic Technician (Maintenance)

CTM1
Cryptologic Technician (Maintenance) First Class

CTM2
Cryptologic Technician (Maintenance) Second Class

CTM3
Cryptologic Technician (Maintenance) Third Class

CTMC
Chief Cryptologic Technician (Maintenance)

CTMCM
Master Chief Cryptologic Technician (Maintenance)

CTMCS
Senior Chief Cryptologic Technician (Maintenance)

CTN
Carton
Center

CTO
Cryptologic Technician (Communications)

CTO1
Cryptologic Technician (Communications) First Class

CTO2
Cryptologic Technician (Communications) Second Class

CTO3
Cryptologic Technician (Communications)

Third Class

CTOC
Cryptologic Technician (Communications)

CTOCM
Master Chief Cryptologic Technician (Communications)

CTOCS
Senior Chief Cryptologic Technician (Communications)

CTR
Cryptologic Technician (Collection)

CTR1
Cryptologic Technician (Collection) First Class

CTR2
Cryptologic Technician (Collection) Second Class

CTR3
Cryptologic Technician (Collection) Third Class

CTRC
Chief Cryptologic Technician (Collection)

CTRCM
Master Chief Cryptologic Technician (Collection)

CTRCS
Senior Chief Cryptologic Technician (Collection)

CTS
Capistrano Test Site
Communications Test Set
Communication Terminals, Synchronous
Contractor Technical Services
Cryptologic Technician Seaman Apprentice

CTSN
Cryptologic Technician Seaman

CTSPTEP
Central Test Site for Personnel and Training Evaluation Program

CTSPTEPDET
Central Trest Site for Personnel and Training Evaluation Program Detachment

CTSS
Compatible Time-Sharing System

CTT
Command Training Team
Cryptologic Technician (Technical)

CTT1
Cryptologic Technician (Technical) First Class

CTT2
Cryptologic Technician (Technical) Second Class

CTT3
Cryptologic Technician (Technical) Third Class

CTTC
Chief Cryptologic Technician (Technical)

CTTCM
Master Chief Cryptologic Technician (Technical)

CTTCS
Senior Chief Cryptologic Technician (Technical)

CTU
Commander, Task Unit

CTV
Control Test Vehicle

CTZ
Control Zone

CU
Common-User
Constructionman
Cube
Cubic
Cumulus

CUB
Cryptologic Unified Build

CUCB
Cumulus and Cumulonimbus (cloud formations)

CUCM
Master Chief Constructionman

CUDIXS
Common User Digital Information Exchange System

CUO
Credit Union Office

CURR
Currency
Current

CURTS
Common User Radio Transmission System

CURV
Cable-Controlled Underwater Recovery Vehicle
Controlled Underwater Recovery Vehicle

CUS
Course

CUST
Custody

CUSTR
Customer

CUT
Cutter

CV
Coefficient of Variation
Multipurpose Aircraft Carrier

CVA
Attack Aircraft Carrier

CVAN
Nuclear-Powered Attack Aircraft Carrier

CVBG
Carrier Battle Group

CVC
Consecutive Voyage Charter

CVE
Escort Aircraft Carrier

CVFR
Controlled Visual Flight Rules

CVHE
Escort Aircraft Carrier (Helicopter)

CVIC
Carrier Intelligence Center

CVL
Carrier Landing
Multipurpose Aircraft Carrier Light

CVLI
Commissioned Vessel Liaison Inquiry

CVM
Seaplane Control Medium Nuclear Carriers

CVN
Multipurpose Aircraft Carrier (Nuclear-Powered)

CVN 21
21st-Century Aircraft Carrier

CVNX
Next-Generation Nuclear-Powered Aircraft Carrier

CVP
Computer Validation Program

CVR
Combat Reconnaissance Vehicle
Controlled Visual Rules

CVR(T)
Combat Vehicle Reconnaissance (Tracked)

CVS
Antisubmarine Warfare Aircraft Carrier

CVSD
Continuously-Variable Slope Delta

CVSG
Carrier Strike Group

CVSGR
Reserve Carrier Antisubmarine Warfare Air Group

CVT
Training Aircraft Carrier

CVU
Utility Aircraft Carrier

CVW
Attack Carrier Air Wing

CVWS
Combat Vehicle Weapons System

CW
Carrier Wave
Chemical Warfare
Chilled Water
Compensating Winding (wiring)
Continuous Wave
Control Work

CWA
Canadian Western Approaches

CWAS
Contractor Weighted Average Share

CWBS
Contract Work Breakdown Structure

CWBW
Chemical Warfare-Bacteriological Warfare
Chemical Warfare-Biological Warfare

CWCS
Common Weapon Control System

CWI
Continuous Wave Illuminator

CWO
Chief Warrant Officer
Chief Watch Officer
Communications Watch Officer

CWPD
Class Work Planning Document

CWRA
Civilian Welfare and Recreation Association

CWS
Chemical Warfare Service
Control Wheel Steering

CWSF
Commander Western Sea Frontier

CWSO
Command Weapons Systems Orientation

CWST
Commander Western Sea Frontier

CWT
Hundred Weight

CWTPI
Conventional Weapons Technical Proficiency

CX
Canister
Control Transmitter

CY
Calendar Year
Cycle Year

CYL
Cylinder

CZ
Combat Convergence Zone
(Panama) Canal Zone
Convergence Zone

CZMA
Coastal Zone Management Act

CZMP
Coastal Zone Management Program

D
Daily (report frequency)
Darkness
Deceased
Development
Dust (weather symbol)
Duty

D&D
Drunk and Dirty

D&F
Determination and Findings

D&I
Disassembly and Inspection

D&P
Development and Production

D&S
Destroyer and Submarine Piers

D&V
Damage and Vulnerability

D-5
Trident Missile

D/A
Digital-to-Analog (converter)

DA
Deaerating
Defense Aid
Delayed Action
Denmark (message traffic)
Dentalman Apprentice
Design Agent
Direction Action (bomb fuze)
Discrete Address
Double-Acting
Double-Attack
Drift Angle

DAA
Data Access Arrangement

Designated Approving Authority

DAAS
Defense Automatic Addressing System

DAASO
Defense Automatic Addressing System Office

DAB
Defense Acquisition Board
Design Appraisal Board
Destroyer Advisory Board
Disbursing/Accounting Branch

DABES
Drug and Alcohol Abuse Education Specialist

DABLC
Director, Advanced Bases Logistic Control

DABOA
Director, Advanced Base Office, Atlantic

DABOP
Director, Advanced Base Office, Pacific

DABRK
Daybreak

DAC
Days After Contract
Design Augmented by Computers
Digital-to-Analog Converter (NNSS)
Duplicate Aperture Card

DACM
Defensive Air Combat Maneuvering

DACOWITS
Defense Advisory Committee on Women in the Service

DADAC
Digital-to-Analog Deck Angle Converter

DADMS
Defense Mapping Agency Automated Distribution Management System

DADS
Deficiency Analysis Data System

DAE
Data Acquisition Equipment

DAES
Drug Abuse Education Specialist

DAF
Data Acquisition Facility
Document Acquisition File

DAGO
District Aviation Gas Office

DAIR
Direct Altitude Identification Readout

DAIS
Director of Automatic Information Service

DAISY
Double Precision Automatic Interpretive System

DALGT
Daylight

DALS
Data Acquisition Logging System
Distress Alerting and Locating System

DALVP
Delay enroute authorized, chargeable as ordinary leave, provided it does not interfere with reporting on date specified and provided individual has sufficient accrued leave

DAM
Damage

DAMA
Demand Assigned Multiple Access

DAMCONTRACEN
Damage Control Training Center

DAME
Distance, Azimuth Measuring Equipment

DA-MON-YR
Day-Month-Year

DAMP
Downrange Antimissile Measurement Project

DAMS
Defense Against Missiles System

DAN
Day Number Entry (NNSS)
Disciplinary Action Notice

DANC
Decontamination Agent, Non-Corrosive

DANTES
Defense Activity for Non-Traditional Education Support

DAO
District Accounting Office
District Aviation Officer
Division Ammunition Office

DAP
Domestic Action Program

DAPA
Drug and Alcohol Program Advisor

DAPF
Data Analysis and Processing Facility

DAPS
Direct Access Programming System

DAR
Defense Acquisition Regulation
Departure Approval Request
Developed Area Ratio (propellers)

DARO
Defense ADPE Reutilization Office

DARPA
Defense Advanced Research Projects Agency

DART
Decentralized Advanced Replenishment Technique
Deployable Automatic Relay Terminal
Detection, Action, Response, Technique
Development Advanced Rate Techniques
Directional Automatic Realignment of Trajectory
Disappearing Automatic Retaliatory Target
Dual-Axis Rate Transducer

DARTS
Air Deployable Acoustic Readiness Training System

DAS
Data Acquisition System
Datatron Assembly System
Defense Audit Service
Digital Analog Simulation

DASA
Defense Atomic Support Agency

DASC
Direct Air Support Center

DASCO
Digital-to-Analog Synchro Converter

DASD
Deputy Assistant Secretary of Defense

DASD(CP)
Deputy Assistant Secretary of Defense (Civilian Personnel)

DASD(EO)
Deputy Assistant Secretary of Defense (Equal Opportunity)

DASD(MP)
Deputy Assistant Secretary of Defense (Military Personnel Policy)

DASH
Destroyer Antisubmarine Helicopter
Drone Antisubmarine Helicopter

DASI
Digital Altimeter Setting Indicator

DASO
Demonstration and Shakedown Operations

DASO CREW EVAL
Demonstration and Shakedown Operations Crew Evaluation

DASPAC
Defense Auditing Service, Pacific

DASSO
Data Systems Support Office

DASSO/FMSO
Data Systems Support Office/Fleet Material Support Office

DAST
Division for Advanced Systems Technology

DASTARD
Destroyer Antisubmarine Transportable Array

DAT
Dependents' Assistance Team
Design Approval Test
Development Assist Team
Distillate Assistance/Advisory Team
Drug Abuse Team

DATA
Defense Air Transportation Administration
Dual Aerosol Transport Apparatus

DATACOL
Data Collection

DATACORTS
Data Correlation and Transfer System

DATANET
Data Network (DCS)

DATC
Development and Training Center

DATE DOS
Date Dependents Arrived at Overseas Station

DATICO
Digital Automatic Tape Intelligence Checkout

DATO
Disbursing and Transportation Office

DATP
Drug Abuse Testing Program

DAU
Daughter

DAVA
Directorate for Audio-Visual Activities (DOD)

DAVC
Delayed Automatic Volume Control

DAWN
Digital Automated Weather Network

DB
Data Bank
Day Beacon
Decibels
Demand Base
Dive Bomber

DBH
Developmental Big Hydrofoil
Diameter at Breast Height
Division Beachhead

DBI
Demand Base Item

DBK
Dominant Battlefield Knowledge

DBL
Double Reduction Gears

DBM
Data Base Manager

DBMS
Data Base Management System

DBO
Data Buoy Office (NOAA)

DBP
Data Buoy Project (USN-USCG)

DBSO
District Base Services Office

D/C
Drift Correction

DC
Damage Control
Damage Controlman
Decagram
Deck Court
Defense Counsel
Dental Corps
Development Characteristics
Digital Computer
Direct Current
Discarded Clothing

DC1
Damage Controlman First Class

DC2
Damage Controlman Second Class

DC3
Damage Controlman Third Class

DCA
Damage Control Assistant
Defense Communications Agency
Defensive Counter-Air
Drift Correction Angle

DCAA
Defense Contract Audit Agency

DCAEUR
Defense Communications Agency, Europe

DCAFLDOFC
Defense Communications Agency, Field Office

DCAOC
Defense Communications Agency Operations Center

DCAP
Deficiency Corrective Action Program

DCAPAC
Defense Communications Agency, Pacific

DCAS
Defense Contract Administration Services

DCASA
Defense Contract Administration Service Area

DCASD
Defense Contract Administration Services District

DCASMA
Defense Contract Administration Service Management Area

DCASO
Defense Contract Administration Services Office

DCASPO
Defense Contract Administration Services Plant Office

DCASPRO
Defense Contract Administration Services Plant Representative Officer

DCASR
Defense Contract Administration Services Region

DC-AUTOMET
Directional Controlled-Automatic Meteorological (compensation)

DCB
Damage Control Booklet
Data Control Board
Defense Communications Board
Design Control Board

DCC
Chief Damage Controlman
Damage Control Central
Data Control Center
Debarkation Control Center
Display Control Console
District Communications Center
Drill, Command, and Ceremony

DC CENTRAL
Damage Control Central

DCCI
Data Converter-Control Indicator

DCCM
Master Chief Damage Controlman

DCCS
Defense Case Control System
Digital Camera Control System
Senior Chief Damage Controlman

DCDCR
Definition of Control, Display and Communications Requirements

DCDP
Defense Center Data Processor

D-CDR
Deputy Commander

DCE
Directorate of Communications-Electronics

DCF
Dependency Certificate Filed
Disaster Control Force
Discounted Cash flow

DCFA
Damage Controlman Fireman Apprentice

DCFEM
Dynamic Cross-Field Electron Multiplication

DCG
Damage Control Group

DCGS-N
Distributive Common Ground Station-Navy

DCH
Damage Control Hulk (Ship)
Data Communications Handler
Depth Charge
District Chaplain

DCI
Damage Control Instructor
Decompression Illness

DCII
Defense Central Index of Investigations

DCL
Data Check List

DCM
Defense Combat Maneuvering
Design Criteria Maneuvering
Directorate for Classified Management

DCMAILSUB
Discharge certificate signed by Secretary of the Navy being retained in NAVMILPERSCOM and will be mailed to member's home subsequent to separation

DCMS
Director, Communications Security Material System

DCN
Design Change Notice
Digital Computer Newsletter (publication)
Document Control Number
Drawing Change Notice

DCNM
Deputy Chief of Naval Management
Deputy Chief of Naval Material

DCNM(D)
Deputy Chief of Naval Management (Development)

DCNM(M&O)
Deputy Chief of Naval (Management and Organization)

DCNM(M&F)
Deputy Chief of Naval Management (Material and Facilities)

DCNM(P&FM)
Deputy Chief of Naval Management (Programs and Financial Management)

DCNO
Deputy Chief of Naval Operations

DCNO(AIR)
Deputy Chief of Naval Operations (Air)

DCNO(D)
Deputy Chief of Naval Operations (Development)

DCNO(FO&R)
Deputy Chief of Naval Operations (Fleet Operations and Readiness)

DCNO(L)
Deputy Chief of Naval Operations (Logistics)

DCNO(MPT)
Deputy Chief of Naval Operations (Manpower, Personnel, and Training)

DCNO(P&P)
Deputy Chief of Naval Operations (Plans and Policies)

DCNO(P&R)
Deputy Chief of Naval Operations (Personnel and Naval Reserve)

DCNO(SW)
Deputy Chief of Naval Operations (Submarine Warfare)

DCNOTEMAILSUB
Discharge certificate signed by Secretary of the Navy and notification concerning Naval Reserve appointment being retained in NAVMILPERSCOM and will be mailed to member's home subsequent to separation

DCO
Depth Cut-Out
Direct Commission Officer
District Clothing Officer
District Communications Officer

DCOFS
Deputy Chief of Staff

DCOIC
Direct Commission Officer Indoctrination Course

DCOP
Direct Commission Officer Program

DCP
Decision Coordinating Paper
Design Change Proposal
Development Concept Paper
Development Concept Plan
Director of Civilian Personnel

DCPA
Defense Civil Preparedness Agency

DCPG
Defense Communications Planning Group

DCPO
Damage Control Petty Officer
District Civilian Personnel Office
DSA Civil Preparedness Office

DCPR
Defense Contractor's Planning Report

DCR
Decrease
Design Certification Review

DCRESMAILSUB
Discharge certificate signed by Secretary of the Navy together with Naval Reserve appointment being retained in NAVMILPERSCOM and will be mailed to member's home subsequent to separation

DCRO
District Civilian Readjustment Office/Officer

DCRP
Disaster Control Recovery Plan

DCS
Defense Communications System
Deputy Chief of Staff

DCSA
Damage Controlman Seaman Apprentice

DCSC
Defense Construction Supply Center

DCSLOG
Deputy Chief of Staff, Logistics

DCSN
Damage Controlman Seaman

DCSP
Defense Communications Satellite Program

DC/SR
Display and Control/Storage and Retrieval

DCSS
Defense Communications Satellite System

DCSTC
Defense Communications Station Technical Control

DCT
Depth-Charge Throwers
Depth Control Tanks
Direct

DCTL
Direct-Coupled Transistor Logic (circuit)

DCTT
Damage Control Training Team

DCU
Device Control Unit
Document Control Unit

DD
Defense Department
Department of Defense
Departure Date
Destroyer
Determination of Dependency
Development Directive
Dishonorable Discharge
Double Drift
Drydock
Duty Driver

DD-21
21st century Land-Attack Destroyer

DD(A&HR)
Deputy Director of Attaché's and Human Resources (DIA)

DDALV
Days delay enroute Authorized, chargeable as Leave

DDALVAHP
Days delay at home or leave address within CONUS authorized, chargeable as leave provided it does not interfere with reporting date as specified. Advanced leave may be granted where necessary.

DDAM
Dynamic Design Analysis Method

DDAS
Digital Data Acquisition System

DD(C)
Deputy Director for Collection (DIA)

DDC
Deck Decompression Chamber
Defense Documentation Center
Defensive Driving Course
Direct Digital Control

DDCFSO
Defense Documentation Center Field Office

DDCPO
Division Damage Control Petty Officer

DDCSTI
Defense Documentation Center for Scientific and Technical Information

DDE
Destroyer (Escort)

DDEP
Defense Development Exchange Program

DDESB
Department of Defense Explosives Safety Board

DDF
Design Disclosure Format

DDG
Guided-Missile Destroyer

DDGC
Dishonorable Discharge, General Court-Martial after Confinement in Prison

DDGI
Dishonorable Discharge, General Court-Martial, Immediate

DDGOS
Deep-Diving Submarines, General Overhaul Specifications

DDGP
Dishonarable Discharge, General Court-Martial after Violation of Probation

DD(I)
Deputy Director of Intelligence (DIA)

DDI
Director of Defense Information

DDIC
Department of Defense Disease and Injury Codes

DD(IS)
Deputy Director for Information Systems (DIA)

DDL
Data Description Language
Data Distribution List

DDN
Defense Data Network

DDO
Deputy Disbursing Officer
District Dental Office/Officer
Dummy Delivery Order

DDOA
Deputy Director of Operations and Administrations

DDP
Design Data Package

DD(PCD&T)
Deputy Director for Personnel, Career Development and Training (DIA)

DDR
Radar Picket Destroyer

DDRE
Director of Defense Research and Engineering

DDRR
Digital Data Regenerative Repeater
Directional Discontinuity Ring Radiator

DD(S)
Deputy Director for Support (DIA)

DDS
Deep-Diving System
Deep Submergency Systems
Design Data Sheet
Design Data Standard
Design Disclosure Standard

DD(S&TI)
Deputy Director for Scientific and Technical Intelligence (DIA)

DDSE
Design Disclosure for Systems and Equipment

DDST
Deputy Director for Science and Technology

DDT&E
Design, Development, Test, and Evaluation

DDTO
District Domestic Transportation Office/Officer

DDU
Document Distribution Unit

DDV
Deep-Diving Vehicle

DDX
Family of Future Surface Warships

D/E
Declared Excess

DE
December
Densimeter
Destroyer Escort
Development Engineering
Dose Equivalent (radiation)
Double-Ended
Pending Detachment (NAPMIS)

DEA
Data Exchange Agreement

DEC
Control Escort Vessel

Deceased
December
Decision
Declination
Decode (NNSS)

DECA
Descent Engine Control Assembly

DECC
Defense Commercial Communications Center

DECCO
Defense Commercial Communications Office

DECEO
Defense Communications Engineering Office (DCA)

DECL
Declared
Declassified
Declassify

DECM
Deception (or Deceptive, or Defense, or Defensive) Electronic Countermeasures

DECMSN
Decommission

DECMSND
Decommissioned

DECOM
Decommission

DECOMD
Decommissioned

DED
Deduct

DEDAD
Data Element Dictionary and Directory

DEE
Digital Evaluation Equipment

DEEPSUBSYS
Deep Submergency Systems

DEEPSUBSYSPROJO
Deep Submergency Systems Project Office/Officer

DEEPSUBSYSPROJTECHO
Deep Submergency Systems Project Technical Office

DEER
Directional Explosive Echo-Ranging

DEERS
Defense Enrollment Eligibility Reporting System

DEF
Defend
Defense

DEFCLOTH&TEXSUPCEN
Defense Clothing and Textile Supply Center

DEFCOM
Defense Command

DEFCOMMSYS
Defense Communications System

DEFCON
Defense Condition

DEFCONSTSUPCEN
Defense Construction Supply Center

DEFELECSUPCEN
Defense Electronics Supply Center

DEFER
Deferred

DEFGENSUPCEN
Defense General Supply Center

DEFINDPLANTEQUIPCEN
Defense Industrial Plant Equipment Center

DEFINDSUPCEN
Defense Industrial Supply Center

DEFINDSUPDEP
Defense Industrial Supply Depot

DEFINTELAGCY
Defense Intelligence Agency

DEFINTELSCOL
Defense Intelligence School

DEFPERSUPPCEN
Defense Personnel Support Center

DEFREMANEDCEN
Defense Resources Management Education Center

DEFSEC
Defense Section

DEFSUBSUPCEN
Defense Subsistence and Supply Center

DEFUELSUPCEN
Defense Fuel Supply Center

DEFWEAPSYSMGMTCEN
Defense Weapons Systems Management Center

DEG
Degree(s)

DEG&DEP
Degaussing and Deperming

DEG/RANGE
Degaussing Range

DEH
Deepwater Escort Hydrofoil

DEIMOS
Development and Investigation of Military Orbital Systems

DEIS
Defense Energy Information System
Draft Environmental Impact Statement

DEL
Delivered

DELCOMBI
Command delivering orders initiate background investigation immediately by submitting forms required by OPNAVINST 5510.1D, as applicable, with ultimate duty station designated as recipient of results.

DELCOMPLYINST
Delivered orders comply with current NAVMILPERSCOMINST 5510.3.

DELGRU
Delaware Group

DELINUS
Provided no excess leave involved, authorized to delay (number of days specified) in reporting, to count as leave, any portion of which may be taken in CONUS.

DELPARTURE
Provided no excess leave involved, authorized to delay (number of days or until date specified), to count as leave, any portion of which may be taken prior to or after departure.

DELREP
Provided no excess leave involved, authorized delay (number of days or until date specified) in reporting, to count as leave (MILPERSMAN 1810360). If member reports before NLT date, may not be paid per diem for period NET date unless authorized IAW NAVMILPERSCOMINST 1320.9. Keep old and new duty station advised of address (MILPERSMAN 1810380). Flag officers also forward itinerary to NAVMILPERSCOM (Code Of). For circuitous travel and leave visits to foreign countries see NAVMILPERSMAN 1810280.6 and 3020420. For leave authorized TEMADD orders, indicate on original orders date and hour TEMADD commenced and was completed.

DELRIVPOE
Delay in Arriving at Port Of Embarkation

DELTA
Detailed Labor and Time Analysis

DELTIC
Delay Line Time Compression

DELURN
Provided no excess leave involved, authorized to delay (number of days or until date specified) in returning to duty station, to count as leave. Keep duty station advised of address. If leave taken, indicate on original orders date and hour TEMADD commenced and completed.

DEM
Demand
Demote
Disability Evaluation

DEMBOMB
Demolition Bomb

DEMC
Defense Electronics Management Center

DEMO
Demolition
Demonstration

DEMOB
Demobilization

DEMON
Demonstration

DEM/VAL
Demonstration/Validation

DEN
Data Element Number

DENBN
Dental Battalion

DENCO
Dental Company

DENT
Dental

DENYG
Denying

DEO(A)
Dependents' Education Office (Atlantic)

DEO(P)
Dependents' Education Office (Pacific)

DEP
Deflection Error Probable
Delayed Entry Program
Depart
Departure
Dependent
Deployment
Depot
Deputy

DEPASSTSECDEF
Deputy Assistant Secretary of Defense

DEPCHNAVMAT
Deputy Chief of Naval Material

DEPCHNAVMAT(MAT&FAC)
Deputy Chief of Naval Material (Material and Facilities)

DEPCOM
Deputy Commander

DEPCOMFEWSG
Deputy Commander Fleet Electronic Warfare Support Group

DEPCOMLANTNAVFACENGCOM
Deputy Commander Atlantic Naval Facilities Engineering Command

DEPCOMOPTEVFORLANT
Deputy Commander Operational Test and Evaluation Force, Atlantic

DEPCOMOPTEVFORPAC
Deputy Commander Operational Test and Evaluation Force, Pacific

DEPCOMPACNAVFACENGCOM
Deputy Commander Pacific Naval Facilities Engineering Command

DEPCOMPT
Deputy Comptroller

DEPCON
Departure Control

DEPDIR
Deputy Director

DEPEVACPAY
Dependents' Evacuation Pay

DEPN
Dependent

DEPNAV
Department of the Navy

DEPNAVSCI
Department of Naval Science

DEPNOTAUTH
Dependents Not Authorized (at overseas duty station)

DEPSUM
Daily Estimated Position Summary

DEPT
Department

DEPTNAVINSTR
Department of Naval Instruction

DER
Radar Picket Destroyer Escort

DERAST
Diesel Engineering Readiness Assistance Team

DERI
Deep Electric Research Investigation

DEROS
Date of Estimated Rotation from Overseas Station
Departing Roster

DERP
Deficient Equipage Reporting Procedures

DES
Data Encryption Standard
Desert
Deserter

Desertion
Desirable
Destroyer

DES ACCTS
Deserter's Accounts

DESC
Defense Electronics Supply Center

DESCHA
Destination Change

DESDEVDIV
Destroyer Development Division

DESDEVGRU
Destroyer Development Group

DESDEVRON
Destroyer Development Squadron

DESDIV
Destroyer Division

DESEFF
Deserter's Effects

DESFLOT
Destroyer Flotilla

DESFLTSURG
Designated Student Naval Flight Surgeon

DESIG
Designated
Designator

DESIGDISBAGENT
Designated special disbursing agent, to remain in force from date of assuming duty until date of detachment

DESNAVAV
Designated Student Naval Aviator

DESO
District Education Office/Officer

DESOIL
Diesel Oil

DESREP
Destroyer Repair
Destroyer Representative

DESRON
Destroyer Squadron

DEST
Destroy

DESTIN
Destination

DET
Design Evaluation Test
Detach
Detachment
Detail
Detainee

DETD
Detached Duty

DETG
Defense Energy Task Group

DETM
Determine

DET PAY
Detained Pay

DETRELBY
When delivered by (officer indicated) detach from duty

DEV
Development
Deviation (request)

DEVNO
Deviation Request Number

DEW
Directed Energy Weapon
Distant Early Warning

DEWIZ
Distant Early Warning Identification Zone

D/F
Direction Finding

DF
Delayed Failure
Delayed Fuze
Direction Finding
Distribution Factor (radiation)

DFA
Designated Field Activity

DFCO
Duty Flying Control Officer

DFD
Digitial Flight Display

DFGO
Inf: Damn Fool Ground Officer

DFH
Developmental Fast Hydrofoil

DFHMA
Defense Family Housing Management Account

DF I
Direction Finding, Phase I (course)

DF II
Direction Finding, Phase II (course)

DFM
Diesel Fuel, Marine

DFQAR
Defense Fuel Quality Assurance Residency

DFR
Dropped from Rolls as Deserter

DFS
Defense Fuel Support
Departure from Specifications
Distance-Finding Station
Dynamic Flight Simulator

DFSB
Defense Force Section Base

DFSC
Defense Fuel Supply Center

DFSTN
Direction-Finding Station

DFT
Deaerating Feed Tank
Direction, Fleet Training

DFU
Drainage Fixture Unit

DFUS
Diffuse

DFW
Diesel Fuel Waiver

DG
Decigram
Defense Grouping
Degaussing
Diesel Generator
Direction Gyro
Downgrade

DGBC
(Polaris) Digital Geoballistic Computer

DGD
Diesel Geared Drive

DGM
Defense Guidance Memorandum

DG-MG
Diesel Geared-Motor Geared

DGO
Degaussing Officer

DGRO
Degaussing Range Officer

DGSC
Defense General Supply Center

DGSE
Developmental Ground Support Equipment

DGTO
Degaussing Technical Officer

DGU
Display Generator Unit

DGUTS
Don't Give Up the Ship

DGV
Digital Generator Video

DGWO
Degaussing Wiping Officer

DGZ
Designated Ground Zero
Desired Ground Zero

DH
Decision Height
Desired Heading
Desired Height
Half-Dozen

DHD
Downwind Hazard Distance

DHE
Data Holding Equipment

DHF
Demand History File

DHO
District Historical Office
District Historical Officer

DHQ
Division Headquarters

DHSS
Data Handling Sub-System

DI
Defense Information
Delayed Ignition (tracer)
Design Integration
Diatom
Digital Inputs
Direct
Direct Impulse
Direction Indicator
Dispenser
District Inspector
Drill Instructor

DIA
Defense Intelligence Agency
Diaphone

DIAC
Defense Industrial Advisory Council

DIADC
Defense Intelligence Agency Dissemination Center

DIAG
Diagonal
Diagram

DIAL
Defense Intelligence Agency Liaison
Deficiency in Allowance List/Listing

DIALGOL
Dialect of Algorithmic Language

DIAN
Decca Integrated Airborne Navigation

DIANE
Digital Integrated Attack and Navigation Equipment
Distance Indicating Automatic Navigation Equipment

DIBC
Digital Integral Ballistic Analyzer

DIC
Dependency and Indemnity Compensation
Detailed Interrogation Center
Dictionary

DICBM
Depressed Trajectory Intercontinental Ballistic Missile

DICNAVAB
Dictionary of Naval Abbreviations

DICOSE
Digital Comunications System Evaluator

DICT
Dictionary

DID
Data Item Description
Digital Information Display

DI/DES
(Vessel) Disposed of by Destruction

DIDS
Data Item Descriptions
Defense Integrated Data System
Digital Information Display System

DIDU
Defense Item Data Utilization (program)

DIECO
Department of Defense Item Entry Control Office

DIER
Department Instrument Equipment Reserve

DIES
Diesel

DIF
Difference
Duty Involving Flying

DIFAR
Direction Low-Frequency Analyzer and Ranging

DIFAX
Digital Facsimile

DIFDEN
Duty in a flying status not involving flying

DIFDENIS
Duty under instruction in a flying status not involving flying

DIFDENREPT
Duty in a flying status not involving flying effective upon reporting

DIFF
Difference

DIF/FLC
Disposition (of vessel by) Foreign Liquida-

tion Corporation

DIFF PAY
Difference in Pay

DIFINSOPS
Duty under instruction in a flying status involving operational or training flights

DIFINSPRO
Duty under instruction in a flying status involving proficiency flying

DIFM
Due in From Maintenance

DIFOPS
Duty under instruction in a flying status involving operational or training flights

DIFOPSDORSE
Detailed to duty in a flying status involving operational or training flights effective such date as hereon endorsed

DIFOPSEXIST
Existing detail to duty in a flying status involving operational or training flights effective upon reporting

DIFOT
Duty in a flying status involving operational or training flights

DIFOTCREW
Duty in a flying status involving operational or training flights as a crewmember

DIFOTDORSE
Duty in a flying status involving operational or training flights as a non-crewmember

DIFOTINSCREW
Duty under instruction in a flying status involving operational or training flights as a crewmember

DIFOTINSNONCREW
Duty under instruction in a flying status involving operational or training flights as a non-crewmember

DIFOTREPT
Duty in a flying status involving operational or training flights upon reporting

DIFOT RVK
Duty in a flying status involving operational or training flights revoked

DIFPRO
Duty in a flying status involving proficiency

DIFTECH
Duty as a technical observer in a flying status involving operational or training flights

DIGOPS
Digest of Operations

DIGS
Defense Information Guidance Series (publication)

DIHEST
Directly-Induced High-Explosive Simulation Technique

DIIC
Dielectrically Isolated Integrated Circuit

DII COE
Defense Information Infrastructure Common Operating Environment

DIIO
District Industrial Incentive Office/Officer

DIIP
Defense Inactive Item Program

DILS
Doppler Inertial LORAN System

DIM
Diminish
District Industrial Manager

DIMATE
Depot Installation Maintenance Automatic Test Equipment

DIMES
Defense Integrated Management Engineering System
Development and Improved Management Engineering Systems

DIMUS
Digital Multi-Beam Steering

DIN
Dingy (USCG)

DINA
Direct Noise Amplifier (airborne radar)

DINFOS
(Department of) Defense Information School

DINO
Deputy Inspector of Naval Ordnance

DI/NT
Disposition (of vessel by) Department of Interior

DIO
Defensive Information Operations
District Intelligence Officer

DIP
Defense Information Procedure
Defense Investigative Program
Deserter Information Point
Display Information Processor
Driver Improvement Program
Dual Inline Package

DIPEC
Defense Industrial Plant Equipment Center

DIR
Direction
Director
Disassembly Inspection Report

DIRAFIED
Director, Armed Forces Information and Education Division

DIRAPCG
Director, Joint Agate Punch Control Group

DIRARFCOS
Director, Armed Forces Courier Service

DIRBY
When directed by

DIRC
Defense Investigative Review Council

DIRDET
When Directed, Detached (duty indicated)

DIREC
Direction

DIRFLDSUPPACT
Director, Field Support Activity

DIR/GEN
Director General

DIRHAVHIS
Director of Naval History

DIRHSG
You are directed to report to the appropriate housing referral office prior to negotiating any agreement for off-base housing

DIRID
Directional Infrared Intrusion Detector

DIRJOAP
Director, Joint Oil Analysis Program

DIRJOAPTSC
Director, Joint Oil Analysis Program Technical Support Center

DIRLAUTH
Direct Liaison Authorized
Direct Line of Authority

DIRMOBSEARAN
Director, Mobile Sea Range

DIRNAVCURSERV
Director, Naval Courier Service

DIRNAVINVSERV
Director, Naval Investigative Service

DIRNAVMARCORMARS
Director, Navy-Marine Corps Military Affiliate Radio Service

DIRNAVPUBPRINTSERV
Director, Navy Publications and Printing Service

DIRNAVRESINTPRO
Director, Naval Reserve Intelligence Program

DIRNAVSECGRUEUR
Director, Naval Security Group, Europe

DIRNAVSECGRULANT
Director, Naval Security Group, Atlantic

DIRNAVSECGRUPAC
Director, Naval Security Group, Pacific

DIRNCPB
Director, Naval Council of Personnel Boards

DIRNCPBDET
Director, Naval Council of Personnel Boards Detachment

DIRNSA
Director, National Security Agency

DIRNSCPO
Director, Navy Secretariat Civilian Personnel Office

DIRPRO
When Directed Proceed

DIRS
Dental Information Retrieval System
Disassembly & Inspection Reports

DIRSDIMA
Director, San Diego (CA) Intermediate Maintenance Activity

DIRSP/PROJMGRFBM
Director, Special Projects/Project Manager Fleet Ballistic Missile

DIRSSP
Director, Strategic Systems Projects

DIS
Defense Intelligence School
Defense Investigative Service
Discharge
Dispatch
Distance
Distant

DISA
Defense Information Systems Agency

DISAL
Disposition (of vessel by) Sale

DISAP
Disapproved

DISB
Disbursing

DISBOFFCOP
Disbursing officer making payment on these orders forward copy of orders with copy of paid voucher to (command indicated)

DISBSUBREPT
Disbursing officer making payment submit monthly letter reports by 10th of following month to NAVMILPERSCOM (Code 33) of pay and allowances earned (including special/incentive pay) in detail. Submit two certified copies of orders when member reports to or is detached from assignment. Also submit two copies of all travel and per diem payment vouchers.

DISC
Defense Industrial Supply Center
Discontinue/Discontinued
Discrepency Identification and System Checkout

DISCH
Discharge

DISCH(BCD)
Bad Conduct Discharge

DISCH(DD)
Dishonorable Discharge

DISCH(HON)
Honorable Discharge

DISCO
Discolored

DISCON
Discontinue
Discrepancy in Shipment Confirmation

DISCORS
Discrepancy in Shipment Cargo Outturn Reporting System

DISCOS
Disturbance Compensation System

DI/SCP
Disposition (of vessel by) Scrapping

DISCREP
Discrepancy Report

DISD
Defense Industrial Supply Depot

DISDEP
Distant Deployment

DISEM
Disseminate

DISEMB
Disembark

DISESTAB
Disestablishment
Upon Disestablishment

DISGOV
Foreign Government Effected Discharge

DISGRAT
Discharge Gratuity

DISI
Defense Industrial Security Institute

DISN
Defense Information Support Network

DISNAV
U.S. Navy or its Agency Effected Discharge

DISNT
Distant

DISOP
Discharge by Operator

DISP
Defense Industry Studies Program
Dispatch
Dispensary
Disposal

DISREPS
Discrepancy in Shipment Report (Transportation)

DIS RET
Disability Retirement

DISS
Dissolve

DIS SERV
Disability Severance

DIST
District

DISTDENTALO
District Dental Officer

DISTEX
District Relief Exercise

DISTMEDO
District Medical Officer

DISTR
Distribute

DISTREAT
Upon Discharge Treatment

DISTRIB
Distribute

DISUB
Duty Involving underway operations in Submarines

DIT
Document Input Transmittal
Dynamic Instrumentation Test

DI/TES
Disposition (of vessel by using as target and) Tests

DI/TRN
Disposition (of vessel by) Transfer to Other Government Agency

DITY
Do It Yourself

DIV
Diversion
Diving
Division

DIVCOM
Division Commander

DIVEDU
Duty Involving the Performance of Diving Duty

DIVERTORD
Diversion Order

DIVINFO
Division of Information

DIVPAY
Diving Pay

DK
Deck
Disbursing Clerk

DK1
Disbursing Clerk First Class

DK2
Disbursing Clerk Second Class

DK3
Disbursing Clerk Third Class

DKC
Chief Disbursing Clerk

DKCM
Master Chief Disbursing Clerk

DKCS
Senior Chief Disbursing Clerk

DKSA
Disbursing Clerk Seaman Apprentice

DKSN
Disbursing Clerk Seaman

D/L
Data Link

DL
Day Letter
Deciliter
Departure Locator

Destroyer Leader
Distance Learning
Frigate (archaic)

DLA
Defense Logistics Agency
Dislocation Allowance
Dual Launching Adaptor

DLC
Diagnostic Coed Laboratory
Direct Lift Control (system)
Dymo Laser Composer

DLCO
Deck Landing Control Officer

DLCR
Drawing List Change Report

DLG
Defense Liaison Group
Guided-Missile Destroyer Leader
Guided-Missile Frigate (archaic)

DLGN
Nuclear-Powered Guided Missile Frigate (or Destroyer Leader)

DLH
Direct Labor Hours

DLI
Deck-Launched Interceptor
Defense Language Institute

DLL
Design Level Logic

DLM
Depot Level Maintenance

DLMP
Depot Level Maintenance Plan

DLMS
Digital Landmass System

DLNC
Deputy Local Naval Commander

DLO
District Legal Office/Officer

DLP
Defense Language Program
Director of Laboratory Programs

DLPT
Defense Language Proficiency Test

DLR
Daily Level Readiness (system)
Depot Level Repairable

DLS
Decoy Launching System

DLSC
Defense Logistics Service Center
Defense Logistics Support Center
Defense Logistics Systems Center

DLSIE
Defense Logistics Studies Information Exchange

DLT
Deck Landing Training

DLTS
Deck Landing Training School

DLVR
Delivery

DLY
Daily

DM
Data Management
Depot Maintenance
Design Manual
Destroyer Minelayer
Draftsman
Dram
Master Diver

D(M&S)
Director for Management and Plans (DIA)

DM&TS
Departure of Mines and Technical Surveys

DM1
Illustrator Draftsman First Class

DM2
Illustrator Draftsman Second Class

DM3
Illustrator Draftsman Third Class

DMA
Defense Mapping Agency
Degraded Mission Assignment
Depot Maintenance Activity
Direct Memory Access (computers)

DMAAC
Defense Mapping Agency Aerospace Center

DMABO
Defense Mapping Agency Branch Office

DMABODET
Defense Mapping Agency Branch Office Detachment

DMADISTRCEN
Defense Mapping Agency Distribution Center

DMAHTC
Defense Mapping Agency Hydrographic/Topographic Center

DMALO
Defense Mapping Agency Liaison Office

DMAODS
Defense Mapping Agency Office of Distribution Services

DMC
Chief Illustrator Draftsman
Decision Module Compiler
Deck Motion Compensator
Defense Manpower Commission
Digital Manpower Commission
Digital Micro-Circuit
Direct Multiplex Control

DMCGS
Descriptive Macro-Code Generation System

DMCM
Master Chief Illustrator Draftsman

DMCS
Senior Chief Illustrator Draftsman

DMDC
Defense Manpower Data Center

DME
Design Margin Evaluation
Diagnostic Monitor Executive
Distance-Measuring Equipment

DMEC
Defense Metals Equipment Center

DMED
Digital Message Entry Device

DMET
Defense Management Education and Training
Distance Measuring Equipment Touchdown

DMFT
Decayed, Missing and Filled Teeth

DMI
Direct Material Inventory

DMISA
Depot Maintenance Interservice Support Agreement

DML
Data Manipulator Language (CODASYL)

DML DY
Demolition Duty

DMM
Domestic Mail Manual

DMMS
Depot Maintenance Management Subsystem

DMO
Data Management Office/Officer
Dependent Meteorological Office
District Marine Officer
District Material Officer
District Medical Officer
District Meteorological Office

DMR
Date Material Required
Defective Material Report
Digital Modular Radio

DMRI
Date Material Required Increasing

DMRR
Defense Manpower Requirements Report

DMS
Defense Management Summary
Defense Mapping School
Defense Materials Service
Defense Materials System
Destroyer Minesweeper

DMSA
Illustrator Draftsman Seaman Apprentice

DMSH
Diminish

DMSL
Defense Message System

DMSMS
Diminishing Manufacturing Sources and Material Shortages

DMSN
Illustrator Draftsman Seaman

DMSO
Directors of Major Staff Offices

DMSP
Defense Meteorological Satelite Program

DMSSB
Defense Material Specifications and Standards Board

DMST
Demonstrate

DMTS
Dynamic Multi-Tasking System

DMX
Data Multiplex Unit (TDDL)

DMZ
De-Militarized Zone

DN
Denied
Dentalman
Down

DNA
Defense Nuclear Agency
Designated National Agency

DNA-AEC
Defense Nuclear Agency-Atomic Energy Commission

DNC
Department of the Navy Civilian
Direct Numerical Control

DNCCC
Defense National Communication Control Center

DnD
Defense-in-Depth

DNDT
Department of the Navy Declassification Team

DNEC
Distribution Navy Enlisted Classification

DNET
Director, Naval Education and Training

DNFYP
Department of the Navy Five-Year Program

DNG
Distinguished Naval Graduate Program

DNI
Director of Naval Intelligence
Division of Naval Intelligence

DNIAS
Day-Night Indirect Attack Seeker

DNL
Director, Navy Laboratories

DNOP
Director of Naval Officer Procurement

DNP
(Reservists) Drill in Non-Pay Status

DNPPS
Director, Navy Publications and Printing Service

DNR
Does Not Run

DNS
Dense
Density

DNT
Director, Naval Telecommunications

D/O
Duty Officer

DO
Defense Order
Delivery Order
Dental Officer
Diesel Oil
Direct Order
Disbursing Officer
Drop Out
Duty Officer

DOA
Date of Award
Day of Ammunition
Dead On Arrival
Director for Operations and Administration
Dissolved Oxygen Analyzer

DOAL
Director of Airlift

DOB
Date of Birth
Defense Office Building

DOC
Data Output Console
Department of Commerce
Direct Operating Costs

DOCC
Defense Operations Communications Complex

DOCU
Document

DOD
Department of Defense
Died of Disease

DODAAD
Department of Defense Activity Address Directory

DODCI
Department of Defense Computer Institute

DODDSLANT
Department of Defense Dependents School, Atlantic

DODDSPAC
Department of Defense Dependents School, Pacific

DODGE
Department of Defense Gravity Experiment

DODI
Department of Defense Instruction

DODIC
Department of Defense Identification Code

DOD-IR
Department of Defense Intelligence Reports

DODISS
Department of Defense Index of Specifications and Standards

DODMERB
Department of Defense Medical Examination Review Board

DODMUL
Department of Defense Master Urgency List

DO DOD
Diagnostic Output Data Additional Development

DODPM
Department of Defense, Military Pay and Allowances Entitlement Manual

DOEIS
Draft Overseas Environmental Impact Statement

DOES
Defense Organizational Entry Standards

DOFL
Diamond Ordnance Fuze Laboratory

DOFS(W)
Director of Stores (Washington)

DOG
Division Officer's Guide (USNI Press)

DOI
Departmental Operating Instructions

DOL
Deep Ocean Laboratory (NCEL)
Dophin

DOMIR
Definition of Operator Maintainer Information Requirements

DON
Department Of the Navy
Dimensionality of Nations

DoN
Department of the Navy

DONADPM
Department of the Navy Automatic Data Processing Management

DONAL
Department of the Navy Occupational Level

DON FEORP
Department of the Navy Federal Equal Opportunity Recruitment Program

DONPIC
Department of the Navy Program Information Center

DONSTPP
Department of the Navy Study Program Plan

DOO
District Operations Officer
District Ordnance Office/Officer

DOOLAR
Deep Ocean Object Location and Recovery

DOOW
Diving Officer-of-the-Watch

DOP
Designated Overhaul Point

DOPMA
Defense Officer Personnel Management Act

DOR
Daily Operational Report
Date of Rank
Dropout Rate
Dropped Own Request

DORA
Diving Operational Readiness Assessment
Dynamic Operator Response Apparatus

DORAN
Doppler Ranging

DORIS
Direct Order Recording and Invoicing System

DOS
Day of Supply
Dependents Arrived at Overseas Station

DOSS
Disk-Oriented Supply System

DOSV
Deep Oceanographic Survey Vehicle

DOT
Deep Ocean Technology
Department of Transportation
Directory of Occupational Titles

DOUCHE
Description of Underwater Contacts Hastily and Exactly

DOV
Disbursing Officer's Voucher

DOVAP
Doppler Velocity and Position

DOW
Died of Wounds

DOWB
Deep Ocean Work Boat

DOZ
Dozen

DP
Data Processing
Detention of Pay
Development Proposal
Dial Pulse
Differential Pressure
(By) Direction of the President
Displaced Person/Persons
Dual-Purpose

DP1
Data Processing Technician First Class

DP2
Data Processing Technician Second Class

DP3
Data Processing Technician Third Class

DPAO
District Public Affairs Officer

DPB
Disaster Preparedness Bill

DPC
Chief Data Processing Technician
Defense Planning Committee
Defense Plants Corporation
Defense Procurement Circulars
Duty Preference Card

DPCA
Displayed Phase Center Antenna

DPCM
Master Chief Data Processing Technician

DPCS
Senior Chief Data Processing Technician

DPD
Data Processing Department
District Port Director

DPDMR
Defense Property Disposal Precious Metals Recovery Office

DPDO
Defense Property Disposal Officer

DPDP
Defense Property Disposal Program

DPDREG
Defense Property Disposal Region

DPDRPACDET
Defense Property Disposal Region, Pacific Detachment

DPDRPACSO
Defense Property Disposal Region, Pacific

Sales Office

DPDT
Double Pole, Double Throw (switch)

DPE
Data Processing Equipment
Director, Planning, and Evaluation

DPICM
Dual Purpose Improved Conventional Munition

DPIR
Detailed Photo Interpretation Report

DPRIS/EMPRS
Defense Personnel Record Imaging System/Electronic Military Personnel Record System

DPSC
Defense Personnel Support Center

DR
Dead Reckoning

DRCT
Direct

DRIBU
Drifting Buoy

DRM
Destructive Readout Memory
Direction of Relative Motion
Direction of Relative Movement

DRMO
District Records Management Officer

DRN
Data Release Notice

DRO
Daily Report of Obligations
Day-Room Orderly
Direct Read-Out

DRP
Dead Reckoning Plotter
Direct Requisitioning Procedure

DRPM
Direct-Reporting Program Manager

DRPR
Drawing Practice

DRRA
Direct-Reading Range Assessor

DRRB
Data Requirements Review Board

DRRI
Defense Race Relations Institute

DRS
Digital Range Safety
Doppler Radar Set

DRSC
Direct Radar Scope Camera

DRSCPO
District Reserve Supply Corps Program

DRSCS
Digital Range Safety Control System

DRSS
Data Relay Satellite System

DRT
Dead-Reckoning Tracer
Disaster Recovery Training

DRTD
Disaster Recovery Training Department

DRU
Demolition Research Unit

D/S
Dropped Shipped

DS
Diver, Salvage
Double Slave (LORAN station)
Double-Stranded

DS1
Data Systems Technician First Class

DS2
Data Systems Technician Second Class

DS3
Data Systems Technician Third Class

DSA
Defense Shipping Authority
Defense Supply Agency
Design Services Allocation
Dial Service Assistance

DSAA
Defense Security Assistance Agency

DSAD
Director, Systems Analysis Division

DSAO
Data Systems Automation Office

DSAP
Defense Security Assistance Program

DSAR
Defense Supply Agency Regulation

DSARC
Defense Systems Acquisition Review Council

DSB
Defense Science Board
Duty Steam or Power Boat

DSBCO
Defense Surplus Bidders Control Office

DSC
Chief Data Systems Technician
Defense Supply Center
Distinguished Service Cross

DSCA
Data Systems Coordinating Activity (DOD)

DSCBO
Defense Surplus Bidders Control Office

DSCC
Defense Supply Center Columbus

DSC IL
Defense Supply Center Indication List

DSCM
Master Chief Data Systems Technician

DSCP
Defense Supply Center Philadelphia

DSCS
Defense Construction Supply Center
Defense Satellite Communications System

DSD
Data Systems Design
Data Systems Division
Defense Systems Division

DSDS
Dual-Source Dynamic Synchro

DSE
Development Support Equipment
Direct Support Equipment

DSEB
Defense Shipping Executive Board

DSFL
Deleted and Superseded FIIN List

DSG
Defense Suppression Group
Designate
Designation

DSIATP
Defense Sensor Interpretation and Training Program

DSIPT
Dissipate

DSL
Deep Scattering Layer

DSLE
Directorate of Security and Law Enforcement

DSM
Distinguished Service Medal

DSMAC
Digital Scene-Matching Area Correlation

DSMG
Designed Systems Management Group

DSMS
Defense Systems Management School

DSN
Defense Switched Network

DSNT
Distant

DSO
DEERS Support Office
District Security Office/Officer
District Service Office/Officer
District Supply Office/Officer

DSOT
Daily Systems Operability Test (SAM)

DSOTS
Demonstration Site Operational Test Series

DSP
Deep Submergence Program
Defense Standardization Program
Designated Stock Point
Dispatch
Dispensary

DSPA
Data Systems Participating Agency

DSPG
Defense Small Projects Group
Drill Service in Paygrade

DSPO
Duty Security Petty Officer

DSRPAC
Defense Subsistence Region, Pacific

DSRV
Deep-Submergence Rescue Vehicle

DSS
Data Systems Specification
Deep Submergence Systems

DSSC
Defense Subsistence and Supply Center

DSSCS
Defense Special Security Communications System

DSSN
Data Systems Technician Seaman
Disbursing Station Symbol Number

DSSO
Defense Surplus Sales Office
District Ship's Service Office/Officer

DSSPO
Deep Submergency Systems Project Office/Officer

DSSPTO
Deep Submergency Systems Project Technical Office

DSSV
Deep Submergence Search Vehicle

DSSW
Defense Supply Service Washington

DST
Destructor
Director for Science and Technology
District

DSU
Data Storage Unit

DSV
Deep Submergence Vehicle

DSVL
Doppler Sonar Velocity Log

DSVOPS
Duty as an operator or crewmember of an operational self-propelled submersible including underseas exploration and research vehicles

DSW
Diesel Sea Water
Differential Shunt Winding (wiring)

DSWS
Diving Salvage Warfare Specialty

D/T
Detector/Tracker

DT
Deep Tank (stowage)
Dental Technician
Developmental Testing
Diagnostic Time (computers)
Dynamic Tear

DT&E
Developmental Test and Evaluation

DT1
Dental Technician First Class

DT2
Dental Technician Second Class

DT3
Dental Technician Third Class

DTA
Differential Thermal Analysis

DTACCS
Director, Telecommunications and Command and Control Systems

DTAS
Data Transmission and Switching

DTB
Destroyer Tactical Bulletin

DTC
Chief Dental Technician
Desert Test Center
Design To Cost

DTCM
Master Chief Dental Technician

DTCS
Senior Chief Dental Technician

DTD
Dated

DTE
Dial Telephone Exchange

DTEAS
Detection, Track, Evaluation, and Assignment

DTF
Data Transmission Facilities
Dental Treatment Facility

DTG
Date-Time-Group

DTH
DMS Transitional Hubs

DTI
Division of Technical Information (AEC)

DTIS
Drill Time in Service

DTL
Detail
Detailed
Diode-Transistor-Logic (circuit)

DTM
Director, Telecommunications Management

DTMB
Defense Traffic Management Branch

DTMF
Dual-Tone Multi-Frequency

DTMS
Defense Traffic Management Service

DTN
Detain

DTNSRDC
David W. Taylor Naval Ship Research and Development Center Detachment

DTNTN
Detention of Pay

DTO
Direct Turn-Over
District Training Office/Officer
District Transportation Office/Officer

DTOC
Division Tactical Operations Center

DT/OT
Development Testing/Operational Testing

DTPEWS
Design-to-Price EW System

DTRA
Defense Technical Review Activity

DTRM
Dual-Thrust Rocket Motor

DTS
Daily Test Schedule
Data Terminal Simulator
Deep Tactical Support
Defense Telephone System
Defense Transportation System

DTS-W
Defense Telephone System-Washington

DTV
Diving Training Vessel

DU
Duty

DUCON
Duty Connection

DUDAT
Due Date

DUE AT DES
Due At Destination

DUFLY
Duty involving flying status

DUFLYTECH
Duty involving flying as a technical observer

DUFLYTECHNAV
Duty involving flying as a technical observer non-pilot navigator

DUINS
Duty Under Instruction

DUINS/TEMDUINS STU
Duty under instruction or temporary duty under instruction as a student

DUKW
Amphibious Truck

DUNC
Deep Underwater Nuclear Counter

DUNS
Deep Underground Support Center

DUP
Duplicate

DUPE
Duplicate

DUR
During

DURELAS
Duty as his relief

DURG
During

DURS
Dockside Underway Replenishment Simulator

DUSD
Deputy Under Secretary of Defense

DUSD(AP)
Deputy Under Secretary of Defense (Acquisition Policy)

DUSD(C^3I)
Deputy Under Secretary of Defense (Communications, Command, Control and Intelligence)

DUSD(PR)
Deputy Under Secretary of Defense (Policy Review)

DUSIGN
To duty assigned by

DUSN
Deputy Under Secretary of Navy

DUSODA
For such other duty as (designated command) may assign

DUSTA
Duty Station

DUT
Duty

DUV
Data Under Voice

(DV)
Qualified as a Diver

DV
Distinguished Visitor

DVC
Direct View Console

DVFR
Defense Visual Flight Rules

DVLP
Development

DVM
Digital Voltmeter

DVNG
Diving Duty

D-VOF
Defense Mapping Agency Vertical Obstruction File

D/W
Dependent Wife

DWA
Died of Wounds Resulting from Action with Enemy

DWC
Damaged Weapons Control
Display and Weapon Control

DWEST
Deep-Water Environmental Survival Training

DWG
Drawing

DWICA
Deep-Water Isotopic Current Analyzer

DWL
Designer's Waterline

DWN
Down

DWNGRD
Downgrading Classification

DWP
Deep-Water Pier

DWPNT
Dew Point

DWS
Design Work Study

DWSMC
Defense Weapons Systems Management Center

DWT
Deadweight Tons

DWV
Drain, Waste, and Vent

DX
Data Extraction
Destroyer, New Construction

Duplex Operation

DX/DXG
New Construction Destroyer Program

DXG
New Construction, Guided Missile Destroyer

DXGN
New Construction, Nuclear-Powered Guided Missile Destroyer

DY
Duty
Dynamotors

DYDAT
Dynamic Data

DYN
Dynamics

DZ
Dozen
Drop Zone

E
East
Eastern
Efficiency (award)
Electrical
Electronic Countermeasures (NAO code)
Equatorial (air mass)
Excellence (award)
Experimental

E&E
Escape and Evasion

E&ML
Environmental and Morale Leave

E&R
Engineering and Repair

E&SP
Equipment and Spare Parts

E&T
Education and Training

E^3
Electromagnetic Environmental Effects

E/A
Enemy Aircraft

EA
Each
Economic Analysis
Educational Advisor
Electronic Attack
Emergency Action
End Article
Engineering Aide
Executive Assistant

EA1
Engineering Aid First Class

EA2
Engineering Aid Second Class

EA3
Engineering Aid Third Class

EAB
Emergency Air Breathing

EAC
Chief Engineering Aid
Emergency Action Console
Expect Approach Clearance

EACA
Engineering Aid Construction Apprentice

EACM
Master Chief Engineering Aid

EACN
Engineering Aid Constructionman

EACS
Senior Chief Engineering Aid

EAD
Effective Air Distance
Enlisted Assignment Document
Entered on Active Duty
Equipment Availability Date

EADEP
Emergency Animal Disease Education Program

EAG
Experimental Auxiliary
Experimental Firing Ship

EAID
Electronic Anti-Intrusion Device

EAM
Electric Accounting Machine
Emergency Action Message
Equipment Acquisition Manual

EAM/EDPM
Electric Accounting Machine and Electronic Data Processing Machine

EAMTMTS
Eastern Area, Military Traffic Management and Terminal Service

EAMU
Electronic Accounting Machine Unit

EAN
Expenditure Account Number

EANS
Emergency Action Notification System

EAOS
Expiration of Active Obligated Service

EAP
Effective Air Path

EAPS
Engine Air Particle Separator

EAPU
Electrical Auxiliary Power Unit

EAR
Electromagnetic Activity Receiver

EARLPRADATE
Earliest Practical Date

EAS
Electronic Altitude Sensor
Equivalent Airspeed

EASTCO
East Coast

EASTCONRADREG
Eastern Continental Air Defense Region

EASTLANTMED
Eastern Atlantic and Mediterranean

EASTOMP
East Ocean Meeting Point

EASTPAC
Eastern Pacific

EASTROPAC
Eastern Tropical Pacific (investigations)

EASTSEAFRON
Eastern Sea Frontier

EASY
Efficient Assembly System

EAT
Environmental Acceptance Testing
Evaporator Assist Team
Expected Approach Time

EATP
Educational Assistance Test Program

EAWS
Enlisted Aviation Warfare Specialist

EB
Early Burst (bomb)
Electric Boat
Enlistment Bonus

EBA
Emergency Breathing Apparatus

EBAP
External Burning Assisted Projectile

EBC
External Baggage Container

EBICON
Electronic Bombardment-Induced Conductivity

EBR
Electron Beam Recorder
Experimental Breeder Reactor (AEC)

EBS
Emergency Broadcast System

EBWR
Experimental Boiling Water Reactor

EC
Electronic Calibration
Electronic Coding
Electronic Component
Engagement Controller
Engineering Construction
Exhaust Close
Exhaust Closed

ECA
Engineering Change Analysis
Engineering Change Authorization
Engineering Cognizance Agreement

ECAC
Electromagnetic Compatibility Analysis Center

ECC
Electronic Control Console
Electronic-Courier Circuit
Engineering Casualty Control
Engineering Control Center
Enlisted Classification Code
Enlisted Correspondence Course

ECCB
Equipment to Computer Converter Buffer

ECCL
Equipment and Component Configuration Listing

ECCM
Electronic Counter-Countermeasures

ECC-OCC
Enlisted/Officer Combined Correspondence Course

ECD
Emergency Category Designation
Estimated Completion Date
Exploratory Career Development

ECDW
Electronic Cooling Distilled Water

E-Cert
Engineering Certification

ECH
Echelon

ECI
Equipment and Component Index
Error Cause Identification
Extension Course Institute

ECL
Emitter Coupled Logic
English Completion Test (DLI)
Equipment Component List

ECM
Electronic Cipher Machine
Electronic Countermeasures

ECMO
Electronic Countermeasures Officer

ECN
Engineering Change Notice
Equipment Component Number

ECN-APL
Equipage Category Numbered Allowance Parts List

ECO
Engineering Change Order

ECP
Emergency Command Precedence
Engineering Change Proposal
Enlisted Commissioning Program

ECPS
Engineering Change Proposal System

ECR
Engineering Change Request
Error Cause Removal (form)

ECRC
Electronic Component Reliability Center

ECRS
Equipage Control Redistribution System

ECU
Environmental Control Unit

ECW
Electronic Cooling Water

ED
Eastern District
Education
Electro-Dialysis
Electron Devices
Engineering Department
Engineering Draftsman
Existence Doubtful (contact)
Extra Duty

EDA
Estimated Date of Arrival

EDAC
Equipment Distribution and Condition
Error Detection and Correction

EDAI
Engineering Design Advance Information

EDATS
Executive Data System

EDAVR
Enlisted Distribution and Verification Report

EDC
Electronic Digital Computer
Engine-Drive Compressor
Engineering Document Control
Enlisted Distribution Commander

EDCMR
Effective Date of Change of Morning Report

EDD
Destroyer (Experimental)
Effective Downwind Direction
Estimated Delivery Date
Estimated Departure Date

EDE
Destroyer Escort (Experimental)

EDED
Electronic and Display Equipment Division

EDF
Effective Downwind Forecast
Engineering Data File

EDG
Exploratory Development Goals

EDGE
Electronic Data-Gathering Equipment
Experimental Display Generation

EDIAC
Engineering Decision Integrator and Communication

EDIS
Engineering Data Information System

EDITAR
Electronic Digital Tracking and Ranging

EDM
Effective Downwind Message
Electrical Discharge Machinery

EDMF
Extended Data Management Facility

EDMICS
Engineering Data Management Information Control System

EDMS
Engineering Drawing Micro-Reproduction System

EDO
Engineering Duty Officer

EDOM
Engineering Department Organizational Manual

EDOSCOL
Engineering Duty Officer School

EDP
Electronic Data Processing
Emergency Defense Plan

EDPAC
Electronic Data Processing and Compiling

EDPC
Electronic Data Processing Center

EDPE
Electronic Data Processing Equipment

EDPM
Electronic Data Processing Machine

EDPS
Electronic Data Processing System

EDR
Electronic Decoy Rocket
Employee Data Record
Engineering Document Record
Equivalent Direct Radiation
Exploratory Development Requirement
Extended Duty Reserve

EDRF
Experienced Demand Replacement Factor

EDS
Electronic Data Systems
Engineering Data Systems
Environmental Data Service (NOAA)

EDSAR
Engineering Drawing Status and Release

ED(SI)
Engineering Department (Ships Installation) (NAEC)

EDSPEC
Education Specialist

EDT
Engineering Design Test
Estimated Delivery Time
Estimated Departure Time

EDTR
Experimental Development Test and

Research

EDTRASUPPDET
Education and Training Support Detachment

EDTRASUPPTRADEV FEO
Education and Training Support Training Device Field Engineering Office

EDU
Experimental Diving Unit

EDUC
Education

EDVR
Enlisted Distribution and Verification Report

EE
End Event
Expiration of Enlistment

EE&H
Electricity, Electronics, and Hydraulics (school)

EE&RM
Elementary Electrical and Radio Material (school)

EEA
External Evidence of Arming

EEAP
Enlisted Education Advancement Program

EEAT
Emergency Expected Approach Time

EEBD
Emergency Escape Breathing Device

EED
Electro-Explosive Device

EEFI
Essential Elements of Friendly Information

EEI
Essential Elements of Information

EELS
Electronic Emitter Location System

EENT
End of Evening Nautical Twilight

EEO
Equal Employment Opportunity (program)

EEOAC
Equal Employment Opportunity Advisory Council

EEOC
Equal Employment Opportunity Commission
Equal Employment Opportunity Coordinator

EEODIRSYS
Equal Employment Opportunity Directives System

EEOO
Equal Employment Opportunity Officer

EEP
Engineering Experimental Phase

EER
Equipment Evaluation Report
Explosive Echo-Ranging

EERC
Explosive Echo-Ranging Change

EES
European Exchange System

EET
Engineering Evaluation Test

EF
Edge Finishing

EFC
Expected Further Clearance

EFD
Engineering Field Division

EFD(MIS)
Engineering Field Division (Management Information System)

EFF
Effective

EFFCY
Efficiency

EFICD
Electrical Fittings Inventory Control Division

EFM
Expeditionary Force Message

EFPROUT
Effecting promotion, procedure outlined in ______ will be followed

EFR
Electronic Failure Report
Equipment Facility Requirement

EFTO
Elementary Flying Training School
Encrypted for Transmission Only

EFW
Effective Fallout Wind

EG
Electro Gas
Escort Group

EGADS
Electronic Ground Automatic Destruct Sequencer

EGL
Equipage Guide List

EGS
Electronic Glide Slope
Exhaust Gas System

EGT
Exhaust Gas Temperature

EH
Exercise Head

E-HA
Enroute High Altitude

EHF
Extremely High Frequency

EHP
Effective Horsepower

EHSV
Electrohydraulic Servo Valve

EI
End Item
Engineering Investigation

EIA
Environmental Impact Assessment

EIB
Electronics Information Bulletin (publication)

EIC
Environmental Information Center
Equipment Identification Code
Exercise Intelligence Center

EICAM
Electronic Installation Change and Maintenance

EICS
Equipment Identification Coded System

EID
End Item Description (PCI)
Estimated Issue Date

EIL
Equipment Identification List
Explosive Investigative Laboratory

EIMO
Engineering Interface Management Office

E INT
Equal Interval

EIOD
Extra Instruction or Duty

EIP
Electronic Installation Plan (ERP)

EIR
Expanded Infrared

EIS
Electronic Installation Squadron
Environmental Impact Statement

EISO
Engineering and Integrated Support Office

EIT
Engineer-in-Training

EJ
Eject

EKMS
Electronic Keying Material System
Electronic Key Management System

EL
Electrical
Electroluminescent
Exchange, Limited

E-LA
Enroute Low Altitude

ELAP
Expanded Legal Assistance Program

ELAT
English Language Aptitude Test

ELDG
Electrical, Defective, Government (GFE)

ELE
Element
Engine-Life-Expectancy

ELEC
Electric
Electrician

ELECT
Electric

ELECTECH
Electronics Technician

ELECTMAINTCO
Electronic Maintenance Company

ELEV
Elevation
Elevator

ELEX
Electronic

ELF
Expeditionary Logistics Facility
Explosive-Actuated Light Filter

ELFC
Electroluminescent Ferroelectric Cell

EL/G
Emergency Landing Ground

ELG
Emergency Landing Ground

ELIG
Eligible

ELIG RET
Eligible for Retirement

ELIM
Eliminate

ELIN
Exhibit Line Item Number

ELINT
Electromagnetic Intelligence
Electronic Intelligence

ELM
Eastern Atlantic and Mediterranean

ELMG
Engine Life Management Group

ELMINT
Electromagnetic Intelligence

ELOM
Electro-Optical Light Modulator

ELOX
Electrical Spark Erosion

ELP
Edge-Lit Panel
Emergency Loading Procedure

ELS
Emergency Lighting Supply
Emergency Lighting System

ELSB
Edge-Lighted Status Board

ELSBM
Exposed Location Single-Buoy Mooring

ELSW
Elsewhere

ELT
Engineering Laboratory Technician

ELTC
Enlisted Loss to Commission Status

EL WICOMATIC
Electrologic Wiring and Connecting Devices, Semi-Automatic

E/M
Electro-Mechanical

EM
Education Manual
Electrician's Mate
Electromagnetic
Electronic Memories
Electron Microscopy
Emission
Energy Management
Engineering Manual
Engine Maintenance
Enlisted Man/Men
Estimated Manhours

EM&D
Engineering, Manufacturing & Development

EM1
Electrician's Mate First Class

EM2
Electrician's Mate Second Class

EM3
Electrician's Mate Third Class

EMALS
Electro-Magnetic Aircraft Launch System

EMAR
Experimental Memory Address Register

EMATT
MK 39 Expendable Mobile ASW Training Target

EMB
Electronic Material Bulletin (publication)
Embark
Embarkation

EMBO
Embarkation Officer

EMBT
Emergency Ballast Tank

EMC
Chief Electrician's Mate
Electromagnetic Compatibility
Electronic Material Change
Electronics Maintenance Center
Engineering Military Circuit

EMCM
Master Chief Electrician's Mate

EMCON
Electromagnetic Radiation Control
Emission Control

EMCS
Senior Chief Electrician's Mate

EMD
Engineering and Manufacturing Development

EMDP
Executive and Management Development Program (DMA)

EME
Environmental Measurement Equipment

EMEC
Electronics Maintenance Engineering Center
Emergency Maintenance Engineering Center

EMER
Electromagnetic Environment Recorder

EMERG
Emergency

EMF
Electromotive Force

EMI
Electromagnetic Interference
Extra Military Instruction

E/ML
Environmental and Morale Leave

EML
Environmental and Morale Leave

EMMP
Equipment Maintenance Management Program

EMO
Electronics Material Officer
Engineering Maintenance Officer
Equipment Management Office

EMP
Electromagnetic Propulsion
Electromagnetic Protection
Electromagnetic Pulse

EMPASS
Electromagnetic Performance of Aircraft and Ship Systems

EMPL
Employ
Employment

EMPRESS
Electromagnetic Pulse Radiation Environment Simulator for Ships

EMPSKD
Employment Schedule

EMR
Electromagnetic Radiation
Estimated Manual Release

EMSA
Electrician's Mate Fireman Apprentice

EMSEC
Emissions Security

EMSF
Fleet Minesweeper Experimental

EMSKED
Employment Schedule

EMSN
Electrician's Mate Fireman

EMSUBS
Equipment Management Subsystem

EMT
Elapsed Maintenance Time
Emergency Medical Technician

EMV
Electromagnetic Vulnerability

EMW
Electromagnetic Wave

EN
Enemy
Engineering Notice
Engineman
Envelope

EN1
Engineman First Class

EN2
Engineman Second Class

EN3
Engineman Third Class

ENC
Chief Engineman
Enclosure
Enlistment Cancelled

ENCL
Enclose
Enclosure

ENCM
Master Chief Engineman

ENCS
Senior Chief Engineman

END
Endorse
Endorsement

ENDG
Ending

ENF
Employment of Naval Forces (course)

ENFA
Engineman Fireman Apprentice

ENFN
Engineman Fireman

ENG
Engineering
Engraving

ENGR
Engineer

ENGRCEN
Engineering Center

ENGREQUIPMAINTRPRPLT
Engineer Equipment Maintenance Repair Platoon

ENGRFAC
Engineering Facility

ENGRMAINTCO
Engineer Maintenance Company

ENGRPLT
Engineer Platoon

ENGRSPTBN
Engineer Support Battalion

ENGSCOLSHIPTRATMLANT
Engineering Schoolship Training Team, Atlantic

ENL
Enlist
Enlistment

ENLDEVDISTSYS
Enlisted Development and Distribution Support System

ENLMAUSTSYS
Enlisted Master File Automated System

ENLTRANSMAN
Enlisted Transfer Manual

ENP3I
Explosive Neutralization Pre-Planned Product Improvement

ENR
En Route

ENS
Ensign

ENSYS
Electromagnetic Environmental Synthesizer

ENT
Enter
Entrance

ENTDISABSEVPAY
Entitled to disability severance pay

ENTERCOPTWO
Enter only on DD Form 214N Copy Two NAVMILPERSCOMINST 1900.2H. If separation processing not at your command, officer will carry copy of this message in sealed envelope addressed to separation activity. This message will not be retained by officer after completion of separation processing. Enter across bottom Block 27, Copy Two: (Authority and separation code indicated). (Reenlistment code if indicated.)

ENTLUMPAY
According Sec. 265, Armed Forces Reserve Act of 1952, as amended, entitled to receive lump-sum readjustment payment computed on basis of two months' basic pay in grade in which service at time of release from active duty for each year of active service, ending at close of eighteenth year, but not to exceed a total of more than two years' basic pay or $15,000, whichever is less. On ______ he completed a total of ______ active service creditable for payment under this Act.

ENTNAC
Entrance National Agency Check

ENTR
Entire

EO
Electro-Optical
Engineering Officer
Engineering Order
Equipment Operator
Executive Order

EO1
Equipment Operator First Class

EO2
Equipment Operator Second Class

EO3
Equipment Operator Third Class

EOA
End of Address
Equal Opportunity Assistant

EOB
Electronic Order of Battle
End of Block
Estimated on Berth
Expense Operating Budget

EOC
Chief Equipment Operator
Electronic Operations Center
ELINT Orientation Course
Emergency Operating Center
Emergency Operations Center
End of Construction
End-of-Course
Extended Operating Cycle

EOCA
Equipment Operator Construction Apprentice

EOCC
Electro-Optics Coordinating Committee
Engineering Operational Casualty Control

EOCM
Master Chief Equipment Operator

EOCN
Equipment Operator Constructionman

EOCS
Senior Chief Equipment Operator

EOD
End of Data
Entering Office Date
Explosive Ordnance Disposal

EODB
Explosive Ordnance Disposal Bulletins (publication)

EODGRU
Explosive Ordnance Disposal Group

EODGRUDET
Explosive Ordnance Disposal Group Detachment

EODGRULANT
Explosive Ordnance Disposal Group, Atlantic

EODGRUPAC
Explosive Ordnance Disposal Group, Pacific

EODMU
Explosive Ordnance Disposal Mobile Unit

EODP
Earth and Ocean Dynamics Program

EODS
Explosive Ordnance Disposal School

EODT&T
Explosive Ordnance Disposal Technology and Training

EODTECHCEN
Explosive Ordnance Disposal Technical Center

EODTEU
Explosive Ordnance Disposal Training and Evaluation Unit

EODTIC
Explosive Ordnance Disposal Technical Information Center

EOF
End of File

EOG
Electrolytic Oxygen Generator

EOGB
Electro-Optical Guided Bomb

EOI
Electronic Operating Instructions

EOID
Electro-Optic Identification

EOISS
Equal Opportunity Information and Support System

EOJ
End of Job

EOLT
End of Logical Tape

EOM
End of Message
End of Month

EOOW
Engineering Officer Of the Watch

EOP
Engineering Operational Procedures

EOPS
Equal Opportunity Program Specialist

EOQ
End of Quarter

EOQI
Equal Opportunity Quality Indicators

EOQT
Economic Order Quality Techniques (course)

EOR
End of Reel
Explosive Ordnance Reconnaissance

EO/RR
Equal Opportunity/Race Relations

EOS
Enclosed Operating Space
Engineering Operating Space
Engineering Operating Station

EOS/MT
Extended Operating System for Magnetic Tapes

EOSS
Engineering Operational Sequencing System

EOT
Electric Overhead Travel (crane)
End of Tape
Engine Order Telegraph
Equal Opportunity and Treatment

EOU
Enemy Objective Unit

EOWT
Electronic Warfare Officer Training

E/P
Effectiveness/Productivity (program)

EP
Enemy Position
Engineering Practice
Estimated Position
Explosion-Proof
Extreme Pressure

EPA
Environmental Protection Agency
Extended Planning Annex

EPABX
Electronic Private Automatic Branch Exchange

EPANS
Enlisted Personnel Allocation and Nomination System of the Naval Military Personnel Command

EPB
Enlisted Performance Branch

EPC
Environmental Policy Center
Equipment Process Card

EPCB
Electric Plant Control Benchboard

EPCER
Experimental Patrol Craft, Escort and Rescue

EPCP
Electric Propulsion Control Panel

EPD
Earliest Practical Date
Eastern Procurement Division
Eastern Production District
Extra Police Duty

EPDB
Environmental Protection Data Base

EPDO
Enlisted Personnel Distribution Office

EPDOLANT
Enlisted Personnel Distribution Office, Atlantic

EPDOPAC
Enlisted Personnel Distribution Office, Pacific

E-PERS
Enlisted Personnel

EPF
Emergency Plant Facilities

EPHC
Eastern Pacific Hurricane Center

EPI
Engine Performance Indicator
Expanded Position Indicator

EPIC
Extended Performance and Increased Capabilities

EPIRB
Emergency Position Indicating Radio Beacon

EPLA
Electronics Precedence List Agency

EPM
Electric/Emergency Propulsion Motor
Equivalents Per Million

EPMAC
Enlisted Personnel Management Center

EPMU
Environmental and Preventive Medicine Unit

EPO
Energy Program Office
Enlisted Programs Officer

EPOR
Electronics Performance and Operational Report

EPP
Effective Program Projections
Emergency Power Package
Energy Policy Project
Environmental (Quality) Protection Program

EPPI
Electronic Programmed Procurement Information

EPPP
Emergency Production Planning Program

EPR
Electronic Requirement Report
Engine Pressure Ratio
Equipment Performance Report
Evaporator Pressure Regulators

EPS
Engineered Performance Standards
Engineering Performance Standards

EPSRG
Exhibit Planning and Study Review Group

EPSS
Electronic Performance Support System

EPTE
Existed Prior to Enlistment (medical condition)

EPU
Electrical Power Unit

EPUT
Events Per Unit Time

EQ
Equator
Equipmentman

EQCC
Entry Query Control Console

EQCM
Master Chief Equipmentman

EQOPPINFOSYS
Equal Opportunity Information and Support System

EQP
Equipment

EQPFOR
Equipment Foreman

EQPMT
Equipment

EQPT
Equipment

EQUIP
Equipment

EQUOPPINFOSYS
Equal Opportunity Information and Support System

ER
Engine room
Enhanced Radiation
Equipment-Related
Error Release
Established Record
Extended Range

ER&SD
Employee Relations and Services Division (IRD)

ERA
Expense for Return of Absentee
Extended-Range ASROC

ERAD
Energy Research and Development

ERATE
Examination Rate

ERBM
Extended-Range Ballistic Missile

E/R/C
Equipage/Repair List/Consumables (code)

ERC
Electronics Research Center

ERCS
Emergency Rocket Communications System

ERD
Engineering Review Diagram
Expense for Return of Deserter

ERDA
Environmental Research and Development Agency

ERDL
Engineering Research and Development Laboratory
Extended Range Data Link

ERF
Emergency Recovery Force

ERFPI
Extended-Range Floating Point Interpretive (code)

ERG
Emergency Recovery Group

ERGM
Extended-Range Guided Munition

ERGS
Enroute Guidance System

ERILCO
Exchange of Ready-for-Issue in Lieu of Concurrent Overhaul

ERL
Environmental Research Laboratories (NOAA)
Equipment Requirements List

ERMA
Electronic Recording Machine Accounting

ERN
Electronic Radar Navigation

ERNT
CNO Executive Review of Navy Training

ERO
Emergency Repair Overseer
Engineering Refueling Overhaul
Equipment Repair Order

EROS
Earth Resources Observation System
Eliminate Range 0 System
Experimental Reflection Orbital Shot

ERP
Effective Radiate Power

Electronic Requirements Plan
Enlisted Requirements Plan
Equipment Requirements Plan

ERPAL
Electronic Repair Parts Allowance List

ERR
Electronic Requirements Report
Engine Removal Report
Error

ERS
Eastern Range Ships
Emergency Recovery Station
Emergency Relocation Site
Engine Room Supervisor
Environmental Research Satellite

ERSA
Electronic Research Supply Agency
Extended-Range Strike Aircraft

ERT
Estimated Repair Time

ERTS
Earth Resources Technology Satellite

ERU
Emergency Recovery Unit

ERW
Elastic Resist Weld

ERY
Early

ES
Echo Suppressor
Electro Slag

ES^3
Environmental Satellite System for the Seventies

ESA
Engineering Support Activity

ESAR
Electronically-Steerable Array Radar

ESAS
Event Sensing and Analysis System

ESC
Echo Suppression Center

ESCAPE
Expansion Symbolic Compiling Assembly Program for Engineering

ESCAT
Emergency Security Control of Air Traffic

ESCWS
Enlisted Seabee Combat Warfare Specialist

ESD
Earth Sciences Division (ONR)
Electronic System Division
Elemental Standards Data
Engineering Standardization Directive
Equipment Statistical Data

ESF
Eastern Sea Frontier
Expeditionary Strike Force

ESFC
Equivalent Specific Fuel Consumption

ESG
Electrostatic Gyroscope
Expeditionary Sensor Grid
Expeditionary Strike Group

ESHP
Equivalent Shaft Horsepower

ESHU
Emergency Ship Handling Unit

ESI
Extremely Sensitive Information

ESL
Electromagnetic Systems Laboratory
Equipment Status Log

ESM
Electronic Support Measures
Electronic Surveillance Measures

ESO
Educational Services Office/Officer
Electronic Supply Office/Officer

ESOC
Emergency Supply Operations Center

ESP
Electromagnetic Subsurface Profiling (radar)
Expendable Stored Projected

ESPAR
Electronically-Steerable Phased Array Radar

ESPC
Expendable Stored Project Contract

ESQ
Enlisted Separation Questionnaire

ESQD
Explosives Safety Quality Distance

ESR
Electron Spin Resonance
Engineering Services Section
Equivalent Service Rounds

ESS
Educational Services Section
Electronic Switching System
Emplaced Scientific Station
Enlisted Submarine Specialist
Submarine Experimental

ESSC
End Sweep Support Carrier

ESSM
Emergency Ship Salvage Material
Evolved Sea Sparrow Missile

ESSNSS
Electronic Supply Segment of the Navy Supply System

EST
Enlistment Screening Test
Epidemiology and Sanitation Technician
Established
Estimate
Estimated

ESTAB
Establish
Establishment

ESU
Electrostatic Unit

ESVR
Examination Status Verification Report

ESWS
Enlisted Surface Warfare Specialist

ET
Elapsed Time
Electronics Technician
Emphemeria Time
End of Tape
Estimated Time
Equipment Test

ET1
Electronics Technician First Class

ET2
Electronics Technician Second Class

ET3
Electronics Technician Third Class

ETA
Estimated Time of Arrival
Exception Time Accounting

ETAS
Estimated True Airspeed

ETB
Enlisted Training Branch
Estimated Time of Blocks

ETC
Chief Electronics Technician
Eco Tracker Classifier
Estimated Time of Completion

ETCG
Elapsed-Time Code Generator

ETCM
Master Chief Electronics Technician

ETCR
Estimated Time of Crew's Return

ETCS
Senior Chief Electronics Technician

ETD
Estimated Time of Departure

ETE
Elapsed Time Enroute
Estimated Time Enroute

ETF
Eastern Task Force
Estimated Time of Flight

ETI
Elapsed Time Indicator
Estimated Time of Intercept
Estimated Time of Interception

ETIC
Estimated Time in Commission

ETM
Elapsed-Time Meter
Enlisted Transfer Manual

ETMH
Estimated Total Manhours

ETMWG
Electronic Trajectory Measurements Working Group

ETN
Electronic Technician (Communications)

ETN1
Electronic Technician (Communications) First Class

ETN2
Electronic Technician (Communications) Second Class

ETN3
Electronic Technician (Communications) Third Class

ETNSA
Electronic Technician (Communications) Seaman Apprentice

ETNSN
Electronic Technician (Communications) Seaman

ETP
Electron Transfer Particles
Elevated Training Platform
Equal-Time Point

ETR
Electronics Technician (Radar)
Engine Transaction Report
Estimated Time of Repair
Estimated Time of Return

ETR1
Electronics Technician (Radar) First Class

ETR2
Electronics Technician (Radar) Second Class

ETR3
Electronics Technician (Radar) Third Class

ETRA
Estimated Time to Reach Altitude

ETRIS
Eastern Test Range Instrumentation Ship

ETRSA
Electronics Technician (Radar) Seaman Apprentice

ETRSN
Electronics Technician (Radar) Seaman

ETS
Educational Training Service
Electronic Test Set
Emergency Throttle System
Engineering and Technical Services
Engineering Time Standards
Enlisted Training Section
Expiration of Term of Service

ETSA
Electronics Technician Seaman Apprentice

ETSD
Education and Training Support Detachment

ETSN
Electronics Technician Seaman

ETS REQ
Engineering and Technical Services Request

ETST
Electronics Technician Selection Test

ETT
Engineering Training Team

ETW
End of Tape Warning

EU
Europe
Exchange, Unlimited

EUCOM
European Command

EUM
European and Mediterranean

EUR
Europe

EUSC
Effective United States Control

EV
Electron Volt
Every

EVAC
Evacuate
Evacuation

EVAL
Evaluation

EVAP
Evaporate
Evaporation
Evaporator

EVC
Electronic Visual Communications

EVE
Evening

EVEA
Extra-Vehicular Engineering Activity

EVID
Evidence

EVSP
Employee Voluntary Support Program

E/W
East/West

EW
Early Warning
Electronic Warfare

EW1
Electronic Warfare Technician First Class

EW2
Electronic Warfare Technician Second Class

EW3
Electronic Warfare Technician Third Class

EWAS
Economic Warfare Analysis Section

EWC
Chief Electronic Warfare Technician
Electronic Warfare Center

EWD
Economic Warfare Division

EWEX
Electronic Warfare Exercise

EWO
Electronic Warfare Officer
Emergency War Orders
Engineering Work Order

EWP
Emergency War Plan
Exploding Wire Phenomena

EWP/E
Electronics, Weapons, Precision, and Electric (facility)

EWQ
Enlisted Women's Quarters

EWR
Early Warning Radar

EWS
Engineering Watch Supervisor

EWSA
Electronic Warfare Technician Seaman Apprentice

EWSN
Electronic Warfare Technician Seaman

EWTG
Expeditionary Warfare Training Group

EX
Electronics
Except
Excess
Exchange
Exercise
Experience
Experiment
Export

EXAMETNET
Experimental Inter-American Meterorological Rocket Network

EXCEL
Excellence Through Our Commitment to Education and Learning

EXCH
Exchange

EXCL
Exclusive

EXCP
Except

EXDIV
Experimental Division

EX/DP
Express/Direct Pack

EXEC
Executive
Executive Officer

EXECASST
Executive Assistant

EXEC ORD
Executive Order

EXECORD
Executive Order

EXLV
Excess Leave

EXOS
Executive Office of the Secretary of the Navy

EXP
Expend
Express

EXPC
Expect

EXPDIVUNIT
Experimental Diving Unit

EXPED
Expeditionary

EXPER
Experience
Experiment

EXPERT
Expanded PERT (program)

EXPL
Explanation
Explosive

EXPLO
Explosive

EXPLOS ANCH
Explosive Anchorage (buoy)

EXPR
Expire

EXREP
Expedious Repair

EXSTA
Experimental Station

EXT
Extend
Extension

EXTENL
Extension of Enlistment

EXTING
Extinguishing

EXTN
Extend
Extension

EXTR
Extruded

EXTRM
Extreme

EXTSV
Extensive

EXTV
Extensive

5VM
Five Vector Model

1STSGT
First Sergeant

F
Bombardier/Navigator
Farad
Final (approach)
Fixed (light)
Flanged (joint)
Fog (weather symbol)
Fordable (body of water)

F&ED
Facilities and Equipment Department (NSC)

F&EDCD
Facilities and Equipment Department's Control Division (NSC)

F&J
Fact and Justification

F&T
Fuel and Transportation

F/A
Fuel/Air

FA
Awaiting Further Assignment (MAPMIS)

Family Allowance
Field Activity
Fireman Apprentice
Flight Attendant
Forces Afloat
Frequency Agility

FAA
Family Allowance, Class A
Federal Aviation Administration

FAAARTCC
Federal Aviation Administration Area Regional Traffic Control Center

FAAB
Family Allowance, Classes A and B

FAAD
Forward Area Air Defense

FAADBTY
Forward Area Air Defense Battery

FAADC
Fleet Accounting and Disbursing Center

FAADCLANT
Fleet Accounting and Disbursing Center, Atlantic

FAADCLANT BRO
Fleet Accounting and Disbursing Center, Atlantic Branch Office

FAADCPAC
Fleet Accounting and Disbursing Center, Pacific

FAAO
Fleet Aviation Accounting Office

FAAOL
Fleet Aviation Accounting Office, Atlantic

FAAOLANT
Fleet Aviation Accounting Office, Atlantic

FAAOP
Fleet Aviation Accounting Office, Pacific

FAAOPAC
Fleet Aviation Accounting Office, Pacific

FAAR
Forward Area Alerting Radar

FAARATCF
Federal Aviation Administration Radar Air Traffic Control Facility

FAARP
Forces Afloat Accident Reporting Procedures

FAB
Fabricate
Fabrication
Family Allowance, Class B
Fleet Air Base

FABIS
Filmless Automatic Bond Inspection

FABU
Fleet Air Base Unit

F/AC
Forward Across the Hatch (stowage)

FAC
Facility
Factory
Final Approach Course
Fleet Activities Command
Fleet Augmentation Component
Forward Air Control
Forward Air Controller
Frequency Allocation Committee
Functional Area Code

FACCON
Facilities Control

FACI
First Article Configuration Inspection

FACR
First Article Configuration Review

FACS
Fast Attack Class Submarine
Federal Automated Career System
Floating Decimal Abstract Coding System

FACSFAC
Fleet Air Control and Surveillance Facility

FACSO
Facilities System Office

FACT
Factory Acceptance Trials
Factual Compiler
Flexible Automatic Circuit Tester
Fully-Automated Compiler-Translator

FAD
Fleet Air Detachment
Flexible Automatic Depot
Force/Activity Designator

FADC
Fighter Air Direction Center

FADM
Fleet Admiral

FAE
Fuel-Air-Explosive

FAETU
Fleet Airborne Electronics Training Unit

FAETUDET
Fleet Airborne Electronics Training Unit Detachment

FAETULANT
Fleet Airborne Electronics Training Unit, Atlantic

FAETUPAC
Fleet Airborne Electronics Training Unit, Pacific

FAF
Final Approach Fix

FAG
Field Artillery Group
Fleet Assistance Group
Forward Air Controller, Ground

FAGAIRTRANS
First available government air transportation

FAGLANT
Fleet Assistance Group, Atlantic

FAGPAC
Fleet Assistance Group, Pacific

FAGT
First available government surface transportation

FAH
Degrees Fahrenheit

FAIR
Fair and Impartial Random (SSS development)
Fleet Air (command)

FAIRDEX
Fleet Air Defense Exercise

FAIRECONRON
Fleet Air Reconnaissance Squadron

FAIRECONRONDET
Fleet Air Reconnaissance Squadron Detachment

FAIRECONRONOPTEAM
Fleet Air Reconnaissance Squadron Operational Team

FAIRINTAUGMU
Fleet Air Intelligence Augmenting Unit

FAIRINTSUPPCEN
Fleet Air Intelligence Support Center

FAIRSUPPU
Fleet Air Support Unit

FAIRTRANS
First available air transportation

FAIRWESTPAC
Fleet Air Wing, Western Pacific

FAIRWG
Fleet Air Wing

FAIRWING
Fleet Air Wing

FAK
Freight, All Kinds

FAMFIRE
Familiarization Firing

FAMHSGASSIGNSY
Family Housing Assignment Application System

FAMHSGRQMTSURVSYS
Family Housing Requirements Survey Record System

FAMIS
Financial and Management Information System

FAMOS
Fleet Air Meteorological Observation Satellite

FAMU
Fleet Aircraft Maintenance Unit

FANDT
Fuel and Transportation

FAO
Fleet Administration Office

FAP
Family Advocacy Program
Family Assistance Plan
Force Personnel Assistance Group

FAPG
Fleet Air Photographic Group

FAPL
Fleet Air Photographic Laboratory

FAPRON
Fleet Air Photographic Squadron

FAR
Federal Aviation Regulation
Fixed-Array Radar
Fleet Alteration Report
Flight Aptitude Rating

FARADA
Failure Rate Data

FARANDA
Failure Rate Data

FARP
Forces Afloat Repair Procedures

FAS
Free Alongside Ship
Fueling at Sea

FASC
Force Automated Services Center

FASDU
Further Assignment to Duty

FASE
Fundamentally Analyze Simiplified English (computer language)

FASO
Field Aviation Supply Office

FASOR
Forward Air Sonar Research
Forward Area Sonar Research

FASOTRAGRULANT
Fleet Aviation Specialized Operational Training Group, Atlantic

FASOTRAGRULANTDET
Fleet Aviation Specialized Operational Training Group, Atlantic Detachment

FASOTRAGRUPAC
Fleet Aviation Specialized Operational Training Group, Pacific

FASOTRAGRUPACDET
Fleet Aviation Specialized Operational Training Group, Pacific Detachment

FASRON
Fleet Aircraft Services Squadron

FAST
Fast Automatic Shuttle Transfer
Fense Against Satellite Threats
Final Acceptance Facility
Fleet Attitude Status
Forward Area Support Team

FASTU
Fleet Ammunition Ship Training Unit

FASTULANT
Fleet Ammunition Ship Training Unit, Atlantic

FASTUPAC
Fleet Ammunition Ship Training Unit, Pacific

FASU
Fleet Air Support Unit

FASWC
Fleet Anti-Submarine Warfare Center

FAT
Fast Automatic Transfer
Final Acceptance Trials

FATCAT
Film and Television Correlation Assessment Technique

FATE
Fuzing, Arming, Test, and Evaluation

FATHOM
Foreign Affairs Theory, Operations, and Monitoring

FATRANS
First available transportation

FATSO
First Airborne Telescopic and Spectrographic Observatory

FATU
Fleet Air Tactical Unit

FAU
Flag Administration Unit

FAV
Favorable

FAVC
Fleet Audio-Visual Center

FAVF
Fleet Audio-Visual Facility

FAW
Fleet Air Wing

FAWPRA
Fleet Air Western Pacific Repair Facility

FAWS
Flight Advisory Weather Service

FAWTU
Fleet All-Weather Training Unit

FAX
Facsimile

FAY
Fleet Activities, Yokosuka

FBA
Fighter Bomber

FBE
Fleet Battle Experiment

FBH
Force Beachhead

FBM
Fleet Ballistic Missile

FBMNAVTESTUNIT
Fleet Ballistic Missile Navigation Test Unit

FBMOPTESTSUPPU
Fleet Ballistic Missile Operation Test Support Unit

FBMS
Fleet Ballistic Missile System

FBMSTC
Fleet Ballistic Missile Submarine Training Center

FBMSTCLANT
Fleet Ballistic Missile Submarine Training Center, Atlantic

FBMSTCPAC
Fleet Ballistic Missile Submarine Training Center, Pacific

FBMTC
Fleet Ballistic Missile Training Center

FBMTLL
Fleet Ballistic Missile Tender Load List

FBMWS
Fleet Ballistic Missile Weapons System

FBMWSS
Fleet Ballistic Missile Weapons Support System

FBP
Fleet Boat Pool

FBR
Feedback Report

FBS
Forward-Based Systems

FBW
Fly-by-Wire

F/C
Facilities Control

FC
Fire Control
Firecontrolman
Fleet Commander
Full Capacity
Fund Code

FC1
Fire Controlman First Class

FC2
Fire Controlman Second Class

FC3
Fire Controlman Third Class

FCA
Field Calibration Activity
Fleet Concentration Area
Flight Control Assemblies

FCAD
Field Contract Administration Division (ONM)

FCB
Foreign Clearance Base

FCC
Chief Fire Controlman
Fleet Command Center

FCCM
Master Chief Fire Controlman

FCCS
Senior Chief Fire Controlman

FCDNA
Field Command Defense Nuclear Agency

FCDSSA
Fleet Combat Direction System Support Activity

FCDSTC
Fleet Combat Direction Systems Training Center

FCDSTCLANT
Fleet Combat Direction Systems Training Center, Atlantic

FCDSTCP
Fleet Combat Direction Systems Training Center, Pacific

FCDSTCPAC
Fleet Combat Direction Systems Training Center, Pacific

FCE
Field Civil Engineer

FCFS
First-Come, First-Served

FCG
Foreign Clearance Guide

FCI
Functional Configuration Identification

FCLP
Field Carrier Landing Practice

FCO
Field Change Order
Flag Communications Officer
Flight Communications Operator
Flying Control Officer

FCO-T
Flight Communications Operator in Training

FCPC
Fleet Computer Programming Center
Flight Crew Plane Captain

FCPCLANT
Fleet Computer Programming Center, Atlantic

FCPCPAC
Fleet Computer Programming Center, Pacific

FCRC
Federal Contract Research Center

FCS
Facility Checking Squadron
Fire Control System

FCSA
Fire Controlman Seaman Apprentice

FCSC
Fire Control System Coordinator
Fleet Command Support Center

FCSN
Fire Controlman Seaman

FCST
Forecast

FCT
Final Contract Trials
Flight Circuit Tester
Functional Context Training

FCTC
Fleet Combat Training Center

FCTCPAC
Fleet Combat Training Center Pacific

FCTG
Fast Carrier Task Group

FCU
Flight Control Unit
Fuel Control Unit

FD
False Deck (stowage)
Fighter Direction
Fire Direction
Frequency Diversity
Functional Description

FDA
Focal-Distance-to-Diameter Ratio

FDAI
Flight Direction and Altitude Indicator

FDB
Forced Draft Blower

FDC
Fire Direction Center
Formation Drone Control

FDCS
Fighter Direction Control School

FDD
Floating Drydock

FDDL
Frequency Division Data Link

FDHDB
Flight Deck Hazardous Duty Billet

FDHDP
Flight Deck Hazardous Duty Pay

FDL
Fast Deployment Logistics

FDLS
Fast Deployment Logistics Ship

FDM
Frequency Division Multiplex

FDNET
Fighter Direction Network

FDNF
Forward Deployed Naval Forces

FDO
Fighter Direction Officer
Flight Deck Officer

FDPM
Final Draft, Presidential Memorandum

FDR
Facts, Discussion, Recommendations
Flight Data Recorder

FDRB
Foreign Disclosure Review Board

FDS
Fighter Direction Ship
Fixed Distributed System

FDSTC
Fleet Combat Direction Systems Training Center

FDT
Fighter Direction Tender

FDW
Feedwater

FDX
Full Duplex (operation)

FE
Far East
Far Eastern
February
Field Engineer
Flight Engineer
Fraudulent Enlistment

FEA
Feather (aircraft engine)

FEB
February
Federal Executive Board
Functional Electronic Block

FEBA
Forward Edge of the Battlefield

FEC
Facilities Engineering Command

FED
Federal

FED LOG
Federal Logistic

FEDSIM
Federal Computer Performance Evaluation and Simulation Center

FEGS
Federation and Employment Guidance Service

FEI
Firing Error Indicator

FEIS
Final Environmental Impact Statement

FEMF
Floating Electronics Maintenance Facility

FEO
Federal Energy Office

FEORP
Federal Equal Opportunity Recruitment Program

FEOS
Forward Engineering Operating Station

FEP
Final Evaluation Period

FEPC
Fair Employment Practices Code

FER
Ferry
Field Engineering Representative

FERON
If transferred, forward this directive immediately to his commanding officer for compliance or further transmittal as

appropriate, notifying originator in each case the activity to which transferred and your action if forwarding.

FERRON
Ferry Squadron

FESO
Facilities Engineering Support Office

FESS
Flight Experiment Shielding Satellite

FE-T
Flight Engineer-in-Training

FET
Field-Effect Transistor
Fleet Evaluation Trial

FEU
Fleet Expansion Unit

FEX
Field Exercise
Fleet Exercise

FF
Failure Factor
Force Flagship
Foreign Flag
Frigate

FFA
For Further Assignment

FFAR
Folding-Fin Aircraft Rocket
Forward-Firing Aircraft Rocket

FFB
Fact-Finding Bodies

FFC
For Further Clearance
Fuze Function Control

FFDO
Force Fighter Director Officer

FFG
Fiscal and Force Capability Guidance
Guided-Missile Frigate

FFL
Fixed and Flashing (light)

FFLOP
Field Fresnel Lens Optical Platform

FFP
Firm Fixed Price
Fleet Frequency Plans
Radar Picket Frigate

FFT
Fast Fourier Transform
For Further Transfer
Frigate (Reserve Training)

FFTF
Fast Flux Test Facility (AEC)

FFW
Failure-Free Warranty

FG
Fine Grain
Fundamentals Graduate

FGO
Flag Gunnery Officer

FGPFL
Fixed and Group Flashing (light)

FHE
Fast Hydrofoil Escort

FHLT
Fleet High-Level Terminal

FHP
Fractional Horsepower
Funded Housing Project

FHTNC
Fleet Hometown News Center

FI
Fabrication Instruction
Face Immersion
Fault Isolation
Field Item
Fiscal Intermediary
Flight Idle

FIANA
File Analyzer and Report Generator

FIAT
Field Information Agency, Technical

FIBI
Filed, But Impracticable to Transmit

FIC
Fault Isolation Checkout
Fleet Intelligence Center

Fleet Issue Control
Flight Information Center
Force Indicator Code
Frequency Interference Control

FIC CATIS
Fleet Intelligence Center Computer-Aided Tactical Information System

FICEURLANT
Fleet Intelligence Center, Europe and Atlantic

FICL
Financial Inventory Control Ledger

FICON
Flight Conveyer

FICPACFAC
Fleet Intelligence Center, Pacific Facility

FIDAC
Film Input to Digital Automatic Computer

FIDO
Flight-Dynamics Officer
Fog, Intensive Dispersal Of

FIES
Federal Information Exchange System

FIFO
First-In, First-Out

FIFOR
Flight Forecast

FIGAT
Fiberglass Aerial Target

FIGHTRON
Fighter Squadron

FII
Federal Item Identification

FIIG
Federal Item Identification Guide
Fligth Instructions Indoctrination Group

FIIN
Federal Item Identification Number

FILG
Filing

FILL
Fleet Issue Load List

FILS
Flarescan Instrument Landing System

Fleet Integrated Logistics Support

FIM
Facing Identification Marks

FIMATE
Field-Installed Maintenance Automatic Test

FIN
Finance
Financial

FIO
Fleet In and Out
Fleet Intelligence Officer

FIP
Fault Isolation Plan
Fleet Improvement Program
Fleet Introduction Program
Flight Indoctrination Program
Flight Information Publication
Force Inspection Procedures

FIPAS
Flight Information Publication, Alaska

FIPC
Financial Information Processing Center

FIR
Financial Inventory Report
Flight Information Report
Flight Information Region
Full Indicator Reading
Functional Item Replacement

FIRE
Feedback Information Request Evidence

FIRE PLAN
Fleet Improved Readiness by Expediting Procurement, Logistics, and Negotiations

FIRFLT
First Fleet

FIRL
Fleet Issue Requirements List

FIRM
Fleet Intensified Repairables Management
Fleet Introduction Replacement Model

FIRMA
Fire and Maneuver

FIRST
Fleet Input and Reserve Support Training

FIS
Fiscal
Fleet Introduction Site
Flight Information Service
Force Information System

FISH
Fully Instrumented Submersible Housing

FISO
Force Information Services Officer

FISSG
Fleet Issue Ship Shopping Guide

FIST
Flight Instruction Standardization and Training

FIT
Fabrication, Integration, Testing (of space systems)
Fighter
Fleet Introduction Team

FITAEWWING
Fighter Airborne Early Warning

FITATKRON
Fighter Attack Squadron

FITC
Fleet Intelligence Training Center
Flight Instructor Training Course

FITCLANT
Fleet Intelligence Training Center, Atlantic

FITCPAC
Fleet Intelligence Training Center, Pacific

FITGO
Floating Input-to-Ground-Output

FITRON
Fighter Squadron

FITRONDET
Fighter Squadron Detachment

FITS
Functional Individual Training System

FITWING
Fighter Wing

FIUL
Fleet Issue Unit Load

FJ
Fighter Jet (pilot code)

FL
Flashing (light)
Flight Level
Full Load
Small Signal Search Light

FLAGADMINU
Flag Administrative Unit

FLAGADMINUCOMNAVAIRLANT
Flag Administrative Unit, Commander Naval Air Forces, Atlantic

FLAGADMINUCOMNAVAIRPAC
Flag Administrative Unit, Commander Naval Air Forces, Pacific

FLAM
Flammable

FLAME
Flame-Launched Advance Material Experiment

FLARE
Florida Aquanaut Research Expedition

FLASH
Factual Lines About Submarine Hazards

FLAT
Foreign Language Aptitude Test

FLAW
Fleet Logistics Air Wing

FLC
Field Logistics Center
Fleet Loading Center
Force Logistics Command

FLCC
Forward Logistics Control Center (LSC)

FLCNAVJUSMAG
Field Logistics Center, Navy Joint United States Military Assistance Group

FLD
Field

FLDARTYGRU
Field Artillery Group

FLDBR
Field Branch

FLDBRBUMED
Field Branch, Bureau of Medicine and Surgery

FLDINTO
Field Intelligence Office

FLDMEDSERVSCOL
Field Medical Service School

FLD RATS
Field Rations

FLDSUPPACT
Field Support Activity

FLE
Fatigue Life Expended
Fleet

FLEA
Flux Logic Element Array (radar)

FLEACT
Fleet Activities

FLEAIRPHOTOLAB
Fleet Air Photographic Laboratory

FLEASWSCOL
Fleet Antisubmarine Warfare School

FLEASWTRACEN
Fleet Antisubmarine Warfare Training Center

FLEASWTRACENLANT
Fleet Antisubmarine Warfare Training Center, Atlantic

FLEASWTRACENPAC
Fleet Antisubmarine Warfare Training Center, Pacific

FLEASWTRAGRU
Fleet Antisubmarine Warfare Training Group

FLEAVNACCTO
Fleet Aviation Accounting Office

FLEAVNACCTOLANT
Fleet Aviation Accounting Office, Atlantic

FLEAVNACCTOPAC
Fleet Aviation Accounting Office, Pacific

FLEAVNMATOPAC
Fleet Aviation Accounting Office, Pacific

FLEBALMISTRACEN
Fleet Ballistic Missile Training Center

FLEBALMISUBTRACEN
Fleet Ballistic Missile Submarine Training Center

FLEBALMISUBTRACENLANT
Fleet Ballistic Missile Submarine Training Center, Atlantic

FLEBALMISUBTRACENPAC
Fleet Ballistic Missile Submarine Training Center, Pacific

FLECOMBDIRSYSTRACEN
Fleet Combat Direction Systems Training Center

FLECOMBDIRSYSTRACENLANT
Fleet Combat Direction Systems Training Center, Atlantic

FLECOMBDIRSYSTRACENPAC
Fleet Combat Direction Systems Training Center, Pacific

FLECOMPRON
Fleet Composite Squadron

FLECOMPRONDET
Fleet Composite Squadron Detachment

FLECOMPUTPROGCEN
Fleet Computer Programming Center

FLECOMPUTPROGCENLANT
Fleet Computer Programming Center, Atlantic

FLECOMPUTPROGCENPAC
Fleet Computer Programming Center, Pacific

FLEHOSPSUPPOFF
Fleet Hospital Support Office

FLEINTROTM
Fleet Introduction Team

FLELO
Fleet Liaison Officer

FLELOGSUPPRON
Fleet Logistics Support Squadron

FLELOGSUPPRONDET
Fleet Logistics Support Squadron Detachment

FLEMARFOR
Fleet Marine Force

FLEMARFORLANT
Fleet Marine Force, Atlantic

FLEMARFORPAC
Fleet Marine Force, Pacific

FLEMATSUPPO
Fleet Material Support Office

FLEMATSUPPODET
Fleet Material Support Office Detachment

FLEMINWARTRACEN
Fleet Mine Warfare Training Center

FLEMIS
Flexible Management Information System

FLENUMOCEANCEN
Fleet Numerical Oceanography Center

FLEOPINTRACEN
Fleet Operational Intelligence Training Center

FLEOPINTRACENLANT
Fleet Operational Intelligence Training Center, Atlantic

FLEOPINTRACENPAC
Fleet Operational Intelligence Training Center, Pacific

FLEOPONTRACENLANT
Fleet Operational Intelligence Training Center, Atlantic

FLESCOP
Flexible Signal Collection and Processing

FLESOAPTEAM
Fleet Supply Operations Assistance Team

FLESONARSCOL
Fleet Sonar School

FLESUBTRAFAC
Fleet Submarine Training Facility

FLETAC
Fleet Tactical Field Office

FLETACSUPPRON
Fleet Tactical Support Squadron

FLETECHSUPPCEN
Fleet Technical Support Center

FLETECHSUPPCENDET
Fleet Technical Support Center Detachment

FLETRACEN
Fleet Training Center

FLETRAGRU
Fleet Training Group

FLETRAGRUDET
Fleet Training Group Detachment

FLETRAGRUWESTPAC
Fleet Training Group, Western Pacific

FLETRAU
Fleet Training Unit

FLEWORKSTUDGRUPAC
Fleet Work Study Group, Pacific

FLEWORKSTUDYGRU
Fleet Work Study Group

FLEWORKSTUDYGRULANT
Fleet Work Study Group, Atlantic

FLEXOPS
Flexible Operations

FLG
Falling

FLIB
Forward Looking Infrared Radar

FLICON
Flight Control

FLIDEN
Flight Data Entry

FLIGA
Flight Incident or Ground Accident

FLIP
Flight Information Publication
Flight-Launched Infrared Probe
Floating Instrument Platform

FLIR
Forward-Looking Infrared (sensor)

FLLDP
First Line Leadership Development Program

FLN
Flown

FLO
French Liaison Office

FLOG
Fleet Logistics

FLOGWING
Fleet Logistics Air Wing

FLOITC
Fleet Operational Intelligence Training Center

FLOLS
Fresnel Lens Optical Landing System

FLOOD
Fleet Observation of Oceanographic Data

FLOP
Fresnel Lens Optical Practice

FLOPF
Fresnel Lens Optical Practice, Fleet

FLOT
Flotilla

FLOTRONCOM
Flotilla or Squadron Commander

FLOT STOR
Floating Storage

FLOX
Fluorine and Oxygen

FLP
Field Landing Practice
Fighting Landplane

FLPA
Flight Level Pressure Altitude

FLR
Field-Level Repairable
Forward-Looking Radar

FLRY
Flurry

FLSD
Fleet Logistics Support Detachment

FLSG
Force Logistics Support Group (GLC)

FLSIP
Fleet Logistics Support Improvement Program

FLSIP-COSAL
Fleet Logistics Support Improvement Program Consolidated Stock Allowance List

FLSU
Force Logistics Support Unit (FLC)

FLT
Fleet
Flight

FLTAC
Fleet Analysis Center

FLTACFO
Fleet Analysis Center Field Office

FLTACREP
Fleet Analysis Center Representative

FLTACT
Fleet Activities

FLTASWCOM
Fleet Antisubmarine Warfare Command

FLTAVCEN
Fleet Audio-Visual Center

FLTAVCENEUR
Fleet Audio-Visual Center, Europe

FLTAVCENLANT
Fleet Audio-Visual Center, Atlantic

FLTAVCENPAC
Fleet Audio-Visual Center, Pacific

FLTAVCOMLANT
Fleet Audio-Visual Command, Atlantic

FLTAVCOMLANTDET
Fleet Audio-Visual Command, Atlantic Detachment

FLTAVCOMPAC
Fleet Audio-Visual Command, Pacific

FLTAVCOMPACDET
Fleet Audio-Visual Command, Pacific Detachment

FLTAVFAC
Fleet Audio-Visual Facility

FLTAVFACLANT
Fleet Audio-Visual Facility, Atlantic

FLTAVFACPAC
Fleet Audio-Visual Facility, Pacific

FLTCERT
Flight Certificate

FLTCINC
Fleet Commander-in-Chief

FLTCM
Fleet Command Master Chief Petty Officer

FLTCOMBATSYSTRAUPAC
Fleet Combat Systems Training Unit, Pacific

FLTCON
Fleet Control
Flight Control

FLTCOORDGRU
Fleet Composite Operational Readiness

Group
Fleet Coordination Group

FLTGUNSCOL
Fleet Gunnery School

FLTINTSUPPCEN
Fleet Intelligence Support Center

FLTMOD
Fleet Modernization

FLTRACKCEN
Fleet Tracking Center

FLTRASUPPRON
Fleet Training Support Squadron

FLTRELSUPPACT
Fleet Religious Support Activity

FLTRELSUPPACTLANT
Fleet Religious Support Activity, Atlantic

FLTRELSUPPACTPAC
Fleet Religious Support Activity, Pacific

FLTSAT
Fleet Satellite

FLTSATCOMSYS
Fleet Satellite Communications Systems

FLTSERVSCOL
Fleet Service School

FLTSIP
Fleet Support Improvement Program

FLTSOUNDSCHOL
Fleet Sound School

FLTSUPPO
Fleet Support Office

FLTTRAGRU
Fleet Training Group

FLTWEPCEN
Fleet Weapons Center

FLW
Follow

FLY DY
Flying Duty

FM
Facilities Maintenance
Fan Marker
Fathom
Financial Management
Foreign Military
Frequency Modulation
From

FMA
Field Maintenance Agent

FMAG
Field Maintenance Assistance Group

FMAG CRUDESLANT CHAR
Fleet Maintenance Assistance Group for Cruiser-Destroyer Force, Atlantic, Charleston (SC)

FMAG CRUDESLANT MPT
Fleet Maintenance Assistance Group for Cruiser-Destroyer Force, Atlantic, Mayport (FL)

FMAG CRUDESLANT NORVA
Fleet Maintenance Assistance Group for Cruiser-Destroyer Force, Atlantic, Norfolk, Virginia

FMB
Federal Maritime Board

FMC
Federal Manufacturer's Code
Fleet Management Center
Forward Motion Compensation
Fuel Management Computer
Fully Mission Capable

FMCDET
Fleet Management Center Detachment

FMCR
Fleet Marine Corps Reserve

FMD
Ferry Movement Directive

FMDCS
Fleet Maintenance Data Collection System

FMEA
Failure Mode and Effects Analysis

FMF
Fleet Marine Force

FMFLANT
Fleet Marine Force, Atlantic

FMFPAC
Fleet Marine Force, Pacific

FMIC
Flight Manual Interim Changes

FMICS
Financial Management Information and Control System

FMIP
Financial Management Improvement Program

FMLP
Field Mirror Landing Practice

FMLS
Fleet Maintenance and Logistics Support

FMO
Fleet Maintenance Officer
Fleet Medical Officer
Fuel Maintenance Officer
Fuels Management Officer

FMP
Family Member Prefix
Field Marching Pack
Fleet Modernization Program
Foreign Material Program

FMR
Field Modification Request

FMS
Field Maintenance Squadron
Fleet Music School
Foreign Military Sales
Fuze Maintenance Spares

FMSAEG
Fleet Missile Systems Analysis and Evaluation Group

FMSAEGANX
Fleet Missile Systems Analysis and Evaluation Group Annex

FMSO
Fleet Material Support Office

FMSS
Fleet Medical Service School

FMTS
Field Maintenance Test Station

FMWTC
Fleet Mine Warfare Training Center

FN
Fireman

FNA
Final Approach

FNC
Future Naval Capabilities

FNH
Flashless Nonhydroscopic

FNMOC
Fleet Numerical Meteorology and Oceanography Center

FNOIO
Fleet Naval Ordnance Inspecting Officer

FNT
Front

FO
Field Order
Flag Officer
Flight Order
Flight Orderly
Font
Foreign Object
Forward Observer
Fuel Oil
Fuels Officer

FOB
Forward Observer Bombardment
Forward Operating Base
Free on Board

FOBS
Fractional Orbital Bombardment System

FOBSTU
Forward Observer Target Survey Unit

FOC
Flight Operating Costs
Free of Charges
Free of Costs
Full Operational Capability

FOCAL
Formula Calculator

FOCC
Fleet Operational Control Center

FOCCEUR
Fleet Operational Control Center, Europe

FOCCLANT
Fleet Operational Control Center, Atlantic

FOCCPAC
Fleet Operational Control Center, Pacific

FOCSL
Fleet-Oriented Consolidated Stock List

FOD
Foreign Object Damage

FOG DET LT
Fog Detector Light

FOG SIG
Fog Signal

FOI
Fleet Operational Investigation
Freedom of Information

FOINTRACEN
Fleet Operational Intelligence Training Center

FOINTRACENLANT
Fleet Operational Intelligence Training Center, Atlantic

FOITC
Fleet Operational Intelligence Training Center

FOITCL
Fleet Operational Intelligence Training Center, Atlantic

FOL
Follow
Following

FOLBY
Followed By

FOMTU
Inf: Fucked Up More Than Usual

FONE
Telephone

FOPINTRACEN
Fleet Operational Intelligence Training Center

FOPINTRACENPAC
Fleet Operational Intelligence Training Center, Pacific

FOR
Fuel Oil Reclaimed

FORAC
For Action

FORCM
Force Command Master Chief Petty Officer

FORFTR
Forfeiture of Pay

FORM
Food Operations Reference Manual

FORN DY
Foreign Duty

FORNN
Forenoon

FOR PAY
Foreiture of Pay

FORSERVSUPPGRU
Force Service Support Group

FORSERVSUPPGRUDET
Force Service Support Group Detachment

FORSTAT
Force Status

FORTRAN
Formula Translation

FORTRANSIT
Fortran Internal Translator

FOS
Full Operational Status

FOSA
Fixed Orifice Sound Attenuator

FOSAT
Fitting-Out Supply Assistance Team

FOSATLANT
Fitting-Out Supply Assistance Team, Atlantic

FOSATPAC
Fitting-Out Supply Assistance Team, Pacific

FOSC
Federal On-Scene Commander

FOSCO
Foreign Officer Supply Corps

FOSDIC
Film Optical Sensing Device for Input to Computers

FOSIC
Fleet Ocean Surveillance Information Center

FOSICPAC
Fleet Ocean Surveillance Information Center, Pacific

FOSIF
Fleet Ocean Surveillance Information Facility

FOSIFWESTPAC
Fleet Ocean Surveillance Information Center, Western Pacific

FOSS
Fiber Optic Sensor System

FOST
Flag Officer Sea Training

FOT
Frequency, Optimum Traffic

FOT&E
Follow-On Operational Test and Evaluation

FOTC
Force Over-the-Horizon Track Coordinator

FOTP
Fleet Operational Telecommunications Program

FOUO
For Official Use Only

FP
Fighter Prop (pilot code)
Final Plan
Fixed Price
Flag Plot
Foreward Peak
Forfeiture of Pay
Forward Perpendicular
Front Panel (NNSS)

FPA
Final Power Amplifier
Flight Path Angle

FPAF
Fixed-Price-Award Fee

FPB
Fast Patrol Boat

FPC
Fixed-Price Contract
Flight Purpose Code

FPDS
Fleet Probe Data System

FPE
Fire Protection Engineering
Fixed Price with Escalation (contract)

FPH
Fast Patrol Hovercraft

FPI
Fixed-Price Incentive

FPIC
Fixed-Price-Incentive Contract

FPIF
Fixed-Price-Incentive Fee

FPIS
Forward Propagation Ionospheric Scatter

FPIST
Fixed Price with Successive Targets

FPJMT
Four-Party Joint Military Team

FPL
Final Protective Line

FPM
Federal Personnel Manual
Feet Per Minute
Flight Path Marker

FPMR
Federal Property Management Regulations

FPO
Fleet Post Office

FPQ
Field Performance Questionnaires

FPR
Federal Procurement Regulations
Fixed-Price Redeterminations (contracts)

FPRC
Fixed-Price Providing for Redetermination of Price Contract

FPS
Feet Per Second
Frames Per Second

FPSO
Forms and Publications Supply Office

FPSTU
Full-Pressure Suit Training Unit

FPT
Fleet Project Team
Full-Power Trial

FPTS
Forward Propagation Tropospheric Scatter

FPU
First Production Unit

FPV
Free Piston Vessel

FQ&P
First Qualities and Performance (branch)

FQN
Family Quarters, Navy

FQT
Frequency

FR
Facilitating Reflex
Federal Register
Fighter Reconnaissance
Fleet Reserve
Flexor Reflex
Food Relief Punt (USCG)
From

FRA
Fleet Readiness Assistants

FRAA
Fleet Repairables Assistance Agent

FRAG BOMB
Fragmentation Bomb

FRAM
Fleet Rehabilitation and Modernization (program)

FRAMP
Fleet Readiness Aviation Maintenance Personnel
Fleet Rehabilitation and Modernization Program

FRAN
Fleet Readiness Analysis

FRAT
Free Radical Assay Technique

FRAUD
Fraudulent

FRAUD ENL
Fraudulent Enlistment

FRB
Federal Reserve Bank

FRC
Facilities Review Committee
Federal Records Center
Fleet Resources Office
Flight Research Center
Full Route Clearance
Functional Residual Capacity

FRCU
Fractocumulus

FRD
Formerly Restricted Data

FRDENL
Fraudulent Enlistment

FREDS
Flight Readiness Evaluation Data System

FREM
Fleet Readiness Enlisted Maintenance

FREN
French

FREQ
Frequency

FRESH
Foil Research Hydrofoil

F REV
Further Review

FRF
Flight-Readiness Firings

FRGS
Force Reports Generation System

FRINGE
File and Report Information Processing Generator

FRISCO
Fast Reaction Integrated Submarine Control

FRM
Form

FRN
Force Requisition Number

FRO
Fleet Records Office
Front

FROF
Freight Office

FRON
Frontier

FROPA
Frontal Passage

FROSFC
Frontal Surface

FRP
Fiberglass-Reinforced Plastic
Fleet Replacement Pilot
Fleet Response Plan
For Record Purposes
Fragmentation Bomb, Parachute
Full-Rate Production

FRR
Flight Readiness Review

FRRS
Frequency Resource Record System

FRS
Federal Reserve System
Fleet Readiness Squadron
Fleet Repair Service

FRSSACS
Free Reaction Sphere Satellite Attitude Control System

FRST
Frost

FRT
Freight

FRU
Fleet Readiness Unit

FRZ
Freeze

FRZER
Freezer (stowage)

FRZN
Frozen

FS
Feasibility
Final Settlement
Firing Set
Fixed Satellite
Flat Seam
Fleet Status
Fleet Support
Flight Service
Fractostratus
Freon Service

FSA
Family Separation Allowance
Federal Security Agency
Fire Support Area

FSAP
Fleet Ships Assistance Program

FSA-R
Family Separation Allowance (Restricted Station)

FSA-S
Family Separation Allowance (Shipboard Operations)

FSA-T
Family Separation Allowance (Temporary Duty)

FSB
Federal Specifications Board
Fire Support Base

FSC
Family Services Center
Federal Stock Class
Federal Supply Catalog
Federal Supply Classification
Federal Supply Code
Fire Support Coordinator
Fixed Satellite Communications (terminal)
Full Systems Capability

FSCC
Fire Support Coordination Center

FSCEN
Flight Services Center

FSCIL
Federal Supply Catalog Identification List

FSCM
Federal Supply Code for Manufacturers

FSCR
First Ship Configuration Review

FSCS
Fleet Satellite Communications Systems

FSD
Federal Systems Division
First Ship Delivered
Foreign Sea Duty
Frequency Shift Demodulator

FSDO
Flight Standards District Office

FSE
Field Support Equipment

FSG
Federal Supply Group

FSI
Federal Stock Item

FSIF
Flight Suit with Integrated Flotation

FSK
Frequency Shift Keying

FSL
Full-Stop Landing

FSM
Frequency Shift Modulator

FSMAO
Field Supply and Maintenance Analysis Office

FSML
Fleet Support Material List

FSMS
Firing Set Maintenance Spares

FSMT
Fleet Service Mine Test

FSN
Federal Stock Number

FSO
Fleet Supply Office/Officer

FSP
Floating Stock Platform

FSPB
Fire Support Primary Base

FS-POWDER
Flashless, Smokeless Powder

FSR
Field Service Representative
Fin-Stablized Rocket
Full Systems Ready

FSS
Federal Supply Schedule
Federal Supply Service (GSA)
Fire Support Station
Fleet Service School
Flight Service Station
Foreign Shore Service
Full-Scale Section

FSSB
Flight Status Selection Board

FSSD
Foreign Service Selection Date

FSSG
Force Service Support Group

FSSGDET
Force Service Support Group Detachment

FS SHIPS
Fire Support Ships

FST
Field Survey Team (NMVO)

FSU
Ferry Service Unit
Fleet Support Unit

FS/UEG
Fleet Staff/Unit Expansion Group

FT
Awaiting Further Transportation (MAPMIS)
Fire Control Technician
Fixation and Transfer
Flight Test
Foot
Fort
Fume Tight

FTAR
Field Training Assistance Representative

FTAS
Fast Time Analyzer System

FTB
Failure To Break
Fire Control Technician (Ballistic) Missile Fire Control

FTB1
Fire Control Technician (Ballistic) Missile Fire Control First Class

FTB2
Fire Control Technician (Ballistic) Missile Fire Control Second Class

FTB3
Fire Control Technician (Ballistic) Missile Fire Control Third Class

FTBC
Chief Fire Control Technician (Ballistic) Missile Fire Control

FT BM
Feet Board Measure

FTBSA
Fire Control Technician (Ballistic) Missile Fire Control Seaman Apprentice

FTBSN
Fire Control Technician (Ballistic) Missile Fire Control Seaman

FTC
Fast Time Constant
Fleet Training Center
Fleet Type Commander
Flight Test Center

FTCM
Master Chief Fire Control Technician

FTCP
Flight Test Change Proposal

FTCS
Senior Chief Fire Control Technician

FTD
Fails to Drive
Field Training Detachment
Force, Type, District (code)
Freight Terminal Department

FTG
Fire Control Technician (Gun Fire Control)
Fitting
Fleet Training Group
Footage

FTG1
Fire Control Technician (Gun Fire Control) First Class

FTG2
Fire Control Technician (Gun Fire Control) Second class

FTG3
Fire Control Technician (Gun Fire Control) Third Class

FTGC
Chief Fire Control Technician (Gun Fire Control)

FTG DIVES
Footage Dives

FTGS
Fittings

FTGSA
Fire Control Technician (Gun Fire Control) Seaman Apprentice

FTGSN
Fire Control Technician (Gun Fire Control) Seaman

FTGWP
Fleet Training Group, Western Pacific

FTHR
Farther
Further

FTI
Fast Tactical Imagery

FTIC
Firm Time in Commission

FTIM
Frequency and Time Interval Meter

FTM
Fire Control Technician (Missile Fire Control)

FTM1
Fire Control Technician (Missile Fire Control) First Class

FTM2
Fire Control Technician (Missile Fire Control) Second Class

FTM3
Fire Control Technician (Missile Fire Control) Third Class

FTMC
Chief Fire Control Technician (Missile Fire Control)

FTMSA
Fire Control Technician (Missile Fire Control) Seaman Apprentice

FTMSN
Fire Control Technician (Missile Fire Control) Seaman

FTOC
Fahrenheit To Celsius

FTP
Field Transport Pack
Fleet Training Publication

FTR
Fails to Respond

Fighter
Flight Test Round

FTS
Federal Telecommunications System
Flight Traffic Specialist

FTSC
Fleet Technical Support Center

FTSCDET
Fleet Technical Support Center Detachment

FTT
Fever Therapy Technician

FTU
Field Torpedo Unit
Fixed Temperature Unit

FTV
Flight Test Vehicle

FU
Follow-Up

FUBAR
Inf: Fucked Up Beyond All Recognition

FUBB
Inf: Fucked Up Beyond Belief

FUE
First Unit Equipped

FUR
Failure and Unsatisfactory Report

FURAS
For Further Assignment

FURASPERS
For further assignment by the Commander Naval Military Personnel Command to (duty indicated)

FURASUB(S)
For further assignment to duty in submarines

FUR/EFR
Failure and Unsatsifactory/Electronic Failure Report

FURN
Furnish

FURNASER
Furnish full names, rates, and social security numbers of personnel transferred in accordance with this directive.

FURORDMOD
Orders further modified

FUT
Fleet Utility

F/W
Fixed Wing (aircraft)

FW
Field Winding (wiring)
Fresh Water

FW/B
Forward toward the Bow (stowage)

FWC
Feedwater Control
Fleet Weapons Center

FWD
Forward

FWDC
Fresh Water Drain Collecting

FWED
Fleet Weapons Engineering Department

FWMAF
Free World Military Assistance Forces

FWP
Final Weight Report

FWS
Fighter Weapons School

FWSG
Fleet Work Study Group

FWSGLANT
Fleet Work Study Group, Atlantic

FWSGPAC
Fleet Work Study Group, Pacific

FW/SIFR
Fixed-Wing Special Instrument Flight Rules

FXP
Fleet Exercise Publication

FXR
Foxer Gear

FY
Fiscal Year

FYDO
Five-Year Design Objective

FYDP
Five-Year Defense Program
Future-Years Defense Plan

FYFS&FP
Five-Year Force Structure and Financial Program

FYI
For Your Information

FYIG
For Your Information and Guidance

FYU
Harbor Utility Unit

FZ
Fire Zone

G

G
Gravel
Gravity
Group
Guilty

G&A
General and Administrative

G&C
Guidance and Control

G&N
Guidance and Navigation

G-1
General Staff, Personnel

G-2
General Staff, Intelligence Section

G-3
General Staff, Operations Section

G-4
General Staff, Supply Section

G-6
General Staff, Civil Affairs Division

G/A
Ground-to-Air

GA
General Average
Ground Attacker (aircraft)

GAA
General Account of Advance
General Agency Agreement
Grease, Automotive, and Artillery

GACTFOSIF
Graphic Analysis Correlation Terminal Fleet Ocean Surveillance Information Facility

GAE
General Classification Test/Arithmetic Test/Electronics Technician Selection Test

GAI
General Accounting Instructions

GAIL
Glide Angle Indicator Light

GAINS
Graphic Administrative Information System

GAM
General Accounting Material
General Aeronautical Material
Guided Aircraft Missile

GAN
Gyrocompass Automatic Navigation

GAO
General Accounting Office
General Administrative Order

GAO NOTE
General Accounting Office Notice of Execution

GAP
Get Ahead Program
Graduate Academic Program

GAPA
Ground-to-Air Pilotless Aircraft

GAPB
General Aptitude Test Battery

GAR
Guided Aircraft Rocket

GARD
General Address Reading Device

GARP
Global Atmospheric Research Program

GASES
Gravity Anchored Space Experiments Satellite

GASSC
Group Aviation Supply Support Center

GAT
General Aviation Transponder (FAA)
Greenwich Apparent Time

GATE
Global Atmospheric Research Program Atlantic Tropical Experiment

GATTC
General Aviation Technical Training Conference

GB
General Board
Government Bunkers
Imperial Gallon

GBI
Gained By Inventory

GBL
Government Bill of Lading

GBLADING
Government Bill of Lading

GBLOC
Government Bill of Lading Office Code

GBRP
General Bending Response Program

GBS
Global Broadcast Service

GBTS
Ground-Based Training System

GBU
Ground Back-Up
Guided Bomb Unit

GBX
Ground Branch Exchange

GC
General Cargo
Graphic Center
Great Circle
Gun Capital

GCA
Ground-Controlled Acquisition
Ground-Controlled Approach
Guidance and Control Assembly

GCBS
Ground Control Bombing System
Guided Control Group

GCC
Ground Control Center
Gun Control Console

GCCS
Global Command and Control System

GCCS-M
Global Command and Control System-Maritime

GCD
General and Complete Disarmament

GCE
Gun Control Equipment

GCFU
Germinal Center-Forming Unit

GCG
Guidance Control Group

GCI
Ground-Controlled Intercept

GCI/ADC
Ground-Controlled Intercept/Air Defense Center

GCM
General Court-Martial
Good Conduct Medal

GCMED
Good Conduct Medal

GCMP
General Court-Martial Prisoner

GCO
Gunfire Control Officer

GCP
General Control Panel
Guidance Control Package

GCR
Gas-Cooled Graphite-Moderated Reactor

GCS
Ground Communications System
Guidance Control Section

GCSS
Global Command Support System

Global Communications Satellite System
Ground-Controlled Space Systems

GCT
General Classification Test

GCU
Gun Control Unit

GD
Guard

GDC
Guidance Display Computer

GDF
Ground Defense Forces

GDH
Ground Data Handling

GDL
Gas Dynamic Laser

GDM
General Development Map

GDP
Gun Director Pointer

GDP(CL)
Gun Director Pointer (Cross Leveler)

GDP(L)
Gun Director Pointer (Leveler)

GDP(P)
Gun Director Pointer (Pointer)

GDP(SS)
Gun Director Pointer (Sight Setter)

GDP(T)
Gun Director Pointer (Trainer)

GDS
General Declassification Schedule

GDU
Garbage Disposal Unit (TDU)

GE
General Expenses

GE&D
General Engineering and Development

GEB
General Engine Bulletin

GECOM
General Compiler

GED
General Education and Development

GEDU
Gun Elevation Displacement Unit

GEEIA
Ground Electronics Engineering Installation

GEFD
Geographical Engineering Field Division

GEISHA
Gun Electron Injection for Semiconductor or Hybrid Amplification

GEK
Geomagnetic Electrokinetograph

GEM
General Effectiveness Model
Green Energetic Materials
Ground Effects Machine
Ground Electronics Maintenance
Guidance Evaluation Missile

GEMD
Ground Electronics Maintenance Division

GEN
General

GEND
General Expenses, Naval Department

GENDET
General Detail

GENOTES
General Notices

GENR
Generate
Generator

GENSPECS
General Specifications

GEO
Geographic

GEOL
Geology

GEON
Gyro-Erected Optical Navigation

GEOREF
Geographic Reference (system)

GEPOL
Generalized Processor for Command-

Oriented Languages

GETOL
Ground Effect Take-Off and Landing

GEX
Government Employees Exchange

GF
Ground Fog (weather symbol)

GFA
Government-Furnished Accessories

GFAE
Government-Furnished Aircraft Equipment

GFCC
Gunfire Control Center

GFCS
Gunfire Control System

GFCS-B
Gunfire Control System-Backup

GFDL
Geophysical Fluid Dynamics Laboratory

GFE
Government-Furnished Equipment

GFEL
Government-Furnished Equipment List

GFI
Government-Furnished Information

GFM
Government-Furnished Material

GFMPL
Geophysics Fleet Mission Program Library

GFO
Geophysical/Geodetic Satellite Follow-On

GFP
Government Furnished Property

GFR
Glomerular Filtration Rates

GFS
Government-Furnished Support
Gunfire Support

GG
Great Gross

GGS
Gravity Gradient Stabilization

GGTS
Gravity Gradient Test Satellite

GH
Grid Heading

GHA
Greenwich Hour Angle

GHE
Ground-Handling Equipment

GHQ
General Headquarters

GHR
Gross Heat Rate

GHSI
General Heat Stress Index

GHz
Giga-Hertz

GI
General Issue
Gill
Government Issue

GIB
General Information Book
Inf: Guy In Back

GIDEP
Government-Industry Data Exchange Program

GIG
Global Information Grid

GIGO
Garbage In, Garbage Out

GIMMIS
G-1 Manpower Management Information System

GIO
Government Information Organization

GIOC
General Input/Output Computer

GIP
Ground Instructor Pilot

GIPS
Ground Information Processing System

GIPSE
Gravity Independent Photo-Synthetic Gas Exchanger

GIRLS
Generalized Information Retrieval and Listing System
Global Interrogation Recording and Location Maps

GIU
General Intelligence Unit

GIUK
Greenland, Iceland, and the United Kingdom (Gap)

GLAKES
Great Lakes (IL)

GLASS
Inf: Good Luck and Smooth Sailing

GLC
Gas Liquid Chromatography

GLDR
Glider

GLI
Glider

GLIPAR
Guideline Identification Program for Antimissile Research

GLO
Gunnery Liaison Officer

GLOBECOM
Global Communications (system)

GLOC
G-induced Loss Of Consciousness

GLOCOM
Global Communications

GLOTRAC
Global Tracking (system)

GLP
Government-Lent Property

G/M
Guided Missile

GM
Geometric Mean
Gram
Guard Mail
Guided Missile
Gunner's Mate

GM&S
General, Medical, and Surgical

GM1
Gunner's Mate First Class

GM2
Gunner's Mate Second Class

GM3
Gunner's Mate Third Class

GMA
Gas Metal Arc

GMAT
Greenwich Mean Astronomical Time

GMC
Chief Gunner's Mate

GMCM
Guided Missile Countermeasures
Master Chief Gunner's Mate

GMCS
Guided Missile Control System
Senior Chief Gunner's Mate

GMD
Ground Meteorological Site

GMDEP
Guided Missile Data Exchange Program

GMFCS
Guided Missile Fire Control System

GMG
Gunner's Mate (Guns)

GML
Guided Missile Launcher

GMLS
Guided Missile Launching System

GMM
Gunner's Mate (Missile)

GMO
General Medical Officer

GMOCU
Guided Missile Operation and Control Unit

GMP
Ground Map Pencil

GMRMR
General Mobilization Reserve Material

Requirements

GMS
General Maintenance System
General Military Subjects
Ground Map Spoiled

GMSA
Gunner's Mate Seaman Apprentice

GMSER
Guided Missile Service Report

GMSN
Gunner's Mate Seaman

GMSR
Guided Missile Service Record

GMST
General Military Subjects Instructor

GMT
General Military Training
Greenwich Mean Time
Greenwich Meridian Time
Gunner's Mate (Technician)

GMT1
Gunner's Mate (Technician) First Class

GMT2
Gunner's Mate (Technician) Second Class

GMT3
Gunner's Mate (Technician) Third Class

GMTC
Chief Gunner's Mate (Technician)

GMTI
Ground Moving-Target Indicator

GMTO
General Military Training Office

GMTS
Guided Missile Test Set

GMTSA
Gunner's Mate Technician Seaman Apprentice

GMTSN
Gunner's Mate Technician Seaman

GMU
Guided Missile Unit

GMV
Government Motor Vehicle

GN
Grain

GNATS
Guidance and Navigational Tracking Satellite

GNC
Global Navigation Chart

GND
Ground

GNDCON
Ground Control

GNDFG
Ground Fog (weather symbol)

GNE
Government Nomenclature Equipment

GNR
Gunnery

GNST
Glossary of Naval Ship Types

GO
General Order

GOAC
Geographic Operational Area Coordinates

GOAR
Ground Observer Aircraft Recognition

GOC
General Officer Commanding

GO/CO
Government-Owned/Contractor-Operated (facility)

GOE
Government-Owned Equipment

GOES
Geostationary Operational Environmental Satellite

GOFAR
Global Ocean-Floor Analysis and Research

GOMAC
Government Microcircuit Applications Conference

GOP
General Operational Plot

GOR
General Operational Requirement

GOS
Geochemical Ocean Studies
Grade-of-Service

GOSS
General Overhaul Specifications, Submarines
Ground Operational Support Equipment

GOTS
Government-Off-The-Shelf

GOV
Government

GOVAIR
Government Aircraft

GOVAIRAUTHOUT
Travel via government aircraft authorized outside CONUS where available. Class _____ priority is certified.

GOVAIRDIR
Travel via government aircraft is directed where necessary.

GOVAIRDIRVAIL
Travel via government aircraft is directed outside CONUS where available. Class _____ priority is certified.

GOVAIRPRI
While travelling via government air outside CONUS Class _____ priority is certified.

GOVCOMAIRAUTH
Travel via government and/or commercial aircraft authorized where necessary to expedite completion of the duty. Class _____ priority is certified for travel via government aircraft.

GOVCOMAIRDIR
Travel via government and/or commercial aircraft as may be elected by him directed where necessary to expedite completion of this duty. Class _____ priority is certified for travel via government aircraft.

GOVT
Government

GP
General Purpose

GPETE
General Purpose Electronic Test Equipment

GPM
Gallons Per Minute

GPS
Global Positioning System

GQ
General Quarters

GR
Group

GREETOUR
Tour of duty to which member ordered is _____ months with dependents. Movement of dependents to new duty station at government expense constitutes your agreement to serve prescribed accompanied tour at new duty station.

GREETOUROBLISERV
Tour of duty to which member ordered is _____ months with dependents. Movement of dependents to new duty station at government expense constitutes your agreement to serve prescribed accompanied tour at new duty station. You have _____ months' obligated service.

GREEXTEND
Orders contingent upon your agreement to extend active duty until (date specified). Execution of these orders constitutes an agreement to serve until date indicated. Member must notify COMNAVMILPERSCOM if he does not desire to execute these orders.

GREN
Grenade

GREPAT
Greenland Patrol

GRIPS
Ground Reconnaissance Information Processing System

GRL
Gross Reference List

GRNC
Groups Not Counted

GRP
Glass-Reinforced Plastic

Group

GRSL
Guam Reference Standards Laboratory

GRTG
Granting

GRU
Group

GRUCOM
Group Command
Group Commander

GRWT
Gross Weight

G/S
General Support

GS
Gas-Turbine System Technician
General Schedule
Glass
Glide Slope
Ground Speed
Guard Ship

GSA
General Services Administration

GSBPP
Graduate School of Business and Public Policy

GSC
Ground Speed Continuing

GSCM
Master Chief Gas Turbine Systems Technician

GSCS
Senior Chief Gas Turbine Systems Technician

GSDA
Ground Speed Drift Angle

GSDF
Ground Self-Defense Force

GSE
Gas Turbine Systems Technician (Electrical)
Government-Specified Equipment
Ground Support Equipment

GSE1
Gas Turbine Systems Technician (Electrical) First Class

GSE2
Gas Turbine Systems Technician (Electrical) Second Class

GSE3
Gas Turbine Systems Technician (Electrical) Third Class

GSEC
Chief Gas Turbine Systems Technician (Electrical)

GSEFA
Gas Turbine Systems Technician (Electrical) Fireman Apprentice

GSEFN
Gas Turbine Systems Technician (Electrical) Fireman

GSEREWORKFAC
Ground Support Equipment Rework Facility

GSESD
Ground Support Equipment Statistical Display

GSF
Gulf Sea Frontier

GSFS
General Specifications for Ships

GSGT
Gunnery Sergeant

GSI
Glide Slope Indicator
Government Source Inspection

GSLL
General Stores Load List

GSM
Gas Turbine Systems Technician (Mechanical)
General Stores Material

GSM1
Gas Turbine Systems Technician (Mechanical) First Class

GSM2
Gas Turbine Systems Technician (Mechanical) Second Class

GSM3
Gas Turbine Systems Technician (Mechanical) Third Class

GSMC
Chief Gas Turbine Systems Technician (Mechanical)

GSMFA
Gas Turbine Systems Technician (Mechanical) Fireman Apprentice

GSMFN
Gas Turbine Systems Technician (Mechanical) Fireman

GSR
General Service Recruit
Ground Speed Returning

GSS
General Specifications for Ships
General Supply Schedule
Geostationary Satellite
Global Surveillance System

GST
General Staff Target
Greenwich Sidereal Time
Greenwich Standard Time

GSTOS
General Specifications for Training Operations and Manuals

GSU
Geographically Separated Units

GT
Gas-Turbine
Great

GTA
Gas Tungsten Arc

GTC
Gas Turbine Compressor

GTCP
Gas Turbine Compressor and Power Plant

GTESM
Gas Turbine Exhaust System Model

GTM
Gas Turbine Model

GTP
Gas Turbine Power
Gas Turbine Propulsion

GTR
Government Transportation Request

GTS
Gas Turbine Ship

GTSS
Gas Turbine Self-Contained Starter

GU
Group
Guam

GUARD
Guaranteed Assignment Retention Detailing

GUARD II
Expanded Guaranteed Assignment Retention Detailing

GUCL
General Use Consumables List

GULFGRU
Gulf Group

GULFSEAFRON
Gulf Sea Frontier

GUN
Gunboat
Gunner
Gunnery

GUPPY
Greater Underwater Propulsion Power

GV
Grid Variation

GVR
Geocentric Vertical Reference

GVWR
Gross Vehicle Weight Rating

GW
General Warning

GWC
Gross Weight Category

GWOT
Global War on Terrorism

GWOTH
Ground Wave Over-the-Horizon (radar)

GWS
Gun Weapons System

GWT
Gross Weight Ton

GY
Gyro
Gyroscope

GZ
Ground Zero

GZN
Grid Azimuth

H
Electronic Countermeasures Evaluator (code)
Haze (weather symbol)
Hull (valve)

H&HS
Headquarters and Headquarters Squadron

H&I
Harrassment and Interdiction (fire)

H&MS
Headquarters and Maintenance Squadron

H24
24-Hour

HA
Headquarters Administration
High Altitude
Home Address
Hospitalman Apprentice
Housing Allowance
Housing Authority

HAA
Height Above Aerodrome

HAAC
Heavy Attack Air Commander

HAACT
Heavy Attack Air Commander Training

HAAW
Heavy Antitank Assault Weapon

HAC
Heavy Antitank Convoy
Helicopter Aircraft Commander

HACS
Hazards Assessment Computer System

HAD
Heat-Actuated Device
High-Altitude Diagnostic

HADES
Hypersonic Air Data Entry System

HAF
Helicopter Assault Forces

HAFC
High-Altitude Forecast Center

HA(HS)
High School Hospitalman Apprentice

HAIIS
Headquarters Administrative Issuance Index

HAIR
High Accuracy Instrumentation Radar

HAL
Height Above Landing
Helicopter Attack Light Squadron
Highly Automated Logic

HALO
High-Altitude, Low-Opening (parachuting technique)

HALS
Hydrographic Airborne Laser Sounder

HAM
Hamlet

HAMS
Headquarters and Maintenance Squadron

HAMSDET
Headquarters and Maintenance Squadron Detachment

HAP
High-Altitude Platform

HAPDEC
Hard Point Decoy

HAR
Harbor Advisory Radar

HARDEX
Harbor Defense Exercise

HARM
High-Speed Anti-Radiation Missile

HARP
Heater Above Reheat Point
High-Altitude Relay Point
High-Altitude Research Project

HARPY
High-Altitude Research Project

HARRS
High-Altitude Relay System

HART
High Acceleration Rocket, Tactical

HART/PGK (JDAM)
Hornet Autonomous Real-Time Targeting/Precision

HASC
House Armed Services Committee

HASP
High-Altitude Sounding Projectile

HAST
High-Altitude Supersonic Target

HAT
Height Above Touchdown

HAT/LANT
Habitability Assistance Team/Atlantic

HAT/PAC
Habitability Assistance Team/Pacific

HATRON
Heavy Attack Squadron

HATS
Helicopter Attack System

HATWING
Heavy Attack Wing

HAV
Heavily Armed Vehicle

HAVHOSP
Naval Hospital

HAVSECGRUMGDAT
Naval Security Group Command Management Data

HAW
Helicopter Assault Wave

HAWK
Homing-All-the-Way Killer

HAWKITS
Hazards Awareness Kits

HAWSEAFRON
Hawaiian Sea Frontier

HB
Heavy Bomber (aircraft)
Horizontal Bands (buoy)
Horizontal Bomber

HBC
Health Benefits Counselor (USHBP)

HBN
Hazard Beacon

H-BOMB
Hydrogen Bomb

HBP
Health Benefits Program
Hospital Benefit Payment

HBPIO
Health Benefits Program Information Officer

HBR
Harbor

HBS
Harbor Boat Service

HC
Health Category
Heavy Clouds
Helicopter Combat Support Squadron
High Capacity
Hydrocarbons

HCA
Headquarters Commitment Authorization
Held by Civil Authorities

HCC
Hand Control Clutch
Helicopter Crash Crane

HCCG
(Discharge under) Honorable Conditions, Convenience of the Government

HCCM
(Discharge under) Honorable Conditions, Convenience of the Man

HCDP
(Discharge under) Honorable Conditions, Dependency Existing Prior to Enlistment

HCDS
Health Care Delivery System

HCEE
(Discharge under) Honorable Conditions,

Expiration of Enlistment

HCF
Highest Common Factor

HCFF
High Capacity Fog Foam

HCFF/AFFF
High Capacity Fog Foam/Aqueous Film-Forming Foam

HCMS
(Discharge under) Honorable Conditions, Medical Survey

HCMU
(Discharge under) Honorable Conditions, Minor Under Age of Consent

HCO
Hangar Control Officer
Helicopter Control Officer

HCP
Hangar Control Position

HCPTR
Helicopter

HCRON
Helicopter Combat Support Squadron

HCU
Harbor Clearance Unit
Helicopter Clearance Unit

HCUDET
Harbor Clearance Unit Detachment

HCUS
(Discharge under) Honorable Conditions, Unsuitable

HD
Harbor Defense
Head (land)
Heat Dissipation (factor)
Helo Direction (nets)
High Drag

HDC
Hangar Deck Control
Harbor Defense Command
Helicopter Direction Center
Helicopter Direction Control

HDCG
Honorable Discharge, Convenience of the Government

HDCM
Honorable Discharge, Convenience of the Man

HDDP
Honorable Discharge, Dependency Existing Prior to Enlistment

HDDR
High Digital Density Recording

HDEE
Honorable Discharge, Expiration of Enlistment

HDF
High Frequency Direction Finder

HDG
Heading

HDGP
High-Drag General-Purpose

HD/HL
High-Demand/Low-Density

HDHVPS
High Density High Voltage Power Supply

HDI
Horizontal Display Indicator

HDMP
Horizon Definition Measurement Program

HDMS
Honorable Discharge, Medical Survey

HDMU
Honorable Discharge, Minor Under Age of Authorized Consent

HDMW
Honorable Discharge, Minor Enlisted Without Consent

HDO
Horizontal Distance Out
Hurricane Duty Officer

HDQTRS
Headquarters

HDR
Home Dockyard Regulations

HDRSS
High Data Rate Storage System

HDX
Half Duplex (operation)

HE
Head
High Explosive
Human Engineering

HEAT
High Explosive Antitank

HEAVYPHOTORON
Heavy Photographic Squadron

HECP
Harbor Entrance Control Post

HECPOST
Harbor Entrance Control Post

HECV
Hose End Control Valve

HED
Headquarters

HEDSUPPACT
Headquarters Support Activity

HEF
High-Energy Fuel

HEFOE
Hydraulic, Engine, Fuel, Oxygen, Electrical

HE-FRAG
High-Explosive Fragmentation

HEI
High Explosive Incendiary (bomb)

HEIT
High Explosive Incendiary Traced (bomb)

HEL
Helicopter
High-Energy Laser

HELANTISUBRON
Helicopter Antisubmarine Squadron

HELANTISUBRONDET
Helicopter Antisubmarine Squadron Detachment

HELATKRON
Helicopter Attack Squadron

HELCOMBSUPPRON
Helicopter Combat Support Squadron

HELI
Helicopter

HELMINERON
Helicopter Mine Countermeasures Squadron

HELMINERONDET
Helicopter Mine Countermeasures Squadron Detachment

HELO
Helicopter

HELOPS
Helicopter Operations

HELOPSUPFAC
Helicopter Operational Support Facility

HELREC
Health Record

HELSRON
Helicopter Antisubmarine Squadron

HELSUPPRON
Helicopter Combat Support Squadron

HELSUPPRONDET
Helicopter Combat Support Squadron Detachment

HELTRARON
Helicopter Training Squadron

HEM
Hemisphere

HEOS
High Eccentric Orbiting Satellite

HEPDEX
High Energy Proton Detection Experiment

HEPS
Helicopter Personnel Escape Protection and Survival

HERALDS
Harbor Echo-Ranging and Listening Devices

HERDESNAVAV
Hereby Designated as a Student Naval Aviator

HERDET
Hereby Detached (duty indicated)

HEREDET
Hereby Detached (duty indicated)

HERO
Hazards of Electromagnetic Radiation to

Ordnance

HERS
Helicopter Expedient Refueling System

HEST
High Explosive Simulation Technique

HET
Heavy Equipment Transport
High Explosive Traced (bomb)

HETS
Hyper-Environmental Test Station

HEX
High Explosive
Hydraulics, External (system)

HF
High Frequency
Human Factor
Hundred Feet

HFDF
High Frequency Direction Finder

HFE
Human Factors Engineering

HFP
Hostile Fire Pay

HFSE
Human Factors and Safety Engineering

HFTE
Human Factors Test and Evaluation

HG
Half Gross

HGR
Hangar

HH
Hedge Hogs
Hogshead

HHE
Household Effects

HHFT
Heavy Helo Fire Team

HHG
Household Goods

HHGLIMIT
Shipment of HHG to overseas duty station indicated is limited to 2000 net pounds or 25 percent of weight limitation authorized by JTR, whichever is greater. This limitation does not apply to hold baggage and professional items.

HHGLIMITFROM
Any restriction on shipment of HHG in orders to present overseas duty station is also applicable in return of HHG from that station.

HHMU
Hand-Held Maneuvering Unit

H-HOUR
Time of landing of the first waterborne assault wave in an amphibious landing

HHS
Headquarters and Headquarters Squadron

HHTR
Hand-Held Tactical Radar

HHV
Higher Heating Value (fuel oil)

HHW
Higher High Water

HI
Height of Instrument
Hide
High

HIALT
High Altitude

HIBEX
High Acceleration Experimental (missile booster)
High Impulse Booster, Experimental

HICAPCOM
High Capacity Afloat Communications (system)

HICOM
High Command

HIDAD
Helicopter Insecticide Dispersal Apparatus, Dry

HIDAL
Helicopter Insecticide Dispersal Apparatus, Liquid

HI-FI
High Fidelity

HIFI
High Fidelity

HIFOR
High Level Forecast

HIFR
Helicopter In-Flight Refueling

HI-HOE
Helium, Hydrogren, and Oxygen (ion measurements project)

HIM
Hill Interaction Matrix

HIMS
Heavy Interdiction Missile System

HINT
High-Intensity (lights)

HIPAR
High-Power Acquisition Radar

HIPEG
High-Performance Experimental Gun

HIPERNAS
High-Performance Navigation System

HIPRI
High Priority

HI-R
High-Intensity Survey Meter

HIR
Handbook of Inspection Regulations
Handbook of Inspection Requirements

HIR CLDS VBS
Higher Clouds Visible

HIRL
High-Intensity Runway Lights

HIS
Hood Inflation System

HI-STEP
High-Speed Integrated Space Transportation Evaluation Program

HIT
Hypervelocity Impulse Tuned

HIVAC
High-Value Asset Control
High-Value Transaction (report)

HK
Hank

H/L
High/Low (limit)

HL
Hard Labor
Heavy Lift
Hectoliter
Hot Line (telephone)

HLF
Half

HLH
Heavy-Lift Helicopter

HLSTO
Hailstones

HLTTL
High-Level Transistor-Transistor Logic (circuits)

HLW
Higher Low Water

HL W/O C
Hard Labor Without Confinement

HM
Hazardous Materials
Hectometer
Helicopter Mine Countermeasures Squadron
Hospital Corpsman

HM&E
Hull, Mechanical, and Electrical (equipment)

HM1
Hospital Corpsman First Class

HM2
Hospital Corpsman Second Class

HM3
Hospital Corpsman Third Class

HMA
Marine Attack Helicopter Squadron

HMC
Chief Hospital Corpsman

HMCM
Master Chief Hospital Corpsman

HMCS
Senior Chief Hospital Corpsman

HMH
Marine Heavy Helicopter Squadron

HMI
Handbook of Maintenance Instructions

HML
Marine Light Helicopter Squadron

HMM
Marine Medium Helicopter Squadron

HMO
Health Maintenance Organization

HMR
Hazardous Material Report
Headquarters/House Modification Request

HMT
Marine Helicopter Training Squadron

HMV
Hydraulic, Main, and Vital (system)

HMW
Height of Max Wind

HMX
Advanced Marine Helicopter Squadron

HN
Hospitalman
Training Helicopter

HND
Hundred

HN(HS)
High School Hospitalman

HN(JC)
Junior College Hospitalman

H/O
Hours of Operation

HO
Observation Helicopter

HOB
Height of Burst

HOBOS
Homing Bomb Systems

HOBS
High Orbital Bombardment System

HOGE
Hover Out of Ground Effect

HOI
Handbook of Overhaul Instructions

HOJ
Home-On-Jam

HOLC
High Order Language Computer

HOMP
Halifax Ocean Meeting Point

HON
Honorable

HOOP
Handbook of Operating Procedures (on Public Works)

HOPM
Hydraulic Oil Power Module

HOR
Home of Record
Horizontal (lights)

HORIZ
Horizontal

HOS
Hospital

HOSP
Hospital

HOSPCO
Hospital Company

HOSP RATS
Hospital Rations

HOST
Hot Spot Tracking

HOUS
Housing

HOV
Hovering (depth control system)

HOVI
Handbook of Overhaul Instructions

HOW
Hercules-Over-Water (C-130 aircraft)

HOWBTRY
Howitzer Battery

HP
High Performance
High Pressure
Horsepower
Hundred Pounds

HP&A
Hull Propulsion and Auxiliaries

HPA
Head of Procuring Activity
High-Power Amplifier

HPAC
High-Pressure Air Compressor

HPB
Harbor Patrol Boat

HPC
Helicopter Plane Commander
High-Pressure Constant
Human Performance Center

HPCBR
High-Pressure Chamber

HPD
Harbor Police Department
Hard-Point Defense
High-Pressure Drain

HP-HR
Horsepower-Hour

HPM
High-Power Multiplier

HPOX
High-Pressure Oxygen

HPP
High-Pressure Pump
Hydraulic Power Plant

HPSM
Human Performance Systems Model

HPSO
Human Performance System Organization

HPT
High-Pressure Test

HPU
Hydraulic Power Unit

HQ
Headquarters

HQBN
Headquarters Battalion

HQBTRY
Headquarters Battery

HQCO
Headquarters Company

HQMTMTS
Headquarters, Military Traffic Management Terminal Service

HQNAVMARCORMARSTA
Headquarters, Navy-Marine Corps Military Affiliate Radio System Station

HQNAVMATCOM
Headquarters, Naval Material Command

HQSQDN
Headquarters Support Squadron

HQSVCBN
Headquarters, Service Battalion

HQSVCCO
Headquarters, Service Company

HR
High Resolution
Hospital Recruit
Hour
Hourly Report
Human Reliability
Transporter Helicopter

HRA
Harness Release Actuator
High-Radiation Area
Human Resources Administration

HRAV
Human Resources Availability Period

HRC
Hydraulics-Resonance Changer

HRD
High Rate Discharge
Human Resources Division

HRDC
Human Resources Development Center
Human Resources Develolpment Command

HRDPO
Human Resources Development Project Office

HR(HS)
High School Hospital Recruit

HRIR
High-Resolution Infrared Radiation

HRM
Human Resources Management

HRMC
Human Resources Management Center

HRMC/D
Human Resources Management Center/Detachment

HRMD
Human Resources Management Detachment

HRMI
Human Resources Management Instructor

HRMS
Human Resources Management School
Human Resources Management Specialists

HRMSS
Human Resources Management Support System

HRMST
Human Resources Management Support Team

HR/MTI
High Resolution/Moving Target Indicator

HRO
Housing Referral Office/Officer

HRPT
High Resolution Picture Transmisson

HRR
High Resolution Radar

HRSCO
Housing Referral Service Coordination Office

HRZN
Horizon

HS
Helicopter Antisubmarine Squadron
Hundred Square Feet

HS&SS
Headquarters and Service Squadron

HSA
Headquarters Support Activity

HSBR
High-Speed Bombing Radar

HSD
Heat Sensing Device
Hydraulic Steering and Diving (system)

HSETC
Naval Health Sciences Education and Training Command

HSF
Hawaiian Sea Frontier

HSG
Housing

HSGREFSVCSYS
Housing Referral Services Record System

HSI
Handbook of Service Instructions
Helicopter Antisubmarine Squadron Light
Horizontal Situation Indicator
Human Systems Integration

HS/JR
High School/Junior College (graduate training program)

HSL
High-Speed Launch
Light Helicopter Antisubmarine Squadron

HSNS
High School News Service (FHTNC)

HSSSM
Highly-Sensitive Ship Synthesis Model

HST
Helicopter Support Team

HSTEC
Health Sciences Education and Training Command

HSTL
Hostile

HT
Heat
Helicopter Training Squadron
High Tensile
Histologic Technician
Homing Terrier (missile)
Hull Maintenance Technician

HT1
Hull Maintenance Technician First Class

HT2
Hull Maintenance Technician Second Class

HT3
Hull Maintenance Technician Third Class

HTA
Heavier-Than-Air

HTC
Chief Hull Maintenance Technician

HTCM
Master Chief Hull Maintenance Technician

HTCS
Senior Chief Hull Maintenance Technician

HTD
Hand Target Designator

HTEXCH
Heat Exchanger

HTFA
Hull Maintenance Technician Fireman Apprentice

HTFN
Hull Maintenance Technician Fireman

HTL
High-Threshold Logic

HTLS
Higher Torque/Low-Speed

HTRE
Heat Transfer Reactor Experiments

HTS
High-Tensile Steel

HT/SZ
Height/Size

HTT
Hydraulics, Turbine Throttle (control system)

HTV
Homing Test Vehicle

HTW
Helicopter Trap Weapon

HU
Hull

HUD
Heads-Up Display

HUDWAC
Heads-Up Display and Weapon Aiming Computer

HUFFDUFF
High Frequency Direction Finder

HUK
Hunter-Killer Force

HUKS
Hunter-Killer Submarine

HULL
High Usage Load List

HUMINT
Human Intelligence

HUMRESMANCEN
Human Resources Management Center

HUMRESMANDET
Human Resources Management Detachment

HUMRESMANSCOL
Human Resources Management Center School

HUMRESMANSCOLDET
Human Resources Management School Detachment

HUMS
Humanitarian Reasons

HUN
Hundred

HURCN
Hurricane

HURR-EVAC
Hurricane Evacuation

HUTRON
Helicopter Utility Squadron

HV
Heavy
High Voltage

HVAC
Heating, Ventilation, and Air Conditioning

HVAP
High-Velocity Armor-Piercing (projectile)

HVAR
High-Velocity Aircraft Rocket

HVAR(HE)
High-Velocity Aircraft Rocket (High Explosive)

HVATKRON
Heavy Attack Squadron

HVD
Hydroviscous Drive

HVDC
High-Voltage Direct-Current

HVDF
Direction Finder, High and Very High Frequency

HVPHOTORON
Heavy Photographic Squadron

HVPS
High-Voltage Power Supply

HVTB
High-Voltage Thermal Battery

HVY
Heavy

HW
Herewith
High Water
Hundred Weight

HWOCR
Heavy Water-Moderated, Organic-Coded Reactor

HWVR
However

HY
Hundred Yards
Hydraulic

HYD
Hydraulic

HYDAT
Hydrodynamic Analysis Tool

HYDR
Hydraulic

HYDROG
Hydrographer
Hydrographic

HYDROLANT
Hydrographic Information for the Atlantic

HYDROPAC
Hydrographic Information for the Pacific

HYDROX
Hydrogen-Oxygen (fuel)

HYFT
High-Yield Fallout Trajectory

HYSAP
Hydrographic Survey Assistance Program

HYSTU
Hydrofoil Special Trials Unit

(I)
To be Inactivated

I
Airborne Intercept (NAO code)
Incendiary (bomb)
Initial (approach)

I&C
Installation and Checkout (spares)

I&EW
Intelligence and Electronic Warfare

I&L
Installation and Logistics

I&R
Instrumentation and Range

I&S
Inspection and Survey

I&SCD
Indoctrination and Special Courses Department

I^2S
Integrated Information System

IA
Identical Additional
Individual Account

Information Assurance
Initial Assessment

IAAA
Integrated Advanced Avionics for Aircraft

IAAB
Interim Aviation Airframe Bulletin

IAC
Initial Approach Course
Integration, Assembly, and Check-Out
International Analysis Code

IACS
Integrated Acoustic Communication System
Integrated Armament Control System

IAD
Initiation Area Discriminator

IADC
Inter-American Defense College

I/ADCSP
Interim/Advanced Defense Communications Satellite Program

IADPC
Inter-Agency Data Processing Center

IADT
Integrated Automatic Direction System

IADWS
Interim Air Defense Weapons System

IAF
(Office of) Information of the Armed Forces
Initial Approach Fix

IAFB
Interim Airframe Bulletin

IAFC
Interim Airframe Change

IAGC
Instantaneous Automatic Gain Control

IAL
International Algebraic Language

IANTN
Inter-American Naval Telecommunications Network Secretariat

IAO
Inter-Agency Committee on Oceanography

IAPG
Inter-Agency Advanced Power Group

IAR
Intersection of Air Routes

IAS
Indicated Airspeed
Integrated Avionics System

IAT
Indicated Air Temperature

IATCB
Interdepartmental Air Traffic Control Board

IATN
Inter-American Naval Telecommunications Network

IAW
In Accordance With

IAYB
Interim Accessory Bulletin

IAZ
Inner Artillery Zone

IB
Incendiary Bomb
Inner Bottom

IBFT
Integrated Battle Force Training

IBN
Identification Beacon

IBOP
International Balance of Payments

IBPDSMS
Improved Basic Point Defense Surface Missile System

IBS
Interbomb Spacing
Integrated Broadcast Service

IBS/JTT
Integrated Broadcast Service/Joint Tactical Terminal

IC
Ice Crystals (weather symbol)
Iceland
In Commission (vessel status)
Index Correction
Individual Counsel
Information Center

Intake Close
Integrated Circuit
Interior Communications
Interior Communications Electrician
Intermediate Course
Inventory Control

IC&RR
Inventory Control and Requirements Review (Board, CNO)

IC1
Interior Communications Electrician First Class

IC2
Interior Communications Electrician Second Class

IC3
Interior Communications Electrician Third Class

ICA
Isolated Code Announcement

ICAF
Industrial College of the Armed Forces

ICAO
International Civil Aviation Organization

ICAP
Improved Capabilities

ICAP III
Improved Capability III (for the EA-6B's AEA system)

ICAS
Interface Control Action Sheet

ICAT
In Commission, Active (vessel status)

ICB
Interior Control Board
International Competitive Bidding

ICBM
Intercontinental Ballistic Missile

ICC
Chief Interior Communications Electrician
Information Control Console
Intermediate Cryptanalysis Course

ICCA
Initial Cash Clothing Allowance

ICCCA
Initial Civilian Cash Clothing Allowance

ICCM
Intercontinental Cruise Missile
Master Chief Interior Communications Electrician

ICCS
Integrated Carrier Catapult System
Integrated Catapult Control System
Interface Configuration Control System
Senior Chief Interior Communications Electrician

ICD
Industrial Cooperation Division
Interface Control Drawing
Inventory Control Department

ICE
Iceland
Increased Combat Effectiveness

ICEDEFOR
Iceland Defense Force

ICEM
Inverted Coaxial Magnetron

ICES
Integrated Civil Engineering System
International Council for Exploration of the Seas

ICFA
Interior Communications Electrician Fireman Apprentice

ICFN
Interior Communications Electrician Fireman

ICG
Icing
Interviewer's Classification Guide

ICGIC
Icing in Clouds

ICGICIP
Icing in Clouds in Precipitation

ICGIP
Icing in Precipitation

ICIR
In Commission, In Reserve (vessel status)

ICM
Improved Capability Missile

ICMA
Initial Clothing Monetary Allowance

ICMS
Integrated Circuit and Message Switch

ICN
Internal Control Number

ICO
In Case Of
In Concern Of
Interagency Committee on Oceanography

ICOR
In Charge of Room

ICOS
Integrated Control System

ICP
Instrument Calibration Procedures
Inventory Control Point

ICR
Intercultural Relations
Item Change Request

ICRC
Interagency Classification Review Committee

ICRL
Individual Component Repair List

ICRM
Intercontinental Reconnaissance Missile

ICS
Intercommunication System
Inverse Conical Scan

ICSB
Interim Command Switchboard

ICSC
Interior Communication Switching Center

ICSMP
Integrated Command System Management Plan

ICSP
In Commission, Special (vessel status)

ICT
Individual Combat Training

ICTEC
Identification of Critical Tasks and Equipment Items

ICV
Individual Cell Voltmeter

ICW
In Conjunction With
In Connection With
Interrupted Continuous Wave

ICWG
Interface Control Working Group

ID
Identification
Identity
Inside Diameter
Intelligence Duties

ID'D
Identified

IDA
Ionospheric Dispersion Analysis
Integrated Disbursing and Accounting

IDAC
Interconnecting Digital-Analog Converter

IDAFMS
Integrated Disbursing and Accounting Financial Management System

IDART
Individual Drill Attendance and Retirement Transaction (card)

IDC
Independent Duty Corpsman
Individual Defense Counsel
Information Design Change
Inner Dead-Center
Interdepartmental Committee

IDCCC
Interim Data Communication Collection Center

IDCS
Integrated Data Coding System

IDCSP
Initial Defense Communications Satellite Program

IDD
Inter-Director Designation

IDDS
Instrumentation Data Distribution System

IDECM
Integrated Defensive Electronic Countermeasures

IDEF
Indefinite

IDENT
Identification

IDF
Iceland Defense Force
Integrated Data File

IDG
Inspector of Degaussing
Integrated Drive Generator

IDGIT
Integrated Data Generation Implementation Technique

IDHS
Intelligence Data Handling System (DOD)

IDLOC
Idle, Waiting for Load

IDMI
Interface Document Master Index

IDNE
Inertial Doppler Navigation Equipment

ID NO
Identification Number

IDO
Initial Defensive Operations

IDP
Individual Development Plan
Integrated Data Processing

IDPM
Initial Draft, Presidential Memorandum

IDQA
Individual Documented Quality Assurance

IDREA
Idle, Other Reasons

IDRL
Intradivision Requirements List

IDRN
Intradivisional Review Notice

IDS
Identification System
Instrument Development Section
Intelligence Data System

IDSCS
Initial Defense Satellite Communications System

IDSOT
Interim Daily System Operational Test

IDT
Inactive Duty Training
Individual Drill for Training

IDTC
Inter-Deployment Training Cycle

IE
In Excess
Initial Equipment

IECI
Industrial Electronics and Control Instrumentation

IECMS
Inflight Engine Condition Monitoring System

IED
Improvised Explosive Device
Independent Exploratory Development

IEM
Inactive Equipment Maintenance

IEP
Information Exchange Project

IER
Individual Education Record

IET
Inport Emergency Team

IETM
Interactive Electronic Technical Manual

IF
Ice Fog (weather symbol)
Insular Force
Intermediate Fix
Intermediate Frequency
Intermittent Frequency

IF-ADD ICMA
Insular Force-Additional Initial Clothing Monetary Allowance

IFARS
Individual Flight Activity Reporting System

IFB
Invitation for Bid

IFBH
Intermediate Force Beachhead

IFBM
Improved Fleet Ballistic Missile

IFCS
Improved Fire Control System

IFD
Inter-Fighter Director

IFF
Identification, Friend or Foe (system)

IFI
In-Flight Insertion

IFIM
International Flight Information Manual

IFIS
Instrument Flight Instructor's School
Integrated Flight Instrument System

IFM
Instantaneous Frequency Measurement

IFMS
Integrated Financial Management System

IFOBRL
In-flight Operable Bomb Rack Lock

IFPM
In-Flight Performance Monitor

IFR
In-Flight Refueling
Instrument Flight Requirement
Instrument Flight Rules

IFREQ
Industrial Forecast Requirements

IFS
Increased Forward Stocking
Inshore Fire Support Ship

IF-SICMA
Insular Force-Special Initial Clothing Monetary Allowance

IFSS
International Flight Service Station

IF TACCA
Intermediate Frequency Time Averaged Clutter Coherent Airborne (radar)

IFTP
Integrated Fight Through Power

IFTRS
Individual Flying Time Report System

IFU
Intelligence Field Unit

IFV
Instantaneous Field of View

IG
Ingot
Inspector General
Interdepartmental Group

IGASS
Integrated Ground-Air Avionics System

IGE
In-Ground Effect

IGFVP
Interservice Group for Flight Vehicle Power

IGL
Installation Group List

IGOS
Inward Grade of Service

IGOSS
Integrated Global Ocean Station System (ICO-WMO)

IGSC
Inspector General, Supply Corps

IHA
Interim Housing Allowance

IHAS
Integrated Helicopter Avionics System

IHCA
In Hands of Civil Authorities
In Hands of Civilian Authorities

IHO
Inspection Hold Order

IHP
Indicated Horsepower
Intermediate High Pressure

IHQ
International Headquarters

IHS
Information Handling System

IHSBR
Improved High-Speed Bombing Radar

IHU
Interservice Hovercraft Unit

I-I
Inspector-Instructor

II
Item Identification

IIDD
Interface Identification Data Document

IIIC
Immediate Imagery Interpretation Center

IIP
Industrial Incentive Plan (NAVFAC)

IIPS
Instantaneous Impact Prediction System

IIPT
Integrating Integrated Product Team

IIR
Integrated Instrumentation Radar

IIS
Intelligence Information System

I/ITSEC
Interservice/Industry Training Simulation and Education Conference

IKA
Information and Knowledge Advantage

IKOR
Instant Knowledge of Results

IL
Intermediate Land

ILA
Instrument Landing Aid
Instrument Landing Approach

ILAAS
Integrated Light Attack Avionics System

I-LAB
Instrumentation Laboratory

ILARTS
Integrated Launch and Recovery Television Surveillance System

ILD
Information Lead Distance

ILE
Integrated Learning Environment

ILLUM
Illuminated
Illuminating

ILM
Integrated Logistic Management

ILMP
Integrated Logistic Management Program

ILMT
Integrated Logistic Management Team

ILO
Integrated Logistics Overhead

ILOSS
Integrated Laser/Optical Sight Set

ILP
International Logistics Program

ILS
Inertial Latching Switch
Instrument Landing System
Integrated Landing System
Integrated Logistics Support

ILSM
Integrated Logistics Support Management

ILSMT
Integrated Logistics Support Management Team

ILSP
Integrated Logistics Support Plan
Integrated Logistics Support Planning
Integrated Logistics Support Procedure
Integrated Logistics Support Program

ILSS
Integrated Life-Support System

ILW
International Low Water

IM
Inner Marker
Insensitive Munitions
Intercept Missile
Intermediate Maintenance
Intramural
Inventory Manager
Item Manager

IM1
Instrumentman First Class

IM2
Instrumentman Second Class

IM3
Instrumentman Third Class

IMA
Intermediate Maintenance Activity

IMAD
Insensitive Munitions Advanced Technology

IMAP
Interactive Manpower Alternatives Processor

IMAT
Information Management and Analysis Team
Interactive Multi-Sensor Analysis

IMBLM
Integrated Medical and Behavioral Laboratory Management

IMC
Chief Instrumentman
Instructional Materials Center
Instrument Meteorological Conditions
Item Management Codes

IMCC
Integrated Mission Control Center

IMC-IFR
Instrument Meteorological Conditions-Instrument Flight Rules

IMCO
Inter-Governmental Maritime Consultative Organization

IMCS
Senior Chief Instrumentman

IMDT
Immediate

IMEP
Indicated Mean Effective Pressure

IMER
Improved Multiple Ejector Rack

IMHE
Industrial Materials Handling Equipment

IMI
Instructor-Managed Instruction

IMIC
Interval Modulation Information Coding

IMINT
Imagery Intelligence

IMIP
Industrial Management Improvement Program

IMM
Integrated Maintenance Management
Integrated Material Manager

IMMDELREQ
Immediate Delivery Required

IMMED
Immediate

IMMIRS
Integrated Maintenance Management Information Retrieval System

IMMP
Integrated Maintenance and Modernization Planning
Integrated Maintenance Management Program

IMMS
Intermediate Maintenance Management System

IMMT
Integrated Maintenance Management Team

IMMUN
Obtain appropriate immunization in accordance with Art. 22-30 NAVMEDDEPT and Current BUMEDINST 6230.1

IMN
Indicated Mach Number

IMO
"I Move Oil" (rotary oil pump)
International Maritime Organization

IMP
Image Projection
Integrated Maintenance Program
Interplanetary Monitoring Platform

IMPACT
Implementation Planning and Control Technique

IMPS
Integrated Master Programming and Scheduling
Interagency Motor Pool System (GSA)
Interplanetary Probes

IMRAN
International Marine Radio Aids to Navigation

IMREP
Immediately Report

IMRL
Individual Material Readiness List

IMS
Industrial Manpower Section
Inertial Measurement Set
In-Flight Management System
Information Management System
Integrated Military Staff
Integrated Military System
International Military Staff
Inventory Management System

IMSA
Instrumentman Seaman Apprentice
Integrated Military Survivor Annuity

IMSN
Instrumentman Seaman

IMSU
Intermediate Maintenance Support Unit

IMT
Immediate

IMU
Inertial Measurement Unit

IN
Inlet
Inspection Notice
Interpreter

INA
Inactivator
Initial Approach
Inspector of Naval Aircraft

INACT
Inactive
Upon Inactivation of (ship or station indication)

INACTFLTLANT
Inactive Fleet, Atlantic

INACTFLTPAC
Inactive Fleet, Pacific

INACTNOTERM
If serving under orders authorizing participation in Naval Reserve Training Program in pay or non-pay status, orders to inactive duty are not terminated, but are not effective during period of temporary active duty. Orders to inactive duty training are effective day following completion of temporary active duty.

INACTSERVCRAFAC
Inactive Service Craft Facility

INACTSHIPDET
Inactive Ship Maintenance Detachment

INACTSHIPFAC
Inactive Ship Maintenance Facility

INACTSHIPSTORFAC
Inactive Ship Storage Facility

INACTV
Inactive

INAD
Inadequate

INA/IC
Inactive-In Commission, In Commission (vessel status)

INA/IS
Inactive-In Service, In Reserve (vessel status)

INA/OC
Inactive-Out of Commission, In Reserve (vessel status)

INA/OS
Inactive-Out of Service, In Reserve (vessel status)

INAS
Industrial Naval Air Station
Inertial Navigation and Attack System

INBD
Inbound

INCAIR
Including Air (travel)

INC BOMB
Incendiary Bomb

INCEP
Interceptor

INCL
Inclose
Include
Including
Inclusive

INCOM
Incomplete

INCOS
Integrated Control System

INCR
Increase
Increment

INCSEA
Incidents On and Over the High Seas

IND
Improvised Nuclear Device
Independent
Index
Information Network Department
Interceptor Director

INDAIR
Identification of Aircraft

INDC
Indicated

INDEBT
Indebtedness

INDEC
Interdepartmental Committee

INDEF
Indefinite

INDFT
Indefinite

INDIV
Individual

INDMAN
Industrial Management
Industrial Manager

INDMGR
Industrial Manager

INDOCNREGREPCEN
Indoctrination Naval Regional Reporting Center

INDT
Induction

INFLAM
Inflammable

INFNT
Iroquois Night Fighter and Night Tracker

INFO
Information

INFOREQ
Information required as to ______

INID/NOD
Immediate Network-In Dial/Network-Out-Dial

INIS
International Nuclear Information System

INIT
Initial
Initiate

INITCCA
Initial Cash Clothing Allowance

INITCCCA
Initial Civilian Cash Clothing Allowance

INIT UNIF ALW
Initial Uniform Allowance

INJ
Injured

INJFACS
Injection Facilities

IN-LB
Inch-Pound

INLS
Individualized Learning System

INM
Inspector of Naval Machinery
Inspector of Naval Material

INMARSAT
International Maritime Satellite

INOP
Inoperative

INOPV
Inoperative

INP
If Not Possible

INR
Intelligence and Research

INREQ
Information Request

INS
Inches
Inertial Navigation System
Insert

Inspect
Inspection
Inspector
Institute of Naval Studies
Insure
Internation Simulation

INSAIR
Inspector of Naval Aircraft

INSAV
Interim Shipboard Availability

INSCAIRS
Instrumentation Calibration Incident Repair Service

INSENG
Inspector of Naval Engineering

INSEREC
Indicate by appropriate entry on pages 9–10 of service record, and in orders, rating for which men have been trained, to insure assignment to appropriate duty.

INSERECAV
Indicate by appropriate entry on pages 9–10 of service record, and in orders, rating for which non-rated men have been trained, to insure assignment to aviation duty.

INSERECSUB
Indicate by appropriate entry on pages 9–10 of service record, and in orders, rating forwhich men have been trained, to insure assignment to submarine duty.

INSGEN
Inspector General

INSHOREBOATU
Inshore Boat Unit

INSHOREPAT
Inshore Patrol

INSHOREUNSEAWARDIV
Inshore Undersea Warfare Division

INSHOREUNSEAWARGRU
Inshore Undersea Warfare Group

INSHOREUNSEAWARSURV
Inshore Undersea Warfare Surveillance Unit

INSHOREUNSEAWARSURVU
Inshore Undersea Warfare Surveillance Unit

INSMACH
Inspector of Naval Machinery

INSMAT
Inspector of Naval Material

INSMATPET
Inspector of Naval Material, Petroleum Products

INSMATPETMIDEASTAREA
Inspector of Naval Material, Petroleum Products, Middle East Area

INSNAVMAT
Inspector of Navigational Material

INSORD
Inspector of Naval Ordnance

INSP
Inspect
Inspection
Inspector

INSPAT
Inshore Patrol

INSPETRES
Inspector of Petroleum Reserves

INSPINSTF
Inspector of Instructor Staff

INST
Installation
Institute
Instruction
Instrument

INSTFURASPERS
For course of instruction and further assignment by Commander Naval Military Personnel Command

INSTL
Install
Installation

INSTR
Instructor

INST RATE
Instrument Rating

INSUPGENCRUIT
In accordance with this assignment, duties are to inspect, supervise, and generally superintend method of recruiting within ___________recruiting district. Authority

to carry out above over all officers and enlisted men detailed to recruiting in the above district is hereby conferred.

INSURV
Inspection and Survey

INT
Individual Needs Test
Interest
International
Interrogatory
Interrupted Quick
Intersection
Interval (NNSS)

INTAC
Intercept Tracking and Control Group

INTAV
Interim Availability

INTCOMBATSYSTESTFAC
Integrated Combat Systems Test Facility

INTCP
Intercept

INTEL
Intelligence

INTELCEN
Intelligence Center

INTELO
Intelligence Officer

INTERCOM
Internal Communications

INTERM
Intermediate

INTERMSTA
Intermediate Station

INTEROBS
International Observations

INTERP
Interpretation

INTERPRON
Interpretation Squadron

INTL
International

INTMED
Intermediate

INTMT
Intermittent

INTO
Intelligence Officer

INTR
Interior

INTRAN
Input Translator

INTRD
Interned

INTREP
Intelligence Report

INTRO
Introduction

INTS
Intense
Intensify

INTSUM
Intelligence Summary

INTSV
Intensive

INTSY
Intensify

INTXN
Intersection

INUS
Inside Continental Limits of the United States

INV
Inventory

INVES
Investigate
Investigation
Investigator

INVOL
Involuntary Extension

INVOLEX
Involuntary Extension

I/O
Input/Output
Instructor/Observer

IO
Information Officer
Information Operations
Intelligence Officer

Intercept Officer
Investigating Officer
Issuing Office

IOA
Instrumentation Operating Areas

IOB
Information Officer Basic (DINFOS)

IOBT
Internal On-Board Trainer

IOC
Initial Operational Capability

IOCS
Input/Output Controllers
Integrated Optical Circuits

IOH
Item on Hand

IOIC
Integrated Operational Intelligence Center

IOIS
Integrated Operational Intelligence System

IOL
Initial Outfitting List

I/OM
Input/Output Multiplexor

IOM
Inert Operational Missile

IOMF
Inactive-Officer Master File

ION
Institute of Navigation

IOP
Inspection Operations Pictorials
Interim Operating Procedures
Items of Priority

IOR
Issue on Request
Issue on Requisition

IOT
In Order To

IOT&E
Initial Operational Test and Evaluation

IP
Ice Plow (USCG)
Impact Point
Implementation of Plan
Information Program
Initial Point
Instructor Pilot
Instrumentation Package
Intermediate Pressure
Internet Protocol
Issuing Point
Items Processed

IPA
Indicated Pressure Altitude

IPB
Illustrated Parts Breakdown
Intelligence Preparation of the Battlespace

IPBM
Illustrated Parts Breakdown Manual

IPC
Iceland Prime Contractor
Illustrated Parts Catalog

IPD
Instructional Program Development
Issue Priority Designator

IPDSMS
Improved Point Defense Surface Missile System

IPE
Industrial Plant Equipment
Industrial Production Equipment

IPER
Industrial Production Equipment Reserve

IP/HHCL
Initial Point/H-Hour Control Line

IPIR
Initial Photo Interpretation Report

IPL
Information Processing Language
Interim Parts List

IPM
Industry Preparedness Measures

IPMS
Integrated Program Management System

IPN
Integrated Priority Number

IPOSS
Interim Pacific Oceanographic Support System

IPP
Industrial Preparedness Planning (program)

IPPB
Intermittent Positive Pressure Breathing

IPPD
Integrated Strategic Capability Plan

IPPP
Industrial Preparedness Planning Program

IPPV
Intermittent Positive Pressure Ventilation

IPR
In-Progress Reviews
Intelligence Production Requirements
Interdepartmental Procurement Request
Interdepartmental Purchase Request

IPS
Integrated Power System
Intercept Pilot Simulator
Interpretative Programming System
Iron Pipe Size

IPSC
Information Processing Standards for Computers

IPSR
Intelligence Priorities for Strategic Planning

IPT
Integrated Process Team

IPU
Immediate Pick-Up

IPV
Improve

IPW
Interpole Winding (wiring)

IPY
Inches Per Year (corrosion rate)

I QK
Interrupted Quick

IQO
Initial Quantity Order

IR
Ice on Runway
Independent Research
Industrial Relations
Informal Report
Information Report
Infrared
Inspection Report
Instruction Register

IR&D
Independent Research and Development

IR&D/B&P
Independent Research and Development/Bidding and Proposal

IR&G
International Relations and Government (DINFOS department)

IRAA&A
Increase and Replacement of Armor, Armament and Ammunition

IRAC
Interim Rapid Action Change

IRAH
Infrared Alternate Head (type Sidewinder missile)

IRAM
Improved Repairables Asset Management

IRAN
Inspect and Repair as Necessary

IRAS
Infrared Automatic System

IRASER
Infrared Amplification by Stimulated Emission of Radiation

IRATE
Interim Remote Area Terminal Equipment

IRB
Industrial Relations Board
Inspection Requirements Branch

IRBM
Intermediate Range Ballistic Missile

IRC
Industrial Relations Counselors
Inspection Record Card
Interservice Recruiting Committees

IRC&M
Increase and Replacement of Construction and Machinery

IRCA
Integrated Readiness Capability Assessment

IRCAT
Infrared Clear Air Turbulence

IRCCS
Intrusion Resistant Communications Cable System

IRCS
Intercomplex Radio Communications System
International Radio Call Sign

IRD
Industrial Relations Department

IRE
International Relations Exercise

IREC
Increase and Replacement of Emergency Construction (ships)

IREPS
Integrated Refractive Effects Prediction System

IRG
Interdepartmental Regional Group
Interactive Response Generator

IRH
Inspection Requirements Handbook

IRIA
Infrared Information and Analysis

IRIG
Inter-Range Instrumentation Graph
Inertial Guidance Integrating Gyro

IR/IOD
Independent Research/Independent Objectives Document

IRIS
Increased Readiness Information System
Infrared Information Symposium
Infrared Interferometer Spectrometer
International Systems Information System

IRL
Information Retrieval Language
Intersection of Range Legs

IRLS
Interrogation, Recording, and Locating System

IRNV
Increase and Replacement of Naval Vessels

IRO
Industrial Relations Office/Officer

IROAN
Inspect and Repair Only as Needed

IR-P
Ice on Runway-Patchy

IRP
Improved Replenishment Program
Industrial Readiness Planning

IR-PERS-REC
Industrial Relations Personnel Records

IRPOD
Individual Repair Parts Ordering Data

IRR
Improved Rearming Rate
Individual Ready Reserve

IRRA
International Routing and Reporting Activity

IRREG
Irregular

IRRP
Improved Rearming Rate Plan

IRSS
Instrumentation and Range Safety Program

IRST
Infrared Search and Track

IRT
Infrared Temperature
In Reference
In Reply
In Response To

IRU
General Individual Reinforcement Unit (USNR)

IRV
Item Rating Value

IS
Information Systems
Instrumentation-Ship's Project
Intelligence Specialist

Intelligence System
Invalidated from Service
Inventory Schedule

IS&MD
Instructional Standards and Materials Division

IS1
Intelligence Specialist First Class

IS2
Intelligence Specialist Second Class

IS3
Intelligence Specialist Third Class

ISA
Inductee Special Assignment
International Security Affairs
International Security Agency

ISAC
In Service, Active (vessel status)

ISAL
Information Service Access Lines

ISAP
Information Sort and Predict

ISAR
Inverse Synthetic Aperture Radar

ISB
Independent Sideband

ISC
Chief Intelligence Specialist
Infiltration Surveillance Center

ISCAS
Integrated Submarine Communications Antenna System

ISCM
Master Chief Intelligence Specialist

ISCP
Integrated Strategic Capability Plan

ISCS
Integrated Submarine Communication System
Interim Sea Control Ship
Senior Chief Intelligence Specialist

ISD
Industrial Survey Division
Initial Search Depth
Initial Ship Design
Instructional Systems Development

ISDS
Integrated Ship Design System

ISE
Independent Ship Exercise

ISED
Information Systems Equipment Division

ISIC
Immediate Superior in the Chain-of-Command

ISINC
Immediate Superior in Command

ISIR
In Service, In Reserve (vessel status)

ISIS
Integral Spar Inspection System

IS/ISD
Instructional Systems/Instructional Systems Division

ISJTA
Intensive Student Jet Training Area

ISL
Inactive Status List
Initial Stock List
Integrated Stock List
Item Survey List

ISLMM
Improved Submarine-Launched Mobile Mine

ISLW
Indian Spring Low Water

ISM
Industrial Security Manual (DOD)
Interim Surface Missile

ISMF
Inactive Ship Maintenance Facility

ISNAC
Inactive Ships in Naval Custody

ISO
Informational Services Office/Officer
Installation Supply Office
Isolate

ISOLD
Isolated

ISP
Integrated Support Plan

ISPO
Instrumentation Ships Project Office

ISR
In-Service Repair
Intelligence, Surveillance, and Reconnaissance

ISRB
Individual Service Review Board

ISS
Industry Sole Source
Inertial Sub System
Information Superiority Sensors
Interservice Supply Support
Issued

ISSA
Intelligence Specialist Seaman Apprentice
Interservice Supply Source Agreement
Intraservice Supply Source Agreement

ISSBN
Improved Fleet Ballistic Missile Submarine

ISSG
Illustrated Shipboard Shopping Guide

ISSM
Interim Surface-to-Surface Missile

ISSN
Intelligence Specialist Seaman

ISSOP
Intra-Fleet Supply Support Operations Program

ISSOT
Intra-Fleet Supply Support Operations Team

ISSP
Information Systems Security Program
Interservice Supply Source Program

ISSR
Information System Service Request

ISSST
Integrated Submarine Sonar Systems Technician

IST
Initial Skills Training
Interswitch Trunk

ISTAR
Image Storage Translation and Reproduction

ISTRS
Index of Submarine Technical Repair Standards

ISUM
Intelligence Summary

ISWR
Current Standing Wave Ratio

IT
Information Systems Technician
Information Technology
Installation Tests
Item Type

IT-21
Information Technology for the 21st Century

IT21
Information Technology for the 21st Century

ITA
Instrument Time, Actual

ITAAS
Integrated Aircraft Armament System

ITAG
Intelligence Threat Analysis Group

ITAL
Initial Trial Allowance List

ITAWDS
Integrated Tactical Amphibious Warfare Data Systems

ITC
Chief Information Systems Technician
Instructor-Training Course (DINFOS)

ITCS
Integrated Target Control System
Senior Chief Information Systems Technician

ITCZ
Intertropical Convergence Zone

ITD
Interim Technical Directive

ITE
Indicated Terminal Efficiency
In The Event Of

ITF
Intermediate Terminal Facility

ITIS
Interactive Terminal Interface System

ITL
Industrial Test Laboratory
Integrate-Transfer-Launch
Intent to Launch

ITLD
Individual Tube Leak Detector

ITM
Index of Technical Manuals

ITNS
International Tactical Navigation System

ITO
Inspecting Torpedo Officer
Installation Transportation Officer
Instrument Take-Off
In Terms Of
International Travel Orders
Invitational Travel Orders

ITOS
Improved TIROS Operational System (NOAA)

ITP
Index of Technical Publications
Initial Trial Phase
Integrated Test Package

ITRO
Integrated Test Requirements Outline
Interservice Training Review Organization

ITRP
Interservice Training Program

ITS
Instrument Time, Standard

ITSA
Information Systems Technician Seaman Apprentice

ITSN
Information Systems Technician Seaman

ITT
Integrated Training Team
Interrogator-Translator Team

ITV
Instructional Television

IU
Instrument Unit
International Unit

IUC
Immediate Unit Commander

IUDS
Independent Variable Depth Sonar

IUS
Interim Upper State

IUWD
Inshore Undersea Warfare Division

IUWG
Inshore Undersea Warfare Group

IUWSU
Inshore Undersea Warfare Surveillance Unit

IVALA
Integrated Visual Approach and Landing Aids

IVN
Intercity Voice Network (FTS)

IVO
In View Of

IVS
Intervoice Communication System

IVVS
Instantaneous Vertical Velocity Indicator

IW
Indications Warning
Information Warfare

IWAR
Integrated Warfare Architecture Requirements

IWC
Individual Weapons Captured

IWCS
Integrated Wideband Communications System

IWD
Intermediate Water Depth

IWHS
Improved Weapons Handling System

IWR
Infrared Warning Receiver

IX
Information Exchange

Unclassified Miscellaneous Ship

IXES
Information Exchange System

IXR
Intersection of Runways

IXSS
Unclassified Miscellaneous Submarine

J
Junction
Radar

JA
January
Judge Advocate

JAAF
Joint Action Armed Forces

JAAP
Joint Aviation Attrition Panel

JAASSM
Joint Advanced Air-to-Surface Standoff Missile

JACC
Joint Airborne Communications Center

JACC/CP
Joint Airborne Communications Center/Command Post

JACCI
Joint Allocation Committee Civil Intelligence (United States-Britain)

JAD
Joint Resource Assessment Data Base

JADM
Joint Direct Attack Munition

JAG
Judge Advocate General

JAGMAN
Judge Advocate General's Manual

JAIEG
Joint Atomic Information Exchange Group

JAMAC
Joint Aeronautical Materials Activity

JAMTO
Joint Airline Military Ticket Office

JAN
January
Joint Army-Navy

JANAID
Joint Army-Navy Air Intelligence Division

JANAIR
Joint Army-Navy Aircraft Instrumentation Research

JANAP
Joint Army-Navy-Air Force Publication

JANAST
Joint Army-Navy-Air Force Sea Transportation (message)

JANCOM
Joint Army-Navy Communications

JANET
Joint Army-Navy Experimental and Testing Board

JANGO
Junior Army-Navy Guild Organization

JANGRID
Joint Army-Navy Grid

JANIC
Joint Army-Navy Information Center

JANIS
Joint Army-Navy Intelligence Studies

JANNAF
Joint Army, Navy, NASA, Air Force

JANOT
Joint Army-Navy Ocean Terminal

JANP
Joint Army-Navy Publication

JAPO
Joint Area Petroleum Office

JARCC
Joint Air Reconnaissance Coordination Center

JASASA
Joint Air Surface Antisubmarine Action

JASCO
Joint Assault Signal Company

JASIG
Joint AUTOVON Subscriber Implementation Group

JASIG-PAC
Joint AUTOVON Subscriber Implementation Group-Pacific

JASMMM
Joint Aviation Supply and Maintenance Material Management

JASSM
Joint Air-to-Surface Standoff Missile

JASU
Jet Aircraft Starting Unit

JATCCS
Joint Advanced Tactical Command and Control Service

JATO
Jet-Assisted Take-Off

JAWPS
Joint Atomic Weapons Publication System

JAX
Jacksonville, Florida

JAYGEE
Junior Grade

JB
Jet Barrier
Jet Boat (USCG)
Jiffy Bag
Joint Army-Navy Board
Inf: Junior Birdman

JBAR
Jet Barrier

JBD
Jet Blast Deflector

JBUSDA
Joint Brazil-United States Defense Commission

JC
Junction

JC2
Joint Command and Control (formerly Global Command and Control System-Maritime, GCCS-M)

JCA
Joint Communications Activity

JCAC
Joint Civil Affairs Committee

JCB
Joint Communications Board

JCC
Joint Communications Center

JCM
Joint Common Missile

JCMPO
Joint Cruise Missile Program Office

JCN
Job Control Number

JCOC
Joint Civilian Orientation Conference (DOD)
Joint Command Operational Center

JCRC
Joint Casualty Resolution Center

JCS
Joint Chiefs of Staff

JCSAN
Joint Chiefs of Staff Alerting Network

JCSNMCC
Joint Chiefs of Staff National Military Command Center

JCSO
Joint Chiefs of Staff Office

JCS(SASM)
Joint Chiefs of Staff (Special Assistant for Strategic Mobility)

JD
Job Description
Joint Determination
Joint Dictionary
Jointed

JDAM
Joint Direct Attack Munition

JDC
Job Description Cards

JDCS
Joint Deputy Chiefs of Staff

JE
June

JEPH
JUMPS Field Procedures Handbook

JEST
Jungle Environmental Survival Training

JET
Jet Engine Trainer

JETCAL
Jet Calibration

JETDS
Joint Electronics Type Designation System

JETMART
Jet Market

JETT
Jettison

JF
Joint Force

JFAI
Joint Formal Acceptance Inspection

JFM
Joint Force Memorandum

JFMCC
Joint Forces Maritime Component Commander

JFMO
Joint Frequency Management and Spectrum Engineering Office

JFN
Joint Fires Network

JFP
Joint Frequency Panel

JFS
Jet Fuel Starter

JG
Jug
Junior Grade

JHC
Joint High Command

JHHGSO
Joint Household Goods Shipping Office

JI
Joint Identification

JIC
Joint Intelligence Center
Joint Intelligence Committee

JICO
Joint Interface Control Officer

JICPAC
Joint Intelligence Center Pacific

JIEP
Joint Intelligence Estimate for Planning

JIFDATS
Joint Services In-Flight Data Transmission System

JIN
Joint Interoperable Networks

JIS
Joint Intelligence Staff

JISPB
Joint Intelligence Studies Publishing Board

JITF
Joint Interface Test Force

JL
July

JLAS
JUMPS Leave Accounting System

JLC
Joint Logistics Committee

JLRB
Joint Logistics Review Board

JLRSS
Joint Long-Range Strategic Study

JMAC
Joint Munitions Allocation Committee

JMAHEP
Joint Military Aircraft Hurricane Evacuation Plan

JMAST
Jont Mobile Ashore Support Terminal

JMBA
Joint Master of Business Administration

JMC
Joint Meterological Committee
Joint Military Commission

JMCIS
Joint Maritime Command Information System

JMCOMS
Joint Maritime Communications Strategy

JMED
Jungle Message Encoder-Decoder

JMEM
Joint Munitions Effectiveness Manual

JMETL
Joint Mission Essential Task List

JMLS
Joint Modular Lighterage System

JMOD
Joint Airborne SIGNINT Architecture Modernization

JMPAB
Joint Military Priorities and Allocation Board

JMPS
Joint Mission Planning System

JMPTC
Joint Military Packaging Test Center

JMRO
Joint Medical Regulating Office

JMTB
Joint Military Transportation Board

JMTC
Joint Military Transportation Committee

JMVB
Joint Military Vessels Board

JNACC
Joint Nuclear Accident Coordinating Center

JNC
Jet Navigation Chart

JNG
Jointing

JNMS
Joint Network Management System

JNROTC
Junior Naval Reserve Officers' Training Corps

JNW
Joint Committee on New Weapons and Equipment

JNWPU
Joint Numerical Weather Prediction Unit

JO
Job Order
Journalist
Junior Officer

JO1
Journalist First Class

JO2
Journalist Second Class

JO3
Journalist Third Class

JOA
Joint Operating Agreement

JOBS
Job-Oriented Basic Skills (program)

JOC
Chief Journalist
Joint Operational Center

JOCM
Master Chief Journalist

JOCS
Senior Chief Journalist

JOG
Joint Operations Graphic

JOIDES
Joint Oceanographic Instructions-Deep Earth Sampling (DOL)

JON
Job Order Number

J-OO
Jet Route ___________

JOOD
Junior Officer Of the Deck

JOOW
Junior Officer-of-the-Watch

JOPREP
Joint Operational Reporting (system)

JOPS
Joint Operational Planning System

JOSA
Journalist Seaman Apprentice

JOSN
Journalist Seaman

JOSPRO
Joint Ocean Shipping Procedures

JOSS
Joint Overseas Switchboard System

JOTS
Joint Operational Tactical System

JP
Jet Penetration
Jet Propulsion

JPA
Job Performance Aides

JPATS
Joint Primary Aircraft Training System

JPB
Joint Planning Board
Joint Purchasing Board

JPC
Joint Planning Committee

JPME
Joint Professional Military Education

JPO
Joint Petroleum Office
Joint Program Office

JPPL
Joint Personnel Priority List

JPPSO
Joint Personal Property Shipping Office

JPRS
Joint Publications Research Service

JPS
Joint Planning Staff

JPSSOWA
Joint Personal Property Shipping Office, Washington (DC) Area

JQR
Job Qualification Requirements

JR
Jar
Junior

JRCC
Joint Rescue Coordination Center

JRDOD
Joint Research and Development Objectives Document

JROC
Joint Requirements Oversight Council

JROTC
Junior Reserve Officers' Training Corps

JRS
Jet Repair Service
Joint Reporting Structure

JS
Joint Staff

JSAF
Joint SIGINT Avionics Family

JSAR
Joint Search and Rescue

JSARC
Joint Search and Rescue Center

JSC
Joint Security Control
Joint Strategic Committee
Joint Support Command

JSCP
Joint Strategic Capabilities Plan

JSESPO
Joint Surface-Effects Ship Program Office

JSF
Joint Strike Fighter

JSI
Joint Support Item

JSIA
Joint Service Induction Area

J-SIID
Joint Service Interior Intrusion Detection (system)

JSIPS
Joint Services Imagery Processing System

JSIPS-N
Joint Service Imagery Processing System-Navy

JSL
Joint Stock List

Joint Support List

JSM
Jump Set Memory (NNSS)

JSN
Job Sequence Number

JSOC
Joint Ship Operations Committee

JSOP
Joint Strategic Objectives Plan

JSOW
Joint Standoff Weapons

JSP
Joint Staff Planners (JCS)

JSR
Journal of Ship Research (publication)

JSS
Joint Support System

JSSC
Joint Strategic Survey Committee

JSSG
Joint Signal Support Group

JSTAFFOFC
Joint Chiefs of Staff Office

JSTP
Joint System Test Plan (IDCSP)

JSTPS
Joint Strategic Target Planning Staff

JT&E
Joint Test and Evaluation

JTA
Job Task Analysis
Joint Tactical Architecture

JTAMD
Joint Theater Air and Missile Defense

JTARS
Joint Tactical Aerial Reconnaissance/Surveillance

JTARS MISREP
Joint Tactical Aerial Reconnaissance/Surveillance Mission Report

JTB
Joint Transportation Board

JTCG
Joint Technical Coordinating Group

JTCG/ME
Joint Technical Coordinating Group for Munitions Effectiveness

JTCTS
Joint Tactical Combat Training System

JTDARMVAL
Joint Test Directorate Advanced Antiarmor Vehicle Evaluation

JTE
Joint Test and Evaluation

JTG
Joint Task Group
Joint Test Group

JTOC
Joint Tactical Operations Center

JTR
Joint Travel Regulations

JTRS
Joint Tactical Radio System

JTSA
Joint Technical Support Activity

JTSTR
Jet Stream

JTT
Joint Tactical Terminal

JTWC
Joint Typhoon Warning Center

JUL
July

JUMP CERT
Jump Certificate
Jump Certified

JUMPS
Joint Uniform Military Pay System

JUMPS/MMS
Joint Uniform Military Pay System/Manpower Management System

JUN
June

JUNC
Junction

JUSMAG
Joint United States Military Assistance Group

JUSPAO
Joint United States Public Affairs Office

JUSSC
Joint United States Strategic Committee

JUTCPS
Joint Uniform Telephone Communications Precedence System

JUWTFA
Joint Unconventional Warfare Task Force, Atlantic

JWICS
Joint Worldwide Intelligence Communications System

K
ASW Tactical Evaluator

KBA
Killed by Aircraft

KCAS
Knots Calibrated Airspeed

KCE
Key Configuration Element

KCMX
Keyset Central Muliplexor

KCN
Kit Control Number

KD
Cord
Knocked-Down

KE
Keg

KEV
Kilo-Electron Volt

KHz
Kilohertz

KIA
Killed in Action

KIAS
Knots Indicated Airspeed

KISS
Inf: Keep It Simple, Stupid

KKV
Kinetic Kill Vehicle

KMU
Kit Munition Unit

KN
Knot

kn
Knot

KNA
Killed, Not Enemy Action

KO
Contracting Officer
Knock-Out

KPA
Keypunch Activity

KPH
Kilometers Per Hour

KPP
Key Performance Perimeter

KR
Carat
Contractor

KS
Cask

KSA
Knowledge, Skills, and Abilities

KSAT
Knowledge, Skills, Abilities, and Tools

KSR
Keyboard Send-Receive

KT
Contract
Kiloton
Kit
Knot(s)

KTAS
Knots True Airspeed

KUDOS
Compliments

K/V
Keypunch/Verify

KW
Kilowatt

KWIT
Key Word in Title

KWOC
Key Word Out of Context

L
Atlantic
Drizzle (weather Symbol)
Locator Beacon
Navigator

L&M
Logistics and Maintenance

L/A
Leave Address

LA
Lighter-Than-Air
Low Altitude

LAA
Light Anti-Aircraft (weapon)

LAACP
Local Alcohol Abuse Control Program

LAAM
Light Antiaircraft Missile

LAAMBN
Light Antiaircraft Missile Battalion

LAAR
Liquid Air Accumulator Rocket

LAAV
Light Airborne Antisubmarine Vehicle

LABIS
Laboratory Information System

LABS
Low-Altitude Bombing System

LAC
Liberal-Academic Complex

LACE
Liquid Air Cycle Engine

LAD
Landing Assistance Device
Los Angeles Division (NAR)

LADAR
Laser Detection and Ranging

LADD
Low-Angle Drogued Delivery (of nuclear weapons)

LADS
Lightweight Air Defense System

LAE NOTE
Licensed Aircraft Engineers' Notice

LAGS
Laser-Activated Geodetic Satellite

LAHS
Low-Altitude High-Speed

LALS
Linkless Ammunition Loading System

LAMP
Logical Analytical Management Program

LAMPS
Light airborne multipurpose system. A helicopter with all its support equipment, including landing platform and the ship carrying it.

LAMPSOP
Light Airborne Multi-Purpose System Standard Operating Procedures Manual

LAN
Local Apparent Noon
Local Area Network

LANCRA
Landing Craft

LANFOR
Landing Force

LANFORTRACOM
Landing Craft Training Command

LANFORTRAU
Landing Force Training Unit

LANG
Language

LANNET
Large Artificial Neuron Network

LANS
Linear Active Two-Part Network

LANSHIPRON
Landing Ship Squadron

LANT
Atlantic

LANTCOM
Atlantic Command

LANTCOMINSGEN
Atlantic Command Inspector General

LANTCOMMBPO
Atlantic Command Military Blood Program Office

LANTCOMOPCONCEN
Atlantic Fleet Commander Operational Control Center

LANTCOMOPSUPPFAC
Atlantic Command Operations Support Facility

LANTFAST
Atlantic Forward Area Support Team

LANTFLEASWTACSCOL
Atlantic Fleet Antisubmarine Warfare Tactical School

LANTFLT
Atlantic Fleet

LANTFLTHEDSUPPACT
Atlantic Fleet Headquarters Support Activity

LANTFLTMATCONOFF
Atlantic Fleet Material Control Office

LANTFLTPEB
Atlantic Fleet Propulsion Examining Board

LANTFLTSOAP
Atlantic Fleet Supply Operations Assistance Team

LANTFLTWPNRAN
Atlantic Fleet Weapons Range

LANTFLTWPNTRAFAC
Atlantic Fleet Weapons Training Facility

LANTFLTWPNTRAVAC
Atlantic Fleet Weapons Training Facility

LANTINTCEN
Atlantic Intelligence Center

LANTIRN
Low-Altitude Navigation and Targeting Infrared at Night

LANTMET
Atlantic Mobile Environmental Team

LANTNAVFACENGCOM
Atlantic Naval Facilities Engineering Command

LANTNAVFACENGCOMBRO
Atlantic Naval Facilities Engineering Command Branch Office

LANTPATRAMID
Atlantic Patrol for the Training of Midshipmen

LANTREPCNAVRES
Atlantic Fleet Chief of Naval Reserve Representative

LANTREPCOMNAVSURFRES
Atlantic Representative for Commander Naval Surface Reserve Force

LANTRESFLT
Atlantic Reserve Fleet

LANTSOC
Atlantic Fleet Signals Security Operations Center

LANTWWMCCS
Atlantic Fleet Worldwide Military Command Control System

LAO
Legal Assistance Office/Officer

LAP
Local Audit Program

LAPES
Low-Altitude Parachute Extraction System

LAPIS
Local Automated Personnel Information System

LAPL
Lead Allowance Parts List

LAPLS
Lead Allowance Parts List System

LAR
Launch Alert Receiver
Liaison Action Record
Liaison Action Request
Liquid Aircraft Rocket
Long-Range Aircraft Rocket

LARA
Light Armed Reconnaissance Aircraft
Low-Altitude Radar Altimeter

LARC
Large Automatic Research Computer

LARC-V
Lighter, Amphibious, Resupply, Cargo-Five Ton

LARP
Launch and Recovery Platform

LARS
Laser-Aided Rocket Systems

LAS
Low-Altitude Satellite

LASER
Light Amplification by Stimulated Emission of Radiation

LASH
Laser Anti-tank Semi-active Homing
Lighter Aboard Ship

LASM
Laser Semi-Active Missile

LASRM
Low-Altitude Supersonic Research Missile

LASSO
Landing and Approach Sysem, Spiral-Oriented

LAST
Last Satellite Position (NNSS)
Low-Altitude Supersonic Target (missile)

LASV
Low-Altitude Supersonic Vehicle

LAT
Latitude
Local Apparent Time

LATKWEPSCOLPAC
Light Attack Weapons School, Pacific

LATR
Lateral

LAU
Launcher Mechanism, Aircraft-Installed Unit

LAV
Light Armored Vehicle

LAW
Library, Amphibious Warfare
Light Anti-tank Weapon
Local Air Wing

LAWRS
Limited Airport Weather Recording Station

L/B
Length/Beam (ratio)
Light Bomber (aircraft)

LB
Lithium Bromide (air-conditioning chemical)
Local Battery

LBA
Limits of the Basic Aircraft

LBCH
Long Beach (CA)

LBH
Leased Bachelor Housing

LBI
Lost By Inventory

LBIR
Laser Beam Image Recorder

LBNS
Long Beach Naval Shipyard

LBP
Length Between Perpendiculars

LBR
Local Base Rescue
Lumber

LBTF
Land-Based Test Facility

LBTS
Land-Based Test Site

L/C
Landing Craft

Learning Curve
Letter Contract

LC
Labor Code
Landing Craft
Legitimate Child
Legitimate Children
Lines of Communication

LCA
Landing Craft, Assault

LCAC
Landing Craft, Air Cushion

LCB
Limited Capability Buoy (NOAA)

LCC
Amphibious Command Ship

LCD
Liquid Crystal Diode

LCDR
Lieutenant Commander

LCM
Landing Craft, Mechanized

LCPL
Landing Craft, Personnel, Large

LCS
Littoral Combat Ship

LCTR
Locator Beacon

LCU
Landing Craft, Utility

LCV
Landing Craft, Vehicle

LCVASI
Low-Cost Visual-Approach Slope Indicator

LCVP
Landing Craft, Vehicle, and Personnel

LCZR
Localizer Beacon

LD
Layered Depth
Line of Departure
Line of Duty
List of Drawings
Long Distance
Low Drag

LDA
Localizer, Directional Aid
Lowest Designated Assembly

LDAPS
Long-Duration Auxiliary Power System

LDATS
Lightening Detection and Tracking System

LDC
Labor Distribution Card

LDD
Letter of Determination of Dependency

LDF
Local Defense Forces

LDG
Landing

LDG LT
Leading Light

LDGP
Low-Drag General-Purpose

LDGSPTBN
Landing Support Battalion

LDHC
Lateral-Homing Depth Charge

LDIN
Lead-In (light system)

LDME
Laser Distance Measuring Equipment

LDMX
Local Digital Message Exchange

LDO
Limited Duty Officer

LDO(T)
Limited Duty Officer (Temporary)

LDR
Leader
Line Driver Receivers

LDS
Line Drawing System

LDSHP
Leadership

LDTTY
Land Line Teletype

LDX
Local Digital Message Exchange
Long Distance Xerography

LE
Low Explosive

LEAD
Launched Expendable Acoustic Decoy

LEAP
Lightweight Exo-Atmospheric Projectile
Limited Education Assistance Program

LEASAT
Leased Satellite (system)

LEG OFF
Legal Officer

LEI
Local Engineering Instruction

LEL
Lower Explosion Limit

LEM
Logistics Element Manager

LEMP
Logistics Element Manager Plan

LEPT
Long-Endurance Patrolling Torpedo

LEROY
Less Errors Rest On You

LERTCON
Alert Condition

LES
Leading-Edge Slots
Leave and Earnings Statement (JUMPS)
Local Engineering Specification

LESS
Least Cost Estimating and Scheduling

LEWP
Line Echo Wave Pattern

LEX
Land Exercise

LF
Landing Force
Line Feed
Linear Foot
Low Frequency

LFA
Low Frequency Active

LFC
Landing Force Commander
Large Format Comparator
Level of Free Convection

LFDM
Low Flyer Detection Modification

LFE
Laboratory for Electronics

LFIC
Landing Force Intelligence Center

LFM
Landing Force Manual

LFOC
Landing Force Operations Center

LFR
Inshore Fire Support Ship
Low-Frequency Range

LFRD
Lot Fraction Reliability Deviation

LFS
Amphibious Fire Support Ship
Landing Force Staff

LFSD
Landing Force Support Weapon

LFSS
Landing Force Support Ship

LFT
Lift

LFTC
Landing Craft Training Command

LFTCPAC
Landing Force Training Command, Pacific

LFTU
Landing Force Training Unit

LG
Land Ground
Left Gun
Length

LGB
Laser-Guided Bomb

LGCOMB
Large Combatant

LGCP
Lexical Graphical Composer Printer

LGT
Light

LGTD
Lighted

LGTR
Laser Guided Training Round

LGW
Laser-Guided Weapon

L/H
Lower Hold (stowage)

LHA
Amphibious Assault Ship (General-Purpose)

LHD
Amphibious Assault Ship (Multipurpose)

LHFT
Light-Helo Fire Team

L-HOUR
Landing of first helicopter assault wave

LHOX
Low and High Pressure Oxygen

LHT
Lightweight Hybrid Torpedo

LHV
Lower Heating Value

LHW
Lower High Water

L/I
Letter of Interest
Line Item

LI
Letter of Interest
Lifted Index
Lithographer

LI1
Lithographer First Class

LI2
Lithographer Second Class

LI3
Lithographer Third Class

LIBEC
Light Behind Camera (technique)

LIC
Atlantic Intelligence Center
Chief Lithographer
License
List of Instruments and Controls
Logistics Indoctrination Course

LICM
Master Chief Lithographer

LICS
Senior Chief Lithographer

LIDAR
Light Detection and Ranging (laser)

LIFESTA
Lifeboat Station

LIF-MOP
Linerally Frequency-Moderated Pulse

LIFO
Last-In, First-Out (inventory)

LIGHTPHOTORON
Light Photographic Squadron

LIM
Limit
Limited
Line Induction Motor
(Compass) Locator at Inner Marker Site

LIMDAT
Limiting Date

LIMDIS
Limited Distribution

LIMDU
Limited Duty

LINS
Lightweight Inertial Navigation System

LIO
Lesser Included Offenses

LIQ
Liquid

LIR
Limited Isolation Requirement (noise control)

LIRSH
Listing of Items Requiring Special Handling

LISA
Lithographer Seaman Apprentice

LISN
Lithographer Seaman

LIT
Light Intratheater Transport
Literacy
Literature

LITH BRO
Lithium Bromide (air-conditioning chemical)

LK
Link

LKA
Amphibious Cargo Ship

LKLY
Likely

LKR
Locker

LL
Load Limit
Long Length
Lower Limit

LLC
Line Load Control
Salvage Craft

LLI
Longitude and Latitude Indicator

LLL
Low-Level Logic
Low-Light Level

LLT
Long Lead Time

LLTM
Long Lead Time Material

LLTV
Low-Light Level Television

LLW
Lower Low Water

LLWS
Low-Level Wind Shear

LM
Land Mine
Legion of Merit
List of Materials

LMDS
Logistics Methodologies Documentation System

L/MF
Low/Medium Frequency

LMFBR
Liquid Metal Fast Breeder Reactor (AEC)

LMG
Light Machine Gun

LMI
Logistic Management Institute

LMM
(Compass) Locator at Middle Marker Site

LMO
Lens-Modulated Oscillator

LMP
Light Marching Pack

LMRS
Long-term Mine Reconnaissance System

LMS
Local Monitor Station

LMSR
Large, Medium-Speed Roll-On/Roll-Off (ship)

LMT
Leadership and Management Training
Limit
Limited
Local Mean Time

LMTD
Log Mean Temperature Difference

LN
Legalman

LN1
Legalman First Class

LN2
Legalman Second Class

LN3
Legalman Third Class

LNB
Large Navigation Buoy

LNC
Chief Legalman

Local Naval Commander

LNCM
Master Chief Legalman

LNCS
Senior Chief Legalman

LNDSPTPLT
Landing Support Platoon

LNG
Liquified Natural Gas
Long
Longitude (NNSS)

LNI
Log Neutralization Index

LNO
Limited Nuclear Operations

LNSA
Legalman Seaman Apprentice

LNSN
Legalman Seaman

LO
Law Officer
Legal Officer
Level Off
Lot
Low
Lube Oil

LOA
Length Overall
Letter of Appreciation
Letter of Offer and Acceptance
Light Off Assessment
Limit Operator Attempts
Local Obligation Authority

LOALT
Low Altitude

LOB
Line of Balance

LOBAR
Long Baseline Radar

LOC
Letter of Commendation
Lines of Communication
Liquid Organic Cleaner
Localizer
Locate
Location

LOCI
List of Cancelled Items
Logarithmic Computing Instruments

LOC LF
Local Line Feed

LOCO TAC
Low-Cost Tactical Radar

LOD
Line of Departure
Line of Duty
List of Drawings

LODE
Large Optics Demonstration Experiment

LODI
List of Deleted Items

LODIG
Loading

LODOR
Loaded, Waiting Orders or Assignment

LOE
Level of Essentiality

LOEC
List of Effective Cards

LOEP
List of Effective Parts (PURS)

LOF
Line of Fire

LOFAR
Low-Frequency Acquisition and Ranging

LOFC
Line of Communications

LOFTI
Low-Frequency Trans-Ionospheric (satellite)

LOFTPS
Lube Oil Fill, Transfer and Purification System

LOG
Logistical
Logistics

LOGAIR
Logistics Aircraft

LOGALGOL
Logical Algorithmic Language

LOGBALNET
Logistical Ballistic Network

LOGEX
Logistics Exercise

LOGICOMP
Logical Compiler

LOGLAN
Logical Language

LOGO
Limitation of Goverment Obligation

LOGREP
Logistics Replenishment
Logistics Representative

LOGREQ
Logistics Request
Logistics Requisition

LOH
Light Observation Helicopter

LOI
Letter of Instruction
Letter of Intent

LOK
Level of Knowledge

LO/LO
Life-On/Lift-Off

LOM
Legion of Merit
(Compass) Locator at Outer Marker Site

LOMMA
List of Mining Materials Available

LONG
Longevity
Longitude

LOO
Letter of Offer

LOPAR
Low-Power Acquisition Radar

LOPU
Logistics Organizational Planning Unit

LO-R
Low-Intensity Range Survey Meter

LORAC
Long-Range Accuracy

LORACTEAM
Long-Range Accuracy Support Team

LORAD
Long-Range Active Detection System

LORAN
Long-Range Navigation

LORAN D
Long-Range Navigation Doppler Inertial

LORAN DM
Long-Range Navigation Double Master

LORAN DS
Long-Range Navigation Double Slave

LORAN S
Long-Range Navigation Slave

LORAPH
Long-Range Passive Homing (system)

LORMONSTA
LORAN Monitor Station

LORSTA
LORAN Station

LOS
Land on Ship
Law of the Sea
Length of Service
Line of Sight
Line of Supply
Local Operating Station

LOSC
Law of the Sea Conference
Local On-Scene Commander

LOSS
Large Object Salvage System
Lube Oil Service System

LOST/A
Vessel Lost by Accident

LOST/E
Vessel Lost by Enemy Action

LOST/P
Vessel Lost Due to Weather/Perils of the Sea

LOT
Large Operational Telescope
Live Operational Training (course)

LOTON
Long Ton

LOTS
Logistics-Over-the-Shore (vehicle)
LORAN Operational Training School

LOU
Letter of Understanding

LOX
Liquid Oxygen

LP
Low Pressure

LPA
Amphibious Transport

LPAC
Low-Pressure Air Compressor

LPCBR
Low-Pressure Chamber

LPD
Amphibious Transport Dock (ship)

LPF
Launch Pontoon Facility

LPG
Liquified Petroleum Gas

LPH
Landing Platform, Helicopter (amphibious assault ship)

LPI
Low Probability of Intercept (communications)

LPM
Lines Per Minute

LPMES
Logistics Performance Measurement and Evaluation System

LPO
Leading Petty Officer

LPR
Amphibious Transport (Small)
Liquid Propellant Rocket

LPS
Linear Programming System

LPSS
Amphibious Transport Submarine

LPT
Low-Pressure Test

LPTV
Large Payload Test Vehicle

LQRR
Low-Quality Recruiting Report

L/R
Latest Revision (issue)

LR
Life Raft
Liter
Long-Range

LRA
Light Replaceable Assembly

LRF
Laser Range Finder

LRIP
Low Rate Initial Production

LRIR
Low-Resolution Infrared Radiometer

LRLAP
Long-Range Land-Attack Projectiles

LRO
Long-Range Objectives

LRP
Long-Range Preparation
Long-Range Preparedness

LRPS
Long-Range Planning System

LRR
Long-Range Radar
Long-Range Requirements

LRRP
Long-Range Reconnaissance Patrol

LR/RT
Long-Range Radio Telephone

LRSTFF
Long-Range Scientific-Technical Planning Program

LRT
Launch and Recovery Transport

LRTP
Long Range Training Plan

LRU
Less-Release-Unit
Line Replaceable Unit
Logistics Support

L/S
Large Screen

LS
Lapped Seam
Light Ship
Logistics Support

LSA
Labor Surplus Area
Logistics Support Analysis
Logistics Support Area
Low Specific Activity

LSAT
Law School Admission Test

LSB
Least Significant BIT
Logistics Support Base
Lower Side Band

LSC
Law of the Sea Conference
Linear Shaped Charge
Logistics Support Center

LSD
Landing Ship, Dock
Large-Screen Display (system)
Lesson Specification Document

LSE
Landing Signal Enlisted

LSFFAR
Low-Spin Folding-Fin Aircraft Rocket

LSG
Landing Support Group

LSG/LSU
Landing Support Group/Logistics Support Unit

LSH/LSF
Landing Ship Helicopter/Landing Ship Fighter Direction

LSI
Large-Scale Integration (MOS display)

LSIC
Large-Scale Integrated Circuit

LSL
Lump-Sum Leave Payment

LSL BP
Lump-Sum Leave Payment, Basic Pay

LSL PMA
Lump-Sum Leave Payment, Personal Money Allowance

LSL QTRS
Lump-Sum Leave Payment, Quarters

LSL SUBS
Lump-Sum Leave Payment, Subsistence

LSM
Landing Ship, Medium
Logistics Support Manager

LSMR
Landing Ship, Medium, Rocket

LSMSO
Landing Ship Material Supply Officer

LSO
Landing Signal Officer

LSP
Logistics Support Plan
Logistics System Proposal
Low Suction Pressure
Lump-Sum Payment

LSR
Logistics Support Requirement (system)
Loose Snow on Runway
Lump-Sum Payment upon Retirement

LSR-P
Loose Snow on Runway-Patchy

LS S
Lifesaving Station

LSS
Life-Support System
Limited Storage Site

LSSB
Light SEAL Support Boat

LSSC
Light SEAL Support Craft

LST
Landing Ship, Tank
Laser Spot Tracker

LST(H)
Landing Ship, Tank (Casualty Evacuation)

LSTH
Landing Ship, Tank (Hospital)

LSU
Landing Support Unit
Logistic Support Unit

LSV
Landing Ship, Vehicle

LT
Lieutenant
Light
Line Telecommunications
Link Terminal
Loader-Transponder
Long Ton

LTA
Lighter-Than-Air
Local Training Authority

LTC
Letdown Terrain Clearance

LTCOM
Lieutenant Commander

LT COMDR
Lieutenant Commander

L/TD
Lower 'tween Deck (stowage)

LTD
Language Training Detachment (DLI)
Limited
Lower 'tween Deck (stowage)

LTDS
Laser Target Designator System

LTDSTD
Limited Standard

LTFRD
Lot Tolerance Fraction Reliability Deviation

LTG
Lighting

LT HO
Lighthouse

LTJG
Lieutenant (Junior Grade)

LTL
Less Than Truckload
Little

LTLCG
Little Change

LTNG
Lighting

LTPD
Lot Tolerance Percent Defective

LTPHOTORON
Light Photographic Squadron

LTR
Later
Letter

LTS
Landfall Technique School

LTST
Indicator Light Test (NNSS)

LTT
Limited Training Team

LT/TN
Long Ton

LUBE
Lubricating (oils)
Lubrication

LUF
Lowest Usable Frequency

LUL
Inf: Language Unseamanlike

LV
Leave
Light Vessel
Live (AFRTS code)

LV&UPK
Leave and Upkeep

LVA
Landing Vehicle, Assault

LVD
Absent on Leave from Ship's duty

LVDT
Linear Variable Differential Transformer

LVG
Leaving

LVL
Level

LVN
Absent on Leave, Not Ship's Company

LVP
Low Voltage Protection

LVR
Line Voltage Regulator

LVRATS
Leave Rations, Sick Leave

LVRATS SL
Leave Rations, Sick Leave

LVRATS SPEC
Leave Rations, Special Leave

LVR(CE)
Low Voltage Release (Continuous Effect)

LVT
Landing Vehicle, Tracked

LVTB
Low-Voltage Thermal Battery

LVTE
Landing Vehicle, Tracked, Engineer

LW
Low Water

LWD
Low Water Datum

LWF
Lightweight Fighter

LWIR
Long Wave Length Infrared

LWL
Length at Waterline
Lightweight Laser
Load Waterline

LWLD
Lightweight Laser Designator

LWM
Low Watermark

LWP
Leave Without Pay

LWR
Lower

LWS
Laser Warning System

LWSC
Local Wage Survey Committee

LWT
Amphibious Warping Tug
Lightweight Type

LY
Lead Yard
Linear Yard

LYFT
Low-Yield Fallout Trajectory

LYR
Layer

LZ
Landing Zone
Loading Zone

LZL
Launch Zero Length

M
Aerology
Machinery
Magnetic (bearing)
Manpower
Model
Monthly (report frequency)
Mud
Muddy

M&ISD
Mathematical and Information Sciences Division (ONR)

M&O
Maintenance and Operation
Management and Organization

M&P
Management and Plans (NTS)

M&R
Maintenance and Repair

M&S
Bureau of Medicine and Surgery
Maintenance and Supply

MA
Machinery
Maritime Administration
Master-at-Arms
Mediterranean Area
Memory Address (NNSS)
Mental Ability
Mercury Atlas (rocket)
Mileage Allowance
Military Attache
Missed Approach
Missile Alert

MA1
Master-at-Arms First Class

MA2
Master-at-Arms Second Class

MA3
Master-at-Arms Third Class

MAA
Master-at-Arms
Maximum Authorized Altitude
Medium Anti-Aircraft (weapon)

MAAG
Military Assistance Advisory Group

MAATC
Mobile Anti-Aircraft Training Center

MABS
Marine Air Base Squadron
Marine Air Base Support
Moored Acoustic Buoy System

MAC
Chief Master-at-Arms
Machine-Aided Cognition
Maintenance Advisory Committee
Management Analysis Course
Maximum Allowable Concentration
Maximum Analysis Course
Mean Aerodynamic Chord
Media Assistance Center
Mid-Atlantic Conference
Military Airlift Command
Military Assistance Command
MIUW Attack Craft
Months After Contract
Multiple Access Computers

MACA
Military Airlift Clearance Authority

MACCS
Marine Air Command and Control System

MACG
Marine Air Control Group

MACH
Machinery
Machinist

MACHGR
Machine Group

MACM
Master Chief Master-at-Arms

MACRI
Mercantile Atlantic Coastal Routing Instructions

MACS
Marine Air Control Squadron
Medium Altitude Communications Satellite
Senior Chief Master-at-Arms

MACTU
Mine and Countermeasures Technical Unit

MACV
Multi-Purpose Air-Transportable Combat-Support Vehicle

MAD
Magnetic Airborne Detection
Magnetic Anomaly Detection
Maintenance, Assembly, and Disassembly
Marine Air Detection
Marine Aviation Detachment
Mathematical Analysis of Downtime
MDCS Analysis Date
Message Address Directory
Mine Assembly Depot
Multi-Apertured Device

MADDAM
Macro-Module Digital Differential Analyzer Machine

MADE
Minimum Airborne Digital Equipment

MADMAN
Master Activity Data Management

MAD-R
Multi-Apertured Device-Resistance

MADRE
Magnetic-Drum Receiving Equipment

MADT
Mean Administrative Delay Time

MAE
Medium Altitude Endurance
Mobile Ammunition Evaluation

MAERU
Mobile Ammunition Evaluation and Reconditioning Unit

MAF
Maintenance Action Form
Marine Amphibious Force

MA/FH
Maintenance Action Per Flight Hour

MAFIA
Microaerofluorometer (NBL)

MAFOG
Mediterranean Area Fighter Operations Grid

MAF/TDC
Maintenance Action Form/Technical Directives Compliance

MAG
Magnetic
Magneto
Marine Aircraft Group
Marine Amphibious Brigade
Marine Assistance Group
Military Assistance Group

MAGBRG
Magnetic Bearing

MAGIC
Master Activity General Information and Control

MAGIS
Marine Air-Ground Intelligence System

MAGLOC
Magnetic Logic (computer)

MAGT
Magnetic Tape (NNSS)

MAGTF
Marine Air Ground Task Force

MAHC
Maximum Allowable Housing Cost

MAI
Material Annex Index

MAID
Merger-Acquistion Improved Decision

MAIDS
Multi-Purpose Automatic Inspection and Diagnostic System

MAINT
Maintenance

MAINTBN
Maintenance Battalion

MAINTSUPOFC
Maintenance Supply Office

MAINTSUPP
Maintenance and Support

MAIP
Maintenance Automatic Integrated Director
Memory Access and Interrupt Program

MAIR
Molecular Airborne Interceptor Radar

MAIRESTLANT
Maritime Air, Eastern Atlantic

MAIRMED
Maritime Air, Mediterranean Area

MAIRU
Mobile Aircraft Instrument Repair Unit

MAKETRANS
When directed by CO make necessary transfers in accordance with (manual designated). Report to CO or command specified in connection with settlement of accounts.

MAL
Master Allowance List

MALE
Multi-Aperture Logic Element

MALI
Material Annex Line Item

MALRE
Marine Aircraft Launch and Recovery School

MALS
Minimum-Approach Light System

MALS/RAIL
Minimum-Approach Light System with Runway Alignment Indicator Lights

MALT
Monetary Allowance in Lieu of Transportation

MAM
Maintenance Assist Module

MAMIE
Minimum Automatic Machine for Interpolation and Extrapolation

MAMOEAST
Marine Aviation Material Office, East

MAMOWEST
Marine Aviation Material Office, West

MAMS
Management of Aviation Maintenance Assistance Modules

MAN
Magnetic Automatic Navigation
Manager
Manual
Military Aviation Notice

MANCAN
Man-Carried Automatic Navigator

MAND
Mandatory

MANFST
Manifest

MANGR
Manager

MANIAC
Mechanical and Numerical Integrator and Computer

MANMEDDEPT
Manual of the Medical Department

MAN/SAFE
Manual/Automatic Separation and Flotation Equipment

MANTRAPERS
Manpower, Training, and Personnel

MAO
Maximal Acid Output

MAOT
Maximum Allowable Operating Time

MAP
Manifold Absolute Pressure
Military Assistance Program
Missed Approach Point
Modular Aviation Package

MAPAD
Military Assistance Program Address Directory

MAP/CIO
Military Assistance Program/Common Item Order

MAPMIS
Manpower and Personnel Management Information System

MAPMISMAN
Manpower and Personnel Management Information System Manual

MAP/OSP
Military Assistance Program Offshore Procurement

MAPS
Multiple Address Processing System
Multivariate Analysis and Prediction of Schedules

MAPSAC
Machine-Aided Planning, Scheduling and Control

MAPTIS
Manpower, Personnel and Training Indoctrination System

MAPUC
Modified Area Production Urgency Committee

MAQ
Money Allowance for Quarters

MAR
Maintenance Analysis Report
March
Marine (Corps)
Memory Access Register
Multi-Function-Phased Array Radar

MARAD
Maritime Administration

MARBKS
Marine Barracks

MARC
Machine Readable Cataloging
Material Accountability and Recoverability Codes

MARCAD
Marine Aviation Cadet

MARCEMP
Manual Relay Center Modernization Program

MARCOMM
Maritime Commission

MARCOMMDET
Marine Communications Detachment

MARCORABSCOLLUNIT
Marine Corps Absentee Collection Unit

MARCORABSCOLLUNITDET
Marine Corps Absentee Collection Unit Detachment

MARCORADMINDET
Marine Corps Administrative Detachment

MARCORHISTCEN
Marine Corps Historical Center

MARDET
Marine Detachment

MARDIV
Marine Division

MARE
Months After Receipt of Equipment

MARENGLAB
Marine Engineering Laboratory

MARENGRLAB
Marine Engineering Laboratory

MARENTS
Modified Advanced Research Environmental Test Satellite

MARES
Maritime Automated Readiness Evaluation System

MARFINCEN
Marine Corps Finance Center

MARI
Mercantile Atlantic Routing Instructions

MARINE
Management Analysis Reporting Information on the Naval Environment (system)

MARIP
Maintenance and Repair Inspection Program

MARISAT
Maritime Satellite (communications)

MARLIS
Multi-Aspect Relevance Linkage Information System

MARLNO
Marine Liaison Office

MARMAP
Maritime Resources Monitoring, Assessment and Prediction (system)

MARP
Manpower Allocation/Requirement Plan
Maximum Authorized for Repair Parts
Months After Receipt of Problem

MARS
Machine Retrieval System
Manned Astronautical Research Station
Military Affiliate Radio System
Mobile Atlantic Range Station
Multi-Aperture Reluctance Switch

MARSA
Military Assumes Responsibility for Separation of Aircraft

MARSPTBN
Marine Support Battalion

MARSREPSYS
Military Affiliate Radio System Repeater System

MARSTELSYS
Military Affiliate Radio System Teletypewriter Relay System

MARTCOM
Marine Training Command

MARTD
Marine Air Reserve Training Detachment

MARV
Maneuverable Reentry Vehicle (Improved MIRV)
Maneuvering Anti-Radar Vehicle

MAS
Machine Accounting School
Marine Advisory Service (NOAA)

MASA
Master-at-Arms Seaman Apprentice

MASAQUE
Major Action Significantly Affecting the Quality of the Human Environment

MA/SB
Motor Antisubmarine Boat

MASC
Magnetic Spin Control

MASER
Microwave Amplification by Stimulated Emission of Radiation

MASF
Military Assistance in Service-Funding (grants)
Mobile Aeromedical Staging Facility

MASG
Military Airlift Support Group

MASH
Manned Antisubmarine Helicopter

MASK
Maneuvering and Sea-Keeping (facility)

MASM
Military Assistance and Sales Manual

MASN
Master-at-Arms Seaman

MASS
Marine Air Support Squadron
Maritime Anti-Standing Sonar System (MARAD)

MASSDAR
Modular Analysis, Speed-Up, Sampling, and Data Reduction

MASSDET
Marine Air Support Squadron Detachment

MAST
Military Assistance for Safety in Traffic (DOD/DOT)
Missile Automatic Supply Squadron
Mobile Ashore Support Terminal

MASTER
Miniaturized Sink-Rate Telemetering Radar
Multiple Access Shared Time Executive Routine

MAT
Material

MATCON
Microwave Aerospace Terminal Control

MATCONOFF
Material Control Office

MATCS
Marine Air Traffic Control Squadron

MATCSDET
Marine Air Traffic Control Squadron Detachment

MATD
Mine and Torpedo Detector

MATEX
Material Expediting (program)

MATL
Material

MATMU
Mobile Aircraft Torpedo Maintenance Unit

MATRED
Material Redistribution (program)

MATSG
Marine Aviation Training Support Group

MATSS
Marine Aviation Training Support Squadron

MATT
Multiple Airborne Target Trajectory System

MATTU
Multiple Airborne Target Trajectory Unit

MAU
Maintenance Augmenting Unit
Marine Amphibious Unit

MAW
Marine Air Wing
Medium Assault Weapon

MAWCS
Mobile Air Weapons Control System

MA/WD
Material Annex/Weapons Dictionary

MAWDET
Marine Aircraft Wing Detachment

MAWS
Missile Approach Warning System

MAWTS
Marine Aviation Weapons and Tactics Squadron

MAX
Maximum

MAX/MIN
Maximum Disclosure/Minimum Delay

M/B
Medium Bomber (aircraft)

MB
Main Battery
Military Band (AFRTS code)
Mooring Buoys
Motor Boat (USCG)

MBBA
Military Benefit Base Amounts

MBC
Magnetic Bias Control

MBFR
Mutual and Balanced Force Reductions

MBL
Mutual Bidders List

MBMU
Mobile Base Maintenance Unit

MBO
Management By Objectives

MBOH
Minimum Break-Off Height

MBR
Member
Multiple Bomb Rack

MBT
Main Ballast Tank
Main Battle Tank
Mobile Boarding Team

M/BVR
Medium Beyond Visual Range Missile

MC
Main Coolant
Maintenance Control
Major Component
Mast Controller
Medical Care, Civilian Source
Medical Corps
Message Center
Miles on Course
Military Characteristics
Mission Capable
(United States) Marine Corps

MC&G
Mapping, Charting, and Geodesy
Mapping, Charting, and Geodetic

MCA
Machinery Condition Analysis
Manning Control Authority
Maritime Control Area
Material Coordinating Agency
Minimum Crossing Altitude

MCAAS
Marine Corps Auxiliary Air Station

MCAC
Military Common Area Control

MCAF
Marine Corps Air Facility

MCAI
Maximum Calling Area Indicator

MCALF
Marine Corps Auxiliary Landing Field

MCAP
Maximum Calling Area Precedence

MCAS
Marine Corps Air Station

MCAT
Medical College Admission Test

MCB
Material Classification Board
Motor Cargo Boat (USCG)
(Naval) Mobile Construction Battalion

MCBETH
Military Computer Basic Environment for Test Handling

MCBF
Mean Cycles Between Failures

MCBL
Motor Cargo Boat (Large) (USCG)

MCC
Machinery Control Console
Mail Classification Center
Main Control Console
Master Control Console

Material Category Code
Material Control Center
Material Control Code
MILCOMS Concentration Center
Military Climb Corridor
Monitored Command Mode
Multiple Computer Complex

MCCDPA
Marine Corps Central Design and Programming Activity

MCCDS
Modified Central Computer Display Set

MCCES
Marine Corps Communications Electronics School

MCCRES
Marine Corps Combat Crew Readiness Evaluation System

MCCRTG
Marine Corps Combat Crew Readiness Training Group

MCD
Maintenance Control Department (PWD)
Marine Corps District

MCEB
Military Communications-Electronics Board

MCF
Master Control File

MCG
Mid-Course Guidance
Mobile Communications Group

MCGS
Microwave Command Guidance System

MCI
Marine Corps Institute

MCIC
Management Control Information Center

MCL
Master Configuration List

MCLWG
Major Caliber Lightweight Gun

MCM
Manual for Courts-Martial
Mine Countermeasures Ship

MCMC
Military Construction, Marine Corps

MCMCC
Marine Corps Movement Coordination Center

MCMWTC
Marine Corps Mountain Warfare Training Center

MCN
Military Construction, Navy

MCNR
Military Construction, Naval Reserve

MCNRF
Military Construction, Naval Reserve Facilities

MCO
Missile Check-Out
Missile Control Officer

MCOI
Minority Centers of Influence

MCON
Military Construction

MCOT
Missile Control Officer Trainer

MCOTEA
Marine Corps Operational Test and Evaluation Activity

MCOY
Military Citizen of the Year

MCP
Main Coolant Pump
Master Construction Project
Master Control Program
Maximum Calling Precedence
Maximum Calling Preference
Military Construction Program
Mission Capability Package
Mutual Change Proposal

MCPO
Master Chief Petty Officer

MCPOC
Master Chief Petty Officer of the Command

MCPOF
Master Chief Petty Officer of the Fleet
Master Chief Petty Officer of the Force

MCPON
Master Chief Petty Officer of the Navy

MCR
Maintenance Requirements Cards

MCRB
Magnetic Compass Record Book

MCRF
Master Cross Reference File

MCRL
Master Component Repair List
Master Cross Reference List

MCRS
Marine Corps Recruiting Station

MCRSC
Marine Corps Reserve Support Center

MCS
Magnetic Card Selecting
Maintenance Control Section
Mine Countermeasures Support Ship
Missile Control Section

MCS-21
Maritime Cryptologic System for the 21st Century

MCSF
Marine Corps Security Force

MCSL
Small Mine Countermeasures Ship

MCSTRANSU
Military Sealift Command Transportation Unit

MCSTU
Military Sealift Command Transportation Unit

MCT
Magnetic Compass Table
Mechanical Comprehension Test

MCTS
Master Central Timing System

MCTSSA
Marine Corps Tactical Systems Support Activity

MCU
Microprogrammed Control Unit (NBL)
Mission Computer Upgrade

MCW
Modulated Continuous Wave

MCXSERV
Marine Corps Exchange Service Branch

M/D
Man/Days

MD
Medical Department
Memory Data Register (NNSS)
Mine Disposal

MDA
Material Data Administrator
Minimum Descent Altitude
Multiple Docking Adaptor

MDAP
Mutual Defense Assistance Program

MDAS
Manpower Data Automated System

M-DAY
Mobilization Day

MDB
Material Distribution Board

MDC
Machineability Data Center
Maintenance Data Collection
Materials Distribution Center
Medium-Frequency Direction Finder

MDCS
Maintenance Data Collection Sub-System
Material Data Collection Sub-System

MDD
Maintenance Due Date
Marijuana Detection Dog

MDDS
Medical or Dental Corps Special Pay

MDEU
Material Delivery Expeditor Unit

MDF
Maintenance Data Form
Master Data File
Mild Detonating Fuze

MDFMR
Mobilization Day Force Material Requirement

MDG
Machinery Defective, Government-Furnished

MDI
Miss Distance Indicator

Mobilization Day Increment

MDL
Management Data List
Master Drawing List
Mine Defense Laboratory

MDM
Manpower Determination Model

MDMAA
Mess Deck Master-at-Arms

MDMS
Miss Distance Measuring System

MDOA
Material Date of Arrival

MDR
Maintenance Data Report
Maintenance Data Reporting
Matter Document Reader

MDRS
Maintenance Data Reporting System

MDS
Maintenance Data System
Malfunction Detection System
Minimum Discernable Signal
Multi-function Display System

MDSAG
Missile Defense Surface Action Groups

MDS-MPOLL
Mail Distribution Scheme/Military Post Office Location List

MDSU
Mobile Diving & Salvage Unit

MDT
Mean Diagnostic Time
Moderate

MDTA
Manpower Development and Training Act

MDU
Mission Data Update
Mobile Development Unit

ME
Magnetoelectric
Meal
Methods Engineering

MEA
Maintenance Engineering Analysis
Minimum Enroute Altitude

MEACONING
Measuring and Confusing

MEAD
Maintenance Engineering Analysis Data
Maintenance Engineering Analysis Division

MEAL
Mobile Equipment Allowance List

MEAR
Maintenance Engineering Analysis Record

MEAS
Measure

MEASURE
Metrology Automated System for Uniform Recall and Reporting

MEAWS
Maintenance Engineering Analysis Work Sheet

MEB
Marine Expeditionary Brigade

MEBD
Medical Examining Board

MEC
Metrology Engineering Center
Military Equipment Code
Military Essentiality Code
Military Essentiality Coding

MECEP
Marine Corps Enlisted Commissioning Education Program

MECH
Mechanic
Mechanical

MECO
Main Engine Cut-Off
Manual Equipment Check-Out

MECP
Medical Enlisted Commissioning Program

MED
Medical
Mediterranean
Medium
Minimal Effective Dose

MEDAL
Micro-Mechanized Engineering Data for

Automated Logistics

MEDBN
Medical Battalion

MEDBR
Medical Branch

MEDCAP
Medical Civic Action Program

MEDDA
Mechanized Defense Decision Anticipation

MEDEVAC
Medical Evacuation

MEDIA
Missile-Era Data Integration Analysis

MEDICARE
(Dependent's) Medical Care

MEDICOS
Mediterranean Instructions to Convoys

MEDIHC
Military Experience Directed Into Health Careers

MEDIUM
Missile-Era Data Integration-Ultimate Method

MEDMAILCOORD
Mediterranean Mail Coordinating Office

MEDOFCOMD
Medical Officer-in-Command

MEDREP
Daily Medical Status Report

MEDSARS
Maintenance Engineering Data Storage and Retrieval System

MEDSERWRNT
Medical Service Warrant

MEDSUPDEP
Medical Supply Depot

MEDT
Military Equipment Delivery Team

MEECN
Minimum Essential Emergency Communications Network

MEEL
Mission Essential Equipment List

MEES
Multi-Purpose Electronic Environment Simulator

MEETAT
Maximum Improvement in Electronics Effectiveness Advanced Techniques

MEF
Marine Expeditionary Force
Middle East Force

MEI
Maintenance and Engineering Inspection
Manual of Engineering Instructions

MEIU
Mobile Explosives Investigative Unit

MEL
Marine Engineering Laboratory
Material Engineering Laboratory

MEL-A
Marine Engineering Laboratory-Annapolis (MD)

MEM
Member

MEMO
Memorandum

MEMQ
Married Enlisted Men's Quarters

MEMRAC
Mission-Essential Material Readiness and Condition

MEN
Master Equipment Number

MENEX
Maintenance Engineering Exchange Program

MENS
Mission Element Need Statement

MENTRAV
Commence travel within (number of days indicated) after completion of physical examination

MEO
Major Engine Overhaul
Management Engineering Office

MEP
Mobile Electric Power

MEPP
Mobile Electric Power Plants

MEPS
Military Entrance and Processing Station

MEQ
Milliequivalent

MER
Maintenance Engineering Report
Multiple Ejector Rack

MERAIR
Including Commercial Air

MERAIRDIR
Commerical air is directed where necessary

MERCAST
Merchant Ship Broadcast

MERCO
Mercantile Communications
Merchant Ship Movement Reports

MERCOMMS
Merchant Marine Communications System

MERCOS
Merchant Codes

MERMUT
Mobile Electronic Robot Manipulator on TV (system)

MERP
Miniature Electronic Repair Program

MERR
Minor Equipment Relocations, Replacements

MERSAIR
Merchant Ship Research and Rescue (manual)

MERSAP
Merchant Ship Auxiliary Program

MERSIGS
Merchant Ships Signal Books
Merchant Signals

MERT
Maintenance Engineering Review Team

MERTRANSUB
Commercial transportation and subsistence authorized

MES
Master Erection Schedule

MESA
Machinery Effectiveness System Analysis
Marine Ecosystems Analysis

MESH
Medical Subject Heading

MESIM
Mission Essential Sub-Systems Inoperative, Maintenance

MESL
Mission Essential Sub-Systems List

MEST
Missile Electrical System Test

MET
Meteorologic
Meteorological
Mine Warfare Exercise and Training (material)
Mission Entry Time
Mobile Environmental Team

METC
Military Electronics Test Center

METCAL
Meteorology and Calibration (program)

METCALANTDETEAST
Atlantic Metrology and Calibration Coordinating Group Detachment, East

METCALANTDETWEST
Atlantic Metrology and Calibration Coordinating Group Detachment, West

METCO
Mobile Engine Tester, Computer-Operated

METG
Middle East Task Group

METIMP
Meteorological Equipment Improvement Program

METLO
Meteorological Equipment and Technical Liaison Officer

METMF
(U.S. Marine Corps) Meteorological Mobile Facility

METOC
Meteorological and Oceanographic

METRI
Military Essentiality Through Readiness

Indices

METRL
Metrology (requirements listing)

METT
Mission, Enemy, Terrain and Weather, and Troops Available

METU
Mobile Electronics Training Unit

MEU
Marine Expeditionary Unit

MEU(SOC)
Marine Expeditionary Unit (Special Operations Capable)

MEV
Million Electron Volts

MEW
Microwave Early Warning (radar)

M/F
Marked For
Mark For

MF
Main Force
Medium Frequency
Millifarad
Multifrequency

MFAR
Modernized Fleet Accounting and Reporting (system)

MFC
Multiple File Concept

MFCS
Missile Fire Control System

MFFV
Mobile Firefighting Vehicle

MFGEL
Master Government-Furnished Equipment List

MFI
Major Force Issue

MFIT
Manual Fault Isolation Test

MFLT
Mean Fault Location Time

MFM
Magneto Fluidmechanic (system)
Mine Firing Mechanism

MFNG
Motion for a Finding of Not Guilty

MFO
Master Frequency Oscillator
Missile Firing Officer

MFP
Minimal Flight Path

MFR
Memo For Record
Multi-Function Radar

MFS
Master Fabrication Schedule
Military Flight Service

MFSS
Missile Flight Safety System

MFTA
Multi-Function Towed Array

MFVU
Mobile Firefighting Vehicle/Unit

MG
Machine Gun
Military Government
Milligram
Motor Generator

MGAS
Motor Gasoline

MGB
Medium Girder Bridge
Motor Gunboat

MGC
Main Gain Control

MGCR
Marine Gas-Cooled Reactor

MGD
Million Gallons per Day

MGDA
Multiple Degaussing Cable

MGE
Maintenance Ground Equipment

MGFEL
Master Government-Furnished Equipment

List

MGGB
Modular-Guided-Glide Bomb

MGM
Mailgram

MGMT
Management

MGR
Manager

MGRS
Military Grid Reference System

MGSE
Missile Ground Support Equipment

MGSGT
Master Gunnery Sergeant

MGU
Military Government Unit

MGZ
Magazine

MH
Magnetic Heading
Man-Hours

MHA
Man-Hour Accounting (card)
Minehunter, Auxiliary
Minimum Holding Altitude

MHAS
Man-Hour Accounting System

MHB
Master Horizontal Bomber

MHC
Minehunter Coastal

MH-CE
Materials Handling and Construction Equipment

MHD
Magnetohydrodynamics (power supply)
Meter Heading Differential

MHDF
Direction Finder (Medium and High Frequency)

MHE
Material Handling Equipment

MH/FH
Man-Hours per Flying Hour

MHHFC
Machine and Hull History File Cards

MHHW
Mean Higher High Water

MHIP
Missile Homing Improvement Program

MHSS
Materials Handling Support System

MHVDF
Direction Finder (Medium, High and Very High Frequency)

MHW
Mean High Water

MHWN
Mean High Water Neaps

MHWS
Mean High Water Springs

MHz
Megahertz

MI
Material Inspection
Medical Illustration
Methods Instruction
Military Intelligence

MIA
Missing in Action

MIAC
Material Identification and Accounting Code

MIAPL
Master Index, Allowance Parts List

MIARS
Maintenance Information Automatic Retrieval System
Micro-film Information and Retrieval System

MIB
Marine Index Bureau
Master Instruction Book

MIBARS
Military Intelligence Battalion Aerial Reconnaissance Report

MIC
Maintenance Index Code
Management Inactivation Center
Management Information Center
Marine Information Center
Material Identification and Control
Military-Industrial Complex

MICA
Macro Instruction Compiler-Assembler

MICFAC
Mobile Integrated Command Facilities

MICR
Magnetic Ink Character Recognition

MICRO
Microfilm File (NARDIS)

MICRO-PAC
Micromodule Data Processor and Computer

MID
Management Information Digest (publication)
Middle
Midshipman
Military Intellilgence Division
Missile Intelligence Directorate

MIDAS
Machine for Information Display and Simulation
Missile Defense Alarm System

MIDATL
Mid-Atlantic

MIDEASTFOR
Middle East Force

MIDIZ
Mid-Canada Identification Zone

MIDN
Midnight
Midshipman

MIDPAC
Middle Pacific

MIDRATS
Midnight Rations
Midwatch Rations

MIDS
Maintenance Index Pages
Movement Information Distribution Station
Multi-Function Information Distribution System

MIDS-LVT
Multifunctional Information Distribution System-Low Volume Terminal

MIG
Metal Inert Gas

MIISA
Management Information and Instructional Systems Activity

MIISADET
Management Information and Instructional Systems Activity Detachment

MIISAU
Management Information and Instructional Systems Activity Unit

MIJI
Meconing, Intrusion, Jamming, and Interference

MIL
Military
Milliradian
Modular Individualized

MILCOMS
Military Commands

MILCOMSAT
Military Communications Satellite

MILCON
Military Construction

MIL CONF
Military Confinement

MILDEPT
Military Department

MILDET
Military Detachment

MILES
Multiple Integrated Laser Engagement System

MILGRP
Military Group

MILGRU
Military Group

MILJUSDOCFILE
Military Justice Docket File

MILPERS
Military Personnel

MILPERSMAN
Military Personnel Manual

MILPERSYS
Military Personnel Information Subsystem

MILPINS
Military Police Information System

MILS
Missile Impact Location System

MILSAT
Military Satellite

MILSCAP
Military Standard Contract Administration Procedure

MILSPEC
Military Specifications

MILSTAAD
Military Standard Activity Address Directory

MILSTAMP
Military Standard Transportation and Movement Procedure

MILSTD
Military Standard

MILSTEP
Military Standard Evaluation Procedure
Military Supply and Transportation Evaluation Procedure

MILSTICCS
Military Standard Item Characteristics Coding Structure

MILSTRAP
Military Standard Transaction Reporting and Accounting Procedures

MILSTRIP
Military Standard Requisition and Issue Procedures

MIM
Maintenance Instruction Manual

MIN
Minimum
Minute

MINAC
Miniature Navigation Airborne Computer

MINCOM
Miniaturized Communications

MINDIV
Mine Division

MINECTRMEASTA
Mine Countermeasures Station

MINEDEFLAB
Mine Defense Laboratory

MINEPACSUPPGRU
Mine Force, Pacific Fleet, Support Group Unit

MINICATS
Miniaturization of the Federal Catalog Systems Publication

MINLANT
Mine Warfare Forces, Atlantic

MINPAC
Mine Warfare Forces, Pacific

MINS
Mare Island Naval Shipyard
Miniature Inertial Navigation System

MINSUPPU
Minecraft Support Unit

MINSY
Mare Island Naval Shipyard

MINWARTECH
Mine Warfare Technician

MINY
Mare Island Naval Shipyard

MIO
Mobile Issuing Office

MIP
Maintenance Index Page
Management Improvement Program
Manual Index Page
Master Improvement Plan
Material Improvement Plan
Maximum Intermittent Power
Methods Improvement Program
Military Improvement Plan

MIPE
Modular Information Processing Equipment

MIPIR
Missile Precision Instrumentation Radar

MIPR
Military Interdepartmental Purchase Request

MIPS
Military Information Processing System

MIR
Material Inspection Report

MIRACL
Mid-Infrared Advanced Chemical Laser

MIRCS
Mechanical Instrument Repair and Calibration Shops

MIRF
Multiple Instantaneous Response File

MIRL
Medium-Intensity Runway Lights

MIRR
Material Inspection and Receiving Report

MIRRER
Microwave Identification Railroad Encoding Reflector

MIRROS
Modulation Inducing Reactive Retrodirective Optical System

MIRS
Micro-Interactive Retrieval System

MIRSI
Monthly Inventory Report of Special Items

MIRTRAC
Missile Infrared Tracking (system)

MIRV
Multiple Independently Targetable Reentry Vehicle

MIS
Management Information Sciences
Management Information Service
Manpower Information System
Material Inspection Service
Metal-Insulator-Semi-Conductor
Military Inspection Service
Mine-Issuing Ship
Missile
Missing
Mission

MISA
Military Industrial Supply Agency

MISC
Miscellaneous

MISD
Management Information System Development

MISDO
Management Information System Development Office

MISEG
Management Information System Executive Group

MISG
Missing

MISIAS
Management Information Systems Inventory and Analysis System

MIS/INAS
Management Information System for Industrial Naval Air Stations

MISL
Manpower Information System Laboratory

MISL REWRK
Missile Rework

MISP
Management Information System Plan

MISR
Minimum Industrial Sustaining Role

MISRAN
Missile Range

MISREP
Mission Report (JTARS)

MISS
Mobile Integrated Support System

MIST
Multi-Input Standard Tape

MISTER
Mobile Integrated System Trainer, Evaluator and Recorder

MISTRAM
Missile Trajectory Measurement

MISTRAULANT
Missile Weapons System Training Unit, Atlantic

MISTRAUPAC
Missile Weapons System Training Unit, Pacific

MIT
Master Instruction Tape

MITAG
Minority Affairs Task Group

MITAGS
Maritime Institute of Technology and Graduate Studies

MITE
Missile Integration Terminal Equipment
Multiple Input Terminal Equipment

MITMS
Military/Industry Technical Manual Specifications

MITO
Minimum Interval Take-Off

MITRE
Authorized to omit or revisit any of the above-mentioned places as necessary

MITREVAR
Authorized to omit or revisit any of the above-mentioned places and to vary above itinerary as necessary

MIUW
Mobile Inshore Undersea Warfare

MIUWSU
Mobile Inshore Undersea Warfare Surveillance Unit

MIW
Mine Warfare

MIZ
Marginal Ice Zone

MJ
Millijoule

MK
Mark

MKR
Marker Radio Beacon

MKSA
Meter-Kilogram-Second-Ampere

ML
Medical Technologist
Middle Level
Military Law
Milliliter
Missile Launch
Money List
Motor Launch (USCG)
Small Minesweeper

ML1
Molder First Class

ML2
Molder Second Class

ML3
Molder Third Class

MLC
Chief Molder
Main Landing Craft
Military Landing Craft
Military Liaison Committee
Motor Landing Craft
Motor Launch, Cabin
Multi-Line Communications Controller

MLCM
Master Chief Molder

MLCS
Senior Chief Molder

MLD
Main Line of Defense

MLDS
Motor Launch, Double Shelter (USCG)

MLF
Multilateral Force

MLFA
Molder Fireman Apprentice

MLFN
Molder Fireman

MLG
Main Landing Gear

MLLW
Mean Lower Low Water

MLM
Multilayer Metallization

ML/MS
Motor Launch/Minesweeper

MLOI
Master List of Outstanding Items

MLP
Mirror Landing Practice
Multi-Level Precedence

Multi-Level Procedure

MLPP
Multi-Level Precedence Preemption

MLR
Main Line of Resistance
Mortar Locating Radar

MLS
Microwave Landing System
Missile Launching System

MLSC
Mobile Logistics Support Concept

MLSF
Mobile Logistics Support Force

M-L-S-R
Missing, Lost, Stolen, or Recovered (government property)

MLT
Medical Laboratory Technician (ASCP)

MLW
Mean Low Water

MLWN
Mean Low Water Neaps

MLWS
Mean Low Water Springs

MM
Machinist's Mate
Memory Multiplexor
Middle Marker
Millimeter

MM1
Machinist's Mate First Class

MM2
Machinist's Mate Second Class

MM3
Machinist's Mate Third Class

MMA
Manual Metal Arc (welding)
Multimission Maritime Aircraft

M-MARP
Mobilization Manpower Allocation/Requirements Plan Allocation

MMART
Mobile Medical Augmentation Readiness Team

MMAT
Mobile Mine Assembly Team

MMC
Chief Machinist's Mate
Minesweeper, Command

MMCC
Military Manpower Claimant Code

MMCM
Master Chief Machinist's Mate

MMCS
Senior Chief Machinist's Mate

MMCSA
Microwave Microminiature Communications System for Aircraft

MMD
Destroyer Minelayer
Manual of the Medical Department

MMES
Master Material Erection Schedule

MMF
Magnetomotive Force
(U.S. Marine Corps) Meteorological Mobile Facility
Minelayer, Fleet
Mobile Maintenance Facility

MMFA
Machinist's Mate Fireman Apprentice

MMFN
Machinist's Mate Fireman

MMFO
Maintenance Management Field Office

MMG
Material Monitoring Guide
Mobile Motor Generator

MMH
Maintenance Man-Hours
Mean Man-Hours

MMH/FH
Maintenance Man-Hours per Flight Hour

MMIS
Maintenance Management Information System

MMM
Maintenance and Material Management (3M)
Marine Multipurpose Missile

MMNIC
Main Mediterranean Naval Intelligence Center

MMNR
Merchant Marine Naval Reserve

MMO
Main Meteorological Office

MMODS
Master Material Ordering and Delivery Schedule

MMP
Maintenance Monitor Panel
MEECN Master Plan
Merchant Marine Personnel Division

MMPC
Mobilization Material Procurement Capabilities

MMPD
Material Movement Priority Designator

MMPNC
Medical Material Program for Nuclear Casualties

MMPR
Missile Manufacturers Planning Report

MMPS
MEECN Message Processing System

MMR
Management Milestone Records
Master Material Record
Maximum Measurable Range
Merchant Marine Reserve
Military Media Review (publication)
Minelayer, River
Mobilization Material Requirements
Monthly Meteorological Records
Multimode Radar

MMRA
Mobilization Material Requirements Adjustment

MMRBM
Mobile Medium Range Ballistic Missile

MMRT
Modified Miniature Receiver Terminal

MMS
Manpower Management System
Master Manpower Schedule
Motor Minesweeper
Munitions Management System

MMSA
Manual Molded Shielded Arc
Military Medical Supply Agency

MMSRC
Mediterranean Maritime Surveillance and Reconnaissance Center

MMU
Mobile Maintenance Unit
Modular Maneuvering Unit

MN
Manual Input (NNSS)
Mineman

MN1
Mineman First Class

MN2
Mineman Second Class

MN3
Mineman Third Class

MNA
Missing-Not as a Result of Enemy Action

MNAO
Mobile Naval Airfield Organization

MNAU
Mobile Naval Airfield Unit

MNC
Chief Mineman

MNCM
Master Chief Mineman

MNCS
Senior Chief Mineman

MNGR
Manager

MNM
Minimum

MNOMU
Mobile Nuclear Ordnance Maintenance Unit

MNOS
Metal Nitrite Oxide Semiconductor

MNPO
Mobile Navy Post Office

MNS
Mine Neutralization System
Mission Needs Statement

MNSA
Mineman Seaman Apprentice

MNSN
Mineman Seaman

MO
Manual Override
Master Oscillator
Medical Officer
Mobile
Modification Order
Month
Monthly Order
Motor

MOA
Management Operations Audit
Matrix Output Amplifier
Memorandum of Agreement
Minute of Angle
Month of Arrival

MOAF
Meteorological and Oceanographic Analyst/Forecaster (course)

MOAT
Missile On Aircraft Test

MOB
Main Operating Base
Make or Buy
Mobile
Mobilization

MOBAS
Model Basin

MOBCON
Mobilization Construction

MOBCONBAT
(Naval) Mobile Construction Battalion

MOBCTR
Mobilization Center

MOBDIVSALU
Mobile Diving and Salvage Unit

MOBIDIC
Mobile Digital Computer

MOBIS
Management-Oriented Budget and Information System

MOBLOGSUPPFOR
Mobile Logistics Support Force

MOBOT
Mobile Robot

MOBS
Mobile Ocean Basing System

MOBSUPPBASE
Mobile Support Base

MOBSUPPGRU
Mobile Support Group

MOBTR
Mobile Trainer

MOC
Mechanical, Operational, Clerical
Missile Operations Center

MOCA
Minimum Obstruction Clearance Altitude

MOCAS
Mechanization of Contract Administrative Services

MOCC
Mobile Operational Command Control Center

MOCEM
Meteorological and Oceanographic Equipment Maintenance (course)

MOCOM
Mobility Command

MOD
Mate of the Deck
Military Obligation Designator
Model
Moderate
Modification
Modification number
Modify
Modulator
Month and Calendar Year of Detachment

MODE
Mid-Ocean Dynamics Experiment
Monitoring Overseas Direct Employment

MODEM
Modulator-Demodulator

MODG
Modifying

MODN
Modification

MODS
Material Ordering and Delivery Schedule
Military Orbital Development System
Models for Organizational Design and Staffing

MOE
Magnetic Anomaly Detection Operational Effectiveness
Measure of Effectiveness

MOE/MOP
Measures of Effectiveness/Measures of Performance

MOEP
Meteorological and Oceanographic Equipment Program

MOETLO
Meteorological and Oceanographic Equipment Technical Liaison Officer

MOF
Months of Operational Flying

MOG
Material-Ordering Guide

MOGAS
Motor Gasoline

MOH
Medal Of Honor

MOIC
Medical Officer-in-Charge

MOJT
Managed On-the-Job Training

MOL
Machine-Oriented Language

MOLAB
Mobile Laboratory

MOL/ACTS
Manned Orbiting Laboratory/Altitude Control and Transmission System

MOLECOM
Molecularized Digital Chamber

MOM
Inf: Man On the Move
Military Overseas Mail

MOMAG
Mobile Mine Assembly Group

MOMAGDET
Mobile Mine Assembly Group Detachment

MOMAGU
Mobile Mine Assembly Group Unit

MOMAT
Mobile Mine Assembly Team

MOMATLANT
Mobile Mine Assembly Team, Atlantic

MOMATPAC
Mobile Mine Assembly Team, Pacific

MOMAU
Mobile Mine Assembly Unit

MOMAULANT
Mobile Mine Assembly Unit, Atlantic

MOMAULANTDETKEF
Mobile Mine Assembly Unit, Atlantic, Keflavik (IC) Detachment

MOMAUPAC
Mobile Mine Assembly Unit, Pacific

MOMCOMS
Man-on-the-Move Communications
Mobile Mine Countermeausures Command

MOMISMAINTU
Mobile Missile Maintenance Unit

MOMP
Mid-Ocean Meeting Point

MOMS
Modified Operational Missile System

MON
Monitor
Month

MONAB
Mobile Naval Air Base

MONIL
Mobile Non-Destructive Inspection Laboratory

MONOB
Mobile Noise Barge (sound laboratory)

MOON
Meeting Our Operating Needs

MOOW
Midshipman Officer-of-the-Watch

MOP
Magnetic Orange Pipe (mine decoy)
McNeil Oblique Plotting
Measures of Performance
Message Output Processor
Mustering Out pay

MOPAR
Master Oscillator-Power Amplifier Radar

MOPSY
Modular Self-Paced Study

MOPTAR
Multi-Object Phase Tracking and Ranging (system)

MOQ
Married Officers' Quarters

M-O-R
Middle of the Road (AFRTS code)

MOR
Management Operation Ratios
Medical Officer's Report
Missile Operationally Ready

MORE
Minority Officer Recruitment Effort

MOREST
Mobile Arresting (gear)

MORG
Movements Reports Generator

MORS
Military Operations Research Society

MORSEAFRON
Moroccan Sea Frontier

MORT
Master Operational Recording Tape
Mortar

MOS
Management Operating System
Marine Occupational Standard
Marking of Overseas Shipments
Master Operating System
Material Ordering Schedule
Metal-Oxide-Semiconductor
Military Occupational Specialty

MOSC
Military Oil Subcommittee (NAEB)

MOS/LSI
Metal-Oxide-Semiconductor/Large-Scale Integration

MOSP
Master Ordnance System Pattern
Medical and Osteopathic Scholarship Program

MOST
Mobile Optical Surveillance Tracker

MOSU
Mobile Ordnance Service Unit

MOSUPPU
Mobile Support Unit

MOT
Maximum Operating Time
Military Ocean Terminal
Motion
Motor

MOTARDES
Moving Target Detection System

MOTARDIV
Mobile Target Division

MOTBA
Military Ocean Terminal, Bay Area

MOTBY
Military Ocean Terminal, Bayonne (NJ)

MOTECS
Mobile Tactical Exercise Control System

MOTG
Marine Operational Training Course

MOTNE
Meteorological Operational Telecommunications Network, Europe

MOTOR
Monthly Throughput Observation Report

MOTSU
Military Ocean Terminal, Sunny Point (Southport, NC)

MOTU
Mobile Ordnance Technical Unit
Mobile Training Unit

MOTUDET
Mobile Ordnance Technical Unit Detachment

MOU
Memorandum Of Understanding

MOV
Material Obligation Validation
Metal Oxide Varistor
Move
Movement

MOVLAS
Manually-Operated, Visual Landing Aid System

MOVREP
Movement Report

MOVSUM
(Daily) Movement Summary

MO-YR
Month and Year

MP
Main Propulsion
Maintenance Period
Manual Proportional (altitude control system)
Marching Pack
Maritime Polar (air mass)
Material Procurement
Military Police
Multiple Punch

MPA
Main Propulsion Assistant
Maritime Patrol Aircraft

MPAR
Maintainability Program Analysis Report

MPB
Merit Promotion Bulletin

MPC
Manpower Priorities Committee
Material Planning and Control
Maximum Permissible Concentration (radiation)
Military Payment Certificate
Multi-Purpose Communications (system)

MPCO
Military Police Company

MPCRI
Mercantile Pacific Coastal Routing Instructions

MPD
Material Property Damage
Medical Pay Date
Military Priority Date
Movement Priority Designator
Multi-Purpose Display

MPDS
Message Processing and Distribution System

MPE
Maximum Permissible Exposure (to radiation)
Monthly Project Evaluation

MP-ER
Multiple Punch, Error Release

MPF
Maritime Prepositioning Forces

MPG
Main Propulsion Gear
Military Products Group

MPI
Mean Point of Impact
Military Procurement Intern

MPM
Maintenance Planning Manual
Major Program Memorandum
Message Processing Modules

MPMS
Missile Propulsion Maintenance School

MPN
Manufacturer's Part Number
Military Pay, Navy
Military Personnel, Navy

MPO
Military Post Office
Motion Picture Operator
Movie Projector Operator
Mustering Petty Officer

MPOS
Movie Projector Operator's School

MPP
Master Program Plan
Merit Promotion Program
Military Pay Procedures
Most Probable Position
Multi-Purpose Processor

MPPLT
Military Police Platoon

MPR
Monthly Production Report

MPRL
Master Parts Reference List

MPS
Maritime Prepositioning Ship
Master Program Schedule
Material Planning Study
Mathematical Programming System
Merit Promotion System
Message Processing System
Miles Per Second
Mission Profile Summary (airborne ASW)

MPSA
Military Petroleum Supply Agency

MPSC
Material Planning Schedule and Control

MPT
Main Propulsion Turbine
Manpower, Personnel, and Training

MPU
Message Processing Unit
Missile Power Unit

MPUL
Military Production Urgencies List

MPWS
Mobile Protected Weapon System

MPX
Multiplexer

MQT
Military Qualification Test

M/R
Map Reading
Memorandum of Receipt
Morning Report
Muster Report

MR
Machinery Repairman
Maintenance Review
March
Material Report
Medium Range
Memory Reference (NNSS)
Migration Ratio
Milli-Roentgen (radiation dose)
Mobilization Regulations
Modification Request
Moon Rise (time)

MR&D
Material Redistribution and Disposal

MR1
Machinery Repairman First Class

MR2
Machinery Repairman Second Class

MR3
Machinery Repairman Third Class

MRA
Minimum Reception Altitude

MRASTU
Marine Reserve Aviation Supply Training Unit

MRB
Material Review Board
Modification Review Board
Motor Rescue Boat (USCG)
Motor Surfboat (USCG)

MRBM
Medium-Range Ballistic Missile

MRC
Chief Machinery Repairman
Maintenance Record Card
Maintenance Requirements Card
Material Redistribution Center
Mathematics Research Center
Movement Report Center

MRCA
Multirole Combat Aircraft

MRCC
Movement Report Control Center

MRCI
Mine Readiness Certification Inspection

MRCM
Master Chief Machinery Repairman

MRCS
Senior Chief Machinery Repairman

MRDAC
Manpower Research and Data Analysis Center

MRDR
Material Receipt Discrepancy Record

MRDS
Malfunction Rate Detection System

MRE
Mean Radial Error

MREM
Milli-Roentgen-Equivalent Man (radiation standard)

MREP
Maneuvering Room Equipment Panel
Medical Remedial Enlistment Program

MRES
Material Requirements Estimation System
Multiple Reentry System

MRF
Maintenance Replacement Factor
Maintenance Requirement Factor
Module Repair Facility

MRFA
Machinery Repairman Fireman Apprentice

MRFN
Machinery Repairman Fireman

MRG
Medium Range

MR/HR
Milli-Roentgens per Hour

MRI
Machine Records Installation
Minimum Release Interval

MRIL
Master Repairable Item List

MRIR
Medium-Resolution Infrared Radiometer

MRIS
Material Readiness Index System

MRL
Master Range List
Master Repair List

MRM
Manpower Reference Model
Medium-Range Missile
Miles of Relative Movement

MRMR
Mobilization Reserve Material Requirements

MRN
Meteorological Rocket Network

MRNG
Morning

MRO
Maintenance, Repair, and Operating Supplies
Management Review Officer
Material Release Order
Mid-Range Objective
Minority Recruiting Officer
Movement Report Office

MRP
Malfunction Reporting Program
Material Reliability Program
Material Review Processing
Mid-Range Plan
Military Rated Power

MR/PA
Make Ready/Put Away

MRPL
Material Requirements Planning List

MRR
Material Rejection Report
Military Rights and Responsibilities
Mission Review Report

MRRC
Material Requirements Review Committee

MRS
Material Routing Sheet
Medium-Range Search (USCG aircraft)
Mobility Requirements Study
Movement Report Sheet

MRT
Maintenance Readiness Training
Mean Active Repair Time
Medium-Range Typhoon (missile)
Military Rated Thrust

MRTFB
Major Range and Test Facility Base

MRTM
Maritime

MRU
Material Recovery Unit
Minimum Replacement Unit

MRV
Multiple Reentry Vehicle

MRWS
Mobile Radar Weather System

MS
Main Steam
Maintenance Support
Management Sciences
Medical Care, Uniformed Services
Medical Survey
Medium Setting
Medium Speed
Medium Steel
Military Service
Military Specification
Military Standards
Milliseconds
Motor Ship

MS1
Mess Management Specialist First Class

MS2
Mess Management Specialist Second Class

MS3
Mess Management Specialist Third Class

MS/A
Midship Abreast (stowage)

MSA
Medical Service Account
Minesweeper, Auxiliary

MSAL
Medical Surveillance Action Level

MSB
Maritime Subsidy Board
Merchant Ship Broadcast
Minesweeping Boat
Mobile Support Base
Most Significant BIT

MSC
Chief Mess Management Specialist
Medical Service Corps
Military Sealift Command
Minesweeper, Coastal
Mobile Satellite Communications

MSCELM
Military Sealift Command, Eastern Atlantic and Mediterranean

MSCFE
Military Sealift Command, Far East

MSCI
Mediterranean Secret Convoy Instructions

MSC IPP
Medical Service Corps Inservice Procurement Program

MSCLANT
Military Sealift Command, Atlantic

MSCLANTDET
Military Sealift Command, Atlantic Detachment

MSCM
Master Chief Mess Management Specialist

MSCO
Military Sealift Command Office
Minesweeper, Coastal

MSCPAC
Military Sealift Command, Pacific

M/S/CPO
Master/Senior/Chief Petty Officer of the Command

MSCREP
Military Sealift Command Representative

MSCS
Merchant Ship Control Office
Senior Chief Mess Management Specialist

MSCSO
Military Sealift Command Service Office

MSCSO-M&R
Military Sealift Command Service Office-Maintenance and Repair

MSCSO-OCPO
Military Sealift Command Service Office-Operations Cargo Passenger Office

MSCSO-SA
Military Sealift Command Service Office-Supply Assistant

MSCU
Military Sealift Command Unit

MSD
Marine Sanitation Device
Material Sciences Division (ONR)
Metering Suction Differential
Minesweeping Drone

MSDG
Multi-Sensor Display Group

MSDI
Modified Ship's Drawing Index

MSDO
Management System Development Office

MSDV
Marine Sanitation Device

MSER
Management System Evaluation Force

MS/F
Midship Forward (stowage)

MSF
Fleet Minesweeper
Moroccan Sea Frontier

MSG
Message

MSGBN
Marine Security Guard Battalion

MSGCEN
Message Center

MSGDET
Message Detachment

MSGP
Mobile Support Group

MSGR
Mobile Support Group

MSGT
Master Sergeant

MSH
Mine Hunter (ship)

MSI
Medium Scale Integration
Minesweeper, Inshore

MSIIP
Missile Systems Installation Interruption for Parts

MSIO
Mass Storage Input/Output (system)

MSIR
Master Stock Item Record

MSL
Master Slave Unit
Mean Sea Level
Minesweeping Launch
Missile

MSLP
Mean Sea Level Pressure

MSM
Medium Minesweeper
Meritorious Service Medal

MS/MS
Mutual Security/Military Sales

MSN
Military Service Number
Mission

MSNAP
Merchant Ship Naval Auxiliary Program

MSNCDRFAIRECONRON
Mission Commander, Fleet Air Reconnaissance Squadron

MSN/SSN
Military Service Number/Social Security Number

MSO
Maintenance Support Office
Mineswpeeper, Ocean (Non-Magnetic)

MSOP
Measurement System Operating Procedure

MSP
Maintenance Support Package
Medium-Speed Printer
Minesweeper, Patrol
Multi-Purpose Semi-Submersible Platform

MSPFW
Multi-Shot Portable Flame Weapon

MSPO
Military Support Planning Officers

MSR
Main Supply Route
Management Summary Report
Master Stock Records
Material Status Report
Missile Site Radar
Monthly Status Report

MS/RM
Manned Storage/Retrieval Machine

MSRT
Mean Supply Response Time

MSS
Manager, System Safety
Military Supply Standard
Minesweeper, Special
Moored Surveillance System

Multiple Secondaries and Selection

MSSA
Mess Management Specialist Seaman Apprentice
Military Subsistence Supply Agency

MSSC
Medium SEAL Support Craft

MSSG
Management System Steering Group
Marine Amphibious Unit Service Support Group

MSSN
Mess Management Specialist Seaman

MST
Missile Supply Standard
Missile System Test
Mobile Service Tower

MSTP
Management Specialist Trainee Program

MSTS
Maritime Sea Transport System

MSU
Material Salvage Unit
Message-Switching Unit

MSV
Main Sea Water

M/T
Measurement Ton

MT
Magnetic Particle Test
Manufacturing Technology
Maritime Tropical (air mass)
Megaton
Military Transport
Missile Technician
Motor Transport
Mount

MT1
Missile Technician First Class

MT2
Missile Technician Second Class

MT3
Missile Technician Third Class

MTA
Military Airlift Command Transportation Authorization
Military Technical Advisor
Minimum Terrain Clearance
Minor Task Authorization

MTAG
Manufacturing Technology Advisory Group

MTB
Maintenance of True Bearing
Marine Test Boat
Motor Torpedo Boat

MTBCM
Mean Time Between Corrective Maintenance

MTBER
Mean Time Between Engine Removal

MTBF
Mean Time Between Failures

MTBMA
Mean Time Between Maintenance Actions

MTBN
Motor Transport Battalion

MTBPER
Mean Time Between Permanent Engine Removal

MTC
Chief Missile Technician
Military Terminal Control

MTCA
Military Terminal Control Area

MTCM
Master Chief Missile Technician

MTCS
Senior Chief Missile Technician

MTD
Maintenance Training Department
Mobile Target Division
Moving Target Division

MTDS
Marine Corps Tactical Data System
Maritime Tactical Data System

MTDT
Magnetic Tape Data Terminal

MTE
Multisystem Test Equipment

MTF
Mechanized Time Fuze
Mechanized Type Fuze
Medical Treatment Facility
Message Text Format

MTFI
Mean Time to Fault Isolate

MTGA
Mean Time to Gain Access

MTI
Moving-Target Indicator

MTIS
Material Turned in to Stock
Material Turned in to Store

MTK
Medium Tank

MTL
Maintenance Test Logic
Mean Tide Level

MTM
Methods Time Measurements

MTMAINTCO
Motor Maintenance Company

MTMTS
Military Traffic Management and Terminal Services

MTMTS-TSP
Military Traffic Management and Terminal Service Transportation Strike Plan

MTNS
Metal Thick Nitrite Semiconductor

MTO
Medical Transport Officer
Mission, Task, Objective

MTOAL
Mobilization Table of Allowance Listing

MTP
Master Typography Program
Multipoint

MTPM
Mean Time to Provide Manpower

MTR
Manpower Training and Recruitment
Mean Time to Restore
Missile Tracking Radar
Motor

MTRE
Missile Test and Readiness Equipment

MTS
Master Training Specialist
Missile Test Set

MTSA
Missile Technician Seaman Apprentice

MTSN
Missile Technician Seaman

MTST
Meter Test (NNSS)

MTT
Medical Training Team
Mobile Training Team (Steam Propulsion)

MTTF
Mean Time to Failure

MTTFF
Mean Time to First Failure

MTTR
Mean Time to Repair

MTTRM
Mean Time to Repair Module

MTU
Magnetic Tape Unit
Maintenance Training Unit
Missile Tracking Unit
Mobile Technical Unit
Mobile Training Unit

MTUN
Manual Receiver Tuning Control (NNSS)

MTV
Marginal Terrain Vehicle

MTW
Major Theater War

MTWR
Mean Waiting Time for Supply Replacement

MTX
Military Traffic Expediting

MU
Musician

MU1
Musician First Class

MU2
Musician Second Class

MU3
Musician Third Class

MUACS
Manpower Utilization and Control System

MUC
Chief Musician
Meritorious Unit Commendation

MUCM
Master Chief Musician

MUCS
Senior Chief Musician

MUF
Maximum Usable Frequency

MUL
Master Urgency List

MULTEWS
Multiple-Target Electronic Warfare System

MULTICS
Multiple Information and Computing Service

MULTOTS
Multiple Unit Link-Test and Operational Training System

MULTS
Mobile Universal Link Translator System

MUNBLDG
Munitions Building

MUOS
Mobile User Objective System

MURS
Machine Utilization Reporting System

MUS
Music
Musician

MUS&T
Manned Undersea Science and Technology (NOAA)

MUSA
Musician Seaman Apprentice

MUSE
Mobile Utilities Support Equipment

MUSEDET
Mobile Utilities Support Equipment Detachment

MUSG
Machine Utilization Report Generator

MUSN
Musician Seaman

MUST
Manned Undersea Science and Technology (NOAA)
Medical Unit, Self-Contained, Transportable
Medical Unit Surgical Team

MUTR
Makai Undersea Test Range

MUX
Multiplexing

MUXIC
Multiplex/Multiple Voice Interior Communications (system)

M/V
Merchant Vessel

MV
Motor Vehicle Mishap (report)
Motor Vessel

MVDF
Direction Finder (Medium and Very High Frequency)

MVFR
Marginal Visual Flight Rules

MVI
Maximum Visual Impact
Merchant Vessel Inspection (Division)

MVO
Money Value Only

MW
Music of the World (AFRTS)

MW&R
Morale, Welfare, and Recreation

MWB
Motor Whaleboat

MWBS
Manufacturing Work Breakdown Structure

MWCS
Marine Wing Communications Squadron

MWDDEA
Mutual Weapons Development Data Exchange Agreement

MWDDEP
Mutual Weapons Development Data Exchange Program

MWE
Mega-Watts Electrical

MWFCS
Multiweapons Fire Control System

MWHS
Marine Wing Headquarters Squadron

MWHSDET
Marine Wing Headquarters Squadron Detachment

MWL
Mean Water Level

MWO
Meteorological Watch Office
Modified Work Order

MWP
Management Work Package

MWR
Morale, Welfare, and Recreation (department, division, or funds)

MWSG
Marine Wing Support Group

MWSGDET
Marine Wing Support Group Detachment

MWWU
Marine Wing Weapons Unit

MY
May
Multi-Year
My

MYDIS
My Dispatch

MYLTR
My Letter

MYMGM
My Mailgram

MYMSG
My Message

MYP
Multi-Year Procurement

MYRAD
My Radio

MYSER
My Serial

MYSPDLTR
My Speedletter

MYTEL
My Telegram

N

N
Naturalization
Navigation (NAO code)
Navy
North
Northern
Nuclear-power

N&MCM
Navy and Marine Corps Medal

N779
Director of Submarine Training

N78
Air Warfare Division, Office of the Chief of Naval Operations

N79
OPNAV code designating the Director of Navy Training

N/A
Not Applicable
Not Available

NA
National Archives
Naval Academy
Naval Air
Naval Attaché
Naval Aviator
North America
Not Applicable

Not Authorized
Not Available

NAA
Naval Attaché for Air

NAAF
Naval Auxiliary Air Field

NAALS
Naval Air Traffic Control and Air Navigation Aids and Landing System

NAAO
Navy Area Audit Office

NAAS
Navy Area Audit Service
Navy Auxiliary Air Station

NAASW
Non-Acoustic Antisubmarine Warfare

NAB
Naval Advanced Base
Naval Air Base
Naval Amphibious Base

NABA
Naval Amphibious Base Annex

NABPARS
Navy Automatic Broadcasting Processing and Routing System

NABS
Nuclear-Armed Bombardment Satellite

NABTC
Naval Air Basic Training Command

NABTRACOM
Naval Air Basic Training Command

NABU
Naval Advanced Base Unit

NAC
National Agency Check
Naval Academy
Navy Activity Control
Naval Air Center
Navy Advanced Concepts

NACAL
Navy Art Cooperation and Liaison

NACF
New Air Combat Fighter

NACIO
Naval Air Combat Information Office/Officer

NACIS
Naval Air Combat Information School

NACO
National Advisory Committee for Oceans (NOAA)
Navy Cool (propellant)

NACOA
National Advisory Committee on Oceans and Atmosphere (NOAA)

NACOMIS
Naval Aviation Logistics Command Management Information System

NACSB
Naval Aviation Cadet Selection Board

NACTU
Naval Attack Combat Training Unit

NAD
Naval Air Depot
Naval Air Detachment
Naval Air Detail
Naval Ammunition Depot

NADC
Naval Air Development Center

NADC/ACEL
Naval Air Development Center/Aerospace Crew Equipment Laboratory

NADC/ACL
Naval Air Development Center/Aeronautical Computer Laboratory

NADC/ASL
Naval Air Development Center/Aeronautical Structures Laboratory

NADC/ED
Naval Air Development Center/Engineering Development Laboratory

NADEC
Navy Decision Center

NADEP
Naval Ammunition Depot
Naval Aviation Depot

NADGE
NATO Air Defense Ground Equipment (project)

NADL
Naval Authorized Data List

NADL/AML
Naval Air Development Center/Aeronautical Materials Laboratory

NAD-LLL
Naval Ammunition Depot-Lwalualei (HI)

NADM
Naval Administration

NADO
Navy Accounts Disbursing Office

NADOP
North American Defense Operational Plan

NADPHRS
Naval Ammunition Depot Hawthorne Police Records System

NADU
Naval Aircraft Delivery Unit

NAEB
Naval Aviation Evaluation Board

NAEC
Naval Air Engineering Center

NAECFO
Naval Engineering Center Field Office

NAEL
Naval Air Engineering Laboratory

NAEL(SI)
Naval Air Engineering Laboratory (Ships Installation)

NAES
Naval Air Experimental Station

NAESU
Naval Aviation Engineering Services Unit

NAESUDET
Naval Aviation Engineering Service Unit Detachment

NAF
Naval Aircraft Factory
Naval Air Facility
Non-Appropriated Funds

NAFAS
Non-Appropriated Funds Accounting System

NAFC
Naval Air Ferry Command
Navy Accounting and Finance Center

NAFEC
National Aviation Facilities Experimental Center

NAFI
Naval Air Fighting Instructions
Naval Avionics Facility, Indianapolis, (IN)
Non-Appropriated Funds Instrumentalities

NAFL
Naval Air Force, Atlantic

NAFMC
Non-Appropriated Funds, Marine Corps

NAFP
Naval Air Force, Pacific

NAFS
Naval Air Fighter School

NAFSA
No American Flag Shipping Available

NAG
Naval Advisory Group
Navy Astronautics Group

NAGARD
NATO Advisory Group for Aeronautical Research and Development

NAGC
Naval Armed Guard Center

NAGCO
Naval Air-Ground Center Office

NAGS
Naval Air Gunner's School

NAICOM/MIS
Navy Integrated Command Management Information System

NAILSC
Naval Aviation Integrated Logistic Support Center

NAIMIS
NAVAIRSYSCOM Integrated Management Information System

NAIRU
Naval Air Reserve Intelligence Unit

NAIS
Navy Attitudinal Information System

NAIT
Naval Air Intermediate Training

NAIT(C)
Naval Air Intermediate Training (Command)

NALC
Navy Ammunition Logistics Code

NALCO
Naval Air Logistics Control Office

NALCOEASTPAC
Naval Air Logistics Control Office, Eastern Pacific

NALCOEURREP
Naval Air Logistics Control Office, European Representative

NALCOLANT
Naval Air Logistics Control Office, Atlantic

NALCOMIS
Naval Air Logistics Command Management Information System

NALCOMIS-OS
Naval Air Logistics Command Management Information System for Operating and Support

NALCOPAC
Naval Air Logistics Control Office, Pacific

NALCOPACREP
Naval Air Logistics Control Office, Pacific Representative

NALCOREP
Naval Air Logistics Control Office Representative

NALCOWESTPAC
Naval Air Logistics Control Office, Western Pacific

NALCOWESTPACREP
Naval Air Logistics Control Office, Western Pacific Representative

NALF
Naval Auxiliary Landing Facility
Naval Auxiliary Landing Field

NALO
Naval Air Liaison Office/Officer

NALSS
Naval Advanced Logistics Support Site

NALTS
National Advertising Lead Tracking System

NAM
Naval Aircraft Modification
Navy and Marine Corps Achievement Medal
North America

NAMA
Naval Aeronautical Material Area

NAMAINTRADET
Naval Air Maintenance Training Detachment

NAMAINTRAGRU
Naval Air Maintenance Training Group

NAMAINTRAGRUDET
Naval Air Maintenance Training Group Detachment

NAMAPUS
Naval Assistant to the Military Aide to the President of the United States

NAMARA
Navy and Marine Corps Appellate Review Activity

NAMB
Naval Amphibious Base

NAMC
Naval Air and Material Center

NAMD
Naval Ammunition Depot

NAMDDU
Naval Air Mine Defense Development Unit

NAMDI
National Marine Data Inventory

NAMDRP
Naval Aviation Maintenance Discrepancy Reporting Program

NAMEDCEN
Naval Aviation Medical Center

NAMESAKES
Naval Aviators Must Energetically Sell Aviation to Keep Effective Strength

NAMF
Naval Aviation Museum Foundation

NAMFI
NATO Missile Firing Installation

NAMI
Naval Aerospace Medical Institute

NAMMOS
Navy Manpower Mobilization System

NAMO
Naval Aircraft Maintenance Orders

NAMP
Naval Aviation Maintenance Program

NAMPS
Naval Manpower Planning System

NAMRI
Naval Aerospace Medical Research Institute

NAMRL
Naval Aerospace Medical Research Laboratory

NAMRU
Navy Medical Research Unit

NAMS
Naval Amphibious School

NAMSO
Naval Maintenance Support Office

NAMT
Naval Aircraft Mobile Trainer
Naval Air Maintenance Trainer

NAMTD
Naval Air Maintenance Training Detachment

NAMTG
Naval Air Maintenance Training Group

NAMTGD
Naval Air Maintenance Training Group Detachment

NAMTRADET
Naval Air Maintenance Training Detachment

NAMTRAGRU
Naval Air Maintenance Training Group

NAMTRATCLOFLT
Naval Air Maintenance Training Type Commander Liaison Office, Fleet

NAMTRATCLOLANT
Naval Air Maintenance Training Type Commander Liaison Office, Atlantic

NAMTRATCLOPAC
Naval Air Maintenance Training Type Commander Liaison Office, Pacific

NAMTS
Navy Afloat Maintenance Training Strategy

NAMU
Naval Aircraft Material (Utility)
Naval Aircraft Modification Unit

NANCF
North Atlantic Naval Coastal Frontier

NANEWS
Naval Aviation News (magazine)

NANFAC
Naval Air Navigation Facility Advisory Committee

NANFORMS
Naval Aviator/Naval Flight Officer Reporting Management System

NANS
Naval Air Navigation School

NANWEP
Navy Numerical Weather Problems Group

NAO
Naval Audit Office
Naval Aviation Observer

NAOC
Naval Aviation Officer Candidate

NAORPG
North Atlantic Ocean Regional Planning Group

NAOT
Naval Air Operational Training

NAOTC
Naval Air Operational Training Center

NAOTS
Naval Aviation Ordnance Test Station

NAP
Naval Academy Preparatory
Inf: Naval Airplane Pusher
Naval Air Priorities
Naval Aviation Pilot

NAPC
Naval Air Photographic Center
Naval Air Priorities Center
Naval Air Propulsion Center

NAPEC
Naval Ammunition Production Engineering

Center

NAPF
Non-Appropriated Funds

NAPI
Naval Aeronautical Publications Index

NAPOG
Naval Airborne Project PRESS (Pacific Range Electromagnetic Signature Studies) Operations Group

NAPP
Naval Aviation Preparatory Program

NAPS
Naval Academy Preparatory School
Naval Academy Primary School
Naval Auxiliary Publications Service

NAPSAC
Naval Atomic Planning, Support, and Capabilities

NAPT
Naval Air Primary Training

NAPT(C)
Naval Air Primary Training (Command)

NAPTC
Naval Air Propulsion Test Center

NAPTCRO
Naval Air Primary Training Command Regional Office

NAPUS
Nuclear Auxiliary Power Unit System

NAR
Naval Air Reserve
Naval Ammunition Reclassification
Notice of Ammunition Reclassification
Numerical Analysis Research

NARAD
Naval Air Research and Development

NARANEXOS
Name, Rate, Social Security Number, and Expiration of Obligated Service

NARANO
Name, Rate, and Social Security Number

NARASPO
Naval Regional Airspace Officer

NARB
Navy Art Review Board

NARC
Naval Air Research Center
Naval Alcohol Rehabilitation Center

NARD
Navy Alcohol Rehabilitation Drydock

NARDAC
Navy Regional Data Automation Center

NARDACWASHDC
Navy Regional Data Automation Center, Washington, District of Columbia

NARDET
Naval Air Reserve Detachment

NARDIS
Navy Automated Research and Development Information System

NARDIV(FA)
Naval Air Reserve Division (Fleet Air)

NAREC
Naval Research Electronic Computer

NARESTRACOM
Naval Air Reserve Training Command

NARESU
Naval Air Reserve Unit

NARETU
Naval Air Reserve Electronics Training Unit

NARF
Naval Air Rework Facility
Navy Aerospace Recovery Facility

NARFFO
Naval Air Rework Facility Field Office

NARFO
Naval Air Rework Facility Office

NARFS
Naval Air Reserve Force Squadron

NARL
Naval Arctic Research Laboratory (ONR)

NARM
Naval Resource Model

NARMC
Naval Aerospace Medical Center

NARMPU
Naval Air Reserve Mobile Photographic Unit

NARMU
Naval Air Reserve Maintenance Unit

NARS
National Archives and Records Service
Naval Air Reserve Staff

NARSTC
Naval Air Rescue Service Training Command

NARTC
Naval Air Reserve Training Command

NARTS
Naval Air Rocket Test Station

NARTU
Naval Air Rescue Training Unit

NARU
Naval Air Reserve Unit

NAS
National Aeronautical Studies
National Aerospace System
Naval Aircraft Standard
Naval Air Station
Naval Audit Service
NSA and APA Items for Stateside Shipment

NASA
National Aeronautics and Space Administration

NASANX
Naval Air Station Annex

NASAP
Navy Alcohol Safety Action Program

NASAPOFF
Navy Alcohol Safety Action Program Office

NASC
Naval Air Systems Command
Naval Aviation Schools Command
Navy Aircraft Standards Committee
Navy AUTODIN Switching Center

NASC FS
Naval Air Systems Command Fleet Support

NASCOM
NASA Communications

NASCRU
Naval Air Systems Command Reserve Unit

NASD
Naval Air Supply Depot

NASDT
Naval Aviators' Speed Discrimination Test

NASEAB
Naval Air Systems Effectiveness Advisory Board

NASIB
Naval Air Station, Imperial Beach (CA)

NASL
Naval Air Station, Lemoore (CA)
Naval Applied Sciences Laboratory

NASLEM
Naval Air Station, Lemoore (CA)

NASMAGS
Naval Air Station Magazines

NASNI
Naval Air Station, North Island (CA)

NASO
National Aeronautics and Space Observatory
Naval Aviation Supply Office

NASP
Naval Air Survivability Program

NASRU
Naval Air Systems Command Reserve Unit

NASS
Naval Air Signal School

NASSIG
Naval Air Station Sigonella

NASTAD
Naval Acoustic Sensor Training Aids Department

NASTC
Naval Air Station, Twin Cities (MN)

NASU
Naval Air Support Unit

NAT
National
Natural
Naval Air Terminal
Naval Air Training
Naval Anthropomorphic Teleoperator
Navigational Aids Technician
North Atlantic

NATB
Naval Air Training Base

NATBASE
Naval Air Training Base

NATC
Naval Air Test Center
Naval Air Training Command

NATCO
Naval Air Traffic Coordinating Office

NATDEC
Naval Air Training Division Engineering Command

NATDS
Navy Automated Transportation Data System

NATEC
Naval Air Training and Experimental Command

NATECHTRA
Naval Air Technical Training

NATECHTRACEN
Naval Air Technical Training Center

NATECHTRAU
Naval Air Technical Training Unit

NATF(SI)
Naval Air Test Facility (Ships Installation)

NATIP
Navy Technical Information Program

NATL
National

NATMILCOMSYS
National Military Commands System

NATNAVDENCEN
National Naval Dental Center

NATNAVMEDCEN
National Naval Medical Center

NATNAVRESMASTCONRADSTA
National Naval Reserve Master Control Radio Station

NATO
North Atlantic Treaty Organization

NATODC
North Atlantic Treaty Organization Defense College

NATOPS
Naval Air Training and Operating Procedures Standardization

NATRA
Naval Air Training Command

NATRACOM
Naval Air Training Command

NATRADIVENGCOM
Naval Air Training Division Engineering Command

NATRI
Naval Training Requirements Information

NATSF
Naval Air Technical Services Facility

NATSFQADIVLANT
Naval Air Technical Services Facility Quality Assurance Division, Atlantic

NATSFQADIVPAC
Naval Air Technical Services Facility Quality Assurance Division, Pacific

NATT
Naval Air Technical Training

NATTC
Naval Air Technical Training Center

NATTCDET
Naval Air Technical Training Center Detachment

NATTCL
Naval Air Technical Training Center, Lakehurst (NJ)

NATTS
Naval Air Turbine Test Station

NATTS/ATL
Naval Air Turbine Test Station/Aeronautical Turbine Laboratory

NATTU
Naval Air Technical Training Unit

NATU
Naval Air Training Unit

NATUS
Naturalized United States Citizen

NATW
National War College

NATWARCOL
National War College

NAU
Naval Administration Unit

NAUT
Nautical

NAUTO
Nautophone

NAUWS
Naval Advanced Undersea Weapons School

NAV
Naval
Navigation
Navy

NAVABSCOLLU
Navy Absentee Collection Unit

NAVACCTGFINCEN
Navy Accounting and Finance Center

NAVACD
Naval Academy

NAVACT
Naval Activities

NAVACTDET
Naval Activities Detachment

NAVADGRU
Naval Administrative Group

NAV-ADMIN
Navigation-Administration

NAVADMINCOM
Naval Administrative Command

NAVADMINO
Navy Administrative Office/Officer

NAVADMINU
Naval Administration Unit

NAVADMINUANX
Naval Administrative Unit Annex

NAVADS
Navy Automated Transport Documentation System

NAVADUNSEAWPNSCOL
Naval Advanced Undersea Weapons School

NAVAERAUDOFC
Navy Area Audit Office

NAVAERAUDSERV
Navy Area Audit Service

NAVAERO(SP)MEDINST
Naval Aerospace Medical Institute

NAVAERO(SP)MEDRSCHINST
Naval Aerospace Medical Research Institute

NAVAERO(SP)MEDRSCHINSTLAB
Naval Aerospace Medical Research Institute Laboratory

NAVAERO(SP)MEDRSCHLAB
Naval Aerospace Medical Research Laboratory

NAVAERO(SP)MEDRSCHLABDET
Naval Aerospace Medical Research Laboratory Detachment

NAVAERO(SP)RECFAC
Naval Aerospace Recovery Facility

NAVAEROSPRECFAC
Navy Aerospace Recovery Facility

NAVAERO(SP)REGMEDCEN
Naval Aerospace Medical Center

NAVAID
Naval Aid

NAVAIDS
Navigational Aids

NAVAIDSUPPUNIT
Navigational Aids Support Unit

NAVAIR
Naval Air Systems Command

NAVAIRBASICTRACOM
Naval Air Basic Training Command

NAVAIRDEVCEN
Naval Air Development Center

NAVAIRENGCEN
Naval Air Engineering Center

NAVAIRENGCENFO
Naval Air Engineering Center Field Office

NAVAIRENGLAB
Naval Air Engineering Laboratory

NAVAIRENGRCEN
Naval Engineering Center

NAVAIRENGRCENFO
Naval Engineering Center Field Office

NAVAIRESCEN
Naval Air Research Center

NAVAIRESFORRON
Naval Air Reserve Force Squadron

NAVAIRESMOPIXU
Naval Air Reserve Mobile Photographic Unit

NAVAIRESTRAU
Naval Air Rescue Training Unit

NAVAIRESU
Naval Air Reserve Unit

NAVAIREWORKFACOFF
Naval Air Rework Facility Office

NAVAIRFAC
Naval Air Facility

NAVAIRLANT
Naval Air Force, Atlantic

NAVAIRLOGOFF
Naval Air Logistics Office

NAVAIRLOGTASKFORREP
Naval Air Logistics Task Force Representative

NAVAIRMAINTRADET
Naval Air Maintenance Training Detachment

NAVAIRMAINTRAGRU
Naval Air Maintenance Training Group

NAVAIRMINDEFDEVU
Naval Air Mine Defense Development Unit

NAVAIRMINEDEFDEVU
Navy Air Mine Defense Development Unit

NAVAIRNEWS
Naval Aviation News (magazine)

NAVAIRPAC
Naval Air Force, Pacific

NAVAIRPROPCEN
Naval Air Propulsion Center

NAVAIRPROPTESTCEN
Naval Air Propulsion Test Center

NAVAIRREWORKFAC
Naval Air Rework Facility

NAVAIRREWORKFACFO
Naval Air Rework Facility Field Office

NAVAIRSTA
Naval Air Station

NAVAIRSUPPU
Naval Air Support Unit

NAVAIRSYSCOM
Naval Air Systems Command

NAVAIRSYSCOMFLEREADREP
Naval Air Systems Command Fleet Readiness Representative

NAVAIRSYSCOMFLESUPREPCEN
Naval Air Systems Command Fleet Supply Representative Center

NAVAIRSYSCOMHQ
Naval Air Systems Command Headquarters

NAVAIRSYSCOMMETSYSDIV
Naval Air Systems Command Meteorological Systems Division

NAVAIRSYSCOMREP
Naval Air Systems Command Representative

NAVAIRSYSCOMREPLANT
Naval Air Systems Command Representative, Atlantic

NAVAIRSYSCOMREPPAC
Naval Air Systems Command Representative, Pacific

NAVAIRSYSCOMREPPNCLA
Naval Air Systems Command Representative, Pensacola (FL)

NAVAIRSYSCOMTARANDSYSDIV
Naval Air Systems Command Target and Range Systems Command

NAVAIRTECHREP
Naval Air Systems Command Technical Representative

NAVAIRTECHSERVFAC
Naval Air Technical Services Facility

NAVAIRTERM
Naval Air Terminal

NAVAIRTESTCEN
Naval Air Test Center

NAVAIRTESTFAC(SHIPINSTAL)
Naval Air Test Facility (Ships Installation)

NAVAIRTRACEN
Naval Air Training Center

NAVAIRTU
Naval Air Training Unit

NAVAIRWARCEN
Naval Air Warfare Center

NAVALREHCEN
Naval Alcohol Rehabilitation Center

NAVALREHDRYDOCK
Navy Alcohol Rehabilitation Drydock

NAVALT
Naval Alteration

NAVAMMODEP
Naval Ammunition Depot

NAVAMPROENGCEN
Naval Ammunition Production Engineering Center

NAVAPSCIENCLAB
Naval Applied Sciences Laboratory

NAVAPSCIENLAB
Naval Applied Sciences Laboratory

NAVARA
Naval Appellate Review Activity

NAVAREAUDOFC
Navy Area Audit Office

NAVAREAUDSERV
Navy Area Audit Service

NAVAREAUDSVC
Naval Area Audit Service

NAVASO
Naval Aviation Supply Office

NAVASTRGRU
Navy Astronautics Group

NAVASTROGRU
Naval Astronautics Group

NAVASTROGRUHQTRINJFAC
Naval Astronautics Group Headquarters, Tracking and Injection Facility

NAVASWDATCEN
Navy Antisubmarine Warfare Data Center

NAVAUDO
Navy Audit Office

NAVAUDODINSCEN
Navy AUTODIN Switching Center

NAVAUDSVC
Naval Audit Service

NAVAUDSVCAP
Naval Audit Service, Capital Area

NAVAUDSVCHQ
Naval Audit Service Headquarters

NAVAUDSVCNE
Naval Audit Service, Northeast Area

NAVAUDSVCSE
Naval Audit Service, Southeast Area

NAVAUDSVCWEST
Naval Audit Service, Western Area

NAVAUTODINSCEN
Navy AUTODIN Switching Center

NAVAVCEN
Naval Audio-Visual Center

NAVAVENGSERVU
Naval Aviation Engineering Services Unit

NAVAVENGSERVUDET
Naval Aviation Engineering Service Unit Detachment

NAVAVIONICSCEN
Naval Avionics Center

NAVAVIONICSFAC
Naval Avionics Facility

NAVAVMEDCEN
Naval Aviation Medical Center

NAVAVMUSEUM
Naval Aviation Museum

NAVAVNENGRSERVU
Naval Aviation Engineering Service Unit

NAVAVNLOGCEN
Naval Aviation Logistics Center

NAVAVNLOGCENDET
Naval Aviation Logistics Center Detachment

NAVAVNLOGCENFSO
Naval Aviation Logistics Center Field Services Office

NAVAVNLOGCENMETALABOPS
Naval Aviation Logistics Center Meteorology Calibration Laboratory Operations

NAVAVNMEDCEN
Naval Aviation Medical Center

NAVAVNWPNSFAC
Naval Aviation Weapons Facility Detachment

NAVAVNWPNSFACDET
Naval Aviation Weapons Facility Detachment

NAVAVSCOLSCOM
Naval Aviation Schools Command

NAVBASE
Naval Base

NAVBCHGRU
Naval Beach Group

NAVBCHPHIBREFTRAGRU
Naval Beach Amphibious Refresher Training Group

NAVBCSTSVCDET
Navy Broadcasting Service Detachment

NAVBCSTSVCDET TASA
Navy Broadcasting Service Detachment Television Audio Support Activity

NAVBCSTSVCWASHDC
Navy Broadcasting Service, Washington, District of Columbia

NAVBEACHGRU
Naval Beach Group

NAVBIODYNLAB
Naval Biodynamics Laboratory

NAVBIOLAB
Navy Biological Laboratory (ONR)

NAVBIOSCILAB
Naval Biosciences Research Laboratory

NAVC
Naval Audio-Visual Center
Naval Aviation Cadet

NAVCAD
Naval Aviation Cadet

NAVCALAB
Navy Calibration Laboratory

NAVCALABANX
Navy Calibration Laboratory Annex

NAVCALABMSG
Navy Calibration Laboratory Meteorology Support Group

NAVCALABOPS
Navy Calibration Laboratory Operations

NAVCALS
Naval Communications Area Local Station

NAVCAMS
Naval Communication Area Master Station

NAVCAMSEASTPAC
Naval Communication Area Master Station, Eastern Pacific

NAVCAMSLANT
Naval Communication Area Master Station, Atlantic

NAVCAMSMED
Naval Communication Area Master Station, Mediterranean

NAVCAMSOAM
Naval Communication Area Master Station, South America

NAVCAMSSPECCOMMDIVEASTPAC
Naval Communication Area Master Station, Special Communications Division, Eastern Pacific

NAVCAMSSPECCOMMDIVLANT
Naval Communication Area Master Station, Special Communications Division, Atlantic

NAVCAMSSPECCOMMDIVWESTPAC
Naval Communication Area Master Station, Special Communications Division, Western Pacific

NAVCAMSWESTPAC
Naval Communication Area Master Station, Western Pacific

NAVCAMSWESTPACRCVRSITE
Naval Communication Area Master Station, Western Pacific Receiver Site

NAVCAP
Naval Combat Air Patrol

NAVCARGOHANBN
Naval Cargo Handling Battalion

NAVCBCEN
Naval Construction Battalion Center

NAVCHAPGRU
Navy Cargo Handling and Port Group

NAVCHAPGRUDET
Navy Cargo Handling and Port Group Detachment

NAVCINTSUPPACT
Navy Counterintelligence Support Activity

NAVCINTSUPPCEN
Navy Counterintelligence Support Center

NAVCINTSUPPGRU
Navy Counterintelligence Support Group

NAVCIVENGLAB
Navy Civil Engineering Laboratory

NAVCLODEP
Naval Clothing Depot

NAVCLOTEXTOFC
Navy Clothing and Textile Office

NAVCLOTEXTRSCHFAC
Navy Clothing and Textile Research Facility

NAVCLOTHTEXOFC
Navy Clothing and Textile Office

NAVCM
Navigation Countermeasures

NAVCOASTSYSCEN
Naval Coastal Systems Center

NAVCOMMDET
Naval Communication Station Detachment

NAVCOMMDETSPECCOMMDIV
Naval Communication Station Detachment, Special Communications Division

NAVCOMMHQ
Naval Communications Headquarters

NAVCOMMOPNET
Naval Communications Operation Network

NAVCOMMSTA
Naval Communication Station

NAVCOMMSTASPECCOMMDIV
Naval Communication Station, Special Communications Division

NAVCOMMSYSHQ
Naval Communications System Headquarters

NAVCOMMSYSSUPPACT
Naval Communications System Support Activity

NAVCOMMTRACEN
Naval Communications Training Center

NAVCOMMU
Naval Communication Unit
Navigation Computer Unit

NAVCOMPARS
Naval Communications Processing and Receiving Station
Navy Automated Message Processing System

NAVCOMPT
Comptroller of the Navy

NAVCOMSTA
Naval Communications Station

NAVCOMSYSSUPPACT
Naval Command Systems Support Activity

NAVCOMSYSSUPPCEN
Naval Command Systems Support Center

NAVCOMSYSTO
Navy Commissary Store

NAVCOMSYSUPPACT
Naval Command Systems Support Activity

NAVCOMSYSUPPCEN
Naval Command Systems Support Center

NAVCON
Naval Schools, Construction

NAVCONSTBAT
Naval Construction Battalion

NAVCONSTRACEN
Naval Construction Training Center

NAVCONSTRAU
Naval Construction Training Unit

NAVCONSTREGT
Naval Construction Regiment

NAVCONTDEP
Navy Contracting Department

NAVCONVHOSP
Naval Convalescent Hospital

NAVCORCOURSECEN
Naval Correspondence Course Center

NAVCORRCUSUNIT
Navy Correctional Custody Unit

NAVCOSSACT
Naval Command Systems Support Activity

NAVCOSSCEN
Naval Command Systems Support Center

NAVCRUITAREA
Navy Recruiting Area

NAVCRUITBRSTA
Navy Recruiting Branch Station

NAVCRUITCOM
Navy Recruiting Command

NAVCRUITCOMORIENTUNIT
Navy Recruiting Command Orientation Unit

NAVCRUITCOMSAT
Navy Recruiting Command Standardization and Audit Team

NAVCRUITCOMYPFLDREP
Navy Recruiting Command Youth Programs Field Representative

NAVCRUITDIST
Navy Recruiting District

NAVCRUITEXHIBCEN
Navy Recruiting Exhibit Center

NAVCRUITEXHIBCENCAT
Navy Recruiting Exhibit Center Catalog

NAVCRUITRACOM
Navy Recruiting Training Command

NAVCRUITSTA
Navy Recruiting Station

NAVCURRSUPPGRULANTFLT
Naval Current Support Group, Atlantic Fleet

NAVCURRSUPPGRUNAVEUR
Naval Current Support Group, Naval Forces, Europe

NAVCURRSUPPGRUPACFLT
Naval Current Support Group, Pacific Fleet

NAVCURSERVDET
Naval Courier Service Detachment

NAVDAC
Navigation Data Assimilation Computer

NAVDAMCONTRACEN
Navy Damage Control Training Center

NAVDATACEN
Naval Data Center

NAVDEFEASTPAC
Naval Defense Forces, Eastern Pacific

NAVDEGSTA
Navy Degaussing Station

NAVDENCEN
Naval Dental Center

NAVDENCLINIC
Naval Dental Clinic

NAVDENSCOL
Navy Dental School

NAVDENTECHSCOL
Navy Dental Technician School

NAVDEPDIRABRES
Navy Deputy Director Advanced Ballistic Reentry Systems Division

NAVDEPNOAA
Naval Deputy National Oceanic and Atmospheric Administration

NAVDEPT
Navy Department

NAVDET
Naval Detachment

NAVDISBAR
Navy Disciplinary Barracks

NAVDISCOM
Navy Disciplinary Command

NAVDISEASEVECTORCONCEN
Navy Disease Vector Control Center

NAVDISP
Naval Dispensary

NAVDIST
Naval District

NAVDISVECTECOLCONCEN
Navy Disease Vector Ecology and Control Center

NAVDIVSALTRACEN
Naval Diving and Salvage Training Center

NAVDIVSALVTRACEN
Naval Diving and Salvage Training Center

NAVDRUGREHCEN
Naval Drug Rehabilitation Center

NAVEARB
Navy Employee Appeals Review Board

NAVEASTOCEANCEN
Naval Eastern Oceanography Center

NAVEDTRA
Naval Education and Training

NAVEDTRACEN
Naval Education and Training Center

NAVEDTRACOM
Naval Education and Training Command

NAVEDTRAPRODEVCEN
Naval Education and Training Program Development Center

NAVEDTRAPRODEVCENCODIV
Naval Education and Training Program Development Center Coordination Division

NAVEDTRAPRODEVCENDET
Naval Education and Training Program Development Center Detachment

NAVEDTRAPROGDEVCEN
Naval Education and Training Program Development Center

NAVEDTRASUPPCEN
Naval Education and Training Support Center

NAVEDTRASUPPCENLANT
Naval Education and Training Support Center, Atlantic

NAVEDTRASUPPCENPAC
Naval Education and Training Program Development Center, Pacific

NAVEDTRASUPPCENPACNCFA
Naval Education and Training Program Development Center, Pacific, Navy Campus for Achievement

NAVELECSYSCOM
Naval Electronic Systems Command

NAVELECSYSCOMHQ
Naval Electronic Systems Command Headquarters

NAVELEM
Navy Element

NAVELEX
Naval Electronic Systems Command

NAVELEXACTS
Naval Electronic Systems Command Activities

NAVELEXDET
Naval Electronic Systems Command Detachment

NAVELEXENGOFF
Naval Electronic Engineering Office

NAVELEXSYSCOM
Naval Electronic Systems Command

NAVELEXSYSCOMDIV
Naval Electronic Systems Command Division

NAVELEXSYSCOMENGCEN
Naval Electronic Systems Command Systems Engineering Center

NAVELEXSYSCOMMIDWESTDIV
Naval Electronic Systems Command, Midwest Division

NAVELEXSYSCOMSEDIV
Naval Electronic Systems Command, Southwest Division

NAVELEXSYSCOMTECHLREP
Naval Electronic Systems Command Technician Liaison Representative

NAVELEXSYSENGCEN
Naval Electronic Systems Engineering Center

NAVELEXSYSTRAPUBMO
Naval Electronic Systems Command Training and Publications Management Office

NAVELEXTECHREP
Naval Electronic Systems Command Technical Representative

NAVEMSCEN
Navy Electromagnetic Spectrum Center

NAVENENVSA
Navy Energy and Environmental Support Activity

NAVENENVSUPPACT
Navy Energy and Environmental Support Activity

NAVENPVNTMEDU
Navy Environmental and Preventive Medicine Unit

NAVENVIRHLTHCEN
Navy Environmental Health Center

NAVENVPREDRSCHFAC
Naval Environmental Prediction Research

NAVENVPVNTMEDU
Navy Environmental and Preventive Medicine Unit

NAVENVRHLTHCEN
Navy Environmental Health Center

NAVENVSUPPCEN
Navy Environmental Support Center

NAVENVSUPPO
Navy Environmental Support Office

NAVEODFAC
Naval Explosive Ordnance Disposal Facility

NAVEODTECHCEN
Naval Explosive Ordnance Disposal Technology Center

NAVETC
Navy Educational Tape Catalog

NAVETOCCOM
Naval Meteorology and Oceanography Command

NAVEUR
Naval Forces, Europe

NAVEURWWMCCS DP
Naval Forces, Europe, Worldwide Military Command Control System Data Processing

NAVEURWWMCCS EMSKD
Naval Forces, Europe, Worldwide Military Command Control System Employment Schedule

NAVEURWWMCCS MOVREP
Naval Forces, Europe, Worldwide Military Command Control System Movement Reports

NAVEURWWMCCS NAVFORSTA
Naval Forces, Europe, Worldwide Military Command Control System Naval Forces Status

NAVEX
Navy Exchange

NAVEXAM
Naval Examining Board

NAVEXAMBD
Naval Examining Board

NAVEXAMCEN
Naval Examining Center

NAVEXAMCENADVAUTHLIST
Naval Examining Center Advancement Authorization List

NAVEXENGLANDCOM
Navy Exchange, England Complex

NAVEXHIBCEN
Naval Exhibit Center

NAVFAC
Naval Facilites

NAVFACCHESDIV
Naval Facilities Engineering Command, Chesapeake Division

NAVFACENGCOM
Naval Facilities Engineering Command

NAVFACENGCOMCHESDIV
Naval Facilities Engineering Command, Chesapeake Division

NAVFACENGCOMCONTR
Naval Facilities Engineering Command Contractor

NAVFACENGCOMHQ
Naval Facilities Engineering Command Headquarters

NAVFACENGCOMLANTDIV
Naval Facilities Engineering Command, Atlantic Division

NAVFACENGCOMNORDIV
Naval Facilities Engineering Command, Northern Division

NAVFACENGCOMPACDIV
Naval Facilities Engineering Command, Pacific Division

NAVFACENGCOMSODIV
Naval Facilities Engineering Command, Southern Division

NAVFACENGCOMWESDIV
Naval Facilities Engineering Command, Western Division

NAVFACENGRCOM
Naval Facilities Engineering Command

NAVFACLANTDIV
Naval Facilities Engineering Command, Atlantic Division

NAVFACNORDIV
Naval Facilities Engineering Command, Northern Division

NAVFACOC
Naval Facility Operational Center

NAVFACPACDIV
Naval Facilities Engineering Command, Pacific Division

NAVFACSODIV

Naval Facilities Engineering Command, Southern Division

NAVFAMALWACT
Navy Family Allowance Activity

NAVFINCEN
Navy Finance Center

NAVFINCEN-CLEVE
Navy Finance Center-Cleveland (OH)

NAVFINCEN-WASH
Navy Finance Center-Washington (DC)

NAVFINOFF
Navy Finance Office

NAVFITWEPSCOL
Navy Fighter Weapons School

NAVFLDINTO
Navy Field Intelligence Office

NAVFLDOPSUPPGRU
Navy Field Operational Support Group

NAVFLITHTDEMORON
Navy Flight Demonstration Squadron

NAVFOODMGTM
Navy Food Management Team

NAVFOODSERVSYSOFC
Naval Food Service Systems Office

NAVFOR
Naval Forces

NAVFOREU
Naval Forces, Europe

NAVFORGER
Naval Forces, Germany

NAVFORJAP(AN)
Naval Forces, Japan

NAVFORKOR
Naval Forces, Korea

NAVFORSTAT
Naval Force Status

NAVFRCOORD
Navy Frequency Coordinator

NAVFROF
Navy Freight Office

NAVFSSO
Navy Food Services Office

NAVFUELDEP
Navy Fuel Depot

NAVFUELSUPO
Navy Fuel Supply Office

NAVGDENSCOL
Naval Graduate Dental School

NAVGEN
Navy General (publications)

NAVGMSCOL
Navy Guided Missile School

NAVGMU
Navy Guided Missile Unit

NAVGRAM
Navy Telegram

NAVGUN
Naval Gun (Factory)

NAVGUNFAC
Naval Gun Factory

NAVHISTCEN
Naval Historical Center

NAVHISTDISPLAYCEN
Navy Historical Display Center

NAVHLTHRSCHCEN
Naval Health Research Center

NAVHLTRSCHCEN
Naval Health Research Center

NAVHOME
(U.S.) Naval Home

NAVHOMERESINFOSYS
Naval Home Resident Information System

NAVHOS
Naval Hospital

NAVHOSINGACT
Naval Housing Activity

NAVHOSP
Naval Hospital

NAVHOSPCORPSCOL
Naval Hospital Corps School

NAVIAR
Naval Air Systems Command

NAVIC
Navy Information Center

NAVICP
Navy Inventory Control Point

NAVIG
Navigation

NAVILCO
Navy International Logistics Control Office

NAVIMAC
Naval Immediate Area Coordinator

NAVINFO
Navy Information Office (CHINFO)

NAVINRELACT
Navy Internal Relations Activity

NAVINSGEN
Navy Inspector General

NAVINTCOM
Naval Intelligence Command

NAVINTEL
Naval Intelligence

NAVINTRELACT
Navy Internal Relations Activity

NAVINTSUPPCEN
Naval Intelligence Support Center

NAVINVSERV
Naval Investigative Service

NAVINVSERVO
Naval Investigative Service Office/Officer

NAVINVSERVOREP
Naval Investigative Service Office Representative

NAVINVSERVRA
Naval Investigative Service Resident Agent

NAVISLO
Naval Interservice Liaison Office

NAVJNTSERVACT
Naval Joint Services Activity

NAVJUSTSCOL
Naval Justice School

NAVLEGSERVOFF
Naval Legal Service Office

NAVLEGSERVOFFDET
Naval Legal Service Office Detachment

NAVLIAGRU
Naval Liaison Group

NAVLINKSTA
Naval Link Station

NAVLIS
Navy Logistics Information System

NAVLOGENGRU
Naval Logistics Engineering Group

NAVLOGSIP
Navy Logistics Support Improvement Plan

NAVLOS
Navy Liaison Officer for Scouting

NAVMAA
Navy Mutual Aid Association

NAVMAC
Navy Manpower Analysis Center

NAVMACLANT
Navy Manpower and Material Analysis Center, Atlantic

NAVMACPAC
Navy Manpower and Material Analysis Center, Pacific

NAVMAG
Naval Magazine

NAVMAINTSUPPO
Naval Maintenance Support Office

NAVMAR
Naval Forces, Marianas

NAVMARCORESCEN
United States Navy and Marine Corps Reserve Center

NAVMAREXHIBCEN
Navy-Marine Corps Exhibit Center

NAVMARJUDACT
Navy-Marine Corps Judiciary Activity

NAVMARTRIJUDCIR
Navy-Marine Corps Trial Judiciary Court

NAVMARTRIJUDCIRBROFF
Navy-Marine Corps Trial Judiciary Court Branch Office

NAVMARTRIJUDIC
Navy-Marine Corps Trial Judiciary

NAVMASSO
Navy Maintenance and Supply Systems Office

NAVMASSODET
Navy Maintenance and Supply Systems Office Detachment

NAVMASSODETPAC
Navy Maintenance and Supply Systems Office Detachment, Pacific

NAVMAT
Naval Material Command

NAVMATCOM
Naval Material Command

NAVMATCOMSUPPACT
Naval Material Command Support Activity

NAVMAT COOPLAN
Naval Material Command Contingency/Emergency Planning

NAVMATDATASYSGRU
Naval Material Data Systems Group

NAVMATDET
Naval Material Command Detachment

NAVMATEVALU
Naval Material Evaluation Unit

NAVMATRANSOFC
Naval Material Transportation Office

NAVMED
Naval Forces, Mediterranean

NAVMEDADMINU
Navy Medical Administrative Unit

NAVMEDATASERVCEN
Navy Medical Data Services Center

NAVMEDCEN
Navy Medical Center

NAVMEDFLDRSCHLAB
Navy Medical Field Research Laboratory

NAVMEDIS
Navy Medical Information System

NAVMEDLAB
Naval Medical Laboratory

NAVMEDLABDET
Naval Medical Laboratory Detachment

NAVMEDMATSUPPCOM
Naval Medical Material Support Command

NAVMEDNPRSCHU
Navy Medical Neuropsychiatric Research Unit

NAVMEDRSCHDEVCOM
Naval Medical Research and Development Command

NAVMEDRSCHINST
Navy Medical Research Institute

NAVMEDRSCHINSTDET
Navy Medical Research Institute Detachment

NAVMEDRSCHINST TOXDET
Navy Medical Research Institute, Toxicology Detachment

NAVMEDRSCHLAB
Navy Medical Research Laboratory

NAVMEDRSCHU
Naval Medical Research Unit

NAVMEDRSCHUDET
Navy Medical Research Unit Detachment

NAVMEDSCOL
Navy School of Medicine

NAVMEDSUPPU
Navy Medical Support Unit

NAVMGTSYSCEN
Navy Management Systems Center

NAVMILPERSCOM
Naval Military Personnel Command

NAVMILPERSCOMINST
Naval Military Personnel Command Instruction

NAVMILPERSCOM SDC
Naval Military Personnel Command Sea Duty Component

NAVMILPERSINST
Navy Military Personnel Instruction

NAVMINEDEFLAB
Navy Mine Defense Laboratory

NAVMINEDEP
Naval Mine Depot

NAVMINENGRFAC
Naval Mine Engineering Facility

NAVMIS
Naval Mission

NAVMISCEN
Naval Mission Center

NAVMMAC
Navy Manpower and Material Analysis Center

NAVMMACLANT
Navy Manpower and Material Analysis Center, Atlantic

NAVMMACPAC
Navy Manpower and Material Analysis Center, Pacific

NAVMOBCONSTBAT
Naval Mobile Construction Battalion

NAVMOBCONSTBN
Naval Mobile Construction Battalion

NAVMORTOFF
Naval Mortuary Office

NavMPS
Naval Mission Planning Systems

NAVMTO
Naval Military Transportation Office

NAVMTONORVA
Naval Military Transportation Office, Norfolk, Virginia

NAVMTOREP
Naval Military Transportation Office Representative

NAVNETDEP
Naval Net Depot

NAVNUPWRSCOL
Navy Nuclear Power School

NAVNUPWRTRAU
Naval Nuclear Power Training Unit

NAVNUPWRU
Naval Nuclear Power Unit

NAVNZ
Naval Forces, New Zealand

NAVOBSY
Naval Observatory

NAVOBSYFLAGSTAFFSTA
Naval Observatory, Flagstaff (AZ) Station

NAVOBSYSTA
Naval Observatory Station

NAVOCEANCOMCEN
Naval Oceanography Command Center

NAVOCEANCOMDET
Naval Oceanography Command Center Detachment

NAVOCEANCOMFAC
Naval Oceanography Command Facility

NAVOCEANCOMMDET
Naval Oceanography Communications Detachment

NAVOCEANO
Naval Oceanographic Office

NAVOCEANOAIRSUPPGRU
Naval Oceanographic Office's Aircraft Support Squadron

NAVOCEANODET
Naval Oceanographic Office Detachment

NAVOCEANOFC
Naval Oceanographic Office

NAVOCEANPROFAC
Naval Ocean Processing Facility

NAVOCEANSURVINFOCEN
Naval Ocean Surveillance Information Center

NAVOCEANSYSCEN
Naval Ocean Systems Center

NAVOCEANSYSCENLAB
Naval Oceans Systems Center Laboratory

NAVOCEANSYSCENLABDET
Naval Ocean Systems Center Laboratory Detachment

NAVOCS
Naval Officer Candidate School

NAVOLF
Navy Outlying Landing Field

NAVOPHTHALSUPPTRACT
Naval Ophthalmic Support Training Activity

NAVOPSUPPGRU
Naval Operations Support Group

NAVOPSUPPGRULANT
Naval Operations Support Group, Atlantic

NAVOPSUPPGRUPAC
Naval Operations Support Group, Pacific

NAVORD
Naval Ordnance

NAVORDENGFAC
Naval Ordnance Engineering Facility

NAVORDFAC
Naval Ordnance Facility

NAVORD ILS/MIS
Naval Ordnance Systems Command Integrated Logistics Support/Management Information System

NAVORDLAB
Naval Ordnance Laboratory

NAVORDLABFIELDIV
Naval Ordnance Laboratory Field Division

NAVORDLIST
Naval Ordnance List

NAVORDMISTESTFAC
Naval Ordnance Missile Test Facility

NAVORDSTA
Naval Ordnance Station

NAVORDSTADET
Naval Ordnance Station Detachment

NAVORDSYSCOM
Naval Ordnance Systems Command

NAVORDSYSCOMHQ
Naval Ordnance Systems Command Headquarters

NAVORDSYSUPPO
Naval Ordnance Systems Support Office

NAVORDSYSUPPOLANT
Naval Ordnance Systems Support Office, Atlantic

NAVORDSYSUPPOPAC
Naval Ordnance Systems Support Office, Pacific

NAVORDTESTU
Naval Ordnance Test Unit

NAVORDU
Naval Ordnance Unit

NAVORECSUPPACT
Naval Officer Record Support Activity

NAVOSH
Navy Occupational Safety and Health (program)

NAVOSTAT
Navigation by Visual Observation of Satellites

NAVPAC
Navigation Packages

NAVPACEN
Navy Public Affairs Center

NAVPBRO
Naval Plant Branch Representative Officer

NAVPECO
Navy Production Equipment Control Office

NAVPECOS
Navy Pentagon Computer Services Division

NAVPERSCEN
Naval Personnel Center

NAVPERSCHACT
Naval Personnel Research Activity

NAVPERSPROGSUPPACT
Naval Personnel Programs Support Activity

NAVPERSRANDCEN
Navy Personnel Research and Development Center

NAVPETOFF
Naval Petroleum Office

NAVPETRAU
Naval Petroleum Training Unit

NAVPETRES
Naval Petroleum Reserves

NAVPETRESO
Naval Petroleum Reserves Office

NAVPGSCOL
Naval Postgraduate School

NAVPGSOL
Naval Postgraduate School

NAVPHIBASE
Naval Amphibious Base

NAVPHIBSCOL
Naval Amphibious School

NAVPHIL
Naval Forces, Philippines

NAVPHOTOCEN
Naval Photographic Center

NAVPLANTDEVU
Naval Plant Development Unit

NAVPLANTREPO
Naval Plant Representative Office/Officer

NAVPLANTTECHREP
Naval Plant Technical Representative

NAVPOLAROCEANCEN
Naval Polar Oceanography Center

NAVPORTCO
Naval Port Control Office

NAVPOSTGRADSCHOL
Naval Postgraduate School

NAVPOSTGRADSCOL
Naval Postgraduate School

NAVPOWFAC
Naval Powder Factory

NAVPRIMSTDEPT
Naval Primary Standards Department

NAVPRIS
Naval Prison

NAVPRO
Naval Plant Representative Office/Officer

NAVPRO
Naval Plant Representative Officer

NAVPROPLT
Naval Propellant Plant

NAVPTO
Navy Passenger Transportation Office

NAVPUBCONBD
Navy Publications Control Board

NAVPUBFORMCEN
Navy Publications and Forms Center

NAVPUBPRINTO
Navy Publications and Printing Office

NAVPUBPRINTSERV
Navy Publications and Printing Service

NAVPUBPRINTSERVDET
Navy Publications and Printing Service Detachment

NAVPUBPRINTSERVO
Navy Publications and Printing Service Office

NAVPUBWKSCEN
Navy Public Works Center

NAVPUBWKSDEPT
Navy Public Works Department

NAVPURDEP
Navy Purchasing Department

NAVPURO
Navy Purchasing Office

NAVPVNTMEDU
Navy Preventive Medicine Unit

NAVRADCO
Naval Regional Active Duty Cryptologic Officer

NAVRADCON
Naval Radiological Control

NAVRADEFLAB
Naval Radiological Defense Laboratory

NAVRADLDEFLAB
Navy Radiological Defense Laboratory

NAVRADRECFAC
Naval Radio Receiving Facility

NAVRADSTA
Naval Radio Station

NAVRADSTA(R)
Naval Radio Station (Receiving)

NAVRADSTA(S)
Naval Radio Station (Sending)

NAVRADTRANSFAC
Naval Radio Transmitting Facility

NAVRECCEN
Naval Recreation Center

NAVRECONTACSUPPCEN
Naval Reconnaissance and Tactical Support Center

NAVRECONTACSUPPCENLANT
Naval Reconnaissance and Tactical Support Center, Atlantic

NAVRECONTECHSUPPCEN
Naval Reconnaissance and Technical Support Center

NAVRECONTECHSUPPCENLANT
Naval Reconnaissance and Technical

Support Center, Atlantic

NAVRECONTECHSUPPCENPAC
Naval Reconnaissance and Technical Support Center, Pacific

NAVRECSTA
Naval Receiving Station

NAVREGAIRCARCONO
Navy Regional Air Cargo Control Office

NAVREGCONTO
Navy Regional Contracting Office

NAVREGCONTODET
Navy Regional Contracting Office Detachment

NAVREGDENCEN
Navy Regional Dental Center

NAVREGDENCENBRFAC
Navy Regional Dental Center Branch Facility

NAVREGDENCLIN
Navy Regional Dental Clinic

NAVREGFINCEN
Navy Regional Finance Center

NAVREGFINCENBRKLN
Navy Regional Center, Brooklyn (NY)

NAVREGFINCENGLAKES
Navy Regional Finance Center, Great Lakes (IL)

NAVREGFINCENNORVA
Navy Regional Finance Center-Norfolk, Virginia

NAVREGFINCENPEARL
Navy Regional Finance Center-Pearl Harbor (HI)

NAVREGFINCENSDIEGO
Navy Regional Finance Center, San Diego (CA)

NAVREGFINCENSFRAN
Navy Regional Finance Center-San Francisco (CA)

NAVREGFINOFC
Navy Regional Finance Office

NAVREGMEDCEN
Naval Regional Medical Center

NAVREGMEDCENBRCLINIC
Naval Regional Medical Center Branch Clinic

NAVREGMEDCENBRHOSP
Naval Regional Medical Center Branch Hospital

NAVREGMEDCENCLINIC
Naval Regional Medical Center Clinic

NAVREGMEDCENDET
Naval Regional Medical Center Detachment

NAVREGPEO
Naval Regional Plant Equipment Office/Officer

NAVREGPROCO
Navy Regional Procurement Office

NAVREGS
Navy Regulations

NAVREL
Navy Relief Society

NAVREPEA
Department of the Navy Representative, Eastern

NAVREPSO
Department of the Navy Representative, Southern

NAVREPSW
Department of the Navy Representative, Southwestern

NAVREPWP
Department of the Navy Representative, Western and Pacific

NAVRES
Naval Reserve

NAVRESCEN
Naval Reserve Center

NAVRESCOMICEDEFOR
Naval Reserve Commander Iceland Defense Force

NAVRESFAC
Naval Reserve Facility

NAVRESFOR
Naval Reserve Force

NAVRESMANPWRCEN
Naval Reserve Manpower Center

NAVRESMGTSCOL
Naval Reserve Management School

NAVRESMIDSCOL
Naval Reserve Midshipmen's School

NAVRESOREACT
Naval Reserve Officer Recording Activity

NAVRESOREP
Navy Resale Systems Office Representative

NAVRESPERSCEN
Naval Reserve Personnel Center

NAVRESREDCOM
Naval Reserve Readiness Command

NAVRESREDCOMREG
Naval Reserve Readiness Command Region

NAVRESSECGRP
Naval Reserve Security Group

NAVRESSECGRU
Naval Reserve Security Group

NAVRESSO
Navy Resale and Services Support Office

NAVRESSOFSO
Navy Resale and Services Support Office, Field Support Office

NAVRESTRA
Naval Reserve Training

NAVRESTRACOM
Naval Reserve Training Command

NAVRESUBDET
Naval Reserve Submarine Detachment

NAVRESUPPOFC
Naval Reserve Support Office

NAVRESUPPOFCDET
Naval Reserve Support Office Detachment

NAVRIIP
Naval Aviation Readiness Integrated Improvement Program

NAVRSCHLAB
Naval Research Laboratory (ONR)

NAVRSCHLABREP
Naval Research Laboratory Representative

NAVSAFECEN
Navy Safety Center

NAVSAR
Naval Search and Rescue

NAVSAT
Navigation Satellite
Navy Navigational Satellite System

NAVSATCOMMDET
Navy Satellite Communications Detachment

NAVSATCOMMFAC
Navy Satellite Communications Facility

NAVSATCOMMNET
Navy Satellite Communications Network

NAVSCIADV
Naval Science Advisor

NAVSCIENTECHINTELCEN
Navy Scientific and Technical Intelligence Center

NAVSCIENTECHINTELCENLANT
Navy Scientific and Technical Intelligence Center, Atlantic

NAVSCIENTECHINTELCENPAC
Navy Scientific and Technical Intelligence Center, Pacific

NAVSCITECHGRUFE
Naval Scientific and Technical Group, Far East

NAVSCOLCEOFF
Naval Civil Engineer Corps Officers School

NAVSCOLCOM
Naval Schools Command

NAVSCOLCONST
Naval School of Construction

NAVSCOLCRYOGENICS
Naval School of Cryogenics

NAVSCOLCRYPTOREP
Naval Cryptographic Repair School

NAVSCOLDEEPSEADIVER
Navy Deep Sea Divers School

NAVSCOLEOD
Naval Explosive Ordnance Disposal School

NAVSCOLHOSPADMIN
Naval Hospital Administration School

NAVSCOLMINWAR
Naval School of Mine War

NAVSCOLPHYDISTMGT
Naval School of Physical Distribution

Management

NAVSCOLTRANSMGT
Naval School of Transportation Management

NAVSCSCOL
Naval Supply Corps School

NAVSCSCOLDET
Naval Supply Corps School Detachment

NAVSEA
Naval Sea Systems Command
Navy Avionics Support Equipment Appraisal

NAVSEAADSO
Naval Sea Systems Command Automated Data Systems Office

NAVSEAADSODET
Naval Sea Systems Command Automated Data Systems Office Detachment

NAVSEACARCO
Navy Sea Cargo Coordinator

NAVSEACARCOORD
Naval Sea Cargo Coordinator

NAVSEACEN
Naval Sea Support Center

NAVSEACENFSO
Naval Sea Support Center Fleet Support Office

NAVSEACENHAWLAB
Naval Sea Support Center, Hawaii Laboratory

NAVSEACENLANTDET
Naval Sea Support Center, Atlantic Detachment

NAVSEACENPACDET
Naval Sea Support Center, Pacific Detachment

NAVSEACENREP
Naval Sea Support Center Representative

NAVSEACOHREP
Naval Sea Systems Command Complex Overhaul Representative

NAVSEADET
Naval Sea Systems Command Detachment

NAVSEAMATREP
Naval Sea Systems Command Material Representative

NAVSEAMQAO
Naval Sea Systems Command Material Quality Assessment Office

NAVSEASYSCOHMQ
Naval Sea Systems Command Headquarters

NAVSEASYSCOM
Naval Sea Systems Command

NAVSEASYSCOMGTOWESTPAC
Naval Sea Systems Command Management Office, Western Pacific

NAVSEASYSCOMREP
Naval Sea Systems Command Representative

NAVSEATECHREP
Naval Sea Systems Command Technical Representative

NAVSEC
Naval Ship Engineering Center

NAVSECENGRFAC
Navy Security Engineering Facility

NAVSECGRUACT
Naval Security Group Activity

NAVSECGRUACTFO
Naval Security Group Activity Field Office

NAVSECGRUACTSPECOMMDIV
Naval Security Group Activity Special Communications Division

NAVSECGRUCOM
Naval Security Group Command

NAVSECGRUDEPT
Naval Security Group Department

NAVSECGRUDET
Naval Security Group Detachment

NAVSECGRUHQ
Naval Security Group Headquarters

NAVSECGRU MIS
Naval Security Group Management Information System

NAVSECMECHSDIV
Naval Ship Engineering Center, Mechanicsburg (PA) Division

NAVSECNORDIV
Naval Ship Engineering Center, Norfolk (VA) Division

NAVSECPHILADIV
Naval Ship Engineering Center, Philadelphia

(PA) Division

NAVSECSDIEGODIV
Naval Ship Engineering Center, San Diego (CA) Division

NAVSECSTA
Naval Security Station

NAVSEEACT
Naval Shore Electronics Engineering Activity

NAVSEEACTLANT
Naval Shore Electronics Engineering Activity, Atlantic

NAVSEEACTPAC
Naval Shore Electronics Engineering Activity, Pacific

NAVSERVSCOLCOM
Naval Service Schools Command

NAVSHIPENGSUPPACT
Naval Ship Engineering Support Activity

NAVSHIPLO
Naval Shipbuilding Liaison Office

NAVSHIPMISENGYS
Naval Ships Missile Systems Engineering System

NAVSHIPREPFAC
Naval Ship Repair Facility

NAVSHIPREPO
Naval Ship Repair Officer

NAVSHIPRSCHDEVCEN
Naval Ship Research and Development Center

NAVSHIPRSCHDEVCENANNA
Naval Ship Research and Development Center, Annapolis (MD) Division

NAVSHIPS
Naval Ships

NAVSHIPSTO
Naval Ships Store Office

NAVSHIPTECHSMAN
Navy Ship's Technical Manual

NAVSHIPWPNSYSENGSTA
Naval Ship Weapon System Engineering Station

NAVSHIPWPNSYSENGSTADET
Naval Ship Weapons Systems Engineering Station Detachment

NAVSHIPWPNSYSENGSTAREP
Naval Ship Weapons Systems Engineering Station Representative

NAVSHIPYD
Naval Shipyard

NAVSHORELECENACT
Naval Shore Electronics Engineering Activity

NAVSHORELECENACTLANT
Naval Shore Electronics Engineering Activity, Atlantic

NAVSHORELECENACTPAC
Naval Shore Electronics Engineering Activity, Pacific

NAVSHORELECENGACTLANT
Naval Shore Electronics Engineering Activity, Atlantic

NAVSHORELECENGACTPAC
Naval Shore Electronics Engineering Activity, Pacific

NAVSHORELECENGCEN
Naval Shore Electronics Engineering Center

NAVSIT
Navy Scholarship Information Team

NAVSO
Navy Staff Offices

NAVSOC
Naval Special Operations Component

NAVSPACEPROJ
Naval Space Project

NAVSPASUR
Naval Space Surveillance

NAVSPASYSAC
Naval Space Systems Activity

NAVSPASYSACT
Naval Space Systems Activity

NAVSPECWARGRU
Naval Special Warfare Group

NAVSPECWARGRUDET
Naval Special Warfare Group Detachment

NAVSPECWARU
Naval Special Warfare Unit

NAVSPECWARUDET
Naval Special Warfare Unit Detachment

NAVSSES
Naval Ship Systems Engineering Station

NAVSSESDET
Naval Ship Systems Engineering Station Detachment

NAVSSI
Navigation Sensor System Interface

NAVSTA
Naval Station

NAVSTAR
Navigation Satellite Tracking and Ranging

NAVSTRIP
Naval Standard Requisitioning and Issue Procedure

NAVSUBBASE
Naval Submarine Base

NAVSUBINSURV
Naval Sub-Board of Inspection and Survey

NAVSUBMEDCEN
Navy Submarine Medical Center

NAVSUBMEDRSCHLAB
Naval Submarine Medical Research Laboratory

NAVSUBOFC
Navy Subsistence Office

NAVSUBSCOL
Naval Submarine School

NAVSUBSUPPBASE
Naval Submarine Support Base

NAVSUBSUPPBASEDET
Naval Submarine Support Base Detachment

NAVSUBSUPPFAC
Naval Submarine Support Facility

NAVSUBTRACENPAC
Naval Submarine Training Center, Pacific

NAVSUP
Naval Supply Systems Command

NAVSUPANX
Navy Supply Annex

NAVSUPCEN
Naval Supply Center

NAVSUPDEP
Naval Supply Depot

NAVSUPDEPT
Naval Supply Department

NAVSUPO
Navy Supply Office

NAVSUPOANX
Navy Supply Office Annex

NAVSUPPACT
Naval Support Activity

NAVSUPPACTDET
Naval Support Activity Detachment

NAVSUPPFAC
Naval Support Facility

NAVSUPPFOR
Naval Support Force

NAVSUPPORANTARCTIC
Naval Support Forces, Antarctic

NAVSUPRANDDFAC
Navy Supply Research and Development Facility

NAVSUPSYSCOM
Naval Supply Systems Command

NAVSUPSYSCOMHQ
Naval Supply Systems Command Headquarters

NAVSURFLANT
Naval Surface Force, Atlantic

NAVSURFLANTREADSUPPGRU
Naval Surface Force, Atlantic Readiness Support Group

NAVSURFPAC
Naval Surface Force, Pacific

NAVSURFPACDAT
Naval Surface Force, Pacific Dependents Assistance Team

NAVSWC
Naval Surface Weapons Center

NAVSWCFAC
Naval Surface Weapons Center Facility

NAVSWCREP
Naval Surface Weapons Center Representative

NAVTACDATASYSDEVSITE
Naval Tactical Data Systems Development and Evaluation Site

NAVTACDOCACT
Navy Tactical Doctrine Activity

NAVTACDOCDEVPRODACT
Navy Tactical Doctrine Development and Production Activity

NAVTACINTEROPSUPPACT
Navy Tactical Interoperability Support Activity

NAVTACINTEROPSUPPACTDET
Navy Tactical Interoperability Support Activity Detachment

NAVTACSAT
Naval Tactical Satellite

NAVTACSUPPACT
Navy Tactical Support Activity

NAVTASC
Naval Telecommunications Automation Support Center

NAVTASCDETLANT
Naval Telecommunications Automation Support Center, Atlantic

NAVTASCDETPAC
Naval Telecommunications Automation Support Center, Pacific

NAVTECHMISEU
Naval Technical Mission in Europe

NAVTECHMISJAP(AN)
Naval Technical Mission to Japan

NAVTECHREP
Naval Technical Representative

NAVTECHTRACEN
Naval Technical Training Center

NAVTECHTRACENDET
Naval Technical Training Center Detachment

NAVTELCOM
Naval Telecommunications Command

NAVTELSYSIC
Naval Telecommunications System Integration Center

NAVTIS
Naval Training Information System

NAVTIS ADS
Naval Training Information System with Automated Data Systems

NAVTORPSTA
Naval Torpedo Station

NAVTRA
Naval Training

NAVTRACEN
Naval Training Center

NAVTRADEVCEN
Naval Training Devices Center

NAVTRADEVICESCEN
Naval Training Devices Center

NAVTRADEVSUPCEN
Naval Training Devices Supply Center

NAVTRAEQUIPCEN
Naval Training Equipment Center

NAVTRAEQUIPCENFEO
Naval Training Equipment Center Field Office

NAVTRAEQUIPCENREPCEN
Naval Training Equipment Center, Representative for the Center

NAVTRAEQUIPCENREPLANT
Naval Training Equipment Center Representative, Atlantic

NAVTRAEQUIPCENREPPAC
Naval Training Equipment Center Representative, Pacific

NAVTRAIDSCEN
Naval Training Aids Center

NAVTRAIDSFAC
Naval Training Aids Facility

NAVTRANSCO
Naval Transportation Coordinating Office

NAVTRAPUBCEN
Naval Training Publications Center

NAVTRASTA
Naval Training Station

NAVTRASUPPDET
Naval Training Support Detachment

NAVTRAU
Naval Training Unit

NAVU
Naval Unit

NAVUARCMSCOL
Navy Unit, Army Chemical School

NAVUDET
Naval Unit Detachment

NAVUSEAMEDINSTITUTE
Naval Undersea Medical Institute

NAVUSEAWARENGSTA
Naval Undersea Warfare Engineering Station

NAVUSEAWARENGSTADET
Naval Undersea Warfare Engineering Station Detachment

NAVUWSEC
Navy Underwater Weapons Systems Engineering Center

NAVUWSYSCEN
Naval Underwater Systems Center

NAVUWTRORDSTA
Navy Underwater Ordnance Station

NAVUWTRSOUNDLAB
Navy Underwater Sound Laboratory

NAVUWTRSOUNDREFLAB
Navy Underwater Sound Reference Laboratory

NAVWAG
Naval Warfare Analysis Group

NAVWARCOL
Naval War College

NAVWEPEVALFAC
Naval Weapons Evaluation Facility

NAVWESTOCEANCEN
Naval Western Oceanographic Center

NAVWESTPAC
Naval Forces, Western Pacific

NAVWPNCEN
Naval Weapons Center

NAVWPNENGSUPPACT
Naval Weapons Engineering Support Activity

NAVWPNEVALFAC
Naval Weapons Evaluation Facility

NAVWPNQUALASSURO
Naval Weapons Quality Assurance Office

NAVWPNSERVO
Naval Weapons Service Office

NAVWPNSTA
Naval Weapons Station

NAVWPNSTRACEN
Naval Weapons Training Center

NAVWPNSUPPACT
Naval Weapons Support Activity

NAVWPNSUPPCEN
Naval Weapons Support Center

NAVWUIS
Naval Work Unit Information System

NAVXDIVINGU
Naval Experimental Diving Unit

NAWAC
National Weather Analysis Center

NAWAS
National Warning System

NAWC
Naval Air Warfare Center

NAWC-TSD
Naval Air Warfare Center-Training Systems Division

NB
Narrow Band
Naval Base
Navy Back (parachute)
Navy Band

NBAD
Naval Bases Air Defense

NBC
Navy Beach Commando
Nuclear, Biological, and Chemical

NBCD
Nuclear, Biological, and Chemical Defense

NBCFD
Naval Base Consolidated Fire Department

NBG
Naval Beach Group

NBL
Navy Biological Laboratory (ONR)
No Bomb Line

NBPA
Navy Board of Production Awards

NBS
National Bureau of Standards
Neutral Buoyancy Simulator

NBSS
Naval Beach Signal Station

NBT
Navigator-Bombardier Training (program)

NBTL
Naval Boiler and Turbine Laboratory

NC
National Course
Navy Chest (parachute)
Navy Counselor
Navy Cross
New Construction
Noise Criteria
Normally Closed
Not Carried
Nurse Corps

NC&B
Naval Courts and Boards

NC1
Navy Couselor First Class

NC2
Navy Counselor Second Class

NC3
Navy Counselor Third Class

NCA
Naval Communications Annex

NCAB
Navy Contract Adjustment Board

NCAC
Navy Combat Art Collection

NCAP
Naval Combat Air Patrol
Navy Common Acoustic Processor

NCAT
Navy College Aptitude Test

NCB
National Competitve Bidding
Naval Communications Board
Naval Construction Battalion
Navy Comptroller Budget

NCBC
Naval Construction Battalion Center

NCC
Chief Navy Counselor
National Climate Center (NOAA)
Naval Command College (NWC)
Naval Communications Command
Navy Command Center
Navy Cost Center
NISTARS Central Controller

NCCCLC
Naval Command Control Communications Laboratory Center

NCCG
Navy Central Clearance Group

NCCM
Master Chief Navy Counselor

NCCMIRS
Navy Civilian Career Management Inventory and Referral System

NCCMP
Navy Civilian Career Management Program

NCCR
Navy Construction/Conversion Requirements (system)

NCCS
National Command and Control System
Senior Chief Navy Counselor

NCD
Naval Construction Division
Navy Cargo Documents
Navy Contracting Directive
Nuclear Commission Date

NCDC
Naval Contract Distribution Center

NCDO
Naval Central Distribution Office

NCDT&EBASE
Navy Combat Demolition Training and Experimental Base

NCDU
Naval Combat Demolition Unit

NCEL
Navy Civil Engineering Laboratory
Navy Contractor Experience List
Nuclear Certified Equipment List

NCF
Naval Construction Force

Navy College Fund

NCFMS
Navy Comptroller, Financial Management Services

NCFSU
Naval Construction Force Support Unit

NCHB
Naval Cargo Handling Battalion

NCHSSP
Navy Campus High School Studies Program

NCI
Navy Cost Inspector

NCIP
Navy Command Inspection Program
Nuclear Career Incentive Pay

NCIRB
Naval Communications Improvement Review Board

NCIS
Navy Cost Information System

NCLT
Night Carrier Landing Trainer

NCM
Navy and Marine Corps Commendation Medal
Navy Correspondence Manual

NCMP
NAVAIDS/Communications Management Office

NCO
Net Control Officer
Network Centric Operations
Non-Commissioned Officer

NCOA
Non-Commissioned Officer's Association

NCOIC
Non-Commissioned Officer-in-Charge

NCOLANT
Net Control Officer, Atlantic

NCOMED
Net Control Officer, Mediterranean

NCOOM
Non-Commissioned Officers' Open Mess

NCOPAC
Net Control Officer, Pacific

NCP
Navy Capabilities Plan
Navy College Program

NCPAC
National Security Agency Central Security Service, Pacific

NCPACE
Navy College Program for Afloat College Education

NCPB
Navy Council of Personnel Boards

NCPC
Navy Civilian Personnel Command

NCPCFD
Navy Civilian Personnel Command Field Division

NCPCFDO
Navy Civilian Personnel Command Field Division Office

NCPD
Navy, Current Procurement Directive

NCPEG
Navy Contractor Performance Evaluation Group

NCPI
Navy Civilian Personnel Instructions

NCR
National Capital Region
Naval Construction Regiment
No Carbon Required

NCS
National Communications System
National Cryptologic School
Naval Communication Station
Naval Communications System
Net Control Station
Nucleus Support Crew

NCSA
Navy Counselor Seaman Apprentice

NCSC
Naval Command Support Center

NCSCC
Naval Security Group Communications

Course

NCSJ
Naval Communication Station, Japan

NCSL
Naval Coastal Systems Laboratory
Naval Code and Signal Laboratory

NCSLO
Navy Control of Shipping Liaison Officer

NCSN
Navy Counselor Seaman

NCSO
Naval Control of Shipping Office

NCSORG
Naval Control of Shipping Organization

NCSP
Naval Communication Station, Philippines

NCSSA
Naval Command Systems Support Activity

NCSSC
Naval Command Systems Support Center

NCSU
Naval Control of Shipping Unit

NCTAMS
Naval Computer and Telecommunications Area Master Stations

NCTC
Naval Construction Training Center

NCTO
Navy Clothing and Textile Office

NCTR
Naval Commercial Traffic Regulations

NCTS
Navy Civilian Technical Specialists

NCU
Naval Communication Unit
Navigation Computer Unit

NCW
Naval Coastal Warfare
Network Centric Warfare

NCWA
Naval Coastal Warfare Area

NCWC
Naval Coastal Warfare Commander

NCWTF
Naval Commander Western Sea Frontier

ND
Naval Dispensary
Naval District
Navy Distillate
Non-Deviation

NDAAC
Naval Drug and Alcohol Advisory Council

NDAC
Nuclear Defense Affairs Committee

NDACP
Navy Drug Abuse Control Program

NDACS
Navy Drug Abuse Counselor School

NDASI
Navy Digital Altimeter Setting Indicator

NDB
Navy Department Bulletin
Navy Disciplinary Barracks
Non-Directional Radio Beacon

NDB(ARF)
Non-Directional Radio Beacon with Airborne Automatic Direction-Finding

NDBDM
Navy Department Board of Decorations and Medals

NDBS
Navy Dispatch Boat Service

NDBULCMED
Navy Department Bulletins, Cumulative Editions

NDC
NATO Defense College
Naval Dental Clinic
Notice of Drawing Change

NDCP
Navy Decision Coordinating Paper

NDD&RF
Naval Drydock and Repair Facility

NDDC
Navy Department Duty Chaplain

NDF
Navy Distillate Fuel
Night Defense Fire

NDFYP
Navy Department Five-Year Program

NDGO
Navy Department General Order

NDI
Non-Destructive Inspection
Non-Developmental Item

NDO
Navy Department Office

NDP
National Disclosure Policy
Navy Department Personnel
Night Defense Position

NDPC
National Disclosure Policy Committee

NDPIC
Navy Department Program Information Center

NDRC
Naval Drug Rehabilitation Center

NDRF
National Defense Reserve Fleet

NDRO
Non-Destructive Read-Out (memory)

NDS
Naval Dental School
Naval Destroyer School
Nuclear Detection Satellite

NDSL
National Defense Student Loan

NDSTC
Naval Diving and Salvage Training Center

NDT
Non-Destructive Test

NDTP
Nuclear Data Tape Program

NDTS/LBTS
Naval Tactical Data System/Land-Based Test Site

NDU
NATO Defense University

NDUSTA
New Duty Station

NDV
No Delay of Vessel
Nuclear Delivery Vehicle

NDW
Naval District Washington (DC)

NE
Northeast
Northeastern

NEACDS
Naval Emergency Air Cargo Delivery System

NEACP
National Emergency Airborne Command Post

NEARNAVDIST
Nearest Naval District

NEASP
Navy Enlisted Advanced School Program

NEAT
Navy Electronics Application Trainer

NEATICC
Northeast Asia Tactical Information Communications Center

NEC
Naval Examining Center
Navy Enlisted Classification Code
Navy Exhibit Center
Necessary
Newspaper Editor's Course
Non-Engineering Change
Not Elsewhere Classified

NECC
Navy Enlisted Classification Codes

NECO
Navy Electronics Commerce Online

NECOS
Navy Enlisted Occupational Classification System

NECP
Non-Engineering Change Proposal

NEDED
Naval Explosive Engineering Department

NEDEP
Navy Enlisted Education Program

NEDN
Naval Environmental Data Network

NEDRECS
Naval Educational Development Records

NEDU
Navy Experimental Diving Unit

NEEO
Naval Electronic Engineering Office

NEES
Naval Engineering Experimental Station

NEESA
Navy Energy and Environmental Support Activity

NEF
Naval Emergency Fund

NEG
Negative

NEGAT
Negative

NEGDET
Navy Enlisted Ground Defense Emergency Force

NEHC
Navy Environmental Health Center

NEL
Naval Electronics Laboratory
Naval Explosives Laboratory

NELATS
Naval Electronics Laboratory Automatic Tester System

NELIAC
Naval Electronics Laboratory International Algor Compilers

NEMEDRI
Northern European and Mediterranean Routing Instructions

NEMO
Naval Experimental Manned Observatory

NEMP
Nuclear Electromagnetic Pulse

NENEP
Navy Enlisted Nursing Education Program

NEO
Navy Exchange Office/Officer
Non-Combatant Evacuation

NEOCS
Navy Enlisted Occupational Classification System

NEODTC
Naval Explosive Ordnance Disposal Technology Center

NEOP
Nuclear Emergency Operations Planning

NEP
Noise Equivalent Power
Nursing Education Program

NEPDB
Navy-wide Environmental Protection Data Base

NEPMU
Navy Environmental and Preventive Medicine Unit

NEPRF
Naval Environmental Prediction Research Facility

NEPSS
Naval Environmental Protection Support Services

NERRA
NALC European Repair and Rework Activity

NERRAREP
NALC European Repair and Rework Activity Representative

NERV
Nuclear Emulsion Recovery Vehicle

NERVA
Nuclear Engines for Rocket Vehicle Applications (program)

NES
Navy Experimental Station
New Enlisted System
Not Elsewhere Specified

NESC
National Environmental Satellite Center
Naval Electronic Systems Command
Navy Electromagnetic Spectrum Center

NESEC
Naval Electronic Systems Engineering Center

NESEP
Navy Enlisted Scientific Education Program

NESIP/POA&M
Navy Explosives Safety Improvement Program/Plan of Action and Milestones

NESN
For Use Among the English-Speaking Nations of NATO

NESO
Navy Electronics Supply Office
Navy Environmental Support Office

NESP
Navy Enlisted Scientific Program
Navy Extremely High Frequency (EHF) Satellite Program

NESTEF
Naval Electronic Systems Testing and Evaluation Facility

NET
Noise Equivalent Temperature
Not Earlier Than
Nuclear Emergency Team

NETC
Naval Education and Training Center
Naval Education and Training Command

NETCOS
Net Control Station

NETFIPC
Naval Education and Training Financial Information Processing Center

NETFIPCBR
Naval Education and Training Financial Information Processing Branch

NETFMS
Naval Education and Training Financial Management System

NETISA
Naval Education and Training Information Systems Activity

NETOPS
Nuclear Emergency Team Operations

NETPDC
Naval Education and Training Program Development Center

NETPDTC
Naval Education and Training Professional Development and Technology Center

NETS
Naval Environmental Training System
Navy Engineering Technical Services
Network Techniques

NETSC
Naval Education and Training Support Center

NETSCEP
Naval Education and Training Support Center, Pacific

NETSCL
Naval Education and Training Program Development Center, Atlantic

NETSCP
Naval Education and Training Support Center, Pacific

NEURS
Navy Energy Usage Reporting System

NEW
Naval Expeditionary Warfare
Net Explosive Weight

NEWENGGRU
New England Group

NEWPOSITREP
New Position Report

NEWRADS
Nuclear Explosion Warning and Radiological System

NEWS
Navy Electronic Warfare Simulator

NEWTS
Navy Electronic Warfare Training Simulator

NEX
Navy Exchange

NEXRAD
Next Generation Radar

N/F
Night Fighter (aircraft)

NF
National Fine (screws & bolts)
Night Fighter (aircraft)

Noise Factor
Noise Figure
Nose Fuze
Nuclear Field

NFA
Naval Fuel Annex

NF/AEF
Nuclear Field and Advanced Electronics Fields (program)

NFB
Naval Frontier Base

NFC
Navy Finance Center
Numbered Fleet Command (ship)

NFC(ALLOT)
Navy Finance Center (Allotments Division)

NFC(CAD)
Navy Finance Center (Central Accounts Division)

NFC-CLEVE
Navy Finance Center-Cleveland (OH)

NFCS
Naval Fires Control System

NFCU
Navy Federal Credit Union

NFC-WASH
Navy Finance Center-Washington (DC)

NFD
Navy Fuel Depot

NFE
Not Fully Equipped

NFEC
Naval Facilities Engineering Command

NFG
No Fucking Good
Non-Functional Gear

NFI
Net Fundable Issues

NFIS
Naval Fighting Instruction School

NFL
No Fire Line

NFLS
Naval Forward Logistic Site

NFMSO
Navy Fleet Material Support Office

NFMT
Navy Food Management Team

NFO
Naval Flight Officer
Navy Finance Office
Normal Fuel Office/Officer

NFO(B)
Naval Flight Officer (Bombardier)

NFO(C)
Navy Flight Officer (Controller)

NFOC
Naval Facility Operational Center
Navy Flight Officer Candidate

NFO(I)
Naval Flight Officer (Radar Intercept)

NFOIO
Navy Field Operational Intelligence Office

NFO(N)
Naval Flight Officer (Navigator)

NFO(S)
Naval Flight Officer (Antisubmarine Warfare)

NFOSG
Navy Field Operational Support Group

NFPS
Naval Flight Preparatory School

NFSN
For Use Among the French-Speaking Nations of NATO

NFSO
Navy Fuel Supply Office

NFSS
National Fallout Shelter Survey

NFSSO
Naval Food Service Systems Office

NFTS
Naval Flight Training School

NFWS
Navy Fighter Weapons School

NG
Natural Gas
No Good
Not Guilty

NGA
National Geospatial-Intelligence Agency

NGCT
Navy General Classification Test

NGF
Naval Gun Factory
Naval Gunfire

NGFS
Naval Gunfire Support

NGL
Nose Gear Launch

NGLO
Naval Gunfire Liaison Officer

NGS
National Geodetic Survey

NGT
Night

NH
Naval Home
Naval Hospital

NHA
Next Higher Assembly
Next Higher Authority

NHDC
Naval Historical Display Center

NHF
Naval Historical Foundation

NHIS
Navy Hazardous Materials Information System

NHOP
National Hurricane Operations Plan

NHRC
Naval Health Research Center

NI
Naval Intelligence
Noise Intensity

NIA
Navy Industrial Association

NIAB
Naval Intelligence Advisory Board

NIAC
NAVSHIPS Industry Advisory Committee

NIB
Not to Interfere Basis

NIC
Naval Intelligence Command

NICAD
Naval Cover and Deception (system)

NICE
Normal Input and Control Executive

NICO
Navy Indochina Clearing Office
Navy Inventory Control Office

NICRAD
NAVAIR/Navy Industry Cooperative Research and Development

NICREP
Naval Intelligence Career Reserve Plan

NICRISP
Navy Integrated Comprehensive Repairable Item Scheduling Program

NID
Naval Intelligence Database
Network Inward Dial

NIDN
Naval Intelligence Data Network

NIDU
Navigation Instrument Developing Unit

NIEHC
Navy Industrial Environmental Health Center

NIF
Navy Industrial Fund

NIFTE
Neon Indicator Flashing Test Equipment

NIG
Navy Inspector General

NIHOE
Nitrogen, Helium, and Oxygen Experiment

NIIN
National Item Identification Number

NILCO
Navy International Logistics Control Office

NILO
Naval Interservice Liaison Office

NIM
Naval Inspector of Machinery

NIMA
National Imagery and Mapping Agency

NIMIS
Naval Intelligence Management Information System

NIMR
Navy Industrial Management Review

NINC
Not Incorporated

NIO
Naval Inspector of Ordnance
Navigational Information Office

NIOD
Network Inward and Outward Dial

NIOSH
National Institute for Occupational Safety and Health

NIOTC
Naval Inshore Operations Training Center

NIP
Naval Institute Press
Navy Interceptor Program

NIPR
Naval Intelligence Products Register

NIPRNET
Nonsecure Internet Protocol Routing Network

NIPS
Naval Intelligence Processing System
NMC Information Processing System

NIPSSA
Naval Intelligence Processing System Support Activity

NIPSTF
Naval Intelligence Processing System Training Facility

NIPSTRAFAC
Naval Intelligence Processing System Training Facility

NIPTS
Noise-Induced Permanent Threshold Shift

NIR
NIS Information Reports

NIRA
Navy Industrial Relations Activity
Navy Internal Relations Activity

NIRPL
Navy Industrial Readiness Planning List

NIS
National Information System
National Intelligence Survey
Naval Inspection Service
Naval Investigative Service
Non-Interference Basis
Not In Service
Not In Store
Not Issued

NISC
Naval Intelligence Support Center

NISMF
Naval Inactive Ship Maintenance Facility

NISO
Naval Investigative Service Office
NAVSEA Industrial Support Office

NISOR
Naval Investigative Service Office Representative

NISP
Navy Integrated Space Program

NISR
Navy Initial Support Requirements

NISRA
Naval Investigative Service Resident Agent

NISREGFORENSICLAB
Naval Investigative Service Regional Forensic Laboratory

NISSO
Naval Investigative Service Office/Officer

NISSU
Naval Investigative Service Satellite Unit

NISTARS
Naval Integrated Storage, Tracking, and Retrieval System

NISW
Naval Inshore Warfare

NITE
Night

NITES
Navy Integrated Tactical Environmental System

NITRAS
Navy Integrated Training Resources and Administration Subsystem

NIW
Naval Inshore Warfare

NJC
Navy Job Classification

NJP
Non-Judicial Punishment

NJPMB
Navy Jet-Propelled Missile Boat

NJROTC
Navy Junior Reserve Officer Training Corps

NJS
Naval Justice School

NL
Natural Logarithm
Navy League
Navy Lighter
Night Letter

NLC
Navy Law Center

NLCEA
Naval Laboratory Centers' Employee Association

NLCP
Navy Logistics Capabilities Plan

NLCP-FY
Navy Logistics Capabilities Plan-Fiscal Year _____

NLD
Navy Lighter Dock

NLDF
Naval Local Defense Force

NLFED
Naval Landing Force Equipment Depot

NLFM
Noise Level Frequency Monitor

NLFS
Nucleus Landing Force Staff

NLG
Nose Landing Gear

NLL
New London (CT) Laboratory

NLM
Navy Learning Model

NLO
Navy Liaison Office/Officer

NLRG
Navy Long-Range Guidance

NLROG
Navy Long-Range Objectives Group

NLRSS
Navy Long-Range Strategic Study

NLSS
Navy Logistics Systems School

NLT
Not Later Than

NLTC
Naval Leadership Training Continuum

NLU
Naval Field Liaison Unit

NM
Nautical Mile
Naval Magazine
Notice to Mariners

NMAA
Navy Mutual Aid Association

NMAB
National Materials Advisory Board

NMAG
Naval Magazine

NMAU
Navy Medical Administrative Unit

NMBR
Number

NMC
Naval Material Command
Naval Medical Center
Naval Missile Center
Naval Mission Center
Navy Mail Clerk
Navy Memorandum Corrections

NMCB
Naval Mobile Construction Battalion

NMCC
National Military Command Center

NMCI
Navy-Marine Corps Intranet

NMCIRD
Naval Material Command Industrial Resources Detachment

NMCJS
Naval Member, Canadian Joint Staff

NMCLK
Navy Mail Clerk

NMCRB
Navy Military Construction Review Board

NMCS
National Military Command System

NMCSA
Naval Material Command Support Activity

NMD
Naval Mine Depot
Navy Marine Diesel

NMDF
Navy Management Data File

NMDL
Navy Management Data List
Navy Management Data Listing
Navy Mine Defense Laboratory

NMDS
Naval Mine Disposal School

NMDSC
Navy Medical Data Services Center

NMDSG
Naval Material Data Systems Group

NMEF
Naval Mine Engineering Facility

NMES
Naval Marine Engineering Station

NMET
Naval Mobile Environmental Team
Navy Mission Essential Tasks

NMETL
Navy Mission Essential Task List

NMETOCD
Naval Meteorology and Oceanography Command Detachments

NMEU
Naval Material Evaluation Unit

NMFC
National Motor Freight Classification (system)

NMFRL
Naval Medical Field Research Laboratory

NMFS
National Marine Fisheries Service

NMG
Navy Metrication Group
Navy Military Government

NMI
Nautical Mile
No Middle Initial

NMIRO
Naval Material Industrial Resources Office

NMIS
Navy Manpower Information System

NMISMAN
Navy Manpower Information System Manual

NMLS
National Microwave Landing System

NMMFO
Navy Maintenance Management Field Office

NMMFO(W)
Navy Maintenance Management Field Office (West)

NMMM
Navy Maintenance and Material Management (system)

NMMMS
Navy Maintenance and Material Management System

NMMSC
Naval Medical Materiel Support Command

NMN
No Middle Name

NMNRU
Naval Medical Neuropsychiatric Research

Unit

NMO
Navy Management Office

NMP
Naval Management Program
Navy Manning Plan

NMPC
Naval Military Personnel Command

NMPCRECSERDIVREGOFF
Naval Military Personnel Command Recreational Services Division Regional Office

NMPEX
Naval Motion Picture Exchange

NMPNC
Naval Medical Material Program for Nuclear Casualties

NMPS
Navy Motion Picture Service

NMPSMOPIXDISTOFF
Navy Motion Picture Service, Motion Picture Distribution Office

NMPX
Naval Motion Picture Exchange

NMR
National Military Representative
Naval Management Review (magazine)

NMR&DO
Naval Material Redistribution and Disposal Officer

NMRC
Naval Material Redistribution Center

NMRDC
Naval Medical Research and Development Command

NMRF
Navy-Marine Corps Residence Foundation

NMRG
Navy Mid-Range Guidance

NMRI
Navy Medical Research Institute

NMRL
Navy Medical Research Laboratory

NMRO
Navy Mid-Range Objectives

NMRS
Navy Manpower Requirements System
Near-Term Mine Reconnaissance System

NMRU
Naval Medical Research Unit

NMS
Navy Meteorological Service
Navy Mid-Range Study

NMSB
Navy Manpower Survey Board

NMSC
Navy Management Systems Center

NMSSO
Navy Maintenance and Supply Systems Office

NMSU
Naval Medical Support Unit

NMTO
Naval Material Transportation Office

NMTS
Naval Mine Testing System

NMVO
Naval Manpower Validation Office

NMVOLANT
Naval Manpower Validation Office, Atlantic

NMVOPAC
Naval Manpower Validation Office, Pacific

NMVP
Navy Manpower Validation Program

NMVT
Navy Manpower Validation Team

NMWS
Naval Mine Warfare School

NMWTS
Naval Mine Warfare Test Station

NNCC
Navy Nurse Corps Candidate

NND
Naval Net Depot

NNDC
National Naval Dental Center

NNMC
National Naval Medical Center

NNPI
Naval Nuclear Propulsion Information

NNPS
Navy Nuclear Power School

NNPTU
Naval Nuclear Power Training Unit

NNPU
Naval Nuclear Power Unit

NNRPB
National Naval Reserve Policy Board

NNSB&DDCO
Newport News Shipbuilding and Drydock Company

NNSS
Naval Navigational Satellite System

NNSY
Norfolk Naval Shipyard

NNYD
Norfolk Naval Shipyard

NO
Naval Observatory
Normally Open
November
Number

NOA
New Obligation Authority

NOAA
National Oceanic and Atmospheric Administration

NOAA-NOS
National Oceanic and Atmospheric Administration-National Ocean Service

NOAA-NWS
National Oceanic and Atmospheric Administration-National Weather Service

NOACT
Navy Overseas Air Cargo Terminal

NOAH
National Ocean Agency Headquarters

NOAP
Naval Oil Analysis Program

NOARA
Navy Overseas Air Routing Activity

NOB
Naval Operating Base
Naval Ordnance Bulletin
Not Observed

NOBC
Navy Officer Billet Codes

NOBS
Naval Operating Base Supplies

NOBSY
Naval Observatory

NOC
Naval Officer Classification (codes)
Naval Operations Center
Not Otherwise Classified
Not Otherwise Coded

NOCF
Naval Oceanography Command Facility

NOCONIT
No Continued Interest

NOCOST
This authorization issued with understanding there will not be an entitled reimbursement for mileage or expenses in connection therewith. In case the individual does not desire to bear this expense, consider this authorization cancelled.

NOCT
Naval Overseas Cargo Terminal

NOD
Network Outward Dial
Night Observation Device

NODAC
Navy Occupational Development and Analysis Center

NODB
NOAA Ocean Data Buoy

NODC
National Oceanographic Data Center
Naval Operating Development Center

NODDES
Naval Oceanographic Data Distribution Expansion System

NODDS
Navy Oceanographic Data Distribution System

NOD/LR
Night Observation Device, Long-Range

NODLR
Night Observation Device, Long-Range

NODS
Navy Overseas Dependents' School

NOE
Notice of Execution

NOEF
Naval Ordnance Engineering Facility

NO EFF
No Effect

NOF
Naval Operating Facility
Naval Ordnance Facility
(International) NOTAM Office

NOFAD
Naval Ocean Floor Analysis Division

NOFORN
No Foreign Eyes Authorized

NOFP
Naval Ocean Processing Facility

NOFT
Naval Overseas Flight Terminal

NOI
Non-Operational Intelligence

NOIBN
Not Otherwise Indexed by Name

NOIC
National Oceanographic Instrumentation Center
Naval Officer-in-Charge

NOIO
Naval Ordnance Inspecting Officer

NOIP
Nuclear Officer Incentive Pay

NOIWON
National Operations Intelligence Watch Officers Net

NOK
Next of Kin

NOL
Naval Ordnance Laboratory

NOLC
Naval Ordnance Laboratory, Coronado (CA)

NOLO
No Line Operators
No Live Operators (on board)

NOLTESTFAC
Naval Ordnance Laboratory Test Facility

NOLTF
Naval Ordnance Laboratory Test Facility

NOMAD
Navy Oceanographic and Meteorological Automatic Device (buoy)

NOMF
Naval Ordnance Missile Test Facility

NOMIS
Naval Ordnance Management Information System

NOMMP
Naval Ordnance Maintenance Management Program

NOMOP
There is no record that he has received previous payment under provisions of the Mustering-Out Payment Act of 1944, Veterans Readjustment Assistance Act of 1952, or Chapter 43 of Title 38, U.S. Code.

NOMTF
Naval Ordnance Missile Test Facility

NONCOM
Non-Commissioned Officer

NONCONST
Non-Consent

NONEG
Negative replies neither required nor desired

NON-FRAG
Non-Fragmentation (bomb)

NON-TOE
Non-Table of Organization and Equipment

NOO
Naval Oceanographic Office

NOP
Naval Oceanographic Program

Naval Ordnance Plant
Navy Operations Plan
Notice of Procurement
Not Operationally Priced
Not Otherwise Provided
Nuclear Ordnance Platoon

NOPCL
Naval Officer Personnel Circular Letters

NOPF
Naval Ocean Processing Facility

NOPHYSRET
Not required to take new physical examination unless material change in physical condition has occurred subsequent to recent physical examination

NOPROCAN
If not already processed, orders (identified by date or DTG) cancelled

NOPS
National Ocean Policy Study
Navigation Operating Procedures

NOR
North
Northern
Notice of Revision
Not Operationally Ready

NORA
Naval Operations Recreation Association

NORAD
North American Air Defense Command

NORAIM
Not Operationally Ready, Aircraft Intermediate Maintenance

NORATS
Navy Operational Radio and Telephone Switchboard

NORBS
Northern Base Section

NORC
Naval Ordnance Research Center
Naval Ordnance Research Computer

NORDA
Naval Research and Development Activity

NORDM
Not Operationally Ready, Depot Maintenance

NORDO
No Radio

NOREAST
North
Northeastern

NOREIMB
This authorization is issued with the understanding that the individual will not be entitled to reimbursement for transportation, per diem, or miscellaneous expenses in connection therewith. In case the individual does not desire to bear this expense, consider this authorization cancelled.

NOREX
Nuclear Operational Readiness Exchange

NORLANT
North Atlantic
Northern Atlantic

NORM
Normal
Normalized
Not Operationally Ready, Maintenance

NORMSHOR
Normal Tour of Shore Duty

NORPAC
North Pacific
Northern Pacific

NORPACREGREPCEN
Northern Pacific Regional Reporting Center

NORRS
Naval Operational Readiness Reporting System

NORS
Not Operationally Ready, Supply

NORSA
Naval Officer Record Support Activity

NORSAIR
Not Operationally Ready, Supply/Aviation Item Reports

NORSG
Not Operationally Ready, Supply/Grounded

NORTHNAVFACENGCOM
Northern Naval Facilities Engineering Command

NORU
Navy Recruiting Orientation Unit

NORVA
Norfolk, Virginia

NORVAGRP
Norfolk, Virginia Group

NORVATEVDET
Norfolk, Virginia Test and Evaluation Detachment

NORWES
Northwest
Northwestern

NORWESSEAFRON
Northwestern Sea Frontier

NORWESSECWESSEAFRON
Northwestern Sector, Western Sea Frontier

NORWEST
Northwest
Northwestern

NOS
National Ocean Service
Naval Ordnance Station
Not Otherwise Specified

NOSC
Naval Ocean Systems Center

NOSCL
Naval Oceans Systems Center Laboratory

NOSIC
Naval Ocean Surveillance Information Center

NOSL
Naval Ordnance Station, Louisville (KY)

NOSR
Naval Oil Shale Reserves

NOSS
National Orbiting Space Station
Nimbus Operational Satellite System

NOSSA
Navy Ordnance Safety and Security Activity

NOSSO
Naval Ordnance Systems Support Office

NOSSOLANT
Naval Ordnance Systems Support Office, Atlantic

NOSSOPAC
Naval Ordnance Systems Support Office, Pacific

NOSSOREP
Naval Ordnance Systems Support Office Representative

NOSTA
Naval Ophthalmic Support Training Activity

NOTAL
Not To All

NOTAMs
Notices to Airmen

NOTAP
Navy Occupational Task Analysis Program

NOTC
Naval Officer Training Center

NOTE
Notice

NOTIP
Northern-Tier Integration Project

NOTS
Naval Ordnance Test Station

NOTU
Naval Operational Training Unit
Naval Ordnance Test Unit

NOTUN
Notice of Unreliability

NOU
Naval Ordnance Unit

NOV
November
NSA Items Only for Overseas Shipment

NP
Naval Prison
Neap (tide)
North Pole
Nuclear Power
Nuclear Powered
Small Patrol Craft

NPA
Navy Purchasing Activity
Network Planning and Analysis
Non-Propulsion Attachment

Numbering Plan Area

NPAB
Naval Price Adjustment Board

NPAM
Navy Priorities and Allocations Manual

NPANX
Naval Potomac Annex

NPAP
Navy Public Affairs Plan

NPBS
Navy Personnel Billeting System

NPC
Naval Personnel Command
Naval Photographic Center
Naval Publications and Forms Center
Nucleus Port Crew

NPCO
Naval Port Control Office

NPD
Navy Procurement Directives
Navy Purchasing Department

NPDC
Naval Personnel Development Command

NPDES
National Pollutant Discharge Elimination System

NPDI
Non-Performance of Duty Because of Imprisonment

NPDI(CIVIL)
Non-Performance of Duty Because of Civil Arrest

NPDU
Naval Plant Development Unit

NPE
Navy Preliminary Evaluation

NPF
Naval Powder Factory
Naval Procurement Fund

NPFC
Naval Publications and Forms Center

N-PFPS
Navy Portable Flight Software

NPG
Naval Proving Ground
Nuclear Planning Group

NPGS
Naval Postgraduate School

NPIC
Navy Photographic Interpretation Center

NPM
Navy Programming Manual

NPMA
Navy Personnel Management Academy

NPN
Negative-Positive-Negative (transistor)

NPO
Naval Petroleum Office
Naval Port Office
Navy Post Office
Navy Program Objectives
Navy Purchasing Office

NPOC
Naval Polar Oceanography Center

NPOESS
National Polar-Orbiting Operational Environmental Satellite System

NPP
Navy Propellant Plant

NPPC
Navy Program Planning Council (CNO)

NPPE
Nuclear Power Propulsion Evaluation
Nuclear Power Propulsion Examination

NPPO
Naval Publications and Printing Office
Navy Program and Planning Office

NPPS
Naval Publications and Printing Service

NPPSBO
Navy Publications and Printing Service Branch Office

NPPSDET
Navy Publications and Printing Service Detachment

NPPSNORDIV
Navy Publications and Printing Service, Northern Division

NPPSO
Naval Publications and Printing Service Office

NPPSSOEASTDIV
Navy Publications and Printing Service, Southeastern Division

NPPSWESTDIV
Navy Publications and Printing Service, Western Division

NPR
Naval Petroleum Reserves
Naval Plant Representative
Navy Payroll
Navy Preliminary Revision
Nuclear Power Reactor

NPRDC
Navy Personnel Research and Development Center

NPRO
Naval Petroleum Reserves Office
Naval Plant Representative Officer

NPS
Naval Postgraduate School
Navy Personnel Survey
Non-Prior Service

NPSC
Naval Personnel Separation Center

NPSCE
Naval Postgraduate School Continuing Education

NPSD
Naval Photographic Services Depot

NPSE
Navy Periodontal Screening Examination

NPSH
Net Positive Suction Head (pump)

NPT
Navy Pointer Tracker
Neuropsychiatry
Nonproliferation Treaty

NPT/E
Navy Parachute Team/East Coast

NPTF
Nuclear Power Task Force

NPTG
Nuclear Power Task Group

NPTR
National Parachute Test Range

NPTRI
Newport, Rhode Island

NPTRL
Naval Personnel and Training Research Laboratory

NPTU
Naval Petroleum Training Unit

NPT/W
Navy Parachute Team/West Coast

NPW
Nuclear-Powered Warship

NPWC
Navy Public Works Center

NPWD
Navy Public Works Department

NPWTC
NAVFAC Public Works Training Center

NQA
Nuclear Quality Assurance

NQC
Nuclear Quality Control

NQE
Nuclear Quality Engineering

NQR
Nuclear Quadropole Resonator

NR
Natural Rubber
Naval Reserve
Navy Regulations
Noise Reduction
Noise Review
Not Ready
Not Required
Nuclear Reactor
Number
Submersible Research Vehicle

NRA
Naval Radio Activity
Naval Reserve Association
Navy Recruiting Area

NRAB
Naval Reserve Aviation Base

NRAC
Naval Reserve Advisory Council

NRACCO
Navy Regional Air Cargo Control Office

NRAF
Naval Reserve Auxiliary Field
Navy Recruiting Aids Facility

NRAMS
Navy Recruiting and Accessions Management System

NRAO
Navy Regional Accounts Office

NRAS
Navy Readiness Analysis System

NRB
Naval Repair Base
Navy Reservation Bureau

NRBS
Navy Recruiting Branch Station

NRC
Naval Radiological Control
Naval Research Company
Naval Reserve Center
Navy Recreation Center
Navy Recruiting Command
Noise Reduction Coefficient

NRCC
Navy Regional Contracting Center
Non-Resident Career Course

NRCHB
Naval Reserve Cargo Handling Battalion

NRCHTB
Naval Reserve Cargo Handling Training Batallion

NRCO
Navy Regional Contracting Office

NRD
Naval Research Development
Navy Recruiting District

NRDC
Naval Drug Rehabilitation Center
Naval Research and Development Center
Navy Regional Dental Center

NRDFS
Naval Radio Direction Finder Service

NRDL
Navy Radiological Defense Laboratory

NRDS
Nuclear Rocket Development Station

NREB
Naval Reserve Evaluation Board

NREC
Navy Recruiting Exhibit Center

NRES
Naval Receiving Station

NRF
Naval Repair Facility
Naval Reserve Facility
Naval Reserve Force

NRFC
Navy Regional Finance Center

NRFC-B
Navy Regional Finance Center-Brooklyn (NY)

NRFC-GL
Navy Regional Finance Center-Great Lakes (IL)

NRFC-N
Navy Regional Finance Center-Norfolk (VA)

NRFC-PH
Navy Regional Finance Center-Pearl Harbor (HI)

NRFC-SD
Navy Regional Finance Center-San Diego (CA)

NRFC-SF
Navy Regional Finance Center-San Francisco (CA)

NRFI
Not Ready for Issue

NRFLTSUPPDET
Naval Research Laboratory Flight Support Detachment

NRFMAU
Naval Reserve Fleet Management Assistance Unit

NRFO
Navy Regional Finance Office

NRFS
Naval Reserve Force Study Group

NRIUW
Naval Reserve Inshore Undersea Warfare

NRL
Naval Research Laboratory

NRLCHESBAYDET
Naval Research Laboratory Chesapeake Bay Detachment

NRLREP
Naval Research Laboratory Representative

NRLSITEDET
Naval Research Laboratory Field Site Detachment

NRLSPECPROJDET
Naval Research Laboratory Special Projects Detachment

NRLUWSREFDET
Naval Research Laboratory Underwater Sound Reference Detachment

NRM
Noise Reduction Manual

NRMC
Naval Records Management Center
Naval Regional Medical Center
Naval Reserve Manpower Center

NRMIUW
Naval Reserve Mobile Inshore Undersea Warfare

NRMOMAGU
Naval Reserve Mobile Mine Assembly Group

NRMS
Naval Reserve Management School
Naval Reserve Midshipmen's School

NRO
National Reconnaissance Office
Navy Retail Office

NROC
Navy Requirements Oversight Council

NROS
Naval Reserve Officers School

N-ROSS
Navy-Remote Ocean Sensing System

NROTC
Naval Reserve Officers Training Corps

NROTCU
Naval Reserve Officers Training Corps Unit

NROTCUNAVADMINU
Naval Reserve Officers Training Corps Unit and Administrative Unit

NRP
Noise Review Program
Notice of Research Projects

NRPAC
Naval Reserve Public Affairs Company

NRPB
Naval Research Planning Board
Naval Reserve Policy Board

NRPC
Naval Reserve Personnel Center

NRPEO
Naval Regional Plant Equipment Office/Officer

NRPIO
Naval Registered Publications Issuing Officer

NRPM
Non-Registered Publications Memoranda

NRR
Naval Research Requirement
Naval Reserve Requirement

NRRC
Naval Reserve Readiness Center
Naval Reserve Research Company

NRRF
Naval Radio Receiving Facility
Naval Reserve Readiness Facility

NRR/O
Naval Reactor Representative/Office

NRS
Naval Radio Station
Naval Reserve Security Division
Navy Recruiting Station
Navy Relief Society
Navy Resale System

NRSC
Naval Reserve Supply Company

NRSG
Naval Reserve Security Group

NRSO
Navy Resale System Office

NRS(R)
Naval Radio Station (Receiving)

NRS(S)
Naval Radio Station (Sending)

NRSSO
Navy Resale and Services Support Office

NRT
Naval Reserve Training

NRTC
Navy Recruit Training Command

NRTD
Near Real-Time Dissemination

NRTF
Naval Radio Transmitting Facility

NRTS
National Reactor Testing Station
Not Repairable This Ship

NRTSC
Naval Reconnaissance and Technical Support Center

NRTSCL
Naval Reconnaissance and Tactical Support Center, Atlantic

NRTSCLANT
Naval Reconnaissance and Technical Support Center, Atlantic

NRTSCPAC
Naval Reconnaissance and Technical Support Center, Pacific

NRX/EST
Nuclear Reactor, Experimental/Engine System Test

N/S
North/South
Not Sufficient Funds

NS
Naval Station
Navy Standard (parachute)
Nimbostratus
Non-Structural
Normally Shut
Nuclear Ship

NS&T
Naval Science and Tactics

NSA
National Security Agency
National Shipping Authority
Naval Support Activity
Navy Stock Account
Navy Supply Annex
Nuclear Science Abstracts

NSACSS
National Security Agency Central Security Service

NSAD
Naval Support Activity Detachment

NSAM
National Security Action Memorandum
Naval School of Aviation Medicine

NSAP
Navy Science Assistance Program

NSA-PC
Naval Support Activity - Panama City

NSAT
NAVMAT Special Assistance Team

NSATS
NAVMAT Selected Acquisitions Tracking System

NSAWC
Naval Strike Air Warfare Center

NSB
Naval Submarine Base

NSC
Naval Schools Command
Naval Sea Cadets
Naval Supply Center
Navy Safety Center
Numeric Sequence Code

NSCC
Naval Sea Cadet Corps
Navy Sea Cargo Coordinator

NSCCLO
Naval Sea Cadet Corps Liaison Officer

NSCD
Nuclear Service Control Date

NSCDET
Naval Supply Center Detachment

NSCF
Naval Small-Craft Facilities

NSCO
Naval Sea Cargo Coordinator
Naval Supply Center, Oakland (CA)

NSCPS
Naval Supply Center, Puget Sound (Bremerton, WA)

NSD
Naval Supply Department
Naval Supply Depot
Navy Support Date

NSDA
Naval Supply Depot Annex

NSDAT
Naval School of Dental Assisting and Technology

NSDAVNDEPT
Naval Supply Depot Aviation Department

NSDDET
Naval Supply Depot Detachment

NSE
Naval Shore Establishment

NSEC
Naval Ship Engineering Center

NSF
Naval Support Force
Navy Stock Fund
Not Sufficient Funds

NSFO
Navy Standard Fuel Oil

NSFS
Naval Surface Fire Support

NSG
National Security Group

NSGA
Naval Security Group Activity

NSGC
Naval Security Group Command

NSGOC
Naval Security Group Orientation Course

NSGTP
Naval Security Group Training Publication

NSHO
Naval Service Headquarters, Ottawa

NSHS
Naval School of Health Sciences

NSHSDET
Naval School of Health Sciences Detachment

NSI
Naval Science Instructor
Non-Standard Item
Non-Stocked Item
Non-Stock Item
Nuclear Status Indicator

NSIC
Next Senior in Command

NSIPS
Navy Standard Integrated Personnel System

NSL
Navy Standards Laboratory
Navy Stock List

NSLI
National Service Life Insurance

NSM
Naval School of Music

NS MCM
Navy Supplement to the Manual for Courts-Martial

NSMG
Naval School of Military Government

NSMG&A
Naval School of Military Government and Administration

NSMP
Navy Support and Mobilization Plan

NSMRL
Naval Submarine Medical Research Laboratory

NSMSES
Naval Ship Missile System Engineering Station

NSN
National Stock Number

NSO
Navy Subsistence Office
Navy Supply Office

NSOC
Navy Satellite Operations Center

NSOOL
NATO Staff Officer Orientation Course

NSP
Navy Safety Program
Navy Support Plan

NSPCC
Navy Ships Parts Control Center

NSPD
Naval Shore Patrol Detachment

NSPF
Not Specifically Provided For

NSPG
Navy Strategic Planning Guidance

NSPO
Navy Special Projects Office

NSPS
Naval Strategic Planning Study

NSR
Naval Supply Requirements

NSRDC
Naval Ship Research and Development Center

NSRDC/A
Naval Ship Research and Development Center, Annapolis, (MD) Division

NSRDCANNADIV
Naval Ship Research and Development Center, Annapolis, (MD) Division

NSRF
Naval Ship Repair Facility

NSRS
Navy Supply Radio Station

NSS
Naval Security Station
Navy Standard Score
Navy Strategic Study
Navy Supply Systems

NSSA
Naval Space Systems Activity

NSSB
Naval Submarine Support Base

NSSC
Naval Sea Support Center
Naval Sea Systems Command
Naval Supply Systems Command

NSSI
Navy System Stock Inventories

NSSMS
NATO Seasparrow Missile System

NSSN
New Attack Submarine

NSSNF
Naval Strategic Systems Navigation Facility

NSSO
Naval Ships Store Office

NSSS
Naval Space Surveillance System

NSS TRD
Navigation, Seamanship and Shiphandling Training Requirements Document

NST
Normal Shore Tour
NSA Items for Stateside Shipment

NSTC
Naval Service Training Command

NSTEP
Naval Scientist Training and Exchange Program

NSTIC
Navy Scientific and Technical Intelligence Center

NSTICLANT
Navy Scientific and Technical Intelligence Center, Atlantic

NSTICPAC
Navy Scientific and Technical Intelligence Center, Pacific

NSTM
Naval Ships Technical Manual

NSW
Naval Special Warfare

NSWC
Naval Surface Weapons Center

NSWSES
Naval Ship Weapon System Engineering Station

NSWTE
Naval Special Warfare Task Element

NSWTG
Naval Special Warfare Task Group

NSWU
Naval Special Warfare Unit

NSY
Naval Shipyard

NSYD
Naval Shipyard

NT
Naval Training
Net Ton
Nighttime
Non-Tight
Normalized and Tempered

NT&DC
Naval Training and Distribution Center

NTAC
Naval Training Aids Center

NTAF
Naval Training Aids Facility

NTAFT
Navy Technical Assistance Field Team

NTBI
Not To Be Incorporated

NTC
Naval Training Center
Navy Test Controller
Notice

NTCC
Naval Telecommunications Center

NTCCDET
Naval Telecommunications Center Detachment

NTCO
Navy Transportation Coordinating Office

NTCSS
Naval Tactical Command Support System

NTDC
Naval Training Devices Center

NTDDPA
Naval Tactical Doctrine Development and Production Activity

NTDI
Non-Destructive Testing and Inspection

NTDO
Navy Technical Data Office

NTDS
Navy Tactical Data System

NTDSC
Naval Training Devices Supply Center

NTE
Navy Technical Evaluation

NTEC
Naval Training Equipment Center

NT FLT CK
Not Flight Checked

NTI
Naval Travel Instructions

NTIS
National Technical Information Service

NTMPS
Navy Training Management and Planning System

NTMT
Navigation Tender Maintenance Training

NTOC
Naval Telecommunications Operations Center

NTOCDET
Naval Telecommunications Operations Center Detachment

NTORS
Naval Torpedo Station

NTP
Naval Technological Projections
Naval Telecommunications Publication
Navy Tactical Publication
Navy Training Plan

NTPC
Navy Training Plan Conference
Navy Training Publications Center

NTPI
Naval Technical Proficiency Inspection

NTP/IDCSP
Navy Test Plan for Initial Defense Communications Satellite Program

NTPS
Near-Term Pre-Positioning Ships

NTS
Naval Target Subdivision
Naval Telecommunications System
Naval Torpedo Station
Naval Training School
Naval Training Station
Naval Transportation Service

NTSA
Naval Telecommunications System Architect
Navy Tactical Support Activity

NTSB
National Transportation Safety Board

NTSP
Navy Training Systems Plan

NTTC
Naval Technical Training Center

NTU
Naval Training Unit
New Threat Upgrade (Terrier missiles)

NTW
Navy Theater-Wide

NTX
Navy Teletypewriter Exchange

NU
Number

NUB
Navy Uniform Board

NUC
Naval Undersea Center
Navy Unit Commendation
Nuclear

NUC FLD
Nuclear Field

NUDETS
Nuclear Detection System

NUFEA
Navy Unique Fleet Essential Airlift

NUHELI
Nuclear Helicopter

NUKE
Nuclear

NULACE
Nuclear Liquid Air Cycle Engine

NUMEC
Nuclear Materials and Equipment Corporation

NUMIS
Navy Uniform Management Information System

NUOS
Navy Underwater Ordnance Station

NUPOC
Nuclear Power Officer Candidate Program

NUPOC-S
Nuclear Power Officer Candidate-Submarine

NUPWR
Nuclear Power
Nuclear Powered

NUPWRU
Nuclear Power Unit

NURIG
Navy Utility Regulatory Intervention Group

NUSC
Naval Underwater Systems Center

NUSCDET
Naval Underwater Systems Center Detachment

NUSL
Navy Underwater Sound Laboratory

NUVEP
NAVSEA Unified Vendor Evaluation Program

NUWATI
Nuclear Work Authorization Technical Instruction

NUWEPSA
Nuclear Weapons Supply Annex

NUWPNSTRACEN
Nuclear Weapons Training Center

NUWPNSTRACENLANT
Nuclear Weapons Training Center, Atlantic

NUWPNSTRACENPAC
Nuclear Weapons Training Center, Pacific

NUWPNSTRAGRU
Nuclear Weapons Training Group

NUWPNSUPANX
Nuclear Weapons Supply Annex

NUWRES
Naval Underwater Weapons Research and

Engineering Station

NV
Non-Vital

NVASS
Night-Vision Aerial Surveillance System

NVCT
Non-Verbal Classification Test

NVGs
Night Vision Goggles

NVII
Navy Vocational Interest Inventory

NVL
Night-Vision Laboratory

NVR
Naval Vessel Register

NW
Northwest
Northwestern
No Wind
Nuclear Warfare

NWA
Navy Wifeline Association

NWAC
National Weather Analysis Center

NWC
Naval War College
Naval Weapons Center

NWCA
Navy Wives Clubs of America

NWC/CS
Naval War College/Command and Staff (course)

NWCF
Naval War College Foundation

NWC/NW
Naval War College/Naval Warfare (course)

NWCP
Navy Weight-Control Program

NWDC
Navy Warfare Development Command

NWEF
Naval Weapons Evaluation Facility

NWEPSA
Nuclear Weapons Supply Annex

NWF
Navy Working Fund

NWFA
Navy-Wide Finance Activities

NWIP
Naval Warfare Information Program
Naval Warfare Information Publication

NWISO
Naval Weapons Industrial Support Office

NWL
Naval Weapons Laboratory

NWL/D
Naval Weapons Laboratory/Dahlgren (VA)

NWP
Naval Warfare Publication
Naval Weapons Plant

NWPSC
Nationwide Postal-Strike Contingency Plan

NWPU
Numerical Weather Prediction Unit

NWRF
Navigational Weather Research Facility

NWS
National Weather Service
Naval Weapons Station

NWSA
Nuclear Weapons Supply Annex

NWSC
National Weapons Satellite Center

NWSF
Northwestern Sea Frontier

NWSO
Naval Weapons Service Office

NWSS
Navy WWMCCS Software Standardization

NWTC
Naval Weapons Training Center
Nuclear Weapons Training Center

NWTCL
Nuclear Weapons Training Center, Atlantic

NWTCP
Nuclear Weapons Training Center, Pacific

NWTD
Non-Watertight Door

NWTG
Nuclear Weapons Training Group

NWTP
Naval Warfare Tactical Publication

NWUIS
Naval Work Unit Information System

NXSR
Non-Extraction Steam Rate

NY
Navy Yard

NYCHARL
Navy Yard, Charleston (SC)

NYK
New York Navy Yard

NYKGRP
New York Group

NYMI
Navy Yard, Mare Island (CA)

NYNOR
Navy Yard, Norfolk (VA)

NYNYD
New York Navy Yard

NYOD
New York Area Office (ONR)

NYPE
New York, Port of Embarkation

NYPH
Navy Yard, Pearl Harbor (HI)

NYPHIL
Navy Yard, Philadelphia (PA)

NYPORT
Navy Yard, Portsmouth (NH)

NYPS
Navy Yard, Puget Sound (WA)

NYWASH
Navy Yard, Washington (DC)

NZLO
New Zealand Liaison Officer

NZSEAFRON
New Zealand Sea Frontier

O

O
Airborne Intercept
Main Oxygen (system)
Obsolescence
Obsolescent
Office
Original (copy)

O&A DATE
Oath and Acceptance Date

O&M
Operations and Maintenance (funds)

O&MMC
Operations and Maintenance, Marine Corps

O&MN
Operations and Maintenance, Navy

O&OS
Overseas Operational Storage Sites

O&R
Overhaul and Repair

O&S
Operations and Support

O/A
Operations Analysis

OA
Shipboard Aviation Operations Division

OAASN
Office of the Administrative Assistant to the Secretary of the Navy

OAC
Operation of Aircraft Costs

OACC
Oceanic Area Control Center

OAD
Officers' Accounts Division
Operational Active Data

Operational Availability Date

OA-DG
Occupational Area Defense Grouping

OA DIV
Operations/Weather Service Division

OADR
Originating Agency's Determination Required

OAL
Order Action List

OAO
Orbiting Astronomical Observatory

OAP
Offset Aimpoint
Overall Average Percentage

OAR
ORDALT Accomplishment Requirement (list)

OARS
Ocean Area Reconnaissance Satellite

OAS
Office of the Assistant Secretary
Other Active Military Service

OASD
Office of the Assistant Secretary of Defense

OASD(HA)
Office of the Assistant Secretary of Defense (Health Affairs)

OASDI
Old Age Survivors and Disability Insurance

OASD(MRA&L)
Office of the Assistant Secretary of Defense (Manpower, Reserve Affairs, and Logistics)

OASIS
Ocean All-Sources Information System
Organic Airborne and Surface Influence Sweep

OASN
Office of the Assistant Secretary of the Navy

OASN(FM)
Office of the Assistant Secretary of the Navy (Financial Management)

OASN(I&L)
Office of the Assistant Secretary of the Navy (Installation and Logistics)

OASN(P&RF)
Office of the Assistant Secretary of the Navy (Personnel and Reserve Force)

OASN(R&D)
Office of the Assistant Secretary of the Navy (Research and Development)

OAT
Outside Air Temperature

OATC
Oceanic Air Traffic Center
Overseas Air Traffic Control

OATS
Optimum Aerial Targeting Sensor

O/B
On Berth

OB
Operating Base
Operating Budget
Operational Base
Ordnance Battalion
Ordnance Board

OBA
Oxygen Breathing Apparatus

OB/CP
Observation/Command Post

OBDB
On Board Data Bank

OBE
Overcome By Events

OBL
Operational Base Launch

OBLISERV
Obligated service of (number of months indicated) required, or execute Form NAVPERS 604

OBLISERVNATRA
Obligated to serve 3-1/2 years following date of completion of training within the Naval Air Training Command

OBLISERVONEASIX
Execution of these orders obligates service-

member to serve on active duty 1 year for each 6 months of schooling or fraction thereof. Obligation to commence upon termination or completion of schooling and is in addition to the remaining time required by any prior active duty obligation

OBLISERVTWOYR
Execution of these orders obligates servicemember to serve on active duty a period of 2 years. Obligation to commence upon termination or completion of schooling and is in addition to the remaining time required by any prior active duty obligation

OBO
Ore/Bunk/Oil (vessel)

OBRP
On Board Repair Parts

OBS
Observation
Observatory
Observe
Obsolete
Obstacle

OBSC
Obscure

OBSHT
Obstacle Height

OBSN
Observation

OBSR
Observer

OBSRON
Observation Squadron

OBSS
Ocean Bottom Scanning Sonar

OBS SPOT
Observation Spot

OBST
Obstruction

OBSTN
Obstruction

OBSY
Observatory

OBT
Onboard Trainer

OBTAINDORSETRANS
If servicemember avails him/herself of leave, obtain endorsement from each TEMADD point as to transportation which would have been available in reporting to next TEMADD point or in returning to duty station via shortest, usually traveled route, giving dates and hours of departure and arrival. Authorized to visit countries specified in leave status

OBTAINFUNDIS
Authorized to obtain funds in accordance with NAVCOMPMAN par. 042352-8, to make cash disbursements to cover actual expenses incurred on account of recruiting

OC
October
Operations Control

OCA
Oceanic Control Area
Offensive Counter-Air
Operational Control Authority

OCAN
Officer Candidate Airman (program)

OCAS
Officer-in-Charge of Armament Supply
Ordnance Configuration Accounting System

OCC
Occulting (light)
Officer Correspondence Course
Operational Control Center

OCCAS
Occasional (light)

OCCSPEC
Occupational Specialties (handbook)

OCCSTANDARDS
Occupational Standards

OCCSTD
Occupational Standards

OCCSTDS
Occupational Standards

OCD
Office of Civilian Defense
Ordnance Classification of Defects

OC DIV
Operations/Aircraft Control Division

OCDM
Office of Civilian and Defense Mobilization

OCE
Office of Chief of Engineers
Officer Conducting the Exercise

OCEANDEVRON
Oceanographic Development Squadron

OCEI
Ocean Construction Equipment Inventory

OCFNT
Occluded Front

OCHAMPUS
Office of the Civilian Health and Medical Program of the Uniformed Services

OCHAMPUSEUR
Office of the Civilian Health and Medical Program of the Uniformed Services in Europe

OCIR
Operational Capability Improvement Request
Out of Commission, in Reserve (vessel status)

OCL
Obstacle Clearance Limits
Occlude
Ordnance Circular Letters

OCLN
Occlusion

OCMM
Office of Civilian Manpower Management

OCNLY
Occasionally

OCONUS
Outside Continental Limits of the United States

OCPO
Operations Cargo Passenger Office

OCPR
Operation and Conversion of Naval Petroleum Reserves

OCPS
Officer Candidate Preparatory School

OCR
Occur
Optical Character Reader
Optical Character Recognition
Overhaul Condition Report

OCRD
Office of the Chief of Research and Development

OCS
Officer Candidate School
Operations Control System
Optimum Coordinated Shipboard Allowance List
Outer Continental Shelf
Outpatient Clinic Substation

OCSOT
Operational Combat Systems Overall Test

OCSP
Out of Commission, Special (vessel status)

OCT
Octane
October
Office of the Chief of Transportation

OCT/RR
Off-Course Target/Remote Reference (display)

OCU
Operations Conversion Unit

O/D
On Deck

OD
Observed Drift
Oil Distribution
On Deck
Optical Density
Ordnance Data
Ordnance Detachment
Outside Diameter

ODA
Operational Data Analysis

ODAR
Optical Detection and Ranging

ODB
Ocean Data Buoy

ODC
Office of Defense Cooperation

Officer Data Card
Other Direct Costs
Outer Dead Center
Overseas Diplomacy Coordinator

ODCR
Officer Distribution and Control Report

ODDR&D
Office of the Director, Defense Research and Development

ODM
Office of Defense Mobilization
Operational Direction Message

ODME
Overseas Diplomacy Mission Element

ODO
Operations Duty Officer

ODP
Officer Distribution Plan
Organized Reservists in Drill Pay Status
Original Departure Point
Overseas Diplomacy Program

ODR
Omnidirectional Range
Omnidirection Range

ODS
Ocean Data Station (USN-USCG)
Ordnance Delivery Schedule

ODSP
Overseas Duty Support Program

ODT
Omnidirectional Transmission
Overseas Diplomacy Training

ODUSD(C^3I)
Office of the Deputy Under Secretary of Defense (Communications, Command, Control, and Intelligence)

OEC
Output Exception Code

OE DIV
Operations Electronics/Material Division

OEDO
Ordnance Engineering Duty Officer

OEF
Operation Enduring Freedom

OEG
Operations Evaluation Group

OEGCMJ
Officer Exercising General Court-Martial Jurisdiction

OEL
Ordnance Equipment List

OEM
Original Equipment Manufacture

OER
Officer's Efficiency Report

OESPCMJ
Officer Exercising Special Court-Martial Jurisdiction

OF
Occupational Fields
Office
Operating Forces
Optional Form
Outfitting and Furnishing

OFC
Office

OFCC
Office of Contract Compliance

OFCOFASSTSECNAV
Office of the Assistant Secretary of the Navy

OFCOFASSTSECNAV(FINMGMT)
Office of the Assistant Secretary of the Navy (Financial Management)

OFCOFASSTSECNAV(INSTALLOG)
Office of the Assistant Secretary of the Navy (Installation and Logistics)

OFCOFASSTSECNAV(PERSRESFOR)
Office of the Assistant Secretary of the Navy (Personnel and Reserve Force)

OFCOFASSTSECNAV(RSCHDEV)
Office of the Assistant Secretary of the Navy (Research and Development)

OFCOFINFO
Office of Information

OFCR
Officer

OFEA
Office of Foreign Economics Administration

OFF
Officer

OFF BUS ONLY
Official Business Only

OFFDEVDISTSYS
Naval Officer Development and Distribution Support System

OFFL
Official

OFFMAUSTSYS
Officer Master File Automated System

OFFNAVHIST
Office of Naval History

OFFPROMSYS
Officer Promotion System

OFF STA
Officer Status

OFGBRO
Officer of the General Counsel Branch Office

OFINDMAN
Office of Industrial Management

OFIT
Occupational Field Implementation Team

OFLD
Offload

OFOFINFO
Office of Information

OFOFLEGAFFAIRS
Office of Legal Affairs

OFP
Operating Force Plan
Operational Flight Program

OFS
Office of Field Service

OFSE
Operating Forces Support Equipment

OFSHR
Offshore

OFT
Often
Operational Flight Trainer

OF/WST
Operational Flight/Weapons System Trainer

OG
Officer-of-the-Guard
Oxygen Generator

OGC
Officer of the General Counsel

OGE
Operational Group Equipment
Out-of-Ground Effect

OGOS
Outward Grade of Service

OGT
Outlet Gas Temperature

OGU
Ongoing Unit

OGW
Overload Gross Weight

O/H
Overhaul

OH
Off Hook
On Hand (quantity)

OHDETS
Over-the-Horizon Detection System

OHF
Overhead Funds

OHH
Operation Helping Hand

OHI
Ordnance Handling Instructions

OHMSETT
Oil and Hazardous Materials Simulated Environment Test Tank

OHO
Ordnance Handling Officer

OHR
Operational Hazard Report

OI
Office of Information
Operating Instructions

OIAF
Office of Information for the Armed Forces

OIC
Officer In Charge

OICC
Officer-in-Charge of Construction

OICCSOWESPAC
Officer-in-Charge of Construction, South Western Pacific

OICMATU
Officer-in-Charge, Marine Air Traffic Control Unit

OICMILDEPT
Officer-in-Charge, Military Department

OI DIV
Operations/Combat Information Center Division

OIF
Operation Iraqi Freedom

OII
Overseas Issues Identification

OIIM
Overseas Issues Identification Meeting

OIL
Ordnance Investigation Laboratory

OINC
Officer In Charge

OIP
Operational Improvement Plan
Ordnance Improvement Plan

OIPT
Overarching Integrated Product Team

OIR
Office of Industrial Relations

OIRS
Operation and Inspection Route Sheet

OIS
Officer Indoctrination School

OIST
Operator Integration Shakedown Test

OJCS
Organization of the Joint Chiefs of Staff

OJT
On the Job Training

OL
Operating Location
Overload

OLA
Office of Legislative Affairs

OL DIV
Operations/Lookout and Recognition Division

OLDS
On-Line Display System

OLF
Outlying Field

OL-IC
Operating Location-Iceland

OLQ
Officer-Like Quality

OLS
Optical Landing System

OLSOR
Object Location and Small Object Recovery

OLSP
Operational Logistics Support Plan

OLSS
Overseas Limited Storage Site

OLTEP
On-Line Text Executive Program

OM
Office Messenger
Operator Maintenance
Organizational Maintenance
Outer Marker
Outfitting Material

OM1
Opticalman First Class

OM2
Opticalman Second Class

OM3
Opticalman Third Class

OMA
Organizational Maintenance Activity

OMB
Office of Management and Budget

OMC
Chief Opticalman

One-Man Control

OMCR
Organized Marine Corps Reserve

OMCS
Senior Chief Opticalman

OMD
Operations Maintenance Division

OMFTS
Operational Maneuver From the Sea

OMI
Ordnance Modification Instructions

OMIGOD
Oh, No!

OML
Overhaul Material List

OMM
Officer Messenger Mail

OMM(S)C
Officer Messenger Mail (Sub) Center

OMP
Overflow Maintenance Program

OMR(E)
Organic Modified Reactor (Experimental)

OMS
Operational Management System
Organizational Maintenance Squadron

OMSA
Opticalman Seaman Apprentice

OMSI
Operating and Maintenance Support Information

OMSN
Opticalman Seaman

OMSTA
Omega Station

OMT
Operational Maintenance Trainer

OMTD
Operator/Maintenance Task Descriptions

ON
Octane Number

ONBD
On Board

ONBOSUB
Onboard a Submarine

ONBOWCOM
Duty on board that vessel when placed in commission

ONBOWSERV
Duty on board that vessel when placed in service

ONC
Operational Navigation Chart

ONDE
Office of Naval Disability Evaluation

ONFE
Operational Aircraft Not Fully Equipped

ON/H
On the Hatch Cover (stowage)

ONH
Office of Naval History

ONI
Office of Naval Intelligence

ONLD
Onload

ONM
Office of Naval Material

ONO
Office of Naval Operations

ONOP
Office of Naval Procurement
Officer-in-Charge, Branch Office of Naval Officer Procurement

ONR
Office of Naval Research

ONRARO
Office of Naval Research Area Research Office

ONRBRO
Office of Naval Research Branch Research Office

ONRDET
Office of Naval Research Detachment

ONREAST

Office of Naval Research, East Coast Regional Office

ONRFE
Office of Naval Research, Far East Regional Office

ONRL
Office of Naval Research, London

ONRREP
Office of Naval Research Representative

ONRRR
Office of Naval Research Resident Representative

ONRWEST
Office of Naval Research, West Coast Regional Office

OOB
Order of Battle

OOC
Out of Commission

OOD
Officer of the Day
Officer of the Deck

OODF
Officer-of-the-Deck (Fleet Task Force Operations)

OODI
Officer-of-the-Deck (Independent)

OOL
Operator-Oriented Language

OOM
Officers' Open Mess

OOO
Out of Order

OOR
Office of Ordnance Research

OOTW
Operations Other Than War

OOW
Officer Of the Watch

OP
Observation Post
Office of Preparedness
Officer Programs
Operating
Operation
Operational
Operational Priority
Operator
Ordnance Personnel
Ordnance Publication
Original Pack

OP&C
Operations Planning and Control

OP&M
Office of Procurement and Material

OPA
Office of Program Appraisal
Overall Probability of Attack

OPAGREE
Operational Agreement

OPAL
Optical Platform Alignment Linkage

OP-AMP
Operational Amplifier

OPANAL
Operations Analysis

OPAREA
Operational Area

OPARS
Optimum Path Aircraft Routing System

OPBY
Operating Authority

OPC
Operational Control Center
Optician
Ownership Purpose and Condition (code)

OPCOM
Operations Communications

OPCON
Operational Control

OPCONCEN
Operational Control Center

OPCTR
Operations Center

OPD
Operations Division
Outpatient Department

OPDAC
Optical Data Conversion (system)

OPDAR
Optical Detection and Ranging

OPDATS
Operational Performance Data System

OPDEVFOR
Operational Development Force

OP DIV
Operations/Air Intelligence Photography Division

OPELINT
Operational Electronic Intelligence

OPER
Operator

O-PERS
Officer Personnel Office

OPEVAL
Operational Evaluation

OPEX
Operational Extension
Operative Extension of Enlistment

OPFS
Offshore Bulk Fuel System

OP/GSA
Office of Preparedness/General Services Administration

OPHOLDS
Operational Holds

OPLAN
Operation Plan

OPLE
Omega Position/Location Equipment

OPM
Operating Plane Month
Operations Per Minute
Overhaul Planning Manual

OPME
Office of Personnel Management Evaluation

OPN
Other Procurement, Navy

OPNAV
Office of the Chief of Naval Operations

OPNAVCOMMO
Office of the Chief of Naval Operations Communications Office

OPNAVSUPPACTDET
Office of the Chief of Naval Operations Support Activity Detachment

OPNAVSUPPACT FIG
Office of the Chief of Naval Operations Support Activity Flight Information Group

OPNAVSUPPACT TCC
Office of the Chief of Naval Operations Support Activity Telecommunications Center

OPNAVSUPPACT WWMCCS DP
Office of the Chief of Naval Operations Support Activity Worldwide Military Command Control System, Data Processing

OPNAVSUPPACT WWMCCS EMPSKED
Office of the Chief of Naval Operations Support Activity Worldwide Military Command Control System, Employment Schedule

OPNAVSUPPACT WWMCCS FORSTAT
Office of the Chief of Naval Operations Support Activity Worldwide Military Command Control System, Force Status

OPNAVSUPPACT WWMCCS MOVREP
Office of the Chief of Naval Operations Support Activity Worldwide Military Command Control System, Movement Reports

OPNAVTCC
Office of the Chief of Naval Operations Telecommunications Center

OPNL
Operational

OPO
Officer Programs Office/Officer

OPORD
Operations Order

OPPE
Operational Propulsion Plant Examination

OPPLAN
Operation Plan

OPQ
Occupying Public Quarters
Other Public Quarters

OPR
Office of Primary Responsibility
Operating
Operator

OPRED
Operational Readiness (plan)

OPREP
Operational Readiness (plan)
Operational Report
Operation Report

OPRG
Operating

OPS
Operations

OPSEC
Operations Security

OPSIG
Operating Signal

OPSKED
Operations Schedule

OPSTAT
Operational Statistics

OPSUB
Operational SUBPAY

OPSUM
Operational Submarine Duty Incentive Pay

OPT
Optician

OPTAG
Optical Aimpoint Guidance

OPTAR
Operational Target (funding)

OPTEMPO
Operational Tempo

OPTEVFOR
Operational Test and Evaluation Force

OPTEVFORDET
Operational Test and Evaluation Force Detachment

OPTEVOR
Operational Test and Evaluation Force

OPTRA
Operational Training

OPTRARON
Operational Training Squadron

OPTRAU
Operational Training Unit

OQ
Order Quantity

OQE
Objective Quality Evidence

O/R
On Request

OR
Operating Room
Operationally Ready
Operational Requirements
Operations Research
Operations Room

ORA
Orbiting Radio Astronomical Observatory

ORC
Officers' Reserve Corps
Outstanding Performance Rating (Cash)

ORCALMIS
Ordnance Calibration Management Information System

ORCON
Operation Report Conversion

ORD
Operational Requirements Document
Order
Orderly
Ordnance

ORDALT
Ordnance Alteration

ORDC
Ordnance Research and Development Center

ORDCAN
Orders (identified by date or message reference numbers following) are cancelled

ORDCONTECH
Ordnance Control Technician

ORDCOR
Orders (identified by date or message reference numbers following) are corrected

ORDENG
Ordnance Engineering

ORDER
Outstanding Requisitions Defeat Endurance Readiness

ORDFAC
Ordnance Facility

ORDIS
Ordnance Discharge

OR DIV
Operations/Radio Communications Division

ORDLIS
Ordnance Logistics Information System

ORDMAINTCO
Ordnance Maintenance Company

ORDMOD
Orders (identified by date or message reference numbers following) are modified

ORDSTA
Ordnance Station

ORDU
Ordnance Unit

ORDVAC
Ordnance Variable Automatic Computer

ORE
Operational Readiness Evaluation
Operational Readiness Exercise

ORG
Ordnance Research Group
Organization

ORI
Operational Readiness Inspection

ORIG
Origin
Original
Originator

ORM
Operational Risk Management

OR/MC
Operational Requirements/Military Characteristics

ORMOD
Orders (identified by date or message reference numbers following) are modified

ORP
Officer Requirements Plan

ORQ
Outstanding Performance Rating with Quality Step Increase

ORS
Operational Reactor Safeguards
Outstanding Requisition System

ORSE
Operational Reactor Safeguards Examination

ORT
Operating Room Technician
Operational Readiness Test
Overland Radar Technology

ORTS
Operational Readiness Test System

ORU
Other than Ship or Squadron Reinforcement Unit (USNR)

O/S
Operating Systems
Out of Service
Outstanding

OS
Operating Systems
Operations Specialist
Ordnance Specifications
Ornamental Stitching
Oxygen Service

OS&D
Over, Short, and Damaged (report)

OS&RP
Onboard Spares and Repair Parts

OS&TD
Ocean Science and Technology Divison (ONR)

OS1
Operations Specialist First Class

OS2
Operations Specialist Second Class

OS3
Operations Specialist Third Class

OSA
Office of Systems Analysis
On-Site Assistance
Open Systems Architecture
Operational Sequence Analysis
Outfitting Stock Activity

OSAP
Ocean Surveillance Air Patrol

OSB
Officer Selection Battery
Operational Stations Book

OSBT
Officer Selection Battery Test

OSC
Chief Operations Specialist
On-Scene Commander
On-Scene Coordinator
Oscillator
Own Ship's Course

OSCAR
Open Systems Core Avionics Requirements

OSCM
Master Chief Operations Specialist

OSCR
Ordnance Systems Component Rework

OSCS
Senior Chief Operations Specialist

OS/D
Over, Short, and Damaged (report)

OSD
Office of the Secretary of Defense
Officer Service Date
Own Ship's Distance

OSDC
Offshore Discharge of Container Ships

OSDOC
Offshore Discharge of Container Ships
Over, Short, and Damaged

OSD/OMB
Office of the Secretary of Defense/Office of Management and Budget

OSF
Ocean Simulation Facility (NCSL)

OSFCO
Office of Solid Fuels Coordinator

OSH
Own Ship's Heading (SINS)

OSHA
Occupational Health and Safety Administration

OSI
Office of Special Investigations
Operating Space Items
Operational Support Inventory

OSILM
On-Site Integrated Logistic Management

OSINT
Open Source Intelligence

OSIP
Operational Suitability Improvement Program
Operation and Safety Improvement Program

OSIR
Out of Service, In Reserve (vessel status)

OSIS
Ocean Surveillance Information System

OSM
Owner-Supplied Material

OSN
Ocean Sciences News (newsletter)
Office of the Secretary of the Navy

OSO
Officer Selection Office
Ordnance Supply Officer
Other Supply Officers

OSOD
Over, Short, and Damaged (report)

OSP
Ocean Survey Program
Offshore Procurement
Outfitting Stock Point
Own Ship's Pitch (SINS)
Own Ship's Position

OSPRO
Ocean Shipping Procedures

OSQ
Officer Separation Questionnaire
Officer Student Quarters

OSR
Office of Scientific Research
Office of Security Review

On-Site Review
Operational Status Release
Operational Support Requirement
Ordnance Status Report
Own Ship's Roll (SINS)

OSS
Ocean Surveillance Satellite
Ocean Survey Ship
Old Submarine
One-Stop Service (FMS)
Operational Sequencing System
Operational Storage Site
Operational Support System

OSSA
Operations Specialist Seaman Apprentice

OSSN
Operations Specialist Seaman

OST
Office of Science and Technology
Operational Suitability Test
Overseas Tour
Own Ship's Track

OSTD
Ordnance Standards

OSU
Optical Scanning Unit
Own Ship's Use

OSV
Ocean Station Vessel (USCG)
On Station Vehicle

OSVEY
Overseas Service Rotation Survey

OT
Ocean Systems Technician
Oil Tight
Operational Testing

OT&E
Operational Test and Evaluation

OT1
Ocean Systems Technician First Class

OT2
Ocean Systems Technician Second Class

OT3
Ocean Systems Technician Third Class

OTA
Office of Technical Assistance
Office of Technology Assessment
Other Than Air (USNR)

OTAC
Ordnance Tank and Automotive Command

OTC
Chief Ocean Systems Technician
Officer in Tactical Command
Officer Training School
Operational Training Command

OTCIXS
Officer in Tactical Command Information Exchange System

OTCLANT
Operational Training Command, Atlantic

OTCM
Master Chief Ocean Systems Technician

OTCN
Officer Training Command Newport

OTCP
Officer Training Command Pensacola

OTCPAC
Operational Training Command, Pacific

OTCS
Senior Chief Ocean Systems Technician

OTD
Official Tables of Distances

OTDA
Office of Tracking and Data Acquisition

OTH
Over-the-Horizon

OTH-B
Over-the-Horizon Back-Scatter (radar)

OTI
Ordnance Technical Instructions

OTIS
Overseas Transfer Information Service

OTL
Operational Time Log

OTLK
Outlook

OTMS
Operational-Technical-Managerial System

OTNP
Other Than New Procurement

OTO NAVSUPPACT
Overseas Transportation Office, Naval Support Activity

OTP
One-Time Pad

OTPI
On Top Position Indicator

OTR
Other

OTRO
Overhaul Test Requirements Outline

OTS
Off The shelf
Operational Training Squadron
Optical Target Simulator
Optical Training Squadron

OTSA
Ocean Systems Technician Seaman Apprentice

OTS-AES
Optical Technology Satellite-Apollo Extension System

OTSN
Ocean Systems Technician Seaman

OTSR
Optimum Track Ship Routing

OTT
Ocean Tactical Targeting
Oral Trade Test

OTU
Operational Training Unit

OUO
Office Use Only

OUSN
Office of the Under Secretary of the Navy

OUTBD
Outbound

OUTCONUS
Outside Continental Limits of the United States

OUTRAN
Output Translator

OUTUS
Outside Continental Limits of the United States

OV
Observation (aircraft)

OVC
Overcast

OVCKD
Overchecked

OVCKD FLD RATS
Overchecked Field Rations

OVHD
Overhead

OVHD PWR CAB
Overhead Power Cable

OVHL
Overhaul

OVPD
Overpaid

OVR
Over

OVRN
Overrun

OVS
Overhaul Specification

OW
Orderwire

OWA
Overhaul Work Authorization

OWC
Ordnance Weapons Command

OWD
Overhaul Work Description

OWP
Overhaul Work Package

OWS
Observation Weather Support
Overhaul Work Scope

OX
Oxygen

OXRB
Oxygen Replacement Bottles

OXY
Oxygen

OY
Overhaul Yard

OYF
Overhaul Yard-Furnished

P
Patchy (runway condition)
Photo/Navigator (NAO code)
Pillar (buoy)
Planning
Polar (air mass)
Popular (AFRTS code)
Priority (message traffic)

P&A
Price and Availability (information)
Procedures and Analysis
Procurement and Assignment

P&E
Planner and Estimator
Planning and Estimating (division)
Procurement and Expedition

P&FM
Program and Financial Management

P&I
Protection and Indemnity

P&O
Plans and Operations

P&P
Packing and Preservation
Payments and Progress
Plans and Policies
Plans and Programs
Process and Print
Process and Proof
Procurement and Production

P&PM
Preservation and Preventive Maintenance

P^3I
Pre-Planned Product Improvement

P A
Position Approximate

PA
Paper
Pattern Analysis (test)
Pending Availability
Permanent Appointment
Pilotless Aircraft
Port Agency
Port Authority
Power Amplifier
Precision Approach
Precomputed Altitude
Procurement Authorization
Program Account
Project Analysis
Public Affairs

PAA
Pay Adjustment Authorization
Percent of Aircraft Available

PAAC
Program Analysis Adaptable Control

PAACS
Prior Active Army Commissioned Service

PAAES
Prior Active Army Enlisted Service

PAAFCS
Prior Active Air Force Commissioned Service

PAAFES
Prior Active Air Force Enlisted Service

PAAT
Personnel and Administration Assistance Team

PAATLANT
Personnel and Administration Assistance Team, Atlantic

PAATPAC
Personnel and Administration Assistance Team, Pacific

P/AB
Port Side Abreast (stowage)

PAB
Policies Allotment Board

Precision Aneroid Barometer
Price Adjustment Bulletin (NRS)
Price Assignment Board

PABX
Private Automatic Branch Exchange

PAC
Pacific
Planned Availability Concept
Privacy Act Coordinator
Program Adjustment Committee
Program Application Code
Project Analysis and Control
Public Affairs Company

PACADIV
Pacific Advanced Headquarters Division

PACAF
Pacific Air Force

PACC
Propulsion and Auxiliary Control Console

PACCOM
Pacific Command

PACCOMOPCONCEN
Pacific Fleet Command Operational Control Center

PACCS
Post Attack Command and Control System

PACDIV
Pacific Division

PACE
Pacific Atoll Cratering Experiment
Performance and Cost Evaluation (program)
Phased Array Control Electronics
Program for Afloat College Education
Project to Advance Creativity in Education

PACED
Program for Advanced Concepts in Electronic Design

PACEE
Propulsion and Auxiliary Control Electronic Enclosure

PACEN
Public Affairs Center

PACENLANT
Public Affairs Center, Atlantic

PACENPAC
Public Affairs Center, Pacific

PACEX
Pacific Exchange (system)

PACFAST
Pacific Forward Area Support Team

PACFASTDET
Pacific Forward Area Support Team Detachment

PACFASTREP
Pacific Forward Area Support Team Representative

PACFIRE
Pre-action Calibration

PACFLT
Pacific Fleet

PACFLTAVCOM
Pacific Fleet Audio-Visual Command

PACFLTCOM
Pacific Fleet Command

PACFLTPROPEXAMBD
Pacific Fleet Propulsion Examining Board

PACGCS
Prior Active Coast Guard Commissioned Service

PACGES
Prior Active Coast Guard Enlisted Service

PACHEDPEARL
Pacific Fleet Headquarters, Pearl Harbor (HI)

PACINTCEN
Pacific Intelligence Center

PACM
Pulse Amplitude Code Modulation

PACMISCEN
Pacific Missile Center

PACMISRAN
Pacific Missile Range

PACMISRANFAC
Pacific Missile Range Facility

PACMISRANFACDET
Pacific Missile Range Facility Detachment

PACMISRANFACREP
Pacific Missile Range Facility Representative

PACMISTESTCEN
Pacific Missile Test Center

PACMISTESTCEN LO
Pacific Missile Test Center Liaison Office

PACNAVCONSTFOR
Pacific Naval Construction Force

PACNAVFACENGCOM
Pacific Naval Facilities Engineering Command

PACNCF
Pacific Naval Construction Force

PACOM
Pacific Command

PACOMBPO
Pacific Command Blood Program Office

PACOMDET
Pacific Command Detachment

PACOMJRO
Pacific Command Joint Medical Regulating Office

PACORNALOG
Pacific Coast Coordinator of Naval Logistics

PACREP
Pacific Representative

PACREPNAVRES
Pacific Representative of the Chief of Naval Reserve

PACRESFLT
Pacific Reserve Fleet

PACS
Pacific Area Communications System

PACSUBDSEC
Pacific Submarine Direct Support Element Coordinator

PACT
Portable Automatic Calibration Tracker
Poseidon Automatic Cable Tester
Production Analysis Control Technique

PAD
Petroleum Administration for Defense
Pilotless Aircraft Division
Pontoon Assembly Detachment
Port, Aft, Down (GQ routing)
Preferred Arrival Date
Preventing Addictive Drugs
Primary Aeronautical Designation
Projects Approval Document
Propellant-Actuated Device
Public Affairs Division

PADAR
Passive Detection and Ranging (radar)

PADD
Planned Active-Duty Date

PADIE
Prevention and Detection of Illegal Entry

PADLOC
Passive Detection and Location of Countermeasures

PA-DRS
Performance Analysis Data Recording System

PADS
Passive Acoustic Display Simulator
Passive-Active Data Simulation
Personnel (Civilian) Automated Data System

PAFCS
Prior Active Foreign Commissioned Service

PAFES
Prior Active Foreign Enlisted Service

PAFSO
Plans and Fleet Support Office

PAGE
Page Generator

PAHEL
Pay and Health Records

PAI
Personnel Accident Insurance

PAINT
Post-Attack Intelligence

PAL
Permissive Action Link
Positive Arming Link
Preliminary Allowance List
Prisoner-at-Large

PALCR
Propulsion Auxiliaries Local Control Rack

PALCRU
Pay and Allowances Accrue from (source listed)

PALS
Permissive Action Link System

PAM
Pressure-Acoustic-Magnetic (minesweeping system)
Priorities and Allocation Manual
Pulse Amplitude Modulation

PAMCCS
Prior Active Marine Corps Commissioned Service

PAMCES
Prior Active Marine Corps Enlisted Service

PAMDS
Price and Management Data Section

PAMIS
Personnel Accounting Machine Installation System

PAMN
Procurement of Aircraft and Missiles, Navy

PAMPA
Pacific Area Movement Priority Agency

PAN
Pilot-Assumed Navigation

PANDL
Pay and Allowances

PANDLCHAR
Pay and allowances chargeable (appropriation and identifying numbers designated)

PANES
Prior Active Navy Enlisted Service

PANGCS
Prior Active National Guard Commissioned Service

PANGES
Prior Active National Guard Enlisted Service

PANS
Procedures for Air Navigation Services

PANSEAFRON
Panama Sea Frontier

PAO
Pilot-Augmented Oscillation
Primary Action Office
Public Affairs Officer

PAP
Patrol Amphibian Plane
Pilotless Aircraft Program

PAPP
Productivity and Pay Plan

P/AR
Problem/Action Report

PAR
Parachute
Parachutist
Perimeter Acquisition Radar
Perimeter Array Radar
Personnel Advancement Requirement
Precision Approach Radar
Problem Analysis Report
Program Adjustment Request
Program Appraisal and Review
Progressive Aircraft Rework
Public Affairs Regulations
Pulse Acquisition Radar

PARA
Parachute
Paragraph

PARC
Periodic Aircraft Reconditioning Cycle

PARD
Pilot Airborne Recovery Device
Pilotless Aircraft Research Division

PAREC
Pay Record

PARESEV
Paraglider Research Vehicle

PARM
Participating Managers

PARR
Performance Analysis Reliability Reporting

PARSEC
Parallax Second

PARSECS
Program for Astronomical Research and Scientific Experiments Concerning Space

PARSYS
Parametric Synthesis

PAR-TEM
Partially Opened-Temporary Pay Record

PARTNER
Proof of Analog Results Through a Numerical Equivalent Routine

PAS
Passenger
Personnel Accounting System
Physically Onboard as a Prisoner
Processing and Analysis Segment
Public Advertising System

PASCALS
Projected Antisubmarine Classification and Location System

PASEP
Passed Separately

PASO
Port Antisubmarine Officer

PASS
Passage
Pay/Personnel Administrative Support System

PASSMAN
Pay/Personnel Administrative Support System Manual

PASTRAM
Passenger Traffic Management (system)

PASU
Patrol Aircraft Service Unit

PAT
Passive Acoustic Torpedo
Patrol
Pattern
Personalized Array Translator
Physically Onboard for Treatment
Political Action Team
Preliminary Acceptance Trials
Proficiency Analytical Testing
Proof and Transit (system)

PAT&E
Production Acceptance Test and Evaluation

PATAO
Personnel and Training Analysis Office (NAVSHIPS)

PAT-C
Position, Altitude, Trajectory Control (system)

PATCO
Professional, Administrative, Technical, Clerical, and Other

PATFOR
Patrol Force

PATN
Pattern

PATRIC
Pattern Recognition, Interpretation, and Correlation

PATRON
Patrol Squadron

PATRONDET
Patrol Squadron Detachment

PATRONSPECPROJDET
Patrol Squadron Special Projects Detachment

PATS
Programmable Automatic Test Set

PATSU
Patrol Aircraft Service Unit

PATWING
Patrol Wing

PATWINGDET
Patrol Wing Detachment

PAU
Pilotless Aircraft Unit

PAV
Pay Adjustment Voucher
Pressure Altitude Variable
Principles and Applications of Value Engineering
Programmed Analysis for Value Engineering

PAW
Powered-all-the-Way

PAWS
Polar Automatic Weather Station

PAX
Passenger
Private Branch Exchange

PAY
Payment

PB
Patrol Boat
Practice Bomb

PBC
Packed by Carrier (household goods)

Practice Bomb Contained

P/BD
Program/Budget Decision

PBD
Program/Budget Decision

PBFT
Planning Board for Training

PBOS
Planning Board for Ocean Shipping

PBR
Patrol Boat, River

PBRA
Practical Bomb-Rack Adapter

PBS
Peninsular Base Section

PBV
Post-Boost Vehicle

PBX
Private Branch Exchange

PC
Paper Copy
Patrol Craft (coastal)
Pay Clerk
Piece
Pitch Cycle
Plane Captain
Plane Commander
Positive Control
Postal Clerk
Power Control (hydraulic system)
Pressure Chamber
Prime Contractor
Printed Circuit
Program Counter (NNSS)
Propulsion Council
Submarine Chaser

PC&D
Planning and Comptroller Department
Planning and Computer Department (NSC)

PC&S
Post, Camp, and Station (contracts)

PC1
Postal Clerk First Class

PC2
Postal Clerk Second Class

PC3
Postal Clerk Third Class

PCA
Personal Cash Allowance
Physical Configuration Audit
Polar Cap Absorption
Position Control Area
Positive Controlled Airspace
Potentially Contaminated Area
Precision Clearing Agent (freon)

PCAM
Punch Card Accounting Machine

PCAMP
Protective Coatings and Metalizing Process

PCAN
Program Change Action Notice

PCB
Parts Control Board
Printed Circuit Board

PCC
Chief Postal Clerk
Patrol Craft, Coastal (control)
Power Control Circuit
Production Compression Capability

PCCL
Pre-Contract Cost Letter

PCCM
Master Chief Postal Clerk

PCCNL
Pacific Coast Coordinator of Naval Logistics

PCCS
Program Change Control System
Senior Chief Postal Clerk

PCD
Polar Cap Disturbance
Program Change Decision

PCDESIG
Plane Captain Designated
Plane Captain Designation

PCE
Patrol Escort
Power Conversion Equipment
Program Cost Estimate
Punch Card Equipment

PCEC
Patrol Vessel, Escort, Control

PCER
Patrol Rescue, Escort

PCF
Patrol Craft, Fast (swift boat)

PCFO
Position Classification Office

PCGOV
Port charges are being paid by foreign government

PCH
Packing, Crating, and Handling
Patrol Craft, Hydrofoil

PCI
Program Configuration Indentification

PCL
Pocket Check List
Power Control Lever
Project Control Ledgers

PCLK
Pay Clerk

PCLO
Passenger Control Liaison Officer

PCM
PASS Consolidation Manual
Penalty Cost Model
Phase-Change Material
Photo-Chemical Machining
Program Change Management
Program Control and Monitor
Pulse Code Modulation
Punch Code Machine

PCMI
Photochromic Microimage

PCN
Parts Change Notice
Production Control Number

PCO
Plastic Chrome Core
Power Change Over
Procurement Contracting Officer
Prospective Commanding Officer

PCOD
Permanent Change of Duty

PCOLA
Pensacola (FL)

PCOP
Port Charges Operator
Port charges are being paid by commercial operator

PCP
Passenger Control Point
Platoon Command Post
Pollution Control Report
Preliminary Definition Plan
Process Control Record
Program Change Proposal
Program Change Record
Program Change Request
Projected Definition Phase
Publications Contract Requirements

PCPN
Precipitation

PCS
Patrol Craft, Submarine
Permanent Change of Station
Primary Control Ship
Propulsion Control Subsystem
Propulsion Control System

PCSA
Seaman Apprentice Postal Clerk

PCSC
Control Submarine Chaser

PCSN
Postal Clerk Seaman

PCSP
Program Communications Support Program

PCT
Percentage
Pharmacy and Chemistry Technician

PCUS
Port charges are being paid by U.S. Army, Navy, or Air Force

PCV
Positive Crankshaft Ventilation
Primary Control Vessel

PCZ
Positive Control Zone

PD
Pad
Paid
Per Diem

Period
Pipe Details
Planning Directive
Point-Detonating
Port Director
Position Description
Position Doubtful
Preference for Duty
Procedures Development
Pulse Doppler
Pulse Duration

PDA
Predicted Drift Angle
Principal Development Activity
Proposed Development Approach
Inf: Public Display of Affection

PDAAP
Program Design and Assurance Plan

PDBA
Personnel Data Base Application

PDBA/SIPM
Personnel Data Base Application/Student Instructor Performance Module

PDC
Personally Developed Contract
Personnel Data Card
Practice Depth Charge
Program Document Control

PDD
Physical Damage Division
Priority Delivery Date
Program Design Data

PDDA
Power Driven Decontamination Apparatus

PDE
Product Design Effort

PDF
Point Detonating Fuze

PDFD
Pulse Doppler Frequency Diversity

PDI
Pre-Deployment Inspection
Product Design Information
Product Design Integration
Product Drawing Index

PDIR
Priority Disassembly and Inspection Report

PDL
Parts Difference List
Pass Down Log
Pass Down the Line

PDLM
Periodic Depot Level Maintenance

PDM
Program Decision Memorandum
Pulse Duration Modulation

P DN
Petition Denied

PDN
Production

PDO
Property Disposal Officer
Publications Distribution Officer

PDP
Program Definition Phase
Programmed Data Processor
Project Definition Phase
Project Definition Plan
Project Development Plan

PDQ
Inf: Pretty Damn Quick

PDR
Periscope Depth Range
Precision Depth Recorder
Preliminary Design Review

PDRC
Professional Recruitment and Career Development

PDRL
Permanent Disability Retirement List

PDRR
Program Definition and Risk Reduction

PDS
Plotter Display System
Production Design Support

PDSMS
Point Defense Surface Missile System

PDT
Processed Directional Transmission

PDT&T
Post Delivery Test and Trial

PE
Patrol Vessel, Eagle
Peck
Personal Effects
Pilot Error
Pistol Expert
Port Engineer
Practical Exercise
Preliminary Evaluation
Probable Error
Procedure Evaluation
Production Engineering
Professional Engineer

PEAC
Photoelectric Auto Controller

PEAT
Priority Equipment Action Tabulation

PEB
Physical Evaluation Board
Pre-Expanded Bin
Propulsion Examining Board

PEBCO
Physical Evaluation Board Counseling Officer

PEBD
Pay Entry Base Date

PEC
Personal Education Counseling
Production Equipment Code
Production Executive Committee

PECE
Proposed Engineering Change Estimates

PECI
Preliminary Equipment/Component Index

PECM
Passive Electronic Countermeasures

PECO
Production Equipment Control Office

PECP
Preliminary Engineering Change Proposal

PED
Personnel Equipment Data
Project Engineering Documentation

PEDC
Personal Effects Distribution Center

PEDIN
Peapod Dingy (USMC)

PEDRO
Pride, Efficiency, Dedication, Reliability, and Order

PEGE
Program for Evaluation of Ground Environment

PEIF
Productivity Enhancing Incentive Fund

PEL
Permissible Exposure Limit
Physiological Exposure Limit

PELSS
Precision Emitter Location Strike System

PEN
Predecessor Event Number

PENAIDS
Penetration Aids (for missiles)

PENO
Prospective Engineering Officer

PEO
Program Executive Office
Program Executive Officer
Prospective Engineering Officer

PEOPLE
Program Enhancing Opportunities for Personal Leadership Effectiveness

PEP
Peak Envelope Power
Performance Effectiveness Program
Personnel Exchange Program

PEPPARD
Propellant, Explosive, Pyrotechnic Pollution Abatement Research and Development

PEPSS
Programmable Equipment for Personnel Subsystem Simulation

PERA
Planning and Engineering for Repairs and Alterations

PERA-CV
Planning and Engineering for Repairs and Alterations-Carrier

PEREF
Personal Effects

PERFMIS
During service as naval attaché perform

under the supervision of the Chief of the Mission such duties as may be assigned by the Navy Department

PERFONSTA
Per diem while on foreign station is payable from locally contributed currency if available, otherwise it is chargeable to (appropriation and identifying numbers designated)

PERGRA
Permission Granted

PERI
Production Equipment Reserve Inventory

PERINTREP
Periodic Intelligence Report

PERISH
Perishable

PERM
Permanent

PERMIC
Personnel Management Information Center

PERMS
Permission

PERNOGRA
Permission Not Granted

PERS
Personnel

PERSCEN
Personnel Center

PERSEPCOMD
Personnel and Separation Command

PERSERVDEPSERVS
Personal Services and Dependents' Services Support System

PERSMAR
Personnel Manning Assistance Report

PERSO
Personnel Officer

PERSOFF
Personnel Officer

PERSRECSYS
Navy Personnel Records System

PERSREHSUPPSYS
Navy Personnel Rehabilitation Support System

PERSRSCHSYSTM
Personnel Management and Training Research Statistical Data System

PERSTEMPO
Personnel Tempo

PERSTRANS
Personal Transportation

PERSTRANSYS
Personal Transportation System

PERSUPPACT
Personnel Support Activity

PERSUPPDET
Personnel Support Detachment

PERT
Pertain
Pertinent
Program Evaluation Review Technique

PERT-CS
Program Evaluation Review Technique-Cost System (expanded PERT)

PERTO
Pertaining To

PES
Production Engineering Specifications

PESD
Program Element Summary Data

PESDS
Program Element Summary Data Sheet

PESM
Precision Electronics Support Measures

PET
Periodic Evaluation Test
Petition
Petroleum

PETE
Portable Electronics Test Equipment

PETRES
Petroleum Reserves

PETRESO
Petroleum Reserves Office/Officer

PETSEC
Petroleum Section

P/F
Practical Factors

PF
Patrol Escort
Performance Factor
Performance Figure (NNSS)
Power Factor
Pre-Fabricated
Protection Factor

PFA
Participating Field Activity

P/FACS
Program/Funds Allocation and Control System

PFAVC
Pacific Fleet Audio-Visual Command

PFB
Pre-Formed Beams (sonar)

PFC
Private First Class

PFCCG
Pacific Fleet Combat Camera Group

PFCO
Position Field Classification Officer

PFD
Pulse Frequency Diversity

PFE
Performance Fitness Examination

PFF
Permanent Family File

PFI
Power Fail Interrupt (NNSS)

PFM
Plan for Maintenance
Pulse Frequency Modulation

PFMPG
Pacific Fleet Mobile Photographic Group

PFN
Pulse-Forming Network

PFP
Primary Failed Part

PFRT
Preliminary Flight Rating Test

PFSV
Pilot to Forecaster Service

PFT
Physical Fitness Testing or Training

PFU
Plan for Use

PG
Package
Patrol Combatant
Pay Grade
Pay Group
Photogrammetry
Postgraduate
Pressure Gradient
Prospective Gain

PGC
Per Gyro Compass

PGH
Patrol Gunboat, Hydrofoil

PGM
Precision-Guided Munitions
Program

PGMG
Guided Missile Motor Gunboat

PG NO DSG
Pay Grade Number Designation

P GR
Petition Granted

PGS
Postgraduate School
Predicted Ground Speed

PGSE
Peculiar Ground Support Equipment

PH
Half Pound
Phase
Photographer's Mate
Plane Handler
Probability of a Hit
Purple Heart

PH1
Photographer's Mate First Class

PH2
Photographer's Mate Second Class

PH3
Photographer's Mate Third Class

PHA
Preliminary Hazards Analysis

PHAA
Photographer's Mate Airman Apprentice

Positive High Angle of Attack

PHAN
Photographer's Mate Airman

PHARM
Pharmacist

PHC
Chief Photographer's Mate

P-HCC
Piston-Hand Control Clutch

PHCM
Senior Chief Photographer's Mate

PHCS
Senior Chief Photographer's Mate

PHD
Pilots' Horizontal Display
Positioning-Head Drum

PHDAN
Physically Dangerous (materials)

PHE
Periodic Health Examination

PHEL
Physiological Heat Exposure Limit

PHER
Photographic Mechanical Equipment Repair (course)

PHGM
Patrol Hydrofoil Guided Missile

PHIB
Amphibious

PHIBCB
Amphibious Construction Battalion

PHIBCORPS
Amphibious Corps

PHIBDET
Amphibious Detachment

PHIBEX
Amphibious Exercise

PHIBFOR
Amphibious Force

PHIBGRU
Amphibious Group

PHIBLANT
Amphibious Forces, Atlantic

PHIBMAINTSUPPU
Amphibious Maintenance Support Unit

PHIBMAINTSUPPULANT
Amphibious Maintenance Support Unit, Atlantic

PHIBMAINTSUPPUPAC
Amphibious Maintenance Support Unit, Pacific

PHIBOPS
Amphibious Operations

PHIBOPTRAU
Amphibious Operations Training Unit

PHIBPAC
Amphibious Forces, Pacific

PHIBRIGLEX
Amphibious Brigade Landing Exercise

PHIBRON
Amphibious Squadron

PHIBTRA
Amphibious Training

PHIBTRABASE
Amphibious Training Base

PHIBTRALANT
Amphibious Training Command, Atlantic

PHIBTRANS
Amphibious Transport

PHIBTRAPAC
Amphibious Training Command, Pacific

PHIBWARTRACEN
Amphibious Warfare Training Center

PHILAGRP
Philadelphia Group

PHILSEAFRON
Philippine Sea Frontier

PH/JO
Photojournalism
Photojournalist

PHK
Probability of a Kill Given a Hit

PHLAGS
Phillips Load-and-Go System

PHM
Patrol Combatant Missile Hydrofoil

PHMRON
Patrol Combatant Missile Hydrofoil Squadron

PHMRON MLSG
Patrol Combatant Missile Hydrofoil Squadron Mobile Logistics Support Group

PHNY
Pearl Harbor Navy Yard

PHONCON
Telephone Conversation

PHONE
Telephone

PHOT
Photograph
Photographer

PHOTO
Photograph

PHOTORON
Photographic Squadron

PHOTOTRIGULANT
Photographic Triangulation Group, Atlantic

PHOTOTRIGUPAC
Photographic Triangulation Group, Pacific

PHST
Packaging, Handling, Storage, Transportation

PHYS
Physical
Physical Examination

PHYSEXAM
Physical Examination

PI
Preliminary Inquiry
Process Interrupts
Programmed Instruction
Proportional Integral (controller)
Public Information

PIA
Primary Insurance Amount

PIACCS
Pacific Integrated Automatic Command and Control System

PIB
Photo Interpretation Brief

PIBAL
Pilot Balloon

PIBALS
Pilot Balloon Reports

PIC
Pacific Intelligence Center
Parent Indicator Code
Payload Integration Center
Photographic Interpretation Center
Picture
Procurement Information for Contracts
Programmed Information Center
Purpose Identification Code
Pursuant to instructions contained in _____

PICA
Procedure for Inventory Control Afloat

PICCOE
Programmed Initiations, Commitments, Obligations and Expenditures

PICM
Master Chief Precision Instrumentman

PICP
Prime Inventory Control Point

PICS
Photographic Information Condensing System

PICT
Picture

PID
Personnel Inquiry/Death/Occupational Illness (report)
Political Intelligence Division
Proportional Integral Derivative (controller)

PIDC
Procurement Intern Development Center

PIDS
Parameter Inventory Display System

PIES
Packaged Interchangeable Electronic System
Procurement and Inventory of Equipment System

PIF
Perpetual Inventory File

PIGA
Pendulous Integrating Gyro Accelerometers

PIID
Prediction Interval Initiation Date

PIIN
Procurement Instrument Identification Number

PIIU
Photo/Imagery Interpretation Unit

PILOT
Piloted-Low Speed Test

PIL STA
Pilot Station

PIM
Point of Intended Movement
Position in Miles
Pulse Interval Modulation

PIMV
Post-Inspection Material Verification

PINS
Persons in Need of Supervision

PINT
Power Intelligence

PIO
Preliminary Inquiry Officer

PIP
Pilot Integrating Pendulum
Problem Improvement Program
Product Improvement Program
Progressive Inspection plan

PIPA
Pulse-Integrating Pendulous Accelerometer

PIPCST
Piping Cost and Weight Analysis Program

PIPMLQ
Pipe Sizing Program for Liquids-Multi-Flow

PIPS
Pneumatically-Induced Pitching System (IBDS)
Pulsed Integrating Pendulums

PIPSAR
Pipe Sizing Program for Air

PIPSLQ
Pipe Sizing Program for Liquids-Single-Flow

PIPSPK
Pipe Sizing Program-Sprinkling

PIPSST
Pipe Sizing Program-Steam

PIR
Periodic Intelligence Report
Problem Identification Report
Procurement Information Reporting
Production Improvement Reports

PIRAZ
Positive Identification Radar Advisory Zone

PIREP
Pilot Report

PIRU
Photographic Interpretation Unit

PIT
Pre-Inspection Testing
Pre-Installation Testing

PITI
Precise Time and Time Interval

PIX
Picture

PIXEL
Picture Element

(PJ)
Qualified as a Parachute Jumper

PJ
Photojournalism
Photojournalist
Procurement Justification
Pulsejet

PJA
Permanent Job Assignment

PJDAM
Precision Joint Direct Attack Munition

PJR
Pipe Joint Record

PK
Package
Position-Keeping

PKI
Public Key Infrastructure

PKP
Purple-K Powder

PKT
Packet

P/L
Packing List
Plain Language

PL
Pail
Patrol Land (pilot code)
Plate
Plumbing (system)
Prospective Loss

PLA
Plain Language Address
Power Level Angle
Practice Landing Approach

PLAA
Positive Low Angle of Attack

PLACE
Position Location and Aircraft Communication Equipment

PLAD
Plain Language Address Directory

PLADS
Parachute Low-Altitude Delivery System

PLANNET
Planning Network

PLANS
Planning Analysis System

PLAT
Pilot Landing Aid Television (system)

PLATF
Plain Language Terminal Forecasts

PLATFS
Plain Language Terminal Forecasts

PLATO
Programmed Logic for Automated Teaching Operation

PLATS
Pilot Landing and Take-Off System

PLAT/VLA
Pilot Landing Aid Television/Visual Landing Aid (system)

PLC
Platoon Leaders Class

PLCC
Propulsion Local Control Console

PLCY
Policy

PLDP
Primary Leadership Development Program

PLI
Pre-Load Indicator

PLICK
Pride, Loyalty, Integrity, Capability, Knowledge

P-LINES
Pole/Power Lines

PLL
Phase-Locked Loop

PLM
Plimsoll Mark
Production Line Maintenance

PLN
Plant

PLNSTD
Planned Standard

PLOP
Pressure Line of Position

PLR
PASS Liaison Representative
Program Life Requirement

PLRS
Position Location Reporting System

PLS
Please

PLSS
Portable Life-Support System

PLT
Plant

PLUS
PERT Life-Cycle Unified System
Programmed Learning Under Supervision

PLYINST
Command delivering orders to command specified comply current NAVMILPERSCOMINST _____

PLYPASSPORT
Application for passport for self (and/or dependents) must be in accordance with NAVMILPERSCOMINST 4650.14 series

PM
Patternmaker
Payload Multiplication (factor)
Permanent Magnet
Phase Modulation
Planned Maintenance (program)
Porous Metal
Position Management
Powered Metal
Preventive Maintenance (program)
Procurement and Material
Program Memo
Project Management
Project Manager
Provost Marshal
Pulse Modulation

PM&ST
Professor of Military Science and Tactics

PM1
Patternmaker First Class

PM2
Patternmaker Second Class

PM3
Patternmaker Third Class

PMA
Permanent Mailing Address
Personal Money Allowance
Political-Military Affairs (unit, USNR)
Principal Management Agreement
Project Manager, Naval Air Systems Command

P-MARP
Peacetime Manpower Allocation/Requirements Plan

PMB
Program Management Branch

PMBR
Practice Multiple Bomb Rack

PMC
Chief Patternmaker
Pacific Marine Center (NOAA)
Pacific Missile Center
Passenger, Mail and Cargo
Procurement, Marine Corps
Procurement Method Coding
Program Management Course (DSMS)
Project Management Course (DSMS)

PMCS
Project Management and Control System

PMDO
Planned Maintenance During Overhaul (program)

PMDS
Point Missile Defense System
Projected Map Display System

PMDU
Projected Map Display Unit

PME
Precision Measuring Equipment
Project Manager, Naval Electronic Systems Command

PMEL
Precision Measuring Equipment Laboratory

PMFA
Patternmaker Fireman Apprentice

PMFC
Post-Maintenance Check-Flight

PMFN
Patternmaker Fireman

PMG
Permanent Magnetic Generator
Political-Military Group

PMI
Program Management Instruction
Proposed Military Improvements

PMIC
Periodic Maintenance Inspection Cards

PMI/MO
Precedence Manual In/Manual Out

PMIP
Post-Maintenance Inspection Pilot

PMK
Performance Mark

PMLFS
Permanent Nucleus Landing Force Staff

PMLO
Philippine Military Liaison Officer

PMM
Permanent Magnetic Synchronous Motors
Planned Maintenance Manual
Pulse Mode Multiplex

PMMP
Preventive Maintenance Management Plan

PMO
Polaris Material Office
Polaris Missile Office
Program Management Office
Project Manager, Naval Ordnance Systems Command
Provost Marshal's Office

PMOLANT
Polaris Material Office, Atlantic

PMOPAC
Polaris Material Office, Pacific

P-MOS
Positive-Metal Oxide Semiconductor

PMP
Program Management Plan
Project Management Plan
Project Master Plan

PMPS
Program Management Planning and Scheduling

PMR
Pacific Missile Range
Planned Maintenance Requirement
Procurement Management Review
Project Manager Representative

PMRA
Projected Manpower Requirements Account

PMRM
Periodic Maintenance Requirements Manual
Projected Manpower Requirements Model

PMRP
Precious Metals Recovery Program

PMS
Performance Measurements System
Planned Maintenance System
Power Management System
Project Manager, Naval Sea Systems Command

PMSV
Pilot-to-Meteorological Service

PMT
Medical Photography Technician

PMV
Private Motor Vehicle

P/N
Part Number

PN
North Pole
Panel
Part Number
Performance Number (fuels)
Personnelman

PN1
Personnelman First Class

PN2
Personnelman Second Class

PN3
Personnelman Third Class

PNA
Passed, but Not Advanced
Price Not Available

PNC
Chief Personnelman

PNCM
Master Chief Personnelman

PNCS
Senior Chief Personnelman

PNEC
Primary Navy Enlisted Classification (code)

PNID
Priority Network In-Dial

PNID/NOD
Priority Network In-Dial/Network Out-Dial

PNNCF
Pacific Northern Naval Coastal Frontier

PNOK
Primary Next of Kin

PNP
Positive-Negative-Positive (transistor)

PNS&T
Professor of Naval Science and Tactics

PNSA
Personnelman Seaman Apprentice

PNSN
Personnelman Seaman

PNUB
Permanent Naval Uniform Board

PO
Permanent Overflow

Petty Officer
Planning Objective
Press Officer
Previous Order
Program Objective
Project Officer
Project Order
Pulse Oscillator
Purchase Order

PO1
Petty Officer First Class

PO2
Petty Officer Second Class

PO3
Petty Officer Third Class

POA
Pacific Ocean Area
Post Overhaul Availability

POA&M
Plan of Action and Milestones

POACS
Prior Other Active Commissioned Service

POAES
Prior Other Active Enlisted Service

POAM
Plan of Action and Milestones

POAN
Procurement of Ordnance and Ammunition, Navy

POAR
Project Order Action Request

POATSC
Pacific Overseas Air Terminal Service Command

POB
Persons Onboard
Projected Onboard

POC
Point of Contact
Privately Owned Convenience
Privately-Owned Conveyance
Production Operational Capability

POCG
Program Operations Coordinating Group

POCL
Power On Clear (NNSS)

POCM
Master Chief Petty Officer

POCP
Program Objective Change Proposal

POCS
Senior Chief Petty Officer

POD
Permissible Operating Distance
Plan of the Day
Port of Debarkation
Port of Discharge
Price, Operation, Decision
Proof of Delivery

POE
Port of Embarkation
Projected Operational Environment

POFA
Programmed Functional Operational Analysis

PO-FY
Program Objectives for Fiscal Year _____

POG
Petty Officer's Guide (publication)
Plant Operating Guide
Propulsion Operating Guide

POIC
Petty Officer In Charge
PO
Petty Officer In Charge

POINTER
Partial Orientation Interferometer

POINTERM
Appointment will be regarded as having terminated upon this date

POINTMAIL
Letter appointment in mail

POL
Petroleum-Oil-Lubricants
Port of Loading

POLCAP
Petroleum Capabilities Report

POLIT
Political

POM
Planned Overseas Movement

Preparation for Overseas Movement
Program Objectives Memorandum

POMA
Petty Officer's Military Academy

POMAR
Positive Operational Meteorological Aircraft Report

POMF
Polaris Missile Facility

POMFLANT
Polaris Missile Facility, Atlantic

POMFPAC
Polaris Missile Facility, Pacific

POMS
Panel on Operational Meteorological Satellites

POMSEE
Performance, Operating, and Maintenance Standards for Electronic Equipment

PONSE
Personnel of the Naval Shore Establishment (report)

PONY
Pride of the Navy Yard

POO
Post Office Order

POOD
Permanent Officer-of-the-Day

POP
Position Operating Procedures

POPR
Pilot Overhaul Provisioning Review

POR
Pay on Return
Proof of Receipt

PORCO
Port Control Office/Officer

PORICH
Port in which (activity designated) may be

PORSE
Post Overhaul Reactor Safeguards Examination

POS
Peacetime Operating Status
Peacetime Operating Stocks
Point of Sale
Position
Preferred Overseas Shore (duty)

POSDCORB
Planning, Organizing, Staffing, Directing, Coordinating, Reporting, and Budgeting

POSIT
Position

POSN
Position

POSS
Passive Optical Satellite Surveillance
Possible
Possibility

POSTER
Post-Strike Emergency Reporting

POT
Potential

POTANN
Potomac Annex

POTS
Pre-Overhaul Tests

POTW
Publically-Owned Treatment Works

POV
Privately-Owned Vehicle

POW
Petty Officer-of-the-Watch
Powder
Prisoner of War

POWP
Preliminary Overhaul Work Package

PP
Page Printer
Plant Procedures
Power Plants (divison)
Preliminary Planning
Pressure Pattern
Pressure Plug
Pressure Proof
Procurement Package

PP&B
Planning, Programming, and Budgeting

PP&C
Production Planning and Control

Program Planning and Control

PP&D
Post Processor and Display

PP&NA
Private Plants and Naval Activities

PP&W
Publicity and Psychological Warfare

PP2P
Patrol Plane Second Pilot

PP3P
Patrol Plane Third Pilot

PPA
Personal Property Activity
Polypropylene Asbestos (seals)

PPAR
Priority Problem Analysis Report

PPB
Provisioning Parts Breakdown

PPBS
Planning, Programming, and Budgeting System

PPC
Partial Pay Card
Patrol Plane Commander
Power Plants Change

PPD
Program Planning Department
Progress Plan Decision
Project Planning Directive

PPDB
Point Positioning Data Base

PPE
Pre-Production Evaluation

PPEA
Plant Performance Evaluation Activity

PPF
Primary Part Failure

PPGBL
Personal Property Government Bill of Lading

PPH
Pounds Per Hour

PPI
Plan Position Indicator

PPL
Preferred Planning List

PPLA
Practice Precautionary Landing Approach

PPM
Parts Per Million
Pulse Position Modulation

PPN
Patrol Plane Navigator

PPNC
Patrol Plane Navigator/Communicator

P PNDG
Petition Pending

PPO
Police Petty Officer
Prior Permission Only
Projected Program Objective
Publications and Printing Office

PPOD
Production Plan of the Day

PPP
Personal Portable Page
Priority Placement Program
Processing and Printing Facility

PPPC
Petroleum Pool Pacific Coast

PPPI
Precision Plan Position Indicator
Projection Plan Position Indicator

PPR
Permanent Pay Record
Prior Permission Required
Production Per Recruiter
Proprietary Procurement Request

PPS
Pre-Position Stocks
Pulse Per Second
Pupil Personnel Services (team)

PPSMEC
Procurement, Precedence of Supplies, Material, and Equipment Committees

PPSO
Personal Property Shipping Office

PPT
Parts Per Thousand

Periodic Production Test
Pre-Production Test

PPTC
Patrol Plane Tactical Coordinator

PPTMR
Personal Property Traffic Management Regulations

PPWO
Propulsion Plant Watch Officer

PQ
Physically Qualified
Previous Question

PQ&MR DIV
Physical Qualifications for Medical Records Division

PQAA
Procurement Quality Assurance Action

PQAP
Planned Quality Assurance Program

PQI
Personnel Quality Index

PQMR
Proposed Qualitative Material Requirement

PQS
Personnel Qualification Standards

PQSDEVGRU
Personnel Quality Standards Development Group

P/R
Planned Requirements

PR
Aircrew Survival Equipmentman
Amphibious Squadron
Precedence Reviewed
Prepare Reply
Press Release
Priority Regulations
Processing and Reporting
Procurement Report
Procurement Request
Public Relations
Purchase Request
Purchase Requisition

PR1
Aircrew Survival Equipmentman First Class

PR2
Aircrew Survival Equipmentman Second Class

PR3
Aircrew Survival Equipmentman Third Class

PRA
Pay Record Access
Personnel Research Activity

PRAA
Aircrew Survival Equipmentman Airman Apprentice

PRAC
Practice

PRAM
Propelled-Ascent Mine

PRAN
Aircrew Survival Equipmentman Airman

PRARS
Pitch, Roll, Azimuth Reference System

PRASD
Personnel Research Activity, San Diego (CA)

PRATE
Present Rate

PRAW
Naval Reserve Research Activity

PRB
Planned Requirements Bureau
Program Review Board

PRBC
Pressure Ratio Bleed Control

PRC
Chief Aircrew Survival Equipmentman
Package Requirements Code
Planned Requirements Conversion

PRCHT
Parachute

PRCM
Master Chief Aircrew Survival Equipmentman

PR/COM
Vessel Delivered in Partially-Completed Status

PRCP
Personnel Readiness Capability Program

PRCS
Senior Chief Aircrew Survival Equipmentman

PRD
Period
Planned Rotation Date
Projected Rotation Date
Public Relations Division

PRDR
Preproduction Reliability Design Review

PRE
Progressive Resistive Exercise

PREC
Precedence

PRECIP
Precipitation

PRECOM
Precommissioning

PRECOMDET
Precommissioning Detail

PRECOMSCOL
Precommissioning School

PRECOMUNIT
Precommissioning Unit

PREF
Preference
Preferred

PREFLT
Pre-Flight

PREFLTSCOL
Pre-Flight School

PREINSURV
President, Board of Inspection and Survey

PRELIM
Preliminary

PRELIMPERSACCT
In accordance with NAVPERSMAN 3860360, activity performing preliminary procedures for separation will carry your separation papers and pay accounts and continue to report you in personnel accounting system until action is taken on proceedings and recommended findings of physical evaluation board

PRELIMSEPRET
Period between date of completion of preliminary procedures incident to separation and date of retirement, discharge, release from active duty, or restoration to duty status, less allowed travel time used in arriving (place designated) will be charged against earned leave

PREMEDU
Preventive Medicine Unit

PREP
Pre-Discharge Education Program
Preparation
Prepare

PREPSCOL
Preparatory School

PRES
Present
President
Pressure

PRESAIR
Pressurized Air Compressors

PRESINSURV
President, Board of Inspection and Survey

PRESPROC
Presidential Proclamation

PRESS
Pacific Range Electromagnetic Signature Studies

PRESTO
Program Reporting and Evaluation System for Total Operation

PREV
Pre-Reenlistment Evaluation
Previous

PREVMEDDIV
Preventive Medicine Division

PREVMEDU
Preventive Medicine Unit

PRF
Pulse Repetition Frequency

PR I
Processing and Reporting, Phase I (course)

PR II
Processing and Reporting, Phase II (course)

PRI
Primary
Priority
Prison
Pulse Repetition Interval

PRIBAG
Priority Baggage

PRI BIL
Primary Billet

PRIDE
Personalized Recruiting for Immediate or Delayed Enlistment

PRIM
Primary
Primary Radar Identification Methods

PRIMAN
Enlisted Primary Manning (codes)

PRIME
Primary Management Efforts
Priority Management Efforts

PRIN
Principal

PRINCE
Parts Reliability Information Center

PRINOBC/NEC
Primary Navy Officer Billet Classification and Navy Enlisted Classification (codes)

PRINT
Pre-edited Interpretive (system)

PRIOR
Program for In-Orbit Rendezvous

PRISE
Program for Integrated Shipboard Electronics

PRISIC
Photographic Reconnaissance Interpretation Section Intelligence Center

PRISM
Program Integrated System Maintenance
Programmed Integrated System Maintenance
Program Reliability Information System for Management

PRITRA
Primary Training

PRIV
Private
Privately

PRIVAUTH
Travel authorized via privately-owned vehicle with understanding that no additional cost to the government is involved

PRIV MAINTED
Privately-Maintained

PRIV PROP
Private Property

PRL
Penetration Records List
Publications Requirements List

PRM GR
Permanent Grade

PRMIS
Printing Resources Management Information System

PRO
Personnel Relations Officer
Price Reduces Overhead
Probation
Procedure
Proceed
Professional
Proficiency
Public Relations Officer

PRO ACCT REC
Property Accountability Records

PROB
Probable
Probably

PROBCOST
Probabilistic Budgeting and Forward Costing

PROBOUT
Proceed on or about

PROC
Photographic Reconnaissance Officers' Course
Procurement

PROCOMP
Process Compiler

PROCON
Request diagnosis, prognosis, present condition, probable date and mode of disposition of following patient(s) reported in your hospital (name, grade, social security number)

PRODAC
Programmed Digital Automatic Control

PROF
Professor
Proficiency

PROFASTRANS
Proceed by first available government transportation

PROF-E
Programmed Review of Operator Functions-Elementary

PROG
Prognosis
Progress

PROGMAINT
Progressive Maintenance

PROH
Prohibit

PROIMREP
Proceed immediately and report

PROJ
Project
Projectile

Project SAIL
Sailor Advocacy Through Interactive Leadership

PROJMGR
Project Manager

PROJMGRASWS
Project Manager, Antisubmarine Warfare Systems

PROJMGRSMS
Project Manager, Surface Missile Systems

PROL
Priority Reconnaissance Objectives List

PROM
Programmable ROM
Prominent
Promote
Promoted

PROMIS
Program Management Information System

PROML
Promulgate

PROMPT
Project Reporting, Organizing and Management Planning Technique

PROMSS
Procedures and Relationships for the Operation of Manual Stations and Spaces

PROM STAT
Promotion Status

PROP
Planetary Rocket Ocean Platform
Propeller
Property

PROPA BAS
Pro-Rated Basic Allowance for Subsistence

PRO-PAY
Proficiency-Pay

PROPORICH
Proceed to port in which (unit located)

PROS
Prosecution
Prospective

PROSIG
Procedures Signal

PROSIGN
Procedure Sign

PROTIMEREP
Proceed in time to report (activity or station designated by group(s) immediately following) not later than (hour and/or date indicated)

PROUS
Proceed to a port in the Continental Limits of the United States

PROV
Provide
Provisional

PROVGR
Proving Grounds

PROVIB
Propulsion System Decision and Vibration Analysis

PROVMAIN
Other provisions to basic orders remain in effect

PROVMAINTCO
Provisional Maintenance Company

PROVMUSTCO
Provisional Medical Unit Self-Contained Company

PROWDELREP
Proceed without delay and report

PRP
Personnel Reliability Program
Physical Readiness Program
Pneumatically-Released Pilot
Production Requirements Plan
Progressive Rework Plan
Public Relations Personnel
Public Relations Plan

PRR
Passenger Reservation Request
Production Readiness Review
Pulse Repetition Rate

PRSEC
Payroll Section

PRST
Persist
Probability Ratio Sequential Test

PRT
Physical Readiness Testing or Training
Power Recovery Turbine
Program Review Team
Pulse Repetition Time

PRT&T
Post Repair Test and Trial

PRTC
Professional Rate Training Course

PRTL
Portable

P/S
Power Section

PS
Patrol Sea (pilot code)
Pistol Sharpshooter
(Coolant) Pressuring System
Program Summary
South Pole

PS&E
Plans, Specifications, and Estimates

PS&M
Personnel Supervision and Management

PS&QS
Planning and Quotas

PS&T
Pay, Subsistence, and Transportation

P/S/A
Port Side Aft (stowage)

PSA
Personnel Support Activity
Post-Shakedown Availability
Project Sensor Abilities
Public Service Announcement

PSANDT
Pay, Subsistence, and Transportation

PSAT
Propulsion Subsystem Availability Test

PSBL
Possible

PSC
Per Standard Compass

PSD
Personnel Support Detachment
Physical Sciences Division
Preferred Sea Duty
Professional Services Dates
Pseudo Stow Document

PSDA
Partial Source Data Automation

PSE
Personnel Support Equipment
Power-Supply Electronics (assembly)

PSEA
Pacific and Southeast Asia

P/S/F
Port Side Forward (stowage)

PSF
Panama Sea Frontier
Philippine Sea Frontier
Private Source Funds

PSG
Passage
Passing

PSGR
Passenger

PSH
Pre-Select Heading

PSI
Periodic Step Increase
Personnel Security Investigations
Pounds per Square Inch
Pressurized Sphere Injection
Programmed Student Input

PSIA
Per-Square-Inch Absolute

PSIB
Preliminary Ship Information Book

PSICP
Program Support Inventory Control Point

PSID
Patrol Seismic Intrusion Detector

PSIG
Per-Square-Inch Gauge

PSK
Phase-Shift Keying

PSK-PCM
Phase-Shift Keying/Pulse-Code Modulation

PSL
Pycnocline Scattering Layer

PSN
Position
Processing Sequence Number (AUTODIN)

PSNCF
Pacific Southern Naval Coastal Frontier

PSNS
Puget Sound Naval Shipyard

PSNSY
Puget Sound Naval Shipyard

PSO
Political Survey Officers
Port Services Office/Officer
Prospective Supply Officer
Publicity Security Officer

PSP
Patrol Seaplane
Perforated Steel Plating
Performance Standards Program
Project Standard Practice

PSR
Packed Snow on Runway
Performance Summary Report
Photo Scale Reciprocal

PSR-P
Packed Snow on Runway-Patchy

PSS
Propulsion Sub-System

PST
Past
Projected Sea Tour

PSTCO
Per Steering Compass

PSTGC
Per Steering Compass

PSTN
Pay, Subsistence, and Transportation, Navy

PSU
Power Switching Unit

PSUM
Phalanx Surface Mode

PSW
Primary Shield Water

PSWR
Power Standing-Wave Ratio

PSYOP
Psychological Operations

PSY-OPS
Psychological Warfare Operations

PSYOPS
Psychological Operations

PSY-S DIV
Psychological Sciences Division (ONR)

PSYWAR
Psychological Warfare

PT
Paper Tape
Particle Test
Patient
Patrol Torpedo Boat
Penetration Test
Period
Physical Therapy or Training
Pint
Point
Primary Target
Proceed Time

PTBL
Portable

PTC
Motorboat, Submarine Chaser
Personnel Transfer Capsule

PTCA
Provisioning Technical Coding Activity

PTCAD
Provision Troop Carrier Airborne Division

PTCCS
Polar Target Card Computer System

PTD
Pilot to Dispatcher
Provisioning Technical Demonstration

PTDP
Preliminary Technical Development Plan

PTF
Fast Patrol Craft
Patch and Test Facility

PTFG
Large Guided Missile Motorboat

PTFMR
Peacetime Force Material Request

PTG
Small Guided Missile Motorboat

PTI
Pre-Trial Investigation

PTL
Patrol
Petroleum Testing Laboratory
Pre-Test Laboratory

PTM
Pulse Time Modulation
Pulse Time Multiplex

PTN
Pattern

PTO
Please Turn Over
Power Take-Off
Project Technical Office

PTR
Painter
Pilot Training Rates

PTS
Perform to Serve
Permanent Threshold Shift
Pre-Flight Test Set
Pressure Test Station

PTT
Part Task Trainers

PTTI
Precise Time and Time Interval (standards)

PTY
Party

PU
Pick Up
Propellant Utilization (system)

PUB
Public
Publication
Publicity
Publish
Published

PUBAFF
Public Affairs

PUBAFF RRU
Public Affairs Ready Reserve Unit

PUBINFO
Public Information

PUBREL
Public Relations

PUBWKS
Public Works

PUBWKSCEN
Public Works Center

PUBWKSDEPT
Public Works Department

PUC
Permanent Unit Code
Port Utilization Committee
Presidential Unit Citation

PUFFS
Passive Underwater Fire Control Feasibility

PUI
Pilot Under Instruction

PULHES
Physical Capacity or Stamina, Upper

Extremities, Lower Extremities, Hearing and Ears, Vision and Eyes, and Psychiatric System

PUM
Per Unit Monthly

PUMA
Precision Underwater Mapping and Navigation

PUMP
Production Upgrade Management Program

PUP
Pull-Up Point

PUR
Purchase
Pursuant

PURA
PACOM Utilization and Redistribution Agency

PURCH
Purchase

PURIF
Purification

PURS
Program-Usage Replenishment System

PUS
Propellant-Utilization System

PV
Prevailing Visibility
Public Volunteer
Public Voucher

PVC
Poly-Vinyl-Chloride (plastic pipe)

PVG
Providing Group
Proving Ground

PVL
Prevail

PVLS
Peripheral Vertical Launch System

PVNT
Prevent

PVST
Port Visit

PVT
Private

PW
Potable Water
Public Works
Pulse Width

PWA
Public Works Administration

PWB
Psychological Warfare Branch
Pulling Whaleboat

PWBS
Product Work Breakdown Structure

PWC
Public Works Center

PWCACE
Public Works Center Activity Civil Engineer

PWCDET
Public Works Center Detachment

PWCMIS
Public Works Center Management Information System

PWCMS
Public Works Center Management System

PWD
Post-Write-Disturb (pulse)
Psychological Warfare Division
Public Works Department

P/WG
Port Wing (stowage)

PWI
Proximity Warning Indicator

PWLA
Public Works Lead Activity

PWM
Public Works Maintenance
Pulse Width Modulation

PWO
Principal Warfare Office/Officer
Public Works Office/Officer

PWOF
Public Works Office/Officer

PWP
Plasticized White Phosphorus

PWR
Power

Pressurized Water Reactor

PWRR
Preposition War Reserve Requirements

PWRS
Preposition War Reserve Stocks

PWS
Performance Work Statement

PWT
Public Works Transportation

PWTC
Public Works Transportation Center

PWU
Public Works Utilities

PXO
Prospective Executive Officer

PY
Planning Year
Program Year
Pyramid

PYPER
Promote Yard Performance Efficiency and Reliability

PYZ
Pickup Zone

Q
Quarterly (report frequency)
Question

Q&A
Questions and Answers

Q&RA
Quality and Reliability Assurance

QA
Quality Assurance
Quick-Acting

QA&R
Quality Assurance and Revalidation

QAB
Quick-Acting Buttons

QAD
Quality Assurance Department
Quality Assurance Division

QAET
Quality Assurance Evaluation Test

QAIP
Quality Assurance Inspection Procedure

QAL
Quarterly Allowance List (aviation)

QAO
Quality Assurance Office

QAP
Quality Assurance Procedures
Quality Assurance Program
Quality Assurance Provisions

QAR
Quality Assurance Representative

QARI
Quality Assurance Receipt Inspection

QAST
Quality Assurance Service Test (nuclear)

QATS
Quarterly Advanced Training Schedule

QAVP
Quality Assurance Verification Procedures

QAWT
Quick-Acting Water-Tight

QC
Quality Control
Quarter Credit

Q CARD
Qualification Card

QCID
Quality Control and Inspection Department

QCR
Quality Control/Reliability
Quality Control/Representative

QDR
Quadrennial Defense Review
Quality Deficiency Record
Quality Deficiency Report

QE
Quality Evaluation

QEAD
Quality Engineering and Assurance Division

QEC
Quick Engine Change

QECA
Quick Engine Change Assembly

QECK
Quick Engine Change Kit

QECS
Quick Engine Change Stand

QEEL
Quality Evaluation and Engineering Laboratory

QEL
Quality Evaluation Laboratory (NTS)

QEST
Quality Evaluation System Test

QF
Quality Factor (radiation dose)

QFA
Qualification Firings Alignment

QFB
Quiet Fast Boat

QFR
Quarterly Force Revision

QFS
Quick-Fit Sea

QI
Quart Imperial

QIB
Quarterly Information Bulletin

QK
Interrupted Quick

QK FL
Quick Flashing (light)

QL
Quintal

QM
Quartermaster

QM1
Quartermaster First Class

QM2
Quartermaster Second Class

QM3
Quartermaster Third Class

QMA
Qualified Military Available

QMAO
Qualified for Mobilization Ashore Only

QMB
Quarterly Management Bulletin (publication)

QMC
Chief Quartermaster
Quartermaster Corps

QMCM
Master Chief Quartermaster

QMCS
Quality Monitoring Control System
Senior Chief Quartermaster

QMOW
Quartermaster Of the Watch

QMS
Quarterly Meteorological Summary

QMSA
Quartermaster Seaman Apprentice

QMSN
Quartermaster Seaman

QM-T
Quartermaster-Trainee

QOH
Quantity On Hand

QOL
Quality Of Life

QOMAC
Quarter-Orbit Magnetic Altitude Control

QOS
Quality Of Service

QPL
Qualified Products List

QPR
Quarterly Program Review
Quarterly Progress Report

QPRS
Quarterly Project Reliability Summary

QR
Qualified Representative
Quantity Requested
Quire

QRA
Quick-Reaction Alert
Quick Replaceable Assembly

QRC
Quick-Reaction Capability
Quick-Reaction Contract

Q/R/M
Quality/Reliability/Maintainability

QRT
Quiet Radio Transmission (sent before SOS)

QS
Quality Surveillance

QSI
Quality Step Increase

QSSI
Quarterly Surprise Security Inspection

QSTOL
Quiet Short Take-off and Landing (aircraft)

QT
Quart
Quenched and Tempered (steel)

QTC
Quick Transmission Change

QTR
Quarter
Quarterly

QTRS
Quarters

QTY
Quantity
Quarterly

QUAD
Quadrant
Quadruplicate

QUAL
Qualification
Quality

QUALREPFLYINS
Upon qualification and completion of academic training and when directed, report as DIFOTINSCREW

QUAR
Quarantine

QUARK
Question and Response Kits

QUES
Question

QUOTE
Quotation

QWR
Quarterly Weight Report

QZ
Quartz

(R)
Receiver

R
Rain
Read
Relay
Religious (AFRTS code)
Repair
Reproducible (copy)
Resistance
Resistor

R&A
Research and Analysis

R&D
Research and Development

R&M
Reliability and Maintainability

R&PT
Rifle and Pistol Team

R & R
Rest & Rehabilitation

R&R
Range and Range-Rate
Rest and Recreation

Rest and Recuperation
Rest and Rehabilitation
Rest and Relaxation

R&SSQ
Repair and Salvage Squadron

R&T
Research and Technology

R&TV
Radio and Television (DINFOS)

R/A
Radius of Action

RA
Radar
Radio Altimeter Setting Height
Ration
Reconnaissance Aircraft
Rental Agreement
Reviewing Authority
Rotary Actuator

RAADC
Regional Accounting and Disbursing Center

RAAN
Repair Activity Accounting Number

RABAL
Radiosonde Balloon (observation)

RABALS
Radar Balloons

RAC
Radar Azimuth Converter
Rapid-Action Change
Reactor Accident Calculation
Refrigerant-Air Condition (system)
Request for Authority to Contract
Responsibility Analysis Chart

RACE
Radiation Adaptive Compression Equipment
Random-Access Computer Equipment

RACEP
Random Access and Correlation for Extended Performance

RACON
Radar Responder Beacon

RA (CONSPIC)
Radar Conspicious (object)

RACS
Recruiting Allocation Control System

RAD
Radial
Radical
Radio
Radius
Rapid Access Disc
Ratio Analysis Diagram
Recruiting Advertising Division
Released from Active Duty
Required Availability Date
Resources Allocation Display

RADA
Random-Access Discrete Address System

RADBN
Radio Battalion

RADCOM
Radar Countermeasures

RADCON
Radar Control
Radiological Control

RADEX
Radar Extractor

RADFAC
Radiating Facility

RADFAL
Radiological Prediction Fallout (plot)

RADFO
Radiological Fallout

RADHAZ
Hazards from Electromagnetic Radiation

RADIDS
Radar Digital Information Display Service

RADINDEF
Notify COMNAVMILPERSCOM not less than six months prior to (date) if member does not desire further ACDU orders. Failure to do so constitutes agreement to accept another tour of duty

RADINJCLRDS
Radiation Injury Claims Records (NAVSEA)

RADINT
Radar Intelligence

RADIST

Radar Distance (indicator)

RADLDEFLAB
Radiological Defense Laboratory

RADM
Rear Admiral
Rear Admiral Upper Half

RADMIS
Research and Development Information Summary

RADMON
Radiological Monitor

RADOB
Radar Observation

RADOP
Radio Operator

RADPLANBD
Radio Planning Board

RADSAFE
Radiological Safety

R/ADT
Registration/Admission, Disposition and Transfer (TRIMIS)

RADU
Ram Air-Driven Unit

RAE
Radio Astronomy Explorer

RAETU
Reserve Airborne Electronics Training Unit

RAF
Radical Awareness Facilitator (school)

RAFLO
Radio Frequency Liaison Office

RAFT
Racial Awareness Facilitators Team
Resource Allocation for Transportation

RAG
Replacement Air Group
River Assault Group

RAI
Random-Access Inquiry

RAID
Radar and Interdiction Device
River Assault Interdiction Division

RAIDS
Rapid Anti-Ship Cruise Missile Integrated Defense System

RAIL
Revised Individual Allowance List
Runway Alignment Indicator Lights

RAILS
Remote Area Instrument Landing Sensor

RAIP
Recruiting Advertising Improvement Program

RAL
Rubber, Air, Lead (sound dampening materials)

RALACS
Radar Altimeter Low-Altitude Control System

RAM
Radio Attenuation Measurement
Random-Access Memory
Readiness and Money
Redeye Air-Launched Missile
Reentry Anti-Missile
Rolling Airframe Missile

RAMAC
Random-Access Methods of Accounting and Control

RAMEC
Rapid-Action Minor Engineering Change

RAMICS
Rapid Airborne Mine Clearance System

RAMP
Repairable-Asset Management Office

RAMPART
Radar Advanced Measurements Program for Analysis of Reentry Techniques

RAMPS
Resources Allocation and Multi-Project Scheduling

RAMS
Recruiting Advertising Management System

RAMSIM
Reliability, Availability, Maintenance, Simulation

RAMTRA
Reserve Air Maintenance Training

RAMUS
Remote Access Multi-User System

RAMVAN
Reconnaissance Aircraft Maintenance Van

RAN
Radar Navigation
Random
Reconnaissance Attack Navigator
Regional Air Navigation
Reporting Accounting Number
Request for Authority to Negotiate

RANCID
Real and Not Corrected Input Data

RANCIN
Retrieval and Analysis of Navy Classified Information

RANCOM
Random Communications (satellite)

RANGECO
Range Company

RAOB
Radar Observation

RAP
Recognize All Potential
Recruiter Assistance Program
Rocket-Assisted Projectile

RAPCON
Radar Approach Control

RAPEC
Rocket-Assisted Personnel Ejection Catapult

RAPIDS
Real-Time Automated Personnel Identification System

RAPLOC
Rapid Acoustic Passive Localization

RAPPI
Random-Access Plan Position Indicator

RAP-TAP
Releasable Assets Program-Transferrable Assets Program

RAPTS
Resource Accounting Project Tracking System

RAR
Radio-Acoustic Range
Record and Report

RARC
Revoked Appointment and Returned to Civilian Status

RA REF
Radar Reflector

RARF
Radome, Antenna, and Radio Frequency (circuitry)

RARI
Reporting and Routing Instructions

RAS
Radar Assembly Spares
Radar Automatic System
Replenishment at Sea
Requirements Audit System

RASAU
Reserve Antisubmarine Warfare Systems Analysis Mobilization Unit

RASC
Radiological Affairs Safety Committee

RASCAL
Random-Access Secure Communications Anti-Jam Link

RASER
Radio Frequency Amplification by Stimulated Emission of Radiation

RASO
Radiological Affairs Support Office

RASOR
Rear Area Stand-Off Repeater

RASP
Radiological Affairs Support Program
Refined Aeronautical Support Program
Reserve Analytical Studies Project

RASTAS
Radiating Site Target Acquisition Study

RAT
Ram Air Turbine
Rocket-Assisted Torpedo

RATAN
Radar and Television Aid to Navigation
Radio and Television Aid to Navigation

RATCC
Radar Air Traffic Control Center

RATE
Remote Automatic Telemetering Equipment

RATIO
Radio Telescope in Orbit

RATO
Rocket-Assisted Take-Off

RATOG
Rocket-Assisted Take-Off Gear

RATPAC
Radar Acquisition Tracking Probe for Active Calibration

RATS
Radar Altimeter Target Simulator
Rations
Recruiting Attrition Tracking System

RATSCAT
Radar Target Scatter

RATT
Radio Teletype

RAU
Retransmission Application Unit

RAV
Restricted Availability

RAVE
Research Aircraft for Visual Environment

RAVIR
Radar Video Recorder

RAWIN
Radar Wind (sounding)

RAWINSONDE
Radar Wind (sounding)

R/B
Radio Beacon

RB
Relative Bearing
Renegotation Board
Rescue Boat
Rubber Block

RBA
Rescue Breathing Apparatus
Revolution in Business Affairs

RBC
Return Beam Vidicon

RBDE
Radar Bright Display Equipment (FAA)

RBE
Relative Biological Effectiveness

RBFC
Retract Before Firing Contractor

RBHB
Red and Black Horizontal Bands (buoy markings)

R BN
Radio Beacon

RBO
Repair Before Operate

RBOC
Rapid-Blooming Off-Board Chaff (missile decoy system)

RBS
Radar Bombing Score
Recoverable Booster System
Regional Briefing Station

RC
Rapid Curing (asphalt)
Reactor Compartment
Reactor Cooling (system)
Reception Center
Reduced Capability
Relay Center
Reserve Component
Resistance Capacitance (time)

RCA
Rating Change Authority
Rating Change Authorization
Reach Cruising Altitude
Repair Cycle Asset
Riot Control Agent

RCC
Recovery Control Center
Rescue Coordination Center
Rescue Coordination Control
Resistance-Capacitance Coupling

RCCA
Recovery Control Center, Atlantic

RCCP
Recovery Control Center, Pacific

RCD
Rocket Cushioning Device

RCDR
Radiological Control Deficiency Report

RCE
Radiological Control Engineering

RCH
Reach

RCL
Ramped Cargo Lighter

RCLM
Reclaim

RCLS
Runway Centerline Light System

RCM
Radar Countermeasures
Radio Countermeasures

RCMA
Reservist Clothing Maintenance Allowance

RCMD
Recommend

RCMP
Recompute Last Fix (NNSS)

RCN
Reconnaissance

RCO
Range Control Officer
Remote Control Officer

RCP
Radar Chart Protector
Request for Contractual Procurement

RCPP
Refrigeration, Compressor and Electrical Power, Airborne Pod Enclosure

RCPT
Reception
Refrigeration, Compressor and Electrical Power, Trailer-Mounted

RCR
Runway Condition Reading

RCRA
Radiologically-Controlled Radiation Area

RCRC
Revoked Commission, Returned to Civilian Status

RCRS
Reserve Combat Replacement Squadron

RCS
Radar Control Ship
Radar Cross Section
Reentry Control System
Report Control Symbol
Rip-Out Control Sheet

RCSS
Random Communications Satellite System
Recruiting Command Support System

RCT
Received Copy of Temporary
Regimental Combat Team
Regional Combat Team
Repair Cycle Time

RCTL
Resistor-Capacitor-Transistor Logic (circuitry)

RCU
Remote Radio Control Unit
Requisition Control Unit

RCV
Receive

RCVD
Received

RCVG
Replacement Carrier Air Group

RCVR
Receiver

RCVW
Readiness Attack Carrier Air Wing

RD
Radar
Radarman
Read
Reference Datum
Replenishment Demand
Restricted Data
Revolutionary Development (team)
Round

RD1
Radarman First Class

RD2
Radarman Second Class

RD3
Radarman Third Class

RDAC
Recruiting District Assistance Council

RDB
Ramped Dump Barge
Research and Development Board

RDC
Chief Radarman
Rapid Development Capability
Recruit Division Commander
Research and Development Center

RDCM
Master Chief Radarman

RDCS
Senior Chief Radarman

RDD
Range Development Department
Required Delivery Date

RDEP
Recruit Depot

RDF
Radio Direction Finder
Rapid Deployment Force
Restoration of Damaged Facilities

RDFSTA
Radio Direction Finder Station

RDG
Ridge

RDI
Reliability Design Index

RDJTF
Rapid Deployment Joint Task Force

RDL
Rapid Draft Letter

RDM
Ramped Dump Barge

RDML
Rear Admiral Lower Half

RDO
Radio
Regional Defense Organization
Research and Development Objective
Runway Duty Officer

RDP
Range Data Processor

RDPM
Revised Draft, Presidential Memorandum

RDS
Rounds

RDSA
Radarman Seaman Apprentice

RDSN
Radarman Seaman

RDSS
Rapidly Deployable Surveillance System

RDT
Reliability Determination Test

RDT&E
Research, Deployment, Test, and Evaluation

RDT&EN
Research, Development, Test, and Evaluation, Navy

RDTE
Research, Development, Test, and Evaluation

RDU
Receipt and Dispatch Unit
Refrigeration Detection Unit

RDVU
Rendezvous

RDY
Ready

RE
Radio, Electronic (system)
Reenlistment (code)

REA
Reactor Enclosure Assembly

REACDU
Recalled to Active Duty

REACOT
Remove Errors and Complete on Time

READ
Radar Echo Augmentation Device
Real-Time Electronic Access and Display

READE
Reduce Errors and Decrease Expense

READI
Rocket-Engine Analyzer and Decision Instrument

READJ
Readjusted

READJPAY
Readjusted Pay

READSUPPGRUDET
Readiness Support Group Detachment

READTRAFAC
Readiness Training Facility

REAF
Responsibility for discharge costs rests with U.S. Air Force or its agent

REALCOM
Real-Time Communications

REB
Radar Evaluation Branch

REC
Receive

RECA
Residual Capacity Assessment

RECBKS
Receiving Barracks

RECCE
Reconnaissance

RECCFO
Received in Connection with Fitting Out

RECCO
Reconnaissance Reporting Code

RECD
Received

RECDUINS
Received for duty under instruction

RECDUT
Received for Duty

RECIP
Reciprocating

RECIPRO
Reciprocating

RECL
Reclamation

RECLUMPSUM
Entitled to receive lump sum payment equal to two months' basic pay multiplied by number of years total commissioned service computed IAW 10 USC 6387 for line officers or 10 USC 6388 for staff corps officers. Payment may not be more than two years' basic pay or $15,000, whichever is lesser. Upon separation he will be entitled to ______ months' basic pay or $15,000, whichever is lesser

RECM
Recommendation

RECNO
This Office has No Record Of

RECO
Remote Command and Control
Remotely Controlled (detonating device)

RECOG
Recognition
Recognize

RECOM
Recommendation

RECOMMTRANSO
Upon receipt of these orders communicate with ______ transportation officer for priority designator via government air transportation if available to (location desired)

RECOMP
Recommended Completion (date)

RECON
Reconnaissance
Reconsideration
Resources Conservation

RECONATKRON
Reconnaissance Attack Squadron

RECONATKWING
Reconnaissance Attack Wing

RECONBN
Reconnaissance Battalion

RECONN
Reconnaissance

RECOVER
Replace Engine Components Vice Engine Return

RECSATSUM
Reconnaissance Satellite Summary

RECSHIP
Receiving Ship

RECSTA
Receiving Station

RECTAD
Received for temporary additional duty

RECTADINS
Received for temporary additional duty under instruction

RECTREAT
Received for Treatment

RED
Record of Emergency Data
Reduction

REDAP
Reentrant Data Processing

REDATKCARAIRWING
Readiness Attack Carrier Air Wing

REDCOM
Naval Reserve Readiness Command

REDOPS
Operational Readiness Report

REDS
Revised Engine-Delivery Schedule

REEL
Radiation Exposure Evaluation Laboratory

REEN
Reenlistment

REENL
Reenlistment

REF
Refer
Reference
Reflector

REFG
Refrigerator

REFRAD
Released from Active Duty

REFRIG
Refrigeration

REFT
Released for Experimental Flight Test

REFTRA
Refresher Training

REFURDIS
Reference Your Dispatch

REFURLTR
Reference Your Letter

REG
Regiment
Region
Register
Registered
Regular
Regulate
Regulation

REGAL
Range and Elevation Guidance for Approach and Landing

REGIS
Register

REGOV
Responsibility for discharge costs rests with foreign government

REGS
Regulations

REGT
Regiment

REH
Rehearing

REHAB
Rehabilitation

REI
Request for Engineering Information

REIL
Runway End Identifier Light (system)

REIMB
Reimburse

REIMBJTR
Reimbursement will be in accordance with Joint Travel Regulations

REIN
Reinforced

REINCC
Resident Engineer-in-Charge of Construction

REINF
Reinforced

REINFS
Reinforcements

REINS
Radar-Equipped Intertial Navigation System

REL
Related
Reliable
Relief

RELACDU
Released from Active Duty

RELBY
When Relieved By

RELDET
When relieved, detached (to duty indicated). (Date on or about which these orders become effective may be indicated.)

RELDIRDET
When relieved and when directed, detached (to duty indicated). (Date on or about which detachment is to be effective may be indicated.)

REM
Registered Equipment Management
Remitted
Roentgen Equivalent Mammal
Roentgen Equivalent Man

REMAD
Remote Magnetic Anomaly Detection

REMD
Remanded

REMG
Remanding

REMS
Responsibility for discharge costs rests with U.S. Navy or its agent

REORG
Reorganize

REP
Range Error Probability
Repair
Report
Reporting Point
Representative
Rework Excellence Program
Roentgen Equivalent Physical

REPERMSG
Report in person or by message

REPFORMAINT
Representative for Maintenance Force

REPISIC
Report to the immediate superior in command, if present, otherwise by message

REPITINERARY
Report by message, or in person, or by other means, to NAVATT or such command specified, giving address and itinerary while in his/their duty area. Indicate on original orders date and method of reporting.

REPL
Replace
Replacement

REPLTR
Report by letter
Reporting by Letter

REPMIS
Reserve Personnel Management Information System

REPMSG
Report by message to (command(s) or person(s) indicated)

REPNAVRESCEN
Upon release you are urged to contact the nearest Naval Reserve Center for information relative to Naval Reserve Training. Participants in Naval Reserve Training may earn retirement points and drill pay if a billet is available.

REPO
Reporting Officer

REPPAC
Repetitvely-Pulsed Plasma Accelerator

REPPT
Reporting Point

REPRO
Reproduce
Reproduction

REPSNO
Report through senior naval officer ___________, if applicable

REPT
Repeat
Report

REPTOF
Reporting Officer

REQ
Request
Require
Requirement

REQFOLINFO
Request the following information to be forwarded to this office

REQN
Requisition

REQNOM
Request Nomination

REQN/OPTAR
Requisition/Operating Target (log)

REQREC
Request Recommendation

REQSI
Request Shipping Instructions

REQUAL
Requalified
Requalify

RER
Rubberized Equipment Repair

RES
Radiation Equivalent Source
Reentry System
Reserve

RESANTISUBCARAIRGRU
Reserve Antisubmarine Warfare Carrier Air Group

RESASWCARAIRGRU
Reserve Antisubmarine Warfare Carrier Air Group

RESASWTRACEN
Naval Air Reserve Antisubmarine Warfare Training Center

RESCAP
Rescue Combat Air Patrol

RESCEN
Reserve Center

RESCOMMIS
Reserve Command Management Information System

RESDESDIV
Reserve Destroyer Division

RESDESRON
Reserve Destroyer Squadron

RESDIST
Reserve District

RESER
Reentry System Evaluation Radar

RESFAC
Reserve Facility

RESFORONS
Reserve Force Squadrons

RESGD
Resigned

RES/IC
Reserve-In Commission (vessel status)

RESIG
Resignation

RES/IS
Reserve-In Service (vessel status)

RESMILCON
Reserve Military Construction

RESO
Regional Environmental Support Office

RESP
Responder
Responsible

RESREP
Resident Representative

RESS
Recruiting Enlisted Selection System

REST
Radar Electronic Scan Technique
Range, Endurance, Speed, and Time (computer)
Restricted

RESTMPS
Reserve Training Management and Planning System

RESTOURSERV
If dependent travel is involved overseas,

submit copy of agreement to remain on active duty, if required, to command having cognizance of transportation.

RESTRACEN
Reserve Training Center

RESTRAFAC
Reserve Training Facility

RESUPSHIP
Resident Supervisor of Shipbuilding Conversion and Repair

RET
Retained
Retired
Returned

RET-ABSTEE
Returned Absentee

RETAN
Retained

RETAT
It is requested that

RETD
Returned

RETDSG
Effective upon being transferred to retired list, designator is changed to ______

RETNDU
Returned to Duty

RETORC
Research Torpedo Configuration

RETRANS
For return transportation to
Report for Transportation

RETRO
Retroactive

RETSER
Retained in Service

RETULSIGN
Retain on board until assignment received

REU
Requesting Expeditor Unit

REURAD
Refer Your Radio Message

REV
Reentry Vehicle
Reverse
Review
Revise
Revolution
Revolve

REVAR
Authorized to revisit any of the above-mentioned places and vary itinerary as necessary

REVD
Reversed
Revised

REVG
Reversing

REVO
Revoke

REV STAT
Revised Status
Revised Statutes

REWARC
Radar Warning Circuit

REWS
Reconnaissance and Electronic Warfare Systems

REWSON
Reconnaissance, Electronic Warfare, Special Operations, and Naval Intelligence Processing System

RF
Radio Frequency
Representative Function

RFA
Radio Frequency Amplifier
Royal Fleet Auxiliary (tankers)

RFB
Reliability Function Blocks

RFBS
Rapid Feedback Message System

RFC
Required Functional Capabilities

RFCS
Radio Frequency Carrier Shift

RFD
Ready for Delivery

RFDC
Reporting Field Designation Code

RFDC C/D
Reporting Field Designation Code Correction/Discrepancy

RFE
Request for Evaluation
Reserve Female Enlistment

RFEP
Reserve Female Enlistment Program

RFER
Reefer (stowage)

RFI
Radio Frequency Interference
Ready for Issue (stock)
Request for Information

RFL
Refuel

RFM
Release for Manufacture

RFNA
Radio Frequency Noise Analyzer

RFO
Radio Frequency Oscillator
Reason for Outage

RFP
Request for Proposals

RFPP
Radio Frequency Propagation Program

RFPS
Requests for Proposal Supplements

RFS
Ready For Sea

RFT
Readiness for Training
Refresher Training

RFU
Ready for Use

RG
Reduction Gearbox
Right Gun

RGA
Reduction Gearbox Assembly

RGE
Range

RGN
Region

RGO
Radio Guidance Operation

RGR
Receipt of Goods Received

RGZ
Recommended Ground Zero

RH
Relative Humidity
Rhumb Line (route)

RHAS
Radiant Heat-Absorbing Surface

RHAW
Radar-Homing and Warning

RHAWS
Radar-Homing and Warning System

RHC
Right-Hand Console

RHI
Range-Height Indicator

RHIO
Rank Has Its Obligations

RHIP
Rank Has Its Privileges

RHIR
Rank Has Its Responsibilities

RHOGI
Radar Homing Guidance Investigation

R/HR
Roentgeens per Hour

RHR
Roughness Height Rating

RHU
Requisition Held Up

RI
Radio Inertial (guiding)
Receiving Inspection
Recruit Induction
Reliability Index
Routing Identification (code)

RIAL
Revised Individual Allowance List

RIB
Receiver Interface Board (NNSS)

RIC
Repairable Item Code
Replaceable Item Code
Representative-in-Charge
Resistance, Inductance, Capacitance (circuitry)

RICL
Receipt Inspection Check List

RICMO
Radar Input Countermeasures Officer

RID
Released to Inactive Duty

RIF
Receipt Inspection Form
Reduction in Force

RIFT
Reactor In-Flight Test

RIIXS
Remote Interrogation Information Exchange System

RIK
Replacement-in-Kind

RIL
Red Indicator Lights

RILOP
Reclamation in Lieu of Procurement

RILSD
Resident Integrated Logistics Support Detachment

RIM
Receipt Inspection Memorandum
Ship-launched intercept-aerial guided missile

RINA
Resident Inspector of Naval Aircraft

RINC
Recruiter-in-Charge

RINM
Resident Inspector of Naval Material

RINO
Resident Inspector of Naval Ordnance

RINS
Resident Inspector

RINSMAT
Resident Inspector of Naval Material

RINSORD
Resident Inspector of Naval Ordnance

RIO
Radar Intercept Officer
Radar Intercept Operator
Retail Issue Outlets

RIOT
Real-Time Input/Output Transducer

RIOTEX
Riot Exercise

RIP
Rapid Installation Procedures
Reduction Implementation Panel
Reenlistment Incentive Program
Reliability Improvement Program

RIPOM
Report in person if present, otherwise by message (command indicated)

RIPS
Radio-Isotope Power Supply
Range Instrumentation Planning Study

RIS
Reading Improvement Specialist
Retail Inventory System

RISE
Reaching Industry with SOS Education
Research in Supersonic Environment

RISIC
Rubber-Insert Sound Isolation Coupling

RISS
Range Instrumentation and Support Systems

RIT
Revolution in Training

RITE
Rapid Information Technique for Evaluation

RIV
River

RIVFLOT
River Flotilla

RIVPATFLOT
River Patrol Flotilla

RIVPATFOR
River Patrol Force

RIVRON
River Assault Squadron

RIVSEC
River Section

RIVSUPPRON
River Support Squadron

RIW
Reliability Improvement Warranty

RJ
Ramjet (engine)

RKO
Range-Keeper Operator

RKT
Rocket

RL
Radiological Lectures
Reel
Report Leaving
Restricted Line (officer)
Roll

RLAD
Radar Low-Angle Drogue

RLCD
Relocated

RLD
Radar Laydown Delivery

RLF
Relevant Labor Force

RLM
Rearward Launched Missile

RLMS
Radar Landmass Simulator

RLO
Repairs Liaison Officer
Restricted Line Officer
Reuseable Learning Object

RLOS
Retention Level of Supply

RLPA
Rotating-Log Periodic Antenna

RLT
Recorder Lead Time
Regimental Landing Team

RLU
Reserve Liaison Unit

R-M
Ready Mariner (program)

R/M
Reliability and Maintainability

RM
Radioman
Ream
Rocket Motors

RM1
Radioman First Class

RM2
Radioman Second Class

RM3
Radioman Third Class

R/M/A
Reliability, Maintainability, Availability

RMA
Reliability, Maintainability, Availability
Request for Manufacturers of Articles
Reserve Maintenance Allowance
Revolution in Military Affairs

RMAL
Revised Master Allowance List

R MAST
Radio Mast

R/MAX
Maximum Range

RMC
Chief Radioman
Reduced Material Condition
Regular Military Compensation
Rod Memory Computer

RMCB
Reserve Mobile Construction Battalion

RMCM
Master Chief Radioman
Return Material Credit Memorandum

RMCS
Senior Chief Radioman

RMI
Radio Magnetic Indicator
Recurring Maintenance Items
Reliability Maturity Index
Routine Manual In

RMI/MO
Routine Manual In/Manual Out

R/MIN
Minimum Range

RMIS
Resource Management Information System

RMKS
Remarks

RML
Rescue Motor-Launch

RMN
Remain
Reserve Material Account, Navy

RMO
Radar Material Office
Radio Material Office

RMP
Radar Modernization Plan
Radar Modernization Program
Reentry Measurements Program
Regional Medical Program

RMS
Radar Maintenance Spares
Radar Manual System
Remote Minehunting System
Resource Management System
Root Mean Square

RMSA
Radioman Seaman Apprentice

RMSN
Radioman Seaman

RMSP
Refractory Metal Sheet Program

RMS VALUE
Root Mean Square Value

RMU
Remote Maneuvering Unit

RN
Residual Number
Ribbon

RNCBC
Reserve Naval Construction Battalion Center

RNCBCDET
Reserve Naval Construction Battalion Center Detachment

RNCR
Reserve Naval Construction Regiment

RND
Round

RNF
Receiver-Noise Figure

RNG
Radio Range
Range

RNID
Routine Network-In-Dial

RNID/NOD
Routine Network-In-Dial/Network-Out-Dial

RNMCB
Reserve Naval Mobile Construction Battalion

RNMCBDET
Reserve Naval Mobile Construction Battalion

RNO
Results Not Observed

RNS
Race, National Origin, and Sex

RNSG
Reserve Naval Security Group

RNSGC
Reserve Naval Security Group Course

RNSSMS
Rearchitectured NATO Seasparrow Missile System

RNVC
Reference Number Variation Code

RNWY
Runway

RNYPO
Regional Navy Youth Programs Officer

RO
Radar Officer
Reactor Operator
Receiving Only

Recruiting Officer
Redistribution Order
Referral Order
Regular Overhaul
Reproducible Ozalid (drawing)
Restricted Operations
Retrofit Order
Rip Out
Rust and Oxidation (oils)

ROA
Recorder Announcement

ROB
Report on Board
Reserve on Board

ROC
Record of Changes
Reduced Operating Costs
Required Obstacle Clearance (height)
Required Operating Capability
Required Operational Capability
Research and Oral Communications
Reserve Officer Candidate

ROCMN
Regional Office of Civilian Manpower Management

ROCOB
Rocketsonde Observation

ROCP
Radar Out-of-Commission for Parts

ROC/POE
Required Operational Capability/Projected Operating Environment

ROD
Range Operations Department (PMR)

ROE
Reflector Orbital Equipment
Rules of Engagement

ROF
Reporting Organization File (system)

ROFOR
Route Forecast

ROG
Receipt of Goods

ROH
Regular Overhaul

ROI
Reports Of Investigation
Return On Investment

ROICC
Resident Officer-in-Charge of Construction

ROICM
Resident Officer-in-Charge of Material

ROID
Report Of Item Discrepancy

ROINC
Resident Officer-in-Charge

ROJ
Range-On Jam

ROM
Read Only Memory
Receive Only-Multipoint
Recruiter Of the Month
Rough Order of Magnitude

ROMACC
Range Operational Mounting and Control Center

ROMP
Radiotelephone Operator Maintenance Proficiency

RON
Receiving Only
Remain Overnight
Squadron

RONLY
Receiver Only

RONS
Reserve Officers of the Naval Service

ROOST
Reusable One-Stage Orbital Space Truck

ROP
Remote Operating Panel
Reorder Point
Run of the Press

ROPEVAL
Readiness Operational Evaluation

ROPS
Roll Over Protection Structure

ROQ
Recruiter Of the Quarter

RORET
Rotational Retention

RO/RO
Roll-On/Roll-Off (transport or trailer)

ROS
Ready Operating Status
Remote Optical Sighting (system)

ROSE
Remote Optical Sensing of the Environment
Rising Observational Sounding Equipment

ROSIE
Reconnaissance by Orbital Ship Identification Equipment

ROT
Rotary
Rotate
Rotating (light)
Rule of Thumb

ROTAD
Required Overseas Terminal Arrival Date

ROTAS
Rotate and Slide

ROTI
Recording Optical Tracking Instrument

ROTLT/BCN
Rotating Light or Beacon

ROT PROJ
Rotation Project

ROTS
Rotary Out-Trunk Switching (AUTOVON)

ROV
Repair of Vessel

ROVNITE
Remain Overnight

ROWP
Reference Overhaul Work Package

RP
Raid Plotter
Reactor Plant
Religious Program Specialist
Reorder Point
Replacement Pilot
Report Passing
Reserve Personnel
Revision Proposal
Rocket Projectile
Rocket Propellant

RP1
Religious Program Specialist First Class

RP2
Religious Program Specialist Second Class

RP3
Religious Program Specialist Third Class

RPA
Radium Plaque Adaptometer

RPAO
Radium Plaque Adaptometer Operator

RPAODS
Remotely-Piloted Aerial Observer Designation System

RPB
Radio Production Branch (AFRTS)

RPC
Chief Religious Program Specialist
Regional-Preparedness Committee
Registered Publications Clerk
Registered Publications Custodian
Repairable Processing Center
River Patrol Craft

RPCM
Master Chief Religious Program Specialist

RPCP
Reactor Plant Control Panel

RPCS
Senior Chief Religious Program Specialist

RPD
Radar Planning Device
Rapid

RPE
Reactor Plant Engineering

RPEP
Register of Planning Emergency Procedures

RPF
Reactor Plant Fueling

RPFI
Reactor Plant Fueling Inspection

RPFW
Reactor Plant Fresh Water

RPG
Radioisotope Power Generator
Report Program Generator
Rocket-Propelled Grenade

RPI
Radar Precipitation Integrator
Real Property Inventory

RPIE
Real Property, Installed Equipment

RPIO
Registered Publication Issuing Office

RPM
Reactor Plant Manual
Registered Publications Manual
Registered Publications Memorandum
Reliability Performance Measure
Revolutions Per Minute
Rounds Per Minute

RPMA
Real Property Maintenance Activities (program)

RPMC
Registered Publications Memorandum Corrections

RPN
Reserve Personnel, Navy

RPO
Registered Publications Officer

RPP
Reactor Plant Planning

RPPI
Remote Plan Position Indicator

RPPS
Retired Pay/Personnel System

RPPY
Reactor Plant Planning Year

RPR
Repair

RPS
Registered Publications Section
Registered Publications System
Revolutions Per Second

RPSA
Religious Program Specialist Seaman Apprentice

RPSN
Religious Program Specialist Seaman

RPS-PL
Repair Parts and Special Tools List

RPT
Reactor Plant Test
Repeat
Report

RPTPT
Reporting Point

RPTS
Reactor Plant Test Section

RPTSO
Reactor Plant Test Support Organization

RPU
Radio Phone Unit
Radio Priority Unit
Registered Publications Unit
Rotatable Pool Unit

RPV
Remotely-Piloted Vehicle

RQD
Required

RQMT
Requirement

RQN
Requisition

RQR
Require
Requirement

RQRD
Required

RQST
Request

RQSTD
Requested

RR
Recruit Roll
Requisition Restriction (code)
Rifle Range

RRB
Regular Reenlistment Bonus

RRC
Readiness Reportable Code

Recognized Rescue Center
Reporting Requirements Code
Requirements Review Committee

RRE
Race-Relations Education (program)

RREB
Race-Relations Education Board

RRF
Regional Relay Facility

RRIS
Remote Radar Integration Station

RRL
Runway Remaining Lights

RRLTU
Recruit Remedial Literacy Training Unit

RRR
Readiness Removal Rate
Repairable Return Rate

RRRR
Recruiting, Readiness, Retention, and Respect

RRS
Readiness Reportable Status
Ready Reserve Status

RR/T
Rendezvous Radar/Transponder

RRT
Remote Reading Thermometer

RRTS
Range-Rate Tracking System

RRU
General Ready Reserve Unit (USNR)

RRVFPA
Red River Valley Fighter Pilots Association

R/S
Report of Survey

RS
Rapid-Setting (asphalt)
Readiness Squadron
Receiving Station
Reconnaissance Strike
Recruiting Station
Repair Services
Revised Statutes

RS&I
Receipt, Storage, and Issue

RSA
Radar Signature Analysis

RSAND
Reserve Systems Analysis Division

RSB
Radiation Safety Booklet
Reduced Size Blueprint

RSC
Rescue Sub-Center
Reserve Service Control
Rework Support Conference
Runway Surface Condition

RSCH
Research

RSCH&DEV
Research and Development

RSCHOPSDET
Research Operations Detachment

RSCS
Rate Stabilization Control System

RSDC
Remote Secure Data Change

RSDU
Radar Storm Detection Unit

RSE
Reference Sensing Elements
Remote Sensing of Environment

RSF
Render Safe Procedure
Requisition Status File

RSFPP
Retired Servicemen's Family Protection Plan

RSG
Rising

RSGN
Reassign
Resign

RSHI
Rough Service, High Impact

R-SI
Restricted-Security Information

RSI
Rationalization, Standardization, and Interoperability

RSL
Remote Spring Missile Launching

RSM
Ready Service Magazine

RSN
Random Sequence Number

RSO
Radiological Safety Officer
Range Safety Officer
Readiness Support Organization

RSOS
Resident Supervisor of Shipping

RSP
Render Safe Procedure
Reserve Stock Point

RSPE
Radar Signal Processing Equipment (course)

RSPL
Recommended Spare-Parts List

RSR
Ready Service Ring
Route Surveillance Radar

RSS
Refrigerant, Ship's Stores

RSSK
Rigid Seal Survival Kit

RSSP
Reporting Secondary Stock Point

RST
Readability, Strength, and Tone (radio transmission)

RSTD
Restricted

RSV
Research Safety Vehicle

RSVP
Restartable Solid Variable Pulse

R/T
Radiotelephone
Radio Terminology
Regular Time

RT
Radiographic Test
Receiving Test
Register Reference (NNSS)
Resistance Thermometer
Right Turn
Route

RTAG
Range Technical Advisory Group

RTB
Return To Base

RTC
Recruit Training Center
Recruit Training Command
Replacement Training Center

RTCC
Real-Time Computer Complex

RTC(W)
Recruit Training Center (Women)
Recruit Training Command (Women)

RTD
Resistance Temperature Detector

RTDP
Real-Time Data Processor (system)

RTDS
Remote Target Designator System

RTE
Route

RTG
Radioisotope Thermoelectric Generator
Rating
Routing

RTI
Radar Target Identification

RTIRS
Real-Time Information Retrieval System

RTL
Resistor-Transistor Logic (circuitry)

RTM
Rapid Turning Magnetron
Receiver-Transistor-Modulator

RTN
Return

RTNEE
Returnee

RTP
Request for Technical Proposal
Requirement and Test Procedures

RTQC
Real-Time Quality Control

RTRD
Retard

RTRN
Return

RTS
Radio Tape Service
Replacement Training Squadron

RTSO
Remote Terminal Security Officer

RTSS
Real-Time Scientific System

RTST
Receiver Self Test (NNSS)

RTT
Radioteletype

RTU
Replacement Training Unit

RTV
Responsive Television
Rocket Test Vehicle
Room Temperature Vulcanizing (silicon rubber)
Route Traffic Via

RTZ
Real-Time Executive

RU
Radio Unit
Release Unit

RUC
Reporting Unit Code
Riverine Utility Craft

RUDAOE
Report of Unsatisfactory or Defective Aviation Ordnance Equipment

RUDM
Report of Unsatisfactory or Defective Material

RUDMINDE
Report of Unsatisfactory or Defective Mine

RUDTORPE
Report of Unsatisfactory or Defective Torpedo Equipment

RUF
Rough

RUG
Radar Upgrade

RUIC
Reserve Unit Identification Codes

RUM
Remote Underwater Manipulator

RUNCIBLE
Revised Unified New Compiler with Internal Translator, Basic Language Extended

RUPPERT
Reserve Unit Personnel Performance Report

RUSNO
Resident United States Naval Officer

RUUWS
Research Underwater-Unmanned Weapons Sensor

R/V
Reentry Vehicle

RV
Recreational Vehicle
Rescue Vessel
Research Vessel
Runway Visibility

RVAH
Reconnaissance Attack Squadron

RVAW
Carrier Airborne Early Warning Training Squadron

RVP
Replacement ASW Patrol Squadron

RVR
Reverse Velocity Rotor
River
Runway Visual Range

RVW
Review

RVWD
Reviewed

RW
Radiological Warfare
Recreation and Welfare

RW BN
Red and White Beacon

RWH
Radar Warning and Homing

RWO
Reimbursable Work Order

RWR
Radar Warning Receiver
Remain Well Right of _____

RWRAT
Replacement Weather Reconnaissance Aircraft

RWY
Runway

RX
Report Crossing

RZ
Reconnaissance Zone
Return-to-Zero (recording)

6YO
Six-Year Obligor

S

S
ASW Tactical Evaluator (NAO code)
Secret
Situational (report frequency)
Snow
South
Southern
Spar (buoy)
Starboard
Straight-In

S&A
Safety and Arming (device)

S&C
Search and Clear (operation)

S&D
Search and Destroy (operations)
Single and Double (reduction gear)

S&E
Supplies and Equipage

S&F
Sound and Flash

S&FSD
Sea and Foreign Service Duty (pay)

S&FSD(A)
Sea and Foreign Service Duty (Aviation)

S&FSD(S)
Sea and Foreign Service Duty (Submarine)

S&M
Sequence and Monitor

S&T
Science and Technology
Scientific and Technical (intelligence)

S^3BP
System Source Selection Board Procedures

S/A
Sub Assembly

SA
Sack
Seaman Apprentice
Semi-Annually (report frequency)
Service Applicability
Servo Amplifier
Ship Alteration
Shipping Agreement
Shop Accessory (drawing)
Sight Angle
Special Agent
Special Assignment
Special Authorization
Superior Achievement (award)
Supervisory Authority
Supplemental Agreement
Systems Analysis

SAA
Small-Arms Ammunition

SAAM
Special Assignment Airlift Mission

SAAP
South Atlantic Anomaly Probe

S/AB
Starboard Side Abreast (stowage)

SAB
Scientific Advisory Board

SABAR
Service Craft and Boat Accounting Report

SABER
SECNAV's Advisory Board on Educational Requirements

SABET
SECNAV'S Advisory Board on Education and Training

SABMAR
Service Craft and Boats Machine Accounting Report

SABMIS
Sea-Based Anti-Ballistic Missile Intercept System

SABOSE
SECNAV's Advisory Board on Scientific Education

SABRE
SAGE Battery Routing Equipment
Secure Airborne Radar Equipment
Self-Aligned Boost and Reentry (missile system)
Shallow Water Assault Breaching

SAC
Security Assistance (program)
Signal Analysis Course
Special Accounting Class
Special Advisory Committee
Standard Aircraft Characteristics
Storeman's Action Copy
Substance Abuse Coordinator
Supporting Arms Coordinator

SACAM
Ship Acquisition Contract Administration Manual (NAVSHIPS)

SACC
Supporting Arms Coordination Center

SACCS
Supreme Allied Command Automated Command Control System

SACE
Semi-Automatic Checkout Equipment

SACEUR
Supreme Allied Commander, Europe

SACLANT
Supreme Allied Commander, Atlantic

SACMED
Supreme Allied Commander, Mediterranean

SACOM
SECNAV's Advisory Committee on Manpower

SACP
Special Assistant for Civilian Personnel

SACP/EEO
Special Assistant for Civilian Personnel/Equal Employment Opportunity

SACR
Semi-Automatic Coordinate Reader

SACS
Sensor Accuracy Check Site

SAD
Search and Destroy
Submarine Anomaly Detector
Support Air Division
Supporting Arms Department
System Analysis Division (USNR)
System Automation Division

SADC
Sector Air Defense Commander

SADIE
Scanning Analog-to-Digital Input Equipment

SADL
Ship's Authorized Data List

SADS
Submarine Active Detection System

SAEC
Support Analysis of an Engineering Change

SAED
Small-Aircraft Engine Department
Submarine Antenna Engineering Division
Systems Analysis and Engineering Department

SA(EF)
Electronics Field Seaman Apprentice

SAES
Special Assistant for Environmental Services

SAEWS
Shipboard Automated Electronic Warfare System

SAF
Shark Attack File
Southern Attack Force
Special Action Force
Support Action Form

SAFE-BAR
Safeland Barrier

SAFECEN
Safety Center

SAFEPLAN
Submarine Air Frequency Plan

SAFOC
Semi-Automatic Flight Operations Center

SAFORD
Safety of Explosive Ordnance Databank

SAG
Self-Aligning Gate (circuitry)
Semi-Active Guidance
Sub-Activity Group
Superior Achievement Group
Surface Action Group
Systems Analysis Group

SAGA
System for Automatic Generation and Analysis

SAGE
Semi-Automatic Ground Environment (system)

SAHR
Semi-Autonomous Hydrographic Reconnaissance Vehicle

SA(HS)
High School Seaman Apprentice

SAIC
Science Applications International Corporation

SAIL
Ship Active Item Listing
Ship Armament Inventory List

SAIMS
Selected Acquisition Information and Management System

SAINTS
Single-Attack Integrated System

SAIP
Ship Acquisition and Improvement Panel
Submarine Antenna Improvement Program

SAL
Salvage
Service Applicability
Ship's Allowance List

SALAD
Shipboard Automatic Liquid Agent Detector

SALTS
Standard Automated Logistics Tool Set
Streamlined Automated Logistical Transmission System

SALV
Salvage

SALVTRA
Specialized maritime diving and salvage training for salvage ships

SALWIS
Shipboard Air-Launched Weapons Installation System

SAM
School of Aviation Medicine
Screen for Aeronautical Material
Seabee Anti-Pollution Movement
Special Air Mission
Surface-to-Air Missile

SAMAR
Ship Activation, Maintenance, and Repair (reserve division)

SAMC
Surface Ammunition Malfunction Control (number)

SAMEM
Sustained-Attrition Minefield Evaluation Model

SAMI
Single-Action Maintenance Instruction

SAMID
Ship Anti-Missile Integrated Defense

SAMIS
Ship Alteration Management Information System

SAMMA
Stores Account Material Management Afloat

SAMMA/SAL
Stores Account Material Management Afloat/Ship Authorization Levels

SAMMS
Standard Automated Material Management System

SAM-NIS
Screen for Aeronautical Material-Not in Stock

SAMOS
Satellite and Missile Observation System

SAMPS
Shore Activity Manpower Planning System

SAMS
Semi-Automatic Meteorological Station
Ship Alteration Management System
Ship Alteration Material Survey

SAM/SAT
South American/South Atlantic (regional area)

SAMSAT
Surface-to-Air Missile Assembly and Test

SAMTEC
Space and Missile Test Center

SAND
Shelter Analysis for New Designs

SANDFSO
Sea and Foreign Service Office

S and SC
Sized and Supercalendered

SA(NSET)
Nuclear Submarine Engineering Technician Seaman Apprentice

SAO
Special Activities Office
Support Air Observer

SAP
Security Assistance Program
Semi-Armor Piercing
Ship Acquisition Project (PMS)
Ship Alteration Package
Soon as Possible
Symbolic Assembly Program

SA(PFE)
Polaris Field Electronics Seaman Apprentice

SA(PFL)
Polaris Field Launcher Seaman Apprentice

SAPIR
System of Automatic Processing and Indexing of Reports

SAPL
System Advanced Parts List

SAPO
Sub-Area Petroleum Office

SAQAD
Submarine Antenna Quality Assurance Directory

SAQAF
Submarine Antenna Quality Assurance Facility

SAQR
Substance Abuse Quarterly Report

SAR
Sea-Air Rescue
Search and Rescue
Selected Acquisition Reports
Selected Air Reserve
Special Aeronautical Requirements
Standard Average and Range
Substance Abuse Report
Supply Activity Report
Synthetic Aperture Radar

SARA
Search and Rescue Aid
Superior Accomplishment Recognition Award

SARBE
Search and Rescue Beacon Equipment

SARDIP
Stricken Aircraft Reclamation and Disposal Program

SAREX
Search and Rescue Exercise

SARIE
Selective Automatic Radar Identification Equipment

SARLANT
Search and Rescue, Atlantic

SARPAC
Search and Rescue, Pacific

SARTEL
Search and Rescue Telephone

SAS
Secure Authentication System
Selection and Appointment System
Ship Alteration Scope
Stability Augmentation System
Supply Accounting Section
Suspended Array System

SASI
Ship and Air Systems Integration

SASITS
Submarine Advanced Signal Training System

SASL
Service Approved Status List

SASM
Special Assistant for Strategic Mobility

SASN
Special Assistant to the Secretary of the Navy

SASS
Spark Chamber Automatic Scanning System
Special Aircraft Service Group
Special Armament Stowage Space
Suspended Array Surveillance System

SASTE
Semi-Automatic Shop Test Equipment

SAT
Safe Air Travel
Satisfactory
Scholastic Aptitude Test
Security Alert Team
Ship Assistance Team
Space Available Travel
Summer Accelerated Training
Systems Approach to Training

SATCOM
Satellite Communications

SATEC
Semi-Automatic Technical Control

SATELLORB
Satellite Simulation Observation and Research Balloon

SATELOON
Balloon Satellite

SATFOR
Special Air Task Force

SAT FOR TEE
System Approach to Training for Transfer Effectiveness Evaluation

SATFY
Satisfactory

SATIN
SAGE Air Taffic Integration

SATIRE
Semi-Automatic Technical Information Retrieval

SATNAV
Satellite Navigation

SATO
Scheduled Airline Traffic Office

SATP
Small-Arms Training Unit

SATS
Short Airfield for Tactical Support

SAU
Search Attack Unit

SAVAC
Simulates, Analyzes, Visualizes, Activated Circuitry

SAVDEP
Savings Depot

SAV-DEP-SYS
Savings Deposit System

SAVE
Shortages and Valuable Excesses

SAVER
Stowable Aircrew Vehicle Escape Rotoseat

SAVI
Sexual Assault Victims Intervention

SAW
Submerged Arc Weld

SAWBET
Supply Action Will Be Taken

SAWRS
Supplementary Aviation Weather Reporting Station

SAWS
Special Airborne Weapons Subsystem
Submarine Acoustic Warfare System

S/B
Should Be

SB
Secondary Battery
Shipbuilding
Slab
Submarine Base
Supply Bulletin
Switchboard

SBA
Sovereign Base Area
Standard Beam Approach

SBAE
Stabilization Bombing Approach Equipment

SBCO
Shipbuilding Company

SBCORP
Shipbuilding Corporation

SBE
Selection Board Eligible

SBI
Selection Board Ineligible
Special Background Investigation

SBL
Space-Based Laser

SBM
Single Buoy Marking

SBMSS
Shore-Based Message Service System

SBN
Subic Bay News (publication)

SBO
Summary Plot Board

SBP
Survivor Benefit Plan

SBPH
Submarine Base, Pearl Harbor (HI)

SBT
Shipboard Test

SBTB
Short Basic Test Battery

SBY
Standby

S-C
Secret and Confidential (files)

SC
Scattered Clouds
Section
Security Code
Separate Contract
Sized and Calendered
Slow Curing (asphalt)
Spacecraft (pilot code)
Step Child/Children
Stratocumulus (cloud formation)
Submarine Chaser
Supply Corps
Surveillance Coordinator

SCA
Service Cryptologic Agency
Software Communications Architecture
Stock Control Activity
Subcontractor Administrator
Superconducting Accelerator
Switching Center, AUTOVON
System Certification Authority

SCAD
Subsonic Cruise Armed Decoy

SCADAR
Scatter Detection and Ranging

SCADS
Scanning Celestial Attitude Determination System

SCAEC
Submarine Classification and Analysis Evaluation

SCAJAP(AN)
Shipping Control Authority, Japan

SCAMP
Scholarships for Children of American Military Personnel
Space-Controlled Array Measurements Program
System/Command Accounting/Monitoring of Projects

SCAN
Switched Circuit Automatic Network
System for Collection and Analysis of Near-Collision (reports)

SCANS
Scheduling and Control by Automated Network System

SCAO
Senior Civil Affairs Officer

SCAP
Silent Compact Auxiliary Power

SCAR
Scientific Committee on Antarctic Research
Sub-Caliber Aircraft Rocket

SCAS
Stability Control Augmentation System

SCAT
Satellite Communications Airborne Terminal
Sequential Component Automatic Test
Service Command Air Transport
Speed Command Altitude/Target
Speed Control Approach/Take-Off
Submarine Classification and Tracking
Submarine Communications Applications and Theory

SCATANA
Security Control of Air Traffic and Air Navigation Aids

SCATER
Security Control of Air Traffic and Electromagnetic Radiations

SCATTOR
Small Craft Assets, Training and Turnover of Resources

SCB
Ships Characteristics Board

SCBA
Self-Contained Breathing Apparatus

SCC
SAGE Control Center
Sequence Control Chart
Ship Control Console
Specification for Contract Change
Speed Control Circuits
Steering Control Console
Stress Corrosion Cracking
Surface Combat Condition

SCCF
Satellite Communications Control Facility

SCC NR
Special Cryptologic Control Number

SCD
Supply, Commissary, and Disbursing
Surface Craft Division
Synchronizing Control Devices

SCDRL
Subcontractor Data Requirements List

SCE
Schedule Compliance Evaluation
Special Conditioning Equipment
Staff Civil Engineer

SCE&PWD
Staff Civil Engineer and Public Works Department

SCEPC
Senior Civil Emergency Planning Committee

SCEPTRON
Spectral Comparative Pattern Recognition

SCERT
Systems and Computers Evaluation and Review Technique

SCF
Support Carrier Force

SCH
School
Sorties Scheduled

SC-HC
Scattered-to-Heavy Clouds

SCI
Sensitive Compartmented Information
Ship-Controlled Intercept
Supervisor Cost Inspector

SCIP
Shipbuilding and Conversion Improvement Program
Ship's Capability Impaired for Lack of Parts

SCIR
Subsystem Capability and Impact Reporting (system)

SCK
Service Change Unit

SCL
Ship Configuration Listing
Standard Components List
Symbolic Correction Loader

SCLK
Ship's Clerk

SCLSIS
Ship Configuration and Logistics Support Information System

SCM
Summary Courts-Martial

SCN
Ship Construction, Navy
Shop Control Number
Southern Command Network (AFRTS)
Specification Change Notice

SCNS
Self-Contained Navigation System

SCO
Scout
Scouting

SCODA
Scan Coherent Doppler Attachment

SCOFOR
Scouting Force

SCOL
School

SCOMA
Shipping Control Office, Marianas

SCOPE
Scientific Cooperation Operational Research Expedition
Subsystem for the Control of Operations and Plan Evaluation
System to Compute Operational Probability Equation

SCOPES
Squad Combat Operations Exercise (Simulation)

SCOR
Special Committee on Ocean Research
Subcommittee on Oceanographic Research

SCORE
Satellite Computer-Operated Readiness Equipment
Selective Conversion and Retention
Signal Communications by Orbiting Relay Equipment

SCORM
Shareable Content Object Reference Model

SCORON
Scouting Squadron

SCOT
System Consolidated Operability Test

SCOTRACEN
Scouting Training Center

SCP
SAGE Computer Program
Ship Control Panel
Special Career Programs
Steam-Condensing Pot

SCPO
Senior Chief Petty Officer

SCPT
SAGE Computer Programming Training

SCR
Silicon Control Rectifier
Sodium-Cooled Thermal Reactor
Sortie Completion Rate

SCRAM
Several Compilers Reworked and Modified
Short-Range Attack Missile
Signal Corps Random-Access Memory
Space Capsule Regulator and Monitor
Spares, Components, Reidentification and Modification Program

SCRAP
Selective Curtailment of Reports and Paperwork

SCRB
Software Change Review Board

SCRIPT
Scientific and Commercial Subroutine Interpreter and Programs Translator

SCS
Satellite Control Satellite
Sea Control Ship
Stabilization and Control Subsystem
Supervisory Control Subsystem

SCSS
Self-Contained Starting System

SCT
Scout
Sector
Special Crew Time
Synchro Control Transformer
System Circuit Test

SCTC
Self-Contained Training Capabilities

SCTD
Scattered (clouds)

SCTOC
Satellite Communications Test and Operations Center

SCTR
Sector

SCTY
Security

SCU
Stock Control Unit

SCUBA
Self-Contained Underwater Breathing Apparatus

SCUP
Spectra Composite Utility Program

SCW
Seabee Combat Warfare

SCX
Subcontractor Equipment

S/D
Seadrome

SD
Safety Destructor
San Diego
Secretary of Defense
Semi-Darkness
Shelter Deck (stowage)
Skid
Special Duty
Standard Deviation
Strength Differential
Supply Department
Surface Danger (zone)
Surveillance Drone
Sympathetic Detonation

SDA
Source Data Automation
Special Duty Assignment

SDAFRS
Source Data Automated Fitness Report System

SDAR
Submarine Departure Approval Request

SDBI
Specifications Drawing Baseline Index

SDC
Signal Data Conversion
Southern Defense Command
Submersible Decompression Chamber

SDCD
Sea Duty Commencement Date

SDCG
Special Data Converter Group

SDCP
Supply Demand Control Point

SDCU
Supply Data Communications Unit

SDD
Special Devices Division
Standard Delivery Date
System Development Department

SDF
Ship Description File
Simplified Directional Facility

SDG
Situation Display Generator
Synchro Differential Generator

SDGE
Situation Display Generator Element

SDGO
San Diego

SDI
Selected Dissemination of Information
Ship's Drawing Index
Situation Display Indicator
Specifications Drawing Index

SDI-KWOC
Selected Dissemination of Information-Key Word Out of Context (system)

SDL
Systems Design Laboratory

SDLM
Standard Depot Level Maintenance

SDO
Special Duty Officer
Squadron Duty Officer
Staff Duty Officer
Station Duty Officer

SDOPR
Sound Operator

SDP
Ship Development Plan
Statistical Data Processing
Status Display Panels
Submarine Distress Pinger

SDR
Special Drawing Rights

SDRN
Supplier Data Review Notice

SDS
Source Data Sheet
Supplemental Data Sheet
System Design Specification

SDSP
Space Defense Systems Program

SDTS
Self-Defense Test Ship

SDV
SEAL Delivery Vehicle
Swimmer Delivery Vehicle

SDVT
SEAL Delivery Vehicle Team
Swimmer Delivery Vehicle Team

SE
September
Set
Signal Ejector
Single-Ended
Single Engine
Southeast
Southeastern
Support Equipment
Systems Engineer
Systems Engineering

SEA
Senior Enlisted Advisor
Sensing Element Amplifiers
Ship/Equipment/Alteration (list)
Ship's Editorial Association
Sonar Evaluation and Assistance
Southeast Asia

SEAC
Seacoast
Southeast Asia Command

SEACALMIS
NAVSEACOM Calibration Management Information System

SEACO
Senior Enlisted Advisor, Communications/Operations

SEACON
Seafloor Construction (NCEL)

SEAD
Suppression of Enemy Air Defenses

SEADU
Sea Duty

SEAFRON
Sea Frontier

SEAL
Sea-Air-Land
Ship Electronic Allowance List

SEAM
Sidewinder Expanded Acquisition Mode

SEAMARF
Southeast Asia Military Altitude Reservation Facility

SEAMOD
Sea Systems Modification and Modernization by Modularity (program)

SEAOPS
Safe Engineering and Operations

SEAR
Systematic Effort to Analyze Results

SEARA
Stockpile Evaluation and Reliability Assessment

SEAS
Sea School

SEATICC
Southeast Asia Tactical Information Communications Center

SEATO
Southeast Asia Treaty Organization

SEAVEY
Sea-to-Shore Rotation Survey

SEAWEA
Sea Weather (report)

SEB
Source Evaluation Board
Support Equipment Bulletin

SEBS
Submarine Emergency Buoyancy System

SEC
Secondary Emission Cathode
Seconds
Sector
Security
Support Equipment Change

SECAS
Ship Equipment Configuration Accounting System

SECBASE
Section Base

SECD
Secondary

SECDEF
Secretary of Defense

SECF
Surface Effect Cruiser Escort

SECFLT
Second Fleet

SEC-FT
Second-Foot

SECGRUHQ
Security Group Headquarters

SECNAV
Secretary of the Navy

SECNAVFIND
The Secretary of the Navy has found that this permanent change of station is required by the exigencies of the service

SECNAVMC
Secretary of the Navy and Marine Corps

SECO
Sustained Engine Cutoff

SECOF
Shipboard Environmental Checkout Facility

SECR
Secret

SECS
Single-Engine Control Speed
Stem-Erected Camera System

SECT
Section
Sector
Submarine Emergency Communications Transmitter

SECTASKFLT
Second Task Fleet

SEC-TREAS
Secretary-Treasurer

SECY
Secretary

SED
Sequence Event Diagram
System Engineering Documentation

SEDPC
Scientific and Engineering Data Processing Center

SEDS
System Effectiveness Data System

SEE/AN
Systems Effectiveness Evaluation Analyzer

SEEDS
Ship's Electrical and Electronic Data Systems

SEEK
System Evaluation Experiment

SEER
Submarine Explosive Echo-Ranging

SEEREP
Ship's Essential Equipment Requisition Expediting Program

SEF
SPECAT Exclusive for

SEFF
Snakeye Free-Fall

SEFIC
Seventh Fleet Intelligence Center

SEFOR
Southwest Experiment Fax Oxide Reactor

SEG
Systems Engineering Group

SEI
Specific Emitter Identification
Stockpile Entry Inspection

SEIE
Submarine Emergency Identification Signal

SEL
Solar Energy Laboratory
Sound Effects Laboratory
Support Equipment List

SELCAL
Selective Calling (system)

SELD
Snakeye Low-Drag

SELRES
Selected Reserve
Selected Reservist

SELS
Severe Local Storm

SELT
SAGE Evaluation Library Tape

SEM
Scanning Electron Microscope
Semaphore
Standard Electronic Module

SEMA
Semaphore

SEMAT
Ship Electronic Module Assembly Test

SEMCA
Shipboard Electromagnetic Computability Analysis

SEMDP
Senior Executive/Management Development Plan

SEN
Senior
Southern European Network (AFRTS)
Successor Event Number

SENAVAV
Senior Naval Aviator

SENDENTALO
Senior Dental Officer

SENG
Single Engine

SENL
Standard Equipment Nomenclature List

SENMEDO
Senior Medical Officer

SENMEM
Senior Member

SENSO
Sensor Operator

SENT
Sentence

SENT CONF
Sentence to be Confined

SENT LP
Sentence to Lose Pay

SENUSNAVOFFNAVBALTAP
Senior United States Naval Officer, Commander Allied Naval Forces, Baltic Approaches

SEOC
Submarine Extended Operating Cycle

SEP
Separate
September
Spherical Error Probable
Surface Electrical Properties

SEPACFOR
Southeast Pacific Force

SEPP
Safety Engineering Program Plan

SEPQUES
Prior to delivery of orders, the CO is directed to complete and return the enclosed Officer Separation Questionnaire to COMNAVMILPERSCOM (Code 402).

SEPROS
Separate Processing
Separation Processing

SEPT
September

SEPTAR
Seaborne Powered Target

SER
Serial
Service
Servicing
Shore Establishment Realignment
SNAP Experimental Reactor
Space Electric Rocket
Support Equipment Requirement

SERANDA
Service record(s), health record(s), pay record(s) and personal effects

SERC
Sonar Environmental Research Card

SERE
Survival, Evasion, Resistance, and Escape

SERET
Snakeye Retarded

SERGRAD
Selected and Retained Graduate

SERL
Services Electronics Research Laboratory

SERNO
Serial Number

SERON
Service Squadron

SERS
Support Equipment Requirements (list)

SERV
Service

SERVDIV
Service Division

SERVFOR
Service Force

SERVGRP
Service Group

SERVHEL
Service record(s) and health record(s)

SERVLANT
Service Force, Atlantic Fleet

SERVMART
Service Market
Service Mart

SERVPA
Service record(s) and pay record(s)

SERVPAC
Service record(s), pay record(s), and health record(s)

SERVREC
Service Records(s)

SERVRON
Service Squadron

SERVSCOLCOM
Service Schools Command

SERVSCOLCOMDET
Service Schools Command Detachment

SES
Sensor Employment Squads
Serving Sentence
Site Environmental System
Strategic Engineering Survey
Surface Effect Ship

SESAME
Service-Sort-and-Merge

SESCO
Secure Submarine Communications

SESE
Secure Echo-Sounding Equipment (sonar)

SESEC
Senior Enlisted Steam Engineering Course

SESI
Shipboard Explosive Safety Inspection

SESPROJ
Surface Effect Ship Project

SESTF
Surface Effect Ship Test Facility

SET
Selective Electronic Training
Sensor Employment Teams
Smoke-Emission Test
Submarine Engineering Technician

SETAF
Southern European Task Force

SETT
Submarine Electronic Technical Training
Submarine Escape Training Tank

SEV
Severe
Surface Effects Vehicle

SEVFLT
Seventh Fleet

SEVR PAY
Severence Pay

SEWT
Simulator for Electronic Warfare Testing

SF
San Francisco
Scouting Force
Ship's Force
Special Forces
Standard Form
Supervisor Furnished
Svedberg Flotation

SFA
Single Frequency Approach

SFAO
San Francisco Area Office (ONR)

SFBNSY
San Francisco Bay Naval Shipyard

SFC
Specific Fuel Consumption
Sub-Functional Code
Surface

SFCP
Shore Fire Control Party

SFDS
Standby Fighter Director Ship

SFEC
Standard Facility Equipment Card

SFEL
Standard Facility Equipment List

SFI
Shop-Fixed Interface

S FL
Short Flashing (light)

SFL
Sequenced Flashing (light)

SFN
Ships and Facilities, Navy

SFNS
San Francisco Naval Shipyard

SFO
Simulated Flameout

SFOB
Special Forces Operating Base

SFOMS
Ship's Force Overhaul Management System

SFPOE
San Francisco, Port of Embarkation

SFPPS
Shore Facilities Planning and Programming System

SFRD
Secret: Formerly Restricted Data

SFRS
Selective File Retrieval Service

SFS
Student Flight Surgeon

SFSD
Star Field Scanning Device

SFSNY
San Francisco Naval Shipyard

SFT
Spray Flammability Temperature

SFTS
Synthetic Flight Training System

SFW
Shunt-Field Winding (wiring)

SFWI
Ship's Force Work Item

SFWL
Ship's Force Work List

SFWL(I)
Ship's Force Work List (Item)

SFWP
Ship's Force Work Package

SG
Qualified for immediate assignment to submarines
Security Group
Snow Grains (weather symbol)
Special Grade
Steam Generator
Surgeon General
Syringe

SGC
Simulation Generator Control

SGCP
Shipboard Gauge Calibration Program

SGD
Special Government Design

SGED
Supervisory Grade Evaluation Guide

SGF
Steam Generator Feedwater

SGLI
Serviceman's Group Life Insurance

SGM
Spark Gap Modulation

SGN
Signed
Standing Group, North Atlantic
Surgeon General, Navy

SGP
School Guarantee Program
Secondary Gun Pointer

SGSE
Standard Ground Support Equipment

SGT
Satellite Ground Terminal
Sergeant

SGTMAJ
Sergeant Major

SGU
Sidewinder Generator Unit

SH
Sheet
Ship's Serviceman

SH1
Ship's Serviceman First Class

SH2
Ship's Serviceman Second Class

SH3
Ship's Serviceman Third Class

SHA
Sidereal Hour Angle

SHAAM
Static Multi-Attribute Assignment Model

SHAC
Small Hydrofoil Aircraft Carrier

SHAPE
Supreme Headquarters, Allied Powers, Europe

SHAPM
Ship Acquisition Project Manager

SHARP
Shared Reconnaissance Pod
Ships Analysis and Retrieval Projects

SHARPS
Ships/Helicopter Acoustic Range Prediction System

SHAVIB
Shaft Alignment and Vibration (check)

SHC
Chief Ship's Serviceman
Superheat Control

SHCM
Master Chief Ship's Serviceman

SHCS
Senior Chief Ship's Serviceman

SHD
Special Handling Designator

SHDCD
Shore Duty Commencement Date

SHE
Special-Handling Equipment

SHEDS
Shipbaord Helicopter Extended Delivery System

SHF
Super High Frequency

SHINE
Self-Help is Necessary Everywhere

SHIP
Self-Help Improvement Program

SHIPALT
Ship Alteration

SHIPALT
Ship Alteration

SHIPDA
Shipping Data

SHIPDAFOL
Shipping Data Follows

SHIPDAT
Shipping Date

SHIPGO
Shipping Order

SHIPIM
Ship Immediately

SHIPMAIN
Ship Maintenance

SHIPMT
Shipment

SHIPOPS
Shipboard Operations

SHIPOSI
Ship Operational Support Inventory

SHIPREPFAC
Ships Repair Facility

SHIPREPFACLANT
Ships Repair Facility, Atlantic

SHIPREPFACPAC
Ships Repair Facility, Pacific

SHIPREPTECH
Ship Repair Technician

SHIPSEPROS
If ship or fleet command from which detached is located in CONUS at the time of detachment, report to the separation processing in accordance with NAVMILPERSMAN 3810260.2 instead of as directed above.

SHIPSEPROSHI
If ship or fleet command from which detached is located in Hawaii at the time of detachment, report for separation processing in accordance with NAVMIPERSMAN 3810260.2 instead of as directed above.

SHIPSTO
Ship Store Office

(SHIPYARD)MIS
Shipyard Management Information System

SHLW
Shallow

SHMD
Shore Manning Documents

SHO
Shore

SHOLS
Single-Hoist Ordnance Loading System

SHOPAT
Shore Patrol

SHORAN
Short-Range Navigation

SHORDU
Shore Duty

SHOROC
Shore Required Operational Capability

SHOROUTPUBINST
Shore duty is required by the public interest

SHOR(T)STAMPS
Shore Requirements, Standards, and Manpower Planning System

SHORVEY
Shore-to-Sea Rotation Survey

SHOT
Senior, Headquarters OPO Team

SHP
Ship Horsepower

SHROC
Shore Required Operational Capabilities

SHSA
Ship's Serviceman Seaman Apprentice

SHSN
Ship's Serviceman Seaman

SHWR
Shower

SI
Selected Intelligence
Self-Instructional (course)
Ship Installation
Showalter Index
Special Intelligence
Specific Impulse
Spot Inventory
Straight-In (approach)

SIA
Standard Instrument Approach
Station of Initial Assignment

SIAP
Single Integrated Air Picture

SIAS
Submarine Integrated Antenna System

SIB
Ship's Information Book
Situation Intelligence Brief
Standard Index Base

SIC
Scientific Information Center
Sonar Intelligence Center

SICB
Senior Interservice Control Board

SICCM
Supervisor Information on Civilian Career Management

SICD
Supply Item Design Change

SICMA
Special Initial Clothing Monetary Allowance

SICMA-CIV
Special Initial Clothing Monetary Allowance-Civilian

SICMA-NAOC
Special Initial Clothing Monetary Allowance-Naval Aviation Officer Candidate

SICMA-NAVCAD
Special Initial Clothing Monetary Allowance-Naval Aviation Cadet

SICR
Specific Intelligence Collection Requirements
Supply Item Change Record

SID
Standard Instrument Departure
Sudden Ionospheric Disturbance
Synchronous Identification System

SIDC
Supply Item Design Change

SIDL
System Identification Data List

SIDMS
Status, Inventory, Data Management System

SIDS
Shrike-Improved Display System
Standard Implementation Document System

SIF
Selective Identification Feature

SIFPPS
Shore Installations and Facilities Planning and Programming System

SIG
Senior Interdepartmental Group
Ship Improvement Guide
Signal
Signature

SIGINT
Signals Intelligence

SIG/IRG
Senior Interdepartmental Group/Interdepartmental Regional Group

SIGMAP
Special Interest Group for Mathematical Programming

SIGMS
Signal Material Supports

SIGNINT
Signals Intelligence

SIGS
Simplified Inertial Guidance System

SIG SEL
Signal Selector

SIG STA
Signal Station

SII
SHIPALT Installation Instruction (PERA)
Statement of Intelligence Interest

SIL
Speech Interference Level (NRP)
Standard Inventory Log

SILO
Security Intelligence Liaison Office

SIM
SAM Intercept Missile (system)
Selected Item Management

SIMA
Ships Intermediate Maintenance Activity

Shore Intermediate Maintenance Activity

SIMAS
Sonar In-suit Mode Assessment System

SIMCOM
Simulator-Compiler

SIMCON
Scientific Inventory Management and Control

SIME
Security Intelligence, Middle East

SIMEX
Secondary Items Military Assistance Program

SIMFAC
Simulation Facility

SIMP
Shipboard Integrated Maintenance Program
Slow Image Motion Processor

SIMSI
Selected Inventory Management of Selected Items

SIMTOS
Simulated Tactical Operations System

SINCGARS
Single Channel Ground and Airborne Radio System

SINEWS
Ship Integrated Electronic Warfare System

SINS
Shipboard Inertial Navigation System

SIO
Specific Instructional Objectives

SIOP
Single Integrated Operational Plan

SIOP-ESI
Safeguarding the Single Integrated Operational Plan-Extremely Sensitive Information

SIP
System Improvement Program

SIPD
Supply Item Provisioning Document

SIPG
Service in Paygrade

SIPM
Student Instructor Performance Module

SIPRNET
Secure Internet Protocol Routing Network

SIR
Selected Item Report
Symbolic Input Routine

SIRCS
Shipboard Intermediate Range Combat System

SIRIN
Single Readiness Information System (NORRS)

SIROS
Specialized Operating System

SIS
SAGE Interceptor Simulator
Screening/Inspection System

SISMS
Standard Integrated Support Management System

SIST
Self-Inflating Surface Target

SIT
Situation
Spontaneous Ignition Temperature
Storage Inspection Test
Storage-In-Transit

SITAP
Simulator for Transportation Analysis and Planning

SITE
Shipboard Information, Training, and Entertainment (system)

SITREP
Situation Report

SITS
Secure Imagery Transmission System (TACSAT)

SIV
Special Interest Vessel

SIXFLT
Sixth Fleet

SIZ
Security Identification Zone

SJP
Shipboard Joint Uniform Military Pay System

SK
Skein
Sketch
Storekeeper

SK1
Storekeeper First Class

SK2
Storekeeper Second Class

SK3
Storekeeper Third Class

SKAMP
Station-Keeping and Mobile Platform

SKB
Skiff, Large (USCG)

SKC
Chief Storekeeper

SKCM
Master Chief Storekeeper

SKCS
Senior Chief Storekeeper

SKD
Schedule

SKED
Schedule

SKI
Skiff, Ice (USCG)

SKILL
Satellite Kill

SKIP
Skill/Knowledge Improvement Program

SKL
Skiff, Light (USCG)

SKM
Skiff, Medium

SKMC
Sickness Due to Misconduct

SKMR
Hydroskimmer

SKOR
Sperry Kalman Optical Reset (SINS)

SKSA
Storekeeper Seaman Apprentice

SKSN
Storekeeper Seaman

SKT
Skill Knowledge Test

S-L
Sound Locator

SL
Search Light
Slide (AFRTS code)
Spool
Support Line

SLAE
Standard Lightweight Avionics Equipment

SLAM
Supersonic Low-Altitude Missile

SLAM-ER
Standoff Land Attack Missile-Expanded Response

SLAMEX
Submarine-Launched Altitude Missile Exercise

SLANG
Systems Language

SLAP
Service Life Assessment Program

SLAR
Side-Looking Radar
Slant Range

SLAT
Ship-Launched Air-Targeted (missiles)

SLATE
Small Lightweight Altitude Transmission Equipment (FAA)

SLBD
Sea Lite Beam Director

SLBM
Submarine-Launched Ballistic Missile

SLC
Side-Lobe Cancellation
Simulated Linguistic Computer
Sonobuoy Launch Tube

SLCC
Ship Life-Cycle Coordinators
Ship Logistic Control Center (LSC)
Summary List of Component Centers

SLCM
Sea-Launched Cruise Missile
Submarine-Launched Cruise Missile

SLCMP
Software Life Cycle Management Plan

SLCU
Standard Landing Craft Unit

SLEP
Service Life Extension Program
State Line End Point

SLEW
Static Load Error Washout

SLF
Special Landing Force

SLGT
Slight

SLIM
Standards Laboratory Information Manual
Submarine-Launched Intercept Missile

SLIS
Shared Laboratory Information System

SLIT
Serial/Lot Item Tracking

SLM
Ship's Logistics Manager
Sound Level Meter
Submarine-Launched Missile

SLMM
Submarine-Launched Mobile Mine

SLMS
Ship-Based Long-Range Missile System

SLNC
Service Life Not Completed

SLO
Slow
Staff Legal Officer

SLOC
Sea Lanes of Communication

SLOE
Special List of Equipment

SLP
Scouting Land Plane
Slope

SLPMS
Single-Level Power Management System

SLR
Side-Looking Radar
Single Lens Reflex (camera)
Slush on Runway

SLRI
Shipboard Long-Range Input

SLR-P
Slush on Runway-Patchy

SLS
Secondary Life Support System
Side-Lobe Suppression

SLT
Sleet
Sonobuoy Launch Tubes

SLTM
Short Lead Time Material

SLV
Satellite Launching Vessel
Standard Launch Vehicle

SLW
Slow

SLWT
Side Loading Warping Tug

S/M
Service Market
Service Mart

SM
Salvage Mechanic
Semi-Monthly (report frequency)
Sheet Metal
Shipment Memorandum
Shop Manufacture
Signalman
Small
Standard Missile
Submarine, Minelaying

SM&DSL
Sector Management and Direct Support Logistics Center

SM&R
Source, Maintenance, and Recoverability (code)

SM&RC
Scheduled Maintenance and Repair Code

SM1
Signalman First Class

SM2
Signalman Second Class

SM3
Signalman Third Class

SMA
Ship's Material Account
Standard Maintenance Allowance (for clothing)
SUBROC Missile Assembly

SMACS
Serialized Missile Accounting and Control System
Simulated Message Analysis and Conversion Subsystem

SMACTRACEN
Small Craft Training Center

SMAF
Shipboard Maintenance Action Form

SMAGOL
Small Computer Algorithmic Language

SMAM
Single Mission Air Medal

SMAR
Summary of Monthly Aerological Reports

SMART
Sailor/Marine American Council on Education Registry Transcript
Source Management of Resources and Time

SMB
Supersonic Manned Bomber

SMC
Chief Signalman
SAGE Maintenance Control
Supply and Maintenance Command

SMCM
Master Chief Signalman
Surface Mine Countermeasures

SMCS
Senior Chief Signalman

SMD
Ship Manning Document

SMEAC
Situation, Mission, Execution, Administrative and Logistics, and Command and Communications (defense tactics)

SMF
Student Master File

SMG
Submachine Gun

SMI
Saturday Morning Inspection
Statute Miles

SMIC
Special Material Identification Code
Study of Man's Impact on the Climate
Submarine Material Identification and Control

SMIPE
Small Interplanetary Probe Experiments

SMIS
(The) Society for Management Information Systems
Supply Management Information System

SMK
Smoke

SML
Small
Support Material List

SMLS
Seaborne Mobile Logistic System

SMMAS
Shipboard Maintenance Manpower Analysis System

SMMR
Specific Mobilization Material Requirement

SMMS
Shipbuilding Material Management System

SMN
Spain-Morocco Network (AFRTS)

SMO
Senior Medical Officer
Ship's Material Office
Stabilized Master Oscillator
Supplementary Meteorological Office

SMOLANT
Ship's Material Office, Atlantic

SMOOS
Shipboard Meteorological and Oceanographic Observing System

SMOPAC
Ship's Material Office, Pacific

SMP
Shipboard Microfilm Program

SMPT
Sound Movie Projector Technician

SMR
Special Money Requisition

SMRB
Senior Material Review Board

SMRL
Station Material Readiness List

SMS
Sequence Milestone System
Shipyard Modernization System
Single Management System
Surface Missile System

SMSA
Signalman Seaman Apprentice

SMSCC
Surface Missile Systems Clearance Committee

SMSD
Submarine Detector, Ship's Magnet

SMSN
Signalman Seaman

SMSP
Senior Medical Student Program
Surface Missile Projects Office

SMT
SUBROC Missile Technician

SMTH
Smooth

SMVLF
Shipboard Mobile Very Low Frequency

SMWHT
Somewhat

SMZ
Southern Maritime Zone

S/N
Stock Number

SN
Seaman
Secretary of the Navy
Serial Number
Signal-to-Noise (ratio)
Stock Number

SNA
Student Naval Aviator

SNAB
Stock Number Action Bulletin

SNAFU
Inf: Situation Normal, All Fucked Up

SNAIAS
Ship's Navigation and Aircraft Inertial Alignment System

SNAME
Society of Naval Architects and Marine Engineers

SNAP
Senior Naval Aviator Present
Shipboard Non-Tactical Automatic Data Processing Program
Student Naval Aviation Pilot

SNB
Small Navigation Buoy

SNCO
Senior Non-Commissioned Officer

SNDL
Standard Navy Distribution List

SNDS
Stock Number Data Section

SNEC
Secondary Navy Enlisted Classification (code)

SN(EF)
Electronics Field Seaman

SNEP FIT
Saudi Naval Expansion Program Project Management Team

SNEP PMT
Saudi Naval Expansion Program Project Management Team

SNEP PROJMGR
Saudi Naval Expansion Program, Project Manager

SNEP PROJMGR TAFT
Saudi Naval Expansion Program, Project Man-

ager, Technical Assistance Field Team

SNF
Systems Noise Figure

SNFL
Standing Naval Force, Atlantic

SNFO
Student Naval Flight Officer

SNFS
Student Naval Flight Surgeon

SNG
Synthetic Natural Gas

SN(HS)
High School Seaman

SNIT
Stock Number Identification Tables

SN(JC)
Junior College Seaman

SN(JCE)
Junior College Technician Electrician Seaman

SN(JCNE)
Junior College Nuclear Field Electronics Seaman

SN(JCNSET)
Junior College Nuclear Submarine Engineering Technician Seaman

SN(JCPE)
Junior College Polaris Field Electronics Seaman

SN(JCPL)
Junior College Polaris Field Launcher Seaman

SN(JCT)
Junior College Technical Electronics Seaman

SNL
Standard Navy (Distribution) List

SNM
Senior Naval Member
Special Nuclear Materials
Subject Named Member

SNMMMS
Standard Navy Maintenance and Material Management System

SN(NFE)
Nuclear Field Electronics Seaman

SN(NSET)
Nuclear Submarine Electronics Technical Seaman

SNO
Subject Named Officer

SNOFORN
Secret: Not Releasable to Foreign Nationals

SNOK
Secondary Next of Kin

SNORT
Supersonic Naval Ordnance Research Track

SN(PFE)
Polaris Field Electronics Seaman

SN(PFL)
Polaris Field Launcher Seaman

SNR
Senior
Signal-to-Noise Ratio

SNS
Stabilized Night Sight

SNSL
Standard Navy Stock List
Stock-Number Sequence List

SNSL-OSI
Stock-Number Sequence List-Operating Space Items

SNSL-SRI
Stock-Number Sequence List-Storeroom Items

SNSN
Standard Navy Stock Number

SO
Seller's Option
Send Only
Shipment Order
Signal Order
South
Southern
Special Order
Submarine Overhaul
Supply Officer
Surface Operating
Systems Orientation

SOA
Safe Operating Area

Speed of Advance
Speed of Approach

SOAC
Submarine Officer Advanced Course

SOAD
Standoff Outside of Area Defense

SOAP
Shaft Optimum Alignment Procedure
Spectographic Oil Analysis Program
Submarine Overhaul Allowance Parts
Supply Operations Assistance Program

SOBDI
Ship Onboard Drawing Index

SOBLIN
Self-Organizing Binary Logical Network

SOC
Serviceman's Opportunity College
Special Operations Cable
Special Operations Craft
Student Origin Code

SOCALSEC
Southern California Section

SOCHINAFOR
South China Force

SOCNAV
Servicemember's Opportunity College - Navy

SOCRATES
Simulator or Creative Reasoning Applied to Education System

SOCUS
Sound Focus

SOD
Small Object Detector
Special Operations Department
Submarine Overhaul Depot

SODAR
Sound Radar

SODAS
Synoptic Oceanographic Data Assimilation System

SODDS
Submarine Oceanographic Digital Data System

SOE
Schedule of Events

SOEAPL
Summary of Effective Allowance Parts List

SOEASTPAC
Southeast Pacific Force

SOES
Special Operations Evaluation System
Station Operations and Engineering Squadron

SOF
Sound On Film
Special Operations Forces
Strategic Offensive Forces
Supervisor Of Flying

SOFAR
Sounding, Fixing, and Ranging

SOFCS
Self-Organizing Flight Control System

SOG
Special Operations Group
Studies and Observation Group

SOGRU
Southern Group

SOH
Safety and Occupational Health

SOI
Space Object Identification

SOIC
Supply Officer-in-Charge

SOINC
Supply Officer-In-Charge

SOIP
Ship Overhaul Improvement Program

SOIS
Shipping Operations Information System

SOJ
Stand-Off Jamming

SOL
Inf: Shit Out of Luck

SOLANT
South Atlantic Force

SOLANTFOR
South Atlantic Force

SOLAS
Safety of Life at Sea

SOLRAD
Solar Radiation (satellite)

SOM
Send-Only-Multipoint
Simulator Operation and Maintenance
Standard Operating Manual
Start of Message

SOME
Secretary's Office, Management Engineer

SOMMTIP
Ship's Overhaul Modernization Manning and Training Information Program

SOMP
Sydney Ocean Meeting Point

SOMS
Standard Operations and Maintenance Squadron
Synchronous Operational Meteorological Satellite

SON
Submitting Office Number

SONAR
Sound Navigation and Ranging

SOND
Secretary's Office, Navy Department

SONOAN
Sonic Noise Analyzer

SONRD
Secretary's Office, Naval Research and Development

SONS
Statistics of Naval Shipyards

SOP
Senior Officer Present
Ship Operational Program
Standard Operating Procedure

SOP(A)
Senior Officer Present (Ashore)

SOPA
Senior Officer Present Afloat

SOPAC
South Pacific

SOPD
Standoff Outside Point Defense

SOPUS
Senior Officer Present, United States Navy

SOQ
Senior Officer's Quarters
Sick Officer's Quarters

SOR
Safety Ordnance Requirements
Specific Operating Requirements
Specific Operational Requirements

SORA
Secretary's Office, Records Administration

SORB
Submarine Overhaul and Refueling Building

SORD
Submerged Ordnance Recovery Device

SORG
Submarine Operations Research Group

SORM
Ship's Organization and Regulations Manual

SORR
Submarine Operations Research Report

SORT
Supply Corps Officer Refresher Training

SORTS
Status of Resources and Training Systems

SOS
Save Our Ship
Save Our Souls
Ship Our Ships (program)
Silicon-On-Sapphire (components)
Source Of Supply
Stamp Out Stock Errors
Supervisor Of Shipbuilding

SOSCAR
Supervisor of Shipbuilding, Conversion, and Repair

SOSED
Secretary's Office, Shore Establishment Division

SOSR
Selected Item Status Report

SOSUS
Sound Surveillance System

SOT
Ship Operational Trainer
Shortest Operational Time
Simulated Operational Training (course)
Sonar Trainer
Superintendent Of Training
Systems Operability Test

SOTB
Secretary's Office, Transportation Branch

SOTD
Stabilized Optical Tracking Device

SOT I
Simulated Operational Training, Phase I (course)

SOT II
Simulated Operational Training, Phase II (course)

SOT III
Simulated Operational Training, Phase III (course)

SOTIM
Sonic Observation of Trajectory and Impact of Missiles

SOUWES
Southwest
Southwestern

SOW
Stand-Off Weapon
Statement Of Work

SOWES
Southwest
Southwestern

SOWESPAC
Southwest Pacific

SOWESSEAFRON
Southwest Sea Frontier

SOWESTPACCOM
Southwest Pacific Command

SOWR
Submarine Overhaul Work Requirement

SOWRA
Submarine Overhaul Work Requirement Authorization

SOWS
Submarine Overhaul Work Scope

S/P
Seaplane

SP
Qualified and screened for submarine training
Secondary Plant
Self-Propelled
Shore Party
Single Purpose
Smokeless Powder
Snow Pellets(weather symbol)
South Pole
Specialist
Special Programs
Speed (NNSS)
Standard Plan
Standard Projects
Steam Plant
Steam Propulsion
Strip
Sub Point
Sub-Professional
Summary Plotter
Symphonic Popular (AFRTS code)

SPAAS
Staff Personnel Accounting and Allocation System

SPACE
Self-Programming Automatic Circuit Evaluation
Symbolic Programming Anyone Can Enjoy

SPACP
Steam Plant Auxiliaries Control Panel

SPALT
Special Projects Alteration

SPALTS
Special Projects Alteration Kits

SPAM
Special Aeronautical Material
Support Production and Multisource

SPAMS
Ship Position and Attitude Measurements System

SPAN
Storage Planning and Allocation

SPANS
Small Passive Navigation System

SPAR
Sea-going Platform for Acoustic Research (NOL)
Symbolic Program Assembly Routine

SPARC
Shore Establishment Planning Analysis and Review Cooperation

SPARM
Solid-Propellant Augmented Rocket Motor

SPARPS
Spares and Repair Parts Support

SPARTA
Special Anti-Missile Research Test-Australia

SPASST
Special Assistant

SPAST
Special Assistant

SPATS
South Pacific Air Transport Service

SPAWAR
Space and Naval Warfare Systems Command

SPC
Shop Process Card
Special Program Code
Still Picture Camera

SPCC
Ship's Parts Control Center
Spill Prevention Control and Countermeasures

SPCL
Special

SPCM
Master Chief Steam Propulsionman
Special Courts-Martial

SPCP
Steam Propulsion Control Panel

SPD
Separation Program Designator
Ship Planning Document
Ship Program Directive
Ship Project Directive
Smokeless Powder, Diphenylamine
Speed
Speed and Heading Coordinate System
Student Pilot Disposition
Superheater Protection Device

SPDB
Smokeless Powder, Diphenylamine, Blend

SPDC
Spare-Parts Distributing Center

SPDF
Smokeless Powder, Diphenylamine, Flashless

SPDLTR
Speedletter

SPDN
Smokeless Powder, Diphenylamine, Nonvolatile

SPDT
Single Pole, Double Throw (switch)

SPDW
Smokeless Powder, Diphenylamine, Reworked

SPE
Signal Processing Element (NRL)
Special-Purpose Equipment
Systems Performance Effectiveness

SPEC
Specialist
Specification
Specify

SPECASTSECNAV
Special Assistant to the Secretary of the Navy

SPECAT
Special Category

SPECK
Safety, Pride, Efficiency, Compatibility, Knowledge

SPECL
Specialize

SPECOM
Special Communications

SPECOMDIV
Special Communications Division

SPECOPS
Special Operations

SPECPROJOUK
Special Projects Liaison Offices, United Kingdom

SPEC(S)
Specification(s)

SPECSERV
Special Services

SPECTRE
Simultaneous Program Executing CATO Transcribed Reruns

SPEED
Self-Programmed Electronic Equation Delineator
Signal Processing in Evacuated Electronic Devices
Special Procedure for Expediting Development
Subsistence Prepared by Electronic Energy Diffusion

SPEEL
Shore Plant Electronics Equipment List

SPEEREBRA
Speech Research Branch

SPENAVO
Special Naval Observer

SPERT
Schedule Program Evaluation Review Technique

SPET
Solid-Propellant Electric Thruster

SPETE
Special Purpose Electronic Test Equipment

SPF
Studded Panel Fastener

SPGE
Steam Plant Gauge

SPGG
Solid-Propellant Gas Generator

SP GR
Specific Gravity

SPH
Statement of Personal History

SPHG
Speed and Heading (NNSS)

SPHQ
Shore Patrol Headquarters

SP HT
Specific Heat

SPI
Ship's Plan Index
Superintendent of Public Instruction

SPID
Submersible, Portable, Inflatable Dwelling

SPIE
Simulated Problem Input Evaluation

SPIL
Ships Parts Integration List

SPINS
Ship Passive Integrated Navigation System

SPINTAC
Special Interest Aircraft (program)

SPIW
Special-Purpose Individual Weapon

SPJTG
Secondary Plant Joint Test Group

SPL
Special

SPLASH
Shipboard Platforms for Landing and Servicing Helicopters

SPLC
Simulated Planetary Landing Capsule

SPM
Scans Per Minute
Secondary Propulsion Motor
Self-Propelled Mount
Steam-Plant Manual

SPMP
Systems Project Master Plan

SPMPS
Submarine Program Management Planning and Scheduling

SPMS
Source Program Maintenance System

SPN
Separation Program Number

SPO
Shore Patrol Officer
Special Projects Office/Officer
Systems Program Office
Systems Projects Office/Officer

SPOC
Single-Point Orbit Calculator

SPOCK
Simulated Procedure for Obtaining

Common Knowledge

SPOD
Ship's Plan of the Day

SPOOK
Supervisory Program(s) Over Other Kinds

SPORT
Support

SPOT
Speed, Positioning, and Tracking
Spot Inventory

SPOTR
Special Projects Officer Technical Representative

SPOTREPS
Significant Occurrences Reports

SPP
Sponsor Program Priorities
Sponsor Program Proposal

SPP&C
Submarine Production Planning and Control

SPR
Small Purchase Request
Solid-Propellant Rocket

SPRINT
Solid-Propellant Rocket Intercept

SPRS
Single Passenger Reservation System

SPS
Ship Planning System

SPST
Single Pole, Single Throw (switch)

SPT
Support

SPTCO
Support Company

SPTF
Signal Processing Test Facility

S/Q
Safety Quotient
Sequential Qualification
Superquick (fuze)

SQ
Squadron
Submarine Qualified

SQA
Submarine Quality Assurance

SQAR
Senior Quality Assurance Representative

SQAT
Ships Qualification Assistance Team

SQD
Squad

SQDN
Squadron

SQDRN
Squadron

SQ/H
Square of the Hatch (stowage)

SQLN
Squall Line

SQMD
Squadron Manning Document

SQN
Squadron

SQ/SD
Special Qualification/Special Designator (code)

SQT
Ship Qualification Trials
Systems Qualification Tests

SQUID
Superconducting Quantum Interference Device

S/R
Shipment Request
Storage and Repair

SR
Seaman Recruit
Service Record
Shaker
Shipment Request
Short-Range
Slant Range
Special Regulation
Standard Range
Study Requirement
Sunrise

Suppressed Range

SR&P
Station Resources and Planning

SR&PO
Station Resources and Planning Office

SRA
Selected Restricted Availability
Shop Replaceable Assembly
Short-Range Attack

SRAD
Ship's Restricted Availability Date
Steerable Right-Angle Drive

SRAM
Short-Range Attack Missile

SRB
Selective Reenlistment Bonus
Specification Review Board
Subspecialty Requirements Board

SRBK
Short-Range Boresight Kit

SRBM
Short-Range Ballistic Missile

SRC
Scheduled Removal Component (program)
Service Record Card
SPECAT Release Code
Stores Reliability Card
Submarine Rescue Chamber

SRCT
Standard Recovery Completion Time

SRD
Secret and Formerly Restricted Data
Selected Record Drawing
Service Revealed Difficulty

SRDS
Shop Repair Data Sheets
Systems Research and Development System

SRE
Surveillance Radar Element

SR(EF)
Electronics Field Seaman Recruit

SRF
Selected Reserve Force
Ship Repair Facility
Submarine Repair Facility

SRFLANT
Ships Repair Facility, Atlantic

SRFPAC
Ships Repair Facility, Pacific

SRG
Short-Range

SRGS
Survivable Radio Guidance System

SRH
Structural Repair Handbook (publication)

SR(HS)
High School Seaman Recruit

SRI
Storeroom Items

SRIP
Ship Readiness Improvement Plan
Specification Review and Improvement Program

SRL
Serial

SRM
Short-Range Missile
Speed of Relative Motion
Speed of Relative Movement

SRMBR
Senior Member

SRN
Satellite Radio Navigation

SR(NFE)
Nuclear Field Electronics Seaman Recruit

SR(NSET)
Nuclear Submarine Engineering Technician Seaman Recruit

SRO
Shop Repair Order
Superintendent of Range Operations

SRP
Selected Records Plan
Shark Research Panel
Standard Repair Procedures
Stern Reference Point
Supply and Repair Parts
Sustained Readiness Program

SR(PFE)
Polaris Field Electronics Seaman Recruit

SR(PFL)
Polaris Field Launcher Seaman Recruit

SRPM
Shaft Revolutions Per Minute

SRPS
Supply and Repair Parts Specifications

SRRT
Simultaneous Rotating and Reciprocating Technique

SRS
Secondary Recovery Ship
Secondary Reference Standard
Simultaneous Reporting System
Substitute Route Structure
Supply Response Section

SRT
Slow-Run-Through (trials)
Space Requirement Travel

SRTS
Short Range Training Schedule

SRTU
Ship Repair Training Unit

SRU
Ship Reinforcement Unit
Ship Repair Unit
Squadron Reinforcement Unit
Submarine Repair Unit

(SS)
Qualified in Submarines

S/S
Same Size
Ship/Store
Spectrum Signature

SS
Secret Service
Selective Service
Ship's Service
Single-Seated
Single Shot
Single-Stranded
Slow-Setting (asphalt)
Special Services
Stack
Submarine
Submarine Service
Submarine Studies
Submarine Warfare (qualification)
Sub Safe (program)
Subsystem
Superimposed Seam
Sworn Statement

SS&CS
Ship's Stores and Commissary Stores

SS1
Ship's Serviceman First Class

SS2
Ship's Serviceman Second Class

SS3
Ship's Serviceman Third Class

SS/A
Starboard Side Aft (stowage)

SSA
Ship's Store Activities
Shipyard Schedule Activity
Source Selection Authority
Submarine, Cargo
Supply Support Agreement

SSAAPP
Surface Ship Acoustic Analysis Proficiency Program

SSADP
Soldier's, Sailor's, and Airman's Deposit

(S)SALS
Simplified Short-Approach Light System

SSAN
Social Security Account Number

SSAS
Self-Scoring Answer Sheets
Signal Assessment System

SSAT
Subsonic Subscale Aerial Target

SSB
Fleet Ballistic Missile Submarine
Single Side Band (radio transceiver)
Source Selection Board
Swimmer Support Boat

SSBC
Stock Status Balance Card

SSBN
Nuclear Powered Ballistic-Missile Submarine

SSBP
System Source Selection Board Procedure

SSC
Chief Ship's Serviceman
Service Schools Command
Shipboard Satellite Communications (terminal)
Ship Safety Council
Ship System Command
Submarine Supply Center
Supply Support Center
Switch Scan Control (NNSS)

SSCB(B)
Submarine Safety Certification Boundary (Book)

SSCDS
Small Ship Combat Data System

SSCM
Master Chief Ship's Serviceman
Sub-Safe Certification Map (JIC)

SSCMA
Special Supplementary Clothing Monetary Allowance

SSCS
Senior Chief Serviceman

SSCT
Special Security Communications Team

S/SD
Ship/Store Department

SSD
Scrap Salvage Division
Specialized Support Depot
Stabilized Ship Detector
Submarine Support Division
Survival Support Device

SSDB
Shore Station Development Board

SSD(F)
Submarine Support Division for Fleet Support

SSD(S)
Submarine Support Division for Shore Facilities

SSDS
Ship Self-Defense System

SSD(ST)
Submarine Support Division for Staff Support

SSE
Special Support Equipment
System Safety Engineering

SS/EAM
Shipboard System/Equipment Acquisition Manual

SSED
Submarine Services Entry Date

SSEE
Ship's Signals Exploitation Equipment

SSEM
Supply Support Element Manager

SSEP
Submarine Support Equipment Program
Submarine Surveillance Equipment Program
System Safety Engineering Plan

SSES
Ship Signal Exploitation Rate

SS/F
Starboard Side Forward (stowage)

SSF
Seconds, Saybolt Furol
Service Storage Facility
Ship's Service Force
Single-Seated Fighter
Special Service Force

SS-FORMS
Special Strike Forms (for nuclear employment)

SSG
Guided Missile Submarine
Service School Guarantee
Strategic Studies Group
Surface Strike Groups

SSGN
Nuclear-Powered Guided-Missile Submarine

SSGT
Staff Sergeant

SSHACS
Small Ships Accounting System

SSI
Standard System Index
Structurally Significant Inspections

SSIC
Standard Subject Identification Code

SSILS
Solid-State Instrument Landing System

SSIP
Sensor System Improvement Program

SSIPS
Shore Signal and Information Processing Segment

SSITF
Standard Shipboard Inspection and Testing Form

SSK
Antisubmarine Submarine
Diesel-powered Submarine
Submarine Hunter-Killer

SSL
SERVMART Shopping List
Severe Storms Laboratory
Solid State Lamp

SSM
Sensor Simulator Materials
Ship's Side Band Modulation
Ship's System Manual
Surface-to-Surface Missile
Systems Supply Manager
Systems Support Manager

SSME
Space Shuttle Main Engine

SSMG
Ship's Service Motor Generator

SSMIS
Special Sensor Microwave Imager/Sounder

SSMR
Single Senior Military Representative

SSN
Nuclear-Powered Attack Submarine
Season and Sunspot Number
Social Security Number
Supply Support Notification

SSO
Ship Safety Officer
Special Security Officer
Submarine Oiler

SSORM
Standard Submarine Operations and Regulations Manual
Standard Submarine Operations and Repair Manual

SSP
Secondary Stock Point
Ship's Stores and Profit
Source Selection Plan
Strategic Systems Project
Sustained Superior Performance

SSPN
Ship's Stores and Profit, Navy

SSPO
Strategic Systems Project Office

SSPOTR
Strategic Systems Project Office Technical Representative

SSPP
System Safety Program Plan

SSR
Safe Secure Rail Car
Spin-Stabilized Rockets
Stock-Status Report
Submarine, Radar Picket
Supply Support Request

SSRNM
Ship's Self Radiated Noise Measurement

SSS
Selective Service System
Service Steam System
Shift Ship Superintendent
Signature Security Service
Storage Serviceability Standard
Strike Support Ship
Supply Screening Section
Synchro Self-Shifting

SSSBP
System Source Selection Board Procedures

SSSCP
Single Supply Support Control Point

SSSP
System Source Selection Procedure

SSSR
SAGE System Status Report

SSSS
Space-Borne Software Systems Study

SSST
Supersonic Sea-Skimming Target

SST
Safe Secure Trailer
Sea Surface Temperature
Shore Survey Team (NMVO)

Substation
Target and Training Submarine (Self-Propelled)

SSTG
Ship's Service Turbine Generator
Ship's Service Turbo Generator

SSTM
SAGE System Training Missile
SAGE System Training Mission

SSTU
SAGE System Training Unit

SSTV
Slow-Scan Television
Submarine Shock Test Vehicle

SSU
Seconds, Saybolt Universal
Semiconductor Storage Unit
Special Service Unit
Squadron Service Unit
Supply Screening Unit
Surveillance System Upgrade

SSURADS
Shipboard Surveillance Radar

SSV
Special Surveillance Vehicle
Submarine Support Vehicle

SSVP
Soviet Ship Vulnerability Program

SSW
Shipboard Safety Watch

S/T
Short Ton
Sonic Telegraphy

ST
Oceanograpic Specialist
Schmidt Trigger
Service Test
Sonar Technician
State
Stratus
Student
Surface Terminal

ST&E
Security Tests and Evaluations

ST1
Sonar Technician First Class

ST2
Sonar Technician Second Class

ST3
Sonar Technician Third Class

STA
Seaman to Admiral
Shuttle Training Aircraft
Station
Stationary
Straight-In Approach

STAAS
Surveillance and Target Acquisition Aircraft System

STAB
SEAL Team Assault Boat Stabilizer

STAFS
Standard Automated Financial System

STAG
Special Task Air Group

STALO
Stabilized Local Oscillator
Stable Local Oscillator

STAMIC
Set Theoretic Analysis and Measurement of Information Characteristics

STAMINRQ
Status During Minimize Required

STAMP
Standard Amphibious Plan

STAN
Standard

STANAG
Standardization NATO Agreement

STANAVFORLANT
Standing Naval Force, Atlantic

STANFLT
Standardization Flight (NATOPS)

STANLANCRU
Standard Landing Craft Unit

START
Strategic Arms Reduction Treaty

STATRAFO
Standard Transfer Order

STBY
Standby

STC
Chief Sonar Technician
Sensitivity Time Control

STCW
Standards of Training, Certification and Watchkeeping for Seafarers

STD
Secondary Test Department
Shift Test Director
Standard
Standing
Submarine Test Department

STDY
Steady

STE
Special Test Equipment

STEAM
Shipboard Training, Education, Advancement, and Morale

STEDMIS
Ship's Technical Data Management Information System

STEIN
System Test Environment Input

STEM
Seabee Tactical Equipment Management
Statistically-Tensioned Extension Mast
Stay Time Extension Module
Storage, Tubular Extendable Member

STEP
Ship Type Electronic Plan
Simple Transition to Electronic Processing
Special Training Enlistment Program
Standardized Tactical Entry Point
Standard Test Equipment Procedures
Supervisory Tape Executive Program
Supplementary Training and Education Program

STERF
Special Test Equipment Repair Facility

STF
Staff
Stiff

STG
Sonar Technician (Surface)
Straggler
Strong

STG1
Sonar Technician (Surface) First Class

STG2
Sonar Technician (Surface) Second Class

STG3
Sonar Technician (Surface) Third Class

STGE
Storage

STGSA
Sonar Technician (Surface) Seaman Apprentice

STGSN
Sonar Technician (Surface) Seaman

STIC
Scientific and Technical Intelligence Center

STID
Ship's Test and Inspection Department

STIK
Striking

STILO
Scientific and Technical Intelligence Liaison Officer

STINFO
Scientific and Technical Information

STINGS
Stellar Inertial Guidance System

STIR
Scientific and Technical Intelligence Register
Submarine Technical Information Record

STK
Stock
Strike

STL
Self-Test Logic (NNSS)
Stock, Time Limitation
Storage Time Limits
Studio-to-Transmitter Link

STLO
Scientific-Technical Liaison Office

STLS
Ship's Transducer Locating System

STM
Service Test Model
Steam
Storm

STMP
Ship Test Management Plan

STM-R
Short-Term Modernization Receiving

STN
Station

STND
Standard

STO
Science and Technology Objective
Ship Test Organization
Short Take-Off
Standard Transfer Order

STOL
Short Take-Off and Landing

STOM
Ship-to-Objective Maneuver

STOP
Special Troop
Standard Temperature and Pressure
Submarine Thermal Reactor

STOPS
Ship's Toxicological Operational Protective System

STOR
Storage

STO/VL
Short Take-Off, Vertical-Landing (aircraft)

STOVL
Short Take-Off and Vertical Landing

STOW
System for Take-Off Weight

STR
Store
Strength

STRAAD
Special Techniques for Repair and Analysis of Aircraft Damage

STRADAP
Storm Radar Data Processor

STRAG
Straggler

STRAP
Star Tracking Rocket Altitude Positioning

STRATANALSUPPGRU
Strategic Analysis Support Group

STRATCOM
Strategic Communications Command

STRAW
Simultaneous Tape Read and Write

STREAM
Standard Tensioned Replenishment Alongside Method

STRESS
Structural Engineering System Solver

STRG
Straggler

STRICOM
(United States) Strike Command

STRINGS
Stellar Inertial Guidance System

STRIP
Specification Technical Review and Improvement Program
Standard Taped Routines for Image Processing
Stock Turn-In and Replenishment Invoicing Procedures

STRS
Submarine Technical Repair Standard

STRUC
Structure

STS
Ship-to-Shore
Sonar Technician (Submarine)
Surface Target Simulator

STS1
Sonar Technician (Submarine) First Class

STS2
Sonar Technician (Submarine) Second Class

STS3
Sonar Technician (Submarine) Third Class

STSA
Sonar Technican Seaman Apprentice

STSC
Shipboard Tactical Satellite Communications

STSN
Sonar Technican Seaman

STSSA
Sonar Technician (Submarine) Seaman Apprentice

STSSN
Sonar Technician (Submarine) Seaman

ST/STE
Special Tooling/Special Test Equipment

STT
Seamanship Training Team
Submarine Tactical Terminal

STTF
Service to the Fleet (newspaper)

STU
Service Trials Unit
Student
Submersible Test Unit (NCEL)

STUD
Student

STUTNG
Student Training

STV
Sensitivity Time Control
Steam Tank Vessel

(SU)
Submarine Qualified

SU
Submarine Qualified
Submarine School Graduate
Sub Unit
Suit

SUADPS
Shipboard Uniform Automatic Data Processing System

SUB
Submarine

SUBAD
Submarine Air Defense (missile system)

SUBBASE
Submarine Base

SUBCAP
Submarine Combat Air Patrol

SUBCERT
Submarine Safety Certification

SUBCH
Subchapter

SUBCOM
Subordinate Command

SUBCONSENT
Assignment to active naval service subject to consent

SUBCOR
Subject to Correction

SUBDIV
Submarine Division

SUBEASTLANT
Submarine Force, Eastern Atlantic

SUBFLOT
Submarine Flotilla

SUBGRU
Submarine Group

SUBIC
Submarine Integrated Control

SUBINSURV
Sub-Board of Inspection and Survey

SUBINSURVLANT
Sub-Board of Inspection and Survey, Atlantic

SUBINSURVPAC
Sub-Board of Inspection and Survey, Pacific

SUBJ
Subject

SUBLANT
Submarine Forces, Atlantic

SUBM
Submerged
Submitted

SUB/MBR
Subcontractor/Material Review Board

SUBNAVPERS
Within 3 days prior to detachment complete applicable items on both sides NAVPERS 7041/1 being forwarded with

confirmation copy of this message, and submit to OIC, Navy Family Allowance Activity (PCSVAD), Cleveland, OH 44199, via CO. (Officers ordered ACDU from home submit direct to OIC, Navy Family Allowance Activity (PCSVAD), Cleveland, OH 44199.) If this order constitutes a modification, do no submit NAVPERS 7041/1 forwarded with previous orders.

SUBNET
Submarine Network

SUBNEWSTA
Complete applicable items on both sides NAVPERS 7041/1 being forwarded with copy of this message to new duty station and submit to OIC, Navy Family Allowance Activity (PCSVAD), Cleveland, OH 44199, via CO.

SUBOR
Subordinate

SUBORCOM
Subordinate Command

SUB-OSC
Submarine Oscillator

SUBPAC
Submarine Forces, Pacific

SUBPAR
Subparagraph

SUBPAY
Submarine Duty Incentive Pay

SUBRESUNIT
Submarine Rescue Unit

SUBROC
Submarine Rocket

SUBRON
Submarine Squadron

SUBRU
Submarine Repair Unit

SUBS
Subsistence

SUBSAFECEN
Submarine Safety Center

SUBSALVEX
Submarine Salvage Exercise

SUBSCOL
Submarine School

SUBSEC
Subsection

SUBS(GM)
Subsisted in a General Mess

SUBSLANT
Submarines, Atlantic

SUBSPAC
Submarines, Pacific

SUBSPEC
Subspecialist

SUBSTD
Substitute Standard

SUBTRAFAC
Submarine Training Facility

SUBTRAP
Submersible Training Platform

SUC
Senior Unit Commander

SUCHTRANS
Via such transportation as (command indicated) designates

SUCHTRANSVAIL
Such transportation as available

SUDAM
Sunk or Damaged (vessel report)

SUDS
Specification Updating and Simplification
Submarine Detection System

SUF
Sufficient

SUM
Summary
Surface-to-Underwater Missile

SUNEC
Seaborne Supply of the Northeast Command

SUP
Supply
System Utilization Procedures

SUPANX
Supply Annex

SUPBN
Supply Battalion

SUPC
Ship Unit Production Code

SUPCOM
Supreme Command

SUPCON
Superintending Contractor

SUPER
Support Program for Extraterrestrial Research

SUPG
System Utilization Procedure Guide

SUPIER
Supply Pier

SUPINSMAT
Supervising Inspector of Naval Material

SUPIR
Supplemental Photo Interpretation Report

SUPO
Supply Officer

SUPP
Supplement
Support

SUPPACT
Support Activity

SUPP BAS
Supplemental Basic Allowance for Subsistence

SUPPL
Supplement

SUPPLOT
Supplemental Plot

SUPPLT
Supply Platoon

SUPPS
(ICAO Regional) Supplementary Procedures

SUPPT
Supply Point

SUPRAD
Supplementary Radio Requirement

SUPSALREPWCOAST
Supervisor of Salvage Representative, West Coast

SUPSHIP
Supervisor of Shipbuilding Conversion and Repair

SUPSYSECGRU
Supply System, Security Group

SUPT
Superintendent

SUPTNAVOBSY
Superintendent, Naval Observatory

SUPV
Supervise
Supervisor

SUR
Surrender
Surrounding
Survivor

SURANO
Surface Radar and Navigation Operator

SURCAL
Surveillance Calibration (satellite)

SURCAP
Surface Combat Air Patrol

SURF
Standard Underway Replenishment Receiving Fixture
Surface

SURFCAST
Surf Forecast

SURFCO
Surf Code

SURGEN
Surgeon General

SURIC
Surface Integrated Control
Surface-Ship Integrated Control (system)

SURORDTECH
Surface Ordnance Technician

SURPICS
Surface Pictures (AMVER)

SURTASS
Surveillance Towed Array Sensor System

SURTEMS
Sea Surface Temperature Measurements System

SURTMPS
Surface Training Management and Planning System

SURTOPS
Surface Training and Operating Procedures Standardization (manual)

SURV
Surveillance
Survey

SURVFOR
Surveillance Force

SURVL
Surveillance

SUS
Saybolt Universal Seconds
Signal Underwater Sound

SUSIE
Surface/Underwater Ship Intercept Equipment

SUSNO
Senior United States Naval Officer

SUSP
Suspect
Suspend

SUU
Suspension and Release Unit

S/V
Surface Vessel

SV
Selective Volunteer
Semi-Vital
Sleeve

SVC
Service

SVCS
Services

SVFR
Special Visual Flight Rules

SVG
Servicing

SVM
Ship's Value Manual

SVR
Severe

SVRL
Several

SVTP
Sound, Velocity, Temperature, and Pressure

SW
Sea Water
Security Watch
Series Winding (wiring)
Short-Wave
Southwest
Southwestern
Steelworker
Surface Warfare
Switch

SW1
Steelworker First Class

SW2
Steelworker Second Class

SW3
Steelworker Third Class

SWA
Southwest Approaches

SWACS
Surveillance, Warning, and Control System

SWAG
Standard Written Agreement

SWAL
Shallow Water Attack-Craft, Light

SWAM
Shallow Water Attack-Craft, Medium

SWAT
Sidewinder Angle Tracking

SWATH
Small Waterplane Area Twin Hull (ship concept)

SWATS
Shallow Water Acoustic Tracking System

SWB
Special Weapons Branch

SWBD
Switchboard

SWBS
Ship's Work Breakdown Structure

SWC
Chief Steelworker
Ship's Weapons Coordinator
Submerged Work Center

SWCA
Steelworker Construction Apprentice

SWCC
Special Warfare Combatant Craft Crewman Specialist

SWCL
Special Warfare Craft, Light

SWCM
Master Chief Steelworker
Special Warfare Craft, Medium

SWCN
Steelworker Constructionman

SWCS
Senior Chief Steelworker

SWDG
Surface Warfare Development Group

SWDI
Shipyard Work Description Index

SWETTU
Special Weapons Experimental Tactical Test Unit

SWFPAC
Strategic Weapon Facility Group, Pacific

S/WG
Starboard Wing (stowage)

SWG
Single-Weight Glossy (photo paper)

SWIM
Ship Weapons Installation Manual

SWIP
Super-Weight Improvement Program

SWIR
Special Weapons Inspection Reports

SWISS
Shallow Water Intermediate Search System

SWL
Safe Working Load
Short-Wave Listeners

SWLIN
Ship's Work Line Item Number

SWM
Shipboard Wave Meter
Short-Wave Meter

SWO
Senior Watch Officer
Surface Warfare Officer

SWOB
Ship Waste Offload Barge

SWO BST
Surface Warfare Officer Billet Specialty Training

SWOD
Special Weapons Ordnance Division

SWOP
Special Weapons Ordnance Publication
Stop Without Pay

SWO PQS
Surface Warfare Officer Personnel Qualification Standards

SWOS
Surface Warfare Officers School

SWOSCOLCOM
Surface Warfare Officers School Command

SWOSCOLCOMDET
Surface Warfare Officers School Command Detachment

SWP
Subordinate Work Package

SWPA
Southwest Pacific Area

SWPF
Southwest Pacific Force

SWR
Standing Wave Ratio

SWS
Strategic Weapons System

SWSA
Steelworker Seaman Apprentice

SWSN
Steelworker Seaman

SWTTEU
Special Weapons Test and Tactical Evaluation Unit

SWU
Special Weapons Unit

SWULANT
Special Weapons Unit, Atlantic

SWUPAC
Special Weapons Unit, Pacific

SXBT
Shipboard Expendable Bathythermograph

SY
Shipyard

SYMPAC
Symbolic Program for Automatic Control

SYNTRAIN
Synthetic Training

SYS
System

SYSARD
System for Automated Reporting (programming)

SYSCOM
Systems Command
Systems Commander

SYSIN
Systems Input

SYSOUT
Systems Output

SYSPLIN
Shipyard Special Purchase Long-Lead Material

SYSRES
Systems-Resistance

SZ
Surface Zero

3M
Standard Navy Maintenance and Material Management System

(T)
Transmitter

T
Tactical (NAO code)
Temporary (personnel status)
Thunderstorm
Time
Trainer (aircraft)
Transformer
True (bearing)
Tug

T&DC
Training and Distribution Center

T&DCEN
Training and Distribution Center

T&E
Test and Evaluation

T&H
Test and Handlng (equipment)

T&MC
Test and Monitor Console

T&RNP
Transportation and Recruiting, Naval Personnel

TA
TACAN Approach
Technical Analysis
Technical Authority
Terrain Avoidance
Transition Agreement
Transition Altitude
Travel Allowance
True Altitude
Tuition Assistance

TAB
Tabulate
Tactical Analysis Branch
Technical Abstract Bulletin
Technological Assessment Board
Training Aids Booklet

TABCASS
Tactical Air Beacon Command and

Surveillance System

TAC
Tactic
Tactical
Tactical Air Command
Tactical Air Controller
Target Acquisition Console
Total Air Control
Training Aids Center
TRANSAC Assembler/Compiler
Transportation Accounting Code

TAC(A)
Tactical Air Coordinator, Airborne

TACA
Tactical Air Coordinator, Airborne

TACAIR
Tactical Air
Tactical Aircraft

TACAMO
Take Charge and Move Out

TACAN
Tactical Air Navigation (system)

TACANCEN
Tactical Air Navigation Control Center

TACC
Tactical Air Command Centers

TACCAR
Time-Averaged Clutter-Coherent Airborne Radar

TACCO
Tactical Coordinator

TACD&E
Tactical Development and Evaluation

TACDEN
Tactical Data Entry

TACDEW
Tactical Advanced Combat Direction and Electronic Warfare

TACDFINSDEN
Temporary active duty under instruction in a flying status not involving flying

TACDIFINSOPS
Temporary active duty under instruction in a flying status involving operational or training flights

TACDIFINSPRO
Temporary active duty under instruction in a flying status involving proficiency flying

TACDIFIPS
Temporary active duty in a flying status involving operational or training flights

TACDIFPRO
Temporary active duty in a flying status involving proficiency flying

TACDIVDEN
Temporary active duty in a flying status not involving flying

TACELECRON
Tactical Electronics Warfare Squadron

TACELECRONDET
Tactical Electronics Warfare Squadron Detachment

TACELECWARON
Tactical Electronics Warfare Squadron

TACGRU
Tactical Air Control Group

TACLAND
Tactical Instrument Landing Program

TACLOG
Tactical Logistics

TACMEMO
Tactical Memorandum

TAC-NAV
Tactical Navigation (system)

TACO
Tactical Coordinator

TACOC
Tactical Air Control Operations Center

TACOSS
Tactical Containerized Shelter System

TACOSS I
Tactical Containerized Shelter System/Detachment Subsistence Unit (Expandable)

TACOSS II
Tactical Containerized Shelter System/Detachment Sanitary Unit (Non-Expandable)

TACOSS IV
Tactical Containerized Shelter System/Provision Storage (Dry, Frozen, Refrigerated)

TACOSS IX
Tactical Containerized Shelter System/Galley Unit, Large (Expandable), 250-man

TACOSS V
Tactical Containerized Shelter System/Equipment and Shop Unit (Expandable)

TACOSS VI
Tactical Containerized Shelter System/Detachment Personnel Unit

TACOSS VII
Tactical Containerized Shelter/Utility Unit (Expandable)

TACOSS VIII
Tactical Containerized Shelter System/Frozen Storage Unit (Non-Expandable)

TACOSS X
Tactical Containerized Shelter System/Sanitary Unit, Large (Expandable), 100-man

TACP
Tactical Air Control Party

TAC/R
Tactical Reconnaissance

TACREDDS
Tactical Readiness Drills

TACRON
Tactical Air Control Squadron

TACS
Tactical Air Control System

TACSAT
Tactical Satellite

TACSATCOM
Tactical Satellite Communications

TACT
Teleprinter Automatic Control Terminal
Transonic Aircraft Technology (program)

TACTAS
Tactical Towed Array System

TACTASS
Tactical Towed Array Sonar System

TACTOM
Tactical Tomahawk

TACTRAGRULANT
Tactical Training Group, Atlantic

TACTRAGRUPAC
Tactical Training Group, Pacific

TACV
Tracked Air Cushion Vehicle

TAD
Tactical Air Direction
Task Analysis Data
Technical Approval Demonstration
Temporary Additional Duty
Theater Air Defense
Training Aids Division

TADC
Tactical Air Direction Center
Training Aids Distribution Center

TADIXS
Tactical Data Information Exchange System

TADL
Tactical Data Link

TADM
Tactical Atomic Demolition Munitions

TADOR
Table Data Organization and Reduction

TADSO
Tactical Digital Systems Office

TADSS
Tactical Automatic Digital Switching System

TADTAR
Temporary Additional Duty Target

T-AE
Ammunition Ship (Military Sealift Command)

TAEG
Training Analysis and Evaluation Group

TAF
Terminal Aerodrome Forecast
Training Aids Facility

TAFMS
Total Active Federal Military Service

TAFOR
Terminal Aerodrome Forecast

T-AFS
Combat Stores Ship (MSC)

TAFT
Technical Assistance Field Team

TAFUBAR
Inf: Things Are Fucked Up Beyond All Recognition

T-AG
Acoustic Survey Ship (MSC)

TAG
Technical Advisory Group
Training Aids Guide
Transport Air Group

TAGIS
Tracking and Ground Instrumentation System

T-AGM
Missile Range Instrumentation/Navigation Test Support Ship (MSC)

T-AGOS
Ocean Surveillance Ship (MSC)

T-AGS
Auxiliary Survey Ship (MSC)

T-AH
Hospital Ship (MSC)

TAIU
Technical Aircraft Instrument Unit

T-AK
Maritime Prepositioning Ship (MSC)

TAK
Military Sea Transport Service AKA

TAKCAL
Tachometer Calibration

TAKD
Military Sea Transport Service LSD

T-AKE
Advanced Auxiliary Dry Cargo Ship (MSC)

T-AKR
Large, Medium-speed, Roll-on/Roll off Ship (MSC)

TAKV
Military Sea Transport Service CVS

TAL
Training Aids Library

TALAR
Tactical Landing and Approach Radar
Talos Activity Report

TALD
Tactical Air-Launched Decoy

TAM
Transistor-Amplifier-Multiplier

TAMD
Tactical Automated Missile Defense

TAMET
Aerodrome Forecast in Units of Metric

TAMI
Technical Information Maintenance Instruction

TAMPS
Tactical Aircraft Mission Planning System
Tactical Automated Mission Planning System

TANKOPINS
Tanker Operating Instructions

TANS
Terminal Area Navigation System

T-AO
Oiler (MSC)

TAO
Military Sea Transport Service Tanker
Tactical Action Officer
Tactical Air Observer
Terminal Arrest Orders

TAOC
Tactical Air Operations Center

T-AOE
Fast Combat Support Ship (MSC)

T-AOT
Transport Tanker (MSC)

TAOW
Time Allowed Off Weapon

TAP
Military Sea Transport Service APA
Target Aircraft Program
Task Area Plan
Technical Alteration Plan
Technical Area Plan
Training Aids Platform
Tuition Assistance Program

TAPE
Tape Automatic Preparation Equipment
Terminal Annual Planning Estimate

TAPER
Temporary Appointment Pending Establishment of Registers (CSC)

TAPIO
Tape Input and Output

TAPIT
Tactical Photographic Image Transmission (subsystem)

TAPS
Time Analysis of Program Status
Trajectory Accuracy Prediction System

TAR
Tactical Aircraft Recovery
Target
Technical Advisory Report
Temporary Active Reserve
Terrain Avoidance Radar
Terrier Advanced Radar
Thrust-Augmented Rocket
Total Accomplishment Requirement
Total Assets Reporting
Training and Administration of Reserves

TARA
Terrain Avoidance Radar

T-ARC
Cable Laying/Repair Ship (MSC)

TARCAP
Target Combat Air Patrol

TARFU
Inf: Things are Really Fucked Up

TARGET
Team to Advance Research for Gas Energy Transformation

TARPS
Tactical Air Reconnaissance Pod System

TARS
Technical and Research Staff

TARSLL
Tender and Repair Ship Load List

TARVH
Aircraft Repair Ship, Helicopter

TAS
Target Acquisition System
Technical Advisory Service
Training Aids Section
Transfer Alignment Set
True Airspeed

TASA
Task and Skill Analysis

TASC
Tactical Articulated Swimmerable Carrier
Training and Support Component (USNR)

TASES
Tactical Airborne Signal Exploitation System

TAS-I
Target Acquisition System-Integrated

TAS/IRAS
Target Acquisition System/Infrared Automatic System

TAS/RMS
Target Acquisition System/Radar Manual System

TASS
Tech Assembly System
Technical Air Armament Study

TAT
To Accompany Troops (cargo)
Torpedo-Attack Teacher
True Air Temperature
Turn Around Time

TATC
Tactical Air Traffic Control

T-ATF
Fleet Ocean Tug (MSC)

TATSA
Transportation Aircraft Test and Support Activity

TATTE
Talos Tactical Test Equipment

TAU
Twin Agent Unit

TAV
Tender Availability

T-AVB
Aviation Logistics Ship (MSC)

TAVE
Thor-Agena Vibration Experiment

TAW
Thrust-Augmented Wing

TAWC
Tactical Air Warfare Center

TB
Technical Bulletin
Torpedo Boat
Torpedo-Bombing
True Bearing
Tub

TBA
Table of Basic Allowances
To Be Activated
To Be Announced
To Be Attacked

TBD
Target Bearing Designator
To Be Determined

TBFU
Shipboard Twin-Ball Fire Fighting Unit

TBH
Test Bed Harness
Test Bench Harness

TBI
Test Best Installation
To Be Inactivated

TBL
Through Bill of Lading

TBM
Theater Ballistic Missile

TBMD
Theater Ballistic Missile Defense

TBN
To Be Named
To Be Nominated

TBO
Time Between Overhaul

TBS
Talk Between Ships
Training Battle Simulation

TBT
Target Bearing Transmitter (system)

TBX
Tactical Ballistic Experimental

T/C
Technical Control
Thermocouple

TC
Temperature and Compression (metal bonding)
Time Charter
Time Check
Total Cost
Training Center
Transceiver Code
Transportation Code
Trial Counsel
True Course
Turret Captain

TCA
Tender-Controlled Approach
Terminal Control Area
Track Crossing Angle

TCARC
Tropical Cyclone Aircraft Reconnaissance Coordinator

TCB
Target Control System Bulletin

TCBM
Transcontinental Ballistic Missile

TCC
Telecommunications Center
Time Compression Coding
Tracking and Control Center
Transportation Control Committee
Travel Classification Code

TCD
Tentative Classification of Defects
Tour Completion Date
Training Control Device

TCDAF
Tenant Command Disciplinary Action File

TCDL
Tactical Common Data Link

TCF
Tactical Control Facility

TCG
Transverse Center of Gravity

TCGR
Track Control Group Replacement

TCMC
Transportation Control and Movement Center

TCMD
Transportation Control and Movement Document

TCMG
Transportable Countermeasures Group

TCN
Transportation Control Number

TCO
Technical Contracting Officer
Telecommunications Certification Office
Termination Contracting Officer

TCP
Total Contract Proposal
Trainer Change Proposal
Training and Certification Program
Transmission Control Protocol

TCS
Tactical Control System
Target Control System
Target Cost System

TCSP
Tactical Communications Satellite Program

TCSS
Tactical Control Surveillance System

TCT
Time Critical Targeting

TCTO
Time Compliance Technical Order

TCU
Tape Control Unit
Torpedo Control Unit
Towering Cumulus (cloud formation)

T/D
Temperature Datum

TD
Target Discrimination
Target Drone
Technical Directive
Temporary Duty
Test Diagram
Testing Device
Touchdown
Transmitter/Distributor
Trimming and Drainage (system)
Tropical Depression

TD&S
Training Development and Support

TDA
Today
Transcript Deserter's Account

TDAS
Tracking and Data Acquisition System

TDBD
Top Down Break Down

TDC
Taiwan Defense Command
Technical Directive Compliance
Through-Deck Cruiser
Top Dead Center
Torpedo Firing Data Computer

TDCF
Technical Directive Compliance Form

TDCO
Torpedo Data Computer Center

TDD
Target Detection Device
Technical Documents Department
Test and Development Director (PERA)

TDDL
Time-Division Data Link

TDDS
Tactical Data Dissemination System

TDH
Total Discharge Head (pumps)

TDI
Target Data Inventory

TDLJMS
Tactical Data Link Joint Message Standard

TDM
Telemetric Data Monitor
Test Development Manager
Time Division Multiplex
Torpedo Detection Modification (sonar)

TDMP
Test Development Management Plan

TDMS
Telegraph Distortion Measuring System

TDN
Travel directed is necessary

TDO
Technical Data Office
Technical Development Objectives
Technical Directives Ordnance

TDOC
Technical Document

TDP
Technical Data Package
Technical Development Plan
Temporary Detention of Pay

TDR
Talos Discrepancy Report
Torque Differential Receiver

TDRL
Temporary Disability Retired List

TDRS
Travelers, Defect Route Sheet

TDS
Tactical Data System
Target Designation System
Total Dissolved Solids
Training Duty Status
Translation and Docking Simulator

TDSA
Technical Directive Status Accounting

TDSO
Training Device Supply Office

TDSS
Tactical Display Support System

TDT
Target Designation Transmitter

TDTG
True Date-Time-Group

TDU
Target Device Unit
Trash Disposal Unit
Traverse Displacement Unit

TDX
Torque Differential Transmitter

TDY
Temporary Duty

TDZ
Touchdown Zone

TDZ/CL
Touchdown Zone/Centerline (light system)

TDZL
Touchdown Zone Light (system)

TE
Task Element
Test Equipment
Trailing Edge
Turbo-Electric
Twin-Engine

TEA
Task Equipment Analysis

TEAM
Tube Earphone and Microphone

TEAMS
Test, Evaluation, and Monitoring System

TEASE
Tracking Errors and Simulation Evaluation

TEC
TOS Evaluation Center
Type Equipment Code

TECG
Test and Evaluation Coordinating Group

TECH
Tactical Exercise Control
Technical
Technician
Technology

TECHAD
Technical Advisor

TECH ASSIST
Technical Assistant

TECHAUTHIND
Technical Paper/Author Cross-Index System

TECHEVAL
Technical Evaluation

TECHMAN
Technical Manual

TECHNOTE
Technical Note
Technical Notice

TECHREP
Technical Representative

TECHTRA
Technical Training

TED
Terminal Eligibility Date
Thermo-Electric Drive
Training Equipment Development

TEDS
Turbine-Electric Drive Submarine

TEG
Tactical Exploitation Group

TEL
Telegram
Telephone
Transporter-Erector-Launcher

TELCOM
Telephone Communications

TELCON
Telephone Conversation
Teletype Conversation

TELEG
Telegram

TELEM
Telemetry

TELEM ANT
Telemetry Antenna

TELERAN
Television and Radar Navigation

TEM
Temporary

TEMAC
Temporary active duty

TEMACDIFOT
Temporary active duty in a flying status involving operational or training flights.

TEMACDIFOTINS
Temporary active duty under instruction in a flying status involving operational or training flights.

TEMACINS
Temporary active duty under instruction

TEMADD
Temporary Additional Duty

TEMADDCON
Temporary additional duty in connection with ___________

TEMADDINS
Temporary additional duty in connection with ___________

TEM-CAS
Temporary-Casualty (pay record)

TEMCON
Temporary duty connection

TEMDIFDEN
Temporary duty under instruction in a flying status not involving flying.

TEMDIFINSOPS
Temporary duty under instruction in a flying status involving operational or training flights.

TEMDIFOPS
Temporary duty in a flying status involving operational or training flights.

TEMDIFOTINS
Temporary duty under instructions in a flying status involving operational or training flights.

TEMDIFPRO
Temporary duty in a flying status involving proficiency flying.

TEMDU
Temporary Duty

TEMDUCON
Temporary duty in connection with ______

TEMDU DIS
Temporary duty pending disciplinary action

TEMDU FFA
Temporary duty for further assignment

TEMDU PAT
Temporary duty as a patient

TEMDU PSI
Temporary duty-programmed student input

TEMDU SEP
Temporary duty pending separation

TEMFLY
Temporary duty involving flying

TEMFLYINS
Temporary duty involving flying under instruction

TEM-GEN
Temporary-General (pay record)

TEMINS
Temporary duty under instruction

TEMP
Tactical Electromagnetic Program
Temperature
Temporary
Test and Evaluation Master Plan
Transportable Electromagnetic Pulse

TEMPATT
Temporarily attached

TEMPDETD
Temporary detached duty

TEMPDU FFT
Temporary duty for further transfer

TEMPLINACT
Temporary duty pending disciplinary action

TEMPLINEAR
Temporary duty pending disciplinary hearing

TEMPROX
Temporary duty will cover approximately _____ days.

TEMPT
Test Equipment, Materials, Parts, and Tools

TEM-RET
Temporary pay record for a retired member called to active duty.

TEMSEPRAD
Temporary duty in connection with separation processing. Upon completion and when directed, detached, proceed home for release from active duty according to instructions.

TEMWAIT
Temporary duty awaiting

TENOC
Ten-Year Oceanographic Research Program

TEP
TAR Enlisted Program
Temperature Extreme Pressure (oil)
Torpedo Ejection Pump
Transportable Equation Program

TEPD
Tasking, Processing, Exploitation, and Dissemination

TER
Terrain
Territory
Triple Ejector Rack

TERCOM
Terrain Comparison
Terrain Contour Mapping

TERCON
Terrain Contour

TERI
Torpedo Effective-Range Indicator

TERM
Terminal
Terminate
Termination

TERMINACTRAORD
If serving under orders authorizing participation in Naval Reserve Training Program in pay or non-pay status, directed to request termination of inactive duty training orders, via appropriate chain of command, to be effective not later than day preceding date of reporting active duty compliance these orders.

TERPACIS
Trust Territory of the Pacific Islands

TERPS
Terminal Instrument Procedures

TERR
Territory

TES
Test and Evaluation Ship (program)

TESE
Tactical Exercise Simulator and Evaluator

TES-N
Tactical Exploitation System-Navy

TESS
Tactical Environmental Support System

TESS/NITES
Tactical Environment Support System/Navy Integrated Tactical Environmental Subsystem.

TEU
Technical Edit Unit

TEV
Turbo-Electric Drive

TEW
Tactical Electronic Warfare

TEWA
Threat Evacuation and Weapons Assignment

TEWDS
Tactical Electronic Warfare Decoy System

TEWS
Tactical Electronic Warfare Systems

TEXGRP
Texas Group

TEXT
Textural File (NARDIS)

TF
Task Force
Terrain-Following (radar)
Turbofan (engine)

TFBR
Technical Feedback Report

TFC
Task Force Commander
Theater Fusion Center

TFCC
Tactical Flag Command Center

TFG
Tactical Fighter Group
Terminal Facilities Guides

TFMMS
Total Force Manpower Management System

TFO
Temporary Flight Orders

TFP
Temporary Forfeiture of Pay

TFR
Terrain-Following Radar
Trouble and Failure Report

TFS
Torpedo Firing System

TFW
Tactical Fighter Wing

TFWC
Tactical Fighter Weapons Center

TFX
Tactical Fighter Experimental

TFZ
Traffic Zone

TG
Task Group
Telegraph
Trunk Group
Turbo-Generator

TGA
Thermogravimeter Analysis

TGBL
Through Government Bill of Lading

TGL
Touch-and-Go Landing

TGM
Training Guided Missile

TGSM
Terminally-Guided Sub-Missile

TGT
Target

TGU
Technical Guidance Unit

TH
Telemetry Head
True Heading

T-HA
Terminal Height Altitude

THA
Total Hydrocarbon Analyzer

THAFE
Thousand Hours Accident Free Each

THAWS
Target Homing and Warning System

THC
True Heading Computer

THD
Thunderhead
Total Harmonic Distortion

THDR
Thunder

THERM
Thermometer

THI
Temperature-Humidity Index
Time Handed In

THIR
Temperature/Humidity Infrared Radiometer

THK
Thick

THOU
Thousand

THP
Thrust Horsepower

THR
Turbine Heat Rate

THRFTR
Thereafter

THRU
Through

THRUT
Throughout

THS
Test History Summary
Thermal Stress

THSD
Thousand

THS-EXPER
Thermal-Stress Experiment

THTN
Threaten

THV
Threshold Limit Value

TI
Test Initiate
Test Instrumentation
Tin
Training Instructor

TIARA
Target Identification and Recovery Aid

TIAS
Target Investigation and Acquisition Study

TIB
Technical Intelligence Brief

TIBS
Tactical Information Broadcast Service

TIC
Target Indication Sight
Technical Information Center
Technical Intelligence Center
Troops in Contact
Type, Intensity, Character (weather)

TICCIT
Time-Shared Computer-Controlled Instructional Television

TICO
Technical Information Contact Officer

TID
Tactical Information Display

TIDB
Technical Information Data Base

TIDOS
Table and Item Documentation System

TIES
Transmission and Information Exchange System

TIF
True Involute Form (gear teeth)

TIFS
Total In-Flight Simulation
Total In-Flight Simulator

TIG
Tungsten Inert Gas

TIIF
Tactical Imagery Interpretation Facility

TIM
Traffic Improvement Memorandum

TIMATION
Time Navigation (satellite)

TIMI
Technical Information Maintenance Instructions

TIMM
Thermonic Integrated Micro-Module

TIMS
Training Integrated Management System

TINSY
Treasure Island Naval Shipyard

TIO
Target Indication Officer

TIP
Technical Information Program
Technical Improvement Plan
Total Information Package
Track Initiation and Prediction

TIPS
Technical Information Procedures
Telemetry Impact-Prediction System
Training Improvement Proposal System (USNR)

TIPSY
Task Input Parameter Synthesizer

TIR
Target-Indicating Room
Technical Information Release
Time in Rate
Total Indicator Reading
Transaction Item Report
Transaction Item Reporting

TIREC
TIROS Ice Reconnaissance

TIROS
Television and Infrared Observation Satellite

TIROS-M
Television and Infrared Observation Satellite-Meteorological (purposes)

TIRS
Tactical Intercept and Recognition System

TIR/SLIT
Transaction Item Reporting/Serial Lot Item Tracking (activities)

TIS
Target Information Section
Technical Intelligence Section
Thermal Imaging System
Time in Service
Tracking and Injection Station

TISEO
Target Identification System Electro-Optical

TISS
Thermal Information Sensor System

TIT
Turbine Inlet Temperature

TIU
Tape Identification Unit

TJS
Tactical Jamming System

TK
Tank

TKBN
Tank Battalion

TKIBU
Transmission-Keying Indicator Buffer

TKOF
Take-Off

TKR
Talker

T/L
Training Literature

TL
Tieline
Trial
Turn Left

T-LA
Terminal Low Altitude (FLIP)

TLA
Temporary Lodging Allowance
Transition Layer

TLAM
Tomahawk Land-Attack Cruise Missile

TLAM-C
Tomahawk Land Attack Missile-Conventional

TLAM-N
Tomahawk Land Attack Missile-Nuclear

TLC
Thin-Layer Chromatography

TLD
Technical Logistics Data
Thermal Luminescent Dosimeter

TLDIC
Technical Logistics Data and Information Program

TLDP
Technical Logistics Data Program

TLI
Tank Level Indicator

TLL
Tender Load List

TLO
Topic Learning Objective
Training Liaison Officer

TLP
Total Loss of Pay

TLQ
Temporary Lodging Quarters
Tender Load Quantities

TLR
Tap Lower Relay
Top-Level Requirement
Trailer
Triangulation-Listening-Ranging (sonar)

TLT
Transportation Link Terminal

TLU
Threshold Logic Usage

TLV
Threshold Limit Value
Transition Level

T/M
Torque Meter

TM
Tactical Missile
Team
Technical Manual
Telemetering
Tone Modulation
Torpedoman's Mate
Training Manual
Type Maintenance

TM&E
Test, Measuring, and Equipment

TM1
Torpedoman's Mate First Class

TM2
Torpedoman's Mate Second Class

TM3
Torpedoman's Mate Third Class

TMA
Target Motion Analysis
Technical Manual Analysis
TRICARE Management Activity

TMC
Chief Torpedoman's Mate
Transportation Material Command

TMCM
Master Chief Torpedoman's Mate

TMCR
Technical Manual Contact Requirements

TMCS
Senior Chief Torpedoman's Mate

TMD
Theater Missile Defense

TMDC
Type Maintenance Due Code

TMDE
Test, Measuring, and Diagnostic Equipment

TMDER
Technical Manual Deficiency/Evaluation Report

TMDL
Technical Manual Data List

TME
Time Entry (NNSS)
Trainee Management Element

TMFA
Torpedoman's Mate Fireman Apprentice

TMFN
Torpedoman's Mate Fireman

TMG
Track Made Good

TMI
Technical Manual Index

TMINS
Technical Manual Identification and Numbering System (NAVELEX)

TML
Terminal

TMMIS
Technical Manual Management Information System

TMO
Total Material Objective
Traffic Management Office

TMP
Temperature
Total Material Package
Transitional Manpower Program

TMPO
Total Material Procurement Objective

TMPRLY
Temporarily

TMPRY
Temporary

TMQAP
Technical Manual Quality Assurance Plan

TMRBM
Tactical Medium-Range Ballistic Missile

TMRP
Target Motion Resolution Processing
Technical Manual Revision Program

T/M/S
Type/Model/Series

TMS
Time and Motion Study
Transportation Management School

TMSA
Torpedoman's Mate Seaman Apprentice
Total Military Service for Advancement

TMSN
Torpedoman's Mate Seaman

TMU
Tabulating Machine Unit
Trainee Management Unit
Transit Monitoring Unit

TMW
Tomorrow

TNCL
Tail Number Configuration List

TNDCY
Tendency

TNG
Training

TNGT
Tonight

TNO
Thermonuclear

TNPO
Terminal Navy Post Office

TNPQ
Temporarily Not Physcially Qualified

TNR
Trainer

TNTV
Tentative

TNW
Theater Nuclear Warfare

T/O
Tactical Organization
Take-Off
Travel Orders

TO
Table of Organization
Tactical Observer
Take-Off
Technical Order
Transportation Officer
Troy Ounce

TO&E
Tables of Organization and Equipment

TOA
Tanker Operations Assistant (MSTS)
Time of Arrival
Total Obligational Authority

TOB
Tanker Operations Branch (MSTS)
Transistor Output Board
Transistor Output Buffer

TOBEDI
To Be Disposed of (vessel)

TOBELE
To Be Leased (vessel)

TOBELN
To Be Loaned (vessel)

TOC
Tactical Operations Center
Tanker Operational Circulate
Total Organic Carbon
Troop Operations Center

TOD
Time of Delivery
Torpedo Operations Department (NTS)

TODE
Transcript of Data Extraction

TOES
Trade-Off Evaluation System

TOF
Test Overflow (NNSS)
Time of Fall
Time of File

TOFC
Trailer on Flat Car (shipping)

T/OFF
Take-Off

TOGW
Take-Off Gross Weight (of missile)

TOJ
Track-On Jamming

TOO
Time Or Origin

TOPLINE
Total Officer Personnel Objective Structure for the Line Officer Force

TOPO ENGR
Topographical Engineer

TOPOPLT
Topographic Platoon

TOPS
The Operational PERT System

TOPSEC
Top Secret

TOR
Technical Override
Time of Receipt

TORP
Torpedo

TORPEX
Torpedo Exercise

TOS
Tactical Operations System
TIROS Operational Satellite

TOSD
Training and Operations Support Department

TOSS
Tape-Oriented Supply System
TIROS Operational Satellite System
Total Operational Submarine Service

TOST
Technical Objectives and Selection Team

TOT
Time of Tape
Time of Target
Time of Transmission
Total
Transportation of Things
Turbine Outlet Temperature

TOTO
Tongue of the Ocean (site of AUTEC)

TOVC
Top of Overcast

TOVR
Turnover

TOW
Take-Off Weight
Tube-Launched, Optically-Tracked, Wire-Command (link guided missile)

TP
Target Practice
Technical Publication
Telephone
Test Procedures
Transport Pack
Turning Point

TP&MS
Turbo Power and Marine Systems

TP&O
Test Plan and Outline

TP&P
Transients, Patients, and Prisoners

TPA
Test Program Analyzer
Test Project Agreement
Transfer of Pay Account
Travel via Privately-owned conveyance Authorized

TPB
Technical Processes Branch

TPC
Tactical Pilotage Chart
Total Price Contract
Training Plans Conference
Transport Plane Commander

TPD
Test Point Data
Training Publications Division

TPDR
Technical Publication Deficiency Report

TPDRS
Time-Phased Downgrading and Reclassification System

TPFDL
Time Phased Force and Development List

TPI
Target Position Indicator
Technical Proficiency Inspection
Tons Per Inch

TPL
Technical Publication Library

TPM
Technical Performance Measurement
Technical Performance Milestone

TPMP
Technical Performance Measurement Plan

TPO
Tentative Program Objectives

TPP
Total Package Procurement

TPPD
Technical Program Planning Document

TPR
Tool Performance Report

TPS
Test Pilot School
Test Program Set
Text Processing System
Threat Platform Simulator

TPT
Tail Pipe Temperature

TPTRL
Time-Phased Transportation Requirements List

TPU
Transient Personnel Unit

TQE
Technical Quality Evaluation

T/R
Transmit/Receive
Transmitter/Receiver
Type of Record (code)

TR
Timing Relay
Torque Receiver
Translation
Transportation Request
Transpose
Travel Request
Tray
Turn Right

TRA
Training
Transfer
Tri-Annually

TRAC
Tracer
Tractor

TRACALS
Traffic Control and Landing System

TRACE
Taxing and Routing of Aircraft Coordinating Equipment
Transportable Automatic Control Environment (system)

TRACEN
Training Center

TRACER
Turnaround Time, Repair Survival Rate, and Cost Evaluation Report

TRACOMD
Training Command

TRACOMDLANT
Training Command, Atlantic

TRACOMDPAC
Training Command, Pacific

TRACOMDSUBPAC
Training Command, Submarines, Pacific

TRACOMDWESTCOAST
Training Command, West Coast

TRAD
Training Administration

TRADAR
Transaction Data Recorder

TRADEC
Training Device Computer

TRADEX
Target Resolution and Discrimination Experiment
Tracking Radar, Experimental

TRADIX
Transistor-Digital Computer

TRAFAC
Training Facility

TRAFOLPERS
Transfer the following enlisted personnel

TRAFS
Torpedo Recognition and Alertment Functional Segment

TRAIF
Torso Restraint Assembly with Integrated Flotation

TRAINMAN
Training Management

TRAM
Target Ranging and Acquisition Multisensor
Target Recognition Attack Multisensor
Test Reliability and Maintainability

TRAMAN
Training Manual

TRAMP
Test Retrieval and Memory Print

TRAMPS
Temperature Regulator and Missile Power Supply

TRAN
Transient

TRANET
Tracking Network

TRANS
Transport
Transportation

TRANSAC
Transistor Automatic Computer

TRANS/DEP
Transportation of Dependents

TRANSDIR
Travel via government aircraft directed outside CONUS where available, otherwise commercial aircraft is directed.

TRANSDIV
Transportation Division

TRANSEC
Transmission Security

TRANSFER
Transportation Simulation for Estimating Requirements

TRANSIM
Transportation Simulator

TRANSITPERSU
Transient Personnel Unit

TRANSLANT
Transports, Atlantic

TRANSMAN
Enlisted Transfer Manual

TRANSMGTSCOL
Transportation Management School

TRANSMONUNIT
Transient Monitoring Unit

TRANSRON
Transportation Squadron

TRANSTEC
Sonar Transducer Test and Evaluation Center (NEL)

TRAP
Tactical Recovery of Aircraft and Personnel
Terminal Radiation Program
Transit, Receive, and Plot

TRAPAC
Training Force, Pacific

TRAPS
Training Requirements and Planning Subsystem

TRARON
Training Squadron

TRASTA
Training Station

TRAT
Torpedo Readiness Assistance Team

TRAU
Training Unit

TRAV
Travel

TRAVCHAR
Cost of travel chargeable (appropriation or department designated in following group(s). Identifying numerals may be added).

TRAVNEC
Subject travel was necessary at this time, and the length of time consumed in administrative channels prevented written orders from being issued prior to departure.

TRAWL
Tape Read and Write Library

TRB
Temperature Resistant Buff
Torpedo Retriever Boat

TRBR
Transportation Branch

TRC
Transmission Release Code

TRCCC
Tracking Radar Center Control Console

TRCVR
Transceiver

T-RDF
Transportable Radio Direction Finding System

TRDP
TRICARE Retiree Dental Plan

TRDTO
Tracking Radar Data Take-Off

TRE
Temperature Resistant Element
Training Readiness Evaluation

TRF
Technical Replacement Factor
Transfer
Tuned Radio Frequency

TR/FLRES
Transferred to Fleet Reserve

TRI
Test Requirement Identification

TRIA
Telemetry Range Instrumented Aircraft

TRICCSMA
Trident Command and Control Systems Maintenance Facility

TRICE
Transistorized Real-Time Incremental Computer

TRIM
Test Rules for Inventory Management
Trail Road Interdiction Mission
Training Records and Information Management System
Training Requirements and Information Management

TRIMIS
Tri-Service Medical Information System

TRIP
Tartar Reliability Improvement Plan

TRIPER
Trident Planned Equipment Replacement

TRIREFFAC
Trident Refit Facility

TRIS
Transmit-Receive Image System

TRI-TAC
Joint Tactical Communications

TRITRAFAC
Trident Training Facility

TRIXS
Tactical Reconnaissance Intelligence Exchange System

TRK
Track
Truck
Trunk

TRL
Time Recovery Loop (NNSS)

TRLFSW
Tactical Range Landing Force Support Weapons

TRLP
Transport Landplane

TRM
Time Release Mechanism

TRML
Terminal

TRMS
Type Commander Readiness Management System

TRN
Train

TRNG
Training

TRNGREP
Training Report

TRNS
Transition

TRO
Test Requirements Outline

TRODI
Touchdown Rate of Descent Indicator

TROP
Tropical
Tropics

TRP
Troop

TRRN
Terrain

TRS
Technical Repair Standard
Transversing Rake System

TRSA
Terminal Radar Service Area

TRSP
Transport Seaplane

TRSR
Taxi and Runway Surveillance Radar

TRSSGM
Tactical Range Surface-to-Surface Guided Missile

TRUMP
Target Radition Unit Measurement Program

T-S
Temperature-Salinity
Terminal Seaplane (ELIP)
Time-Sharing

TS
Tank Scope
Temperature Switch
Test Set
Test Squadron
Test Station
Time Shack
Top Secret
Inf: Tough Situation
Training Station
Transmitting Station
Tropical Storm
Tube Size

TSAF
Typical Systems Acquisition Flow

TSAM
Test Set Antenna Maintenance
Trainer, Surface-to-Air Missile
Trident Support Activities, Mechanicsburg (PA)

TSAPG
Telecommunications Systems Architecture Planning Group

TSC
Tactical Support Center
Tandem Switching Center
Transmitter Start Code
Transportable Satellite Communications (terminal)

TSCC
Top-Secret Control Channel

TSCM
Technical Surveillance Countermeasures

TSCO
Top-Secret Control Officers

TSCP
Top-Secret Control Procedures

TSCS
Top-Secret Control Section

TSD
Tactical Situation Display
Technical Support Division
Toured Sea Duty

TSF
Training Summary File

TSFC
Tactical Support Functional Component

TSG
Technical Specialty Group

TSGM
Terminally-Guided Submersible

TSHWR
Thundershower

TSI
Technical Standardization Inspection

TSL
Tri-Service Laser
Troop Safety Line

TSMC
Technical Supply Management Code

TSN
Time Since New

TSO
TACAMO Systems Operator
Test-Site Office
Time Since Overhaul

TSOR
Tentative Specific Operating Requirement
Tentative Specific Operational Requirement

TSOS
Time-Sharing Operational Requirement

TSO-T
TACAMO Systems Operator in Training

TSP
Teleprocessing Services Program
Tri-Sodium Phosphate (pipe cleaner)

TSPR
Total System Performance Responsibility

TSR
Telecommunications Service Request

TSRI
Technical Skill Reenlistment Incentive

TSS
Telecommunications Switching System
Thrust-Sensitive Signal
Time-Sharing Supervisor

TSSC
Target Systems Service Change

TSTA
Tailored Ship Training Availability

TSTD
Total Ship Test Director

TSTM
Thunderstorm

TSTP
Total Ship Test Program

TSTP/AFS
Total Ship Test Program for Active Fleet Ships

TT
Tablet
Target Towing (aircraft)
Teletypewriter
Test and Trials
Trust Territory of the Pacific Islands

TTA
Trials Test Assurance

TTAB
Technical Training Acceptance Board

TTAT
Torpedo Tube Acceptance Trials

TTC
Transportable Telephone Communications

TTCP
The Technical Cooperation Plan

TTE
Technical Training Equipment

TTEE
Transfer of Training Effectiveness Evaluation

TTF
Training Task Force

TTI
Time To Intercept

TTL
Transistor-Transistor Logic

TTM
Tactical Target Material
Two-Tone Modulation

TTPI
Torpedo Technical Proficiency Inspection
Trust Territory of the Pacific Islands

TTR
Tactical Test Station
Target Track Radar
Time-Temperature Recorder

TTS
Temperature Test Station
Temporary Threshold Shift
Test and Training Satellite
Transitional Training School

TTSA
Transitional Training School, Atlantic

TTSP
Transitional Training School, Pacific

TTSU
Trunion Tile and Angle of Sight Unit

TTT
Time to Turn
Time, Transformation, Temperature (diagram)

TTWCS
Tactical Tomahawk Weapon Control System

TTY
Teletype
Teletypewriter

TU
Task Unit
Thank You
Thermal Unit
Training Unit
Tube

TUPC
Transfer Underwater Pressure Chamber

TURB
Turbine

TURBC
Turbulence

TURPS
Terrestrial Unattended Reactor Power System

TUSLOG
Turkish-United States Logistics Group

TUSLOGDET
Turkish-United States Logistics Group Detachment

TVC
Thrust Vector Control

TVDS
Television Distribution System

TVG
Temperature-Voltage-Gasses
Time Variation of Gain
Well Done (old code)

TVIG
Television Inertial Guidance

TVIS
Turbine Vibration Indicator System

TVL
Travel

TVP
Tri-Vertiplane

TVT
Television Translator

TV TR
Television Tower

TVX
Target Vehicle, Experimental

T/W
Thrust/Weight (ratio)

TW
Tele-Weekly (AFRTS code)

TWA
Time-Weighted Average

TWAES
Tactical Warfare Analysis and Evaluation System

TWAH
This Week at Headquarters (NAVSHIPS publication)

TWD
Toward

TWEB
Transcribed Weather Broadcasts

TWIX
Teletypewriter Exchange

TWK
Total Work Content

TWLT
Twilight

TWPL
Teletypewriter, Private Lines

TWR
Torpedo Weapons Receiver

Tower
Transceiver

TWS
Track While Scanning

TWT
Telephone-Teletypewriter Exchange
Traveling Wave Tube
Two-Week Training (USNR)

TWX
Teletypewriter Exchange

TWY
Taxiway

TYCOM
Type Commander

TYCOMSLANT
Type Commands, Atlantic

TYCOMSPAC
Type Commands, Pacific

TYDAC
Typical Digital Automatic Computer

TYT
Type Training

TZ
Time Zone

U

U
Union
Unit

U/A
Units per Application

UA
Unauthorized Absence
Unauthorized Absentee

UAB
Until Advised By

UACC
Upper Air Control Center

UACTE
Universal Automatic Checkout Control and Test Equipment

UADPS
Uniform Automatic Data Processing System

UADPS-ICP
Uniform Automatic Data Processing System for Inventory Control Point

UADPS-INAS
Uniform Automatic Data Processing System for Industrial Naval Air Station

UADPS-SP
Uniform Automatic Data Processing System for Stock Points

UAG
Upper Atmosphere Geophysics

UALI
Universal Automatic Laser Interferometer

UAM
Underwater-to-Air Missile

UAN
Unidentified Atmospheric Noise

UAP
Utility Amphibious Plane

UAR
Upper Air Route

UAV
Unmanned Aerial Vehicle

UBFC
Underwater Battery Fire Control

UBITRON
Undulating Beam Interaction Electron (tube)

UB/MS
Utility Boat, Minesweeper

UBST
Unbonded Spool Type

U/C
Unclassified

UC
UCA Summary Account Code
Under Construction
Unit Cost

UCA
Uniform Chart of Accounts

UCCS
Universal Camera Control System

UCL
Upper Control Limit

UCLAR
Rocket Launcher Control Unit

UCLS
Underwater Crash Locator System

UCM
Uniform Code of Military Justice

UCMJ
Uniform Code of Military Justice

UCO
Universal Weather Landing Code

UCT
Underwater Construction Team

U/D
Upper Deck

UD
Underway Demonstration
Undesirable Discharge
Unit Diary

UDATS
Underwater Damage Assessment Television System

UDCA
Undesirable Discharge, Trial by Civil Authorities

UDDE
Undesirable Discharge, Desertion Without Trial

UDFE
Undesirable Discharge, Fraudulent Enlistment

UDL
Urine Disposal Lock

UDM
Unassigned Direct Material

UDMU
Universal Decoder Memory Unit

UDOFIT
Universal Digital Operational Flight Trainer Tool

UDR
Urgent Data Request
Urgent Data Requirement

UDT
Underwater Demolition Team

UDTPHIBSPAC
Underwater Demolition Team, Amphibious Forces, Pacific

UDU
Underwater Demolition Unit

UDUF
Undesirable Discharge, Unfitness

UEG
Unit Expansion Group

UEL
Upper Explosion Limit

UEPH
Unaccompanied Enlisted Personnel Housing

UEQ
Unaccompanied Enlisted Quarters

UER
Unsatisfactory Equipment Report

UERT
Universal Engineer Tractor, Rubber-Tired

UETA
Universal Engineer Tractor, Armored

UF
Under Frequency (controller)

UFA
Until Further Advised

UFCG
Underwater Fire Control Group

UFCS
Underwater Fire Control System

UFN
Until Further Notice

UFO
Ultra High Frequency Follow-On

UFOP
Ultra-Fast-Opening Parachute

UFSS
Unmanned Free Swimming Submersibles

UFU
Utility Flight Unit

UG
Undergoing

UHF
Ultra High Frequency

UHS
Unit Handling System

UHT
Unit Horizontal Tail

U/I
Unidentified
Unit of Issue

UI
Under Instruction

UIC
Unit Identification Code

UICP
Uniform Inventory Control Point (system)

UIEV
Universal Imagery Exploitation Viewer

UIR
Upper Flight Information Region

UKN
Unknown

UL
Upper Level

ULCC
Ultra-Large Crude Carrier (ship)

ULMS
Undersea Long-Range Missile Submarine
Underwater Long-Range Missile System

ULO
Unrestricted Line Officer

ULP
Utility Landplane

ULTSIGN
Ultimate Assignment

UM
Underwater Mechanic

UMA
United Maritime Authority

UMBR
Universal Multiple Bomb Rack

UMC
Unspecified Minor Construction (program)

UMIPS
Uniform Material Issue Priority System

UMM
Universal Mission Module

UMMIPS
Uniform Material Movement and Issue Priority System
Uniform Military Material Issue Priority System

UMMMIPS
Uniform Military Material Movement and Issue Priority System

UMPAR
Unit Mobilization Personnel Assignment Report

UMRS
Unsatisfactory Material Reporting

UMT
Universal Military Training

UMV
Unmanned Vehicles

UN
Unit

UNA
Use No Abbreviations

UNAMACE
Universal Automatic Map Compilation Equipment

UNASGN
Unassigned

UNAUTH
Unauthorized

UNAUTHD
Unauthorized

UNB
Universal Navigation Beacon

UNCINCSO
United States Commander-in-Chief, South-

ern Command

UNCLAS
Unclassified

UNDELORDCAN
Undelivered orders (identified by date or message reference numbers following) cancelled.

UNFAV
Unfavorable

UNFTP
Unified Navy Field Test Program

UNIDENT
Unidentified

UNIF
Uniform
Uniformity

UNITAS
United International Antisubmarine Warfare (exercise involving South American and United States navies).

UNITOPOS
Unit to which ordered will operate in an overseas area for a contemplated continuous period of 1 year or more.

UNITREPS
Unit Reports

UNIV
Universal

UNK
Unknown

UNKN
Unknown

UNL
Unlimited

UNLGTD
Unlighted

UNLOD
Unload

UNLTD
Unlimited

UNO
United National Organization

UNODIR
Unless otherwise directed

UNORCAN
Unexecuted portion of orders (identified by date or message reference numbers following) cancelled.

UNPAREN
End of Parentheses

UNQUAL
Unqualified

UNQUOTE
End of Quotation

UNREL
Unreliable

UNREP
Underway Replenishment

UNRSTD
Unrestricted

UNSAT
Unsatisfactory

UNSECNAV
Under Secretary of the Navy

UNSTBL
Unstable

UNSTDY
Unsteady

UNSVC
Unserviceable

UNT
Undergraduate Navigator Training

UNW
Underway

UOES
User Operational Evaluation System

UOPH
Unaccompanied Officer Personnel Housing

UOQ
Unaccompanied Officers Quarters

U/P
Unit Price

UPA
Unauthorized Precedence Announcement

UPDATE
Universal Prefabricated Depot Automatic Test Equipment

UPH
Unaccompanied Personnel Housing

UPIR
Uniform Photo Interpretation Report

UPK
Upkeep

UPLR
Unplanned Loss Report

UPP
Upper

UPS
Uninterruptible Power System
Universal Polar Stereographic (grid)

UPSTART
Universal Parachute Support Tactical and Research Target

UPWARD
Understanding Personal Worth and Racial Dignity

UR
Unsatisfactory Report
Your

URACTY
Your Activity

URAD
Your Radio

URDIS
Your Dispatch

UREST
Universal Range, Endurance, Speed, and Time

URFO
Universal Radio Frequency Oscillator

URG
Underway Replenishment Group
Universal Radio Group
Urgent

URGP
Underway Replenishment Group

URI
Unexpected Real Incapacitation

URL
Uniform Resource Locator
Unrestricted Line (officer)

URLTR
Your Letter

URMGM
Your Mailgram

URMSG
Your Message

URO
Unrestricted Operation(s) (overhual)

URSER
Your Serial

URSPDLTR
Your Speedletter

URTEL
Your Telegram

URV
Undersea Research Vehicle

U/S
Unserviceable

US
Uncle Sam
United States
Unserviceable

USA
United States of America

USA/ATL
Undersecretary of Defense for Acquisition, Technology, and Logistics

USADO
United States Defense Attaché Office

USADP
Uniform Shipboard Automatic Data Processing

USAG
Underwater Sound Advisory Group

USARP
United States Antarctic Research Program

USB
United States Band
Upper Sideband

USBATU
United States-Brazil Aviation Training Unit

USBER
United States Mission, Berlin

USBS
Unified S-Band System

USC
United States Citizen
United States Code

USCENTCOM
United States Central Command (unified command)

USCG
United States Coast Guard

USCGC
United States Coast Guard Cutter

USCINCMEAFSA
United States Commander-in-Chief, Middle East, South Asia and Africa South of the Sahara

USCMA
United States Court of Military Appeals

USCOMEASTLANT
United States Commander, Eastern Atlantic

USCOMEASTLANT ERS
United States Commander, Eastern Atlantic Emergency Relocation Site Commander

USCOMSOLANT
United States Commander South Atlantic Force

USCOMSUBGRUEASTLANT
United States Commander Submarine Group, Eastern Atlantic

USDAO
United States Defense Attaché Office

USDELMC
United States Delegation to the NATO Military Committee

USDLG
United States Defense Liaison Group

USDOCO
United States Documents Officer

USDR
United States Defense Representative

USD(R&E)
Under Secretary of Defense (Research and Engineering)

USEES
United States Naval Engineering Experimental Station

USELMCENTO
United States Element, Central Treaty Organization

USER
User Interest File (NARDIS)

USEUCOM
United States European Command (unified command)

USF
United States Fleet

USFORAZ
United States Forces, Azores

USFR
United States Naval Fleet Reserve

US/FRG
United States/Federal Republic of Germany

USFSPA
Uniformed Services Former Spouse Protection Act

USG
United States Government

USGLI
United States Government Life Insurance

USGPO
United States Government Printing Office

USGRDR
United States Government Research and Development Report

USGS
United States Geographical Service
United States Geological Survey

USGW
Undersea Guided Weapon

USHBP
Uniformed Services Health Benefit Program

USIC
Undersea Instrumentation Chamber

USIO
Unidentified Submerged Illuminated Object
United States Institute of Oceanography

USL
Underwater Sound Laboratory

USLO
United States Liaison Office/Officer

USM
Underwater-to-Surface Missile

USMAC
United States Military Assistance Command

USMAP
United Services Military Apprenticeship Program

USMC
United States Marine Corps

USMCEB
United States Military Communications Electronics Board

USMMA
United States Merchant Marine Academy

USMS
United States Maritime Service

USMSOS
United States Maritime Service Officers

USMSTS
United States Maritime Service Training School

USMTF
United States Message Text Format

USN
United States Navy

USN&USMCRC
United States Navy and United States Marine Corps Reserve Center

USNA
United States Naval Academy

USNAVFORCONAD
United States Naval Forces, Continental Air Defense Command

USNAVMILCOMUN
United States Navy Representative, Military Staff Committee United Nations

USNAVMIS
United States Naval Mission

USNAVREGDENCEN
United States Naval Regional Dental Center

USNAVREGMEDCEN
United States Naval Regional Medical Center

USNAVSO
United States Naval Forces, Southern Command

USNDD
United States Navy Drydock

USNFR
United States Naval Fleet Reserve

USNH
United States Naval Hospital
United States North of Hatteras

USNI
United States Naval Institute

USNIP
United States Naval Institute Press

USNLO
United States Navy Liaison Officer
United States Navy Logistics Office

USNM
United States Naval Mission

USNMPS
United States Naval Motion Picture Service

USNMRC
United States Naval Manpower Center

USNMTC
United States Naval Missile Test Center

USNO
United States Naval Observatory

USNOBSYSUBSTA
United States Naval Observatory, Time Service Sub-Station

USNOO
United States Naval Oceanographic Office

USNORTHCOM
United States Northern Command (unified command)

USNPGS
United States Naval Postgraduate School

USN-R
United States Navy-Retired

USNR
United States Naval Reserve

USN-RET
United States Navy-Retired

USNR-R
United States Naval Reserve-Retired

USNR-S1
United States Naval Reserve-Standby 1 (mobilization)

USNR-S2
United States Naval Reserve-Standby 2 (mobilization)

USNRTC
United States Naval Recruit Training Center

USNS
United States Naval Ship
United States Naval Station

USNSA
United States Naval Sailing Association

USNSCC
United States Naval Sea Cadet Corps

USNSPO
United States Navy Special Projects Office

USNTI
United States Navy Travel Instructions

USNTPS
United States Naval Test Pilot School

USNUSL
United States Navy Underwater Sound Laboratory

USO
United Services Organization
United States Presidential Order

USOM
United States Operations Mission

USP
United States Property
Utility Seaplane

USP&FO
United States Property and Fiscal Office/Officer

USPACOM
United States Pacific Command (unified command)

USPS
Unified Shipbuilding Specifications

USRD
Underwater Sound Reference Division (ONR)

USREPO
United States Navy Reporting Officer

USRL
Underwater Sound Reference Laboratory

USRO
United States Routing Office

USS
United Seamen's Service
United States Ship
Undersea Surveillance System

USSBS
United States Strategic Bombing Survey

USSDP
Uniformed Services Savings Deposit Program

USSOUTHCOM
United States Southern Command (unified command)

USSP
United States Special Program

USSPA
Uniformed Services Special Pay Act

USSSO
United States Sending State Office

UST
Universal Subscriber Terminal

USTDC
United States Taiwan Defense Command

USUHS
Uniformed Services University of Health Services

USW
Undersea Warfare

USWB
United States Weather Bureau

USWDIV
Undersea Warfare Division

UT
Ultrasonic Test
Underway Trials
Utilitiesman
Utility

Utility Boat (USCG)

UT1
Utilitiesman First Class

UT2
Utilitiesman Second Class

UT3
Utilitiesman Third Class

UTA
Upper Control Area

UTC
Chief Utilitiesman
Unit-Type Code
Universal Time Coordinated

UTCA
Utilitiesman Construction Apprentice

UTCM
Master Chief Utilitiesman

UTCN
Utilitiesman Constructionman

UTCS
Senior Chief Utilitiesman

U/TD
Upper 'tween Deck (stowage)

UTD
Upper 'tween Deck (stowage)

UTIL
Utilities

UTL
Utility Board, Light (USCG)

UTM
Universal Test Message
Universal Transverse Mercator

UTML
Utility Motor Launch (USCG)

UTNOTREQ
Utilization of government facilities not required as it is considered such utilization would adversely affect the performance of assigned temporary duty.

UTRANSRON
Utility Transport Squadron

UTRC
United Technique Research Center

UTRON
Utility Squadron

UTS
Universal Time Standards

UTSA
Utilitiesman Seaman Apprentice

UTSN
Utilitiesman Seaman

UTTAS
Utility Tactical Transport Aircraft System

UTU
Underway Training Unit

UUM
Underwater-to-Underwater Missile

UUT
Unit Under Test

UUV
Unmanned Underwater Vehicle

UV
Ultraviolet (light)
Under Voltage (controller)

UVASER
Ultraviolet Amplification by Stimulated Emission of Radiation

UVHFDS
Ultraviolet Hydrogen Fire Detection System

U/W
Underway

UW
Underwater

UWAYTUNORVA
Underway Training Unit, Norfolk, Virginia

UWCS
Underwater Weapons Control System

UWORDTECH
Underwater Ordnance Technician

UWS
Underwater Segment

UWSEC
Underwater Weapons Systems Engineering Center

UXO
Unexploded Explosive Ordnance

V
Photo Navigator
Variable
Variables
Varies (reporting frequency)
Vital

V&R
Vent and Replenishing

VA
Attack Squadron
Value Analysis
Visual Aids
Visual Approach

V-AC
Value-Acceleration

VAC
Vacant
Vacate
Vacuum

VADM
Vice Admiral

VAF
Voluntary Application Fill

VAH
Heavy-Attack Squadron

VA(J)
Jet Attack Squadron

VAK
Aerial Refueling Squadron

VAL
Heavier-Than-Air, Attack, Light
Light-Attack Squadron
Vertical Assault Lift

V-AM
Valve-Amplifier

VAN
Advanced

VAND
Vacuum-Air-Nitrogen Distribution (system)

VAO
Voting Assistance Officer

VAPI
Visual-Approach Indicator

VAQ
Tactical Electronic Warfare Squadron

VAR
Variation
Visual-Aural Range

VAS
Vertical Atmospheric Sounder
Visual Audit Sheet

VASI
Visual-Approach Slope Indicator

VAST
Versatile Avionics Shop Test

VAT
Village Assistance Team

VATE
Versatile Automatic Test Equipment

VATS
Versatile Avionics Test, Shop

VAW
Carrier Airborne Early Warning Squadron

VAX
Heavier-Than-Air, Attack, Experimental

VB
Vertical Beam

VBSS
Visit, Board, Search, and Seizure

VC
Fleet Composite Squadron
Variable Contrast (photo paper)
Vector Control
Voice Control
Voyage Charter

VCA
Vacant Code Announcement

VCG
Vertical Center of Gravity

VCMR
Variable Change-to-Mass Ratio

VCNM

Vice Chief of Naval Management

VCNO
Vice Chief of Naval Operations

VCNTY
Vicinity

VCO
Voltage-Controlled Oscillator (NNSS)

V-CP
Valve-Course Pilot

VCS
Vehicle Control System

VCTY
Vicinity

VCXO
Voltage-Controlled Crystal Oscillator (NNSS)

VD
Photographic Squadron
Van Dyke (reproducible drawing)

VDC
Vendor Data Control
Volts-Direct Current (NNSS)

VDF
Very-High-Frequency Direction Finder

VDG
Vertical Displacement Gyro
Vertical Display Generator

VDI
Vertical Display Indicator

VDL
Video Display Logic (NNSS)

VDP
Volunteer Reservists in Drill Pay Status

VDS
Variable-Depth Sonar

VDT
Video Display Terminal (NNSS)

VE
Air Evacuation Squadron
Value Engineering

VEAP
Veterans Education Assistance Program

VECO
Venier Engine Cutoff

VECP
Value Engineering Change Proposal

VEH
Vehicle

VEI
Value-Engineered Indicator

VEL
Velocity

VER
Verify
Vertical Ejection Rack

VER DUP
Verify Duplication

VERLOT
Very-Long-Range Tracking Radar

VERT
Vertical

VERT-2-EXP
Vertical Double-Expansion (engine)

VERT-3-EXP
Vertical Triple-Expansion (engine)

VERT CL
Vertical Clearance

VERTOL
Vertical Take-Off and Landing

VERTREP
Vertical Replenishment

VERT-R-EXP
Vertical Quadruple-Expansion (engine)

VES
Vessel(s)

VESCA
Vessel(s) and cargo

VET
Veteran

VEWS
Very Early Warning Satellite

VF
Fighter Squadron
Video Frequency
Voice Frequency
Voltage Frequency

VFI
VF Radar Intercept Officer (code)

VFM
Volt Frequency Monitor

V-FP
Valve-Fine Pilot

VFP
Light Photographic Squadron

VFTG
Voice Frequency Terminal Group

VG
Very Good
Voice Grade

VGLI
Veterans Group Life Insurance

VH
Helicopter (pilot code)
Rescue Squadron

VHA
Variable Housing Allowance

VHF
Very High Frequency

VHLH
Very Heavy Lift Helicopter

VHRR
Very-High-Resolution Radiometer

VHSIC
Very-High-Speed Integrated Circuits

VI
Vial

VIC
Variable Instrument Computer
Vicinity

VICI
Velocity Indicating Coherent Integrator

VID
Video

VIDA
Ventricular Impulse Detection and Alarm

VIDAR
Velocity Integration, Detection, and Ranging

VIDEC
Vibration Analysis and Detection Concept

VIDS
Visual Information and Display System

VIL
Village

VIMS
Verification Information Management System

VIO
Visual Intercept Officer

VIOL
Violation

VIP
Variable Information Processing
Versatile Information Processor
Very Important Person
Visual Information Processor
Vocational Interviewing and Placement
Volunteer Informant Program

VIPP
Variable Information Processing Package

VIPRE FIRE
Visual Precision Fire (control)

VIPS
Voice Interruption Priority System

VIR
Vendor Information Report

VIS
Visibility
Visual
Visual Instrument Subsystem

VISSR
Visible Infrared Spin-Span Radiometer

VIXS
Video Information Exchange System

VLA
Vertical Launch ASROC
Very Large Array
Very Low Altitude
Visual Landing Aid

VLBI
Very Long Baseline Interferometry

VLCC
Very Large Crude Oil Carrier (ship)

VLF
Very Low Frequency

VLR
Very Long Range

VLS
Vertical Launch System

VLT
Vendor Lead Time

VM
Velocity Modulation

VMA
Marine Attack Squadron

VMA(AW)
Marine All-Weather Attack Squadron

VMAQ
Marine Tactical Electronic Warfare Squadron

VMAT
Marine Attack Training Squadron

VMAT(AW)
Marine All-Weather Attack Training Squadron

VMC
Visual Meterorological Conditions

VMFA
Marine Fighter Attack Squadron

VMFAT
Marine Fighter Attack Training Squadron

VMFP
Marine Tactical Reconnaissance Squadron

VMFPDET
Marine Tactical Reconnaissance Squadron Detachment

VMGR
Marine Aerial Refueler Transport Squadron

VMO
Marine Aerial Refueler Transport Squadron

VMR
Volunteer Military Rejectee

VMRS
Vessel Movement Reporting System

VMS
Velocity-Measuring System

V/N
Vital/Non-Vital (code)

VN
Velocity North-Velocity East (NNSS)

VO
Observation Squadron
Verbal Order

VOCAL
If you desire a voluntary recall to active duty, comply NAVMILPERSMAN 1820320. Contact the nearest naval activity or district for assistance.
Vessels Ordnance Coordinating Allowance List

VOCO
Verbal Order of the Commanding Officer

VOCOM
Voice Communications

VOCOM/AUTOSERVOCOM
Voice Communications/Automatic Secure Voice Communications

VOD
Vertical Onboard Delivery

VODAT
Voice-Operated Device for Automatic Transmission

VOG
Observation Plane Squadron

VOIS
Visual Observation Instrumentation Subsystem

VOL
Volunteer

VolEd
Voluntary Education

VOLMAIN
If you desire to remain on active duty, comply NAVMILPERSMAN 1830150

VOLMET
Meteorological Information for Aircraft in Flight

VOM
Volt-Ohm-Meter

VOR
VHF Omnidirectional Radio
VHF Omnidirectional Range
Visual Omnidirectional Range

VOR/DME
VHF Omnidirectional Radio/Distance-

Measuring Equipment

VORTAC
VHF Omnidirectional Radio and Tactical Air Navigation

VOSA
Variable Orifice Sound Attenuator (system)

VOSL
Variable Operating and Safety Level

VOU
Voucher

VOU DED
Voucher Deduction

VOWF
Value-Operated Water Flash (nuclear reactor)

VOY
Voyage

VP
Patrol Squadron
Variable-Pitch (propeller)
Vertical Planning

VPB
Vertical Plot Board

VPM
Volts Per Minute

VPR
Virtual PPI Reflectoscope

VPR-NMP
Virtual PPI Reflectoscope with Navigational Microfilm Projector (radar)

VPT
ASW Tactical Coordinator (code)

VQ
Fleet Air Reconnaissance Squadron

VQE
VA ESM/SIGINT Evaluator (code)

V/R
Very Respectfully

VR
Air Transport Squadron
Fleet Tactical Support Squadron
Visual Reconnaissance
Voltage Regulator (tubes)

VRA
Veteran's Readjustment Appointment

VRB
Variable Reenlistment Bonus
Voice Rotating Beacon

VRBL
Variable

VRC
Air Transport Squadron

VRE
Volume Review Exercises

VRF
Aircraft Ferry Squadron
Visual Flight Rules

VRS
Visual Reference System

VRU
Utility Transport Squadron

VS
Air Antisubmarine Squadron
Vertical Stripes (buoy)
Visual Sign
Visual Signal

VSB
Visible

VSBY
Visibility

VSCF
Variable-Speed Constant-Frequency (electrical power circuit)

VSD
Vertical Situation Display

VSF
Antisubmarine Fighter Squadron

VSFI
Vertical Scale Flight Indicator

VSG
Vocational School Graduate (program)

VSI
Vertical Speed Indicator

VSM
Vestigial Sideboard Modulation

VSMF
Vendor Specification Microfilm File
Visual Search Microfilm Files

VSOM
Velocity Sensor Oscillator Multiplier

VSS
Variable Stability System
Volume Search Sonar
V/STOL Support Ship

VST
VS-ASW Tactical Coordinator (code)

V/STOL
Vertical Short Take-Off/Landing (aircraft)

VSTT
Variable-Speed Training Target

VSWF
Voltage Standing-Wave Frequency

VSWR
Voltage Standing-Wave Radio

VT
Training Squadron
Variable Thrust
Variable Time (fuze)
Ventilation
Virbo Tool (markings)

VTC
Video Teleconferencing

VTF
Variable Time Fuze

VTM
Voltage Turnable Magnetron

VTO
Visual Training Officer
Vocational Training Officer

VTOHL
Vertical Take-Off and Horizontal Landing (aircraft)

VTOL
Vertical Take-Off and Horizontal Landing (aircraft)

VTOL/STOL
Vertical Short Take-Off/Landing (aircraft)

VTR
Tracked Recovery Vehicle
Video Tape Recorder

VTS
Vessel Traffic Services
Vessel Traffic System
Video Tape System

VTU
Voice Terminal Unit
Voluntary Training Unit

VTUAV
Vertical Take-off and Landing Tactical Unmanned Aerial Vehicle

VTVM
Vacuum Tube Voltmeters

VU
Voice Terminal Unit

VW
Airborne Early Warning (pilot code)
Fleet Air Reconnaissance Squadron

VWC
VW Airborne Intercept Controller (code)

VWS
Ventilated Wet Suit

VX
Air Development Squadron

VXN
Oceanographic Development Squadron

W
Watts
Weapon(s)
Weekly (report frequency)
West
Western

W/
With

W&R
Welfare and Recreation

WA
Weld, Attachment (JIC)
Word After
Work Authorization

WAA
Wide Aperture Array

WAACP
Western Atlantic Airlift Command Post

WAC
Weapon Assignment Console
World Aeronautical Chart

WAE
When Actually Employed

WAFFLE
Wide-Angle Fixed-Field Locating Equipment

WAG
Miscellaneous Auxiliary (USCG)

WAGB
Icebreaker (USCG)

WAGL
Buoy Tender (USCG)

WAGO
Oceanographic Cutter (USCG)

WAGR
Miscellaneous Auxiliary (USCG)

WAI
Wide-Angle Indicator

WAITORDERS
If, after earned leave has expired, final action on proceedings and recommended findings of physical evaluation board has not been taken, continue in an awaiting orders status with pay and allowances until final action is taken.

WALP
Weapons Assignment Linear Programming

WAM
Weapons Assembly Manual

WAML
Work Authorization Material List

WAMTMTS
Western Area, Military Traffic Management and Terminal Service

WAN
Wide Area Network

WAO
Oiler (USCG)

WAP
Weighted Average
Work Assignment Procedure

WARES
Workload and Resources Evaluation System

WAS
Worked All States (ARRL)

WASP
War Air Service Program (CAB)

WATPL
Wartime Traffic Priority List

WATS
Wide-Area Telephone Service

WB
Weld, Butt (JIC)
Word Before

WBC
Weather Broadcast Center

WBLC
Waterborne Logistics Craft

WB/MC
Wide Band and Master Control

W BN
White Beacon

WBS
Work Breakdown Structure

WB SIG STA
Weather Bureau Signal Station

W/C
Work Center

WC
Work Center

WCAFCO
West Coast American Flag Berth Operators

WCBSU
West Coast Base Service Unit

WCC
Weapons Control Console
Wing Command Center
Work Center Code

WCD
Weapons Classification of Defects

WCDS
West Coast Naval Publications Distribution Center

WCN
Workload Control Number

WCP
Weapons Control Panel

WD
When Directed

WDC
Washington Document Center
Work Definition Conference

WDE
Weapons Designation Equipment
Weapons Direction Equipment

WDI
Weapons Data Index
Work Description Index

WDLY
Widely

WDN
Work Description Number

WDS
Weapon(s) Direction System

WEA
Weather
Weather Advisory

WEARCON
Weather Observation and Forecasting Control (system)

WEARECONRON
Weather Reconnaissance Squadron

WEAX
Route Weather Forecasts
Weather

WEC
Water Export Control

WEDGE
Weapon Development Glide Entry

WEE
Work Experience Education

WEFT
Wings, Engines, Fuselage, Tail (aircraft recognition system)

WEIS
World Event/Interaction Survey

WEL
Weapons Equipment List

W/ENCL
With Enclosure(s)

WEP
Weapon

WEPSYS
Weapons System

WEPTRAEX
Weapons Training Exercise

WEPTU
Weapons Training Unit

WES
West
Western
Wing Engineer Squadron

WESCAR
Western Carolines

WESCOSOUNDSCOL
West Coast Sound School

WESDET
Wing Engineer Squadron Detachment

WESPAC
Western Pacific

WESTDIVNAVFACENGCOM
Western Division Naval Facilities Engineering Command

WESTLANT
Western Atlantic

WESTOMP
Western Ocean Meeting Point

WESTPAC
Western Pacific

WESTPACDET
Western Pacific Detachment

WESTPACTRAMID
Western Pacific Training Program for Midshipmen

WESTSEAFRON
Western Sea Frontier

WET
Wet Environmental Trainer
Wet Environment Trainer

WF
Waffer
Weld, Fillet (JIC)
White Falcon (publication)

WFN
Weapons and Facilities, Navy

WG
Wine Gallon

WGBT
Wet Bulb Globe Temperature

WGM
Weight Guideline Method

WGS
Wideband Gapfiller Satellite
World Geodetic Survey (DOD)

WHAM
Work Handling and Maintenance

WHAP
Where/When Applicable

WHB
Waste Heat Boiler

WHCA
White House Communications Agency (DCA)

WHEC
High-Endurance Cutter (USCG)

WHIIP
Weapons Installation Interrupted for Parts

WHIST
Worldwide Household Goods Information System

WHLS
Wheels

WHP
Water Horsepower

W-HR
Watt-Hour

WHS
Warehouse

WHY DFTFT
What Have You Done for the Fleet Today?

WI
Weapons Instrumentation

WIA
Wounded In Action

WICOMATIC
Wiring and Connective Device, Semi-Automatic

WIE
With Immediate Effect

WILCO
I Understand and Will Comply

WIN
Women in the Navy (workshop)
WWMCCS Intercomputer Network

WIP
Work In Progress

WIR
Weapons Inspection Report

WIRE
Weapons Interference Reduction Effort (program)

WISE
Weapons Installation System Engineering

WISP
Wartime Information Security Program

WISS
Weekly Induction Schedule System

WISSA
Wholesale Interservice Supply Support Agreement

WIT
Witness

WITHOUTACCTDATA
Issuance of this order is without accounting data since it appears orders can be executed without cost. If costs or entitlements will accrue, member must request and receive written authorization including accounting data from COMNAVMILPERSCOM prior to execution.

WIX
Training Cutter (USCG)

WK
Week
Work
Wreck

WKD
Weekday

WKR
Worker

WL
Water Line
Weld Seal (JIC)

WLB
Seagoing Buoy Tender (USCG)

WLC
Weapons Launching Console

WLD
West Longitude Date

WLI
Inland Buoy Tender, Large (USCG)
Inland Buoy Tender, Small (USCG)
Work List Item

WLIC
Construction Tender (USCG)

WLM
Coastal Buoy Tender (USCG)

WLR
River Buoy Tender, Large (USCG)
River Buoy Tender, Small (USCG)

WLV
Lightship (USCG)

W/M
Weight or Measurement

WM
Weld, Bimetallic (JIC)

WMEC
Medium-Endurance Cutter (USCG)

WMO
World Meteorological Organization

WMX
Worldwide Military Command and Control System

WN
Weld, Nozzle (JIC)

WNG
Warning

WNTF
Western Naval Task Force

W/O
Without

WO
War Orientation
Warrant Officer
Weapons Officer
Work Order

WOA
Weapons Orientation, Advanced

WOC
Without Compensation

WOCS
Women Officer Candidate School

WOD
Wind-Over-Deck
Without Compensation

WOG
Water, Oil, Gal (valverating)

WOM
Write-Only Memory

WOP
Without Pay

WOQ
Women Officer's Quarters

W OR
White and Orange (buoy)

WORP
Work Order Resource Plan

WOS
Women Officer School

WOSAC
Worldwide Synchronization of Atomic Clocks

WOSD
Weapons Operational Systems Development

WOW
War On Wastefulness

WOWAR
Work Order and Work Accomplishment Record

W/P
Waypoint

WP
Weapon

White Phosphorous
Work Punt (USCG)

WPB
Patrol Boat (USCG)
Weapons Procurement, Navy

WPBC
Western Pacific Base Command

WPLO
Water Port Logistics Office

WPM
Words Per Minute

WPN
Navy Weapons Procurement Appropriation
Weapon

WPNS
Weapons

WPNSCO
Weapons Company

WPNSPLT
Weapons Platoon

WPNSTRNGBN
Weapons Training Battalion

WPPG
Working Plan Preparation Guide

WPRB
Weapons Personnel Research Branch (EISO)

WPRD
Weapons Personnel Research Division

WPWOD
Will Proceed Without Delay

W/R
Washroom
Work Request

WR
Ward Room
War Reserve
War Room
Washroom
Weapons Requirement
Weld, Rooter Boss (JIC)
Wet Runway
Women's Reserve
Work Request

WRA
Weapons Replaceable Assembly

WRAP
Weapons Readiness Aircraft Program
Weapons Reliability Assurance Program

WRB
Wide-Range Burner

WRC
Weapon Release Computation
Weather Relay Center

WRCS
Weapons Release Computer System

WR MESS
Wardroom Mess

WRNT
Warrant

WR-P
Wet Runway-Patchy

WRR
Water/Surface/Underwater Radio

WRT
Water Round Torpedo (tank)
With Respect To

WS
Weapons Specifications
Weapons System
Weld, Socket (JIC)
With System (SWBS)

WSAM
Weapons System Acquisition Management (NPGS)
Weapons System Acquisition Manager (NPGS)

WSAT
Weapons Systems Acceptance Tests
Weapons Systems Acceptance Trials

WSC
Western Sea Frontier Command

WSE
Weapons and Support Equipment

WSEF
Weapon System Effectiveness Factor

WSEG
Weapons System Evaluation Group

WSEIAC
Weapon System Effectiveness Industrial Advisory Committee

WSESRB
Weapon System Explosives Safety Review Board

WSET
Weapon System Evaluation Test

WSF
Western Sea Frontier

WSHFT
Wind Shift

WSIM
Water Separation Index, Modified

WSMR
White Sands Missile Range

WSO
Weapons System Officer

WSP
Working Steam Pressure (valve rating)

WSPACS
Weapons Systems Programming and Control System

WSPD
Weapons System Planning Data
Weapons System Planning Document

WSPO
Weapons System Project Office

WSS
Wholesale Storage Site

WSSG
Weapons System Safety Guidelines

WST
Weapons System Test
Weapons System Trainer

WSTH
Weapons System Tactical Handbook

W/T
Water-Tight (integrity)
Wireless Telegraphy

WT
Water Tender
Weight
Weld, Support (JIC)

WTA
Work-Task Agreement

WTCA
Water Terminal Clearance Activity

WTCON
Weight Control

WTCSS
West Coast Off-Shore Tactical Control Surveillance System

WTD
Watertight Door

WTF
Western Task Force

WTGB
Icebreaking tug (USCG)

WTI
Water-Tight Integrity

WTR
Reserve Training Cutter (USCG)
Water
Western Test Range

WTRP
Watch Team Replacement Plan

WTS
Wing Transportation Squadron

WTSDET
Wing Transportation Squadron Detachment

WTV
Water Tank Vessel

WUC
Work Unit Code

WUT
World Utility Transporter

W/V
Wind Vector
Wind Velocity

WVD
Waived

W/W
Worldwide

WW
Weather Wing
Wire Way

WWC
World Weather Center

WWMCCS
Worldwide Military Command and Control System

WWRI
Worldwide Mobile Communications Routing Index

WWSP
Worldwide Surveillance Program

WWW
World Weather Watch

WX
Weather
Weather Advisory

WXR
Weather Radar

WYTL
Harbor Tug, Small (USCG)
Harbor Tug, Small, Wood (USCG)

X

X
Cross (as in X-OVER)
Experimental
Index Register (NNSS)
Special Projects
Submersible Craft (Self-Propelled)

X&DFLOT
Experimental and Development Flotilla (landing craft)

XBT
Expendable Bathythermograph

XC
Experimental Cooling

XCOM
Executive Committee
External Communications

XCS
Excess

XDECK
Crossdeck

XDPU
Expanded Data Processing Unit (NNSS)

XEO
Experimental Engineering Orders

XERB
Experimental Environmental Reporting Buoy

XFER
Transfer

XFM
Expeditionary Force Message

XFMR
Transformer

XLR
Experimental Liquid Rocket

XMAP
Sweeper Device (vessel)

XMIT
Transmit

XMPT
Exempt

XMS
Experimental Development Specification
Transmission

XMSN
Transmission

XMT
Exempt

XMTL
Transmittal

XMTR
Transmitter

XO
Executive Officer

XP
Transmitter Pressure

XPC
Inshore Patrol Cutter

XPG
Converted Merchant Ship

XREP
Auxiliary Report

XRL
Extended Range Lance (missile)

XSIT
Transit

XSV
Expendable Sound Velocimeter

XTND
Extend

XTRAN
Experimental Translation Crystal

XTRM
Extreme

Y
Year
Yearly

YA
Ash Lighter

YAG
Miscellaneous Auxiliary Service Craft

YAGR
Ocean Station Radar Ship

YAGT
Floating Target

YBD
Bowdock

YC
Coal Barge
Open Lighter (Non-Self-Propelled)

YCD
Fueling Barge

YCF
Car Float (Non-Self-Propelled)

YCK
Open Cargo Lighter

YCS
Years Commissioned Service

YCSS
Cargo Semi-Submersible Barge

YCV
Aircraft Transportation Lighter (Non-Self-Propelled)

YD
Floating Crane ((Non-Self-Propelled)
Yard

YDG
Degaussing Vessel

YDT
Diving Tender (Non-Self-Propelled)

YE
Aircraft Homing System
Ammunition Lighter (Self-Propelled)

YEN
Ammunition Lighter (Non-Self-Propelled)

YF
Covered Lighter (Self-Propelled)
Freight Lighter

YFB
Ferryboat or Launch (Self-Propelled)

YFD
Yard Floating Drydock (Non-Self-Propelled)

YFN
Covered Lighter (Non-Self-Propelled)

YFNB
Large Covered Lighter (Non-Self-Propelled)

YFND
Drydock Companion Craft (Non-Self-Propelled)

YFNX
Lighter (Special-Purpose)

YFP
Floating Power Barge (Non-Self-Propelled)

YFR
Refrigerated Covered Lighter (Self-Propelled)

YFRN
Refrigerated Covered Lighter (Non-Self-Propelled)

YFRT
Covered Lighter Range Tender (Self-Propelled)

YFU
Harbor Utility Craft (Self-Propelled)

YG
Garbage Lighter (Self-Propelled)

YGN
Garbage Lighter (Non-Self-Propelled)

YH
Ambulance Boat

YHB
Houseboat

YHLC
Salvage Lift Craft, Heavy (Non-Self-Propelled)

YHT
Heading Scow

YLA
Open Landing Lighter

YLLC
Salvage Lift Craft, Light (Self-Propelled)

YM
Dredge (Self-Propelled)

YMN
Dredge (Non-Self-Propelled)

YMP
Motor Mine Planter

YMS
Motor Minesweeper

YMT
Motor Tug

YN
Yeoman

YN1
Yeoman First Class

YN2
Yeoman Second Class

YN3
Yeoman Third Class

YNC
Chief Yeoman

YNCM
Master Chief Yeoman

YNCS
Senior Chief Yeoman

YNG
Gate Craft (Non-Self-Propelled)

YNSA
Yeoman Seaman Apprentice

YNSN
Yeoman Seaman

YNT
Net Tender (Tug Class)

YO
Fuel Oil Barge (Self-Propelled)

YOB
Year Of Birth

YOG
Gasoline Barge (Self-Propelled)

YOGN
Gasoline Barge (Non-Self-Propelled)

YON
Fuel Oil Barge (Non-Self-Propelled)

YOS
Oil Storage Barge (Non-Self-Propelled)

YOSS
Submersible Oil Storage Barge

YP
Yard Patrol (craft)

YPD
Floating Pile Driver (Non-Self-Propelled)

YPK
Pontoon Storage Barge

YPT
Torpedo Retriever

YR
Floating Workshop (Non-Self-Propelled)
Yard Repair
Year
Yearly
Your

YRB
Repair and Berthing Barge (Non-Self-Propelled)

YRBM
Repair, Berthing, and Messing Barge (Non-Self-Propelled)

YRC
Submarine Rescue Chamber

YRDH
Floating Drydock Workshop (Hull) (Non-Self-Propelled)

YRDM
Floating Drydock Workshop (Machine) (Non-Self-Propelled)

YR FLN
Year Flown

YRL
Covered Lighter Repair

YRR
Radiological Repair Barge (Non-Self-Propelled)

YRST
Salvage Craft Tender (Non-Self-Propelled)

YS
Stevedoring Barge
Yankee Station

YSD
Seaplane Wrecking Derrick (Self-Propelled)

YSP
Salvage Pontoon

YSR
Sludge Removal Barge (Non-Self-Propelled)

YTB
Large Harbor Tug (Self-Propelled)

YTD
Large Harbor Tug (Self-Propelled)
Year-to-Date (payroll records)

YTL
Small Harbor Tug (Self-Propelled)

YTM
Medium Harbor Tug (Self-Propelled)

YTR
Small Rescue Tug

YTRES
Yankee Tractor Rocket Escape System

YTT
Torpedo-Testing Ranging
Torpedo Trials Craft

YV
Drone Aircraft Landing Craft

YW
Water Barge (Self-Propelled)

YWN
Water Barge (Non-Self-Propelled)

Z

Z
Tactical
Zenith
Zone

Z/A
Zone of Action

ZA
Zone of Action

ZAP
Zero Anti-Aircraft Potential

ZAR
Zeus Acquisition Radar

ZBB
Zero-Based Budgeting

ZD
Zenith Distance
Zero Defects
Zone Description

ZELL
Zero-Length Launch

ZEM
Zero-Error Mentally

Z/F
Zone of Fire

ZGS
Zero-Gradient Synchrotron

ZI
Zone of Interior

ZIP
Zone Inspection Program

ZMAR
Zeus Multifunction Array Radar

Z-MKR
Zone Marker

ZMKR
Zone Marker

ZOR
Zone Of Reconnaissance

ZPA
Zeus Program Analysis

ZPEN
Zeus Project Engineer Network

ZPO
Zeus Project Ofice

Z/R
Zone of Responsibility

ZR
Zone of Responsibility

ZSL
Zero Sight Line

ZT
Zone Time

About the Authors

Deborah W. Cutler and Thomas J. Cutler are a husband-and-wife team that has long worked together on books, oral histories, magazine articles, lesson plans, and speeches pertaining to naval matters. Tom's name has appeared on many of these products, while Debbie has worked largely behind the scenes until now. Together, they have worked on such titles as *The Bluejacket's Manual*, *A Sailor's History of the U.S. Navy*, and *Brown Water, Black Berets: Coastal and Riverine Warfare in Vietnam*.

Debbie is a recognized professional in the field of oral history transcription and developmental editing. Besides his writing, Tom is well known throughout the Navy as a teacher and lecturer, having taught at the U.S. Naval Academy for nine years and currently serving as a Fleet Professor with the Naval War College.